As pratical information
and admission times and charges
are liable to alteration,
the information printed in this publication
is for guidance only.

Travel Publications

38 Clarendon Road - WATFORD Herts WD1 1SX - U.K.
Tel. (01923) 415 000
www.michelin-travel.com
TheGreenGuide-uk@uk.michelin.com

Manufacture française des pneumatiques Michelin

Société en commandite par actions au capital de 2 000 000 000 de francs
Place des Carmes-Déchaux – 63000 Clermont-Ferrand (France)
R.C.S. Clermont-Fd B 855 200 507

© Michelin et Cie, Propriétaires-éditeurs, 2001
Dépôt légal avril 2001 – ISBN 2-06-000887-5 – ISSN 0763-1383

Printed in France 03-01/3.1

Typesetting : MAURY Imprimeur S.A., Malesherbes
Printing and binding : AUBIN Imprimeur, Ligugé.

Cover design : Carré Noir, Paris 17ᵉ

THE GREEN GUIDE:
The Spirit of Discovery

*The exhilaration of new horizons,
the fun of seeing the world, the
excitement of discovery: this is what
we seek to share with you. To help you
make the most of your travel experience,
we offer first-hand knowledge and turn
a discerning eye on places to visit.
This wealth of information gives
you the expertise to plan your own
enriching adventure. With THE GREEN
GUIDE showing you the way, you can
explore new destinations with confidence
or rediscover old ones.
Leisure time spent with THE GREEN
GUIDE is also a time for refreshing
your spirit, enjoying yourself,
and taking advantage of our selection
of fine restaurants, hotels
and other places for relaxing.
So turn the page and open a window
on the world. Join THE GREEN GUIDE
in the spirit of discovery.*

Contents

Canal-side house in Amsterdam

Vadim/DIAF

R. Mazin/DIAF

Delftware

4

Sights 84

Letterbox, Zaanse Schans

Irises (1890), Vincent van Gogh

Maps and plans

COMPANION PUBLICATIONS

Plan of Amsterdam no 36 and spiral-bound atlas of Amsterdam no 2036:
– a complete street map of the city (1cm=150m) with all major thoroughfares, one-way streets, large car parks, major public buildings, cycle lanes, etc.
– a street index
– practical information

Map of the Netherlands no 908

A 1:400 000 scale map:
– detailed information about the road network, intersections, border crossings, etc.
– indication of distances
– list of place names
– enlarged map of Amsterdam and Rotterdam

Map of the northern Netherlands no 210

A 1:200 000 scale map:
– detailed information about the road network, intersections, border crossings, etc.
– indication of distances
– list of place names
– enlarged map of Amsterdam

Map of the southern Netherlands no 211

A 1:200 000 scale map:
- detailed information about the road network, intersections, border crossings, etc.
- indication of distances
- list of place names
- enlarged map of The Hague and Rotterdam

LIST OF MAPS AND PLANS

Plans of districts

Plans of sites and museums

Local maps

Using this guide

● The summary maps at the front of this guide have been designed to assist you in planning your trip. The **Map of principal sights** identifies major attractions, classified according to Michelin's star system, while the **Map of touring programmes** proposes a number of driving itineraries.

● The guide is divided into four sections: **Practical Information, Introduction, Sights** and **Admission Times and Charges.**

● The **Practical Information** section includes information on transport, where to stay and where to eat, sports, a bibliography and a calendar of events.

● The **Introduction** gives information on the geographical, historical and cultural background of the country.

● The principal natural and cultural attractions in the Netherlands are presented in alphabetical order in the **Sights** section. The clock symbol ⊘ placed after the name of a sight indicates that opening times and prices for visiting that sight are included in the **Admission times and charges** section at the back of the guide.

● The **Travellers' addresses** sections, listed under a number of towns and cities within this guide, give selected hotel and restaurant recommendations, along with practical information for that specific location (guided tours, boat trips, stores, markets and festivals).

● The **Index** at the back of this guide contains a comprehensive list of specific place names, historical figures and and other important information.

We greatly appreciate comments and suggestions from our readers. Contact us at:

Michelin Travel Publications, 38 Clarendon Road, Watford, Herts WD1 1SX, England.
☎ 01923 415 000
Fax 01923 415 250
TheGreenGuide-uk@uk.michelin.com
www.michelin-travel.com

Lighthouse, Ameland

Key

	Sight	Seaside Resort	Winter Sports Resort	Spa
Worth a journey	★★★	≌ ≌ ≌	✳ ✳ ✳	♱ ♱ ♱
Worth a detour	★★	≌ ≌	✳ ✳	♱ ♱
Interesting	★	≌	✳	♱

Tourism

⊙	Admission Times and Charges listed at the end of the guide		►►	Visit if time permits
⊙➡	Sightseeing route with departure point indicated		AZ B	Map co-ordinates locating sights
♠♦♠♦	Ecclesiastical building		🛈	Tourist information
▨ ⛨	Synagogue – Mosque		⚰ ⁞	Historic house, castle – Ruins
▰	Building (with main entrance)		∪ ☼	Dam – Factory or power station
▪	Statue, small building		☆ ∩	Fort – Cave
✝	Wayside cross		⚲	Prehistoric site
◎	Fountain		▼ ۷	Viewing table – View
●—●—■	Fortified walls – Tower – Gate		▲	Miscellaneous sight

Recreation

🏇	Racecourse		🚶	Waymarked footpath
⛸	Skating rink		◆	Outdoor leisure park/centre
≋ ▨	Outdoor, indoor swimming pool		⛹	Theme/Amusement park
⚓	Marina, moorings		🦌	Wildlife/Safari park, zoo
⛺	Mountain refuge hut		🌳	Gardens, park, arboretum
▫—▪—▫	Overhead cable-car		🐦	Aviary, bird sanctuary
🚂	Tourist or steam railway			

Additional symbols

▬▬ ▬	Motorway (unclassified)		✉ ◉	Post office – Telephone centre
❶ ❶	Junction: complete, limited		✉	Covered market
⊏▭▬	Pedestrian street		⁙	Barracks
⌶=====⌶	Unsuitable for traffic, street subject to restrictions		⚠	Swing bridge
⸬ ----	Steps – Footpath		∪ ✕	Quarry – Mine
🚆 🚌	Railway – Coach station		B F	Ferry (river and lake crossings)
▫+++++▫	Funicular – Rack-railway		🚢	Ferry services: Passengers and cars
— ◉	Tram – Metro, Underground		⛴	Foot passengers only
Bert (R.)...	Main shopping street		③	Access route number common to MICHELIN maps and town plans

Abbreviations and special symbols

G	Police station (Marechaussee)		**POL.**	Police station (Politie)
H	Town hall (Stadhuis)		**T**	Theatre (Schouwburg)
J	Law courts (Gerechtshof)		**U**	University (Universiteit)
M	Museum (Museum)		⟷	Landing stage
P	Provincial capital (Hoofdplaats provincie)		🏛	Outstanding frontage
P	Provincial council (Provinciehuis)		🅿	Park and Ride

Principal sights

GLOSSARY

Afsluitdijk	barrier dam
Bollenvelden	bulb fields
Brug	bridge
Dam	barrage
Eiland(en)	island(s)
Hunebed(den)	dolmen(s), covered passage grave(s)
Kanaal	canal
Land	land, countryside
Meer, Meren	lake, lakes
Openluchtmuseum	open-air museum
Plassen	pools
Stormvloedkering	storm surge barrier
Streek	region
Terp(en)	settlement mound(s)
Vaart	waterway
Zee	sea

Touring programmes

IJsselmeer 500km-310 miles:
7 days including 2 days in Amsterdam

The cities of Central Netherlands 550km-342 miles:
10 days including 2 days in Amsterdam

Delta and Southern Netherlands 500km-310 miles:
7 days including 1 day in Den Haag (The Hague)

Overnight stop

Name under which a route is described.
See the index for page number.

★★★ = ☆☆☆   ★★ = ☆☆   ★ = ☆

★★★ = ☆☆☆   ★★ = ☆☆   ★ = ☆

0   30 km

Practical
Information

Planning your trip

WHEN TO GO

The Netherlands is a land for all seasons and although the country is uniformly flat it is never dull, as there is a constantly changing play of light between sea and sky.

Spring – Without doubt the outstanding attractions are the bulb fields, a kaleidoscope of dazzling colours in season *(from mid-April to end of May)*. The main bulb-growing areas are between Haarlem and Leiden and in the vicinity of Alkmaar. In spring the foliage of the countryside is a fresh green and the trees along the canalside add a splash of colour to townscapes.
The Betuwe region is a delight when the cherry orchards are in blossom *(mid-April to end of May)* and the bright yellow of the fields of oil seed rape makes a vivid picture in the provinces of Friesland, Groningen, Overijssel and Flevoland *(mid-May to early June)*.

Summer – The great stretches of sandy beach along the North Sea coast are popular with holidaymakers and locals alike. Here as in other popular resorts and holiday areas (Drenthe and Southern Limburg) it is always wise to book in advance as accommodation is scarce during the summer season. The many lakes, reservoirs, canals and waterways make this ideal sailing country and good for water sports.
Throughout spring and summer flowers are everywhere: towns and villages are bright with well-tended public gardens and parks and cheerful flower boxes and window displays enhance even the plainest façades.

Autumn – By late August and early September the dunes and heathlands are bright with the purple of heather in bloom. The forests like those of the Veluwe start to sport their autumnal hues.

Winter – The winter landscapes have a charm of their own, as captured by past generations of Dutch artists, and even the towns take on an uncanny stillness as they lie muffled under their first mantle of snow. In the Netherlands, frozen lakes and canals are an irresistible invitation to skate and children are not the only ones to take it up.

FORMALITIES

Although the Netherlands signed the Schengen Agreement ending internal border controls between member countries, which came into effect in 1995, travellers should nonetheless be equipped with proof of identity. This may take the form of a European Identity Card (for nationals of EU member states) or a **passport**. Holders of British, Irish and US passports require no visa to enter the Netherlands, although visas may be necessary for visitors from some Commonwealth countries, and for those planning to stay for longer than three months. Visitors are advised to check visa requirements with their travel agent or with their local Dutch embassy or consulate. US citizens should obtain the booklet **Your Trip Abroad**, which provides useful information on visa requirements, customs regulations, medical care etc for international travellers. Apply to the Superintendent of Documents, PO Box 371954, Pittsburgh, PA 15250-7954, ☎ (202) 512 1800; Fax (202) 512 2250; www.access.gpo.gov

Customs regulations – Since the birth of the single European market and the abolition of the duty-free system on certain goods, allowances for various commodities within the EU have changed. A free leaflet, **Duty Paid**, is available from HM Customs and Excise, Finchley Excise Advice Centre, Berkeley House, 304 Regents Park Road, London N3 2JY, ☎ (020) 7865 4400. The US Customs Service offers a free publication **Know Before You Go** for US citizens, ☎ (202) 927 6724; www.customs.gov

Travel insurance – British citizens should apply for **Form E 111**, issued by the Post Office, which entitles the holder to urgent treatment for accident or unexpected illness in EU countries. This form should be presented to the relevant medical services prior to receiving treatment. For further information in the UK, contact the Department of Health and Social Security ☎ (0191) 218 7777. Visitors are strongly advised to take out additional travel insurance to cover against any expenses not covered by form E 111, as well as lost luggage, theft, cancellation, delayed departure etc.
Non-EU travellers are advised to check with their insurance companies about taking out supplementary medical insurance with specific overseas coverage.

Pets (cats and dogs) – A general health certificate and proof of rabies vaccination should be obtained from your local vet before departure.

BY AIR

Various airline companies operate regular services to the international airports in the Netherlands (Amsterdam-Schiphol, Rotterdam, Eindhoven and Maastricht). These include:
KLM: ☎ 0990 074 074; www.klm.com; flights from London and from regional airports around the UK to Amsterdam.
British Airways: Waterside, PO Box 365, Harmondsworth, UB7 0GB, England; ☎ 0845 77 333 77; www.britishairways.com; flights from London airports to Amsterdam.
Reservations within the US and Canada: ☎ 1-800-AIRWAYS.
EasyJet: ☎ 0870 6000 000; www.easyJet.com; flights from London Luton, Belfast, Edinburgh and Liverpool to Amsterdam.

BY FERRY

There are numerous cross-Channel services from the United Kingdom and Eire. It may be preferable to sail to France or Belgium and then drive to the Netherlands. For details apply to travel agencies or to:
Brittany Ferries: ☎ 0870 901 2400; Fax 01752 600 698; www.brittany-ferries.co.uk. Sailings from the UK and Eire to various ports in France. **Plymouth-Roscoff; Poole-Cherbourg; Portsmouth-St Malo; Portsmouth-Caen; Cork-Roscoff.**
Seafrance: ☎ 08705 711 711; Fax 01304 828 405; www.seafrance.com. **Dover-Calais.**
Hoverspeed: ☎ 0990 240 241 (reservations), 01304 865 000 (switchboard); Fax 01304 865 111; www.hoverspeed.co.uk. **Dover-Ostend.**
P&O Stena Line: ☎ 0990 980 980; Fax 01304 863 464; www.posl.com. **Dover-Calais.**
P&O North Sea Ferries: ☎ 08701 296 002 (reservations); Fax (01482) 706 438; www.ponsf.com. **Hull-Rotterdam; Hull-Zeebrugge.**
DFDS Seaways: ☎ 08705 333 000; Fax 01255 244 382; www.dfdsseaways.co.uk. **Newcastle-IJmuiden (Amsterdam).**
Stena Line UK: ☎ (01233) 647 022; Fax (01233) 202 231; www.stenaline.com. **Harwich-Hoek van Holland.**

BY RAIL

Eurostar runs direct high-speed passenger trains from London to Paris and London to Brussels. The service takes only 3hr to travel from London Waterloo to Paris Nord and 2hr 40min from London Waterloo to Bruxelles Midi. ☎ (0990) 186 186, www.eurostar.com
From Brussels it is possible to take one of the frequent InterCity trains to Amsterdam. In the UK **Rail Europe** will make bookings for train journeys between Brussels and the Netherlands. They can be contacted at 179 Piccadilly, London W1, ☎ 08705 848 848; www.raileurope.co.uk
Eurotunnel runs passenger and freight services which link Folkestone to Calais in just 35min. ☎ 08705 353 353; www.eurotunnel.com

BY COACH

Eurolines operates coach services to Amsterdam, Arnhem, Breda, Eindhoven, The Hague, Nijmegen, Rotterdam and Utrecht. For details and reservations, contact Eurolines UK, 4 Cardiff Road, Luton, Bedfordshire, England, LU1 1PP; ☎ (01582) 404 511; Fax (01582) 400 694; www.eurolines.co.uk

---

The Channel Tunnel

This tunnel under the sea is the realisation of dreams of linking Britain to mainland Europe which date back over 200 years. The Channel link consists of two single-track rail tunnels (7.6m/24ft in diameter) for passenger and freight transport, and one service tunnel (4.8m/15ft in diameter) for safety and ventilation. The tunnels are 50.5km/31mi long, 37km/23mi of which are under the Channel. Most of the tunnel is 40m/131ft beneath the seabed, in a layer of blue chalk. The trains (800m/2 624ft long) have two levels for passenger cars (capacity 118 cars per shuttle) and one level for coaches and caravans. Special services operate for heavy goods vehicles. British, French and Belgian trains, including French TGVs, also use the tunnel. Journey time through the tunnel is ideally 35min, 28min of which are in the tunnel at a maximum speed of 130kph/80mph.

BY ROAD

When driving to the continent the ideal ports of entry for the Netherlands are Vlissingen, Rotterdam and Hoek van Holland. Depending on the point of departure it may be more convenient to land at Hamburg (seasonal service from Harwich), Zeebrugge (from Felixstowe and Kingston-upon-Hull), Ostend or Calais (both from Dover) and then drive on to the Netherlands. To choose the most suitable route between one of the above ports and your destination, use the Michelin Road Atlas of Europe, or consult the Michelin route-planning service on the Internet (www.michelin-travel.com).

Calais to Rotterdam via Antwerp: *305km/190mi* - 3hr 30min.
Calais to Amsterdam via Antwerp and Rotterdam: *379km/235mi* - 4hr 30min.
Hamburg to Amsterdam via Bremen: *472km/290mi* - 4hr 50min.

Travelling in the Netherlands

BY CAR

Car hire – Cars can be hired in most major towns and resorts. The minimum age limit is 21 although some companies maintain a minimum age of 23 and possession of a valid licence for a minimum of one year. A current driving licence is required. It is cheaper to reserve in advance rather than to pay on the spot. All the major companies (Avis, Hertz, and Europcar) are to be found in the main Dutch cities as well as local companies. The telephone numbers below are for the rental offices based at Schiphol airport in Amsterdam:
Avis ☎ 020 655 6050; www.avis.com
Europcar ☎ 020 316 4190; www.europcar.com
Hertz ☎ 23 567 0747 or 0800 2354 3789 (toll-free); www.hertz.com

Documents – Nationals of the European Union require a valid **national driving licence**. Nationals of non-EU countries should obtain an **international driving licence**, available in the US from the American Automobile Association, US$18 for members and US$20 for non-members. The AAA can be contacted at AAA National Headquarters, 1000 AAA Drive, Heathrow, FL 32746-5080, ☎ (407) 444 7000. Other documents required include the vehicle's current **log book** and a **green card** for insurance.

Insurance – Those motorists entering the Netherlands in their own vehicles should ensure that their insurance policy includes overseas cover. Visitors are advised to check with their respective insurance companies prior to travel. Motorists are also advised to take out adequate accident and **breakdown** cover for their period of travel overseas. Various motoring organisations (AA, RAC etc) will be able to provide further details on options available. Bail bonds are no longer necessary, although travellers may wish to take this precaution (consult your insurance company). Members of the American Automobile Association should obtain the free brochure, *Offices to Serve You Abroad*, which gives details of affiliated organisations in the Netherlands.

Accidents – In the event of an accident the emergency number for ambulance and police is ☎ 112. Emergency telephones are to be found alongside the main roads.

Signposting – In the Netherlands the names of certain foreign towns are often signposted in Dutch:
Belgium: Luik for Liège;
France: Parijs for Paris, Rijsel for Lille;
Germany: Aken for Aachen.
For useful motoring terms see Glossary.

Tourist routes – The ANWB has organised and signposted about 40 itineraries ranging in distance from 80-150km/50-100mi. These routes have hexagonal signposts and take in the most picturesque regions and interesting towns. Leaflets showing the routes and main points of interest are available from the ANWB offices. Other tourist and heritage trails are organised by local authorities.

Driving regulations – Traffic in the Netherlands drives **on the right**. The minimum age for driving is 18 for cars and motorcycles and 16 for mopeds. Children under 12 are not allowed to travel in the front seat as long as there is room for them in the back. Seatbelts are compulsory in the back as well as the front of the car.

Maximum **speed limits** for cars, caravans and small trailers are 50kph/31mph in built-up areas, 80kph/50mph on the open road, and 120kph/75mph on motorways (minimum speed on motorways is 70kph/45mph). Motorways *(autosnelweg)* are toll-free and all motorway junctions are numbered *(see the Michelin map series)*. There are however tolls for certain bridges and tunnels (Kiltunnel and Prins Willem Alexander Brug).

Priority must be given to cars coming from the right at junctions and on roundabouts, unless shown otherwise. Give way also to trams, pedestrians boarding or alighting from trams, and pedestrians crossing the road into which you are just turning. Only pass trams on the right unless there there is insufficient room. Trams generally have priority. Cyclists will pass on the right and have priority over motorists when the latter want to turn off the road.

The regulation **red warning triangle** must be carried, and displayed in the event of a breakdown.

Road maps – Michelin map 907 covers all the Benelux countries at a scale of 1:400 000. Map 908 covers the Netherlands at a scale of 1:400 000 and has a comprehensive index as well as enlarged inset maps of the conurbations of Amsterdam and Rotterdam. The Netherlands is also covered at a scale of 1:200 000 by maps 210 (northern half) and 211 (southern half) which give both road and tourist information. Map 210 has a detail map of Amsterdam and map 211 of The Hague and Rotterdam. Maps at a scale of 1:100 000 are available from the ANWB and the VVV.

Route planning – Michelin has created a web site to help motorists plan their journey. The free route planning service covers the whole of Europe – 21 countries and one million kilometres of highways and byways – enabling browsers to select their preferred route such as the fastest, the shortest or that recommended by Michelin.
The description of the itinerary includes the distances and travel times between towns, as well as information on hotels and restaurants en route.
The network is updated three times weekly, integrating road works, detours, new motorways and snowbound mountain passes.
Consult the web site at **www.michelin-travel.com**

Petrol – The following kinds of petrol are on sale in the Netherlands:

Super	Super gelood
Super (unleaded, only 95 octane)	Super (loodvrij)
Diesel	Diesel
Euro (Unleaded, onlu 95 octane)	Euroloodvrij
LPG	Gas

Credit cards are sometimes accepted at petrol stations, but visitors are still strongly advised to have other means of payment with them.

Breakdown service – The main organisation is the ANWB (Koninklijke Nederlandsche Toeristenbend), the Royal Dutch Touring Club, which operates road patrols (*Wegenwacht*) on main roads. If no patrol happens to pass then phone for assistance from one of the roadside telephones to the nearest ANWB office (*alarmcentrale*) ☎ 0800 08 88. This breakdown service operates 24hr a day. The receptionist usually speaks several foreign languages. Foreign visitors who are not in the possession of a valid membership card of a club affiliated to the AIT (Alliance International du Tourisme) must pay the cost of membership. Members of the Automobile Association (AA) with a valid International Circular Letter of Credit (IRK) obtain free assistance.
ANWB, PO Box 93200, 2509 BA The Hague, ☎ (070) 314 71 47.

BY BUS, TRAM OR METRO

Tickets – A strip card (*strippenkaart*), valid for buses, trams and metros throughout the Netherlands, can be bought from post offices, railway stations and from shops displaying the *strippenkaart* logo. It works out cheaper than buying a single ticket each time you travel by bus, tram or metro. You should either feed it into a punching machine on board the vehicle, or get the driver to stamp it, cancelling one strip per journey and one strip per zone being travelled through. Once stamped the strip is valid for one hour, during which you can change vehicle without having to get it restamped. City centres are one zone, and the surrounding zones are shown on maps at bus, tram and metro stops. Information on times, routes and fares is available on ☎ 0900-9292 or at www.ov9292.nl

BY TRAIN

Tickets and fares – The Dutch railway system is run by the Netherlands Railways (NS). Further information and reservations are available from Holland Rail, ☎ (01962) 773 646; Fax (01962) 773 625; info@hollandrail.com; www.hollandrail.com. Within the Netherlands, information about times, fares (day-tickets and weekly tickets, season tickets), taking a bike onto the train, special offers, etc. can be obtained by phoning the public transport information office ☎ 0900-9292 or by consulting the public transport information web site at www.ov9292.nl
The Netherlands has an extensive and efficient railway network. There is an InterCity network of express trains linking major cities. It is not possible to reserve seats on national train services. There are two classes (first and second). A day return is cheaper than two singles. There are numerous organised day trips and group tickets (multi, family and teenager) at reduced rates.
If you arrive in a city or town by train, you can use the **Train Taxi** service to travel into the centre. These are operated in 111 towns and cities, and charge a set fare regardless of the distance travelled. The taxi driver will wait (normally not for more than 10min) until he has enough passengers before setting off. Further information is available at railway stations.

BY AIR

The main airports in the Netherlands are Amsterdam-Schiphol, Rotterdam, Eindhoven and Maastricht. For information on internal flights, contact KLM, ☎ 0990 074 074; www.klm.com

BY FERRY

Ferries run from the Dutch mainland to the Wadden islands, with services from Holwerd to Ameland, Lauwersoog to Schiermonnikoog, Harlingen to Vlieland and Terschelling and Den Helder to Texel. Further information on these services is available from the Netherlands Board of Tourism at www.holland.com

General information

Currency – The unit of currency in the Netherlands is the guilder (usually abbreviated to fl, from its old name "florin", although it is indicated internationally by NLG) comprising 100 cents. In December 2000, the exchange rate was 3.60fl to the British pound (2.50fl to the US dollar). Coins come in the following denominations: 5 cents *(stuiver)*, 10 cents *(dubbeltje)*, 25 cents *(kwartje)*, 100 cents/1fl *(gulden)*, 2.50fl *(rijksdaalder)* and 5fl, with notes in 10, 25, 50, 100, 250 and 1 000fl values. Prices are rounded up or down to the nearest 5 cents as there are no 1 cent coins.
From 1 January 2002 the euro will replace the guilder.

Changing money, credit cards – Travellers' cheques and foreign cash can be exchanged at post offices, banks and exchange offices (GWK) and in some coastal VVV offices. Rates of commission can vary considerably between exchange bureaux so check before changing your money. GWK offices are found throughout the country, at major border crossing points and Amsterdam-Schiphol airport. They are usually open Monday to Sunday, early morning to late at night. The following GWK offices are open 24hrs a day: Amsterdam Central Station, Schiphol Plaza (NS-station), Antwerp-Breda border (E 19), Cologne/Oberhausen-Arnhem border (E 35), Osnabrück-Oldenzaal border (E 30).
Most GWK offices also offer a hotel booking service, tickets to major attractions, maps, tourist guides and telephone cards.
International credit cards (American Express, Diners Club, Eurocard, Visacard, Access and MasterCard) are accepted in most shops, hotels and restaurants. Visitors can also obtain cash from bank machines using credit and debit cards. A pin number will be required to use this service.
Lost or stolen credit cards or Eurocheques should be reported to the following numbers as soon as possible:
      Visa: ☎ 0800 022 41 76
      Mastercard/Eurocard: ☎ (030) 283 55 55/283 60 00
      American Express: ☎ (020) 504 85 04/504 86 66
      Diners Card: ☎ (020) 654 55 11.
You should also report the loss or theft to the local police and your bank.

Banks – These are generally open Monday, 1-4pm or 5pm and Tuesday to Friday, 9am-4pm or 5pm. However, opening times vary a great deal from one place to another, and from one branch to another. Some banks stay open during late-night shopping.

Time – The time in the Netherlands is usually Central European Time (GMT + 1hr).

Post offices and postal rates – Post offices are open Monday to Friday, 8.30am-5pm and Saturday, 8.30am-noon. The postage for letters and postcards is as follows:
      letters and postcards within Europe = 1.10fl
      letters to the USA = 1.60fl (0-20g)/2.80fl (20-50g)
      postcards to the UK and USA = 1.10fl.
Some post offices house telephone facilities.

Telephones – To phone abroad from the Netherlands dial:
      GB: 00 44   **Australia**: 00 61
      USA: 00 1   **Eire**: 00 353
      Canada: 00 1
followed by the area code without the 0 and subscriber's number.
Dutch dialling codes are given in **The Red Guide Benelux**. The code for Amsterdam is 020, The Hague 070, Rotterdam 010, Utrecht 030 and Maastricht 043. Telephone numbers beginning with 0800 are toll-free; those beginning with 0900 are charged at a special rate.
In the Netherlands the phone boxes are green. Public telephones take both coins (25 cent, 1fl and 2.50fl pieces) and phonecards. Phonecards, in units of 10, 25 or 50fl, are available from Primafoon (Dutch Telecom outlet), bookshops, newsagents, VVV offices, railway stations and post offices.

When calling the Netherlands from abroad, dial the international access code, followed by 31 for the Netherlands, then the area code without the first 0 and the subscriber's number.

Telecenters – Amsterdam has two telecenters (Raadhuisstraat 48 close to the Dam and a second at Schiphol airport). These centres provide facilities for making phone calls, sending telegrams, sending and receiving fax or telex messages and making photocopies. They stock stamps and telephone cards. They are open Monday to Sunday, 8am-2am.

Shops – Shops are usually open Tuesday to Saturday, 9am-6pm (they tend to close earlier on Saturday, at 5pm), and are closed on Sunday and Monday mornings (sometimes all day Monday).
In many towns there is late-night shopping on Thursday or Friday evening, when most shops stay open until 9pm. In Amsterdam and Rotterdam the large shops and department stores in the city centre are open on Sunday from 1-5pm. **Supermarkets** are open Monday to Friday, 8am-8pm, Saturday, 8am-6pm and on late-night shopping nights until 9pm. They are closed on Sunday.
GWK offices are open Monday to Saturday, 8am-8pm and Sunday, 10am-4pm.

Pharmacies – Pharmacies are open Monday to Friday, 9.30am-5.30pm; lists of chemists on call in the evening, at night or at the weekend are shown on the door.

Monuments, museums and churches – An annual **museum card** (*Museumjaarkaart*) gives entry to more than 440 museums all over the Netherlands. This can be bought at most affiliated museums, VVV offices and all Netherlands Boards of Tourism. The card costs 30fl for young people under 25 and 70fl for adults.
The **Under 26** European cultural pass gives reduced rates for museums, theatres, concerts. For further information apply to Under 26, 52 Grosvenor Gardens, London SW1W 0AG, ☎ (020) 7823 5363.
The **Nederland Museumland** guide, updated annually, lists all the museums, castles and zoos in the Netherlands. Each entry gives a brief description as well as the admission times and charges. The guide is for sale at bookshops, major museums and ANWB and VVV offices.
Details on museums and exhibitions in the Netherlands can be obtained from the following web sites:
www.hollandmuseums.nl: the museum web site of the Netherlands Tourist Board (NBT/Nederlands Bureau voor Toerisme);
www.museumland.nl: the on-line version of the *Nederland Museumland* guide (in Dutch only)
www.museumserver.nl: links to all the museums that have their own web site; includes the on-line Museumkr@nt (museum news; mainly in Dutch)
For specific opening times of monuments and museums, consult the Admission Times and Charges section of this guide.

Tipping – For hotels, restaurants and shopping, the bill is usually inclusive of service charge and VAT. For taxi fares, although the price shown on the taxi meter includes the service charge, it is customary to give an extra tip of around 10%.

Public holidays – 1 January, Good Friday, Easter Sunday and Monday, 30 April (Queen's Day or National Day), Ascension Day, Whit Sunday, Whit Monday, 5 May (Liberation Day), 25 and 26 December.
Local festivals (*see Calendar of events*) can also mean that various public facilities will be closed.

Electrical current – 220 volts AC. Plugs are two-pin.

Water – Water is generally safe to drink although mineral water is also widely available.

Accommodation

Travellers' addresses – This section, which has been added to a number of towns and cities in this guide, offers a choice of hotels in three categories to suit all budgets. Hotels have been selected for their convenient location, character or value for money. Prices are based on a double/twin room:
– The **Moderate** category includes rooms at less than 150fl (195fl for Amsterdam). These are usually small, simple hotels with a basic level of comfort.
– The **Mid-range** category covers hotels with rooms at between 195fl and 325fl with a certain amount of character.
– In the **Luxury** category we have included hotels with particular charm, offering a high degree of comfort and ensuring a memorable stay. Naturally, the cost of these hotels is in keeping with the high level of facilities provided.

Hotels – When choosing a stopover for a few hours or a few days, the current edition of *The Red Guide Benelux* is an indispensable complement to this guide. It is updated every year and offers a range of hotels and restaurants with an indication of their standard of service and comfort, their location and their prices. The prices listed are for the current year. The red symbol ⑤ indicates that the hotel is particularly pleasant or peaceful.

Towns underlined in red on the Michelin maps are listed in the current edition of *The Red Guide Benelux* with a choice of hotels and restaurants.

Visitors may also like to consult the **Michelin web site** (www.michelin-travel.com).

Booking accommodation – A wide range of accommodation can be reserved through Bookings NL, an organisation which offers an on-line booking service. Contact Bookings NL, Weteringschans 28-4, 1017 SG Amsterdam, ☎ (020) 695 59 80; Fax (020) 695 59 43; info@bookings.nl; www.bookings.nl. Please note that reservations can only be made on line. Once in the Netherlands, contact a VVV tourist office, which also offers an accommodation service.

Rented accommodation – A wide range of accommodation (bungalows, log cabins, holiday cottages, flats and apartments) from the luxurious to the rustic is available for visitors. Contact the Netherlands Board of Tourism *(see Useful addresses)* or regional VVV offices for further information. Accommodation may also be booked through the Netherlands Board of Tourism web site, www.holland.com, the ANWB web site, www.anwb.nl (in Dutch only), or through the Netherlands Reservation Centre (Nationaal Reserverings Centrum), Postbus 404, 2260 AK Leidschendam, ☎ (070) 419 55 00; Fax (070) 419 55 19; www.hotelres.nl

Youth hostels – These are open to young and old alike, who are members of their own national youth organisation or have an international card, and offer facilities for individuals, families and groups. Further information is available from Stichting Nederlandse Jeugdherberg Centrale (NJHC), Postbus 9191, 1006 AD Amsterdam ☎ (020) 551 31 55, www.njhc.nl

Camping and caravanning – Camp sites are indicated by the symbol Δ on Michelin maps 908, 210 and 211. A list of camp sites in the Netherlands is available from VVV tourist offices or from the Netherlands Board of Tourism. Information on camping in the grounds of country houses and castles is available from Vereniging Gastvrije Nederlandse Landgoederen en Kastelen LKC, Nevenlandsehof 14, 7312 EX Apeldoorn ☎ (055) 355 88 44; www.lkc.nl (in Dutch only).

Dutch camp sites are classified under the auspices of the Stichting Classificatie Kampeer-en Bungalowbedrijven. The number of stars allocated (1 to 5) refers to sanitary facilities, and the number of flags (1 to 5) concerns general and recreational facilities.

Camping in places other than official camp sites is not allowed in the Netherlands. However landowners may obtain exemptions from this law from their local councils. Many camp sites in the Netherlands have **hikers' cabins** *(trekkershut)*, which can normally accommodate four people and offer rudimentary facilities. A maximum of three nights can be spent in any one cabin during the high season. Contact the ANWB or VVV for a brochure, or book through the Nationaal Reserverings Centrum, Afdeling Trekkershutten (hikers' cabins section), Postbus 404, 2260 AK Leidschendam, ☎ (070) 419 55 251; Fax (070) 419 55 19; www.trekkershutten.nl

Bed and Breakfast – Most VVV offices have listings of families offering bed and breakfast style accommodation. Reservations can also be made through Bed & Breakfast Holland, Theophile de Bockstraat 3, 1058 TV Amsterdam, ☎ (020) 615 75 27; Fax (020) 669 15 73 (bookings only); www.bedandbreakfast.nl

Rural accommodation – Visitors interested in staying on a farm should contact **Hoeve-Logies Nederland**, Postbus 73, 2390 AB Hazerswoude-dorp, ☎/Fax (0172) 58 63 40; www.dutch-farmholidays.com. This organisation publishes a guide entitled *Natuurlijk...logeren op de boerderij*, which lists addresses of farms, B&Bs and apartments in the countryside.

Holiday villages – The ANWB publishes a guide (also at www.anwb.nl, *Bungalowwijzer*, in Dutch only) listing the addresses of holiday villages where bungalows may be rented. These are classified under the auspices of the Stichting Classificatie Kampeer- en Bungalowbedrijven. The number of stars allocated (1 to 5) refers to the level of comfort in the bungalows and the number of flags (1 to 5) to the facilities offered in the villages. Bookings may be made through the ANWB and VVV offices.

For historical background on the region see the Historical Table and Notes in the Introduction

Eating out

A wide variety of food is served in the Netherlands, from good local dishes to delicious foreign cuisine. Asia is represented particularly well, with Indonesian, Chinese, Japanese and Indian restaurants. The Dutch tend to have a hearty breakfast and eat a light lunch around 12.30pm. The evening meal is usually eaten between 6pm and 7pm.

Restaurants – The usual opening times for lunch are from 11am-2.30pm or 3pm and for dinner from 5.30-10pm or 11pm. There are some late-opening restaurants in the larger cities.

P. Hussenot/TOP

Indonesian restaurant

Travellers' addresses – The restaurants listed in the **Travellers' addresses** section of several towns and cities in this guide have been selected for their surroundings, ambience, typical dishes or unusual character. For a wider selection of restaurants and more detailed gastronomic information, consult **The Red Guide Benelux**. The red Bib Gourmand ⊛ found in the guide indicates a good meal at a reasonable price.

Neerlands Dis – The 140 restaurants of this nationwide chain are easily recognisable by their red, white and blue soup tureen emblem. They offer a selection of traditional Dutch dishes.

Tourist Menu – The restaurants displaying a blue wall plaque with a white fork serve a three course meal (starter, main course and dessert) at a reasonable price. A booklet is available from VVV offices.

Brown Cafés (Bruin café) – These traditional dark panelled bars are famous for their atmosphere, conviviality and comfort, more typical of a cosy sitting room. They are a sharp contrast to the chrome and glass designer bars popular with trendy clientele.

The **cafés** of Amsterdam and other large towns are known for the friendly atmosphere during their cocktail hour when drinks are accompanied by small cubes of cheese and the famous small hot meatballs (*Bitterballen*).

Many so-called **coffee shops** specialise in the sale and consumption of soft drugs. Those in search of tea or coffee should look instead for tearooms.

Useful addresses

Dutch Embassies and Consulates abroad

Australia: Consulate General of the Netherlands, Level 19, Bondi Junction Plaza, 500 Oxford Street, Bondi Junction NSW 2022, ☎ 02 9387 6644; Fax 02 9387 3962; www.netherlandsconsulate.org.au

Eire: Royal Netherlands Embassy, 160 Merrion Road, Dublin 4, Ireland, ☎ 01 269 3444; Fax 01 283 9690; www.netherlandsembassy.ie

New Zealand: Royal Netherlands Embassy, PO Box 840, Cnr. Ballance & Featherston Street, Wellington, ☎ 04 471 6390; Fax 04 471 2923; nlgovwel@compuserve.com; www.netherlandsembassy.co.nz

UK: Royal Netherlands Embassy, 38 Hyde Park Gate, London SW7 5DP, ☎ (020) 7590 3200; Fax (020) 7225 0947; london@netherlands-embassy.org.uk; www.netherlands-embassy.org.uk

USA: Royal Netherlands Embassy, 4200 Linnean Avenue NW, Washington, DC 20008, ☎ (202)-244-5300; Fax (202)-362-3430; www.netherlands-embassy.org

Foreign Embassies and Consulates in the Netherlands

Australia: Carnegielaan 4, 2517 KH Den Haag, ☎ (070) 310 8200; Fax (070) 310 7863; www.australian-embassy.nl

Canada: Sophialaan 7, 2500 GV Den Haag, ☎ (070) 311 1600; Fax (070) 311 1620.

Eire: Dr. Kuyperstraat 9, 2514 BA Den Haag, ☎ (070) 363 0993; Fax (070) 361 7604; www.irish.embassy.demon.nl

New Zealand: Carnegielaan 10, 2517 KH Den Haag, ☎ (070) 346 9324; Fax (070) 363 2983.

UK: Lange Voorhout 10, 2514 ED Den Haag, ☎ (070) 427 0427; Fax (070) 427 0345; www.britain.nl

USA: Lange Voorhout 102, 2514 EJ Den Haag, ☎ (070) 310 9209; Fax (070) 361 4688; www.usemb.nl. NB: for information on passports and visas, contact the American Consulate at Museumplein 19, 1071 DJ Amsterdam, ☎ (020) 575 5309.

Dutch National Tourist Offices

UK & Ireland – Netherlands Board of Tourism, 18 Buckingham Gate, London SW1 (postal address : PO Box 523, London SW1E 6NT), ☎ 0891 871 7777 (calls charged at premium rate) or (020) 7828 7900; Fax (020) 7828 7941; hollandinfo-uk@nbt.nl; www.holland.com/uk

USA – Netherlands Board of Tourism, 355 Lexington Avenue, New York, NY 10017, ☎ (212) 370 7360; Fax (212) 370 9507; go2holland@aol.com; www.holland.com

Canada – Netherlands Board of Tourism, 25 Adelaide Street East, Suite 710, Toronto, Ontario M5C 1Y2, ☎ (416) 363 1577; Fax (416) 363 1470; nbtor@aol.com; www.holland.com

Amsterdam: Netherlands Board of Tourism (NBT): Vlietweg 15, 2266 KA Leidschendam, ☎ (070) 370 57 05; Fax (070) 320 1654; www.holland.com/nl

Dutch Regional Tourist Offices

ANWB – The **ANWB** (Koninklijke Nederlandse Toeristenbond) Royal Dutch Touring Club has offices throughout the country. ANWB, Wassenaarseweg 220, 2596 EC Den Haag, ☎ (070) 314 71 47; www.anwb.nl

Tourist Information Centres – In the Netherlands the **tourist information centres** are indicated by ▯ or **VVV**, three blue V's on a white triangle. These offices supply information on a wide range of subjects, including hotels, restaurants, camp sites, rented accommodation, youth hostels, local events, cycling, sailing, sightseeing, opening hours and entertainment. They also sell tourist, cycling and walking maps and provide exchange facilities as well as a nationwide hotel reservation service. The addresses and phone numbers of the VVV offices in the main towns are given in the Admission Times and Charges section at the end of this guide (many are also listed in *The Red Guide Benelux*) and they are located on all town plans by the symbol ▯. Most VVV's are open Monday to Friday, 9am-5pm and Saturday, 10am-noon. In summer the offices in major towns are usually open for a few hours on Sundays. Information can also be obtained from the Netherlands Board of Tourism web site, www.holland.com

Disabled visitors – Most public buildings, museums, galleries and theatres provide good facilities for the disabled and the sights accessible to wheelchair users are indicated by the symbol ♿ in the Admissions Times and Charges section at the back of the guide. *The Red Guide Benelux* also indicates rooms and facilities suitable for the disabled. Further information is available from Nederlands Instituut voor Zorg en Welzijn ☎ (030) 230 66 03 and the information department for the disabled of the ANWB ☎ (070) 314 14 20. The ANWB publishes a brochure entitled *Reiswijzer voor gehandicapten* (Travel Guide for the Disabled) which provides useful information on tourism, leisure activities and sports facilities suitable for the disabled. The brochure is aimed at Dutch tourists with a disability but is also useful for foreign tourists.

The Netherlands Railways offer a comprehensive service for the disabled traveller hich includes a free escort service. The train timetables are available in braille.

Useful numbers

Dutch Directory Enquiries – ☎ 06 8008

International Directory Enquiries – ☎ 06 0418

Weather information – ☎ 0900-8003

Emergency Services – ☎ 112

Breakdown service (24hr a day) – ☎ 0800-0888

Traffic reports – ☎ 0900-8855

Public transport travel information – ☎ 0900-9292

Entertainment

Theatre, Dance and Music – The title of cultural capital goes to **Amsterdam** with its 62 museums, 60 art galleries, 32 theatres and 12 concert halls. The 1986 Muziektheater, part of the modern Stopera development in its attractive riverside setting, provides state-of-the-art facilities for the **Nederlandse Opera** and the **Nationale Ballet**. The vitality of the ballet company owes much to its founder, the Russian choreographer Sonia Gaskall, and the choreographer Hans van Manen and its repertoire consists of traditional, classical and romantic ballets. In summer musicians from the two orchestras give free lunchtime concerts. Since its resplendent refurbishment the 100-year old Concertgebouw is the perfect setting for the performances of the famous **Koninklijk Concertgebouworkest** under the baton of Riccardo Chailly. Berlage's famous Beurs building has been refurbished to serve as a cultural centre and provides a home to the **Netherlands Philharmonic** and **Chamber Orchestras**. In summer, the open-air theatre in Vondelpark is the venue for free concerts.
The Hague is home to the more contemporary culture of the **Nederlands Dans Theater** acclaimed for its adventurous performances in modern dance under the Czech-born artistic director, Jiri Kylian. The Anton Philipszaal is home to the city's **Residentie Orkest**.
The refurbished Circustheater (1904) in Scheveningen now serves as a venue for musical extravaganzas while the redecorated Schouwburg Theatre concentrates on drama. The North Sea Jazz Festival is a well known international event and welcomes as many as 1 000 musicians.
Rotterdam boasts the **Scapino Ballet** with its narrative ballet repertoire while the **Rotterdam Philharmonic** plays at the Doelen.

Tickets – Tickets for major events (concerts, theatre, sports etc) can be obtained through most VVV offices. They can also be purchased from the **Ticket Service** on ☎ 0900-300 12 50 or at **www.ticketservice.nl** (currently in Dutch only). This useful web site has three categories (theatre, concert and cinema) in which you can search by date, venue or title, and also has numerous links to cinema, theatre and concert venues all over the Netherlands.

Casinos – The official gambling palaces (Holland Casinos) offer an afternoon or evening of gambling where you can try your hand at Blackjack, Punto Banco, American or French Roulette or the jackpot machines in pleasant surroundings. There are casinos in Amsterdam, Breda, Eindhoven, Groningen, Nijmegen, Rotterdam, Scheveningen, Schiphol, Utrecht, Valkenburg and Zandvoort. Guests must be 18 years of age, carry a valid identity card and be appropriately dressed. Casinos are usually open from 1.30pm-2am. Further information is available at www.hollandcasino.nl (currently in Dutch only).

Cinemas – Most films are shown in the original version with Dutch sub-titles. In larger towns there are usually two performances (6.45pm and 9.30pm).

Festivals – In the summer months many colourful and cultural **festivals** are held *(see Calendar of Events and Travellers' addresses)*.

Leisure activities

Cycling

The Netherlands is traditionally the land of the bicycle and there is no better way to discover the country at your leisure. There are approximately 16 million bicycles in the country, outnumbering the population.

Cycle lanes and paths – The Netherlands has many special lanes and paths for cyclists (about 15.000km/9 320mi). Follow the special lanes – marked by a white bicycle on a blue sign – to be found in both towns and the countryside and you won't be bothered by other traffic. Normally cyclists are not allowed on footpaths, not even if they are only leading their bike.

Cycling rules and special signs – Keep to the right and overtake other bicycles or mopeds on the left. Other traffic must be overtaken on the right. Use clear hand signals to indicate a change of direction. It is in the interest of cyclists as well as motorists to be able to recognise the main signs:
– blue circular sign with a white bicycle: bicycles *(fietsen)* and mopeds *(bromfietsen)* must use this lane;
– rectangular sign with the mention **Fietspad** or **Rijwielpad**: an optional cycle lane for cyclists, but mopeds using their engine power are prohibited;
– sign with **Fietsers oversteken**: give way crossing point for bicycles and mopeds.

Gears are not necessary in a flat country like the Netherlands so do not be surprised if your bike has none! Many bicycles have the traditional Dutch braking system where you have to back-pedal: you push backwards on the pedals to stop the back wheel. Practice is necessary for foreigners used to doing this to change gear.

Bicycle hire – Bicycles can be hired from most railway stations (in approximately 100 stations). Look for the blue and white square sign, which indicates there is a **NS-Rijwielshop**, where train travellers can hire a bicycle for 7.50fl a day and 30fl a week. In towns there are numerous bicycle hire firms but cycle dealers and repair shops also have bicycles for hire *(fietsverhuur)*.

Parking – It is advisable to lock your bike, especially in towns, and it is preferable to leave it in a guarded cycle park.

Cycle routes – The ANWB has marked out about 250 cycle tours with an average of 40km/25mi for bicycles and mopeds. These routes are marked with blue rectangular road signs which have a white hexagonal sign with a bicycle or by hexagonal white signs with indications in red. Descriptive leaflets are available for the different routes.

The **Stichting Landelijk Fietsplatform** has waymarked over 6 000km/3 730mi of national cycle routes (**LF-routes**). These routes follow cycle paths or quieter local roads and are marked with rectangular signs with green lettering. The association publishes two main guides – one for the northern and central part of the country and the other for central and southern Netherlands and northern Flanders – and the **Fietsideeënkaart**, which lists all the recreational cycling facilities in the Netherlands. For information contact Stichting Landelijk Fietsplatform, Postbus 846, 3800 AV Amersfoort, ☎ (033) 465 36 56; Fax (033) 465 43 77; www.fietsplatform.nl (currently in Dutch only). VVV offices also provide information on local cycle routes. Mountain bike enthusiasts can explore the special network of ATB-routes.

Morand-Grahame/HOA QUI

Waymarked cycling and walking routes

Cycling events – *See Calendar of Events.* Information is available from Nederlandse Toer Fiets Unie (NTFU), Postbus 326, 3900 AH Veenendaal, ☎ (0318) 58 13 00; www.ntfu.nl (currently in Dutch only).

Rambling

Rambling is popular in the Netherlands and there are numerous annual meetings. The Four Day Walk takes place in Apeldoorn and Nijmegen *(see Calendar of Events)*, and the Tour of the Eleven Towns of Friesland leaves from Leeuwarden.

State-owned forests – Most of the forests and woods are owned by the State *(staatsbossen)* and are administered by the **Staatsbosbeheer**, a department of the Ministry of Agriculture, Nature Conservation and Fisheries. The recreational facilities provided usually include cycle paths, picnic areas and footpaths. Many trails are waymarked and differentiated by colour. Signs give the time required for each tour. Detailed information about these trails is available from: Staatsbosbeheer, Princenhof Park 1, 3972 NG Driebergen, ☎ (030) 692 61 11; Fax (030) 692 29 78.

Areas of outstanding natural beauty – The **Vereniging Natuurmonumenten** association (Postbus 9955, 1243 ZS 's-Graveland, ☎ (035) 655 99 33) can provide information and booklets on walking routes, wildlife and the landscape in these areas

(*Wandelen met Natuurmonumenten* by Harm Piek). The association also publishes a handbook, which is a useful reference for walkers (*Natuur- en wandelgebieden in Nederland*).

Long-distance footpaths – The Netherlands offers a network (total length approximately 6 000km/3 750mi) of 33 long-distance footpaths (**langeafstandswandelpaden** or LAW) of 100km/60mi or longer, waymarked in white and red. The footpaths marked in yellow and red are **streekpaden**, which are shorter walking routes (80km/50mi to 260km/160mi) and, as the name suggest, take ramblers through a particular region or specific landscape. Information is available from **Stichting Wandelplatform-LAW**, Postbus 846, 3800 AV Amersfoort, ☎ (033) 465 36 60; Fax (033) 465 43 77; www.wandelnet.nl (currently in Dutch only, with some English links).

Theme parks, fun-fairs and zoos

Over recent years theme and leisure parks have attracted a surge of interest throughout Europe. The Netherlands has its fair share of amusement parks. Not all of the parks listed below are described in the guide.

Bird watching

The wetlands (Biesbosch National Park, the Frisian Lakes), the Wadden Islands, the many low-tide mudflats and the polderlands provide a variety of ecological habitats rich in birdlife, ideal for the amateur bird-watcher. For those interested in bird watching the address to contact locally is Vogelbescherming Nederland, Driebergseweg 16c, 3708 JB Zeist, ☎ (030) 693 77 00.

Animal parks

Name	Theme	Location
Apenheul/Berg en Bos	Monkeys	Apeldoorn
Artis	Zoo	Amsterdam
Aqualutra	Otters	Leeuwarden
Avifauna	Birds	Alphen aan den Rijn
Beekse Bergen	Safari park	Hilvarenbeek
Blijdorp	Zoo	Rotterdam
Burgers' Zoo	Zoo	Arnhem
Dolfinarium	Sea-life park	Harderwijk
Sealife Scheveningen	Sea-life park	Scheveningen

Leisure parks

Name	Theme	Location
Archeon	Archaeology	Alphen aan den Rijn
Autotron	Cars	Rosmalen
Duinrell	Amusement park	Wassenaar
De Efteling	Amusement park	Kaatsheuvel
Hellendoorn	Adventure park	Hellendoorn
Land van Ooit	Amusement park	Drunen
Madurodam	Miniature town	The Hague
Six Flags Holland	Amusement park	Biddinghuizen
Slagharen	Amusement park	Slagharen

Skating

When snow lies thick on the ground and frost has set in, the many waterways and lakes are ideal for skating.

Steam trains

Tourist trains are operated between Apeldoorn and Dieren, Hoorn and Medemblik as well as Goes and Oudeland.

Sports

Water sports

The Netherlands, with its rivers, canals, waterways, broads, lakes, reservoirs and the sea, provides ample opportunities for water sports, and with their tradition of being a sea faring nation the Dutch are enthusiastic sailors. There are over 300 000 boat owners (ie approximately one boat per 50 inhabitants) and at least 950 marinas or pleasure boat harbours throughout the country. Few places are far from a navigable waterway and one of the unexpected charms of sailing in Holland is that it is possible to sail into or through many of the town centres with their networks of canals.

The most popular sailing areas are the IJsselmeer (high seas possible), the lakes bordering the IJsselmeer polders (calmer waters), the lakes of South Holland, the Utrecht lake district (Loosdrechtse and Vinkeveense) and the Frisian Lakes.

Customs formalities – On arrival and departure visiting sailors with boats over 5.4m/18ft must report to the nearest customs harbour office which will issue the necessary sailing certificate. Boats capable of travelling at more than 20kmph/12mph should be registered at a post office and have a licence. Yachts measuring 15m/50ft in length must also carry a licence. Insurance cover is compulsory with a legal liability of a minimum of 250 000fl. To use a sea-scooter you must be over 18 and have a Dutch licence to navigate.

Restrictions and regulations – Yachts with high fixed masts must look out for fixed bridges with a limited headroom and remember that some bridges only open at certain hours. Many lakes have restrictions for craft with a deep draught. There are speed limits on many waterways and some even prohibit motor boats. At movable bridges there is often a fee to pay, usually well indicated, and the bridgekeeper will lower a clog (*klomp*) for you to put the fee into.

For other regulations consult the Almanac for Water Tourism (*Wateralmanak*); Part I contains general shipping rules and regulations and Part II gives information on tide timetables, opening times of bridges and locks and facilities offered by the various marinas. These almanacs have introductions in English and are available from the ANWB and some specialised bookshops. Both the ANWB and the Netherlands Hydrographic Services (Hydrografische Dienst, Badhuisweg 169-171, 2597 JN Den Haag, ☎ (070) 316 28 01) publish **hydrographic charts** which can be purchased from ANWB and VVV offices.

Boat hire – Motor boats and sailing boats can be hired in a number of locations in Friesland. Tjalks (flat-bottomed boats), fishing smacks and clippers are also available for hire. For lists of companies chartering boats apply to the Netherlands Tourist Board, ANWB, VVV offices or Top of Holland Yachtcharter, Postbus 330, 9200 NL Drachten, ☎ (0512) 58 50 82; www.topofhollandyachtcharter.nl

Schools for sailing, windsurfing and motor-boating – Almost all resorts with water sports facilities have sailing schools. Addresses are available from ANWB and VVV offices or from Koninklijk Nederlands Watersport Verbond (*see below*).

Water skiing – This sport is subject to strict regulations and can only be practised in authorised areas. In some cases authorisation must be obtained from the local authorities.

Canoeing – The calm waterways of the Netherlands provide ideal conditions for this sport. The VVV offices can provide more information on request.

Surfing – Again the opportunities are varied. Experienced surfers will enjoy the rougher waters of the IJsselmeer or the North Sea waves. The inland waters of the Utrecht Lakes and the lakes bordering the polders are also suitable for surfing.

Boat trips – For those who prefer to take it easy there are numerous boat trips to choose from. For towns with a good canal network this is a relaxing way to sightsee and ideal for admiring all the canal houses. The following towns offer boat trips on the canals: Alkmaar, Amsterdam, Delft, Groningen, Leiden and Utrecht. Others such as Enkhuizen, Harderwijk, Kampen and Urk organise trips on the IJssel Lake while Leiden (Rhine), Maastricht (Meuse to the Belgian border), Nijmegen (Waal), Rotterdam (Rhine), Venlo (Meuse) and Zierikzee (Eastern Scheldt) propose river excursions.

Fishing – Two documents are necessary: a fishing licence (*sportvisakte*) and a permit (*vergunning*). The first is on sale in post offices, VVV offices and angling shops and associations, while the second can be obtained from the local angling associations (Hengelsportverenigingen) and angling shops – addresses of these are available from

Dior/CEDRI

The Frisian lakes

the **Nederlandse Vereniging van Sportvissersfederaties** or **NVVS** (Postbus 288, 3800 AG Amersfoort, ☎ (033) 463 49 24; www.nvvs.org (currently in Dutch only). Local information on fishing facilities is available from the VVV offices.

Useful addresses – **Koninklijk Nederlands Watersport Verbond** (KNWB; Water sports Federation), Postbus 87, 3980 CB Bunnik, ☎ (030) 656 65 50; www.knwv.nl (currently in Dutch only); **ANWB vakgroep Watersport** (Water sports Section), Wassenaarseweg 220, 2596 EC Den Haag, ☎ (070) 314 71 47; www.watersportnet.nl (currently in Dutch only).

GOLF

The Michelin maps 210, 211 and 408 locate the country's golf courses, many of which welcome visitors. The Dutch Golf Federation's headquarters are at: Nederlandse Golf Federatie, Rijnzathe 8, 3454 PV De Meern, ☎ (030) 662 18 88.

Further reading

History

Dutch Revolt – Geoffrey Parker (Penguin Books 1990)

Amsterdam – Geert Mak, Philipp Blom (Trans) (Harvill Press 1999)

The Netherlands: Revolt and Independence, 1550-1650 – Martyn Rady (Hodder & Stoughton Educational 1990)

A Bridge Too Far – Cornelius Ryan (Wordsworth Editions Ltd 1999)

Arnhem – Christopher Hibbert (The Windrush Press 1998)

The Diary of a Young Girl – Anne Frank, Otto Frank (Ed), Mirjam Pressler (Ed), Susan Massotty (Trans) (Penguin Books 1997)

The Battle of the Bulge – Charles B MacDonald (Phoenix Press 1998)

Patriots and Liberators – Simon Schama (Fontana 1992)

The Embarrassment of Riches: An Interpretation of Dutch Culture in the Golden Age – Simon Schama (Fontana 1988)

Travel

Through the Dutch and Belgian Canals – P Bristow (A & C Black)

Of Dutch Ways – H Colijn (Harper & Row)

Holland – A Hopkins (Faber & Faber)

Art and architecture

Mondrian – John Milner (Phaidon Press 1994)

Vincent: the Complete Self Portraits – Bernard Denvir (Courage Books 1997)

From Rembrandt to Vermeer – Jane Turner (Ed) (Macmillan Reference Books 2000)

Rembrandt – Michael Kitson (Phaidon Press 1992)

The Paintings of Willem Van De Veldes – MS Robinson (Philip Wilson Publishers 1990)

From Van Eyck to Brueghel (Phaidon Press 1998)

Dutch Painting – Christopher Brown (Phaidon Press 1993)

Dutch Painting – RH Fuchs (Thames and Hudson 1978)

Dawn of the Golden Age : Northern Netherlandish Art 1580-1620 – Ger Luijten, Ariane Van Suchtelen, Reinier Baarsen (Rijksmuseum 1994)

Dutch Art – Sheila D Muller (Ed) (Garland Publishing Inc 1994)

Rembrandt's Eyes – Simon Schama (The Penguin Press 1999)

De Stijl 1917-1931: The Dutch Contribution to Modern Art – HLC Jaffe (Harvard University Press 1986)

Fiction

Headlong – Michael Frayn (Faber Paperbacks 2000)

Tulip Fever – Deborah Moggach (Heinemann 1999)

Girl with a Pearl Earring – Tracy Chevalier (HarperCollins 1999)

An Empty House – Marga Minco (Peter Owen 1986)

The Black Tulip – Alexandre Dumas, David Coward (Ed), Franz Demmler (Trans) (Oxford Paperbacks 2000)

The Assault – Harry Mulisch, Claire White (Trans) (Random House 1986)

The Two Hearts of Kwasi Boachi – Arthur Japin, Ina Rilke (Trans) (Chatto & Windus 2000)

Calendar of events

Listed below are the most important of the many festivals held in the Netherlands; others are mentioned in the descriptions of towns and cities in the alphabetical section of the guide.

A detailed calendar of festivals appears in leaflets produced annually by the VVV (tourist information centre) and any further information and phone numbers can be obtained from VVV offices.

January-February
Rotterdam .... International Film Festival

In February or March during Lent
Breda .... Carnival★
Bergen op Zoom .... Carnival
Eindhoven .... Carnival
Venlo .... Carnival
's-Hertogenbosch .... Carnival
Maastricht .... Carnival★
Sittard .... Carnival

March
Maastricht .... The European Fine Art Fair★★, ☎ (073) 614 51 65

1 April
Brielle .... Historical Festival

Last Saturday in April
Noordwijk-Haarlem .... Procession of floral floats

Mid April to mid September
Alkmaar .... Cheese Market★★

May to late September, Sundays
Tegelen .... Passion Plays *(2005; every five years)*

Late May (around Ascension Day)
Breda .... Jazz Festival

Saturday before Whitsun
Exloo .... Shepherds' Feast

Whitsun
Utrecht .... *Stoom*

May/June
Scheveningen .... Sand sculpture festival

June
Amsterdam .... Holland Festival★ (concerts, opera, ballet, theatre). To reserve apply to: Holland Festival, Kleine Gartmanplantsoen 21, 1071 RP Amsterdam; ☎ (020) 530 71 10 or to large travel agencies abroad

The Hague .... Pasar Malam Besar (Indonesian market)

Terschelling .... *Oerolfestival*

Tilburg .... Festival Mundial

Late June to late August, Thursdays
Schagen .... Market *(West-Friese Marktdagen)*

July
Haarlem .... International Organ Festival *(every other year: 2002)*, ☎ (023) 516 05 74

Den Helder .... National Navy Days *(Vlootdagen)*

Kerkrade .... International Music Competition *(2001: every four years)*

Leiden .... Leiden Drapers' Festival

Nijmegen .... International 4-day walking event *(Wandelvierdaagse)*

Rotterdam .... Summer Carnival (street parade)

Tilburg .... Kirmess: fair to celebrate local patron saint's day

Second weekend in July
The Hague .... North Sea Jazz Festival, ☎ (015) 214 89 00

Third Sunday in July
Exloo .... International Festival of Ancient Handicrafts

July-August (2 weeks)
Frisian Lakes .... Regattas: *Skûtsjesilen*

July and August, Wednesdays
Edam .... Cheese Market

July and August, Saturday afternoons
Kinderdijk .... Windmill Days

A floral float in the procession

Early August
Sneek .... Sneekweek Regattas

3rd Saturday in August
Rijnsburg-Noordwijk 908 E 5 Procession of floral floats

Mid August
Yerseke .... Mussel Day

Late August
Maastricht .... *Preuvenemint* (Burgundian Food Festival)
Harlingen .... Fishing Days

Late August-early September
Breda .... Nationale Taptoe: military tattoo
Utrecht .... Holland Festival of Ancient Music★, ☎ (030) 236 22 36

1st Saturday in September
Aalsmeer .... Procession of floral floats

1st Sunday in September
Zundert 908 E 7 .... Procession of floral floats

Early September
Rotterdam .... *Wereldhavenfestival* (festival celebrating the port)

2nd weekend in September
Tiel .... Fruit Parade

3rd Tuesday in September
The Hague .... State Opening of Parliament: the Queen arrives in a golden coach

4th Wednesday in September
Odoorn .... Sheep market

Late September
Utrecht .... Netherlands Film Festival (*Golden Calf award*)

35

Celebrations for
the Queen's birthday

3 October (following Monday if the 3rd is a Sunday)
Leiden .... Leidens Ontzet: historical procession

1st Wednesday in October
Leeuwarden .... Show of prize Frisian bulls

3rd Saturday before 5 December
Amsterdam .... St Nicholas' official arrival *(Prins Hendrikkade)*

From 1st Sunday of Advent to 1 January
Denekamp, Ootmarsum ..... Blowing of midwinter horns

Nationwide events

National Museum Weekend 3rd weekend in April
**Queen's Birthday
Celebrations** .... 30 April (on 29 April if 30th is a Sunday)
National Mill and Cycle Day 2nd Saturday in May
Open Monument Day .... 2nd weekend in September

Skûtsjes regatta

Sports Competitions

Automobile and motorcycle races – The Dutch Grand Prix takes place in Assen on the last weekend in June.
Cross-country motorcycling is very popular and races on ice are held in ice skating rinks.

Cycling events – The Regional Cycle Day is held every year on the second Saturday in May. The tour of 11 Friesland towns (depart from Bolsward) is held Whit Monday; Drenthe's 4-Day Cycling Event (Rijwielvierdaagse) is held in late July and Nijmegen's 4-Day Event in early August.

Water sports competition – Across the country different water sports activities are held throughout the summer. The most spectacular are the **skûtsjesilen**, *skûtsjes* regattas on the Frisian Lakes (late July). Among the other activities are Delta Week (Zierikzee) in late June and early July and Sneekweek in early August.

Walking – A 4-Day Walking Event takes place in Nijmegen (3rd or 4th week in July). The Frisian 11-Town Walking Event (late May) lasts five days (depart from Leeuwarden). The **6-day event** from Hoek van Holland to Den Helder is held in July.

Traditional sports – *See also Introduction, Traditions and folklore.* Archers processions *(boogschieten)* are held on the second Sunday in July in many towns in the Limburg province as part of the **Oud Limburgs Schuttersfeest**. Those who like ball games can watch **kaatswedstrijden** held in Frisian villages (May to September); the most important meet is held in Franeker on the fifth Wednesday in July. Annual pole vaulting championships *(fierljeppen)* are held in Friesland in late August.

Other events – The **Amstel Gold Race**, an international cycle race leaving from and returning to Maastricht, is held in April. The **Rotterdam Marathon** follows a course through the city centre in late April.

Help us in our constant task of keeping up-to-date.
Send us your comments and suggestions to

Michelin Travel Publications
38 Clarendon Road
Watford
Herts WD1 1SX
England
Tel. 01923 415 000
Fax 01923 415 250
TheGreenGuide-uk @ uk.michelin.com
www.michelin-travel.com

Glossary

Common words

NB: for restaurant terminology, consult the current edition of The Red Guide Benelux.

U	you	goedemorgen	good morning
mijnheer	Mr	goedemiddag	good afternoon
mevrouw	Mrs, Ms	goedenavond	good evening
juffrouw	Miss	tot ziens	goodbye
rechts	right	alstublieft	please
links	left	dank u (wel)	thank you (very much)
ja	yes	nee	no
postkantoor	post office	postzegel	postage stamp
hoeveel/		wat? waar?	what? where?
wat kost dit?	how much?	en BTW	and VAT
inclusief bediening	service included	ziekenhuis	hospital
apotheek	pharmacy		

Numbers

een	one	zes	six
twee	two	zeven	seven
drie	three	acht	eight
vier	four	negen	nine
vijf	five	tien	ten

Towns and provinces

's-Gravenhage, Den Haag	The Hague	Leiden	Leyden
Noord-Brabant	North Brabant	Vlissingen	Flushing
Noord-Holland	North Holland	Zuid-Holland	South Holland

Road vocabulary

autosnelweg	motorway	parkeerschijf	parking disk
doorgaand verkeer	through traffic	verplicht	obligatory
eenrichtings-		richting	direction
verkeer	one-way street	uitrit	exit
inhaalverbod	no overtaking	verboden	prohibited
knooppunt	junction	verboden toegang	no entry
let op! gevaar!	caution! danger!	voorrang geven	give way
niet parkeren	no parking	werk in uitvoering	roadworks
omleiding	diversion	zachte berm	soft verge
overstekende wielrijders	cyclists path crossing		

Tourist vocabulary

abdij	abbey	Onze Lieve Vrouwe	Our Lady
begraafplaats	cemetery	oost	east
berg	mountain, hill	opengesteld	open, accessible
Beurs	stock exchange	orgel	organ
bezienswaardigheid	sight	oud	old
bezoek	visit	oudheidkamer	antiquities (museum)
boerderij	farm	paleis	palace
boot	boat	plas	lake
brug	bridge	plein	square
dam	dam	poort	gate (to town)
dierenpark	zoo	raadhuis	town hall
dijk	dike	rederij	shipping company
duin	dune	Rijks-	of the State
eiland	island	rondvaart	boat trip
gasthuis	hospice, old hospital	scheepvaart	navigation
		schilderij	painting, picture
gemeentehuis	town hall	schouwburg	theatre
gracht	canal (in town)	singel	ring canal
groot, grote	great	slot	castle, fortress
grot	grotto, cave	sluis	lock
gulden	florin	stad	town
haven	harbour, port	stadhuis	town hall
heilige	saint	state	castle (in Friesland)
heuvel	hill		

hof	court, palace	*stedelijk*	municipal
hofje	almshouse	*straat*	street
ingang	entrance	*tegel*	earthenware
jachthaven	pleasure boat		tile
	harbour	*tentoonstelling*	exhibition
kaai, kade	quay	*toegang*	entrance
kasteel	castle	*tuin*	garden
kerk	church	*uitgang*	exit
kerkhof	churchyard	*veer*	ferryboat
kerkschat	treasury	*vest*	rampart
klooster	convent	*vogel*	bird
koninklijk	royal	*vuurtoren*	lighthouse
markt	market, main square	*waag*	weigh house
meer	lake	*wal*	rampart
molen	(wind) mill	*wandeling*	walking tour
museum	museum	*weg*	path, road
natuurreservaat	nature reserve	*west*	west
noord	north	*zee*	sea
		zuid	south

Introduction

Description of the country

The area of the Netherlands, which includes huge stretches of water such as IJsselmeer and the Waddenzee, is 41 863km²/16 163sq mi, of which 9 896km²/3 820sq mi is reclaimed land. The longest distance from one end of the country to the other is 310km/193mi, ie from Rottum Island in the north of the province of Groningen to the south of Limburg. The Netherlands has a total population of 15 863 950 (2000 census). With a density of 465 persons per km² or 1 187 per sq mi, it is one of the most densely populated countries in the world (the United Kingdom, by comparison, has a density of 236 per km² or 612 per sq mi). The population distribution is very uneven, and the highest densities are in the provinces of Noord- and Zuid-Holland. Together with the province of Utrecht these form the **Randstad**, a large conurbation encompassing the country's four main cities: Amsterdam, The Hague, Rotterdam and Utrecht.

Agriculture in the Netherlands is highly intensive and productive, but represents only a small percentage of the gross national product. Stock-raising is well suited to the fertile reclaimed areas. Industry, especially chemicals, metallurgy and food processing, is concentrated within the Randstad area, the Twente, Noord-Brabant and Limburg. The Netherlands relies heavily on imported raw materials and the export of its manufactured goods. Because of its privileged geographical location trade, especially goods in transit between Europe and the rest of the world, plays an important role in the Dutch economy.

Holland and the Netherlands – Over the years the name **Holland** has come to designate the whole of the Netherlands. In fact, this old province, separated since 1840 into Noord-Holland and Zuid-Holland, supplanted the other regions of the United Provinces in the 17C due to its economic prosperity and political supremacy. Napoleon I ratified the primacy of Holland by creating the short-lived kingdom of Holland in 1810. In fact, as early as the late Middle Ages the plains stretching from Friesland to Flanders were called **Lage Landen** or **Nederlanden** (Low Countries). In 1581 the United Provinces of the Netherlands (Verenigde Provinciën der Nederlanden) came into being. In 1815 this was still the name used when William I became ruler of the kingdom, which included part of Belgium. The name has remained unchanged – Netherlands – despite the secession of Belgium in 1830, and Queen Beatrix has the title of Queen of the Netherlands (Koningin der Nederlanden). The country now has 12 provinces.

Climate – A cloudy sky pierced by a few timid rays of sunshine or a misty horizon are typical of the climate, and were beautifully captured by the landscape artists of the 17C. The oceanic climate is humid and cool. An average of 750mm/30in of rain falls each year, spread over more than 200 days. The temperature is fairly cool in summer without being too harsh in winter. Winters are warmer than in the past, as proved by Avercamp's delightful 17C skating scenes; in 1795, too, the town of Den Helder fell after the French took advantage of the fact that the Dutch fleet was frozen into the ice. The westerly winds are often strong, and many of the farmhouses are protected by a screen of poplar trees.

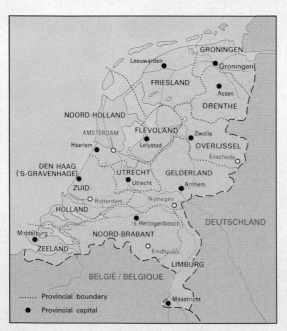

Provincial boundary
● Provincial capital

A "LOW COUNTRY"

The name Netherlands, from the Dutch *Neder-land*, is very apt (*neder* = low, *land* = country). The sea is a constant threat, since more than one third of the country is below sea level. Without the protection of dunes and dikes more than half the country would be under water during surge tides or when the rivers are in spate. The lowest point, 6.5m/21ft below sea level, is at Alexanderpolder, near Rotterdam.

There is a marked difference between east and west. The west of the country is a low-lying plain with an average altitude of less than 5m/16ft. This is the most densely populated area. In the east, on the other hand, the Veluwe Hills rise to a height of 106m/348ft at Zijpenberg to the northeast of Arnhem, and **Drielanden-punt** (321m/1 053ft), at the junction of the Dutch, Belgian and German frontiers, is the highest point. The Netherlands represents a depressed area of the earth's crust which has subsequently been infilled by alluvial deposits from the rivers and depositions from the sea.

A land of water – The land above sea level represents only five sixths of the total area. The country is criss-crossed by a network of rivers, whose estuaries form an immense delta. In addition, the large freshwater lake, the IJs-selmeer, created by the Zuiderzee Project, covers an area of 120 000ha/ 296 400 acres. Elsewhere

ALTITUDE

Over 20 m/66 ft/

5 to 20 m/16 to 66 ft/

Under 5 m/16 ft/

Below sea level

ponds, small lakes, canals, streams and ditches abound, especially in Friesland, whose flag has water lily leaves as its emblem. The percentage of land above sea level increases with the altitude from west to east. In the east the land is relatively well drained, while water tends to accumulate in the low-lying plains and polders of the west.

LANDSCAPE

Apart from a few hilly regions, the Netherlands consists of an immense plain with little diversity of soil, resulting in a corresponding lack of variety in the landscape. The polder lands are the result of man's determined intervention throughout the ages, but they also give a somewhat monotonous appearance to the countryside. However, they are one of the quintessential aspects of the country and their peacefulness, light and colour give the landscape a poetic dimension.

Vast sandy tracts – Sand covers 43% of the land with the main areas in the south and the east, notably the Kempenland of Noord-Brabant, which is a continuation of the Belgian Kempenland, the **Veluwe** and the north of the provinces of Overijssel and Drenthe. In addition to agricultural land there are moorlands of heather, broom and gorse and forests (in the **vicinity of Breda** and the the Veluwe, with its pines). The great Scandinavian glaciers left tracts of **morainic material** with their telltale erratics in the undulating Utrechtse Heuvelrug and the Veluwe. The glaciers were also responsible for deflecting the course of the Rhine and Maas rivers westwards.

There are several areas of **marshland** (De Peel and Biesbosch) and lakes, for example in the south of Friesland. Unlike those in the province of Holland, these have not been reclaimed due to the infertility of their sandy soil.

Dunes – Coastal currents have caused offshore sand bars to form along the coast. The coastal **sand dunes** are of the utmost importance, as they provide protection against the high tides. Marram grass is planted to stabilise the dunes, which are carefully monitored by local authorities. Public access is restricted in certain sectors to prevent further erosion and damage to this fragile ecosystem. In some cases the chain of dunes is strengthened by a dike. The dunes also act as reservoirs for the rainwater which then filters down to the water table. The vast sandy beaches beyond the dunes and dikes are a valuable asset for the local seaside resorts.

In the north the Wadden Islands form an important offshore barrier. They are lashed on the north and west by the waves of the North Sea, with the calmer waters of the Waddenzee on the landward side.

Alluvial deposits – Marine deposited clays cover 28% of the country, especially in the Delta area, around the great coastal estuaries and bays, and in those which have been reclaimed as polders such as the Lauwerszee and the Middelzee, which once reached as far inland as Leeuwarden. The **fluvial clays** which cover 10% of the Netherlands are associated with the many rivers in the centre of the country and the Maas Valley, to the south of Venlo.

Peat bogs – In the Netherlands there are two types of peat bog. The first has formed in the lagoons on top of marine sediments. Once the peat was extracted, lakes then formed which were drained and used for agricultural purposes. In the upland region peat formed in the marshy areas; here again it was used for fuel and the land was then given over to agriculture. The provinces of Groningen and Drenthe were known for the peat colonies *(veenkoloniën)* which flourished from the 16C to 19C.

Limestone plateau – The limestone landscapes of southern Limburg provide a sharp contrast to the rest of the country. Some parts of the bedrock are silt-covered (loess), as in the Hesbaye region of Belgium, while others appear as rocky outcrops more akin to the ancient (Hercynian) Ardennes Massif, again in Belgium.

All mining activity has now ceased in the Limburg coalfields, which are a continuation of the coal seams of Kempenland in Belgium.

THE FIGHT AGAINST THE SEA

The history of the Netherlands tells of man's continuous struggle with the elements, against the sea, storm surges and rivers in spate. The first dunes were formed to the south of Haarlem around 5 BC, and by AD 1000 a sand bar stretched from the Scheldt to the Eems. The bar was breached at several points, creating the chain of islands now known as the Wadden Islands, and the sea inundated the peat bogs lying inland to form the **Waddenzee**.

First steps: terps and dikes – Around 500 BC the **Frisians**, the earliest inhabitants of the coastal areas, were already engaged in their struggle with the sea. They built artificial mounds or **terps** to protect their settlements from the encroaching water. As early as AD 1200 they were building dikes and had drained a few areas of land – the very first polders – between Leeuwarden and Sneek. During the 13C there were at least 35 great floods, and large tracts of land were inundated, creating the Dollard and **Lauwerszee** in the north and the **Zuiderzee**, now IJsselmeer, in 1287.

Windmills: the first polders – In the 14C **windmills** were being used to drain lakes and marshes. By the 15C the rivers of Zeeland had already carved out an intricate network of peninsulas and islands, and the coastal dunes were crumbling under the assaults of the waves. The overall lack of protection was responsible for the catastrophic **St Elizabeth Flood** in 1421. Following this disaster, windmills were increasingly used in the threatened low-lying areas. Thus in Noord-Holland small **polders** appeared in Schagen in 1456 and in Alkmaar in 1564. Many of the coastal dikes of the time were the work of **Andries Vierlingh** (1507-79).

17C: a series of polders – In the 17C, much of the draining of inland tracts of water was carried out by **Jan Adriaenszoon Leeghwater** (his name means low water). Leeghwater supervised the successful draining of the **Beemstermeer** to the north of Amsterdam in 1612 with the help of 40 windmills. *(The Beemsterpolder has been inscribed on the UNESCO World Heritage List since 1999.)* The success of this initial project encouraged the Dutch to continue reclamation work, and they built the polders of **Purmer** in 1622 and **Wormer** in 1626. In 1631 the town of Alkmaar started reclaiming the **Schermermeer** in accordance with Leeghwater's instructions. This time 50 windmills were used and the work was completed in 1635. Another of Leeghwater's projects (never completed) was the draining of Haarlem Lake. As early as 1667, Hendrik Stevin proposed a project to drain the Zuiderzee "to evacuate the violence and poison of the North Sea". The project was only completed in the 20C. In the 18C autonomous water boards **(waterschappen)** were invested with the responsibility for building, maintaining and monitoring the country's dikes, canals and locks. These bodies still exist, but today they fall under the authority of the **Ministry of Transport and Waterways**. Steam power was introduced just before 1800, and this proved capable of pumping water over high dikes, thus replacing several rows or gangs of windmills. Pumping operations no longer depended on the vagaries of wind power.

The ambitious projects of the 19C and 20C – The most spectacular period of land reclamation began in 1848 with the draining of **Haarlem Lake** which was completed four years later. Three large pumping stations were built, including that of Cruquius, which has now been converted into a museum *(see HAARLEM, Outskirts)*.

After the great floods of 1916 it was the turn of the Zuiderzee itself. This great arm of the sea was closed off by the barrier dam or **Afsluitdijk** in 1932, creating the outer Waddenzee and an inland freshwater lake now known as the IJsselmeer. Once enclosed, work began on draining several polders around the edge (Wieringermeer, Noordoost, Zuidelijk Flevoland and Oostelijk Flevoland). The fifth polder **(Markerwaard)** was abandoned in 1986.

N.A.P.

PUMPING STATION

MINOR CANAL

POLDER

RING DIKE

The N.A.P. (Normaal Amsterdams Peil) or "Normal Amsterdam Level" was created in the 17C as a reference measurement against which to calculate sea level in the Netherlands and Europe.

THE FIGHT AGAINST THE SEA

■ Polders: 14-18C   ■ Polders: 19C to the present   〰 Dike: coastal or fluvial

Other polders reclaimed in the 19C and 20C are the Prins Alexander Polder (1872) near Rotterdam and the Lauwersmeer Polder.

The most recent disaster occurred during the night of 31 January 1953, when gale force winds swept landwards at high tide. 1 865 people died and 260 000ha/642 200 acres were inundated. The success of the Zuiderzee Project encouraged engineers to find a similar way of protecting the islands of Noord- and Zuid-Holland. The outcome was the **Delta Plan** *(see DELTA)*, work on which began in 1954. This vast project was not completed until 1998, with the building of the storm surge barrier in the Nieuwe Waterweg.

Conquering the sea – Since the 13C about 7 050km²/2 745sq mi have been reclaimed from the sea. Coastal dikes have been responsible for creating 4 000km²/2 400sq mi, the IJsselmeer for another 1 650km²/644sq mi and a further 1 400km²/546sq mi has been reclaimed by other means.

However, at the dawn of the 21C, some parts of the Dutch landscape may undergo a radical change. New EU farming regulations, the surplus of floral and market garden products, and the critical level of pollution – partly caused by large-scale pig breeding – led the Dutch government to pass a bill in 1993 stipulating that one tenth of arable land should be left fallow.

NATURE CONSERVATION

In this highly industrialised and densely populated country, certain groups are very active in the protection of the environment. The Nature Conservation Society (Vereniging Natuurmonumenten) is a private organisation which acquires and preserves unspoilt coastal and rural areas. The Society currently manages more than 300 nature reserves **(natuurmonumenten)** covering a total area of 78 000ha/192 700 acres of varied habitats, including woodlands, moors, dunes and marshes. In general visitors are welcome to the reserves, and some have visitor centres, nature trails and bird hides, but there are usually restrictions *(see also Practical Information)*. There are also 84 national heritage sites and 13 National Parks. State-owned forests and woodlands are managed by the Forestry Commission (Staatsbosbeheer). Recreation is encouraged and the facilities include picnic sites, nature trails and camp sites.

Birds

The great variety of habitats provided by the Netherlands' seasides, hills, waters and woodlands attracts many bird species, both native and migratory *(illustrations: see WADDENEILANDEN)*.

One of the most common species is the **lapwing** with its plaintive "pee-wit" cry, which is almost considered the national bird. This plump little bird is about 30cm/12in in length, with lustrous bronze plumage, and prefers grassy areas, especially in Friesland. Its eggs are considered a delicacy, but plans are afoot for a ban on their sale, and Queen Juliana ended the tradition whereby the first lapwing's egg to be found each year is given to the queen.

The seashores are home to **terns**, **seagulls** and other **gulls**, particularly the black-headed gulls, which often nest inland. Colonies of **oyster catchers**, a small black and white wader, nest along the shores while the **grey heron** can be seen along the canals. The **spoonbill** is rarer but can be seen in shallow estuaries, while the **whlte stork** is protected to prevent its extinction.

All sorts of **ducks** abound in the canals, ponds and marshes: the wild duck or mallard and the sheldrake with multicoloured plumage are the most common.

The country's numerous **nature reserves** provide protection for a variety of species and their coastal and inland habitats. The reserves provide safe breeding and feeding grounds and facilities for scientific study. Public access is limited and usually prohibited during the breeding season (April to August).

Historical table and notes

Prehistory

30000 BC	Earliest traces of human settlement in the east of the country.
4500	Agriculturists settle in Limburg; their pottery belongs to the Spiral Meander Ware culture.
3000-2000	The megalithic Hunebed culture flourishes in the Drenthe area.
2200	A nomadic people settles to the north of the great rivers; stroke ornamented pottery ware.
2000	Bell-Beaker civilisation, notably in the Drenthe. New settlements in the alluvial areas of the delta.
1900	Bronze Age. The dead are buried in burial mounds.
800	In the east the people incinerate their dead and bury them in urnfields.
750-400	First Iron Age: Hallstatt Period.
500	First **terps** are built in Friesland and the Groningen area *(see LEEUWARDEN, Terp Region)*
450	South of the Great rivers, Second Iron Age: La Tène Period.
300	Germanic and Celtic tribes arrive in the area south of the Rhine.

Romans – Vikings

57-51	South of the Rhine, **Caesar** defeats the Menapii and Eburones, Celtic tribes belonging to the Roman province of Gallia Belgica.
12	The Germanic tribe the **Batavi** settle the banks of the great rivers.
AD 69-70	Batavian uprising against the Roman garrisons.
3C	Incursions by Germanic tribes: the **Franks** settle the banks of the Rhine. At this time the main tribes occupying the territory are the Franks, **Saxons** and **Frisians**.
Late 3C	The area south of the Rhine belongs to the Roman province of Germania Secunda (capital: Cologne).
4C	Power struggle between the Salian Franks and the Romans.
382	St Servatius transfers his bishopric from Tongeren to Maastricht and the region's gradual conversion to Christianity begins.
Early 6C	The Merovingian kingdom under Clovis (465-511) extends from the north of Gaul to the Rhine.
561	The Merovingian kingdom is divided into Neustria (west of the river Scheldt) and Austrasia (east of the Scheldt; the present Netherlands).
Late 7C	The Northumbrian missionary **Willibrord** evangelises Friesland.
800	**Charlemagne** is crowned Emperor of the West, a territory which covers the whole of the country and is centred on Aachen.
834	First of the **Viking** raids at Dorestad *(see AMERSFOORT, The Woodlands and Heathlands of the Utrechtse Heuvelrug).*
843	**Treaty of Verdun.** The Carolingian Empire is divided into three kingdoms: Germania, Francia and, between the two, a Middle Kingdom stretching from the North Sea to the Mediterranean and including the present-day Netherlands. The Middle Kingdom (Lotharingia) was short-lived and Lothair II received only the northern part.
879-882	Viking invasions: from their base in Utrecht they make raids into the surrounding countryside.
925	The German King Henry I, the Fowler, annexes **Lotharingia**.
959	Lotharingia is divided into Upper Lotharingia (Lorraine) and Lower Lotharingia, covering nearly all the present country.

Counties and Duchies

10C	Bishop Balderic (919-76) extends the **See of Utrecht**.
Early 11C	The **Duchy of Brabant** is founded by Lambert, Count of Leuven.
11C	Creation of the county of Gelderland.
Late 11C	The county of **Holland** is extended at the expense of the county of Flanders (in Zeeland) and the See of Utrecht.
Early 13C	Zutphen and Veluwe become part of the county of Gelderland.
Late 13C	**Floris V**, Count of Holland conquers West Friesland.

1323	Zeeland passes from Flanders to Holland.
1350	Start of the civil war between the **Hooks** (*Hoeken* – backed by Margaret of Bavaria) and the **Cods** (*Kabbeljauwen* – backed by her son William V).

Consolidation of Burgundian power

Late 14C	The Duchy of Burgundy is extended northwards when **Philip the Bold** acquires Limburg and certain rights over Brabant.
1428	Philip the Good deposes **Jacoba** and makes himself ruler of Holland and Zeeland.
1473	**Charles the Bold** acquires Gelderland; the only territory not in Burgundian hands is Friesland.

The Habsburgs

1477	Death of Charles the Bold; his daughter and heir Mary of Burgundy marries Maximilian of Austria, one of the Habsburgs.
	Mary is forced to sign the Great Privilege, a charter conferring far-reaching local powers.
1494	Philip the Fair, their son, inherits the Low Countries when Maximilian is elected Holy Roman Emperor.
1515	Charles I of Spain, son of Philip the Fair, inherits the Low Countries. In 1516 he becomes King of Spain, and then in 1519 Emperor of Germany as **Charles V**. He adds **Friesland** to the Low Countries in 1523; the See of Utrecht in 1527; Overijssel in 1528; and takes Groningen and Drenthe by force in 1536.
1543	The Duke of Gelderland cedes his dukedom to Charles V, who thus rules over nearly the whole of Europe.
1548	Charles V groups the 17 provinces of the Low Countries and the Franche-Comté into the independent Burgundian Kreis.

The Spanish Netherlands

1555	Charles V abdicates his claim to the Low Countries in favour of his son Philip II, soon to become King of Spain.
1555-79	The **Revolt of the Netherlands**; the rise of Protestantism.
1566	The **Breda Compromise** also known as the Compromise of the Nobility; the Beggars protest against the Inquisition *(see BREDA)*.
	The **Iconoclasm**, involving riots and destruction of Church property.
1567	The Duke of Alba is appointed Governor of the Low Countries.
1568	**William the Silent** raises an army; beginning of the Eighty Years' War.
1572	**Capture of Brielle** by the Sea Beggars *(see BRIELLE)*; Vlissingen and Enkhuizen follow.
1579	**Union of Arras** is signed by Catholic Hainaut, Artois and Douai, pledging allegiance to Philip; in reply the northern Protestant provinces form an essentially military alliance and sign the **Union of Utrecht**.

William the Silent (detail of a stained glass window in St.-Janskerk, Gouda)

The United Provinces

1581	Creation of the **Republic of the Seven United Provinces**, a federation of seven provinces, independent of Spanish rule; Philip II is deposed.
1584	William the Silent is assassinated in Delft.
1585	His second son, Maurice of Nassau, succeeds his father as Stadtholder of Holland and Zeeland. He becomes undisputed leader of the United Provinces in 1618 on the death of his elder brother.
1596	Cornelis de Houtman establishes trading relations with Java.
1598	Edict of Nantes.
1602	**Dutch East India Company** founded to trade with Asia.
1609-21	**Twelve Years' Truce** with Spain. Henry Hudson sails up the American river later named after him in his ship the *Half Moon*, while on a voyage for the Dutch East India Company.
1614	The name New Netherland is first used for the colony founded in the New World.
1618	**Synod of Dort**. Reprobation of the Remonstrants.
1619	Founding of **Batavia** (Jakarta) in the Dutch East Indies.
1620	The Pilgrim Fathers arrive on the **Mayflower** and establish Plymouth Colony.
1621	Founding of the **Dutch West India Company** to trade with America. Renewal of hostilities with Spain.
1624-54	Colonisation of northeast Brazil.
1625	The Dutch trading post on Manhattan Island is called Nieuw Amsterdam.
1626	Peter Minuit of the Dutch West India Company buys Manhattan from the Indians for the equivalent of $24.
1634	Dutch West India Company establishes a trading post in Curaçao in the Antilles.
1648	Treaty of Westphalia ends the Thirty Years' War, also called the Eighty Years' War. In the **Peace of Münster** Philip IV of Spain recognises the independence of the United Provinces.
1651	The English Navigation Act augurs ill for Dutch trade.
1652	Jan van Riebeeck founds the Cape Colony.
1652-54	**First Anglo-Dutch War**: commercial and colonial rivalry lead to what is essentially a war at sea; the Dutch fleet is commanded by Admiral Tromp *(see BRIELLE)*.
1653-72	Stadtholderless Period: the statesman **Johan de Witt** *(see DORDRECHT)* governs as Grand Pensionary.
1658-1795	Colonisation of Ceylon (Sri Lanka).
1664	The English seize New Netherland and rename its capital New York after the Duke of York, later James II.
1665-67	**Second Anglo-Dutch War**. Admiral de Ruyter earns distinction as commander of the Dutch fleet. Under the **Treaty of Breda**, Dutch Guiana (Surinam) is ceded to the Dutch in exchange for control of New Netherland.
1667-68	War of Devolution led by Louis XIV; Treaty of Aachen.
1672	**William III** becomes Stadtholder of Holland and Zeeland.
1677	William marries Mary, the daughter of James II.
1672-78	War with France.
1678-79	**Peace of Nijmegen**
1685	Revocation of the Edict of Nantes.
1688	Glorious Revolution: British crown offered jointly to William and Mary following the flight of James II.
1689	William becomes King of England.
1701-13	Spanish War of Succession: alliance of several countries, including the United Provinces, against Louis XIV. **Treaty of Utrecht**.
1702	Stadtholder William III dies without an heir. The title of Prince of Orange passes to the Frisian Stadtholder, Jan Willem Friso.
1702-47	Stadtholderless Period.
1747	**William IV**, the son of Jan Willem Friso, is the first elected Stadtholder of the United Provinces.
1751-95	**William V**, William IV's son, is Stadtholder.

French domination

1795	A French army under General Pichegru overruns the country; William V flees to England; the United Provinces become the **Batavian Republic** (1795-1806).
1806	**Louis Bonaparte** becomes king of the **Kingdom of Holland** with Amsterdam as the capital.
1810-13	Louis Bonaparte abdicates; the country becomes part of the **French Empire** under Napoleon.

Union with Belgium

Dec. 1813	William VI of Orange, son of William V, becomes last Stadtholder of the Netherlands.
1815	Battle of Waterloo and the fall of Napoleon. The Congress of Vienna recognises William VI, Prince of Orange, as the King of the Netherlands (including Belgium) under the name **William I**. In addition, he becomes Grand Duke of Luxembourg.
	The Western seaboard of New Guinea is colonised.
1830	Brussels Revolution leads to Belgium's independence.

Kingdom of the Netherlands: an independent kingdom

1831	Parts of Limburg and Brabant are ceded to Belgium but William I only ratifies the treaty in 1839.
1839	The first **railway** line is built between Haarlem and Amsterdam.
1890-1948	Reign of **Queen Wilhelmina** (b 1880).
1932	Zuiderzee Project.
May 1940	The country is invaded by the German army. The Queen and her family leave for London.
5 May 1945	German army surrenders *(see ARNHEM)*, and the Queen returns.
1948	Queen Wilhelmina abdicates in favour of her daughter **Juliana** (b 1909). Economic Union of Benelux.
Dec. 1949	Independence of the Dutch East Indies which become the Republic of **Indonesia**.
1954	Autonomy of Dutch Guiana or Surinam and the archipelago of the Dutch Antilles.
1957	The Netherlands joins the **EEC**.
1960	The **Benelux** economic union comes into effect.
Nov. 1975	Dutch Guiana becomes independent as the Republic of **Surinam**.
30 April 1980	Queen Juliana abdicates in favour of her daughter **Beatrix**.
1 Jan. 1986	**Aruba** is separated from the Netherlands Antilles and becomes an internally self-governing integral part of the Netherlands realm.
1986	Flevoland becomes the 12th province.
1987	Inauguration of the Oosterschelde storm-surge barrier.
1992	**Treaty of Maastricht** signed by the twelve EC members.
1998	Completion of the Delta Plan.
2000	The Netherlands and Belgium co-host the **Euro 2000** football championships.

TIES BETWEEN THE BRITISH AND THE DUTCH

The Netherlands and Britain were two small seafaring nations with a strong Protestant tradition, in an otherwise predominantly Catholic world. They were linked politically, religiously, commercially, intellectually and artistically long before William III's reign, though it was during his time that their friendship reached its peak. **William III, Prince of Orange**, was the nephew and son-in-law of King James II (1685-88) of England, and Stadtholder of the United Provinces. He married Mary, James's daughter, in 1677. James set about establishing Catholicism, which created nationwide unrest and dissent. The British wrote to William in June 1688 asking him to restore peace and unity to the country. William landed in October 1688, James abdicated, and Mary, the nearest Protestant claimant to the throne, was crowned jointly with William in April 1689. During their reign (1689-1702) a vogue for all things Dutch developed.

Political decisions were closely linked to commercial interests, and the Dutch, English and Scots had been exchanging naval techniques and trading together for years, in areas such as the wool and shipbuilding industries.

Once commercial links had been established between the two countries, Dutch goods and influences began appearing in Britain. These included bricks and gables, sash windows, Dutch-style gardens, marine painting and portraits, and interior decoration. Dutch influence reached its peak during William and Mary's reign with the transformation of Hampton Court and Kensington Palace, where the influence of their Dutch residence, Het Loo, is apparent. They employed Grinling Gibbons to do carvings, Daniël Marot as their architect and interior decorator, and Sir Godfrey Kneller to paint portraits; all were in some way connected with the Netherlands. Many stately homes, such as Belton, Ashdown and Easton, contained Dutch-style decorative features including carvings, tulip vases, lacquerware cabinets, and upholstered cabriole-legged chairs, and reflected Mary's great love of porcelain and William's for gardens.

The Dutch tradition of religious tolerance and freedom of expression also attracted political and religious refugees from Britain. With the reign of William and Mary, a wave of tolerance spread through Britain, rendering exile to the Netherlands unnecessary.

OVERSEAS EXPANSION

In the middle of the 16C, Amsterdam traders went to Antwerp to obtain goods brought back from the Indies by Portuguese ships. Since the mouth of the Scheldt was cut off by the Sea Beggars, the traders started sailing to Lisbon in 1580, the same year that Philip II of Spain invaded Portugal. In 1585 he placed an embargo on Dutch trade in Spain and Portugal. The Dutch merchants, forced to handle shipments themselves, clashed with the Spanish, Portuguese and above all the English, who were fearsome competitors in the overseas markets.

The route to the East – While looking for a passage to India from the north of Europe, **Willem Barents** *(see WADDENEILANDEN, Terschelling)* discovered Novaya Zemlya in 1594 and Spitsbergen in 1596. In the same year, **Cornelis de Houtman** landed in **Java**. **Jacob van Neck** conquered the island of Mauritius in 1598. After the establishment of Batavia (now Jakarta) by **Jan Pieterszoon Coen** *(see HOORN)* in 1619, Java became a Dutch colony. In 1641, **Malacca** was wrested from the Portuguese, and in the following year the explorer **Abel Janszoon Tasman**, an explorer working for the East India Company, discovered the islands of **Tasmania** and **New Zealand**. Australia was first mapped by Dutch cartographers, who called it **Nieuw-Holland**. **Jan Anthoniszoon van Riebeeck** established the **Cape Colony** (South Africa) in 1652, and **Ceylon** was occupied in 1658.

The East India Company – To coordinate the large number of trading companies sailing to the East, Johan van Oldenbarnevelt founded the **United East India Company** or **VOC** *(see AMSTERDAM)* in 1602. The Company obtained a monopoly over shipping and trade to the east of the Cape of Good Hope and west of the Strait of Magellan, and very soon became the biggest trading company of the 17C, with trading posts all over Asia. From these settlements, the VOC brought back costly spices (nutmeg,

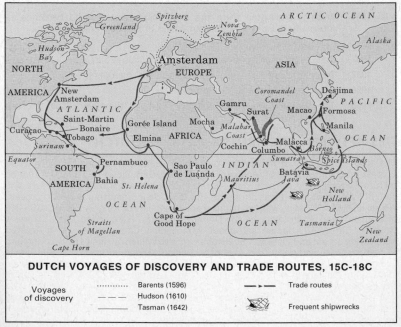

DUTCH VOYAGES OF DISCOVERY AND TRADE ROUTES, 15C-18C

Voyages of discovery	.... Barents (1596)	——►— Trade routes
	— — — Hudson (1610)	
	———— Tasman (1642)	Frequent shipwrecks

pepper, cinnamon, saffron, ginger and cloves) and Chinese porcelain; these were largely replaced by tea, coffee, silk and cotton from the 18C onwards. The journey from the Netherlands to Java took eight months, and to coordinate all these expeditions a central administration was set up in **Batavia**. Here, all products from Sumatra, Borneo, the Moluccas, and also India, China, Japan and Persia,were centralised for transportation to the home country. Here, they played a major part in creating the prosperity that was the Golden Age. The VOC was finally disbanded in 1789.

The Americas – In the 17C, Dutch trade also turned towards the New World. The first expedition was that of **Hudson** *(see AMSTERDAM)* in 1609; Amsterdam merchants established a factory in **Surinam** in 1613, and **Willem Schouten** *(see HOORN)* discovered Cape Horn in 1616.

The **Dutch West India Company (WIC)**, created in 1621, traded both with Africa and the Americas; the "commodities" included slaves. It set up trading posts on the coasts of both continents, and also conquered many islands in the Caribbean: Bonaire, Tobago, **Curaçao**, Sint-Maarten and the other Antilles.

In **Brazil**, **Johan Maurits van Nassau** (1604-79) was appointed governor-general (1636-44). He was a great patron of the arts and sciences, and assembled a team of academics and artists who documented the country in great detail.

The WIC concentrated mainly on southern America, but in 1624 it established a settlement known as **Nieuw Amsterdam** on the east coast of North America, and the Dutch colonialist **Peter Stuyvesant** became its governor shortly afterwards. Under his rule, Nieuw Amsterdam developed rapidly, but in 1664 it was taken by the English and renamed New York.

Colonies – Many of the Dutch conquests in Asia and America were only temporary. However, they succeeded in establishing lasting settlements in **Indonesia** (until 1949) and **Surinam** (until 1975). The **Netherlands Antilles** (Curaçao, Bonaire, St Eustatius, Saba and St Martin) and **Aruba** still form part of the Kingdom of the Netherlands, having become an internally self-governing integral part of the Netherlands in 1954 and 1986 respectively.

Language and literature

The Dutch language is spoken by about 22 million people throughout the world: in the Netherlands itself, in part of Belgium, and in the Netherlands Antilles and Surinam. Dutch is one of the western branches of the Germanic family of languages, and resembles both German and English. Frisian is not a dialect of Dutch, but a language in its own right. It was only on 29 January 1993 that Dutch was recognised by law as being the official national language, and Frisian was accorded the status of the second governmental language.

Literature: the Middle Ages – Although most literature until the Middle Ages was written in Latin, a number of mystical works were published in Dutch during the 13C, by authors including Jan van Ruusbroeck and Hadewych. Other works written in Dutch were those of the Flemish poet Jacob van Maerlant, the anonymous animal epic **Reynard the Fox**, the miracle play **Mariken van Nieumeghen**, the morality play **Elckerlyc** (Everyman) and the works of Thomas à Kempis.

16C-17C – The great 16C and 17C humanists wrote in Latin; they included **Erasmus**, **Jansenius** (1585-1638), the theologian Hugo de Groot or **Grotius**, and the jurist and Jewish philosopher **Spinoza** (1634-77). The country, and especially Amsterdam, became known for its liberal attitude; many foreign scholars and philosophers, such as John Locke, Descartes and Pierre Bayle, sought shelter in the Netherlands and found freedom to publish. The two great figures in Dutch literature of the period were the poet and historian **PC Hooft** (1581-1647), and the poet and dramatist **Joost van den Vondel** (1587-1679); both belonged to the **Muiderkring**, a circle of artists, writers and musicians founded by Hooft.

18C: the Age of Enlightenment – The Dutch presses continued to print the uncensored works of great foreigners, including such prophets of enlightenment as Voltaire and Diderot, but for Dutch literature this was a period of decline.

19C – **Eduard Douwes Dekker**, known under the pseudonym of **Multatuli**, gained an international reputation with his novel *Max Havelaar*, a satire on colonial life in the Dutch East Indies. **Louis Couperus** was an important novelist of the 1880 literary revival, and is best known for *Eline Vere,* dealing with contemporary life in The Hague, and *Old People and the Things That Pass.*

20C – Other writers of the early 20C include the historian **Johan Huizinga**, known for the lively style of his book *The Waning of the Middle Ages*, the prolific novelist **Simon Vestdijk** who wrote several works on middle-class provincial life, and **Simon Carmiggelt**. The post-war generation included **Willem Frederik Hermans**, **Gerard Reve**, **Cees Nooteboom** and **Harry Mulisch**. The prevalence of the war theme in post-war Dutch literature is evident in Jeroen Brouwer's *Sunken Road* (1981), Willem Frederik Hermans' controversial novels, including *The Tears of the Acacias* and *The Dark Room of Damocles*, Gerrit Kouwenaar's *I Was Not a Soldier* (1951) and Harry Mulisch's *The Assault*. Two other important figures are the poet **Ida Gerhardt** and **Hella Haasse**, renowned for her historical novels.

The new avant-garde or *Revisor* writers reacted against realism: they included Dirk Ayelt Kooiman *(A Romance)*, Doeschka Meijsing *(Tiger, Tiger!)*, Frans Kellendonk *(Letter and Spirit)* and Nicholas Matsier *(The Eternal City)*.

The **Raster** writers formed an even more influential group named after the literary magazine of the same name. These representatives of "the alternative prose" were a less homogeneous group and represented several generations. The Flemish writers Louis Paul Boon and Hugo Claus influenced their younger compatriots.

Other writers remained outside the mainstream of Dutch literature: the traditional realist storyteller Maarten 't Haart, Jeroen Brouwers, Joost Zwagerman *(Gimmick)*, who portrayed a tarnished image of the Amsterdam art world, and Willem Jan Otten. The old guard produced best-selling works such as Hugo Claus' much-acclaimed *The Sorrow of Belgium* (1983) and Harry Mulisch's *The Discovery of Heaven*. Kellendonk's very topical *Mystic Body* caused considerable controversy when it was published in 1986.

Frisian literature – The highly gifted poet **Gysbert Japicx** (1603-66) is the first to use the Frisian language in literature; a literary prize named after him is awarded in Bolsward every two years.

Architecture

RELIGIOUS ARCHITECTURE

'S-HERTOGENBOSCH – Ground plan of St.-Janskathedraal (1380-1580)

Bay: transverse section of the nave between two pillars

Pillar

Transept arm

Ambulatory: extension of the side aisles around the chancel; in pilgrimage churches it allowed the faithful to file past the relics

Axial chapel

Chevet: French term for the far (usually east) end of the chancel, on the church exterior; the interior far end is known as the **apse**

Nave

Transept crossing

Side aisle

Side doorway

Chancel

Radiating or **apsidal chapels**

HAARLEM – Grote Kerk or St.-Bavokerk (Chancel)

The inclusion of an ambulatory and the length of the chancel are unusual in a Gothic church in the Netherlands, suggesting French influence. The architect chose cedar wood for the stellar vaulting.

Keystone

Lierne: auxiliary rib

Rib

Quarter or **cell**

Capital

Formeret: rib against the wall in a rib-vaulted ceiling

Tierceron: auxiliary rib (subdivision of a lierne)

Stellar vaulting (in cedar)

Upper window

Triforium: passage above the nave and chancel, below the clerestory and opening into the nave

Great arch, separating the nave from the side aisle

Engaged column

Chancel railing

Fresco in a tapestry design

AMSTERDAM – Westerkerk (1619-31)

The Westerkerk is the last and most imposing of the three Mannerist churches built by Hendrik de Keyser commissioned by the city of Amsterdam. The two churches which predate it are the Zuiderkerk and the Noorderkerk.

Imperial crown, added to the city's coat of arms by Maximilian I

Bell chamber

Amsterdam city coat of arms

Belfry-porch

Fronton

Niche

Dormer window or **lucarne:** admits light to the attic storey

Tracery

Upper window

Window (late 18C)

Mullion: vertical element dividing a window opening

Buttress: external support for a wall, built against it or projecting from it

M. Guillou/MICHELIN

56

MILITARY ARCHITECTURE

AMERSFOORT – Koppelpoort (c 1400)

This fortified gateway is a remnant of the second enceinte around Amersfoort. It is a unique combination of a town and water gate; the latter houses a double fulling mill.

Watch tower

Amersfoort town coat of arms

Loophole (gun)

Arrow slit

Embrasure

Merlon: in battlements one of the solid sections in between embrasures

Hip roof

Dormer window

Polygonal roof

Fixed bridge

Town gate

Water gate on the Eem

Machicolation: overhanging structure with holes in the floor through which missiles could be dropped on attackers

Mullion window

BOURTANGE – Stronghold (late 16C and 17C)

The stronghold at Bourtange was designed by Adriaan Anthonisz. and dates from the late 16C; the fortifications were extended and strengthened in the following century. It is one of the best examples of a fortress in the Old Dutch style.

Grain mill (for feeding the occupants of the stronghold)

Counterscarp: outside wall of the moat

Crown-like outwork consisting of three bastions

Scarp: inside wall of the moat

Latrines

Wooden drawbridge

Access road

Demi-lune: projecting outwork reinforcing a bastion

Battered wall: sloping at the foot to deflect missiles

Water-filled moat

Ravelin: projecting outwork reinforcing a curtain wall

Bastion: a round or polygonal defence work projecting from the outer wall of a fortification

Curtain wall

Exterior moat

Powder magazine

M. Guillou/MICHELIN

CIVIL ARCHITECTURE

AMSTERDAM – 18C merchant's house

The beautiful town houses along the canals of Amsterdam were built on pilotis (free-standing piles). Those commissioned by merchants in the 18C consist of a "downstairs", where the domestic staff were housed, an "upstairs", where the merchant and his family lived, and a loft in which merchandise was stored.

Upper door (access to loft)

Curved pediment

Projecting beam with pulley

Volute in the form of a claw

Upper door with wrought-iron railing

Cartouche: decorative medallions

Roof timbers

Gable roof

Festoon or **garland**

Late 18C window

Fanlight

Straight flight of steps

"Down-stairs"

Pilotis: the building's mass is in fact resting on firm ground 13m/40ft below ground level

Partition wall

Layer of **sand and clay**

Layer of **sand and peat**

Layer of **peat**

Layer of **sand**

M. Guillou/MICHELIN

58

HILVERSUM – Town Hall (1927-31)

Hilversum town hall won international renown for architect WM Dudok. Giant cuboid forms sit on top of or next to one another, giving rise to a harmonious interplay of vertical and horizontal lines. A tall clock tower overlooks the complex.

Roof overhang, designed to accentuate the horizontal and create a play of light and shade

Tall, thin **brick;** bricks with this dimension (24 x 11.5 x 4.5cm/9.4 x 4.5 x 1.8in) came to be known as "Hilversum format"

Canopy

Tower

WM Dudok's **office** with a large corner window

Gallery

Tall, narrow **windows,** surmounted by a small projecting roof; the openings are reminiscent of those in a bell tower

Row of small windows directly beneath the roof, making it seem to be floating in thin air

Long row of windows with tiny square panes

Triangular **balcony,** breaking up the line of the walls

Balcony from the council chamber

Lake, in which the building is reflected

Path leading to the entrance; in bad weather visitors can reach the building along a covered walkway running parallel to the path

ROTTERDAM – Erasmusbrug (1996)

This 802m/2 630ft long single pylon bridge is the work of Ben van Berkel. It was inaugurated in 1996 and consists of two approach ramps joined in the middle by a fixed metal cable bridge and a steel bascule bridge.

Cable

Pylon (139m/456ft high); this has give the bridge its nickname "The Swan"

Roadway (30m/100ft wide and 2.3m/7.5ft thick)

Pillar

Bascule bridge in steel

Approach ramp

M. Guillou/MICHELIN

The arts

Over the centuries, the Netherlands has made a major contribution to Western art. Sculpture occupies a relatively modest place in the Dutch artistic heritage, perhaps due to a shortage of materials until the 20C, and so does music. But the country's architecture has been outstanding during some periods of its history, and its paintings, too, make the Netherlands a place of pilgrimage and inspiration.

ARCHITECTURE AND SCULPTURE

Romanesque art and architecture

Examples of Romanesque art and architecture can be seen throughout the country.

Rhenish-Mosan Art – This form of Romanesque developed in the Maas Valley and in particular at Maastricht, which belonged to the diocese of Liège. The style is very similar to that of the Rhine Valley; hence its name (Mosan being the adjective for Maas or Meuse).

Maastricht was an important town in the Roman era and then a place of pilgrimage where the relics of St Servatius, who died in 384, were venerated. The town has some magnificent buildings, such as the St-Servaasbasiliek and the Onze Lieve Vrouwe-basiliek. In its early days, Mosan art borrowed a great deal from **Carolingian architecture**. Apart from the St-Nicolaaskapel at Nijmegen, whose shape imitated the octagonal basilica of Charlemagne in Aachen Cathedral, Carolingian churches usually have two chancels, an imposing westwork, and a court chapel. Inside, there is a flat wooden ceiling and square pillars. Construction of the **St-Servaasbasiliek** began in about 1000, starting with a westwork with two large towers decorated with Lombard arcading. The **Onze Lieve Vrouwebasiliek**, dating from the same period, also has a massive westwork, flanked by round turrets *(photograph: see MAASTRICHT)*. The St-Amelbergakerk at **Susteren**, built in the second half of the 11C, is very plain.

In the 12C, Mosan architecture mellowed and became more decorative, and sculpture started appearing on the capitals, low reliefs and portals. It was during this period that both the St-Servaasbasiliek and the Onze Lieve Vrouwebasiliek were altered, and the chancel of the latter, viewed from the nave, is one of the most beautiful Romanesque achievements in the country. The original trefoiled plan of **Rolduc Abbey** in Kerkrade also shows a Rhenish influence. The Onze Lieve Vrouwe Munsterkerk at **Roermond**, although restored, retains some Rhenish-Mosan characteristics. The crypts of these Romanesque churches are often very beautiful.

Other centres – **Utrecht**, which was an important bishopric in the Middle Ages, became a centre of Romanesque church architecture at an early stage. However, apart from the Pieterskerk dating from 1148, there are only a few remains of the fine Romanesque buildings erected by Bishop Bernulphus. Among the churches in the diocese of Utrecht, the Grote Kerk at **Deventer** has preserved the remains of a double transept and a westwork which links it to Mosan churches. At **Oldenzaal**, the great St-Plechelmusbasiliek is later (early 12C) and has a nave with groined vaulting supported by powerful pillars. Beginning in the mid-12C, regional versions of the Romanesque style appeared in **Friesland** and in the **province of Groningen**, where **brick decoration** was used on the outside walls of village churches *(see GRONINGEN and LEEUWARDEN, Excursions)*; inside, there are often the remains of frescoes.

Gothic architecture

Gothic architecture appeared in the Netherlands during the 14C and 15C. Many churches, and some town halls, date from this period.

Churches – Noord-Brabant, a province where the majority of the inhabitants are Catholic, has most of the large churches and **cathedrals** in the country. These were built in the **Brabant Gothic style**, which resembles Flamboyant Gothic and is found in many buildings in Belgium. Their exteriors have open-work gables and crocket spires, tall windows, flying buttresses, and a tall belfry, while the interiors have a slender central nave with pointed vaulting resting on round columns with crocket capitals and a triforium.

The Grote Kerk in **Breda** *(illustration: see BREDA)* is a typical example of Brabant Gothic, as is the St-Janskathedraal in **'s-Hertogenbosch** *(illustration: see Architecture, p 55 and 'S-HERTOGENBOSCH)*, which was begun in the 14C and is one of the most beautiful pieces of architecture in the country, as well as being the largest. Unlike other buildings, its vaults rest not on columns but on a cluster of small columns without capitals. Brabant Gothic influenced the style of many other churches in the country. In Noord- and Zuid-Holland, the stone vault was rare and churches had flat or barrel-vaulted wooden ceilings; the only exception is the Grote Kerk in Dordrecht. Other beautiful Gothic buildings include the Hooglandse Kerk in Leiden, the Grote Kerk in Alkmaar, the Nieuwe Kerk in Amsterdam, the St-Janskerk in Gouda, and the St-Bavokerk in Haarlem *(illustration: see Architecture, p 55)*. The cathedral in Utrecht unfortunately did not survive the great storm of 1672, but its elegant bell-tower, the **Domtoren**, still stands, and influenced many other bell-towers around the country, including that of Amersfoort. In the same diocese, the Gothic St-Nicolaaskerk in Kampen is also interesting.

Town halls (Stadhuizen) – Two town halls in the Flamboyant Gothic style are particularly remarkable. That of **Gouda** is delightful, its façade a mass of pinnacles and slender spires. The town hall in **Middelburg** *(photograph: see MIDDELBURG)* is sumptuous; it was built by the Belgian architect family Keldermans and shows the influence of Brussels town hall.

Vaults of St.-Janskathedraal, 's-Hertogenbosch

Lescourey/PIX

Sculpture – Although this is not as abundant as in Belgium, there are some interesting 15C and early 16C woodcarvings. The groups by **Adriaen van Wesel** (late 15C) displayed in the Rijksmuseum in Amsterdam are carved with a remarkable sense of composition and a great strength of expression. The Brabant altarpieces are triptychs in the Flamboyant style, with a carved central panel showing very lively scenes. This is flanked by two painted panels. The altarpieces can be seen at St.-Janskathedraal in 's-Hertogenbosch and Onze Lieve Vrouwe Munsterkerk in Roermond. There are some fine examples of choir stalls, often carved with satirical themes, in churches including the Martinikerk in Bolsward and the Grote Kerk in Breda.

The Renaissance and Mannerism

The Renaissance reached the Netherlands at a relatively late stage, and its pure Italian form appears hardly at all. However, Mannerism (a transitional form between Renaissance and Baroque) flourished, particularly in Holland.

Architecture – This was not influenced by the Renaissance until the mid 16C. The style was brought here by Italian artists such as **Thomas Vincidor da Bologna**, who designed Breda Castle; it was then taken up by local architects. In fact, Renaissance elements were used without making major architectural changes, and the traditional Gothic plan was often retained. They were mainly apparent in details, such as shell-shaped window tympana, dormer windows with pinnacles, and octagonal turrets.

Hans Vredeman de Vries (1527-c 1603) was a great advocate of Renaissance decoration applied to architecture, but did not do much work in his own country. His theoretical writings had an important influence on the architecture of the Low Countries. The Fleming **Lieven de Key** worked a great deal in Haarlem, where he was the municipal architect. The old meat market, or Vleeshal (1603), is his finest work. **Hendrick de Keyser** (1565-1621) was both a sculptor and architect. He built several churches, mainly in Amsterdam (including the Zuiderkerk and Westerkerk; *illustration, see Architecture, p 56*) and large town houses (Huis Bartolotti)). De Keyser's mannerist style, like that of Lieven de Key, also contained Baroque elements; his buildings were more monumental, with an imposing feeling of line.

Renaissance influences were particularly apparent in **Friesland**, where the penchant for geometric decoration and playful detail, which was already apparent in Romanesque churches, spread to many other buildings. The new style was used in town halls, such as those of Franeker and Bolsward, law courts (the Kanselarij in Leeuwarden), and town gateways (the Waterpoort in Sneek; *illustration: see SNEEK*). The east and west of the country were less affected by these influences, though the weigh-house in Nijmegen is a good example of the Renaissance style.

Sculpture – Increasing numbers of **funerary monuments** were made in the Italian Renaissance style. Thomas Vincidor da Bologna made the tomb of Engelbert II of Nassau in Breda. Hendrick de Keyser continued this trend in the early 17C with the tomb of William the Silent in Delft. He also designed the bronze statue of Erasmus in Rotterdam. In **Friesland**, the Renaissance style was expressed in woodwork. Some churches, such as the Martinikerk in Bolsward and the Grote Kerk in Dokkum, have **pulpits** whose panels are carved with symbolic scenes. The remarkable 17C choir stalls of Dordrecht's Grote Kerk are also inspired by the Renaissance, and the magnificent stained glass of the St-Janskerk in Gouda is one of the finest examples of Renaissance art.

The Golden Age

In the middle of the 17C, the playful ornamentation of mannerism began to disappear. Architecture became dominated by symmetry and proportion, although this was much more restrained in the Netherlands than the Baroque style of other countries, and is sometimes called "**Classicism**".

Mauritshuis, The Hague

One of the most famous architects of the Golden Age was **Jacob van Campen** (1595-1657), designer of **Amsterdam's town hall** (1648), which subsequently became the royal palace. This is square in shape, with severe lines softened a little by the slightly projecting façade, sculpted pediments and small tower. It is a majestic work which greatly influenced architecture throughout the country. **Pieter Post** (1608-69), who built the royal palace (Huis ten Bosch) and the Mauritshuis in The Hague based on plans by Van Campen, and the town hall in Maastricht, continued this trend. **Jacob Roman** built Het Loo Palace in Apeldoorn in a similar style in 1685. This stately architectural style, reflecting the Golden Age, is also apparent in the **town houses** along Amsterdam's main canals *(illustration: see AMSTERDAM)*. One of the most beautiful examples is the Trippenhuis built by **Justus Vingboons** (c 1620-98), who worked a great deal with his brother Philips.

Many of the Protestant **churches** of this period are circular, often with a dome; one example is the Nieuwe Kerk, or Ronde Lutherse Kerk, in Amsterdam (1671). In the south of the country, some buildings were constructed using the more extravagant Baroque style; one example is the Jezuïtenkerk in Maastricht.

18C and 19C

The French-born architect and decorative designer **Daniël Marot** (1661-1752) built a number of elegant town houses in The Hague. From now on, the French influence and the Louis XV and XVI styles predominated; the Rococo or **Louis XV** style was mainly apparent in the external sculpture, and in the grilles and imposts used to decorate the doors, though it also appeared in stucco interior decoration.

In the early 19C, architects began once again to seek their inspiration in the past; first ancient Greece and Rome (**neo-Classicism**), and later the Middle Ages and Renaissance (**neo-Gothic** and **neo-Renaissance**). In **Eclecticism**, these stylistic elements were used together. One of the most important architects in this period, **PJH Cuypers** (1827-1921), introduced a form of neo-Gothic to his buildings, which included the Rijksmuseum and the central railway station in Amsterdam, and carried out radical restorations of several medieval buildings such as Kasteel De Haar. Although the architecture of earlier eras provided such a major source of inspiration for that of the 19C, it was also during this period that new materials such as cast iron and steel were first used *(see below, Industrial heritage)*.

20C

During the 20C, architecture has experienced something of a renaissance in the Netherlands, and there has also been a renewed interest in sculpture.

Architecture – **HP Berlage** (1856-1934), who built Amsterdam's Stock Exchange (1897-1903), was the precursor of Rationalism, an architectural movement which placed a great deal of emphasis on materials and function. **KPC de Bazel** (1869-1923) worked in a similar way with his building for Algemene Bank Nederland, Amsterdam.

The **Amsterdam School** (c 1912-23) strove for a less austere architecture than that of Berlage, and **Michel de Klerk**, **Peter Kramer** and **JM van der Mey** were the great masters of urban renewal; their work made expressionistic use of brick. **WM Dudok** stood slightly apart from the Amsterdam School; he was influenced by Frank Lloyd Wright and is best known as the designer of the town hall in Hilversum *(Illustration: see Architecture, p 59).*

Ph. Lau/EUREKA SLIDE

Amsterdam – Spaarndammerplantsoen (M de Klerk)

At the same time, the **De Stijl movement** was being founded by the painters **Piet Mondrian** and **Theo van Doesburg** and the architect **JJP Oud**. Architects such as **Gerrit Rietveld** (who also designed furniture), **J Duiker** and **B Bijvoet** also gained their inspiration from the movement, using concrete skeletons and superimposing and juxtaposing cube-shaped spaces to form a whole. This was known as **Nieuwe Bouwen** (New Building) or Functionalism, and was at its height from 1920-40. One of the highlights of this style is the Van Nelle factory in Rotterdam by the architects **Brinkman** and **Van der Vlugt**, a masterpiece in steel, glass and concrete.

Around 1950, particularly during the rebuilding of **Rotterdam**, urban planners began taking more account of local people's needs. The Lijnbaan (1952-54), designed by JH Van den Broek and **JB Bakema**, was the first pedestrian precinct in Europe. The Forum generation, as it was called, also included **Aldo van Eyck** (who built the Burgerweeshuis and Moederhuis in Amsterdam), **Herman Hertzberger** (responsible for the Vredenburg in Utrecht and the VROM building in The Hague), and **Piet Blom**, the

The Netherlands has a leading international reputation for modern architecture and urban planning. Top Dutch and foreign architects have worked on such major projects as the Resident and Kop van Zuid developments in The Hague and Rotterdam respectively. The latter, in particular, is an absolute must for visitors interested in contemporary architecture, and more new projects are in progress there. A number of museums are also important works of architecture in their own right; they include the Groninger Museum in Groningen, the Bonnefantenmuseum in Maastricht, and Nemo in Amsterdam.

architect of the famous cube-shaped apartments and the building known as Het Potlood, both in Rotterdam. **Wim Quist** built the Willemswerf, an office block in the same city, and various museums including the Museum Beelden aan Zee, the seaside sculpture museum in The Hague.

Rem Koolhaas (b 1944) is one of the country's leading contemporary architects. He established a firm of international architects, the Office for Metropolitan Architecture, in Rotterdam in 1975. Koolhaas has become famous in the Netherlands for buildings such as the Nederlands Danstheater in The Hague and the Museumpark and Kunsthal in Rotterdam. He has also gained an international reputation for work such as his urban plan for the French city of Lille. The local environment and traditional building styles play an important part in the work of **Jo Coenen** (b 1949), whose most important project has been the Nederlands Architectuurinstituut in Rotterdam. Finally, among the younger generation of architects, **Ben van Berkel** (b 1957) designed Rotterdam's Erasmusbrug, or Erasmus Bridge, completed in 1996.

Sculpture – Most Dutch towns and cities have used sculpture in a wide variety of materials to enliven their pedestrian precincts and parks. Many modern buildings have façades decorated with mosaics, coloured ornamentation or bronze figures.

Mari Andriessen (1897-1979) was one of the greatest Dutch sculptors of the 20C. He created the statue of a docker near the Portuguese Synagogue in Amsterdam, the monument in the Volkspark in Enschede, and the statue of Queen Wilhelmina in the Wilhelminapark in Utrecht.

Other leading contemporary sculptors are the **Fortuyn/O'Brien** duo, whose light, elegant compositions feature wooden slats wrapped in paper or silk. **Carel Visser** (b 1928) was one of the first Dutch sculptors to work in metal, and made collage sculptures, including a wide variety of found objects. His recent work is more detailed and intricate. **Henk Visch** (b 1950) is mainly known for his figurative sculptures, often consisting of contemplative human or animal figures with poetic titles.

Groninger Museum (1995), designed by the Coop Himmel(1)bau cooperative

MILITARY ARCHITECTURE

All over the Netherlands there are the remains of fortifications built over the centuries to defend the country against invasion.

In the Middle Ages, defensive works initially consisted of walls of earth surrounded by a ditch and a ring of stakes; later on, castles and fortresses were built. Some of the finest examples are the fortress in **Leiden**, the **Muiderslot**, and **Slot Loevestein**. As towns began to develop, so earthworks were replaced by stone walls with towers and impressive gateways. Parts of these walls can still be seen in **Amersfoort** (*illustration: see Architecture, p 57*) and **Elburg**. Typical features included machicolations and parapet walks along the tops of walls and towers, and crenels and other holes through which stones and burning pitch could be thrown.

The walls of fortified towns were not able to withstand the cannons introduced in the early 15C, and so the high walls and towers were lowered and provided with moats or earthworks which could not be breached by these weapons. The **Spanjaardsgat** in Breda is an example of this kind of construction.

Breda – the Spanjaardsgat

The next step was to build bigger but less tall towers known as **roundels**; a fine example of these is **De Vijf Koppen** in Maastricht. However, their round shape was not very practical, since there was not enough room for armaments at the top and there was a blind spot straight in front of the roundel. As a result, Italian engineers in the early 16C developed the bastion, a five-sided projecting fortification intended to overcome the drawbacks of roundels. This new structure was soon adopted in the Netherlands. During the Eighty Years' War, a variety of Italian-inspired changes resulted in the development of a new form of defence known as the **Old Dutch System**. The Flemish engineer **Simon Stevin** (1548-1620) developed the theoretical basis for this system. The fortifications were made of earth, so that cannon balls would simply become lodged in them, and were nearly always surrounded by a ditch in which small islands known as demilunes. The leading builder of fortifications at this time was **Adriaan Anthoniszoon** (c 1543-1620), who worked on nearly 30 towns and forts around the country. The best-preserved examples of these are at Willemstad, Heusden, and **Bourtange** *(illustration: see Architecture, p 57)*. Naarden, whose fortifications are better preserved than any other in the country, was built using the so-called **French System**, with larger bastions and a double ring of defences. In 1685, **Colonel Menno van Coehoorn** (1641-1704) designed the **New Dutch System** exemplified by Hellevoetsluis and Bergen op Zoom. This had large bastions placed close together, making the walls between them (known as curtain walls) shorter and shorter, eventually resulting in the **tenaille system** of star-shaped fortifications formed by a succession of bastions with no curtain walls **(Linie van Doesburg)**.

The development of longer-range artillery meant that fortifications had to be built at increasing distances from the towns they were built to defend. Forts were built in a circle around the fortifications, as in the **Nieuwe Hollandse Waterlinie** (1840-60) around Utrecht. The main purpose of these "water lines" was to flood the land to a depth of about 40cm/16in to slow the enemy down; this was done using a system of sluices and quays. Forts were built in places which could not be flooded, such as the huge fort at Rijnauwen, near Bunnik. The circle of some 40 forts that form the **Amsterdam Citadel** is an average of 12km/8mi from the capital; one is the island fort of **Pampus** in the IJsselmeer. This famous citadel has been a UNESCO World Heritage site since 1996. The earlier citadel of **Den Helder** was built by Napoleon in 1811.

After the First World War, defensive lines of concrete bunkers were built; the best known are the **Grebbelinie** and the bunkers on the Afsluitdijk near De Oever and Kornwerderwand (now a museum). The most prominent Second World War fortifications in the Netherlands are the long series of bunkers along the coast, which formed part of the German **Atlantic Wall**. The most recent are the Rijn-IJssellinie, built in 1951 as part of NATO defences. The project was cancelled in 1954 as a result of changes in NATO's strategic plans.

INDUSTRIAL HERITAGE

The **Industrial Revolution** did not take place in the Netherlands until the end of the 19C. **Factories** were built, steam power began to be used, as were iron and steel. But as far back as the 17C, the Netherlands had Europe's biggest industrial area, the **Zaanstreek** *(see ZAANSTREEK)*, where nearly a thousand windmills were used to manufacture paper, dye, and foodstuffs.

Factories and workers' housing – The first factories were built in Twente and Noord-Brabant, making such products as cotton and wool. Many of these were subsequently demolished, but some have been put to new uses, such as the 19C wool factory in Tilburg, which is now the **Nederlands Textielmuseum**, and the **Jannink spinning mill** in Enschede. In the early 20C, the use of concrete, glass and steel enabled larger factories to be built, such as the **Wiebengahal** of the former Sphinx Céramique factory in Maastricht and Rotterdam's **Van Nelle factory** (1926-30). Examples of whole districts built specially to house the multitude of workers include the **Agnetapark** in Delft and **Philipsdorp** in Eindhoven.

Minerals – There are still some impressive **limekilns** to be seen here and there (such as in the Zuiderzeemuseum in Enkhuizen); these were bottle-shaped structures used to burn shells to make lime. There are some fascinating remains of Zuid-Limburg's **coal industry**, including the Nulland pit in Kerkrade and the Oranje Nassau mine in Heerlen. The reconstructed **mine at Valkenbrug** gives a first-hand view of how coal was dug.

Stations – The oldest surviving railway station in the Netherlands is the building at **Valkenburg**, dating from 1853. **Amsterdam**'s Centraal Station was designed by PJH Cuypers (1827-1921), and the elegant Art Nouveau station at **Haarlem** is by the architect Margadant. The enormous iron roofs of such stations as 's-Hertogenbosch and The Hague were also a major technological innovation. The history of railways is chronicled in the **Nederlands Spoorwegmuseum** in Utrecht.

Ports – Amsterdam still has a 19C wharf with cast iron roofs, 't **Kromhout**. In Rotterdam, which was largely destroyed in 1945, there are still some old warehouses such as **De Vijf Werelddelen** (now a shopping and entertainment centre). The former headquarters of the **Holland-Amerika shipping line** (1901) on Wilhelmskade has been converted into a hotel. **De Hef**, an old lifting railway bridge, is on permanent display in the raised position.

Steam-operated pumping stations – The first time that steam pumping stations were used was in the draining of the Haarlemmermeer *(see p 44, The fight against the sea)*. One of these was the **Cruquius**, which is now a museum. These stations were used in increasing numbers in the second half of the 19C; they included the **Vier Noorder Koggen** (now the Nederlands Stoommachinemuseum), and the **Ir Lely station** at Medemblik and the steam pumping station near **Halfweg**, now a museum. The **Ir. D.F. Wouda steam pumping station** just outside Lemmer is the largest in Europe; this highly impressive structure was built in 1917 and has been a UNESCO World Heritage Site since 1998.

Water towers and lighthouses – The oldest water tower in the country is in **Rotterdam** and dates from 1873. The oldest lighthouse, the **Brandaris** on the island of Terschelling, was built in 1594. The brick lighthouse at **Haamst-ede** is depicted on the 250fl banknote. The **Waterleiding-museum**, situated in Utrecht's oldest water tower, describes the history of the mains water supply in the Netherlands. The neo-Gothic water tower of **Schoonhoven** is the centre of the Zilver in Beweging initiative.

PAINTING

Dutch painting was initially very similar to that of Flanders, and was later influenced by Italian art. It reached its peak in the 17C, reflecting the country's increasing prosperity.

Ph. Gajic/MICHELIN

De Cruquius steam pumping station

Pre-Renaissance

One of the greatest of all Dutch artists was **Hieronymus Bosch**, who was active in 's-Hertogenbosch in the late 15C. His work was extraordinarily imaginative for its time *(illustration: see 's-HERTOGENBOSCH)*. Although his vision of a world dominated by the spectre of sin was a medieval one, his realism presaged that of 17C painting, and his work has many features of modern Surrealism. Other artists had more in common with the Flemish primitives. The work of **Geertgen tot Sint Jans** is akin to miniature art. **Cornelis Engebrechtszoon** painted lively, colourful scenes full of people; a number of his works can be seen in the Stedelijk Museum De Lakenhal in Leiden. Another of the early Dutch painters was **Jan Mostaert**.

Museum Boijmans Van Beuningen, Rotterdam

The Assumption of the Virgin Mary, Geertgen tot Sint Jans

Renaissance

Jan van Scorel, a pupil of **Jacob Corneliszoon van Oostsanen**, introduced the Renaissance to the northern Netherlands when he returned from Rome in 1524. He was the first Dutch painter to be influenced by Italian art, and painted portraits of great sensitivity, such as the *Portrait of a Young Scholar* in the Museum Boymans-van Beuningen in Rotterdam, as well as rather mannerist religious pictures. One of his pupils was **Maarten van Heemskerck**. **Lucas van Leyden**, a pupil of Cornelis Engebrechtszoon, was also influenced by the Renaissance. He painted large, carefully composed canvases such as the *Last Judgement* in the Stedelijk Museum De Lakenhal in Leiden. **Pieter Aertsen** was not at all influenced by Italian art. This great Amsterdam artist, who also lived in Antwerp for a time, painted subtle landscapes and interior scenes with still life compositions in the background. Antoon Mor became famous under the Spanish name of **Antonio Moro**, since he was the court painter to Charles V and Philip II of Spain. He later worked at the English court.

The Golden Age

The 17C may have been dominated by such great figures as Rembrandt, Hals, Vermeer and Ruisdael, but it had many other highly talented artists. While the Flemish continued to paint large numbers of religious scenes, Dutch art was more secular and varied, since much of it was painted for well-off middle-class homes. It also provides a remarkable record of the daily life of the period.

Group portraits – During the Golden Age, there was a considerable demand for group portraits from bodies such as guilds, companies of the civic guard, groups of surgeons, and the governing bodies of almshouses. **Bartholomeus van der Helst** painted many traditional, formal portraits of wealthy citizens and members of the House of Orange, as well as numerous group portraits. **Frans Hals** had the nonconformist style that came with genius. Most of his large group portraits are in the Frans Hals Museum, in his home town of Haarlem. He also painted striking and lively individual portraits, such as *The Jolly Drinker*, now in the Rijksmuseum.

Rembrandt and his pupils – **Rembrandt** also painted group portraits such as the famous *The Anatomy Lesson of Doctor Tulp* which is in the Mauritshuis in The Hague, but the best-known example is the *Night Watch*, in the Rijksmuseum. This museum has an excellent collection of Rembrandt's work, notably Biblical scenes, portraits and self-portraits, with brightly lit, solemn figures against dark backgrounds. Rembrandt had a number of pupils: **Gerard Dou**, who did chiaroscuro genre paintings; **Ferdinand Bol**, one of the closest to Rembrandt in style; **Nicolaes Maes** who used warm colours to paint calm interior scenes; **Samuel van Hoogstraten**; **Aert van Gelder**; **Carel Fabritius**, who died young, but was the most gifted of all; and **Philips Koninck**, who was mainly a landscape painter.

Landscape and seascape painters – Although Rembrandt produced many landscape drawings and etchings, he painted few landscapes. Many artists specialised in this genre ; these included **Hercules Seghers, Salomon van Ruysdael** and **Jan van Goyen**. They painted luminous, serene compositions with wide horizons, still rivers, sunlight filtering through the clouds, and silhouetted trees, churches and windmills. The greatest landscape painter of the time, **Jacob van Ruisdael**, had a penchant for romantic scenes.

Meindert Hobbema painted tall trees with vivid green sunlit foliage, while **Cornelis van Poelenburgh** preferred Italian-style landscapes and sunsets. Sometimes landscapes were a pretext to depict human figures, as with **Albert Cuyp**; elsewhere, they included shepherds and their flocks in the case of **Nicolaes Berchem**, cows and horses in the case of **Paulus Potter**, and horses and their riders in the paintings of **Philips Wouwerman**. **Hendrick Avercamp** was slightly different: his paintings were similar to miniatures, with subtle colours bringing to life the picturesque world of ice-skaters. **Aert van der Neer** also painted winter scenes and rivers by moonlight.

Willem van de Velde the Elder, and more especially his son **Willem the Younger**, were remarkable marine painters, as were **Ludolf Bakhuizen, Jan van de Cappelle** and the Ghent painter **Jan Porcellis**. **Pieter Saenredam** and **Emanuel de Witte** whose work was highly appreciated during their lifetime, depict church interiors in carefully studied compositions. **Job Berckheyde** and his younger brother **Gerrit** were also painters of architecture.

Rijksmuseum-Stichting, Amsterdam

A Black Squall, Willem van de Velde the Younger

Genre pieces – Apart from some of Rembrandt's pupils, many other painters specialised in domestic interiors. **Gerard Terborch, Frans van Mieris the Elder** and **Gabriel Metsu** recreated domestic scenes with delicate brushwork, while **Pieter de Hooch**, a remarkable colourist and virtuoso of perspective, depicted the daily lives of the wealthy. **Vermeer** was neglected for a long period, but is now regarded as one of the greatest of all artists. He mainly painted interior scenes, which were realistic but extraordinarily poetic. Although simple in appearance, they make highly sophisticated use of colours, composition and light. **Adriaen van Ostade** was a painter of rollicking peasant scenes, and was influenced by the Flemish artist Adriaen Brouwer. Van Ostade's pupil **Jan Steen** painted similarly cheerful and humorous pictures, though with a moral message.

In Utrecht, the Italian influence which was widespread in the 16C made itself felt in the work of **Abraham Bloemaert**. One of his pupils, **Hendrick Terbrugghen**, introduced "Caravaggism" to the Netherlands along with **Gerard van Honthorst**. Their work is characterised by strong light-dark contrasts, half-length portraits of ordinary people, and people playing music. **Judith Leyster**, a pupil of Frans Hals, was also clearly influenced by Caravaggio.

Still life with Cheeses, Floris Claeszoon van Dijk, Rijksmuseum, Amsterdam

Still-life paintings – The tradition of still-life painting had its origins in Flanders, in the work of artists such as Fyt and Snyders. It was taken up in Haarlem by **Pieter Claeszoon** and **Willem Claeszoon Heda** and **Floris Claeszoon van Dijck**. Their favourite subject was a table covered with the remains of a meal, and glasses and dishes reflecting the light. Their paintings were less crowded than those of their Flemish predecessors, with flatter colours and strictly geometrical compositions. The works of **Willem Kalff**, **Abraham van Beyeren** and **Jan Davidszoon de Heem** were more colourful and Baroque.

Drawings and prints – 17C painters also produced very large numbers of drawings and prints, particularly etchings, and **Rembrandt** excelled in this form of art *(illustration: see Admission times and charges at the back of the guide)*.

18C, 19C and 20C

In the 18C, a decline set in. One notable exception was **Cornelis Troost**, an Amsterdam painter whose work was inspired by the theatre, and evokes Watteau and Hogarth. **Jacob Wit** was known for his *grisailles* (in Dutch: *witjes*), which were popular forms of household decoration among the wealthy. **Wouter Joannes van Troostwijk** immortalised the streets of Amsterdam in his paintings.
In the 19C, with **The Hague School** led by **Jozef Israëls**, Dutch art enjoyed a rebirth. Nature, beaches, dunes and the lives of fishermen provided an inexhaustible source of inspiration for the artists of this school *(illustration: see Den HAAG)*.
JB Jongkind was a precursor of the Impressionists, and his paintings were full of light and atmosphere. This was also true of **George Hendrick Breitner**, who is known for his pictures of horsemen and of old Amsterdam *(illustration: see AMSTERDAM)*. **Isaac Israëls**, the son of Jozef, painted beach scenes and numerous portraits.
Vincent van Gogh was the greatest figure of the late 19C. His early paintings were sombre, but under the influence of Impressionism his canvases became lighter and more colourful. From 1886 onwards he worked mainly in Paris and near Arles in Provence. Many of his masterpieces can be seen in the Kröller-Müller Museum, near Arnhem, and the Van Gogh Museum in Amsterdam.
Jan Toorop was born in Java. He began his career as an Impressionist, before turning to Symbolism, a movement in which he held an important place in Europe along with **Johan Thorn Prikker**. Later, Toorop briefly allied himself with the pointillists and divisionists, and also took an interest in the Art Nouveau movement, painting a large number of posters in this style.
Piet Mondrian *(illustration: see AMERSFOORT)* was one of the greatest innovators of his time. He was the driving force behind the **De Stijl** movement (1917-31) and its magazine of the same name, along with **Theo van Doesburg** and **JJP Oud**. In so doing, he helped to found the constructivist movement.
One of the most intriguing artists of the inter-war period was **Herman Kruyder**, whose work is highly enigmatic. **Jan Wiegers** was the leader of the Expressionist movement **De Ploeg** (1918-30), characterised by dramatic contrasts in colour. **Hendrik Werkman** is now regarded as the most important member of De Ploeg; he introduced radical

Counter-composition of Dissonants XVI (1925), Theo van Doesburg
Haags Gemeentemuseum, The Hague

innovations in woodcuts and typography. After a brief Expressionist period, **Charley Toorop**, the daughter of Jan Toorop, subsequently adopted a realist style of painting. **Kees van Dongen** *(illustration: see ROTTERDAM)* became a famous artist in Paris.

The main exponents of **magic realism** (or **new objectivity**; 1920-30) in the Netherlands were **Raoul Hynckes**, **Pyke Koch** and **Carel Willink**. Their strange, near-photographic realism, tinged with surrealism, influenced many young artists. One of their contemporaries was **MC Escher** (1898-1972), the Netherlands' leading graphic artist, whose ingenious play on spaces and dimensions became world-famous *(illustration: see LEEUWARDEN)*.

The international group of experimental artists **CoBrA** (1948-51) was named from the initial letters of Copenhagen, Brussels and Amsterdam. Its main members were the Dane Asger Jorn, the Belgian artist Dotremont and three Dutchmen, **Karel Appel** *(illustration: see EINDHOVEN)*, **Constant** and **Corneille**. The movement advocated free, spontaneous creation, often inspired by children's drawings.

The year 1960 saw the creation of the Dutch group **Nul** (Zero) whose three principles were impersonality, detachment and objectivity. Its most important representative was **Jan Schoonhoven**, best known for his monochrome reliefs.

During the 1970s, **Jan Dibbets** and **Ger van Elk** used photography as a means of expression; Dibbets turned reality into abstraction by creating trick montages characterised by a strong sense of perspective. **Rob van Koningsbruggen** uses unconventional techniques to produce his quasi-monochrome pictures: he takes canvases painted in black, white or primary colours and rubs one or more unpainted canvases over them.

The leading artistic figures of the 1980s were **Rob Scholte** and **Marlene Dumas** who, despite their different styles, both draw inspiration from the visual imagery generated by newspapers, magazines and other media.

DECORATIVE ARTS

Pottery and porcelain

The Museum Het Princessehof in Leeuwarden has a comprehensive collection of Dutch pottery and porcelain.

From sandstone and majolica to delftware – The majolica technique was brought to Antwerp and other parts of northern Europe by Italian potters in the 16C. After the fall of Antwerp in 1585, many potters moved to the Netherlands, where majolica production subsequently flourished. Very soon, this technique replaced the traditional Rhine sandstone pottery.

In the early 17C, large quantities of **Chinese eggshell porcelain** were imported by the United East India Company. These damaged the domestic market and bankrupted many potters. Some majolica-makers switched to making tiles or domestic objects not made by the Chinese, such as mustard pots and apothecaries' jars, often imitating oriental styles of decoration. Others tried to discover the secret of eggshell porcelain, but initially they had no success. However, a few manufacturers in **Delft** and **Haarlem** did manage to make a better-quality product than traditional majolica to compete with porcelain from the Far East. This new technique, called **faience**, used a different mixture of clays to make thinner ceramics. The lead glaze was replaced by a white tin glaze closely resembling white porcelain, and the pieces were decorated with both Chinese and Dutch motifs; Italian-inspired decoration was also popular.

When imports of Asian porcelain declined around 1650 as the result of a civil war in China, delftware enjoyed a huge success. Delft potters responded quickly to the gap in the market, and specialist faience factories began producing on a larger scale *(see DELFT)*.

Frisian majolica – In the second half of the 17C, **Makkum** *(see MAKKUM)* and **Harlingen** became the centres of Frisian majolica production, consisting mainly of tiles and tableware. This bore considerable similarities to the pottery produced in Delft, but was simpler in style and less imitative of Chinese porcelain. Also, the Frisian pieces rarely bore a manufacturer's mark; most were inscribed with the name of the client for whom they were made. Plates made in the **port of Lemmer** were particularly distinctive. The **Tichelaar factory** in Makkelum was established in the late 17C and is still in operation.

Dutch porcelain – True porcelain was first successfully produced in the German town of Meissen in the early 18C, and other west European countries began making it shortly afterwards. Porcelain was made in the Netherlands only for a short period of about 50 years, mainly in imitation of the German variety. The typically Dutch **porcelain cabinet** was designed to display and protect these costly objects; it consisted of a tall, flat display case on a base.

The first Dutch factory was established in **Weesp**, producing Rococo forms with multicoloured decoration, but this closed ten years later. Its equipment and stock were acquired by a priest in Loosdrecht to provide jobs for poor people in his area, and the **Loosdrecht** factory produced beautifully painted tableware and ornaments between 1774 and 1784. After the priest's death, the factory moved to **Ouder-Amstel**, where it produced its own Louis XVI-style designs between 1784 and 1809. In that year it moved to **Nieuwer-Amstel** and continued making Empire-style porcelain until it closed in 1814.

Hague porcelain was made in The Hague from 1776 to 1790; porcelain imported mainly from Ansbach and Tournai was used and then painted.

Dutch porcelain was of reasonably high quality, but high production costs and a limited market meant that large-scale production was not possible.

Dutch Art Nouveau – In the second half of the 19C, Petrus Regout's factory in **Maastricht** made mainly white dinner services, sometimes with printed decoration; these were strongly influenced by, and sometimes copied from, Wedgwood and other British manufacturers.

Art Nouveau did not become widespread in the Netherlands until the end of the 19C. The **Rozenburg** delftware factory in The Hague made pottery with stylised, often fanciful flower and plant motifs. The designer **TAC Colenbrander** was a great innovator who devised some highly imaginative forms and decorations. Another very successful product of the Rozenburg factory, under **JJ Kok**, was **eggshell porcelain** with very fine, naturalistic decoration. In Gouda, too, brightly coloured ceramics, known as **Gouds plateel**, were made between 1900 and 1930.

Modern ceramics – Despite increasing Industrialisation at the beginning of the 20C, smaller-scale production of stoneware and earthenware has continued, and ceramics have become unique works of art. Leading modern Dutch ceramists include Chris Lannooy, Bert Nienhuis, WC Brouwer, Johan van Loon and Jan van der Vaart.

Tiles

The Nederlands Tegelmuseum in Otterlo and Museum Het Princessehof in Leeuwarden have a comprehensive collection of Dutch tiles.

Like majolica, tiles arrived in the Netherlands in the 16C via Italy and Flanders. They were initially used as **floor tiles**, but the thin tin glaze was easily damaged, and soon **wall tiles** were being made instead. These were initially painted in bright colours and decorated with geometric motifs, animals and fruit. Later, under the influence of Chinese porcelain, they were often decorated entirely in blue.

After 1750, the demand among townspeople for painted tiles tailed off almost to nothing; they preferred to decorate their walls with expensive fabrics. In the countryside, however, they remained a popular form of decoration. They depicted mainly craftsmen and women, imaginary sea creatures, children playing, soldiers and ships. Later on in the 18C, biblical and **pastoral scenes** became increasingly popular. After 1800, however, interest declined as people began using wallpaper, and also machine-produced tiles from England.

Tile pictures – Huge tile pictures were made in the Netherlands from about 1620 until well into the 18C. These were placed either against the back of a fireplace or in other positions such as in **passageways**, on **walls** or above the **hearth**. They included beautifully painted vases of flowers; in the 18C, a wider variety of motifs was produced, including scenes from rural life, allegorical pictures, naval battles, townscapes, dogs and parrots. Tile pictures enjoyed a small-scale revival at the beginning of the 20C; they were made mainly for commercial purposes such as **shop interiors** or **advertising** on the outsides of buildings.

Tile (c 1625)

Vase, Chris Lanooy (1927)

Haarlem dish (c 1660)
and Delft water jug (c 1650-70)

Porcelain candle-holder,
Rozenburg Den Haag (1920)

Dish of Italian inspiration,
Haarlem (c 1660)

Porcelain soup tureen, Loosdrecht (c 1780)

Furniture

The Rijksmuseum in Amsterdam has a comprehensive collection of furniture.

Middle Ages and Renaissance – The late-Gothic period produced carved oak chests, small side-tables with shelves and dressers decorated with **letterbox motifs**. From 1550 onwards, the Italian Renaissance inspired ornamentation with carved panels depicting medallions and grotesques, and heavy tables in the Flemish style (*bolpoottafels*) with turned feet widening into vase-like shapes.

Chests in the Golden Age – The most beautiful items of furniture from the late 16C and the Golden Age were linen chests. The **Dutch chest** (*Hollandse kast*) was perhaps the most common kind. It had very varied decoration: lion's heads, caryatids, friezes of foliated scrolls, grotesque masks, etc. The chest had a wide plinth, four doors and a heavy cornice decorated with a frieze of plants. Its uprights

Dutch chest

consisted of pilasters, and subsequently columns: it was then called a columned chest (*kolommenkast*).

By the second half of the 17C magnificent chests in various kinds of wood were being made, known as **bombé chests** (*kussenkast*) because of the bulging shape of their panels, usually veneered with ebony. The chest rested on enormous ball feet. A set of five delft vases would often be placed on the cornice.

Marquetry and inlaid work – In the 17C and 18C, marquetry and inlays of ebony, tortoiseshell, metal and ivory became increasingly popular. Both in the Netherlands and in Flanders, they were used on inkstands and **cabinets** with numerous drawers used to store precious objects.

Bombé chest

18C and 19C chests – The Louis XV style, imported by the French Huguenots, was very much in vogue in the 18C, though it was freely adapted. **18C cabinets** had two doors and a base with drawers, which in the middle of the century acquired a characteristic bulge, and undulating cornices on their tops. Inlays and marquetry remained popular during this period.

At the end of the 18C, the influence of the more austere Louis XVI style became apparent; this was much more faithfully reproduced. In the 19C, the Empire style became popular following the arrival in the Netherlands of King Louis Napoleon and his wife Hortense, both of whom were very fond of Parisian fashions.

Zeeland chest

Painted furniture – The north of the country specialised in the production of painted furniture in the 18C. This was mainly made by fishermen in the Zuiderzee ports during the months when they did not fish, and they used methods they had seen during their travels in the Baltic or the East. This furniture was elaborately carved, and painted in bright colours in a style reminiscent of naive popular art. Many different objects were painted in this manner: chests, box beds, cradles, chairs, and even children's wooden satchels. There are fine collections of this form of furniture in the **Zuiderzeemuseum** in Enkhuizen, the **Hidde Nijland Stichting** in Hindeloopen, and the **Nederlands Openluchtmuseum** in Arnhem.

Clocks

After the famous scholar Christiaan Huygens invented the pendulum clock in 1656, clocks became a great deal more accurate, and **long-case** or **grandfather clocks** became increasingly popular in well-off households. These had a tall ornamented plinth containing the weights and pendulum, with the mechanism contained in a case above this and an arched pediment at the top. The dial was often painted with pictures of the night sky and moving human figures or boats; some showed the month, the day of the week, the date and the phase of the moon as well as the time. Amsterdam was a great clock-making centre in the 18C, and wall clocks in Louis XV style were also popular.

Many Dutch museums have a decorative arts section with recreations of rooms furnished in the style of a particular period or region. Some also have **doll's houses** which are detailed reproductions of the interiors of wealthy Dutch homes during the Golden Age.

The provinces of Friesland, Groningen and Drenthe had their own distinctive form of clocks known as **stoeltjesklokken**. These had ornate openwork decoration, similar to that of the painted furniture described above, and the mechanism rested on a console. Zaandam clocks were more elegant.

Several museums have very fine clock collections, in particular the **Nederlands Goud-, Zilver- en Klokkenmuseum** in Schoonhoven and the **Museum van het Nederlandse uurwerk** in the Zaanse Schans to the north of Amsterdam

Gold and silverware

Romanesque period – All over the bishopric of Liège in Belgium, the **gold and silversmiths of the Maasland** produced many masterpieces. The **shrine** of St Servatius in the St.-Servaaskerk in Maastricht, for example, is made of copper gilt decorated with enamel and precious stones, with depictions of Christ, St Servatius and the apostles around it. The Museum Catharijneconvent in Utrecht contains examples of **gold and silverware** that reflect the prosperity of bishops in the region during the Romanesque period; they include monstrances, pyxes, shrines, processional crosses, and books.

Stichting Schatkamer St.-Servaas

The shrine of St Servatius

The Golden Age – In the 16C, and even more so in the 17C, it was a common practice among town councils, guilds and well-off ordinary people to commission finely engraved and chased silver objects to commemorate particular events. Most museums have collections of these items; they include large and small goblets, dishes, water jugs, **nautilus-shell cups** (made with a nautilus shell on a silver base), chains of office and other ceremonial items. The churches also owned much gold and silverware. Many beautiful **brandy bowls** were made during this period. They were oval in shape, with handles, and were highly decorated. The most famous silversmiths were the **Van Vianen** brothers.

A distinctive feature of the 17C interiors of Holland are the **brass candelabras**, also prevalent in churches.

MUSIC

Musicians – One famous Renaissance musician was **JP Sweelinck**, who was organist of the Oude Kerk in Amsterdam, and composed vocal and instrumental works. During the same period, the poet and diplomat **Constantijn Huygens** composed a number of pieces of music, as well as writing about the subject.

In the 19C, the composer and conductor **Johannes Verhulst** made an important contribution to music in the Netherlands, as did **Richard Hol**, a conductor, pianist and composer of cantatas and symphonies. One of Hol's students was **Johan Wagenaar**, an organist who composed works in his own very distinctive style. Wagenaar in turn taught the composer **Willem Pijper**, who was also known for his essays on music.

Today, the Netherlands has two of the world's leading orchestras: the Royal Concertgebouw Orchestra in Amsterdam, and the Residentie Orchestra in The Hague. The first conductor of the Concertgebouw Orchestra was **Willem Mengelberg**, who had a particular interest in the works of contemporary composers such as Mahler. Under his leadership, the orchestra became known for its exceptionally high standard of performance, and he was succeeded by Eduard van Beinum, Bernard Haitink and Riccardo Chailly.

Organs – This instrument was first developed in Byzantium, imported into Western Europe in the 9C, and played an important part in Catholic worship from the 12C onwards. The instrument was also used in people's homes from an early stage, and therefore escaped the destruction wrought by the iconoclasm of the 16C. However, organ music was at first condemned by the Calvinist religion, and it was only in the mid 17C that it spread into Protestant churches. Numerous instruments were made during this and the following century. The sons of the famous German organ-builder **Arp Schnitger**, who had moved to Groningen, perfected the instrument in the Netherlands and built the great organ in **Zwolle's** Grote Kerk. The impressive 18C organ of St-Bavokerk in **Haarlem**, built by **Christiaan Müller**, is one of the best-known in the world.

Most of the organ cases date from the Baroque era, and are sumptuous achievements with statues and carvings above the pipes. Where regular organ concerts are held, this is mentioned under the heading for the locality in this guide.

The organ case – Oude Kerk, Amsterdam

Ph. Gajic/MICHELIN

Mechanical organs – The first such instrument was a **barrel organ**, probably invented by an Italian in the 18C. A barrel covered in pins and turned by a handle raises levers which admit air to a set of organ pipes. Wheeled organs of this kind became widespread in 19C Europe. In 1892, Gavioli built the first mechanical organ to use a **perforated paper roll** instead of a barrel. Turning the handle moves a continuous sheet of perforated paper across a keyboard. The organ's repertoire was almost unlimited, since the paper rolls were interchangeable. The mechanical-organ builder **Carl Frei** established a business in Breda in 1920, but most of the instruments were imported from abroad, from Belgium (Mortier) and France (Gasparini and Limonaire Frères). At the end of the 19C, the **dance-hall organ** became popular; this was an impressive instrument with a beautifully ornamented front. The beginning of the 20C saw the introduction of the **fairground organ**, which produced loud music intended to be heard above the hubbub of the fair. Finally, in 1945, an **electric dance-hall organ** appeared, with many built-in automatic instruments imitating the sound of a full orchestra.

The **Museum van Speelklok tot Pierement** (museum of mechanical music) in Utrecht has an interesting collection of mechanical organs.

Carillons – Countless churches and town halls in the Netherlands have carillons. These are believed to have been first used in the 15C, and are operated by barrels in a similar way to mechanical organs.

In the 17C, **François and Pierre Hemony**, famous bell-founders from Lorraine, played a very important role in the development of the carillon in the Netherlands. Of the many carillons they made, the best-known are those of the Onze Lieve Vrouwe Toren in Amersfoort, the Martini Toren in Groningen and the Domtoren in Utrecht. In 1941, a bell-founder in Heiligerlee, in Groningen province, invented an **electromagnetic system** to replace the barrel. In 1953, the Netherlands Carillon School was established in Amersfoort.

The town of Asten has an interesting **National Carillon Museum** (*see EINDHOVEN: Excursions*). Details of carillon concerts are given in the descriptions of individual towns.

Admission times and charges for the sights described are listed at the end of the guide. Every sight for which there are times and charges is identified by the symbol ⊘ in the Sights section of the guide.

Traditions and folklore

COSTUMES

In the past, the Netherlands had a great variety of local costumes. Today, apart from Marken and Volendam where many people wear traditional costume during the tourist season, there are few places where it is regularly worn, and then it is mostly confined to older women.

Women's costumes – In spite of their variety, there are common features shared by all women's costumes. They consist of a skirt, an apron and a jacket done up at the front, usually with short sleeves. Over the jacket some women wear a stiff bodice or a shawl. The costume worn on Sundays is always more elegant than that of other days, and on Whit Sunday in particular, women usually dress up in their finest clothes and jewellery.

Caps – Although many foreigners immediately think of the typical **Volendam lace cap**, there is a wide variety of other forms of cap throughout the country. Those worn on the island of South Beveland are particularly eye-catching and can still sometimes be seen on weekly market days in Goes.

Cap brooches are widely worn; these are usually made of silver, and have ornamented ends which vary from one place to another. In Scheveningen, they are oval and decorated with filigree; in Walcheren, Axel and Arnemuiden they are spiral-shaped, and those of Urk bear the figures of animals' heads. Two gold pins with pearl heads are used to hold the brooch in place. The lacework on all these caps is exceptionally beautiful.

Woman in Middelburg costume

Morand-Graham/HOA QUI

Men's costumes – Nowadays, these are worn only in a few coastal areas, such as Urk, Volendam and Zuid-Beveland. They are nearly always black, whereas in the past brighter colours were worn. The costume consists of a jacket, often double-breasted, and wide trousers or, around the Zuider Zee, knickerbockers. The shirt, which is rarely visible, is made of brightly coloured cotton with a striped or checked pattern, and has a straight collar with two gold buttons. These are the costume's only ornaments, except in Zuid-Beveland, where two attractive chased silver buckles are used to hold up the trousers. Men also wear a small cotton scarf knotted round the neck, and a black hat; this is often a simple cap, but in Urk it resembles a kepi, and a round hat is worn in Zeeland. Wooden clogs are usually worn as well.

Fabrics – Women's jackets and shawls, and also men's shirts worn under their black jackets, were made out of traditional, brightly coloured textiles patterned with stripes, checks, or flowers; the latter were most often **chintz**. From the 17C onwards, the Dutch East India Company imported enormous quantities of chintz from the East. This cotton cloth was hand-decorated with a coloured pattern, using a special technique, and its suppleness, lightness and bright colours and designs made it hugely popular in the Netherlands. It was used for interior decoration in the form of bedspreads, curtains and wall hangings, and to make clothes of all kinds. The women of Hindeloopen in Friesland used chintz to make the traditional jacket and elsewhere women replaced their plain jackets with brightly-coloured chintz. In the late 17C, chintz began to be machine-made in the Twente.

Where to see local costumes – The main centres where costumes are worn daily by local men, women and children are **Volendam** and **Marken**, but this is less common in winter than in summer. In **Staphorst** and the neighbouring village of **Rouveen**, women wear traditional clothes every day, as do some female inhabitants of **Bunschoten** and **Spakenburg**. On the islands of **Walcheren** and **Zuid-Beveland** in Zeeland, a number of women still retain a strong allegiance to their costume, to the extent that in 1975 they strongly protested against a law requiring motorcyclists to wear crash helmets. Other places where costumes are still sometimes worn are **Scheveningen**, **Urk**, and various towns and villages in Overijssel such as Rijssen, Dalfsen, and Raalte.

These are brought out for special occasions such as church services, market days and festivals. More details of local costumes can be found under the headings for individual places in the guide. In addition, various Dutch museums have departments devoted to costumes from a particular area or areas.

FARMHOUSES

The lovely farmhouses which are scattered over the countryside are part of the country's familiar landscape. They are largest in the polder areas.

Frisian farmhouses – These buildings with huge roofs can be seen all over Friesland, in areas which were formerly part of Friesland such as the north of the province of Noord-Holland, and in the province of Groningen.

Pyramid-roofed farmhouses (*Stolpboerderijen*) – There are many of these in the north of the province of Noord-Holland. Their enormous pyramid-shaped roofs are reminiscent of haystacks, and the stables, barn and living quarters are all under one roof. On one side of the roof, the thatch is partially replaced by tiles forming a decorative pattern. Sometimes, in the more elaborate farmhouses, the façade has a richly decorated brick pediment. Similar buildings which are rectangular are found in southern Friesland.

"Head-neck-trunk" farmhouses (*Kop-hals-rompboerderijen*) – These can be seen in the north of Friesland and the province of Groningen. These are made up of three parts: the living quarters (the "head") are linked by a narrow section (the "neck") to a large building (the "trunk"), which includes the cowshed, barn, and in some cases a stable. Traditionally, the living quarters have a tiled roof, whereas the barn is thatched. This kind of farmhouse is often built on a mound (*see LEEUWARDEN, Terp Region*). At either end of the ridge of the barn roof, there is an ornamental triangular board with holes in it, which were placed there to allow owls to fly in and out of the building, nest in the hay and catch mice (*illustration: see Admission times and charges at the back of the guide*). The boards are often decorated with carved wooden motifs depicting two swans.

"Head-neck" farmhouses (*Kop-rompboerderijen*) – These are found in the same areas as "Head-neck-trunk" farmhouses, and are similar to them except that, although the living quarters have a tiled roof, there is also some living accommodation in the thatched section. Sometimes, the back of the house gradually widens out to form the barn.

Oldambt farmhouses – These are named after the region of **Oldambt**, in the east of Groningen province, where they were first built. They can now be seen all over the province, and have staggered side walls which merge into those of the barn. The tall, wide living quarters often have stucco mouldings around the front door, making the building look very elegant. There are small windows in the attic, and the living quarters have a tiled roof, while the barn is usually thatched. Sometimes a second or even a third barn would be attached to the first to cope with large harvests.

Hall-houses (*Hallenhuizen*) – These are the most widespread type found in the Netherlands, particularly in the provinces of Drenthe, Overijssel, Gelderland and Utrecht; they can also be seen in Zuid-Holland and in the Gooi. Inside, the ceiling rests on two rows of piles connected by crossbeams. These divide the interior into a wide central "nave" and two narrower "side aisles".

All hall-houses derived from *losse hoes* or open houses. The interior consisted of one large room with no partitions and with an open fireplace; the family and cattle shared the same space, and the hay was stored on the beams beneath the roof. A separate living area for the parents was sometimes built on to the side of the house. This type of farmhouse can still be found in Twente.

Twente farmhouses (*Twentse boerderijen*) – In Twente and around Winterswijk (Gelderland), there are still some **half-timbered farmhouses**. The walls were formerly made from woven wicker and clay, but are now made of brick. The buildings have two-sided roofs with wooden gable ends.

Drenthe farmhouses (*Drentse boerderijen*) – These are elongated in shape, with a usually thatched four-sided roof to both the house and the barn and stable section. At the back of the building, the roof has a section taken out of it to create sufficient height for the stable doors, so that haycarts can pass through. From the 18C onwards, some farmhouses in southwest Drenthe and to the north of Overijssel had the stable doors at the back replaced by side doors in order to increase the space in the barn.

Southern Limburg farmhouse

Frisian head-neck-trunk farmhouse

Kop-romp farmhouse

Drenthe farmhouse

Pyramid-shaped Frisian farmhouse

T-shaped farmhouse

M. Guillou/MICHELIN

Stage mill

Hollow post mill

Mill with rotating cap

Post mill

Tjasker

Winter in Kinderdijk

T-shaped farmhouses *(T-huizen)* – In the Achterhoek, the IJssel area, the provinces of Utrecht and Zuid-Holland, and in Gooi, the house is set crosswise to the barn, creating a T shape. This design owes its existence to the prosperity of farmers in the fertile areas along the main rivers, who extended their houses on either side. Carts entered through the back of the building, which had a single long roof.

Local variations on the hall-type farmhouse can also be seen in Staphorst and Giethoorn. They also exist in the Krimpenerwaard and Alblasserwaard *(see ROT-TERDAM, Excursions)*, where the living quarters have a raised floor because of the risk of floods. In the provinces of Utrecht Zuid-Holland, cheese-making farms had a dairy and a cheese storage area in the basement of the house.

Transverse farmhouses *(Dwarshuizen)* – These farmhouses have their longest side at the front, and the rooms are side by side, with the living quarters set at right angles to the barn. They can be seen in Limburg and in the eastern part of Noord-Brabant.

Limburg – This is the only province in the Netherlands where farmhouses have a square enclosed courtyard, which is reached from the outside via a large gateway. In Southern Limburg, some of the buildings often have black and white **half-timbered walls**.

Noord-Brabant – This province has a distinctive long-fronted style of farmhouse, **langgevelboerderijen**, with the doors and windows facing the road and a long thatched or tiled roof. Because these farmhouses often provided limited space, a Flemish barn would often be built beside them, with wooden walls and a thatched roof.

Zeeland – Here, the various buildings were kept separate. The largest was the wooden barn, which had tarred walls and white door and window frames.

WINDMILLS

There are still some 1 000 windmills in the Netherlands, and they are one of the most distinctive features of the landscape. Some overlook the old walls of towns and dikes; others stand at the entrances to villages or beside lakes. The most famous group of windmills is at Kinderdijk.

The language of windmills – The sails of a windmill turn anti-clockwise. When stationary, their position could be used to send messages to the people of the surrounding area, as follows:
– two vertical sails (+): windmill is at rest, but ready to be operated again.
– two diagonal sails (×): polder windmill, at rest for a longer period.
– upper sail just to the right of vertical (ᐃ): a sign of celebration.
– upper sail just to the left of vertical (�): a symbol of mourning.

Windmill decorations – Many wooden windmills are painted green with white edging. The windshaft, where the sails cross, is often painted with a red and yellow or blue and white star, with a decorative board underneath stating the windmill's name and the date of its construction. When a wedding took place, the sails would be abundantly decorated with garlands and symbolic motifs.

80

CPA STOCK/HOA QUI

Main types of windmills – There are two main kinds of windmills: polder mills and industrial mills. **Polder mills** were used for drainage purposes, and there are none in the east of the country, where the height above sea level ensures natural drainage of water. **Industrial mills** were used for a wide variety of purposes, such as milling wheat, extracting oil, hulling rice and peppercorns, and sawing wood. Some of these are still in use.

The oldest type of windmill – Originally, the only mills in the Netherlands were the watermill and the horse-powered treadmill. The first windmills appeared in the mid 13C, and may have derived from the stone-built ones used in Persia to mill corn. The body and sails rotate round a heavy fixed wooden post made out of a tree trunk, so that the mill is always facing into the wind. When the sails turn, they rotate the grindstones inside. Outside, on the side opposite the sails, a tail pole joined to the post and operated by a wheel enables the windmill to be turned round. The ladder fixed to the main body of the windmill also turns with it. Few windmills of this type remain in the country.

The first polder mills – The first windmill used for drainage, in about 1350, was a post-mill adapted specifically for the purpose by replacing the solid central post with a hollow one, through which the drive-shaft was placed. This was known as a **hollow post-mill**; the earliest known example dates from 1513. This had a smaller tower and a larger base to allow space for a scoop, resembling a paddle-wheel, which was used to lift the water. In most cases, however, the scoop was on the outside and the base was used as living accommodation, particularly in Zuid-Holland.

The **sleeve windmill** (*kokermolen*) was easier to turn into the wind: the wooden spindle was replaced by a sleeve, around which the sails and the top part of the windmill rotated. In Friesland, there is a smaller version of the hollow post-mill known as the **spinnekop** (spider's head) because it looks like a spider from a distance. The **weidemolentje** of Noord-Holland is even smaller. In Friesland and Overijssel, there are still a few examples of the **tjasker**, a simply constructed windmill with a tilted spindle.

Mills with rotating caps – Turning the whole windmill into the wind was heavy work, and the Dutch invention of the **smock mill** represented a major improvement. This had a small rotating cap and sails on a large fixed tower. The wheel used to turn the cap and sails was usually on the outside, though there was also a form in Noord-Holland where the wheel was inside the mill, making it larger.

These mills were built of wood. They often had a **thatched roof** and an octagonal shape, in which case the base was made of stone. Sometimes, the wooden frame was clad in **brick**, giving it a **truncated cone shape**.

Industrial mills – *Illustration: see ZAANSTREEK.* In the 16C, the windmill was adapted for industrial purposes. The first oil windmill began operation in Alkmaar in 1582. In 1592, Cornelis Corneliszoon of Uitgeest built the first **sawmill**, which subsequently underwent many improvements and resulted in the first **post-mill** used for sawing, which rotated on its base. Next, **hulling mills** were built to hull first barley and then, when the Dutch began trading in the Far East, rice. The first of these was built in 1639 in Koog aan de Zaan. **Paper mills** were first used in about 1600, and became more widespread in 1673 when French paper manufacturers relocated to the **Zaanstreek**.

It was here that the greatest concentration could be found until the 19C; they were specially built for making paper and sawing wood for boat-building. Most of the other different types of windmills developed in this area; they included tobacco snuffmills, hemp mills for

A few proverbs about windmills:
Hij heeft een klap van de molen gehad
He was struck by a windmill (He's a little crazy)
Hij loopt met molentjes
His mind runs on little windmills (He's rather simple-minded)
Dat is koren op zijn molen
It's grain for his windmill (It's all grist to the mill)

making ropes, tanning mills for leather, spice mills mainly for mustard, and fulling mills for textiles. Most of these were very tall, with a balcony around the side and a workshop at the bottom.

Tower mills – Industrial windmills were often built in towns, and had to be several storeys high if they were to catch the wind. Because they were so tall, the sails could not be set from the ground, and so this was done from a balcony halfway up the windmill; the miller's accommodation and the storage area were below this. Alternatively, instead of a balcony, an earth wall was built around the windmill and served the same purpose. Most tower mills were made of stone and were a truncated cone shape. In Groningen province, they had octagonal bases made of brick, and in the Zaanstreek there was a workshop in the wooden base.

TRADITIONAL SPORTS

Many sports from earlier times are being kept alive, and in some cases are highly popular. **Archery** is one such example; it is particularly widely practised in **Limburg**, and dates from a time when citizens felt it necessary to arm themselves against possible enemies. Members of a large number of local societies or guilds of archers congregate at an annual gathering, the Oud Limburgs Schuttersfeest (Old Limburg Archers' Festival) and give a colourful demonstration of their sport. In Friesland, **kaatsen** is a traditional ball game similar to fives, with six players divided into two teams, and the **skûtsjesilen** are spectacular annual regattas using traditional boats called *skûtsjes (see SNEEK)*. Pole-vaulting (known as *fierljeppen* in Frisian) is another equally exciting traditional sport. It originates from the time when people hunting birds' eggs in the fields used to cross the many canals with the help of a long pole. In the Zeeland town of Middelburg, the sport of **ringrijderijen** has been revived. This is a tournament where riders on horseback gallop past and try to place their lances through a ring.

Skating was not only a traditional sport and pastime, but also a practical means of transport in the harsh winters of years gone by. The delightful winter scenes of the 17C Dutch master Hendrick Avercamp show how popular skating was at the time, and how sleighs were also used on the ice. Another activity that Avercamp portrayed in his paintings is **kolf**. This game was also played on ice with a club (*kolf*) and ball, and the aim was to hit a pole stuck into the ice. This game has been a subject of controversy between the Dutch and the Scots for centuries. The Dutch claim that it was the origin of the game of golf. However, the Scots claim that the early ball-and-stick version of golf was already being played on the sandy links of Scotland in 1457, when an Act of the Scottish Parliament was passed requiring that "futeball and the golfe be utterly cryit down" in favour of church attendance and archery practice *(see The Green Guide Scotland)*. The tradition of the **Friese Elfstedentocht**, or Eleven Towns Race *(see LEEUWARDEN)*, is thought to go back to the 18C.

World Heritage List

In 1972, the United Nations Educational, Scientific and Cultural Organization (UNESCO) adopted a Convention for the preservation of cultural and natural sites. To date, more than 150 States Parties have signed this international agreement, which has listed over 500 sites «of outstanding universal value» on the World Heritage List. Each year, a committee of representatives from 21 countries, assisted by technical organizations (ICOMOS – International Council on Monuments and Sites; IUCN – International Union for Conservation of Nature and Natural Resources; ICCROM – International Centre for the Study of the Preservation and Restoration of Cultural Property, the Rome Centre), evaluates the proposals for new sites to be included on the list, which grows longer as new nominations are accepted and more countries sign the Convention. To be considered, a site must be nominated by the country in which it is located.

The protected cultural heritage may be monuments (buildings, sculptures, archaeological structures etc) with unique historical, artistic or scientific features; groups of buildings (such as religious communities, ancient cities); or sites (human settlements, examples of exceptional landscapes, cultural landscapes) which are the combined works of man and nature of exceptional beauty. Natural sites may be a testimony to the stages of the earth's geological history or to the development of human cultures and creative genius or represent significant ongoing ecological processes, contain superlative natural phenomena or provide a habitat for threatened species.

Signatories of the Convention pledge to cooperate to preserve and protect these sites around the world as a common heritage to be shared by all humanity.

Some of the most well-known places which the World Heritage Committee has inscribed include: Australia's Great Barrier Reef (1981), the Canadian Rocky Mountain Parks (1984), The Great Wall of China (1987), the Statue of Liberty (1984), the Kremlin (1990), Mont-Saint-Michel and its Bay (France, 1979), Durham Castle and Cathedral (1986).

In the Netherlands, UNESCO World Heritage sites are:

The former island of Schokland (1995)

The Defense Line of Amsterdam (1996)

Kinderdijk windmills (1997)

Ir. D.F. Wouda steam pumping station (1998)

The Beemsterpolder, Noord-Holland (1999)

Zandhoek, Amsterdam

Sights

AALSMEER★

Noord-Holland
Population 22 513
Michelin maps 908 F 5 and 211 N 9

Aalsmeer is on the edge of the Haarlemmermeer Polder (*see HAARLEM*) and the large lake, the Westeinder Plassen. The town is mainly known as the home of the world's largest flower auction, where most Dutch florists buy their flowers and, thanks to the proximity of Schiphol airport, foreign buyers as well.

The **Bloemencorso** is a famous annual procession of floral floats from Aalsmeer to Amsterdam and back (*see Calendar of events*).

SIGHTS

★★ **Bloemenveiling Aalsmeer** ⊙ – *Legmeerdijk 313.* The flower auction takes place in a huge complex of halls (766 000m²/922 891sq yd) decorated with a stylised red tulip, the headquarters of the Aalsmeer Flower Auction, the **VBA** (Verenigde Bloemenveilingen Aalsmeer).

Visitors are advised to arrive early. The auction is open to visitors from 7.30 to 11am, but the best time to visit is before 9am. Mondays are usually the busiest days and Thursdays the quietest. Inside there is a **gallery** from where visitors are able to watch the auction and the activity down below on the shop floor.

Some of the halls are reserved for the arrival of cut flowers, which takes place the day before or early in the morning. The flowers are packed and loaded onto trucks elsewhere. At the centre of the halls are the **auction rooms**: four of these amphitheatres are used for selling cut flowers and can be viewed. The retail buyers sit in tiers facing dials linked to a computer. A trolley carrying a lot, or batch, of flowers is brought to the foot of one of the dials. On the dial a number indicates the product, the producer, the quality, the size of the lot and the currency. As soon as the buyer sees the price he wants to pay come up on the dial, he presses a button to stop the countdown on the dial. The fastest – and therefore the highest – bidder gets the lot for which he has just bid. The successful bidder's number then appears on the dial as well as the number of lots bought.

Westeinder Plassen – This large lake is one of the most popular watersports centres near Amsterdam. The road that runs round it via Kudelstaart provides lovely views.

Selling flowers at the VBA

The biggest flower market in the world

It is fair to say that the sales figures of the VBA are impressive. A total of 19 million cut flowers and 2 million pot plants are sold every day. Roses are the greatest seller with 1.7 billion units, leaving tulips (569 million), chrysanthemums (421 million), gerberas (272 million) and carnations (178 million) trailing far behind. The Aalsmeer Flower Auction is the largest market in the Netherlands with an annual turnover of almost 3 billion guilders (1999). An average of 50 000 transactions are concluded every day.

ALKMAAR*

Noord-Holland
Population 92 902
Michelin maps 908 F 4 and 210 N 7

The historic town of Alkmaar is best known for its picturesque weekly cheese market *(from mid-April to mid-September)*.
Inside its surrounding moat, formed partly by the Noordhollandskanaal, the old town has more or less preserved its 17C plan and a number of old façades. The old fortifications have been transformed into a garden. Alkmaar is now the main market town for the agricultural regions of the Noord-Holland peninsula.

HISTORICAL NOTES

Alkmaar was founded in the 10C in the middle of marshes and lakes. Its name derives either from *elk meer* or "each lake", or from *alken meer* or "auk lake", after the name of the bird which lived in the marshes.

The siege of Alkmaar – During the Eighty Years' War, which began in 1568, Alkmaar was besieged in August 1573 by 16 000 Spaniards commanded by Don Federico of Toledo, the son of the Spanish governor, the Duke of Alba.
Heavy autumn rain flooded the surrounding countryside and forced the assailants to withdraw on 8 October, after a seven-week siege. Alkmaar was therefore the first town to resist the Spanish, and for centuries it has been said that victory began in Alkmaar.

Boat trips ⊙ – Tours on offer include Alkmaar's canals as well as excursions to Amsterdam and the Zaanstreek.

The famous cheese porters of Alkmaar

★★ KAASMARKT ⊙ *30min*

This traditional market, known since the early 17C, is held on Waagplein every Friday in summer. Early in the morning, trucks and cars bring the Edam and Gouda cheeses to the square, where they are carefully piled up. At 10am the buyers start tasting and comparing the different cheeses and haggling; they then seal their agreement with the seller by slapping hands. Next, the famous **cheese porters** *(kaasdragers)*, wearing the traditional white clothes and straw hats, take over. The porters belong to an ancient guild, which is divided into four companies each identified by a different colour (green, blue, red, and yellow) and consisting of six porters and a weigher or stacker *(tasman)*.
Once a batch of cheese is sold, it is placed on a barrow in the company's colour. With the public looking on with great interest, the porters then run with the load (weighing up to 160kg/353lb) to the weigh-house, where the *tasman* officiates. Finally, the cheese is taken to the trucks.

ALKMAAR

ADDITIONAL SIGHTS

Waag – The weigh-house is the former Chapel of the Holy Ghost, built at the end of the 14C and converted in 1582. On the east side, the chancel has been replaced by a Renaissance building with a finely worked gable, which since the 19C has been decorated with a painting on Auvergne lava, representing trade and industry. The tower, which was built at the end of the 16C, was modelled on that of the Oude Kerk in Amsterdam and has a carillon and working models of knights engaging in a joust every hour.

Hollands Kaasmuseum ⊙ – *In the Waag. Visit starts on second floor.* The Dutch Cheese Museum includes a collection of tools and other objects, such as decorative carved wooden cheese moulds, illustrating the history and making of cheese and butter. The display on the first floor shows how cheese is made on farms and in dairies, and explains the importance of dairy products to the Dutch economy.

Nederlands Biermuseum De Boom ⊙ – *Houttil 1.* A beer museum in a 17C brewery, chronicling the history of brewing. There is a tasting area in the cellar.

Huis met de Kogel – This building, the "house with the cannonball", overlooks the canal and has a corbelled wooden façade. Embedded in the gable is a Spanish cannonball from the battle of 1573.
From the neighbouring bridge there is a fine **view** of the weigh-house.

Mient – On this square and along the canal there are numerous old façades. To the south is the fish market, Vismarkt.

Langestraat – This pedestrian precinct is the town's main shopping street.
Stadhuis ⊘ – The town hall's charming Gothic façade with its flight of steps is flanked by an elegant octagonal tower with streaks of white limestone. The adjoining building is 17C. The town hall has a collection of porcelain.

Grote Kerk or St.-Laurenskerk ⊘ – This is a beautiful church with three naves, a transept and an ambulatory dating from the late 15C and early 16C. It was built by members of the Keldermans family, famous architects from Mechelen in Belgium. The imposing interior has wooden vaults with beautiful 17C chandeliers. Under the chancel vault there is a painting, the *Last Judgement*, by **Cornelis Buys** (15C-16C), known as the Master of Alkmaar. The **great organ case**★, made in 1645 by Jacob van Campen, is decorated with panels depicting the Triumph of King Saul. The **small organ**★ on the north side of the ambulatory dates from 1511; it is one of the country's oldest such instruments. Over 1 700 gravestones are embedded in the floor. The church also contains the memorial tomb of Count **Floris V**, who was assassinated in 1296. Since 1996, the building has been used for events such as organ concerts, exhibitions, trade fairs and conferences

Stedelijk Museum ⊘ – The municipal museum houses several interesting collections pertaining to the history of the town: 16C and 17C paintings, including a great many portraits of companies of the civic guard *(schuttersstukken)*, and works by Maerten van Heemskerk, Pieter Saenredam, Gerard van Honthorst, Willem van de Velde the Elder and Allart van Everdingen. The museum also has a collection of silver and pewter, memorial stones and statues, and an interesting display of toys dating from around 1900. Temporary exhibitions from the museum's collection of modern art are held here, including works from the Bergen School *(see below)*.

EXCURSIONS

Broek op Langedijk – *8km/5mi north of Alkmaar*. This is the home of Europe's oldest "drive-through" vegetable auction, the **Broeker Veiling** ⊘. From 1887 to 1973, market gardeners from the "Kingdom of the Thousand Islands", as the watery surrounding area is called, transported their produce to auction by boat. Instead of wasting time loading and unloading the produce, they would simply moor at the water's edge. In 1903, the system was changed so that they were actually able to sail into the auction room! Today, visitors can buy vegetables themselves using an auction dial, or enjoy a boat tour through the fields.

Graft-De Rijp – *17km/11mi to the southeast*. These two localities merged and became one municipality in 1970. **Graft** has kept its beautiful town hall built in 1613, with crow-stepped gables.

De Rijp was an important centre for herring fishing and whaling in the 16C and 17C. It has a town hall (1630) designed by **Jan Adriaenszoon Leeghwater** (1575-1650), the famous hydraulic engineer, who was born in De Rijp. There are also a number of houses built in the regional style with wooden gables. The Dutch Reformed Church or Hervormde Kerk has 17C stained-glass windows.

Beemster, a masterpiece of 17C creative planning

When the problem of high water levels and a lack of good farming land came to a head in the early 17C a group of Amsterdam merchants, enlisting the ingenious talent of hydraulic engineer **Jan Adriaenszoon Leeghwater**, decided to drain the Beemstermeer. This ambitious project was completed in 1612, providing 7 200ha/17 790 acres of fertile land. In accordance with 17C Renaissance aesthetic ideals of order, cohesion and harmony, the reclaimed land was divided into perfect squares, which in turn were divided into parcels, 185m x 930m or 203yd x 1 021yd, which was deemed ideal for farming. The geometrical landscape of roads, ditches, dikes and trees has been preserved almost intact. This explains the exceptional interest of this area. Among the fields and farmhouses with pyramidal roofs, the Amsterdam landowners had luxury country-houses built, where they came to escape the stench of the city in the summer. Some of these houses have been preserved.

De Beemsterpolder – *22km/14mi to the southeast.* The Beemster Polder was declared a UNESCO World Heritage Site in 1999, as a result of its perfectly straight parcels of land and exceptional history of development. In Middembeemster the local museum, **Museum Betje Wolff** ⊙, is housed in the parsonage where the Enlightenment authoress Betje Wolff lived and worked between 1759 and 1777.

The Dunes – *Round tour of 35km/22mi – about 2hr. Leave Alkmaar via Scharlo.*

Bergen – Also known as Bergen-Binnen (*binnen*: inner), as opposed to the neighbouring seaside town, Bergen is an agreeable holiday resort where substantial villas stand in rows along tree-lined avenues. It has a university department of extramural studies, located in the former manor house of the lords of Bergen.

The **Bergen School** of artists was founded around 1915; its members played an important part in propagating the influence on Dutch art of artists such as Cézanne and Le Fauconnier. The **Museum Kranenburgh** ⊙ *(Hoflaan 26)* contains work by artists including Leo Gestel, Matthieu and Piet Wiegman and Charley Toorop.

Bergen still attracts numerous artists, whose work is exhibited in a space behind the Kunstenaarscentrum Bergen *(on Plein)* and in open-air markets in the summer.

The entrance to the **Noordhollands Duinreservaat** ⊙ is at the junction with the Egmond road. This is a nature reserve of 4 760ha/11 757 acres owned by the provincial water company, and a large number of bird species nest in the dunes.

Bergen aan Zee – This pleasant seaside resort has a coastline with long beaches and high dunes dotted with villas. From the promenade there is an extensive view over the dune landscape, with trees lining the horizon.

The **Zee Aquarium Bergen aan Zee** ⊙ has 43 aquariums with exotic fish and crustaceans, a large collection of shells and a touch tank. The 14-m/45ft-long skeleton is that of one of the sperm whales stranded on the Frisian island of Ameland in November 1997.

Egmond aan de Hoef – This village is set in the bulb field area to the south of Alkmaar. To the east, on the old Alkmaar road, beyond the church and close to the Slotkapel, the ruins of the moated **Slot van Egmond** (or Slot op den Hoef) can be seen. Only the red-brick foundations surrounded by water are still visible. One of its better-known owners was the famous Count of Egmond, executed in 1568 in Brussels *(see DELFT).*

≊ **Egmond aan Zee** – This small seaside resort is in the middle of the dunes. At the foot of the lighthouse a statue of a lion symbolises the heroism of **Lieutenant Van Speijk**, who on 5 February 1831 blew up his gunboat with all on board on the Scheldt near Antwerp, rather than surrender to the Belgians.

Return to Egmond aan de Hoef.

Egmond-Binnen – The famous **abbey** of Egmond was destroyed by the Beggars in 1573 and was only rebuilt in 1935.

Return to Alkmaar.

AMERSFOORT*

Utrecht

Population 123 367
Michelin maps 908 H 5 and 211 R 10
Plan of the conurbation in the current edition of The Red Guide Benelux

Amersfoort stands at the confluence of two waterways which form the navigable River Eem in the Gelderse Vallei. In the surrounding area, woodland and moorland cover the poor glacial soils, while the hills to the south, the **Utrechtse Heuvelrug**, are moraines deposited by the Scandinavian ice sheets.

Amersfoort is a delightful medieval town encircled by a double ring of canals. The whole of the town centre is a protected architectural area. In the modern northern suburb of **Kattenbroek**, there are a number of buildings designed by leading contemporary architects, including Ashok Bhalostra, Babet Gallis, Jan de Graaf, Leo Heijdenrijk, Jan Poolen, Rudy Uytenhaak and Kas Oosterhuis.

HISTORICAL NOTES

The town grew up around its 12C castle, and in 1259 it was granted civic rights. The first town wall, with its girdle of canals, dates from the 13C.

Amersfoort prospered in the 15C and 16C thanks to its thriving trade in wool and cloth and to a growing brewing industry. A second town wall was built c 1400 and reinforced by a ring of canals, now partially replaced by the wide circular boulevard, the Stadsring. The town gate known as the Koppelpoort and other foundations at the far end of the main street, Kamp, are all that remain of the second city wall.

AMERSFOORT

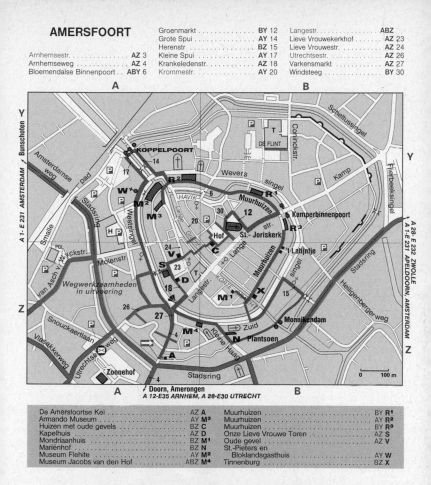

Johan van Oldenbarnevelt – Amersfoort was the birthplace of **Johan van Oldenbarnevelt** (1547-1619), the **Grand Pensionary** or political leader of Holland, the most important of the United Provinces. Oldenbarnevelt was one of the founding figures of the independent Netherlands, and strove constantly to achieve peace and prosperity. He was responsible for the Twelve Years' Truce with Spain in 1609, and was one of the founders of the Dutch East India Company in 1602.
Unfortunately he clashed with Prince Maurits of Nassau, the son of William the Silent and Stadtholder from 1584 onwards, who had him imprisoned in 1618. Oldenbarnevelt was beheaded in May 1619.

★ OLD TOWN 4hr

The recommended itinerary follows the line of the first town wall, where the famous **Muurhuizen**★, or wall houses, were built in the 15C. These houses are a distinctive feature of Amersfoort, and are so called because they are built into the town wall.

De Amersfoortse Kei – A park on the Stadsring is the final resting-place of this enormous **glacial boulder** weighing 9t. It was originally found in a nearby wood, where it had been deposited by the Scandinavian ice sheet. In 1661 it was moved to the Varkensmarkt in the centre of town before it was finally transferred to its present site.

Varkensmarkt – This was the site of the pig market. From the bridge over the canal there is a lovely view to the left over the tree-shaded canal to the tower, Onze-Lieve-Vrouwe Toren.

Krankeledenstraat – There are numerous old houses in this street; note in particular the late-Gothic **Kapelhuis** or chapel-house.

★ **Onze-Lieve-Vrouwe-Toren** ⊘ – This beautiful 15C Gothic tower dedicated to Our Lady stands in a large peaceful square, Lieve Vrouwekerkhof. It is 98m/326ft high and has an onion-shaped dome and a carillon. The tower is all that remains of a church destroyed in 1787 by an explosion.
There is an attractive old house on the corner of Lieve Vrouwestraat. A flower market is held every Friday morning on Lieve Vrouwekerkhof.

Piet Mondrian and De Stijl

Pieter Cornelis Mondrian was born in Amersfoort in 1872. After experimenting with many different forms of painting, and a stay in Paris (1911-14) where he discovered the Cubism of Picasso, Braque and Léger, Mondrian returned to Amersfoort to look after his sick father.

During the First World War he came into contact with artists such as **Bart van der Leck**, **Theo van Doesburg** and **JJP Oud**, with whom he founded the abstract art movement called **De Stijl** ("The Style"). He passionately expounded his theories in the art periodical of the same name.

From then on his painting abandoned all subjectivity, and he used vertical and horizontal lines and the three primary colours, red, blue and yellow, together with neutral blacks, whites and greys.

Mondrian unremittingly pursued his experimentation in this genre, which is known as **Neo-Plasticism**. After a second period in Paris from 1919 to 1938, he moved to New York in 1940, and died there four years later.

Mondrian is regarded as one of the founders of geometric abstraction. His last, unfinished painting, *Victory Boogie Woogie*, was bought by the Dutch national art collections fund in September 1998 for 80 million guilders, making it one of the ten most expensive artworks ever. The painting was given to the Gemeentemuseum Den Haag, which owns the world's largest collection of works by Mondrian.

His influence can also be seen in architecture; buildings designed by **Gerrit Rietveld** (1888-1964), such as the 1959 **Zonnehof** ⊙ *(Zonnehof 8; now a centre for modern art)* and the Rietveld Schröderhuis in Utrecht *(illustration: see UTRECHT)* are directly inspired by his theories.

Collectie Haags Gemeentemuseum

Self-portrait (1919), Piet Mondrian

Take the small footbridge to cross the canal, the Lange Gracht, which divides Amersfoort in two.

Hof – This spacious square is still bordered by some old houses (eg no 24) and is the scene of a lively market on Friday mornings and Saturdays.

St.-Joriskerk ⊙ – The Romanesque **church** of St George, dating from 1243, was destroyed by fire in 1370. It was rebuilt and then extended in 1534 into a hall church with a nave and two aisles.

The tower in the right aisle and a few superimposed arcades are all that remain of the original building. A finely sculpted sandstone **rood screen**, in the late 15C Gothic style, separates the nave from the chancel. The capitals and consoles in the chancel depict people and animals. At the far end of the left aisle is a memorial to **Jacob van Campen** (1595-1657), the architect of Amsterdam's old Town Hall, now the Royal Palace.

Other items worthy of attention include wall paintings, a 14C baptismal font beside the pulpit and – against the Romanesque tower – a jack-o'-the-clock (Klockman) dated 1724. In the Gothic portal is a 17C surgeons' room (chirurgijnskamer).

Groenmarkt – Several of the old houses in this pleasant square have been beautifully restored, in particular those near the adjoining square, Appelmarkt.
Follow Langestraat to Kamperbinnenpoort.

Kamperbinnenpoort – This 13C brick gateway with its octagonal turrets stood just outside the inner town wall on the road to Kampen.
In the street to the west are some of the smaller wall houses, **Muurhuizen**, which have been well restored.

Havik – This is Amersfoort's old port, situated near the ford where the town was founded (Amersfoort means "ford on the Amer").
Continue along Muurhuizen

There are some interesting and quite impressive **Muurhuizen**★ between nos 217 and 243.

Armando Museum ⊙ – *Langegracht 36.* This museum was once a church, the Elleboogkerk, and is now the showcase for the work of the very versatile Dutch artist **Armando** (1929). Exhibits include drawings, paintings, sculptures, poems and music. Temporary exhibitions are also held here.

★ **Koppelpoort** ⊙ – *Illustration: see Architecture, p 57.* This beautiful double gate, built c 1400, includes a fortified bridge or water-gate over the Eem, a double treadmill in the centre and the gateway proper, flanked by polygonal towers. The Bag-Carriers' Guild used this as their meeting place and today it is occupied by a **puppet theatre** ⊙.
Some of the houses in **Grote Spui** and **Kleine Spui** have interesting facing stones.

Museum Flehite ⊙ – The collections in this museum, which is housed in three wall houses, cover the history, archaeology and decorative arts of the town and the Flehite area (the eastern part of the province of Utrecht). There is also a section devoted to the famous local figure, Johan van Oldenbarnevelt *(see above)*.

Opposite the museum, on the Westersingel, is the chapel of the **St.-Pieters en Bloklands Gasthuis**, with the restored **Mannenzaal** ⊙ behind it. This almshouse was built in 1530, and until 1907 the sick and poor of Amersfoort could stay here at the expense of local benefactors, sleeping in one of the curtained wooden beds.
Return to the Varkensmarkt via the Westsingel, the last part of which is pedestrianised. Cross the square.

Museum Jacobs van den Hof ⊙ – This small, privately-owned museum contains sculpture and drawings by Gijs Jacobs van den Hof (1889-1965). The fine house opposite is the School of Music and Dance (Muziek- en Dansschool).
Turn right into Kleine Haag, to reach the town walls.

Mariënhof – This beautifully restored 16C convent now houses two restaurants. A herb garden has been created in the old convent garden.

Plantsoen – The footpath and cycle path along the top of the town ramparts lead to the Monnikendam.

Monnikendam – This graceful water-gate (1430) formed part of the outer fortifications, and overlooks the leafy gardens of patrician houses.
Take Herenstraat back to Zuidsingel and follow this to the left.

The lovely shaded **canal**, the Zuidsingel, runs beside the gardens of the wall-houses. Cross the canal back to the wall-houses. The bridge over the **Kortegracht** is in a very picturesque **location**★, with a view of the 15C wall-house, **Tinnenburg**.

Mondriaanhuis ⊙ – *Kortegracht 11.* In the house where Piet Mondrian was born and the adjoining school where his father used to be headmaster, a permanent retrospective of his work has been set up.

Ph. Gajic/MICHELIN

Water-gate, Monnikendam

This follows the main phases in the artist's career, from the time when he painted pictures from nature to his "neoplastic" phase, in which line and colour were equally important. There is a particularly interesting reconstruction of the studio in Paris where Mondrian worked from 1921 to 1936; he adapted this five-sided room to suit his own ideas of how spaces and surfaces should be divided up, using panels in primary colours where necessary.

't Latijntje – Also known as the Dieventoren or the Plompetoren, the 13C tower on the right is a relic of the first town wall. Past this tower, there is a very fine series of Muurhuizen★ on the right before you reach Langestraat.

EXCURSIONS

Dierenpark Amersfoort ⊙ – *3km/2mi to the west. Leave Amersfoort via Van Asch Van Wijckstraat.* Surrounded by woodland, Amersfoort's zoo features animals from all over the world. Visitors can watch the lynxes through underground glass pipes, walk over a bridge overlooking a savannah landscape, look at the cranes in the Japanese garden, have coffee among the parrots, and more. The Ancient City (Stad der Oudheid) with its Roman gate, arena, ziggurat (Mesopotamian stepped tower) and Egyptian temple is a place where crocodiles, tigers, lions and baboons roam. The adventure playground (Speel-O-Droom) has climbing towers and rope bridges, and in the Amersfoort Ark a collection of curiosities is on display.

★ Bunschoten – *12km/8mi to the north via the N 199. Leave Amersfoort via Amsterdamseweg.* Bunschoten forms one conurbation with Spakenburg, a small port on the edge of the freshwater lake, Eemmeer, once famous for its eel fishing.
The two villages line a street for more than 2km/1mi, which divides in the north to form the quays of a canal. The canal then widens into a dock where old boats, typical of the Zuiderzee, are still sometimes moored in the old shipyard.
The two villages are famous for the fact that some of the older women still wear the traditional costume★. The skirt is long, black and covered with a black apron. The distinctive feature of the costume is the stiff, flowered panels, often of chintz, on either side of the tartan band which marks the centre of the bodice. Widows wear a violet or black bodice for the rest of their lives unless they remarry. Under this they wear a black shirt with short check sleeves. A small white crocheted bonnet is perched on the back of the head. These costumes can be seen on Saturday afternoons when the market is being held, and on the last two Wednesdays of July and the first two Wednesdays of August (known as Spakenburg Days), when handicrafts are on sale in the marketplace and around the port.
The Museum 't Vurhuus ⊙ gives a picture of what everyday life used to be like in Bunschoten-Spakenburg. It includes old shops, a herring smokehouse, a farmhouse and a fisherman's house.

The woodlands and heathlands of the Utrechtse Heuvelrug

41km/26mi to the south – about 3hr 30min. Leave Amersfoort to the south via Arnhemsestraat.

The road crosses the heathland known as the Leusder Heide and the woodlands of the Utrechtse Heuvelrug, the southern part of which has been designated a National Park.
Turn right at the Utrecht-Woudenberg junction of the N 227.

Piramide van Austerlitz (Austerlitz Pyramid) – In 1804, Napoleon ordered his unemployed troops to build a sand pyramid here. It was restored in 1894, and a flight of steps and a small memorial were added.

Kasteel Huis Doorn ⊙ – *South of Doorn along the N 227.* Surrounded by moats, set in the middle of a lovely park, this castle was the home of the ex-Kaiser of Germany Wilhelm II from 1920 to his death in 1941. Forced into exile after he refused to abdicate in November 1918, he was first given refuge in Kasteel Amerongen (*see below*). Then, in May 1920, he and the Empress Augusta Victoria moved into Doorn Castle, which he had acquired. His wife died the following year. In 1922 he married Hermine, Princess of Reuss. The original castle was built in the 14C by the Bishop of Utrecht to defend his territory and altered in 1780. The tower on the southwest side is part of the medieval castle. Now a museum, the castle contains souvenirs of Wilhelm II, who brought back collections★ (paintings, tapestries) from the imperial palaces. These are displayed in a setting which has remained unchanged since the Kaiser's death. One room is devoted to Frederick the Great (King Frederick II of Prussia, 1712-86), the most famous representative of the Hohenzollern family, who was a great art lover and collected paintings and pastels of the French School (Nicolas Lancret, Watteau's contemporary) as well as snuffboxes. There is also a fine collection of family silver, consisting mainly of presents received by the Hohenzollerns in the 19C and 20C as well as a good collection of uniforms, helmets, boots and ceremonial sabres which belonged to Wilhelm II. Kaiser Wilhelm's mausoleum stands in the park.

Wijk bij Duurstede – This small town on the River Lek is on the site of **Dorestad**, a great trading centre which was abandoned after its destruction by the Vikings in 863. The town developed again in the 15C after the Bishop of Utrecht chose it as his residence. Marktplein, the market square, is overlooked by the church, **Grote Kerk**, with its incomplete square tower, and the town hall (1662). In Muntstraat no 42 is a museum, the **Museum Dorestad** ⊙, which traces the history of the town and the excavations on the site of Dorestad. Beside the Lek is a **windmill** (Molen Rijn en Lek).

On the outskirts of town, the ruined moated castle, **Kasteel Duurstede**, still has the remains of an outwork (1270) and a 15C round tower. The grounds are now a listed monument and the castle is hired out for special functions.

Amerongen – A peaceful place in the area between the Rhine and the Utrechtse Heuvelrug, where tobacco was formerly cultivated; typical wooden tobacco-drying sheds can still be seen here and there. The Gothic **church** has a tall 16C tower with limestone courses. On the square, with its lovely restored rustic houses, an oak tree was planted in 1898 in honour of Queen Wilhelmina's coming of age. The **Amerongs Historisch Museum** ⊙ is housed in an old drying shed and gives an insight into the history of tobacco-growing in the area.

Not far away, in Drotestraat, stands the famous castle, **Kasteel Amerongen** ⊙. The first castle was built on the foundations of a medieval fortress dating from 1286. After it was destroyed by the French army in 1673, its owner Godard van Reede had a new castle with double moats built on the same site. Kaiser Wilhelm II of Germany lived here from 1918 to 1920, before abdicating and moving to Doorn. The rooms inside feature splendid furniture, tapestries and paintings, and the grounds are open to the public.

Near **Leersum**, the lakes known as **De Leersumse Plassen** ⊙ are favourite breeding grounds with birds. Here the landscape is made up of heathland and fens, which used to cover a large part of the Utrechtse Heuvelrug.

AMSTERDAM***

Noord-Holland

Population 727 053
Michelin maps 908 F 4 folds 27 and 28 (inset),
210 J 8 and folds 19 and 20 (inset) and 211 J 8 – Local map see IJSSELMEER
Plan of the conurbation in the current edition of The Red Guide Benelux

Amsterdam, the biggest city in the Netherlands, lies on the banks of two rivers, the IJ and the Amstel. One of the best ways of getting to know this unique metropolis is by strolling along the picturesque canals with their narrow brick houses, some of them gradually sinking because they are built on piles to cope with the marshy subsoil. The numerous houseboats moored on the canals reflect the difficulty of building new housing in the old city centre. The lack of tall buildings and wide roads gives Amsterdam a small-town atmosphere, and another of its most striking features is the dominance of the bicycle as a means of transport. Hiring a bike is the ideal way of exploring the city's byways.

Apart from its international importance as a port, Amsterdam is a city of great cultural wealth, including major exhibitions in the Rijksmuseum and the Stedelijk Museum, numerous art galleries in and around Nieuwe Spiegelstraat, concerts by the world-famous Concertgebouw Orchestra, the Hollandfestival of theatre, music and other genres, the Prinsengrachtfestival outside the Pulitzerhotel in summer, and the Uitmarkt, heralding the beginning of the new theatre season.

The city has some of the best nightlife in the world: cosy "brown cafés", trendy alternative bars, discos, night-clubs, and of course the infamous red-light district, the Walletjes.

Amsterdam is a very outward-looking and tolerant city. As elsewhere in the Netherlands, many coffee shops sell soft drugs quite legally.

HISTORICAL NOTES

Legend has it that Amsterdam was founded by two Frisian fishermen, who landed on the shores of the Amstel in a small boat with their dog. In fact, the first documented mention of the city dates from 1275, when Count Floris V of Holland granted toll privileges to this herring-fishing village, situated on two dikes joined by a dam, at the mouth of the Amstel River. Amsterdam developed in stages round the original village centre, the present-day Dam square. It was awarded its city charter in about 1300, and was annexed by William III to the county of Holland in 1317.

In 1345, following a miracle in which a Eucharistic host was left undamaged in a fire, Amsterdam became an important place of pilgrimage. In 1428 the town, together with the county of Holland, passed into the hands of the Duke of Burgundy,

Amsterdam in winter

Philip the Good. The use of the imperial crown in the city's coat of arms was sanctioned in 1489 by Emperor Maximilian for the support given by the city to the Habsburg monarchs.

The beginning of prosperity – A period of great affluence began in the late 16C. After Antwerp had been pillaged by the Spanish in 1576, the town's rich merchants took refuge in Amsterdam, bringing their diamond industry with them. Once Amsterdam had been freed from Spanish rule by the Union of Utrecht in 1579, the town became very prosperous, not least because of the large-scale influx of immigrants. Later, at the end of the 16C, the Marranos arrived from Spain and Portugal; these were Jews who had been forcibly converted to Catholicism but continued to practise their own religion in secret. The authorities granted them extensive privileges in order to encourage their trading activities.

The Golden Age – The 17C marked the height of Amsterdam's powers. Following in the wake of the Portuguese, the Dutch began a period of overseas expansion, and only a few years later their sailing ships were trading all over the Far East. In 1602 they founded the East India Company (Verenigde Oostindische Compagnie, or VOC), followed in 1621 by the West India Company. A Dutch settlement was established at Nieuw Amsterdam; this was later renamed New York by the British.

The Wisselbank, created in 1609, was one of Europe's first banks, and the Stock Exchange was built in 1608 by Hendrick de Keyser.

In 1610 it was decided to build the three main canals, the Herengracht, Keizersgracht and Prinsengracht, and these were soon lined with the mansions of wealthy merchants. The town was surrounded with a high wall on which a number of windmills were built.

Rembrandt, who was born in Leiden, came to live in Amsterdam in 1630, and was buried in the Westerkerk in 1669.

In 1648, when the Treaty of Münster ended the Eighty Years' War with Spain, the independence of the United Provinces was officially recognised.

The growth of navigation led to an increased demand for maps and globes, and their manufacture became one of Amsterdam's specialities. The city acquired a leading reputation in this area, partly as a result of the work of famous geographers such as Hondius, who published a new edition of Mercator's famous atlas in 1605.

The Revocation of the Edict of Nantes in France in 1685 resulted in the arrival of a large number of Huguenots, who contributed to the city's prosperity. By the end of the 17C, however, Dutch maritime power was on the decline, as was textile manufacturing.

French occupation – Such was Amsterdam's accumulated wealth that for a long time it withstood the effects of the economic decline of the 18C. Although the city had contrived to repel an attack by Louis XIV's troops in 1672 by opening the locks which protected it, it could do nothing in 1795 against Pichegru's army. In 1806, Napoleon made his brother Louis Bonaparte King of Holland. Louis settled in Amsterdam, which became the capital of the kingdom. The country became a part of France in 1810, and was decreed by Napoleon to be the third city of the French Empire and seat of the local government of the Zuiderzee *département*. However, Amsterdam was seriously hit by Napoleon's blockade of Britain, the Continental System, which ruined its trade. In November 1813, the population revolted and recognised the Prince of Orange, William I, as their sovereign on 2 December.

Economic reawakening – It was only in the second half of the 19C that the city emerged from a long period of economic lethargy. The city walls were demolished and the opening of the Noordzeekanaal in 1876 provided a major boost to overseas trade. In 1889 the Centraal Station was built. The diamond industry also began to flourish again.

The early 20C – In 1903 the new Stock Exchange by **Berlage** was completed, marking the beginning of a new era of architecture.
Shortly before the First World War, the city began expanding and new suburbs were built. The **Amsterdam School** of architecture developed a new style of building, mainly after the First World War. The central figure of this movement was **Michel de Klerk**. He, along with **Peter Kramer** and **JM van der Mey**, designed a great deal of local authority housing, particularly to the south of **Sarphatipark** and to the west of **Spaarndammerstraat** *(illustration: see Introduction, The arts)*. They tried to break the monotony of façades by using asymmetry and differences in level, and to reduce the severity of straight lines by introducing sections of curving walls.
The last war hit the city badly. Under the five-year German occupation, nearly 80 000 Jews were deported to concentration camps; only 5 000 survived.

Amsterdam after 1945 – Since the war, Amsterdam has staged a magnificent recovery from its ordeal. It is now a major industrial city, part of the huge **Randstad conurbation**. Its industries include medical technology, metals, printing, food, and of course tourism. The **RAI**, built on Europaplein in the 1960s, hosts many international congresses and trade fairs, and the **World Trade Centre** near the Station Zuid was inaugurated in 1985.
The canal from Amsterdam to the Rhine (Amsterdam-Rijnkanaal), completed in 1952, has contributed to the development of the port. The completion of a road tunnel under the IJ in 1968 improved communication between the city centre and the area to the north of the port; the first Metro line was opened in 1976. The town has seen the development of such modern suburbs as **Buitenveldert** to the south and **Bijlmermeer** to the south-east. However, the housing problem remains acute, and the city is continuing to expand **(Java-eiland, KNMS-eiland)**. Another typical feature of the city are the 2 400 picturesque houseboats lining 36km/22mi of quays. Amsterdam has two universities and numerous higher educational institutions.

WHERE TO STAY

The Red Guide Benelux gives a detailed list of hotels in each area. The following hotels have been selected for their facilities, location, character or value for money. They have been divided into three categories:
– **MODERATE**: Small, simple but comfortable hotels charging less than 195fl for a room.
– **MID-RANGE**: Pleasant hotels with their own distinctive charm, costing between 195fl and 350fl per night.
– **LUXURY**: Very comfortable and well located luxury hotels with prices to match.

Youth Hostels

Non-members can stay in youth hostels on payment of a supplement, and there is no age limit. Information from www.njhc.org

NJHC Stadsdoelen – *Kloveniersburgwal 97, 1011 KB,* ☎ *(020) 624 68 32. 184 beds.* Right by the red-light district.

NJHC Vondelpark – *Zandpad 5, 1054 GA,* ☎ *(020) 589 89 96. 493 beds.* The busiest and best-located youth hostel.

Hotels

MODERATE

Aalders – *Jan Luijkenstraat 13-15, 1071 CJ,* ☎ *(020) 673 40 27, Fax (020) 673 46 98. www.hotelaalders.nl. 53 rooms.* Simple but comfortable hotel close to the Stedelijk Museum, the Van Gogh Museum and the Rijksmuseum.

Amstel Botel – *Oosterdokskade 2-4, 1011 AE,* ☎ *(020) 626 42 47, fax (020) 639 19 52. www.amstelbotel.com. 176 rooms.* This cruise ship with 176 cabins lies right by the station (Centraal Station) and is well-appointed.

Nicolaas Witsen – *Nicolaas Witsenstraat 4, 1017 ZH,* ☎ *(020) 623 61 43, Fax (020) 620 51 13. 31 rooms.* Comfortable hotel in a quiet street at walking distance from the main museums and the busy area around Rembrandtplein and Leidseplein.

MID-RANGE

Ambassade – *Herengracht 341, 1016 AZ,* ☎ *(020) 555 02 22, fax (020) 555 02 77. www.ambassade-hotel.nl. 59 rooms.* This stylish hotel is superbly located in a group of 17C houses on the Herengracht, close to the tourist centre. Start the day in style in the beautiful breakfast room.

Arena – *'s-Gravesandestraat 51, 1092 AA,* ☎ *(020) 694 74 44, fax (020) 663 26 49. www.hotelarena.nl. 121 rooms.* This hotel near Oosterpark is housed in a former orphanage dating from 1890. The rooms are spacious, the fixtures and fittings are simple and modern. A café-restaurant with a terrace overlooking the garden and a night-club also form part of the same complex. The hotel has its own private car park.

Canal House – *Keizersgracht 148, 1015 CX,* ☎ *(020) 622 51 82, Fax (020) 624 13 17. www.canalhouse.nl. 26 rooms.* This very elegant 17C hotel is full of antiques; each room is furnished differently. Breakfast is served in the dining room overlooking the garden.

X. Richer/HOA QUI

The dining room, Canal House Hotel

La Casaló – *Amsteldijk 862, 1079 LN, ☎ (020) 642 36 80, Fax (020) 644 74 09. 4 rooms.* Each of the rooms in this floating hotel is in a different style: Dutch, oriental, African and Caribbean. You can have breakfast outside in fine weather.

Piet Hein – *Vossiusstraat 53, 1071 AK, ☎ (020) 662 72 05, fax (020) 662 15 26. www.hotelpiethein.nl. 37 rooms.* Comfortable hotel right by Vondelpark and the main museums.

Toro – *Koningslaan 64, 1075 AG, ☎ (020) 673 72 23, Fax (020) 675 00 31. 22 rooms.* This early 20C villa on the edge of Vondelpark has a pleasant atmosphere and an attractive lake view from the terrace.

LUXURY

American – *Leidsekader 97, 1017 PN, ☎ (020) 624 53 22, Fax (020) 556 30 00, fax (020) 556 30 01. www.amstelhotel.nl. 186 rooms.* Well known hotel on Leidseplein. Its magnificent Art Deco-style brasserie is frequented mainly by politicians and leading figures in the arts.

Amstel – *Prof. Tulpplein 1, 1018 GX, ☎ (020) 622 60 60, Fax (020) 622 58 08. www.amstelhotel.nl. 64 rooms.* This luxury hotel on the banks of the Amstel has one of the Netherlands' most famous restaurants, La Rive. It also boasts a fitness club complete with pool, jacuzzi, sauna, gymnasium and steam room.

Europe – *Nieuwe Doelenstraat 2, 1012 CP, ☎ (020) 531 17 77, Fax (020) 531 17 78. www.leurope.nl. 94 rooms.* This famous hotel of Victorian grandeur is close to the historic centre of Amsterdam. The Excelsior restaurant, known for its outstanding wine cellar, has a unique view of the Amstel. The hotel also has a heated indoor pool, a solarium and a fitness club.

Pulitzer – *Prinsengracht 315-331, 1016 GZ, ☎ (020) 523 52 35, Fax (020) 627 67 53. www.pulitzer.nl. 222 rooms.* This magnificent hotel on Prinsengracht was created from twenty-five 17C and 18C houses. It has an inner courtyard, a restaurant, a piano bar and a café.

The Grand – *Oudezijds Voorburgwal 197, 1012 EX, ☎ (020) 555 31 11, Fax (020) 555 32 22. www.thegrand.nl. 169 rooms.* This luxury hotel is housed in the former Prinsenhof. The rooms overlook either the canal or the inner courtyard.

WHERE TO EAT

The capital offers a huge variety of eating experiences. The following restaurants have been selected for their food, decor and/or distinctive setting. **The Red Guide Benelux** contains a larger selection of restaurants, with a gastronomical emphasis.

MODERATE

Cobra – *Museumplein, ☎ (020) 470 01 14.* Everything about this café-restaurant is inspired by the Cobra art movement: the artwork on the walls, the chairs, even the floor and the wine labels. The tableware was designed by Corneille, founder member of the movement. Also a sushi bar, shop and a large terrace in the summer months.

De Rode Leeuw (Hotel Amsterdam) – *Damrak 93, ☎ (020) 555 06 66.* Brasserie on the busy Damstraat, serving Dutch specialities such as *kapucijners*, kidney beans served with bacon and onion.

Haesje Claes – *Spuistraat 275, ☎ (020) 624 99 98.* Simple Dutch food, generous portions, and excellent value for money.

Indrapura – *Rembrandtplein 40, ☎ (020) 623 73 29.* Indonesian restaurant.

Kantijl & De Tijger – *Spuistraat 291-293, ☎ (020) 620 30 74.* Indonesian.

MID-RANGE

Bordewijk – *Noordermarkt 7, ☎ (020) 624 38 99.* Open evenings only. Trendy restaurant in the Jordaan serving contemporary cuisine.

Café Roux – *Oudezijds Voorburgwal 197, ☎ (020) 555 35 60.* This restaurant, on the ground floor of The Grand hotel *(see above)*, serves good food in a beautiful Art Deco setting. By the entrance is a mural by Karel Appel.

De Gouden Reael – *Zandhoek 14, ☎ (020) 623 38 83.* Superbly located restaurant on the old harbour; a weekly changing menu of French local dishes.

De Vijff Vliegen – *Spuistraat 294-302, ☎ (020) 624 83 69.* Dutch cooking in an atmospheric, typically Amsterdam setting; a jumble of little rooms, beautifully decorated in 17C style.

Le Garage – *Ruysdaelstraat 54-56, ☎ (020) 679 71 76.* Modern brasserie with an artsy atmosphere and international clientele. The owner has a cooking programme on Dutch television.

In de Waag – *Nieuwmarkt 4*, ☎ *(020) 422 77 72*. This pleasant café-restaurant is in the city's historic weigh-house *(waag)*. The menu emphasises fish from the IJsselmeer, and there is also a wine bar, a reading table and a large terrace in summer.

Sea Palace – *Oosterdokskade 8*, ☎ *(020) 626 47 77*. Floating Chinese restaurant with a great view of Amsterdam.

Tom Yam – *Staalstraat 22*, ☎ *(020) 622 95 33*. Stylish restaurant with a Zen garden and an exotic mixed cuisine.

OUT AND ABOUT IN AMSTERDAM

Amsterdam is believed to have around a thousand cafés, renowned for their friendly and cosy atmosphere. Some serve snacks and simple meals.

The area around **Leidseplein** and Rembrandtplein is particularly busy in the evenings. The Stadsschouwburg, or municipal theatre, is located on the former; the area also has a wealth of small theatres, cafés, cinemas and discos, as well as the Holland Casino. **Rembrandtplein** is mainly known for its restaurants, its large terrace cafés, and its clubs.

Drinking

BROWN CAFÉS

Brown cafés are a typically Dutch phenomenon, so named because of their nicotine-stained ceilings and wooden interiors. They are often not very large, and so tend to get crowded quickly. The most authentic brown cafés are in the city centre and the Jordaan.

Café Hoppe – *Spui 18-20*. A meeting place for writers, journalists and other denizens of the literary world; in summer, customers also spill out onto the pavement.

De Admiraal – *Herengracht 563*. This café makes its own gin in one of Amsterdam's oldest distilleries.

't Papeneiland – *Prinsengracht 2*. This is one of the city's most romantic brown cafés, with Delft tile decoration, an old-fashioned stove and a delightful waterside location.

't Smalle – *Egelantiersgracht 12*. A tiny café with a terrace overlooking the canal.

PROEFLOKALEN

Proeflokalen are a relic of the 17C, when merchants came to sample drinks being sold by importers; *proeflokaal* simply means "tasting place". Today, you can taste gin and other spirits here before making a purchase.

De Drie Fleschjes – *Gravenstraat 18*. This proeflokaal is always pleasantly busy, with a throng of people at the bar, and walls lined with carafes of exotically named drinks like crème de roses, parfait amour and ratafia.

Ph. Gajic/MICHELIN

A proeflokaal: "De Drie Fleschjes"

Wynand Fockink – *Pijlsteeg 31 (near Dam)*. Wynand Fockink offers a wide selection of gin and other local spirits, with the chance to try before you buy. There is also an attractive courtyard.

CAFÉS

Café Américain – *Leidsekade 97 and Leidseplein 26*. An Amsterdam institution; despite its rather high prices, this wonderful brasserie is a must for lovers of Art Deco.

Café Dantzig – *Zwanenburgwal 15*. Large café with a terrace on the Amstel and a separate reading area. A good place to put your feet up after a visit to the Waterlooplein flea market.

Café Luxembourg – *Spui 22*. Actually somewhere part-way between a brown café and a French-style café; at its best in the late morning, though it also serves a great breakfast.

De Jaren – *Nieuwe Doelenstraat 20-22*. This huge modern café is particularly popular with young locals; its delightful two-level terrace on the Amstel gets packed in fine weather.

De Kroon – *Rembrandtplein 17*. This is an Amsterdam landmark, with a very varied clientele. The room on the first floor is a sight in itself, and the terrace has an enjoyable view of the square.

BARS

Café de Sluijswacht – *Jodenbreestraat 1*. This cheerful little waterside café lies opposite the Rembrandthuis, and the terrace offers a view of the Oude Schans. Don't worry if you've had a glass or two and things look a little strange; it's the building that's leaning at an angle, not you.

De Prins – *Prinsengracht 124*. Pleasant café with terrace, right by the Anne Frank Huis.

Walem – *Keizersgracht 449*. Attractive designer interior with a garden at the back.

Morlang – *Keizersgracht 451*. Next door to Café Walem. An often busy place, with a youngish clientele and a scenic waterside terrace.

VOCafé in de Schreierstoren – *Prins Hendrikkade 94-95*. This café has two rooms, one furnished with antiques and the other used as a reading room. It also has two terraces, one beside the water.

COFFEE SHOPS

Although you can actually go into a coffee shop just for a drink, their main purpose is to sell legal soft drugs such as hashish and marijuana.

Nightlife

What's on in Amsterdam is published every three weeks, and gives full listings of music, dance, theatre and other events. It is available in VVV tourist offices and some bookshops.

You can book tickets direct or through **VVV Theatre Ticket Service** (Centraal Station, Leidseplein or Stadionplein) or **Amsterdams Uit Buro: AUB Ticketshop** in the theatre (Stadsschouwburg) on Leidseplein *(every day 10am-6pm)* or through the **Uitlijn** ticket line, ☎ *0900 0191 (every day 9am-9pm)*.

Clubs – **Escape**, *Rembrandtplein 11*, is Amsterdam's biggest club; **iT**, *Amstelstraat 24*, is an extravagant venue with go-go girls, drag queens, and special gay evenings.

Casino – **Holland Casino**, *Max Euweplein 64*, ☎ *(020) 620 10 06*.

Jazz, rock, pop concerts – **Amsterdam ArenA**, *Huntum 2*, ☎ *(020) 311 13 33*, performances by big international names; **Bimhuis**, *Oude Schans 73*, ☎ *(020) 623 13 61*, a must for jazz lovers; **De Melkweg**, *Lijnbaansgracht 234*, ☎ *(020) 531 81 81*, concerts and dance nights in an old dairy; **Paradiso**, *Weteringschans 6*, ☎ *(020) 626 45 21*, dancing and rock concerts in a former church.

Classical music and opera – **Koninklijk Theater Carré**, *Amstel 115-125*, ☎ *(020) 625 52 25*, circus, variety, musicals; **Muziektheater (Stopera)**, *Amstel 3*, ☎ *(020) 625 54 55*, performances by the Nederlandse Opera, the Nationale Ballet and the Nederlands Dans Theater; **Stadsschouwburg**, *Leidseplein 26*, ☎ *(020) 624 23 11*; **Beurs van Berlage**, *Damrak 213*, ☎ *(020) 627 04 66*, concerts by the Netherlands Philharmonic Orchestra and others; **Concertgebouw**, *Concertgebouwplein 2-6*, ☎ *(020) 671 83 54*, home of the world-famous Royal Concertgebouw Orchestra; **Felix Meritis**, *Keizersgracht 324*, ☎ *(020) 623 13 11*, classical concerts in a magnificent 18C auditorium.

Shopping

Most shops are closed on Monday mornings. Many, particularly in the city centre, are open until 9pm on Thursdays.

Department stores and shopping centres – De Bijenkorf, *Damrak 1*, department store; **Magna Plaza Center**, *Nieuwezijds Voorburgwal 182*, an upmarket indoor shopping centre with some 40 shops; **Metz & Co**, *corner of Keizersgracht and Leidsestraat*, design, gifts etc; **Vroom and Dreesmann**, department store, *Kalverstraat 201*.

Fashion – There are plenty of exclusive and trendy fashion stores, luxury shoe shops and jewellers in the **Museum District**, and particularly in P.C. **Hooftstraat** and **Van Baerlesstraat**. The pedestrianised **Kalverstraat** and Nieuwendijk have many more down-to-earth clothes shops.

Diamond factories – Ten of these are open to the public. Information from the VVV, ☎ *0900 400 40 40*.

Antiques – Most of the antique shops are located around the main canal area (Singel, Herengracht, Keizersgracht and Prinsengracht), and more especially in **Spiegelstraat**, **Nieuwe Spiegelstraat** and **Kerkstraat**.

Markets

Even if you don't buy anything, the markets are a great place for people-watching.

Albert Cuypmarkt – *Albert Cuypstraat; Mondays to Saturdays, 9.30am to 5pm*; general goods.

Flower market – *Singel, between Muntplein and Koningsplein; Mondays to Saturdays, 9.30am to 5pm.*

Book market – *Oudemanhuispoort, Mondays and Saturdays, 10am to 4pm; Spui, Fridays, 10am to 6pm.*

Flea market – *Waterlooplein; Mondays to Saturdays, 9am to 5pm.*

Antiques market – *Nieuwmarkt; May to September, Sundays, 9am to 5pm.*

Indoor flea market – *Looiersgracht 38, Saturdays and Sundays, 11am to 5pm.*

Ch. Bastin et J. Evrard

The flower market

PRACTICAL INFORMATION

General information – The VVV tourist office has branches in and opposite the **Centraal Station**, on the corner of **Leidseplein** and **Leidsestraat**, on **Stadionplein** and at **Schiphol**. These are all open daily, ☎ 0900 400 40 40; their web site is at www.visitamsterdam.nl. The City of Amsterdam (local authority) also has an interesting web site with many useful tips and links: **www.amsterdam.nl**

Parking – Parking is very difficult and expensive in Amsterdam, and is free only after 11pm. If you break the rules, you risk getting ticketed or even clamped; in the latter case, call the **clamping assistance** line on ☎ (020) 667 10 01. You can avoid all these problems by buying a daily parking permit from your hotel or using one of the (equally expensive) **multi-storey car parks**. There is free parking at the **park and ride centres** on the outskirts of the city, though their isolated location means that parking here at night is not recommended.

Public transport – Information and tickets, including one-day travelcards and strippenkaarten (strips of tickets), are available from the VVV tourist office. The **Circle-Amsterdam Ticket** is valid for one to nine days and allows unlimited use of trams (including express services), buses and the metro. The **Circle-tram** is particularly useful, as it serves most of the main sights and hotels.

Guided tours – The VVV organises a great variety of guided tours. Some take in the main sights in the city, others visit Jordaan or the old Jewish quarter.

Boat trips – Boat trips on the canals leave from various points in the city. *For further information, see below and under Admission times and charges at the back of the guide.*

Alternative transport – Renting a **bicycle** ⊘ is definitely the best way of getting around and avoiding parking problems. **Canal bikes** ⊘ are available for hire in various places.
The **Museum Boat** ⊘ and **Canal Bus** ⊘ follow a circular route from the station (Centraal Station) and stops near all the main museums.

Events – Amsterdam has a constant succession of festivals and similar events *(see Calendar of events at the front of the guide for dates and phone numbers, or contact the VVV).* They include the **Holland Festival**, the **open-air theatre** season in **Vondelpark**, the **Prinsengracht Concert**, the **Bloemencorso** or flower parade from **Aalsmeer to Amsterdam**, and the **official entry of Santa Claus** into the city. A number of important annual trade fairs take place at the **RAI** exhibition and conference centre.

If you've still got time...

The following sites are marked on the town plans; details are given in *The Green Guide Amsterdam.*

OUDE ZIJDE: Hash Marihuana Museum – Koffie- en Theemuseum – Prinsenhof – Tattoo Museum

THE CANALS: Amstelkerk – De Appel – De Duif – De Krijtberg – Leidsegracht – Max Euwe Centrum – Multatuli Museum – Torensluis – West-Indisch Huis – Woonbootmuseum

MUSEUM DISTRICT: Vondelkerk

JORDAAN: Elandsgracht – Lauriergracht – Lindengracht – Theó Thijssen Museum

DE PLANTAGE: De Gooyer windmill

THE PORT: Haarlemmerpoort – Java-eiland – Open Haven Museum – Vereniging Museumhaven Amsterdam – Werf 't Kromhout

PIJP: Gemeentearchief Amsterdam

OUTSKIRTS: Amstelstation – Amsterdam ArenA – Bosmuseum visitor centre – Electrische Museumtramlijn Amsterdam – Van Leers office building – Olympic Stadium – Peter Stuyvesant Stichting – Rembrandt Tower

OUDERKERK A/D AMSTEL: Oudheidkamer – Portuguese-Israeli cemetery – St.-Urbanuskerk

---

★★★ OLD AMSTERDAM

★★ Nieuwe Zijde

Centraal Station – The huge central station on three artificial islands in the River IJ aroused great controversy when it was built between 1881 and 1889, mainly because it blocked off the view of the port. Designed by the architects **PJH Cuypers** and **AL van Gendt**, it is now one of the city's best-known buildings.
The busy Damrak leads to the Beurs.

★ **Beurs (Commodities Exchange)** – Built between 1897 and 1903, this is the principal work of **Berlage**, the ardent functionalist and pioneer of modern architecture in the Netherlands. It has a simple brick exterior, and inside, the open steel framework supports a glass roof.

Since 1987, it has been used as a cultural centre for exhibitions, conferences and concerts. The **Beurs van Berlage Museum** ⊙ contains a small permanent exhibition dealing mainly with the construction of this distinctive building.
The 1913 **Stock Exchange** is also on Beursplein.

★ **Dam** – The Dam, Amsterdam's main square, is at the junction of the two large central thoroughfares, **Damrak** and Rokin, on the site of the dam across the Amstel. Overlooking this very busy square are the Royal Palace and the Nieuwe Kerk.
The **Nationaal Monument** (1956, Raedeker) symbolises humanity's suffering in times of war and has become a popular meeting-place.

★ **Koninklijk Paleis (Royal Palace)** ⊙ – In 1648, Jacob van Campen began building a new town hall to replace the old Gothic one destroyed by fire in 1652. The town hall became the Royal Palace in 1808 during the reign of Louis Bonaparte. This imposing classical building was built on 13 659 wooden piles. The east and west façades are topped by tympana carved by Artus I Quellin, of Antwerp, who also decorated the interior. On the ground floor is the **Vierschaar**, the courtroom where death sentences used to be passed. The public could watch the proceedings through grilles.
In the **Burgerzaal★** (citizens' room) on the first floor, the floor decoration depicts the eastern and western hemispheres. There is also a famous sculpture by Artus I Quellin of Atlas holding the celestial globe on his shoulders. It was in the Council Room **(Schepenzaal)** that Queen Juliana abdicated in 1980.

★★ **Nieuwe Kerk** ⊙ – The Protestant New Church is the national church of the Netherlands. It is here that the country's sovereigns are crowned; Queen Wilhelmina's coronation was held here on 6 September 1898, that of her daughter Juliana 50 years later to the day, and Queen Beatrix on 30 April 1980. This lovely late-Gothic building was pillaged and gutted by fire several times. After the fire in 1645 its tower, designed by Jacob van Campen, remained unfinished. Today the building is used as a cultural centre, where all kinds of activities are organised, including major **exhibitions**.
The church has a massive mahogany **pulpit★★** carved by Vinckenbrink in 1649, and a copper **chancel screen★** which is a masterpiece of Johannes Lutma, the Amsterdam gold and silversmith. The main **organ case★★** (c 1650) was designed by Van Campen. The church contains the tombs of several Dutch admirals, including that of **Michiel de Ruyter★**, the commander of the fleet in the Second and Third Anglo-Dutch Wars, by the Belgian sculptor Rombout Verhulst. The poet Vondel and the famous bell-founders François and Pierre Hemony were also buried here.

Madame Tussaud Scenerama ⊙ – *Dam 20*. Here modern technology, including audio-animatronics, is used to create a fascinating museum illustrating mainly life during the Golden Age, as depicted in the paintings of Rembrandt, Vermeer and Jan Steen. There is also a fine **revolving model** of 17C Amsterdam. The exhibition ends with many well-known figures from the Netherlands and abroad.

Magna Plaza – *Nieuwezijds Voorburgwal 182*. Behind the Koninklijk Paleis is a former post office designed by CG Peters in 1899. This was converted in 1990 into an upmarket shopping centre with some 40 stores.

Kalverstraat – This bustling pedestrian precinct is the most important shopping street in Amsterdam.

★★ **Amsterdams Historisch Museum** ⊙ – *Access via Kalverstraat 62, Sint-Luciënsteeg 27 or Gedempte Begijnensloot (Gallery of the Civic Guards)*. This museum is housed in a 15C former orphanage. On the left of the entrance in Kalverstraat is the boys' playground; the cubbyholes where they used to keep their belongings are in the east wing. Opposite, a building in the classical style hosts temporary exhibitions. In **St.-Luciënsteeg** a small gateway is surmounted by the city's coat of arms. On one wall there is a large collection of picturesque **façade-stones**, and there is also a free **gallery of schutterstukken★**, group portraits of companies of the civic guard.
The entrance to the museum is through the second courtyard, formerly reserved for the girl orphans.
Follow the rooms in numerical order; these are spread over several floors and retrace the history of Amsterdam chronologically and thematically.

An illuminated map shows the city's remarkable expansion. The city was built on sand, erected a town hall and fairly rapidly began to trade with the rest of the world. In 1345 a miracle made it a centre of pilgrimage, and then Amsterdam was subjected to Spanish rule. During this period it began to extend its influence around the world. The ships and merchandise from the Dutch East India Company and other companies flooded the city. At its peak, it built a new town hall, the present Royal Palace. The city began attracting many artists, who were commissioned by the rich merchants to paint portraits and landscapes. Large numbers of buildings were constructed, including several churches. Although the town had become wealthy, it did not forget those living in poverty: charitable institutions abounded, and their regents, or governors, liked having their portraits painted. In the 18C, despite strong competition from foreign countries, Amsterdam still occupied a prominent position in the world of the arts. In 1795 the French arrived; the towns lost their independence but the country was unified. At the end of the 19C, Amsterdam experienced something of a population explosion. New developments sprang up, including the Rijksmuseum. After the horrors of the Second World War, Amsterdam went back to being the dynamic city it had once been and it has remained so ever since. As you leave, visit the **17C Regents' Room** left of the entrance; this is where the directors of the orphanage met.

Ph. Gajic/MICHELIN

Beguine convent

★★ **Begijnhof** – The Beguine convent is a haven of peace in the heart of the city. Founded in the 14C, it is one of the few such institutions remaining in the Netherlands *(see BREDA)*. Beguines are women belonging to a lay sisterhood; although they take no vows, they devote themselves to religious life and wear a habit. The tall 17C and 18C houses with small front gardens are arranged around an area of grass where the former church of the Beguines stands. This has belonged to the English Presbyterian community since 1607. Nos 11, 19, 23 and 24 have beautiful sculpted façade-stones, while the tall and elegant house at no 26 was that of the mother superior of the Beguinage. At no 29 there is a hidden Catholic chapel, built by the Beguines in 1665. Not far away is the city's oldest house, no 34, dating from the 15C and with a wooden **façade**★; note the large number of façade stones incorporated into the wall of the courtyard on the left.

Rokin – This dock is situated at the far end of the Amstel, the continuation having been filled in. At the far end of the dock stands an **equestrian statue** of Queen Wilhelmina by Theresia van der Pant.

Langebrugsteeg leads into Amsterdam's oldest quarter, Oude Zijde, around which the city developed.

★★ Oude Zijde

Sint-Nicolaaskerk – This domed neo-Baroque-style Catholic church is situated very close to the Centraal Station. The church was built in 1887 and designed by AC Bleys.

Schreierstoren – This tower, known as the "weeping tower", formed part of the city wall. Legend has it that sailors' wives came to say goodbye to their husbands; hence the name.

There is a bronze plaque commemorating the Englishman, **Henry Hudson**, who discovered the American river which bears his name while working for the Dutch East India Company in 1609.

Huis Leeuwenburg – *14 Oudezijds Voorburgwal*. This picturesque 17C house has a stepped gable of rust-coloured brick. A carved façade-stone depicts a fortified castle sheltering a lion.

From the bridge over the lock where the two canals meet, there is an attractive **view**★: on one side, the Oudezijds Kolk, and the dome of the Catholic Sint-Nicolaaskerk, and on the other side the Oudezijds Voorburgwal, with its lovely series of old façades, and the Oude Kerk in the distance.

* **Museum Amstelkring Ons' Lieve Heer op Solder (Amstelkring Museum of Our Lord in the Attic)** ⊙ – After the Union of Utrecht in 1579, when the Catholics were driven out of their churches by the Reformation, they were forced to celebrate mass in private houses. Although this was officially prohibited, in practice the authorities turned a blind eye (a 17C example of Amsterdam's spirit of tolerance and liberalism). This secret chapel fitted out in the attics of two houses was used for Catholic worship from 1663 until the construction of the new St.-Nicolaaskerk in 1887. Services and concerts are sometimes held here.

The staircase leading to the 2nd floor passes in front of the hall, which is in pure 17C Amsterdam style, and the curate's room with a box bed. The **church**, whose two superimposed galleries occupy the 3rd and 4th floors of the houses, has interesting 18C furnishings. In the rooms behind and below the church there is an interesting exhibition of church silver.

The hall, Museum Amstelkring Ons' Lieve Heer op Solder

Ph. Gajic/MICHELIN

* **Oude Kerk** ⊙ – The present Old Church, dedicated to St Nicholas, was built in 1306. It is the oldest in the city. In the 16C the bell-tower was topped by an elegant spire whose carillon was in part cast by François Hemony; there is an excellent **view**★★ from here.

The church's interior was seriously damaged by Calvinist iconoclasts, but its Lady Chapel still has three fine **stained-glass windows**★ (1555). The **organ loft**★ above the entrance to the nave was made in 1724 by Jan Westerman. In 1642 Rembrandt's wife Saskia was buried here, and the church is the final resting-place of many famous people, including the painter Pieter Aertsen, the writer Roemer Visscher, the architects Justus and Philips Vingboons and the composer JP Sweelinck.

The church hosts various cultural events, such as organ recitals, exhibitions and theatre performances.

** **The Walletjes** – *The area between Warmoesstraat, Damstraat, Oude Doelenstraat, Kloveniersburgwal, Nieuwmarkt and Geldersekade.* Amsterdam's **red-light district**. The locals sometimes use the word *"Walletjes"* to describe this district frequented by seafarers from the 14C onwards. The word means "small walls" and refers to the fact that the shop windows displaying the ladies' charms are sometimes half-concealed in old, very narrow streets (particularly to the south of Oude Kerk). The days of the seafarers and distilleries have gone, however, and today the industry, although equally colourful, has become much less light-hearted, with a mass of sex shops and stores selling pornographic videos. The area is not dangerous – indeed avoiding it would mean missing out on a large section of the historic centre – but visitors should nevertheless be on their guard as the area is well known for pickpockets and bag-snatchers.

Nieuwmarkt – Amsterdam's oldest market square is between the Chinese district *(Zeedijk and the surrounding area)* and the red-light district.

Waag or St.-Anthoniespoort – This imposing fortified gateway (1488), flanked by towers and turrets, was converted into a weigh-house (waag) in 1617 and restored in 1996. The top floor served as an anatomy theatre, where surgeons and their students could attend public dissections, often on the corpses of criminals who had been condemned to death. Rembrandt's famous painting, *The Anatomy Lesson of Dr Jan Deyman* (now in the Amsterdams Historisch Museum), documents the lecture given by Dr Deyman in 1656. The building also has a café-restaurant.

Index of streets included in the maps of Amsterdam

SIGHTSEEING WITH AMSTERDAM STREET MAPS

(M) = See **Museums**   (T) = See **Theatres**

Trippenhuis – *Kloveniersburgwal no 29*. This elegant classical edifice was built in 1662 by Justus Vingboons for the Trip brothers, who were cannon manufacturers; the chimneys are in the shape of mortars. The small picturesque house next door at **no 26** is thought to have been built for the Trip brothers' coachman, using the stone left over from the main house

Oudemanhuispoort – A covered passage between Kloveniersburgwal and Oudezijds Achterburgwal, once the site of a home for elderly men (oudemanshuis) and now a book market.

Universiteitsmuseum de Agnietenkapel – *Oudezijds Voorburgwal 231*. Near the Oudemanhuispoort, the **Agnietenpoort** leads to this chapel, once the home of the Athenaeum Illustre of 1632, a predecessor of the university. The buildings are currently being used by the university, and temporary exhibitions are held here.

Grimburgwal – This canal was built in the early 14C and marked the southern boundary of the city. The beautiful **Huis op de Drie Grachten**★ (House on the Three Canals), dating from 1609, stands at the confluence of the Oudezijds Voorburgwal, the Oudezijds Achterburgwal, and the Grimburgwal.

★ **Allard Pierson Museum** ⊙ – This archaeological museum, part of Amsterdam University, has a remarkable collection of antiquities. The first floor contains items from Egypt (such as **funerary masks**★, sculptures and Coptic textiles), the Middle East (Iranian pottery and jewellery), Syria, Anatolia, Palestine and Mesopotamia (including cylinder-seals and cuneiform writings). The second floor is devoted to Greece, Etruria and the Roman empire. The collection includes the **Amsterdam Kouros**★ (c 590 BC), ceramics (including **red-figure jars**★), a Roman sarcophagus (c AD 300) and various items of Etruscan earthenware and sculpture.

Nearby is the **Nes** theatre district, with the **Engelenbak** and **Frascati** theatres and the Flemish Cultural Centre **De Brakke Grond**.

Between the flower market★★ and Rembrandtplein★

Muntplein – This busy square is dominated by the Mint Tower, **Munttoren**. The tower, the remains of a 17C gateway, has a Baroque spire which was added by Hendrick de Keyser and which has a **carillon**. In 1672, during the war against France, money was minted here.

★★ **Bloemenmarkt (Flower Market)** – This colourful market is located at the southern end of the Singel. It has been a floating market since 1862, offering passers-by a wide selection of cut flowers and bulbs as well as clogs and other souvenirs.

Ph: Gajic/MICHELIN

Tuschinskitheater - Art Deco detail

Tuschinskitheater – *Reguliersbreestraat 26-8.* This beautiful cinema in genuine Art Deco style was built in 1921 by HL de Jong. Note particularly the expressive **front façade**, the very beautiful **carpet** in the foyer, and the overwhelming **interior**★ of the Tuschinski 1 auditorium. Opposite, the building that was once the Cineac cinema (1934, J Duiker) has now become a restaurant (Planet Hollywood). The exterior is a good example of the differences between Art Deco and Functionalism.

★ **Rembrandtsplein** – This square is a popular destination for local people out for an evening stroll. There are many large cafés around the square, with its statue of **Rembrandt** by Royer (1852).

Thorbeckeplein – With its many night-clubs, this square is very busy in the evenings.

In and around Waterlooplein

Waterlooplein – On this large square, which has a lively **daily market** (second-hand clothes and furniture, ethnic jewellery, textiles etc), stands the **Mozes-en Aäron Kerk**. This Catholic church (1837-41) is used for exhibitions and concerts. The southern part of the square is occupied by the highly controversial **Stopera** (1987) (from *stadhuis* and *opera*). This modern complex includes the **Muziektheater** and the **Stadhuis**, or city hall, both designed by the Austrian architect Wilhelm Holzbauer and the Dutchman Cees Dam. The 1 689-seat theatre is home to the Nederlandse Opera and the Nationale Ballet. In the passage between the stadhuis and the opera house is a replica of the Normaal Amsterdams Peil (standard watermark).

The black marble **monument** standing in front of the city hall at the corner of the Amstel and the Zwanenburgwal commemorates the resistance by Jewish citizens who lost their lives during the Second World War.

★ **Museum Het Rembrandthuis** ⊙ – *Jodenbreestraat 4-6.* Rembrandt's house is situated at the heart of the old Jewish quarter. **Rembrandt** bought it in 1639 for 13 000 guilders and lived and worked here, producing large numbers of works in his studio on the first floor, until his creditors sold the house and contents by auction in 1658. The interior has been faithfully reconstructed using the inventories made up at the time of the sale. The various rooms evoke the way in which Rembrandt lived and show where he received his clients and sold his paintings, where he found his inspiration (in the Kunst Caemer), and where he introduced his pupils to painting and etching.

The new wing has a rotating exhibition of about 290 etchings *(illustration: see Admission times and charges at the back of the guide).* The rooms open to the public will convince even the most hardened detractor of etchings that Rembrandt was an exceptionally talented engraver, whose work was depicted with unadulterated realism.

Temporary exhibitions exploring various aspects of his work and examining the work of his contemporaries (Dirck Sandvoort, Ferdinand Bol and Pieter Lastman) are also held.

Holland Experience ⊙ – *Next door to the Rembrandthuis.* An audio-visual display and "odorama" lead visitors on a journey of discovery through the Netherlands.

★ **Oude Schans** – The **Montelbaanstoren** stands on this attractive canal. This tower, along with the St.-Anthoniespoort, was part of the city walls in the 16C.

Zuiderkerk ⊙ – The first church built in Amsterdam after the Reformation was designed by Hendrick de Keyser and constructed between 1603 and 1611; it is flanked by a **tower**★ (1614). At present, the church is used as an information centre for the department of housing and town and country planning.

Further along, at 69 St-Antoniesbreestraat, is the beautiful **Huis de Pinto**, which was built c 1680 and once belonged to a rich Jewish merchant.

★ **Joods Historisch Museum** ⊙ – The Museum of Jewish History is housed in a complex of four synagogues on Jonas Daniël Meijerplein. The first one on the site was the Grote Synagoge, built in 1671, but as the congregation expanded new

ones were built on neighbouring plots: the upstairs or Obbene Sjoel in 1685, the third or Dritt Sjoel in 1700 and the new or Nieuwe Synagoge in 1752. The latter is recognisable by the Ionic columns at the entrance and by the domed roof.
The **Nieuwe Synagoge** examines five aspects of the "Jewish identity": religion ; Israël and Zionism; war, persecution and survival ; history ; and mixing of cultures.
The **Grote Synagoge**★ or Grand Synagogue still has the marble Ark of the Covenant given to the community in 1671. Various themes, such as the Jewish Year and its feast days and the Bar mitzvah, are explained through displays of items used in worship and ceremonials (silver plate, lamps, clothes, decorations for the Torah). The galleries are devoted to the socio-economic history of the Jewish people in the Netherlands. The renovation work brought to light a **mikveh**★, a bath used for ritual purification.

★ **Portugees-Israëlitische Synagoge** ◷ – This massive brick building, lit by tall windows, was built in 1675 by Elias Bouman as a place of worship for three Portuguese congregations which had just united.
The interior remains as shown in Emmanuel de Witte's painting in the Rijksmuseum, with wide wooden barrel vaults supported by very high columns, galleries for the women, the Ark of the Covenant, and large **copper chandeliers**. There is no curtain (Parochet) in this synagogue, as this feature was unknown in the Jewish tradition of Spain and Portugal.
Sand is regularly sprinkled on the floor to absorb the humidity and muffle the noise of footsteps and, just as in the 17C, the synagogue has no electricity or heating. One of the most important Jewish libraries in the world is attached to this place of worship.
De dokwerker, the statue of a docker by **Mari Andriessen** in the square in front of the synagogue, commemorates the strike launched by the dockers on 25 February 1941 in protest against the deportation of Amsterdam's Jewish population.

Blauwbrug – The "blue bridge" dates from 1883 and is a copy of the Alexandre III Bridge in Paris; it has a view of the Magere Brug to the south.

★ **Magere Brug** – The "thin bridge" is a picturesque wooden drawbridge across the **Amstel**, dating from the end of the 17C and still manually operated. It is attractively lit at night during the summer months. The wooden 18C **Amstelsluizen** or Amstel sluices refresh the water in the city's canals twice a week in winter and four times a week in summer. The large building to the east of the Magere Brug is the **Koninklijk Theater Carré**, which dates from 1887.

Gables

There are countless different forms of gables. Late medieval houses were made of wood, an had simple **pointed gables (A)**. Later on, they were built with pinnacles or **crow steps (B)** *(see Huis Leeuwenburg above)*. A pitched roof was hidden behind the gable.

Later on, gables became taller, and **Dutch gables (C)** and **neck gables (D)** were used. These had triangular or curved pediments, often elaborately sculpted on either side.

The finest houses had broader façades and a roof running parallel with the street. The roof was hidden by a large pilaster gable ending in a triangular pediment or an **emblazoned balustrade crowned with statues and a coat of arms (E)**.

Finally, a large type of house developed with pilasters and a **triangular carved pediment (F)**. The façade was sometimes made of stone and decorated with garlands. The many warehouses mostly have a simple, undecorated **spout gable (G)**.

M. Guillou/MICHELIN

★★★ THE CANALS

In 1586, the town council decided to launch the building of the **Grachtengordel** (*gracht* means "canal" and *gordel* "belt"), a vast ring of four concentric canals to the west and south of the historic town centre. The plan included, first the widening of the existing **Singel** and then the digging of the **Herengracht** (1586-1609), the **Keizersgracht** (1612) and the **Prinsengracht** (1612) respectively. These canals, 25m/8ft wide, then stretched from the Brouwersgracht to the current Leidsegracht, which was dug in 1664. As the population continued to grow, work on extending the ring of four canals eastwards began in 1662. It was completed in 1665.

The canal-side houses – *Illustration, see Architecture, p 58.* Most of the houses which line the canals in the centre of the city were built in the 17C and 18C by wealthy merchants.

Although somewhat similar in appearance, with their narrow façades and front steps, they differ in colour and in the way their gables are decorated. Beams with pulleys project over the pediments: the narrow staircases make it impossible to bring in furniture.

★ **Boat tours** ⊘ – A boat tour gives an excellent view of the most important canals as well as part of the port. The route varies according to which locks are open.

★★ Singel

Nieuwe Kerk or Ronde Lutherse Kerk – The high-domed New Church or Round Lutheran Church from 1671 has been converted into a **concert hall** ⊘ and **conference centre**.

No 7 – This house, the width of a door, is often said to be the narrowest in the city. It is in fact the rear access to a house in Jeroenensteeg.

★ **Bloemenmarkt** – The flower market is at the end of the Singel (*see above*).

★★★ Herengracht

This is the most important of the four canals and is where wealthy merchants came to live. The houses vie with one another in their rich decoration, and particularly that of their gables.

Number 168: Theatermuseum ⊘ – The theatre museum forms part of the Netherlands Theatre Institute and is located in four houses along the Herengracht

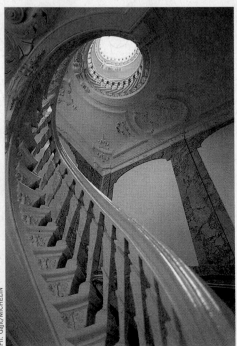
Staircase in the Theatermuseum

(*nos 168-174*). No 168 has a fine stone **neck gable**★ designed by **Philips Vingboon**. It dates from 1638 and is the oldest of its kind in Amsterdam.

The **interior**★★, in Louis XIV style, is richly decorated with stucco, murals and ceiling paintings, many of them by **Jacob de Wit**. There is also an ornamental spiral **staircase**★ leading from the basement to the attic.

The museum's permanent display includes costumes, posters, props and an audio-visual archive. Temporary exhibitions are also held here.

The **Huis Bartolotti**★ next door at no 170 was built by Hendrick de Keyser around 1617. The combination of brick and freestone on the frontage is typical of what is referred to as the Dutch Renaissance style.

★ **Nos 364 and 370: Crom-houthuizen** – Philip Vingboons built this fine row of four houses with neck gables in 1662. The gracious buildings, Baroque as regards their decoration, were commissioned by Catholic merchant Jacob Cromhout *(see the façade-stone at no 366)*. No 366 houses the **Bible Museum** ☉.

* **Nos 386 to 394** – A lovely series of façades. At no 394, below a graceful gable, a **façade-stone** depicts the four sons of Aymon, mounted on their horse Bayard.

Gouden Bocht – The large, elegant houses on the second bend in the Herengracht are known collectively as the "Golden Bend". In the 17C, this was the area favoured by wealthy Amsterdam citizens who could afford double-fronted houses; these are now mostly occupied by banks and consulates.

During the period when these houses were built, façades were becoming wider, and although the new classical style meant that pediments were flatter, they were still richly decorated.

* **No 475** – This house (1731) with a stone façade was built by **Daniël Marot** and decorated by Jan van Logteren.

No 497: Kattenkabinet ☉ – The Cat Gallery, located in a beautiful 17C house, holds temporary exhibitions consisting mainly of works of art depicting cats.

* **No 476** – This elegant mansion was built around 1740. It has a very fine façade with six Corinthian pillars and decorative festoons. The open-work attic above the main part of the building has a balustrade decorated with the owner's blazon and an eagle above.

The **ABN-AMRO Bank** building (1923) on the corner of Vijzelstraat is by the architect De Bazel, a contemporary of Berlage.

No 502: Huis met de Kolommen – This 17C "house with the columns", which was altered in 1791, has been the **official residence of the city's mayor** since 1927.

* **No 605: Museum Willet-Holthuysen** ☉ – This mansion, built between 1685 and 1690, has a series of elegantly furnished rooms evoking the lifestyle of rich merchants of the time. The kitchens, the men's smoking room, the bedroom and the collector's room contain paintings, pottery, glassware and gold and silver. The **garden**★ has been restored to the original design of **Daniël Marot**.

★★ Keizersgracht

* **No 123: Huis met de Hoofden** – This attractive restored brick house dates from 1622. Its façade is similar to that of the Huis Bartolotti *(see above)*, and is decorated with six sculpted heads of Roman gods; hence its name, "house of the heads".

* **No 672: Museum Van Loon** ☉ – This stately mansion was built in 1671 by Adriaan Dortsman, and has been altered on various occasions since; it once belonged to the painter **Ferdinand Bol** (1616-80). It has a stairwell decorated in stucco with magnificent **banisters**★ from the second half of the 18C, and numerous portraits. There is also a small Classical-style coach house in the lovely French-style **garden**★.

★★ Prinsengracht

* **Westerkerk** ☉ – *Illustration: see Architecture.* This Renaissance church was built between 1620 and 1631 by **Pieter de Keyser**, based on the plans of his father Hendrick. It is the largest Protestant church in the city.

The remarkable carillon in the 85m/280ft **bell-tower**★★ dates from 1638 and is the work of **François Hemony**. The tower is topped by the imperial crown, commemorating Emperor **Maximilian of Austria**, who gave permission in 1489 for it to be added to the city's coat of arms. The fine **view**★ from the top of the tower takes in the central canals and the Jordaan district.

The church **interior** is very plain; the nave has wooden barrel vaulting and the twelve chandeliers are copies of the original ones. The magnificent painted organ panels are the work of **Gerard de Lairesse**.

Rembrandt was buried here in 1669, one year after his son Titus, though the exact location of his tomb is not known.

On the pavement behind the church **Westermarkt** stands the **Homomonument**, commemorating gay men and women who died in the Nazi concentration camps.

★★ **Anne Frank Huis** ☉ – This narrow building erected in 1635 extends back a considerable way, and has an extension behind it which was enlarged in 1740. It was here that **Anne Frank**'s father, a German Jew who emigrated in 1933, hid seven members of his family and friends in July 1942. They were betrayed, arrested and sent to Auschwitz in August 1944; only the father returned. The moving diary kept by his 13-year-old daughter was found in the house, and displays a rare sensitivity.

A revolving bookcase reveals a secret passage which leads to the bare rooms where the family hid. In the attic and in an adjoining house are exhibitions on Anne's life, and on war, National Socialism and anti-Semitism, as well as temporary displays related to these issues.

★ Reguliersgracht

This delightful canal built in 1664 provides one of the most attractive **views★★** of any of Amsterdam's waterways. From the bridge spanning the canal beside Kerkstraat, the view encompasses the seven bridges across the Reguliersgracht.

★ Leidseplein

This is possibly the liveliest square in Amsterdam. There are many theatres in the area, including the well known municipal theatre, the **Stadsschouwburg**, as well as restaurants and night-clubs. The **American Hotel**, dating from 1902, combines elements of Art Nouveau and the Amsterdam School, as well as a beautiful art deco café.

Max Euweplein is the home of the **Holland Casino**.

Further on, at no 6 Weteringschans, is the **Paradiso**, a disused church which is now a popular venue for musical events. Behind the Stadsschouwburg (municipal theatre) a former dairy now houses the **Melkweg** cultural centre (*Lijnbaansgracht 234a*).

The long and pleasant pedestrian street **Leidsestraat** links Leidseplein to the city centre.

THE MUSEUM DISTRICT *allow 1 day minimum*

★★★ Rijksmuseum ⊘

The famous national museum was founded by Louis Napoleon, the brother of Napoleon Bonaparte, in 1808. The present building was constructed between 1876 and 1885 by PJH Cuypers in a style combining neo-Gothic and neo-Renaissance features. It includes an exceptional collection of 15C-17C paintings, including magnificent works by Rembrandt and Vermeer, and also has important departments of sculpture and decorative arts, Dutch history, prints, Asiatic art, costumes and textiles.

★★★ **Dutch paintings (15C to 17C)** – *First floor, east wing; room numbers appear in brackets.* The collection of **pre-Renaissance** paintings includes works by **Geertgen tot Sint-Jans** (room 201), such as his *Adoration of the Magi*; Jan Mostaert, whose painting of the same subject (202) is set amid an Italian Renaissance scene; the

RIJKSMUSEUM

EAST WING

THE NIGHT WATCH

Woman at her Toilet
View of Haarlem
The Syndics of the Drapers' Guild
Portrait of a Young Girl Dressed in Blue
THE KITCHEN MAID, WOMAN IN BLUE READING A LETTER
Portrait of Maria Trip
Landscape with Two Oaks
Summer and Winter
Isaac Massa and his Wife, The Jolly Drinker
The Seven Works of Compassion
To ground floor

- ℹ Information desk
- 🏠 Shop
- 🎧 Audio Guide
- ↕ Lift
- 🚻 Toilets

Master of Alkmaar, famous for his *Seven Works of Charity* (202); and Jacob Corneliszoon van Oostsanen, whose ornamental style is apparent in his triptych of the *Adoration of the Magi* (203).

In the **Renaissance** section, **Lucas van Leyden**'s *Adoration of the Golden Calf* (204) shows great mastery of composition; **Jan van Scorel** depicts a *Mary Magdalene* (205) of very Italian elegance. In room 206, the art of Pieter Aertsen is more realistic, while Antonio Moro's portraits show considerable restraint. Both Cornelis Corneliszoon van Haarlem and Abraham Bloemaert are representatives of **Mannerism**. There is also a still-life with flowers by Jan ("Velvet") Brueghel as well as some lovely landscapes by the Antwerp painter, Joos de Momper.

In the **Golden Age**, painting styles varied a great deal. Hendrick Avercamp specialised in winter scenes, such as *Winter Landscape* (207). **Frans Hals** (209, 210) produced outstanding portraits such as that of *Isaac Massa and his Wife*, while the vivid and rapid brushwork of *The Jolly Drinker* is reminiscent of Impressionism.

Several rooms are devoted to the work of the great master **Rembrandt**. *The Stone Bridge* (211) is one of the few landscapes he painted, and dates from 1638. It is interesting to compare the 1631 portrait of Rembrandt's mother meditatively reading the Bible (211) to the painting of a similar subject by his pupil Gerrit Dou, which is more austere in style. Rembrandt painted his portrait of the elegantly dressed *Maria Trip* (211) in around 1640. Frans Hals's pupil **Judith Leyster** is represented by a genre piece, *The Serenade* (213).

Pieter Saenredam specialised in churches and other interiors, such as that of Amsterdam's old town hall (214).

There were numerous artists painting landscapes; these included **Van Goyen**, with his *Summer and Winter* (213) and *Landscape with Two Oaks* (214), and Salomon van Ruysdael, who painted a *Landscape with Ferryboat* (214).

During this period, portraits were also very much in vogue; the beautiful *Portrait of a Young Girl in Blue* is by **JC Verspronck**.

Paulus Potter chose to depict animals, while **Jan Steen** specialised in cheerful domestic scenes (*The Feast of St Nicholas*, 216; *Woman at her Toilet*, 219).

Other leading landscape artists included **Jacob van Ruysdael** (*The Windmill at Wijk bij Duurstede*, 217, and *View of Haarlem*, 218) and **Meindert Hobbema** (*Watermill*, 217). Adriaen van Ostade was more interested in villagers and their daily lives (*Peasants in an Interior: The Skaters*, 218).

Also on display are some outstanding seascapes and naval battles by **Willem van de Velde the Younger** (220).

WEST WING

FIRST FLOOR

ARIA
Documentation Centre

Delftware

The Jewish Bride

Dutch Painting

Sculpture and decorative arts

Temporary exhibitions

Closed

261

256

To ground floor 259   258   257   255

260

229

258ª   254

253

231   Auditorium   253ª   252   Noah's Ark

233   250   250ª   Terracotta bust

251   The Triumph of Fame

235   249   248   251ª

247   246

To ground floor   238 239 240 241 242   243 244 245   Annunciation of the Virgin Mary

Bookshop   Bronze statuettes   Dormition of the Virgin Mary

RIJKSMUSEUM, AMSTERDAM

The Feast of St Nicholas by Jan Steen

The four works (221a) by **Vermeer** are all masterpieces: *The Little Street* (c 1658), painted from the windows of his house; *The Milkmaid* (c 1658), pouring milk with a measured gesture; *Woman in Blue Reading a Letter* (c 1662), in luminous blue tones; and finally *The Love Letter* (c 1666).

Room 222a presents portraits by Terborch, a *Self-portrait with Pipe* by Gerrit Dou, and a sentimental scene by Metsu, *The Sick Child*. **Pieter de Hooch** is famous for his geometric interiors (*The Pantry*, 222). Also in this room is *Girl at a Window: The Daydreamer* by Nicolaes Maes.

Room 224 contains Rembrandt's *The Militia Company of Captain Frans Banning Cocq and Lieutenant Willem van Ruytenburch*, known as **The Night Watch**. Commissioned by a company of the civic guard, this enormous group portrait was completed in 1642 and displayed in the company's headquarters in Kloveniersburgwal, before being transferred to Amsterdam's town hall in 1715. At that time, it was made smaller by cutting large strips off the edges. During the Second World War, it was hidden in caves near Maastricht *(see MAASTRICHT, Outskirts)*. It owes its name to the darkened varnish, which was cleaned in 1947, but the painting in fact depicts the company in broad daylight.

The guards are shown in great agitation, as though taken by surprise; the captain is giving the signal to depart, and some of the guards have their faces half hidden, resulting in a very original group portrait. There are a number of details which add to the feeling of spontaneity: the little girl with a bird attached to her belt walking through the group, the barking dog, the dwarf running, and the man with a helmet covered with leaves. Spots of bright colour offset the rather grey tones of the guards' uniforms: the bright yellow of the girl's and the lieutenant's costumes, the red outfit of the guard reloading his gun, and the captain's red scarf.

The pictures from the **Italian School** include numerous Primitives, such as a remarkable *Madonna of the Lily* by Fra Angelico and a *Mary Magdalene* by Crivelli. There are some interesting portraits by the Florentine painter Piero di Cosimo and views of Venice by Guardi. Works from Spain include a lovely *Virgin and Child* by Murillo. The Flemish paintings include two works by **Rubens**.

The **Gallery of Honour** (229-236) contains major paintings by Dutch masters from the second half of the 17C; the late works by Rembrandt are particularly noteworthy. The *Portrait of Titus in a Monk's Habit* dates from about 1600. The *Self-Portrait as the Apostle Paul* (1661) shows Rembrandt as a disillusioned old man (229), while the portrait of a couple known as *The Jewish Bride* (1668-69) is full of light and tenderness (229). The *Syndics*, a masterpiece dating from 1662, shows the inspectors of the Drapers' Guild grouped behind a table with a warm red tablecloth. Although their expressions are serious, this portrait is full of life (230).

Room 231 has a work by Nicolaes Maes, a contemporary of Rembrandt: *Old Woman at Prayer*. Another of his pupils who was greatly influenced by the master was Aert de Gelder (*Portrait of Ernst van Beveren*, 232). Albert Cuyp was a very versatile landscape painter whose compositions featured shepherds, cattle and small human figures (234).

★★★ **Sculpture and Decorative Arts** – *First floor, ground floor and basement, west wing*. This important section takes up numerous rooms, and has a rich collection of furniture and works of art from the 15C to the 20C.

Particularly worthy of note among the collection of sculpture from the Low Countries are the series of **bronze statuettes** (Brabant, 1476) used to decorate the tomb of Isabella de Bourbon (239), representing the mourning family of the deceased, and **Adriaen van Wesel**'s *Death of the Virgin* (242) from the same period, as well as a rood screen made in about 1500 (248). The **Annunciation of the Virgin Mary** (245) by the German sculptor **Tilman Riemenschneider** is typically late Gothic, while the 16C Brussels wall tapestry *The Triumph of Fame over Death* (248) shows the influence of the Italian Renaissance. Other notable 17C works include the tapestry *Noah's Ark*, produced in Brussels (250) and a terracotta bust by **Hendrick de Keyser** (250a). The **treasury** (251) contains fine goblets, bowls, dishes and jewellery. Note the map of the Iberian Peninsula and the **chess set**. Other items of interest are a Renaissance oak cabinet (252), engraved glassware (253), a Colonial ebony bed (253a), delftware (255-257), a bombé chest (260) and a lacquer cabinet (261). Of particular interest on the ground floor are: the finely detailed **doll's houses** (164), the 18C canopy beds (165/169); the 1730 **apothecary's chest** thought to originate from Delft (168); the **Meissen porcelain** (170/1); the fine inlaid bureau (176) and the enamelled snuffboxes (179).

The basement has displays of engraved glass (24), 18C furniture (25/27), Art Nouveau jewellery (34), a 1909 Art Nouveau drawing room (35) and porcelain from Weesp and Loosdrecht (32).

★★ **Dutch history** – *Ground floor, east wing*. Here, art is used in an interesting and pleasant way to retrace the history of the Netherlands from the Eighty Years' War through to the Second World War. Room 102 is devoted to the Golden Age and contains model ships, paintings and weaponry. The **VOC-Galerij** (102a) tells the story of the East India Company through the eyes of the men who sailed its ships. The Netherlands were a formidable power at sea and this was mainly due to admirals such as Maarten Tromp and Michiel de Ruyter (104). The works in room 107, which include a Japanese roller painting depicting cannibals and Dutch naval officers, bear witness to the Dutch presence in the East. The painting by the French artist Pierre-Paul Prud'hon, *Rutger Jan Schimmelpenninck, his Wife and Children* (109) was painted in 1802. Schimmelpenninck was the Ambassador of the Batavian Republic in Paris. The huge painting, *The Battle of Waterloo, 18 June 1815* by JW Pieneman (110) recalls the victory over Napoleon. The chair used by William III at his inauguration in the Nieuwe Kerk in 1849 is on display in room 112.

★★ **Prints room (Rijksprentenkabinet)** – *Ground floor, west wing*. The museum possesses over a million drawings and engravings from the 15C to the present day, including the largest collection of etchings by **Rembrandt**, a rare collection of engravings by **Hercules Seghers** and a large number of oriental woodcuts. These are all shown in temporary themed exhibitions.

Girl in Kimono (detail, 1894), by George Breitner

Rijksmuseum-Stichtung, Amsterdam

Vincent van Gogh

Born in Zundert, near Breda, Van Gogh began sketching as a child, but only became conscious of his vocation at the age of 27. He then threw himself into drawing, before taking up oil painting the following year in The Hague.

At first, Van Gogh was inspired by the dark landscapes and thatched cottages of the Drenthe region. Later on, he and his parents moved to a presbytery in the village of Nuenen (see EINDHOVEN, Excursions). Here, he produced a series of portraits of peasants, with strikingly intense expressions, which served as studies for The Potato Eaters (1885).

After a stay in Antwerp, the artist moved to Paris in February 1886. During 1887 and 1888, under the influence of the Impressionists, he began using brighter colours in his paintings. Examples include View of Paris from Theo's Room, Cornfield with a Lark, Road beside the Seine at Asnières, and numerous self-portraits, including Self-Portrait at the Easel. Van Gogh also painted landscape paintings influenced by Japanese art.

During the period from 1888 to 1889, he strove to reproduce the bright, contrasting colours he saw in Arles, with paintings of Provençal orchards, The Zouave, Pont Langlois with Road beside the Canal and Sunflowers.

Van Gogh, Self-portrait with a straw hat (1887)

VAN GOGH MUSEUM

The first signs of mental illness began to be reflected in his paintings of windswept cornfields and twisted olive trees and cypresses, all in more muted colours. This illness resulted first in a stay in Arles hospital and then in his admission to the mental hospital at St-Rémy-de-Provence from 1889 to 1890, where he painted his room in Arles as he remembered it. In 1890, after a quiet period in Auvers-sur-Oise, near Paris, Van Gogh painted the moving Cornfield with Crows. On 27 July of the same year, he shot himself in a fit of depression, and two days later the artist's stormy life came to a premature end.

* **Dutch painting (18C-19C)** – *First floor, south wing. Can also be reached direct via the entrance at Hobbemastraat 19.* The 18C paintings are hung in rows one above the other, as was customary at the time when they were painted; this is illustrated in the work by Adriaan de Lelie *The Gallery of Brentano in his house on Herengracht.* Most of these paintings are rather formal portraits of elegant women, and men in wigs. The works by Cornelis Troost deserve special attention. The pastels room (14) includes works by the Swiss artist Jean-Etienne Liotard and portrait miniatures. The rooms dedicated to the 19C (16-21) cover the Napoleonic era (PG van Os), Dutch Romanticism (Barend C Koekkoek; WJJ Nuyen's *Shipwreck on a Rocky Coast*) and the Hague School (Weissenbruch; J Maris's *Feeding the Chickens*; Josef Israëls; and A Mauve, *for illustration, see Den HAAG*). George Breitner, Isaac Israëls and Jacobus van Looy (*Summer Luxury*) are important representatives of Amsterdam Impressionism.

Costume and textiles – *First floor, south wing; room 15.* A changing selection of items from the collection is on display, including 18C and 19C Dutch costumes, oriental carpets, lace and linen damask.

* **Asiatic art** – *Ground floor, south wing; can also be reached direct via the Hobbemastraat 19 entrance.* The nine rooms of this particularly interesting department display a changing selection of more than 500 objects from the Indian subcontinent, Cambodia, Indonesia, Japan and China. The 12C bronze, *Shiva,*

King of Dance, represents India. One of the most striking small sculptures is the 7C or 8C *Buddha Shakyamuni* found in Indonesia. The Chinese sculptures include an elegant, relaxed-looking seated Buddha, and some magnificent porcelain. Highlights of the Japanese collection include ceramics for the tea ceremony, lacquer items and delicately painted screens.

★★★ Van Gogh Museum ⊙

This museum opened in 1973, and was designed by the architect **Gerrit Rietveld**. It has a collection of over 200 **paintings** and around 600 **drawings** by Vincent van Gogh (1853-90), as well as the **letters** he wrote to his brother Theo and **works by contemporaries** such as Toulouse-Lautrec, Gauguin, Chaval and Redon. The painting collection traces the artist's development from the sombre canvases of his early career to the violent tonalities of his last years. In the oval pavilion behind the museum (1999, Kischo Kurokawa), temporary exhibitions of late 19C art are held, which seek to give a greater insight into the world of art in Van Gogh's time.

★★★ Stedelijk Museum ⊙

Built in 1895 and enlarged in 1954, this modern art museum has a very varied collection covering the period from 1850 to the present day. This includes paintings, sculpture, drawings and prints, applied art and industrial design, posters and photographs. There are also paintings by artists such as Cézanne, Kandinsky, Malevitch, Chagall, Mondrian, Picasso, De Kooning and Lichtenstein. Recent trends in European and American art are also well represented, and the museum also holds major exhibitions and other events.

IN AND AROUND THE VONDELPARK

Vondelpark – This park (48ha/120 acres), named after the famous 17C Dutch poet and dramatist Joost van den Vondel, is located between Singelgracht and Amstelveenseweg. It was laid out between 1864 and 1874.
It is popular with walkers, cyclists and horse-riders, and has a fine collection of over 120 kinds of tree, including chestnuts, oaks, poplars, swamp cypresses and catalpas, as well as vast lawns, a rose garden and sparkling lakes and fountains. In summer, free concerts are given in the open-air theatre **(openluchttheater)**, and the **Filmmuseum** ⊙ is also located in the park.

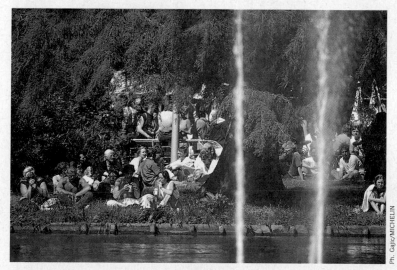

Ph. Gajic/MICHELIN

The Vondelpark

Concertgebouw – The famous concert hall (1888) is the home of the Royal Concertgebouw Orchestra; the title "Royal" was bestowed by Queen Beatrix to mark the orchestra's centenary.

Hollandse Manege – AL van Gendt, the architect of this riding school dating from 1882, was clearly influenced by the Spanish Riding School in Vienna. The neo-Classical building is decorated with stucco and cast iron and is still in use.

⋆ THE JORDAAN

This area dates from the 17C, and has been thoroughly restored over recent years. Its many warehouses have been converted into apartments, and the area is full of attractive shops and cafés. The Jordaan's picturesque nature has made it very popular with students, artists, and the well-off middle classes. It was originally inhabited by French immigrants, and its name is believed to derive from the French word *jardin*, a term thought appropriate given the many flower and vegetable gardens dotted across the area. It is tempting to agree since many of its canals and streets are named after flowers.

Noorderkerk – Built in 1623 by Hendrick de Keyser, this church is in the shape of a Greek cross. A **farmers' market**, selling organic fruit and vegetables, is held in Noorderplein on Saturday and on Mondays there is a **general market**.

⋆ **Brouwersgracht** – The Brewers' Canal is lined with attractively restored warehouses. Nos 172 to 212 are particularly interesting. No 118, the De Kroon warehouse, has a carved stone on its façade depicting a crown, which is what its name means. There is a row of houses with crow-stepped gables dating from 1641 near the bridge where Brouwersgracht and **Prinsengracht** meet. The popular Papeneiland, a small brown café, is located here.

Karthuizerhofje – *Entrance via Karthuizerstraat no 173 or after no 85.* These delightful almshouses, the biggest in Amsterdam, were built in 1650 by the municipal architect, Daniël Stalpart.

Claes Claeszoon Hofje – A 17C almshouse *(entrance at Eerste Egelantiersdwarsstraat no 3)* with a picturesque inner courtyard.

⋆ **Egelantiersgracht** – This canal, with its beautiful 17C and 18C houses, has retained the typical charm of yesteryear.

⋆ **Bloemgracht** – This canal, sometimes ironically called the Herengracht of the Jordaan, used to be occupied by dyers and paint makers. There are three magnificent houses with stepped gables, nos 87 to 91, and many others have **façade stones**, including nos 19 (a pelican), 23 (a unicorn), 34 (a trout) and 77 (a sower).

Façade stones

After the huge fire of 1452, all new houses were required to be built of stone with tiled roofs. In the absence of house numbers, a small sculpted façade stone was used, showing the emblem of the owner or the symbol of their trade. This practice ended when house numbering was introduced by the French. Such façade stones are still sometimes used today; this example in mirror writing dates from 1972.

Ph. Gajic/MICHELIN

⋆ THE PLANTAGE

This eastern residential area was developed in the 19C, and takes its name from the area's many parks.

Hortus Botanicus ⊘ – The botanical garden was created in 1682 for the cultivation of medicinal plants. In addition to the outdoor part of the garden, there is also a greenhouse representing three different climatic zones, and a palm house.

Nationaal Vakbondmuseum ⊘ – The national trade union museum is located in the headquarters of the Dutch diamond workers' union, founded in 1894 by Henri Polak. The imposing building was designed in 1900 by **Hendrik Petrus Berlage**, and soon gained the nickname of Burcht van Berlage (Berlage's Castle). The magnificent **staircase**⋆, council chamber and boardroom are particularly worth seeing, and the museum itself is devoted to the history of the trade union movement.

★★ **Artis** ⓥ – Founded in 1838, this is one of Europe's oldest zoos. It has some 6 000 animals including small mammals, big cats, insects, sea-lions, gorillas and polar bears. A few sections are of particular interest: the new **African Savannah**, the reptile pavilion, the ape enclosure, the noisy aviary and the "Jungle by Night". The newly restored **aquarium**★ brings to light the colourful world of the coral reefs as well as showing what lives in Amsterdam's canals. In the **Zoological Museum** in the same building, temporary exhibitions are held. The lecture theatre contains the **Heimans Diorama**, where the dune ecosystem is explained in a 15-minute presentation. Artis also has a **Geological Museum**, with exhibitions on the Earth's history and collections of minerals, precious stones and crystals, a **planetarium** with shows specially adapted to children, hothouses, and an animal sanctuary.

Artis

Ph. Gajic/MICHELIN

★ **Verzetsmuseum** ⓥ – This interactive museum uses film and sound recordings, photographs and a wide range of authentic objects to lead visitors on a journey through the occupied Netherlands of the Second World War. The terror and horror as well as the daily lives of the people during that wartime period are vividly brought to light. As visitors walk through the reconstructed streets and houses they are given answers to questions such as what happened on the ground during an air raid; how did the propaganda machine of Nazi Germany operate; how did the resistance movement manage to get secret messages through; and how were false documents made? The letters of farewell thrown from the deportation trains and the yellow Stars of David recall the deportation of more than 100 000 Jews. And the resourcefulness and creativity of people during times of war are illustrated through items such as radios, chess sets and small Christmas trees, all made by prisoners of war during their confinement.

Hollandse Schouwburg ⓥ – This former theatre was used during the war as a transit camp for Jews, and has a memorial to those who died.

Muiderpoort – This gate (1771) is the one through which Napoleon entered the city.

★ **Tropenmuseum** ⓥ – The Museum of the Tropics is part of the Royal Tropical Institute, and is an excellent source of information about the cultures of Africa, Asia, the Middle East, Oceania and Latin America. The displays include works of art, a wide variety of everyday objects, reconstructions of homes and shops, and photographs, slide shows and music, all working together to give visitors an insight into life in tropical and subtropical countries. The Kindermuseum, or **children's museum**, holds two-year exhibitions for young people aged six to twelve.

THE PORT AREA

Oosterdok

★★ **Nederlands Scheepvaartmuseum** ⓥ – The Netherlands Shipping Museum is located in the arsenal of the Dutch Navy, an impressive building in the Oosterdok dating from 1656. It has interesting collections of items relating to Dutch maritime history, including maps, globes and atlases, model ships, nautical instruments, paintings and prints.
Among the boats moored along the quays is the **Amsterdam**★★, a replica of an 18C merchant ship belonging to the Dutch East India Company. From April to October visitors are given an insight into the crew's living conditions and way of life on board ship, when a series of scenes are acted out.

★ **Nemo** ⊙ – Bright green and shaped like the bow of a ship, this science and technology centre was designed by the Italian architect **Renzo Piano**. It provides hands-on displays on subjects as varied as medicine and money, and is particularly suitable for children. There is a beautiful **view**★★ of the city from the roof.

Prins Hendrikkade – On the corner of this quay and the Binnenkant is the impressive **Scheepvaarthuis**★, or Shipping House. This was built in 1916 by the principal architects of the Amsterdam School, Van der Mey, Michel de Klerk and PL Kramer, and is the first example of their style. From the bridge to the east, there is a fine **view** of the Montelbaanstoren (1512).

Entrepotdok – On this canal stand 84 warehouses dating from between 1708 and 1829 and rebuilt in the 1980s for use as offices, low-cost housing, and cafés. The development is a fine example of sensitive urban renewal.

Westerdok

Realeneiland – This is one of the "islands" in the western part of the port, lined with warehouses. On **Zandhoek**, overlooking the Westerdok, is a row of restored 17C houses with attractive facing-stones.

Spaarndammerbuurt – *Corner of Zaanstraat and Oostzaanstraat*. This beautiful low-cost housing area was designed in the 1920s by **Michel de Klerk**. It is one of the finest creations of the Amsterdam School of architecture. The **Het Schip**★ apartment block in Hembrugstraat has an expressionist-style tower.

THE PIJP

This area is actually an island linked to the rest of the city by 16 bridges. It was a working-class area in the 19C, and its long, narrow streets (in fact filled-in canals) have given it its nickname of the "pipe", while its cosmopolitan population has also led it to be called the Latin Quarter of Amsterdam. The Pijp is a lively area full of cafés, restaurants and shops.

Heineken Brewery ⊙ – The brewery was built in 1864, and has been open to the public since 1988. There is a tour *(in English only)* describing the history of the company and the methods used to brew beer; a free sample is available at the end.

★ **Albert Cuypmarkt** – This colourful and multi-racial market in the 3km/1.5mi long Albert Cuypstraat has been in existence since 1904, and sells just about anything, from fruit to clothing, from all over the world.

★ **De Dageraad** – *Area around Pieter Lodewijk Takstraat*. This complex of 350 workers' apartments was built between 1919 and 1922 by **Michel de Klerk** and Piet L Kramer for the De Dageraad housing association. Its unusual forms, undulating orange-tiled roofs and rounded beige brick façades make it one of the finest products of the **Amsterdam School**.

EXCURSIONS

Ouderkerk aan de Amstel – This picturesque village is a popular Sunday outing for people from Amsterdam. To the north is a **stage mill**.

Amstelveen – A modern commuter district which has been the home of the **Cobra Museum voor Moderne Kunst**★ ⊙ *(Sandbergplein 1)* since 1995. This surprisingly light building designed by **Wim Quist** houses a fine collection of modern art, including works by the **CoBrA movement**. This international movement (its name derives from **Copenhagen, Brussels, Amsterdam**) was established in Paris in 1948 by a Dane, **Asger Jorn**; two Belgians, **Christian Dotremont** and **Joseph Noiret**; and the Dutch artists **Appel, Constant** and **Corneille**. They sought to break away from the dullness of neo-traditional post-war art by taking their inspiration from folk and primitive art and, most importantly, from drawings by children and mentally ill people. This resulted in spontaneous, experimental, colourful and often cheerful works. The museum does not have a permanent exhibition; the pieces are shown in rotation. Related movements, such as the Dutch groups **Vrij Beelden** and **Creatie**, are also represented. Together, they give an excellent overview of abstract and semi-abstract art in the Netherlands between 1945 and 1955. The museum also holds exhibitions of contemporary art.

Amsterdamse Bos – This is Amsterdam's main woodland area, an immense park strewn with lakes offering boating, and fishing with a permit.

Schiphol – Amsterdam's international airport, one of Europe's leading transit points for air travellers, lies 4.5m/14ft below sea level in what used to be a bay of the Haarlemmermeer.

Not far from the runways is the **Aviodome** ⊙, a distinctive building with an aluminium domed roof, housing a collection of items from the National Aviation Museum. The history of air travel is traced using models, and special attention is given to Dutch aircraft constructor **AHG Fokker** and his work. There is a cinema in the basement.

Sloten – This village, which grew up in the 11C, still has a boundary post dating from 1794 laying down the outer limit beyond which the city of Amsterdam must not expand. The **Molen van Sloten** ⊙ is a polder mill from 1847 erected here in 1989. There is a tour explaining how it works; the screw is capable of raising 60 000l/13 000 gallons of water a minute through a difference in level of 1.5m/5ft. A slide show and some wax figures describe the life of that famous miller's son, **Rembrandt**.

Round tour north of Amsterdam

65km/40mi – About 4hr. Leave Amsterdam by Mauritskade. After the second bridge (Schellingwouder Brug), turn off towards Schellingwoude, then pass under the road towards Durgerdam.

Just before **Durgerdam** there is an excellent **view**★ of the village. The houses are painted in different colours; some have wooden gables. There is also an attractive square church with a pyramid-shaped roof and a clock tower.

Past Durgerdam, the narrow, winding road across the dike offers fine views of what used to be the Zuiderzee.

Durgerdam

★ **Marken** – *See MARKEN.*

Monnickendam – This small port was formerly renowned for its eels. The town is overlooked by the 16C brick tower, the **Speeltoren** ⊙. Opposite, the town hall or **stadhuis** is an 18C patrician house with a decorated pediment; note the snake-shaped balustrades. In the same street (Noordeinde) and in Kerkstraat, several houses have picturesque gables and façade stones.

Nearby, in Middendam, stands the weigh-house or **Waag**, a small building dating from about 1600 with pilasters and an elaborately carved gable. To the south, the Gothic **Grote Kerk or St.-Nicolaaskerk** is a triangular hall church with a fine 16C carved wooden choir screen.

★ **Volendam** – *See VOLENDAM.*

Edam – *See EDAM.*

Broek in Waterland – This village of brightly painted 17C and 18C houses is full of flowers in summer, and has a long-established reputation for being clean and tidy. Some of the 17C houses are U-shaped, and some have two doors, the front door being used only for weddings and funerals.

On the edge of the lake, the Havenrak, is the small white pagoda-shaped pavilion where Napoleon was received when he visited the village in 1811, the **Napoleonhuisje**. The **church** by the canal was burned down by the Spaniards in 1573, and rebuilt between 1585 and 1639. In the north aisle, there is an interesting stained-glass window (c 1640) recalling these events.

Return to Amsterdam via the S 116.

APELDOORN

Gelderland

Population 152 860.

Michelin maps 908 I 5 and 211 U 9

Town plan in the current edition of The Red Guide Benelux

The town of Apeldoorn, with its broad, shady lanes and many parks, lies in the heart of the Veluwe *(see Introduction)*.

In the past, agriculture and the paper industry were the main sources of income here. From 1870 onwards, the paper mills were unprofitable and were converted into laundries. This industry continued to expand thanks to the pure spring water found locally, and by 1921 Apeldoorn had 66 laundering businesses.

A market is held in the square outside the new town hall on Mondays, Wednesdays, and Saturdays.

A tourist steam train, the **Veluwsche Stoomtrein** ⊘, runs southwest from Apeldoorn to Dieren *(23km/14mi)*.

*** **Nationaal Museum Paleis Het Loo** – *See Nationaal Museum Paleis Het LOO.*

Historisch Museum Apeldoorn ⊘ – The local museum is located in the old town hall; it documents the history of the town and the surrounding area. Particularly interesting items include objects and documents relating to the paper industry.

Gemeentelijk Van Reekum Museum ⊘ – This is the local museum of modern and contemporary art, which houses mainly post-1960s Dutch art and work by non-western artists, as well as a substantial collection of modern jewellery. The museum holds a dozen or so exhibitions a year.

Apenheul/Berg en Bos ⊘ – *4km/2mi to the west. Leave Apeldoorn via Kennedylaan and JC Wilslaan.* **Apenheul** means "apes' refuge", and most of the apes here, representing 30 different species, are able to roam free in the woodlands. They include rare woolly monkeys, over 120 squirrel monkeys, Barbary apes and half-apes from Madagascar, which spend their time swinging through the trees or crowding round visitors. They are also accomplished pickpockets, and visitors are given special bags to put their belongings into. The larger animals, such as the **gorillas**, the orang utans and the bonobos live on separate islands. Feeding time is a particularly good time to see them. There is also a separate tropical animals section for children, **Dajak Farm**. The **Berg en Bos** (hill and forest) nature reserve is ideal for walks.

EXCURSION

Kasteel Cannenburch ⊘ – *In Vaassen; 9km/6mi north of Apeldoorn via the road to Zwolle towards Epe.* This moated castle was built in 1543 in Renaissance style by **Maarten van Rossum**, the bloodthirsty commander of Karel van Gerle's army. After his death the castle was occupied by the Van Isendoorn family, who extended and refurbished it during the 17C and 18C. The interior, now fully restored to its 18C appearance, is an excellent example of a stately home that has been inhabited by the same family for centuries.

ARNHEM

Gelderland Ⓟ

Population 137 222

Michelin maps 908 I 6 and 211 U 11

Plan of the conurbation in the current edition of The Red Guide Benelux

Arnhem is the capital of the province of Gelderland, which used to be called **Gelre** when it was a duchy. Situated on the Neder Rijn or Lower Rhine, by the confluence with the IJssel, Arnhem is an important road junction and a major industrial and retailing centre. It is, however, first and foremost an administrative centre. Also referred to as the **Tuinstad** or **Garden City** because of its many green spaces and its favourable position at the southern foothills of the **Veluwe** *(see Introduction, Description of the country)*, Arnhem is a pleasant place to explore on foot, in particular the pedestrianised area in the city centre and the parks.

Arnhem is also known for its **Arnhemse meisjes**, biscuits made of sweet puff pastry.

Boat tours ⊘ – On the Gelderland rivers.

HISTORICAL NOTES

A coveted duchy – Arnhem was a prosperous town trading in goods along the Rhine and the IJssel, and belonged to the Hanseatic League. Gelre became a duchy in 1339. Arnhem was taken by Charles the Bold in 1473, and then by Emperor Maximilian (Charles the Bold's son-in-law) in 1505. Invaded by Emperor Charles V, the duchy was defended by **Charles of Egmont**, who was killed in battle in 1538. His successor ceded his rights to the duchy to Charles V in the Treaty of Venlo (1543). In 1585, under the reign of Philip II (Charles V's son), the town was taken from the Spanish. It passed to the French during the 1672-74 war, and then to the Austrians between 1795 and 1813.

Prior to the Second World War, Arnhem was one of the favourite retirement places for colonials returning from Indonesia; their substantial residences are dispersed throughout the woods.

The Battle of Arnhem (17-27 September 1944) – The name Arnhem is associated with one of the most tragic episodes in the liberation of the Netherlands. The aim of **Operation Market Garden** was to gain access to the Ruhr via a corridor north from the Belgian border across the three great rivers. On 17 September 1944 more than 10 000 English soldiers were parachuted into **Oosterbeek**, west of Arnhem. They were to march on Arnhem to take the bridge over the Neder Rijn, and hold it until the 20 000 Americans and the 3 000 Poles parachuted to the south were able to cross the Maas at Grave and the Waal at Nijmegen. General Montgomery, who directed Operation Market Garden, counted on surprise to disorganise the enemy. Unfortunately the plan was not successful. On the 18th thick fog enveloped Arnhem, making help impossible. Only a few battalions of parachutists from Oosterbeek had reached the town. After nine days of desperately hard fighting the **Red Devils**, who had not managed to capture the bridge, left 2 000 dead and more than 5 000 wounded or missing in the ruins of the town. On the other hand 500 soldiers were given shelter by the townspeople and 2 300 were evacuated towards the south during the night of 25-26 September. In the meantime the progress of armoured divisions effecting a junction had been held up by several German attacks. The crossing of the Maas at **Grave** (on 19 September) and the Waal at **Nijmegen** (on the 20th) made it possible for the Allies to come within sight of Arnhem, but it was too late. The bridge over the Neder Rijn was, according to Browning, "a bridge too far". For more details read *A Bridge Too Far* by Cornelius Ryan. Arnhem was liberated by the Allies on 8 April 1945, shortly before the German capitulation.

SIGHTS IN THE CITY CENTRE

Markt – This long square is bordered by the Law Courts, the **Paleis van Justitie** and, at the end, by the Gelderland seat of government, the **Huis der Provincie**. This was destroyed during the war and a simple new building with an inner courtyard was constructed by JJM Vegter in 1954. Adjoining it is the **Sabelspoort**, a 14C fortified gateway (altered in 1645), which is all that remains of the town's ramparts.

Grote Kerk or Eusebiuskerk ⊘ – This 15C church by the square (Markt) was destroyed during the Battle of Arnhem. Both the church and its tower (93m/305ft) were rebuilt in the neo-Gothic style; the upper part is in a more modern style.

The tower has a new 53-bell carillon, the largest in western Europe, and a small carillon of seven bells. A panoramic glass lift takes visitors up between the bells to a height of 73m/240ft, where there is a magnificent **view**★ of the town and the surrounding area.

The richly decorated **mausoleum** of Charles of Egmont, the last Duke of Geldern, dates from 1538. Look out for the "man in the box" against the pillar beside the tomb. Also of interest is the tomb of Jodocus Sasbout (1546) to the right of the large Salvator Clock. The inscription "Homo Bulla" (man is a soap bubble), the young woman and the decaying body all symbolise the transience of life.

Duivelshuis – The Renaissance Devils' House was built in 1545 and greatly restored in 1829; it suffered no damage during the war. It takes its name from the strange statues and grotesque heads which decorate its walls. The building was the last dwelling place of the bloodthirsty general **Maarten van Rossum**, chief of the armies of the Duke of Gelderland, Charles of Egmont, and adversary of Emperor Charles V. According to legend, Van Rossum had these demons carved to offend the magistrates of Arnhem, who refused to allow him to pave his front steps with gold. Formerly the town hall, the house is still occupied by various municipal departments.

Behind is the new **stadhuis**, or town hall, built in 1964 and designed by JJ Konijnenburg. In the distance is the restored 14C **St.-Walburgiskerk**, which has two different towers.

★ **Historisch Museum Het Burgerweeshuis** ⊘ – This beautifully restored 18C mansion was used as a public orphanage (burgerweeshuis) from 1844 to 1920. Today, it houses a rich collection of decorative arts: 15C Arnhem **guild silverware**★, oriental porcelain, glass, rare local pottery and 17C paintings. The **Rococo-style regentenkamer** (boardroom) has oil-painted wall-hangings showing three episodes from the life of Alexander the Great. The picture of Pallas Athene and Mercury (the god of trade) on the stucco ceiling reminds us that the mansion was built for a successful soap dealer. The first floor, where temporary exhibitions are also held, houses a collection relating to local topography and a collection of 19C paintings, silverware and tobacco boxes. The top floor chronicles the story of Arnhem using archaeological finds, paintings, photographs and videos.

SIGHTS OUTSIDE THE CITY CENTRE

★ **Museum voor Moderne Kunst** ⊙ - A former 19C men's club, standing on a hill overlooking the Rhine, houses Arnhem's museum of modern art. The museum has interesting collections of modern and contemporary art, with the emphasis on Dutch artists, and has a policy of ensuring that at least half its acquisitions are by women artists. The museum holds around 20 exhibitions a year. The permanent collection includes work by **magic realists** (Carel Willink, Raoul Hynckes, Pyke Koch) and **contemporary artists** such as Dick Ket, Wim Schuhmacher and Charley Toorop. There are also a number of fine paintings by the artist Jan Mankes (1889-1920) and by the **New Figuratives** (Roger Raveel, Reinier Lucassen, Alphons Freymuth). The new garden room houses the post-war applied art and design section. This includes ceramics, glass and other design, as well as the country's largest collection of Dutch post-1960 **jewellery**. The garden, which also has a beautiful view of the Rhine, has a collection of old and contemporary sculpture.

★ **Sonsbeek Park** - This park of 75ha/185 acres, together with the adjoining Zypendaal and Gulden Bloem Parks, is one of the most beautiful landscaped parks in the Netherlands. It was declared a national monument in 1963. It is an undulating area with woodlands, large meadows, a string of streams, lakes, a castle and a 16C watermill, De Witte Molen. The barn beside this houses a visitors' centre. Elegant turn-of-the century houses are located around the park.

★★ **Nederlands Openluchtmuseum** ⊙ - The open-air folklore museum is set in 44ha/109 acres of splendid wooded parkland. Around 80 authentic farmhouses, cottages, barns, windmills, workshops, a schoolhouse, a church and a steam-operated dairy factory (see Introduction, Industrial heritage) have been assembled here to illustrate rural architecture and life in the past. The buildings, from all over the Netherlands, are decorated and furnished authentically. Demonstrations of a variety of handicrafts add interest to the visit. The buildings from some of the provinces are grouped together, as in the case of the handsome half-timbered farmsteads from Limburg (nos 100 to 104) or the farmhouses from Gelderland (nos 1 to 19). However the most picturesque corner is probably the one representing **Zaanstreek** with its very characteristic houses. The green-painted buildings with variously-shaped gables are attractively decorated with white trims. The calm waters of the nearby pond are reminiscent of the Zaan and are spanned by a wooden lever-bridge and bordered by two windmills.

Visitors first arrive at the **entreepaviljoen**, a recently renovated pavilion affording a splendid view of the park and several windmills - the taller ones are grain mills while the smaller ones are typical examples of polder mills. Like the **Collectie Centrum**, it contains a number of exhibition rooms where temporary exhibitions of pottery, ornamental folk art, traditional costumes, farming tools and other items are held on a rotational basis. On the lower floor is the entrance to the spectacular **HollandRama**, a simulator-type capsule in which visitors are

NEDERLANDS OPENLUCHTMUSEUM

▬▬▬ Blue itinerary (4 hr)	🏚 Gelderland	🏠 Zaanstreek
▬▬▬ Red itinerary (2 hr)	🏚 Limburg	🏚 Other provinces

taken on a virtual sightseeing tour. Film, sound, light, smell and even temperature-changes bring to life a variety of landscapes, towns and cities, and interiors.

★★ **Burgers' Zoo** ⊙ – In this exceptional zoo ("burgers'" means "people's") artificial ecosystems have been created so that visitors can see animals in their natural habitat.

Burgers' Desert (7 500m²/9 036sq yd) recreates the North American desert, complete with rocks, sand dunes and cactuses. This is home to turkey vultures, lynxes, collared peccaries, and colourful hummingbirds. A cave area containing nocturnal animals and an "abandoned mineshaft" lead from the desert to the tropics.

Nederlands Openluchtmuseum – Inside a typical Marken fisherman's cottage

Burgers' Bush – This enormous greenhouse recreates the ecosystem of a tropical forest, with trees and plants from Asia, Africa and South America. These include rice, sugar cane, pineapple, vanilla, banana and coffee plants as well as mahogany and rubber trees. Amid this colourful vegetation, complete with a waterfall and suspension bridges, live the more timid animals such as butterflies, exotic birds, manatees and caimans.

The next stage in this journey of discovery is the tropical beach and lagoon of **Burgers' Ocean**. A coral cave provides a first-hand view of an extraordinary undersea world: corals, sponges, sea anemones, starfish and a wealth of other creatures. Hundreds of colourful fish accompany the visitor on to an impressive 20m × 6m (66ft × 20ft) panorama showing life in the dark depths of the ocean, where sharks, rays, and jellyfish lurk. Finally, **Burgers' Safari** is a place where giraffes, zebras, ostriches, rhinoceroses and antelopes roam freely. The wild animal enclosure is home to lions and cheetahs. There is also a group of chimpanzees (which is being closely studied), large numbers of birds of prey, a nocturnal animal house and **Burgers' Mangrove**.

*NATIONAAL PARK VELUWEZOOM

Round tour of 20km/12mi. Leave Arnhem by Beekhuizenseweg.

The Veluwezoom National Park is a vast area (4 600ha/11 362 acres) of pine and silver birch forest and undulating heathland situated to the north of Arnhem on the edge (zoom) of the Veluwe. The park has many footpaths and cycle routes, and there are several car parks.

Kasteel Rosendael

Rozendaal – A small 18C castle, **Kasteel Rosendael** ⊙, flanked by a 14C tower, stands on the edge of a lake in the heart of its own **park** ⊙. Several furnished rooms are open to the public. The gallery of shells is also worth a visit.

The road climbs and descends as it crosses the forest, goes through the hamlet of **Beekhuizen** and then climbs to an altitude of approximately 100m/330ft to the **Posbank** where several viewing points offer good **panoramas**★ of the rolling heathland stretching away to the horizon. There are many footpaths and the area makes good walking country.

The road then descends to Rheden.

The **Visitor Centre** ⊙ (Bezoekerscentrum Veluwezoom) occupies an old farmhouse on Heuvenseweg. Ramblers will be able to find detailed maps here. The exhibition introduces visitors to the beauty of this area through the eyes of a badger, a black woodpecker and a red deer.

On the N348, turn left towards Dieren.

De Steeg – To the east of the village the 17C **Kasteel Middachten*** ⊙ is surrounded by a double moat. There is a fine view of the castle from the large garden. Inside, the original furnishings have been preserved, including portraits, miniatures, and a library.

Returning to Arnhem by the N348, there is another moated castle, **Kasteel Biljoen**, on the left just before Velp.

THE SOUTHERN VELUWEZOOM
25km/16mi to the west – 2hr 30min. Leave by ⑤ on the town plan.

Oosterbeek – To the north of this small town, on the road to Warnsborn, just after the railway, is the **Airborne Kerkhof** war cemetery. This is the last resting place of the Allied troops who fell during the Battle of Arnhem; there are more than 1 700 gravestones (1 667 British and 79 Polish).

The Huize Hartenstein (Utrechtseweg 232) was the headquarters of General Urquhart, the commander of the 1st British Airborne Division, in September 1944. It houses the **Airborne Museum** ⊙, which covers Operation Market Garden and the Battle of Arnhem. General Urquhart's headquarters have been reconstructed in the cellar.
To the south, on the banks of the Rhine, the terraces of the **Westerbouwing** (restaurant) offer a fine view over the river and the Betuwe with its orchards.

Drive towards the north bank of the Rhine.

Doorwerth – This village was badly damaged in 1944 during the Battle of Arnhem.
Kasteel Doorwerth, in its riverside setting, dates originally from 1260 but was enlarged c 1600. This massive square castle and its outbuildings are still encircled by moats. In the north and east wings several furnished rooms and exhibition rooms are open to visitors. The south wing houses the **Museum voor Natuur- en Wildbeheer** ⊙, or museum of nature and game conservation, with exhibitions on the various aspects of hunting and game. The fine collections of weapons, stuffed animals, pictures and photographs are attractively displayed.

Continue towards Renkum and pass under the motorway to take the road to Wageningen.

Wageningen – Thanks to its **agricultural college**, Wageningen is known as one of the largest centres of agrarian science in Europe. It lies in the heart of orchard and market gardening country.

On the **Grebbeberg**, 5km/3mi west of Wageningen, there is a **Dutch military cemetery** commemorating the battle that took place here in 1940. A path opposite leads to the **Koningstafel** or "king's table", which has a view over the Rhine and the Betuwe. It was one of King Frederick V of Bohemia's favourite walks; he took refuge in the Netherlands after having been defeated by the Austrians in 1620.

Rhenen – Rhenen is known for its large zoo, the **Ouwehands Dierenpark** ⊙, with over 1 600 animals. A large aviary of exotic birds, a primate house, a dolphinarium and an aquarium add to the interest of the visit. There is also a bear forest in which 11 brown bears and six wolves roam free and can be observed from a walkway, and a tiger forest, where Amur tigers are bred. Also a children's play area, a lake and children's farm. The beautiful clock tower of the **Cunerakerk** ⊙ has been restored since it was bombed in 1945.

ASSEN
Drenthe Ⓟ
Population 57 376
Michelin maps 908 K 2 and 210 Y 5
Town plan in the current edition of The Red Guide Benelux

Assen owes its existence to a nunnery, founded in the 13C, of which one can see the chapel (the old town hall) on the main square or Brink. Today, this modern and spacious town is laid out beside **Asserbos**, a pleasant woodland area to the south. The area is known for its many megalithic monuments *(see HUNEBEDDEN)*.
Until 1602 members of the States or Provincial Assembly of Drenthe met out of doors, in the Germanic style, at the Balloërkuil *(see below)* where they dispensed justice. Due to its central location Assen was chosen as capital of the Drenthe in 1809 during the reign of Louis Bonaparte. To the south of Assen, a motorcycle **racing circuit** (TT Circuit) is used for the Dutch Grand Prix.

Drenthe

For a long time this province was ill-favoured. The Scandinavian glaciers, which spread over the north of the Netherlands, left a sandy and not very fertile soil. In places it is covered with **heathland** with a few clumps of oak or pine. In the wetter areas, **peat** developed on the poor morainic soils left by the glaciers. Drenthe was at one time the largest peat-producing region and local peat working has left a dense network of canals, built to transport the peat. Today much of the area has been brought into cultivation, by clearing and the judicious use of fertilisers, and the region now has a very different aspect. Sheep moors have given way to pastures or plantations of conifers. Well fertilised peat bogs, with sand and the upper layer of peat, can make good arable land for growing potatoes, cereals and market garden produce; many ex-colonials have taken over farms in the area. The farmhouses in Drenthe are very picturesque with their vast thatched roofs, and are for the most part hall farmhouses *(see Introduction, Farmhouses)*.

SIGHTS

★★ **Drents Museum** ⊘ – *Brink 1.* The Drents Museum is housed in a complex of historic buildings: the former Provinciehuis or provincial government building (1885), the abbey, the Drostenhuis or sheriffs' building, and the **Ontvangershuis**★, the former home of the receiver-general. The museum has a very wide-ranging collection which is attractively presented with the help of audio, video and interactive media.

There is a particularly interesting historical and **archaeological section**★ with an outstanding display on prehistoric times. This includes a large number of artefacts from the local burial mounds known as hunebedden *(see HUNEBED-DEN)*, fields of funerary urns, and objects preserved by peat bogs, such as a canoe from 6300 BC (discovered in Pesse, south of Assen) and 3C and 5C bodies including that of a strangled girl from Yde. In the **Discovery Room**, children can explore the daily lives of prehistoric people for themselves.

The extensive collection of **decorative arts** (furniture, everyday objects and ceramics), as well as the local **silver**, **period rooms** and **textile collection**, provide a detailed picture of local life, while the paintings by the **Hague masters** and the selection of prints and drawings from the historical topographic atlas show the Drenthe landscape at its best. The **GeoExplorer** section shows how this landscape was created, taking visitors on a spectacular journey back to the beginning of the Earth's history.

Bartje

Finally, the museum has an important collection of **art from around 1900**, in which Art Nouveau and Art Deco are particularly well represented. In addition, it holds regular temporary exhibitions.

Behind the garden of the Ontvangershuis, there is a charming statuette of the young **Bartje**, the famous character of the local novelist Anne de Vries (1904-64). The statue was the work of Suze Berkhout (the original is in the town hall).

OUTSKIRTS

Rolde – *6km/4mi to the east – local map see HUNEBEDDEN.* In a wood to the west of Rolde is a former place of assembly, **Balloërkuil**, an open clearing several metres below ground level. Beyond the church, turn left onto a paved path signposted *"hunebeddden"*. In a wood there are two of these **burial mounds** (D 17/18); one of them is covered with seven slabs. Both have their entrances on the south side.

Hooghalen – *9km/5mi to the south.* In Hooghalen, turn left onto the Amen road. The **Herinneringscentrum Kamp Westerbork** ⊘ commemorates the war and the persecution of Jews in the Netherlands using photographs, films, drawings, objects and monuments. Anne Frank was deported from Westerbork to Auschwitz.

EXCURSION

Norg, Leek and Midwolde – *27km/17mi via the N 373; turn right after 3km/2mi.*

Norg – This charming Drenthe village with numerous thatched cottages is built around the Brink, a large shady square. It has a small Gothic church with a saddleback roof.

Nationaal Rijtuigmuseum, Kasteel Nienoord

Nationaal Rijtuigmuseum, Kasteel Nienoord

Leek – To the north of town the moated manor of **Kasteel Nienoord** stands in extensive parkland. It was rebuilt in 1887 and it now houses the National Carriage Museum, or **Nationaal Rijtuigmuseum** ⊙. This includes many unique carriages (some drawn by goats), royal children's carriages and 17C to 20C sledges. Paintings and travel requisites (saddles, whips, harnesses, livery coats) also form part of the collection. During the summer season the carriages in the outbuildings are occupied by costumed figures.

There is a further collection of stagecoaches in a modern building, which stands beside a delightful shell-covered pavilion dating from c 1700.

Midwolde – The small brick **church** with a saddleback bell-tower contains a fine **marble tomb**★ made by Rombout Verhulst in 1669 for Anna van Ewsum. The young woman is shown leaning gracefully over the mortal remains of her husband. The cherubs in white marble represent the couple's children. In place of the seventh cherub there is now a statue of Anna van Ewsum's second husband; this statue by Bartholomeus Eggers was added in 1714.

Note the carved pulpit (1711), the tall choir stalls (c 1660-70) and the small organ (1630) with lead pipes.

BERGEN OP ZOOM

Noord-Brabant

Population 64 663

Michelin maps 908 D 7 and 211 K 14 – Local map see DELTA

Town plan in the current edition of The Red Guide Benelux

In the Middle Ages Bergen op Zoom was already the venue for two important annual fairs, and in 1287 it became the chief town of an independent fiefdom. The old port, today partially filled in, was once linked to the Oosterschelde. The town was long regarded as invincible after withstanding two sieges by the Spanish: in 1588 by the Duke of Parma, Alessandro Farnese, then again in 1622 when it was besieged by Spinola's troops. The town's fortifications were strengthened c 1700 by **Menno van Coehoorn** (1641-1704), an engineer who had already designed numerous strongholds throughout the country. However, Bergen was unable to withstand the French army in 1747, during the Austrian War of Succession. The ramparts were demolished in 1868 and the boulevards mark their former location.

Situated in a forested area of heathland and dunes of drifting sand, Bergen op Zoom has become renowned for its asparagus. Its carnival is also well known *(see Practical information at the front of the guide).*

SIGHTS

Grote Markt – The **Stadhuis** ⊙ (town hall) stands on Grote Markt and comprises three buildings; the one in the middle and the one on the right have attractive limestone fronts and date from 1611. They have a perron bearing the **town's coat of arms**; two savages support the coat of arms crowned by a coronet, and the arms themselves show three St Andrew's crosses and three hills (Bergen means "hills"). The city theatre **De Maagd** is housed in a former church.

Near Grote Markt, there is a massive **bell-tower** (14C), which locals call De Peperbus (the Pepperpot). The tower belonged to the **St.-Gertrudiskerk** which was destroyed in 1747 by the French *(see above)*; although the church was rebuilt it was destroyed by fire in 1972. All that remains of the original building is the outside walls (15C-16C).

Markiezenhof

★ **Markiezenhof** ⊘ - *Steenbergsestraat 8.* Antonie and Rombout Keldermans, from the famous family of architects in Mechelen, built this 15C and
16C palace for the marquises of Bergen op Zoom. The palace remained in
the family until 1795 and has been restored; it is one of the finest late-
Gothic town palaces in western Europe. The main façade is of brickwork,
patterned with string courses. The palace is now a cultural centre and includes
a **museum**, an art gallery, a library and a restaurant. There is also a small,
picturesque arcaded courtyard. The **Hofzaal** or great hall is remarkable for the
carved stone chimneypiece (depicting St Christopher) of 1522, and for its
paintings, furniture and silverware, giving an idea of the elegant environment
in which the marquises lived. In the garden wing, which was rebuilt in 1706 in
the Classical style, there are lovely period rooms. The second floor is devoted
to the history of Bergen op Zoom, and includes a scale model of the town's
fortifications and a **fairground** collection, which children will find particularly
appealing.

Gevangenpoort or Lieve Vrouwepoort - *Accessible via Lieve Vrouwestraat,
opposite the Markiezenhof.* This 14C gateway is all that remains of the
town's medieval ramparts. The brick façade facing inwards is flanked by two
bartizans, or lookout turrets; two enormous stone towers stand outside the
gateway.

Ravelijn "Op den Zoom" - *To the north-east of the town.* This small moated
outwork is one of the last remaining parts of the fortifications built by Van
Coehoorn. Opposite it is an attractive park, A. van Duinkerkenpark, laid out
around a lake.

WOUW AND ROOSENDAAL *15km/9mi via A 58*

Wouw - This Gothic **church** ⊘ contains some fine 17C Baroque statues. These
formed part of the choir stalls, which disappeared during the war. They are now
on consoles in the chancel, and in the aisles on either side of the confessional
boxes. The stained-glass window on the west side of the tower, depicting the
Resurrection, is by Joep Nicolas (1937).

Roosendaal - This town is an important railway junction and industrial
centre. The **Streekmuseum De Ghulden Roos** ⊘ is a local museum in the 18C
presbytery, **Tongerlohuys** *(Molenstraat 2).* It contains an interesting collection
of tableware, local hats, and toys. There is also a reconstruction of a village
shop.
Nearby are several nature reserves, notably **Landgoed Visdonk** and **Rucphense Heide**
(1 200ha/2 965 acres).

BOLSWARD*

Fryslân

Population 9 334
Michelin maps 908 H 2 and 210 S 4
Local map see SNEEK

Bolsward, or Boalsert in Frisian, is one of the eleven towns of Friesland. The date of its foundation is inscribed on a façade stone of the town hall: 713. Its name is believed to mean "the land of Bodel, surrounded by water"; the ending "ward" or "werd" refers to a small mound *(see LEEUWARDEN, Terpenland)*.

In the past Bolsward was linked to the Zuiderzee and it grew rapidly to become a prosperous and powerful town. In the 11C it was granted the privilege of minting coins and became a Hanseatic town. Today it is a peaceful place in the middle of an area of rich pastureland.

Every three years, it awards a prize for Frisian literature named after **Gysbert Japicx** (1603-66) who was the first literary writer to use Frisian; written Frisian had been obsolete for many years.

SIGHTS

* **Stadhuis** ⊘ – The town hall is an elegant Renaissance construction dating back to the years 1614-17. The centre of the street front has a gable surmounting a fine 18C perron decorated with two lions bearing the town's coat of arms. At the top there is a tall octagonal clock tower with **a carillon**. In the **council room** there is a splendid carved door by the cabinetmaker Japick Gysberts, who also undertook the decoration of

Choir stalls (detail), Martinikerk

the lovely wooden chimney piece framed by stone telamones. One of the rooms on the first floor, with great timber beams supporting the weight of the tower, houses a collection of antiquities, including Frisian silverwork, traditional costumes, and artefacts from archaeological excavations.

Martinikerk ⊘ – This large Gothic church was built in the middle of the 15C and, like most Frisian churches, has a saddleback roof. Inside, great round piers support the vaulting of the three naves. The **choir stalls*** (late 15C) have interesting wood-carvings combining realism with a degree of naïvety. The scenes which are shown on the lateral partitions are particularly noteworthy. Equally interesting are the figures on the high backs, the picturesque illustrations of parables shown on the misericords, the figures on the cheekpieces, and the grotesque figures of the lecterns. The **pulpit*** (17C), with a tiered canopy, is decorated with elegant motifs in the Frisian style. The central panel depicts a Bible and the signs of the Zodiac; the other panels depict the seasons. The organ was made in 1775 by Hinsz of Groningen. The church's remarkable acoustics make it a popular venue for recording music. Note the church floor embedded with tombstones.

EXCURSION

Witmarsum – *10km/6mi to the northwest.* Near the main road there is a statue of **Menno Simonszoon** (1496-1561). He was born in Witmarsum and became vicar of Pingjum, then the parish priest of his native town and, finally, in 1536, turned his back on Catholicism to become an Anabaptist. He founded the *doopsgezinden* brotherhood or **Mennonites**. In 1539 he summarised his doctrine, which was more pacific than that of John of Leiden: belief in the Bible, rejection of the baptism of children, an emphasis on personal piety, and a refusal to obey all the established Church's dogma. The Mennonite religion spread to Germany, Switzerland and North America, where it still has its adherents.

The Mennonites of Witmarsum meet in a small church, the **Menno-Simonskerkje** ⊙, which was rebuilt in 1961. The prayer area has a portrait of Menno Simonszoon, and the sacristy has various objects commemorating him.

Further down the street is a monument to his memory, located on the site of his first church.

BOURTANGE

Groningen

Michelin maps 908 M 2 and 210 X 4

Bourtange, close to the German border, is one of the best-preserved fortified villages in the Netherlands. Lying on the extensive marshes to the east of Groningen, it was built during the Eighty Years' War by **Adriaan Anthoniszoon** for Prince William of Orange, who hoped that it would enable him to free Groningen from Spanish occupation. Bourtange was not completed until 1593 through lack of money. When Groningen surrendered a year later, Bourtange became part of the frontier fortifications. Because of its strategic position, it was considerably expanded and reinforced.

Until 1851, Bourtange was a military fort permanently occupied by some 300 soldiers and their families. Later it was turned over to civil use and the fort fell into disrepair.

Bourtange was made a listed monument in 1967, and extensive rebuilding has restored it to its appearance in 1742, when it was at its largest.

TOUR ⊙ *Illustration: see Architecture, p 57*

Bourtange is a classic example of a fortress in the style of the **Old Dutch System** (*see The Arts, p 65*). The core consists of a bastioned pentagon surrounded by two moats.

The only access to the fort is via two narrow paths following a complicated route of bridges and outworks to the Marktplein, or market square. From here 10 streets radiate outwards to the bastions and the main ramparts. This layout made it possible for troops to move around quickly and to be seen by their commanders.

The **Museum De Baracquen**, a reconstructed barracks, contains items found in the fortress.

The **protestant church**, the former synagogue, an officer's apartment and the horse mills can also be visited, and the former powder magazine has an informative slide show about the fortress.

BREDA★

Noord-Brabant

Population 159 042

Michelin maps 908 F 7 and 211 N 13

Plan of conurbation in the current edition of The Red Guide Benelux

At the confluence of the Mark and the Aa, Breda was formerly one of the country's main fortified towns and the centre of an important barony. Today it is a dynamic city and a great commercial and industrial centre. Benefiting from its position on one of the main access routes into the country, it is a welcoming stopping place with large pedestrian precincts.

With numerous parks, Breda also has very attractive suburbs and large areas of woodland, such as the **Liesbos** to the west and the **Mastbos** to the south. To the east, **Surae** is a recreational park with a bathing area.

In February (*see Calendar of events*), Breda holds its well-known **carnival★**. In May there is the International Jazz Festival and at the end of August the Taptoe, a military music festival (*see Calendar of events*). The month of October brings the Breda Flower Show, held in the Grote Kerk.

HISTORICAL NOTES

The residence of the House of Nassau – Breda obtained its city rights in c 1252. It became part of the Breda barony, but in 1404 this passed to the Nassau family, who adopted Breda as their family seat. The 13C fortifications were rebuilt (c 1535) by Count Henry III of Nassau, and the ring of canals mark the former alignment of the walls, which were destroyed shortly after 1870.

The Compromise of Breda – Although the treaty was actually concluded in the month of September at Spa (now Belgium), the Compromise of the Nobility or of Breda was signed in Breda Castle in 1566. Its aim was to abolish the Inquisition. Following this meeting a delegation of about 300 nobles set out for Brussels to petition the Governor, Margaret of Parma, to convene the States General and change the edicts against heretics (i.e. the Protestants). She burst into tears; her counsellor, the Count of Berlaymont, responded in jest with the phrase: "What, Madam, afraid of these *gueux* (beggars)?" This taunt did not displease the Calvinists, who from then on took the name **beggars** for their movement and the beggar's bowl as the symbol of their fight against Spanish rule. The Calvinists' actions then knew no bounds: in August the **Iconoclasm** was unleashed, and churches were pillaged and statues destroyed. In 1567 Philip II of Spain sent the tyrannical Duke of Alba as governor-general to punish the rebels, root out heresy and re-establish royal authority in the Spanish Netherlands.

An ardently disputed stronghold – In 1581 Breda was pillaged by the Spanish, who occupied the castle, the family seat of William the Silent.

In 1590, Maurice of Nassau took the town by surprise, 70 of his men having been able to enter by hiding under a load of peat in a barge belonging to Adriaan van Bergen.

In 1625, after a long siege, Breda surrendered to the Spanish commanded by the Marquis of Spinola. This episode was immortalised by Velázquez in *The Surrender of Breda-Las Lanzas* (1634-35). The town was recaptured in 1637 by the Prince-Stadtholder Frederick Henry.

The **Treaty of Breda** of 1667 ended the Second Anglo-Dutch War (1665-67) and confirmed English possession of Nieuw Amsterdam, which became New York. The Dutch retained Guiana (now Surinam). The negotiations and the signing of the treaty took place in the castle.

During the French Revolutionary Wars, the town was taken by Dumouriez in 1793. He was forced to evacuate it after the defeat of Neerwinden (Belgium). Breda was once again under siege in 1794, this time by Pichegru, but only surrendered when the whole country was occupied. It became part of the Deux-Nethes *département* (with Antwerp as its county town) until 1813: that year, at the approach of the Russian vanguard, the French garrison sallied out but the population of Breda prevented their return.

On 11 and 12 May 1940 Breda marked the most northerly point of the Allied advance into the Netherlands; the Dyle Manoeuvre, a Franco-British operation to force a breakthrough to the north, was a failure. The soldiers had to hastily withdraw to Belgium, and Breda was liberated by the Allies in October 1944.

★ GROTE KERK OR ONZE-LIEVE-VROUWEKERK ⊙ *45min*

The church is an imposing 15C-16C edifice in the Brabant Gothic style. With three naves, it was enlarged in the 16C by the addition of a number of chapels and an ambulatory. Its tall **bell-tower**★ of 97m/318ft with a square base and octagonal top is surmounted by an onion-shaped dome. The **carillon** has 49 bells.

The interior, with its typical Brabant Gothic-style columns – their capitals decorated with crockets – and with a triforium, contains numerous tombs. The most striking one is the **tomb**★ of Engelbracht II of Nassau (1451-1504) and his wife in the Chapel of Our Lady, to the north of the ambulatory. This Renaissance alabaster monument was probably designed by Thomas Vincidor of Bologna. The recumbent statues lie under a slab held up by four figures; they depict Julius Caesar (representing military courage), Regulus (magnanimity), Hannibal (perseverance) and Philip of Macedonia (prudence). Engelbracht's armour lies on top of the slab. The vault under the tomb contains the mortal remains of **René de Chalon**, Henry III of Nassau and Anna van Buren, William of Orange's first wife. In the ambulatory is the 15C tomb of Engelbracht I and his son Jan van Nassau.

The 15C wooden chancel stalls are carved with satirical motifs illustrating vices, proverbs etc. Other unusual reliefs were added after 1945. In the north transept there is a triptych by Jan

Grote Kerk, Breda

BREDA

van Scorel whose central panel illustrates the *Finding of the True Cross*. At the end of the south aisle there is a bronze baptismal font (1540) made in Mechelen, Belgium, of Gothic construction with Renaissance motifs. The organ case is decorated with a 17C painting depicting David and Goliath and the Ark of the Covenant. The organ, a fine instrument with its oldest parts dating from the 16C, can be heard when **concerts** ⊘ are held.

ADDITIONAL SIGHTS

Leave from the point where Nieuwe Prinsenkade becomes Prinsenkade.

From here you have a lovely view of the Grote Kerk's bell-tower.

Het Spanjaardsgat – These remains of the fortifications, known as the Spanish Gap, consist of two large towers with small onion-shaped domes flanking a watergate, which was used to drain the moat.

Hidden behind the thick walls is the **castle** ⊘, an immense building with numerous windows, surrounded by a moat; the north façade (visible from the Academiesingel) is flanked by octagonal turrets. Since 1828 it has been occupied by the Royal Military Academy. This old fortified castle was redesigned from 1536 onwards by **Thomas Vincidor da Bologna**, and was William the Silent's favourite retreat until his departure for the revolt which was declared in 1567. It was here that the Compromise of Breda *(see above)* was signed by the nobles.

The castle's present aspect dates from between 1686 and 1695, under Stadholder William III of Orange, who continued Vincidor's original plan.

Havermarkt – This charming little square in front of Grote Kerk was at one time the hay market. There are several busy cafés around the square.

★ **Valkenberg** – This pleasant park with its magnificent trees was once part of the castle grounds. Nearby the Beguine convent, or **Begijnhof** (1535), comprises simple houses arranged round a courtyard with a herb garden and a chapel.

The Beguines are a Catholic community, but unlike nuns they do not make any vows.

At the entrance is the covent's former chapel, which has become a Walloon Church, **Waalse Kerk**. The Frisian, **Peter Stuyvesant** (1592-1672) was married here; he was the last Dutch governor of Nieuw Amsterdam (New York) from 1647-64.

Grote Markt – From the middle of this large square there is a fine view of the Grote Kerk. On Tuesday and Friday evenings a general market is held here and a flea market on Wednesdays.

The **stadhuis** ⊙ (town hall), dating from the 17C, was rebuilt in 1767. It contains a copy of Velázquez's painting, **The Surrender of Breda**, the original of which is in the Prado Museum in Madrid.

Opposite, on the corner of Reigerstraat, there is a lovely house with a crow-stepped gable.

To the south of the square, at no 19, is **Het Wit Lam** (The White Lamb), the former meat hall and premises of the crossbowmen's guild. The pediment of the façade bears the date 1772 and a depiction of St George slaying the dragon.

De Beyerd ⊙ – This former almshouse has been transformed into a centre for the visual arts (Centrum voor beeldende kunst). The centre also organises temporary exhibitions on architecture, ceramics, photography and graphic design.

Breda's Museum ⊙ – The rich history and archaeology of the barony of Breda is chronicled in this former police barracks. The story of Breda as a bishopric is also traced in an important collection of religious art, including statues of saints, paintings, church silver and richly decorated textiles. There is a display of local arts and crafts, and temporary exhibitions are held.

OUTSKIRTS

Kasteel Bouvigne ⊙ – *4km/3mi. Leave to the south along Duivelsbruglaan before turning right.* This castle stands on the edge of the **Mastbos**, a lovely wood criss-crossed with cycle paths and rides. The moated castle was built in 1612, and it is flanked by a high octagonal turret with an onion-shaped dome. The gardens are open to visitors.

EXCURSIONS

① **Baarle-Nassau**
37km/23mi to the south-east via Gen. Maczekstraat.

This village is both Dutch and Belgian; the Belgian part, Baarle-Hertog, consists of some thirty enclaves on Dutch soil. In the 12C the village of Baerle was divided in two; the southern part was ceded to the Duke of Brabant (Baarle-Duc or Baarle-Hertog), and the northern part was united to the Breda barony and called Baarle-Nassau. At present each community has its own town hall, church, police station, school and post office. The border is so complicated that houses of different nationalities stand side by side: a small flag alongside the house number indicates the nationality of each household.

② **From Hoeven to Willemstad**
Round tour of 50km/31mi to the west. Leave by Haagweg, the N 58, and turn right towards Etten-Leur.

Hoeven – In the observatory, **Quasar, Het heelal dichtbij** ⊙, visitors are invited – as the name suggests – to take a close look at the universe and all its secrets. The building also comprises a **planetarium** and telescopes.

Oudenbosch – This village, also known as Klein (Little) Rome, is overlooked by the enormous **Basiliek van de HH Agatha en Barbara**. It was built by PJH Cuypers in 1867-80, as a smaller version of St Peter's in Rome. The dome, however, is 68m/224ft high. The façade (1892) is a copy of the west front of the Basilica of St John Lateran in Rome. The interior was decorated by an Antwerp sculptor.

The **Nederlands Zouavenmuseum** ⊙, or Museum of Pontifical Zouaves, tells the story of the 3 200 Dutch people who, in the 19C, volunteered to defend the Papal States in Italy.

Beyond Standdaarbuiten take the A 59 and then the A 29 to reach Willemstad.

Willemstad – This fortified town in the shape of a seven-pointed star dates from 1583. It is one of the finest example of a fortress in the Old Dutch style and owes its name to its founder, William of Orange. Willemstad was designed by **Adriaan Anthoniszoon**. Today it has a marina which is very popular with holidaymakers. The **Prinsenhof** or Mauritshuis *(now the home of the tourist information office)* was built for Prince Maurice of Orange. It stands in its own park within the old town walls, which have remained intact. There is a small historical collection. The octagonal **church, Koepelkerk**, was completed in 1607 and claims to be the first Protestant church in the Netherlands. The 17C **former town hall** stands close to the harbour, and a little further along is the **d'Orangemolen**, a tall white-walled mill dating from 1734.

★ ③ From Raamsdonksveer to Biesbosch
50km/31mi to the north via St Ignatiusstraat.

Raamsdonksveer – The **Nationaal Automobielmuseum**★ ⊙ is near the Geertruiden-berg exit of the A 27 motorway. With over 200 vehicles on display, it traces the history of the car from its origins to the present day. A number of carriages, sledges and motorcycles add to the interest of the main collection. The hall to the left of the entrance contains cars by the Dutch manufacturer Spijker. The company was operational from 1899 to 1925 and its vehicles were popular with the Dutch royal family in the early years of the 20C. The Ahrens-Fox fire engine is American-built, and Elvis Presley owned the bright red Cadillac (1976). The area to the right of the entrance includes such pioneers of the road as the Peugeot Double Phaeton (1894), the Benz Victoria (1899) and the Panhard & Levassor (1895). There is also a 1907 steam-operated street-sweeping machine which belonged to the city of Amsterdam. Among the serried ranks of models and racing cars in the other halls, look for the magnificent **Auburns, Duesenbergs and Cords**★★★ of the 1920s and 1930s produced by the American manufacturer and advocate of front-wheel drive, Errett Lobban Cord. The superb 1932 Bugatti Type 50 is one of only two remaining examples. There is a comprehensive section on Japanese car manufacturers, especially Toyota.

Geertruidenberg – This small fortified town on the Amer is organised round a triangular **square** overlooked by the massive tower of St.-Geertruidskerk. The town hall, or **stadhuis**, has a lovely 18C façade overlooking the square. Nearby a Baroque fountain splashes.

Drimmelen – Drimmelen stands on the banks of the Amer and has become an excellent water-sports centre attracting increasing numbers of tourists; it is also popular with anglers. The **marina** can accommodate up to 1 400 boats. The **Biesbosch Informatiecentrum** provides information on the **Biesbosch** national park.

★ **De Biesbosch** – Biesbosch (or Biesbos) was made a National Park in 1994 and consists of three parts, stretching across the area of Noord-Brabant and Zuid-Holland *(see also DORDRECHT, Excursions)*. The **boat tours**★ ⊙ give a good overall view of the region.
This area of 40 000ha/98 000 acres suffered badly during the St Elisabeth Flood in 1421. The important diking work reduced the submerged area to a mere 7 100ha/17 544 acres. Although very busy with pleasure boats, the Biesbosch is rich in birds. Reeds, rushes and grassland are the main vegetation on the many small islets. Recreational facilities in the Biesbosch include rowing, sailing and canoeing.
In the **Biesbosch Museum** ⊙ *(Hilweg 2, 12km/7.5mi west of Werkendam)* visitors can find out about the origins of the area and its wealth of flora and fauna as well as the products Biesbosch used to produce (rushes, reeds and willow) and the three reservoirs that supply the Rotterdam and Dordrecht regions with water.

BRIELLE
Zuid-Holland
Population 15 795
Michelin maps 908 D 6 and fold 23 (inset) and 211 J 11

Brielle, generally known as Den Briel (pronounced bril), stands on the island of Voorne. This fortified historic town was once a busy port at the mouth of the Maas. On 1 April 1572 the Sea Beggars *(Gueux de Mer* or *Watergeuzen)*, with the support of William the Silent, left England and landed at Brielle. This was the signal for the uprising of Holland and Zeeland against the Spanish occupation. In July, 19 priests were executed in Brielle of which 16 had just been made prisoners by the Sea Beggars at Gorinchem. Known as the "martyrs of Gorkum", they have been canonised. Each year, on 1 April, Brielle commemorates the taking of the town by the Sea Beggars with a costumed parade and a series of plays.
Brielle was the birthplace of Admiral **Maarten Tromp** (1598-1653), famous for his victory against the Spanish at the Battle of the Downs in 1639.
Today, it is a tourist centre benefiting from the proximity of **Brielse Meer**, to which it is linked by a ferry for pedestrians and cyclists.

SIGHTS

Reminders of the past include fortifications, laid out as an esplanade, and peaceful quays bordered with old houses, like **Maarland** to the north of the town. At the far eastern end of Maarland, beyond a bridge, there is a fine **view** over the docks and the tower of the Gothic church, St.-Catharijnekerk.

Historisch Museum Den Briel ☉ – Behind the 18C stadhuis, on the **picturesque Wellerondom** square, this small museum, installed in a former prison and weigh-house, is devoted to the turbulent history of the town and the island of Voorne.

Grote Kerk or St.-Catharijnekerk ☉ – Although this church was started in the Brabant Gothic style in the 15C, it remains unfinished. It has a massive stone tower 57m/187ft high. The carillon, cast in 1660 by one of the Hemonys, has been enlarged and now has 48 bells.

DELFT★★

Zuid-Holland
Population 95 268
Michelin maps 908 E 5, fold 24 (inset) and 211 L 10
Plan of the conurbation in the current edition of The Red Guide Benelux

The town of Delft is known the world over for its blue and white ceramics, delftware. With its tree-lined canals, famous monuments and museums, Delft is also one of the Netherlands' most charming towns. It was the home town of the jurist **Grotius**, as well as the artist **Vermeer** and the naturalist **Antonie van Leeuwenhoek** (1632-1723) who, thanks to the microscopes which he perfected, made a multitude of discoveries in both botany and zoology.

HISTORICAL NOTES

A prosperous city – Delft, which means moat, was probably founded in 1074. Count William II of Holland granted the city its charter in 1246, and Delft reached the peak of its prosperity in the 13C and 14C based on the cloth trade and its brewing industry. At the end of the 14C the town's authorities decided to build a canal linking the city to the Maas to facilitate the transportation of its products. Slowly the small town of Delfshaven grew up around the newly established port, which became part of Rotterdam in 1886. In 1428 Jacoba or Jacqueline of Hainaut *(see GOES)* signed the **Treaty of Delft** by which she gave her territories of Holland, Zeeland and Hainaut to Philip the Good, while keeping the title of countess. The ramparts were built in the

---

William the Silent

William was born in 1533, in Dillenburg Castle in Germany, to Count William of Nassau and Juliana of Stolberg. On the death of his cousin **René de Chalon** (1544) William the Silent *(illustration: see Introduction, Historical table and notes)* inherited his possessions in France and in the Low Countries, and took his title of **Prince of Orange** as well as his motto *Je maintiendrai* (I shall maintain). In 1559, Philip II of Spain made him **Stadtholder** of the provinces of Holland, Zeeland and Utrecht.

Philip II took measures to repress the Calvinists and in so doing encouraged the growth of an opposition movement, which was led by William of Orange and the **Counts of Egmont and Hornes**. In 1566 the Iconoclasm *(see BREDA)* began. William, convinced he was under threat, fled to Dillenburg (1567). The Counts of Egmont and Hornes were less lucky, they were executed in Brussels in 1568. In 1570 William, who had been brought up as a Catholic, became a Calvinist and he then began to give open support to the Beggars campaigns, both on land and sea. The capture of Brielle by the Sea Beggars on 1 April 1572 was only the beginning of a long and bitter conflict. The States of Holland met in Dordrecht in July and approved the revolt and acknowledged William of Orange as Stadtholder *(see DORDRECHT)*.

From 1572 onwards the prince often resided in Delft. In 1579 by the Union of Utrecht the provinces of Holland, Zeeland, Utrecht, Gelderland and Zutphen decided to join the fight; the other provinces followed suit fairly soon afterwards.

In 1581 Philip II offered a reward for the assassination of the prince; William of Orange retaliated with the well-known *Apologie*. He sought support from François of Anjou, brother of King Henri II of France, but the latter died (1584) before he could help. On 10 July 1584 William the Silent was assassinated in the Prinsenhof *(see below)* in Delft.

15C. Delft was extensively damaged by the large fire of 1536 and it has few edifices dating from before the 16C. In 1654, the explosion of a powder magazine completed the destruction.

Today Delft is an intellectual centre, due to its schools of Natural Sciences, its hydraulic laboratories and its Technical University. A nuclear reactor was built in 1963 for research and development purposes. The modern university buildings are in the southwest of the town.

The father of international law – **Hugo de Groot** or **Grotius** (1583-1645), one of the greatest intellectuals of his time, was born in Delft. He was a theologian, philosopher, politician, diplomat and poet, but is best known for his legal writings and notably his *De Iure Belli ac Pacis* (*On the Law of War and Peace* – 1625) which became the accepted authority on matters of civil rights and earned its author the sobriquet "father of International law". Following the Synod of Dort, Grotius, who was a Remonstrant and follower of Oldenbarnevelt, was imprisoned in Slot Loevestein. He managed to escape and went to live in Paris, where in 1634 he became the Swedish Ambassador to France.

Johannes Vermeer (1632-75) – Delft and its townspeople were the whole universe of Vermeer, one of the Netherlands' greatest Old Masters, who was born and died in Delft.

Early on he applied himself to painting scenes of daily life, and he is one of those who, without giving up the realism current at the time, revolutionised pictorial art. Vermeer avoided the anecdotal and his subject matter tended to be banal and everyday, however he displayed an extraordinary sense for composition, geometry, for the use of unctuous matter, vivid tones (lemon yellow, sky blue) remarkably blended, and above all, for the marvellous light effects for which Vermeer is the great virtuoso. This play of light is particularly fine in the famous *View of Delft* or in the portraits of women suffused with light and grace like the *Girl with a Pearl Earring* (*illustration: see Den HAAG*) and *The Lacemaker*. The Mauritshuis in The Hague and the Rijksmuseum in Amsterdam have the greatest number of works by Vermeer, who was not in fact a prolific artist.

His contemporary, **Pieter de Hoogh** or **Hooch** (1629-84) was born in Rotterdam and spent a long time in Delft before going to Amsterdam. He depicted the life of the well-to-do bourgeois seen in interiors with open doors and windows, creating clever perspectives and light effects on the floor.

Delftware – *Illustration, see Introduction, The arts*. In the second half of the 17C Delft acquired a reputation for making ceramics which soon spread over all of Europe. Heir to the Italian majolica techniques, delftware is tin-glazed earthenware and characterised by its remarkable lightness and its particularly shiny aspect, due to the application of a translucent coating.

At first Delft was known for its monochrome painting of blues on a white background; this is still one of the characteristics of delftware today **(Delfts blauw)**.

At the end of the 17C the production became more varied, polychromy appeared, and there was not a design or shape, coming from China or Japan, which the Delft artists did not try out in order to satisfy the tastes of European clients fascinated by the Orient. In the 18C the influence of Sèvres and Meissen porcelain expressed itself in objects with mannered outlines and decoration, while some of the pieces remained faithful to traditional Dutch scenes where one sees small boats sailing on the canals spanned by humpback bridges.

At the beginning of the 18C delftware reached its peak. But a decline set in rapidly, caused mainly by English competition and porcelain, made first in Germany and later throughout Europe. However, production continues today in several local factories.

Ch. Sappa/HOA QUI

Decorating delftware

145

WHERE TO STAY

This beautiful old town has many hotels in historic buildings; the following is a selection.

MODERATE

De Plataan – *Doelenplein 10, 2611 BP,* ☎ *(015) 212 60 46, fax (015) 215 73 27. www.hoteldeplataan.nl. 25 rooms.* This is a hotel with a great deal of character. The rooms – and in particular the bridal suites – are furnished with refreshing originality: beds in the shape of a sycamore leaf (the hotel is called the Sycamore [plane-tree]), and entire rooms decorated in Turkish style. The hotel also has apartments for guests who wish to stay for longer periods. Breakfast is served in the welcoming Living Room Café Quercus.

Herberg de Emauspoort – *Vrouwenregt 9, 2611 KK,* ☎ *(015) 219 02 19, fax (015) 214 82 51. www.emauspoort.nl. 12 rooms.* The rooms in this family hotel are pleasantly furnished in the Old Dutch style. For those who are looking for something slightly out of the ordinary, however, two old-fashioned gypsy caravans have been set up in the inner courtyard, fully equipped with shower, toilet and television. And a breakfast of fresh home-baked rolls ensures that guests start the day on the right footing.

Leeuwenbrug – *Koornmarkt 16, 2611 EE Delft,* ☎ *(015) 214 77 41, fax (015) 215 97 59. 38 rooms.* This hospitable and typically Dutch hotel is located in two mansions in the heart of the town, and has comfortable rooms of various sizes.

MID-RANGE

Johannes Vermeer – *Molslaan 18-22, 2611 RM,* ☎ *(015) 212 64 66, fax (015) 213 48 35. 25 rooms.* Set in a quiet location, the Johannes Vermeer lives up to its name, with large reproductions of the Old Master's work decorating the walls of the brasserie. The rooms are comfortable and look out over the old town centre at the back. The restaurant is fitted out in the typical style of Holland, with a wonderful array of copper kettles suspended from the ceiling.

Bridges House – *Oude Delft 74, 2611 CD,* ☎ *(015) 212 40 36, fax (015) 213 36 00. www.delfthotels.nl/bridgeshouse. 7 rooms.* This fine canalside building is where Jan Steen lived between 1654 and 1656. Today it is a small but elegant luxury hotel. The hotel and the spacious rooms are tastefully decorated in the English style.

Museumhotel & Residence – *Oude Delft 189, 2611 HD,* ☎ *(015) 214 09 30, Fax (015) 214 09 35. www.museumhotel.nl/Delft. 28 rooms in the Residence.* The Residence, the splendid annexe of the Delft Museumhotel, is housed in a row of smart 17C canalside houses with an attractive courtyard. It is full of antique and modern objets d'art, and the modern rooms, lounge and garden contain displays of contemporary ceramics. Almost a museum, and also a top-class hotel.

WHERE TO EAT

L'Orage – *Oude Delft 111b,* ☎ *(015) 212 36 29.* Arts restaurant with good food and a beautiful town-centre location. Good value for money.

Le Vieux Jean – *Heilige Geestkerkhof 3,* ☎ *(015) 213 04 33.* Typically Dutch decor, but typically French cuisine.

De Klikspaan – *Koornmarkt 85,* ☎ *(015) 214 15 62.* Excellent food served in an old canalside warehouse. The restaurant is called "the telltale" after the resident parrot, but don't worry; the bird is the very model of discretion.

Van der Dussen – *Bagijnhof 118,* ☎ *(015) 214 72 12.* This trendy restaurant is housed in the superb 13C Bagijnhofje, or almshouses, and offers tasty exotic cuisine in a historic setting.

De Zwethheul – *Rotterdamseweg 480 (5km/3mi southeast of Delft),* ☎ *(010) 470 41 66.* Although this restaurant is outside the centre, it is worth a detour. Apart from its superb view of passing boats, and its pleasant terrace, the food is excellent. Treat yourself!

PRACTICAL INFORMATION

General information – VVV Delft, *Markt 83-85, 2611 GS Delft,* ☎ *(015) 212 61 00.* www.vvvdelft.nl has information on sights, excursions, cultural events, restaurants, maps, etc. It also publishes a brochure listing the town's hotels, pensions and campsites.

Transport – All parking in the town centre is either metered or pay and display. **Daily parking permits** are available for 5, 10 or 15fl at the VVV. The main sights in the historic town centre are within walking distance of one another.

Tours and walks – A 1hr 30min **walking tour** of the town leaves the VVV on Wednesdays and Fridays at 2pm from early April to late September. There is also a **tour by horse-drawn tram**, departing from outside the town hall in Markt; reservations are required on ☏ (015) 256 18 28.

Boat trips – Touring the historic town centre, these leave from outside Koornmarkt 113, ☏ (015) 212 63 85, daily from April to the end of October.

Markets – A **general market** takes place on Markt on Thursdays, while the **Brabant Peat Market** takes place on Saturdays. Plant and flower sellers set out their wares on Hippolytusbuurt on Thursdays, and a **flea market** is held along the canals every Saturday from mid-April to the end of September. An **art market** also takes place on Heilige Geestkerkhof from mid-April to mid-September.

Delft specialities – The town still has a few factories making delftware using traditional methods. The following are open to the public: **De Koninklijke Porceleyne Fles Anno 1653 Royal Delft**, Rotterdamseweg 196, ☏ (015) 251 20 30; **De Delftse Pauw**, Delftweg 133, ☏ (015) 212 49 20; **Aardewerkatelier de Candelaer**, Kerkstraat 14, ☏ (015) 213 18 48.

Almshouses – Delft's beautiful old hofjes are worth a visit: the **Bagijnhof** and the Old Catholic Church, Bagijnhof 21; **Hofje van Gratie**, Van der Mastenstraat 26-38; the **Pauwhofje**, Paardenmarkt 54-62; the **Klaeuwshofje**, Oranje Plantage 58-77.

Night-life – **Theatre** and **dance**: Theater de Veste, Vesteplein 1, ☏ (015) 212 13 12. **A special night out**: Stadsherberg De Mol, one of Delft's oldest buildings (1563), is at Molslaan 104, ☏ (015) 212 13 43. It is now a restaurant serving medieval dishes in suitably old-fashioned surroundings.

De Koninklijke Porceleyne Fles Anno 1653 Royal Delft

★★ HISTORIC CENTRE *allow half a day*

Markt – This long, narrow square stretches from the Nieuwe Kerk to the Stadhuis. In the middle stands a statue of Grotius *(see above)*.

★ **Nieuwe Kerk** ⊙ – This Gothic church (1381) has a brick tower crowned with a stone spire whose top has weathered to black. The carillon has bells cast by one of the Hemonys. The church contains the crypt of the princes of the House of Orange. Only a few members of this family were not buried here: Stadtholder and King of England, William III, lies in Westminster Abbey, John William Friso in Leeuwarden, Philip-William, eldest son of William the Silent, in Diest (Belgium). The interior is plain, with three naves and squat columns supporting wooden arches. The well-lit nave contrasts with the more sombre light reflected by the rich stained-glass windows (1927-36, WA van Konijnenburg) of the transept and the wide ambulatory. The glazing depicts figurative motifs in warm colours. The exception is the stained-glass window portraying Grotius, in the north transept, by the master **Joep Nicolas** (1897-1972) with its muted grey and blue tones.

The **mausoleum of William the Silent**★ stands in the chancel, above the royal crypt. This imposing Renaissance edifice in marble and black stone was made by Hendrick de Keyser from 1614-21. In the middle of a peristyle quartered by great allegorical figures, the prince lies in full-dress uniform, under the eyes of a bronze Fame. At his feet lies his ever-faithful dog. At the head of the recumbent marble statue, a bronze statue depicts William the Silent in armour.

In the centre of the chancel, the entrance to the House of Orange's crypt is indicated by a large emblazoned slab. In the ambulatory, paved with tombstones, is the mausoleum of King William I by William Geefs (1847) and further on a simple monument to Grotius (1781), and another by the Italian sculptor Canova to Prince Willem George Frederik, can be seen.

From the penultimate platform of the **tower** ⊙ there is a **panorama**★ over the new town which lies beyond the ring canal. Both the Technical University and the nuclear reactor are quite easy to pick out, and away on the horizon are Rotterdam and The Hague.

Stadhuis – The old town hall burnt down in 1618, and it was rebuilt two years later by Hendrick de Keyser. Since the 1960s restoration it has recovered its 17C aspect with its mullioned windows set in lead and its low shutters. The shell-decorated façade fronting the square is dwarfed from behind by the old 15C keep, all that remains of the original stadhuis. There is a fine view of the Nieuwe Kerk and its tower at the far end of the square.

The stadhuis and statue of Hugo de Groot

Waag – The weigh-house (1770) has been transformed into a café. Nearby is the meat hall, **Vleeshal**, the façade of which is appropriately adorned with two ox heads (1650).

Koornmarkt – *Cross the canal.* This is the landing stage for the boat trips mentioned above. At no 81 there is a lovely Renaissance-style house with medallions, called De Handboog (the bow). At no 67 the 18C patrician house, where the painter **Paul Tetar van Elven** lived (1823-96), is now a **museum** ⊙ containing furniture, paintings by Van Elven and his contemporaries, and ceramics.

★ **Legermuseum** ⊙ – *Enter through Korte Geer, the continuation of Koornmarkt.* The two former arsenals housing the Army Museum date from 1602 and 1692; they used to belong to the States of Holland and Western Friesland. The third building was used as a warehouse by the Dutch East India Company.

The historical exhibition in the "gebouw 1692" (1692 building) retraces the evolution of the Dutch army through the ages. Impressive collections illustrate the different stages of development of national military history: weapons, armour, uniforms, headgear, banners, trappings, means of transport, paintings and scale models. These cover the Roman and medieval periods, the Eighty Years' War, in which the army reformer Maurice of Orange and his half-brother

DELFT

Frederick Henry distinguished themselves, the French domination (1795-1813) and its upheavals, the Belgian Revolution (1830), and the two World Wars. The post-war events relative to Indonesia and the Cold War are also represented.

The 1602 building focuses more specifically on V-weapons, and holds temporary exhibitions.

* **Oude Delft** – The sombre water of the canal shaded by lime trees, the humpbacked bridges and the elegant façades make an attractive picture. At no 39 the lovely house of the Dutch East India Company, **Oostindisch Huis**, has been restored. The façade carries the company's coat of arms and its initials: VOC. The weathervane is shaped like a ship.

Turn back and follow the quay.

One soon sees the slightly leaning spire of the Oude Kerk. Built of a sombre-coloured brick, it is flanked by four pinnacles, and is crooked, earning it the nickname of Scheve Jan, Crooked Jan. On the opposite quay there is the charming Gothic chapel, Kapel van het H Geestzusterhuis.

149

From Nieuwstraat Bridge there is a fine view★ over the canal. At no 167 the Delft Water Board, **Hoogheemraadschap van Delfland**, an old patrician house (c 1520), displays a sumptuous Renaissance stone façade decorated with sculptured tympana. The portal is topped with polychrome armorial bearings.

No 169, **Het Wapen van Savoyen**, has a fine façade emblazoned with the arms of the House of Savoy and contains the local archives.

★ **Prinsenhof** ⊙ - *No 183. Enter from St Agathaplein, reached through a gateway on Oude Delft.* The relief above one of the former gates on Oude Delft is a reminder that in the 17C the Prinsenhof was converted into a cloth market. It originally included a convent **(St Agatha)** before becoming, in 1572, the residence of **William the Silent**, who was assassinated here on 10 July 1584 by Balthazar Gerard. The Moordhal, or Assassination Hall, still has two bullet holes at the bottom of the stairs to the first floor. The palace (Prinsenhof: the Prince's Court) now houses a **museum** with important historical collections relating to the Eighty Years' War and the House of Orange-Nassau. The Historical Room on the first floor has angel figures on the ceiling and numerous portraits on the walls. The museum also has many still-lifes and schutterstukken (portraits of companies of the civic guard) and some fine tapestries. The buildings, in late-Gothic style, date from the 15C and 16C and are grouped around two courtyards. After the Reformation, the chapel of the old monastery was given to the Wallonian Reformed Church and services were held in French for Protestants who had fled from the southern Netherlands.

Volkenkundig Museum Nusantara ⊙ - Nusantara means "island kingdom between two hemispheres", and the museum's collection is devoted to the history and cultures of Indonesia. It includes such items as statues, masks, weapons, textiles, brassware, shadow puppets, jewellery and Javanese *gamelan* instruments.

★ **Museum Lambert van Meerten** ⊙ - This beautiful 19C canalside mansion has a magnificent collection of **Dutch and foreign tiles**★ from the 16C to 19C. The attractive little passageway from the hall to the vestibule is decorated with Gothic and Renaissance-style motifs, while the monumental staircase depicts a naval battle between French, English and Dutch ships. Other tiles and tile pictures depict flowers, animals, and traditional crafts. The museum also has collections of delftware, furniture and other items from the estate of the industrialist Lambert Van Meerten (1842-1904).

Oude Kerk ⊙ - This 13C church is reflected in the waters of the Oude Delft canal. Since the 16C it has three chancels and the beginning of a transept. The tower, which leans, embedded in the main nave, is built on the foundations of a watch tower. It has the second biggest bell in the Netherlands (9t). Numerous memorial slabs are set in the pavement. The finely carved Renaissance pulpit resembles the one in the Grote Kerk in The Hague. The stained-glass windows (1972) were made by **Joep Nicolas**. Several famous people are buried in this church. In the main chancel Admiral Piet Hein is shown lying in full armour; it is the work of Pieter de Keyser, the son of Hendrick. In the chapel near the north chancel is the Baroque mausoleum of Admiral Tromp by Rombout Verhulst. The low relief depicts the naval battle of Terheyde, where the admiral was killed in 1653. To the north of the tower, near the stained-glass window depicting William the Silent, there is the monument to the naturalist Van Leeuwenhoek.

Hippolytusbuurt - This tree-lined canal is one of the oldest in Delft. On the corner of Hippolytusbuurt and Camaretten is the fish market (still in operation), next to which stands the former meat market. Opposite this is a 16C house (Kaaskop) with crow-stepped gables.

Voldersgracht - This is a picturesque canal, lined on the south side by a few corbelled houses. From the second bridge, there is a fine view of the Nieuwe Kerk's tower.

ADDITIONAL SIGHTS

★ **Oostpoort** - Formerly called St Catherine's Gate, it is the only one remaining from the town walls. It is a lovely brick construction, flanked with two slender turrets dating from the 15C and 16C. There is a fine view from the picturesque white lever bridge. A canal passes under the annexe.

Cultuurtuin voor technische gewassen ⊙ - This botanical garden has been used to grow a wide variety of plants for Delft Technical University since 1917. Its purpose is purely scientific and educational. It has glasshouses with tropical and subtropical plants, and there are also two short walking routes for visitors to the tree and herb garden.

Techniek Museum Delft ⊙ – This museum is located in the former mechanical engineering laboratory of the Technical College, and consists of three very large halls dating from about 1910. These provide an overview of technology past and present, including steam-operated machinery and engines. Hall 3 contains the **Museum IJkwezen**, or weights and measures museum, with a collection of measuring and weighing equipment.

Graf van Naundorff – The tree-lined square at the far end of Noordeinde canal, the continuation of Oude Delft, is the last resting place of the pretender Naundorff. Until recently it was claimed that he was the son of Louis XVI, but this has now been disproved by DNA testing.

DELTA*

Zuid-Holland – Zeeland

Michelin maps 908 and 211

In the coastal provinces of Zuid-Holland and Zeeland the estuaries of the Rhine, Maas and Scheldt form a complicated network of islands, headlands and channels known as the Delta.

HISTORICAL AND GEOGRAPHICAL NOTES

At the mouth of three great rivers – The **Rhine** divides into two branches as it crosses the Netherlands, the Neder Rijn and the Waal. The **Neder Rijn** (Lower Rhine) becomes the Lek, then the Nieuwe Maas before entering the Nieuwe Waterweg. The **Waal**, the main arm of the Rhine, flows into the Lek and the Maas. The **Maas**, which also has several names (Bergse Maas, Amer) flows into the Hollands Diep. The Oosterschelde is a former estuary of the **Schelde** (Scheldt), which presently flows into the Westerschelde. The rivers thread their way between the islands, some of which have become peninsulas.

A region under constant threat – The islands built up slowly towards the end of the Middle Ages as the rivers deposited sediments. They are generally very low-lying, many below Amsterdam Reference Level and most under 5m/16ft. The coastline is protected by high dunes while the banks of the rivers are strengthened by dikes. Several times throughout history these have proved vulnerable when the great surge tides swept inland.

On the feast day of **St Elisabeth** (19 November) 1421 the flood waters inundated the entire Delta and swept as far inland as Dordrecht and the Biesbosch area. Six villages were inundated and 10 000 lost their lives.

There was another great disaster on the night of 31 January 1953 when, under the combined effects of low atmospheric pressure and high tides, the water breached the dikes in several places. Once again the islands were inundated; 1 835 died and a further 500 000 were left homeless.

The effects were felt as far inland as the Hollandse IJssel.

The Delta Plan – Three years after the tidal wave of 1953, two options were under discussion to prevent the recurrence of similar tragedies: heighten the existing dikes or dam the major estuaries and inlets of the Delta. In 1958 the Delta Plan was incorporated in an Act of Parliament.

Four main dams, two with locks, closed off the inlets of the North Sea and several secondary dams closed off the estuaries further inland. The **secondary dams** afforded initial protection from high tides during the construction of the main dams. Once the main dams were finished the importance of the secondary ones diminished, although they proved a considerable asset to the road network.

The completion in May 1997 of the storm barrier in the Nieuwe Waterweg, which flows through Rotterdam, meant that the Delta Plan had been implemented in full after nearly forty years. The Westerschelde, which gives access to the port of Antwerp, is now the only inlet remaining open.

The dams have many advantages: they shorten the coastline by approximately 700km/435mi, and they form freshwater lakes (ie Haringvlietdam and further to the east two auxiliary dams, Philipsdam and Oesterdam). They reduce the seepage of salt water into the water table, limit the risk of floods, form ideal stretches of water for recreational purposes, improve the road network and encourage the development of the region.

The Delta Plan also included the raising and strengthening of existing dikes along navigable waterways and the development of the Biesbosch area.

The Scheldt-Rhine Canal, to the east of the Delta, was completed in 1975 and links Antwerp to the Volkerak, a distance of 37km/23mi.

Dams and bridges – Already by 1950 the Brielse Maas, downstream from Rotterdam, had been transformed into a lake called the Brielse Meer *(see BRIELLE)*. Since it was necessary to leave the New Waterway open for navigation a storm

Boat trips

Boat trips are available in the northern part of the Delta, leaving from Rotterdam *(see ROTTERDAM)* and Willemstad, or further along the Oosterschelde from Zierikzee *(see ZIERIKZEE)* or WaterLand Neeltje Jans *(see below)*.

surge barrier, **Stormvloedkering Hollandse IJssel**, was built between 1954 and 1958 on the Hollandse IJssel near Krimpen aan de IJssel in the eastern suburbs of Rotterdam. The reserve lock (120 x 24m/394 x 79ft) alongside is for larger vessels and ships in general when the gates of the storm surge barrier are closed. Following the completion of the storm barrier in Nieuwe Waterweg in 1997, the Rotterdamse Waterweg can now also be fully closed *(see ROTTERDAM, Excursions)*. The Haringvliet estuary was closed off by the **Haringvlietdam** while further inland the secondary **Volkerakdam** linked Overflakkee to the province of Noord-Brabant. Built between 1957 and 1969, the dam has three large sluice caissons and is itself linked to **Haringvlietbrug** which spans the waterway to the north towards Beijerland.

To the west, the Brouwershavense Gat Channel is closed by the **Brouwersdam**, with inland the **Grevelingendam** on the waterway of the same name. The latter links Duiveland and Overflakkee, and when it was built in 1958-65, 170 000 tons of rubble were tipped as infill from the gondolas of a cableway. The **Philipsdam** is a prolongation to the southeast.

The year 1986 saw the completion of the Oosterschelde Storm Surge Barrier, **Stormvloedkering in de Oosterschelde**. In the event of a bad storm or when the water level reaches a critical point, it is now possible to close off this estuary, the widest

(9km/6mi) and the deepest (40m/130ft) in the Delta. Two dams east of the estuary, **Oesterdam** (1986) and Philipsdam *(see above)* protect the Scheldt-Rhine Canal from tidal flow. The Oosterschelde is also spanned by the **Zeelandbrug**.

The saltwater channel, Veerse Meer, to the south of Noord-Beveland is closed off by **Veerse Gatdam**, which is backed up by a secondary dam, **Zandkreekdam**, on the saltwater Zandkreek channel between Noord-and Zuid-Beveland. Built between 1956 and 1960, the 800m/2 625ft long dam has a lock (140 x 20m/459 x 65ft) spanned by a swing bridge for traffic.

Two companies provide regular boat services across the estuary. There is a project under discussion to build a tunnel.

★★ THE STORM SURGE BARRIER

Construction of the storm surge barrier began in 1976, and was completed ten years later. The road running along the dam was opened in 1987. This gigantic and unique structure is 3km/2mi long. It is built across three tidal channels of the Oosterschelde and two artificial islands which were originally used as construction bases.

The original project involved the river being completely closed off, but this was changed to keep the link with the sea open. The barrier consists of 65 prefabricated concrete piers and 62 sliding steel gates. Each pillar is 30 to 38m/99 to 125ft high, and weighs up to 18 000 tonnes. The gates are normally raised, but can be closed in less than an hour in the event of high water or a storm. This construction preserves 75% of the tidal flow in the Oosterschelde and thus the unique estuary habitat with its fish and its oyster and mussel beds.

Ir. Topshuis on the former artificial island of Neeltje Jans (also home to the theme park **WaterLand Neeltje Jans** ⊘) houses the central control room as well as the **Delta-Expo** exhibition, which gives an idea of the importance of the Delta Project to the area as a whole and the history of land reclamation and hydraulic engineering in the Netherlands. A working model reproduces the 1953 floods and explains the safety measures implemented since then. The film *Delta Finale* recounts the successive stages of the development of the dam: the making of the different prefabricated elements, the preparation of foundations in the sandy channel bed, the floating and sinking into position of the concrete piers and finally the fitting of the computer-controlled sluice gates. The tour of one of the pillars of the dam is also worthwhile, particularly at high tide; access to the upper girder is through the control room. Note the powerful current: in the Oosterschelde each tide displaces 800 million cubic metres of water. The futuristic **Waterpaviljoen** uses light, sound and image effects to show the cycle of water movements. In summer, there are nature walks on the island, and it is also possible to climb one of the pillars or go on a tour of the Oosterschelde. And for children there is the **Waterspeelplaats** (water playground).

HELLEVOETSLUIS TO VEERE

99km/62mi – allow a day

Hellevoetsluis – This small village on an inlet of the sea, Haringvliet, has a marina.

★★ **Haringvlietdam** – This major civil engineering project was undertaken from 1955 to 1971.

Initially an artificial construction site was built in the middle of the estuary and surrounded by an encircling dike. A cableway was used in the final stages, a method that had already been used on the Grevelingendam. Concrete blocks were tipped from the gondolas into the final channel to be dammed. All of 5km/3mi long, the Haringvlietdam has 17 drainage sluices of 56.50m/185ft, the largest in the world. Their gates take 20min to open using a hydraulic press system with 68 presses set within the

Oosterschelde storm surge barrier

16 pillars and the abutment piers. Normally these sluice gates are closed and the water is forced back to the Nieuwe Waterweg. The drainage locks help to achieve a balance between fresh and saltwater.

A shipping lock has been made near the small port to the south. At **Expo Haringvliet** ⓥ visitors are shown how the locks are constructed and how they work. They also get a chance to look around one of the engine rooms.

Brouwersdam – The dam was built from 1963 to 1972 between the islands of Goeree and Schouwen; there is no lock. To complete the north channel, Springerdiep, sluice caissons were made, the same system which had been used for the first time when building the Veerse Gatdam. The south channel, Brouwershavense Gat, was filled in using the cableway system whereby 15-tonne loads of concrete blocks were dropped each time by the gondola. Between the Brouwerdam and Grevelingendam is the saltwater but tideless lake, Grevelingenmeer.

Renesse – This small village on the north coast of the island of Schouwen has a lovely sandy beach. Just to the east is a fine 16C-17C manor, **Slot Moermond**, which is now a hotel and restaurant.

Den Osse – This recent marina is well hidden by the dikes.

Brouwershaven – This was originally a prosperous port trading in beer from Delft (*brouwer*: brewer); however life today revolves around its small pleasure boat harbour.

This was the home town of the statesman, **Jacob Cats** (1577-1660), nicknamed Father Cats, who was Grand Pensionary of Holland and West Friesland from 1635 to 1651. He was also known for his poetry.

Brouwershaven has a lovely Gothic church, the **Grote Kerk or St.-Nicolaaskerk** ⓥ. The pulpit and font screen are in the Rococo style. The town hall **(stadhuis)** of 1599 has a highly decorated Renaissance façade.

★ **Zierikzee** – See ZIERIKZEE.

★★★ **Storm Surge Barrier** – See above.

★ **Zeelandbrug** – *Illustration: see Admission times and charges at the back of the guide*. In 1955 this bridge was built to link Zierikzee to the former island of Noord-Beveland. The crossing was paralleled with the opening of the road along the Oosterschelde Barrier. This impressive feat of engineering bridges the 5 022m/ 16 476ft waterway in 50 arches at a height of 17m/56ft above water level. The swing bridge on the Schouwen-Duiveland side gives passage to boats with tall masts.

Veerse Gatdam – This dam was built (1958-61) from a point west of Veere on the island of Walcheren to the former island of Noord-Beveland. It is 2 700m/8 858ft long, and in spite of protection from a sandbank is very exposed to storms, due to its north-westerly orientation. It was the first dam to use sluice caissons; these were placed on the bed of the channel and the sluice gates were then closed at slack water, which prevented the formation of a destructive current. Another small saltwater and tideless lake, the Veerse Meer, lies between this dam and the Zandkreekdam to the east.

★ **Veere** – See VEERE.

154

DEVENTER★

Overijssel

Population 82 621

Michelin maps 908 J 5, 210 W 9 and 211 W 9

Plan of the conurbation in the current edition of The Red Guide Benelux

Deventer stands on the east bank of the IJssel in the south of the province of Overijssel. This former Hanseatic town has a historic centre full of character which is witness to a rich past. Today it is a lively university town and commercial centre, and the home of the famous gingerbread, **Deventer Koek**.

HISTORICAL NOTES

As early as the 9C Deventer was a prosperous port. At the end of the 9C, the town became the residence of the Utrecht bishops, who fled from their city threatened by the Vikings. The remains of an 11C episcopal palace have been found in Nieuwe Markt. The town soon played an important religious role. The theologian **Gerhard Groote** (1340-84), born in Deventer, was the innovator of a spiritual movement, the **Devotio Moderna** (modern devotion). One of his pupils, following the wishes of his master, founded in Deventer c 1384 the first monastery for the **Order of the Brethren of the Common Life**, a community devoted to the education and care of the poor, which had a great intellectual influence in Europe. Those who passed through this school included Thomas à Kempis *(see ZWOLLE)*, Pope Adrian VI *(see UTRECHT)*, Erasmus in 1475-76 and Descartes in 1632-33.

In the 16C the artist Hendrick Terbrugghen was born in Deventer. At the end of the 17C, the painter Gerard Terborch, born in Zwolle, came to work here, dying in 1681.

155

In the 16C and 17C printing was an important enterprise in the town; many incunabula had already been produced here in the 15C.

Today, on the first Sunday in August, Deventer hosts the great book market, **Grootste Boekenmarkt van Europa**. Deventer is also an Old Catholic Episcopal See *(see UTRECHT)*.

Bussink's Koekwinkel (gingerbread shop)

TOWN CENTRE 2hr

Brink – This is the name given to the main square of the town and is typical of all localities of Saxon origin. A market is held here on Friday mornings and Saturdays, and the many outdoor cafés provide a pleasant place to linger in the summertime. At nos 11 and 12 there is an early 17C façade decorated with shells. The richly decorated **Penninckhuis** (no 89) dates from 1600. No 84 is the original **Bussink's Koekwinkel**, where Deventer's delicious gingerbread is still sold.

*Waag – This is a large, slightly leaning weighhouse built in 1528 in the late Gothic style and complemented in 1643 by the addition of a tall perron resting on arcades. On the right side wall hangs a huge cauldron in which, it is said, counterfeiters used to be boiled.

The building contains the **Historisch Museum De Waag** ⊘, displaying several collections related to the town's history. Note the *Four Evangelists* by Hendrik ter Brugghen, the remnants of a 17C majolica oven and the bicycles, believed to be the oldest in the Netherlands.

De Drie Haringen – This merchant's house (1575), known as the House of the Three Herrings, has a fine Renaissance façade decorated with a façade stone depicting three herrings.

Speelgoed- en Blikmuseum ⊘ – The biggest public collection of toys in the country has been set up in two medieval houses. Most of the exhibits were made after 1860: construction sets, train sets, dolls, games and mechanical toys. One section presents a range of packaging tins, manufactured in the Netherlands between 1800 and 1980.

Retrace your steps and turn right into Bergstraat.

Bergstraat – This street, in the **Medieval Bergkwartier**★★ (Berg meaning hill) comprises several beautifully restored old houses in the Gelder-Overijssel style, which is a mixture of Gothic and Renaissance. It affords a lovely view of the two towers of the Bergkerk *(see below)*.

St.-Nicolaas or Bergkerk ⊘ – Building started c 1200 and the two great west front towers date from that period. In the 15C the rest of the building was remodelled in the Gothic style. In 1991 the church was turned into an exhibition space, forming an elegant setting for the **13C paintings**★ that are on display.

Return to Brink via Kerksteeg – at the end of Kerksteeg, turn around and stop a moment to take in the view – and Menstraat. Polstraat then leads to Grote Kerkhof.

Grote Kerkhof – The Grote Kerk and Stadhuis are both on this square.

Stadhuis ⊘ – The town hall complex (greatly restored) is in three parts: the Raadhuis, the Wanthuis (also giving on to Polstraat), and the Landshuis. The latter has a brick façade (1632) topped by a pinnacled gable. The joint façade of the Raadhuis and the Wanthuis dates from 1693; its architect Jacob Roman also designed Het Loo Palace in Apeldoorn.

In the hall several 17C and 18C group portraits of guilds are exhibited. A room on the first floor of the Raadhuis has a lovely canvas by Terborch: entitled **The Aldermen's Council**, it was painted in 1657.

Bussink's Deventer Koekwinkel

Grote Kerk or St.-Lebuïnuskerk ⊙ – It bears the name of Lebuin, the Saxon apostle, who built a church here in the 8C.

The Romanesque church was converted after 1235 and then again in the 15C in the Gothic style. It is a vast building flanked to the west by a tower topped with a lantern designed by Hendrick de Keyser.

Its carillon, which was cast by one of the Hemonys, can be heard during **concerts** ⊙. From the top of the **tower** ⊙ (219 steps) there is a lovely view of the town.

In the hall-type interior the remains of a double transept can still be seen. The stellar vaulting has paintings round the keystones (16C). Other paintings can be seen, notably under the porch near the tower; the *Bearing of the Cross* dates from the 16C. The 19C great **organ** has 3 000 pipes.

The Romanesque crypt (1040), under the chancel, is remarkable with its six short pillars, cabled or decorated with geometric motifs.

ADDITIONAL SIGHT

Buyskensklooster – This early 15C building has recovered its brickwork walls. It is the former convent of St Agnes where the Sisters of the Common Life lived, following the rules set down by Gerhard Groote. It contains the town archives, **Gemeentelijke Archiefdienst** (no 3) and a library, the **Atheneumbibliotheek** ⊙.

EXCURSION *26km/16mi to the east via Snipperlingsdijk*

Holten – This town, situated in the Salland region, attracts many tourists, drawn by the wooded and sandy heights of the **Holterberg** (alt 60m/200ft), which marks the southern limit of the Scandinavian glaciers.

On the Holterberg, there is the **Natuurdiorama Holterberg★** ⊙. About 10 large **dioramas★** bring to life ecosystems and their fauna, many of which are still to be found locally .

In a nearby clearing is the **Canadian military cemetery**, with 1 496 graves of Canadians killed in the Second World War.

Markelo – At the beginning of the 20C an important field of funeral urns *(see Introduction, Historical table and notes)* was found north of Markelo.

Markelo has an **open-air theatre**, De Kösterskoele.

DOESBURG

Gelderland

Population 11 370

Michelin maps 908 J 5 and 211 V 10

At the confluence of the IJssel and the Oude IJssel, Doesburg, an old stronghold of the Zutphen earldom, was a prosperous commercial town in the Middle Ages and a member of the Hanseatic League in 1447. This lovely town in the Achterhoek *(see ZUTPHEN, Excursion)* has kept several of its Gothic and Renaissance façades.

SIGHTS

Grote Kerk or Martinikerk ⊙ – This Gothic church dedicated to St Martin (15C) is lit by tall Flamboyant windows. Its high **tower** was destroyed in 1945, but has been rebuilt and has a carillon. Organ concerts are given in summer.

Waag – Now a restaurant – and an inn for as far back as the 15C – this attractive weigh-house (1478) has tall picture windows with painted shutters, topped by tympana and a gable decorated with pinnacles. Inside, in a typical setting, the weigh-house scales can be seen.

There are other interesting houses in the same street, notably the **Baerkenhuizen** (nos 29-31), two Renaissance buildings of 1649.

Stadhuis – Opposite the Waag, the town hall dates from the 15C. Of particular interest are its front and rear façades.

The **Streekmuseum De Roode Tooren** ⊙ is at nos 9-13 in the same street. Reconstructions include a room where a cigar-maker chopped tobacco and an old grocer's shop. Note the scale model of a pontoon bridge: near Doesburg the banks of the IJssel were linked by this type of bridge until 1952.

Doesburgsch Mosterd- en Azijnmuseum ⊙ – *Boekholtstraat 22.* In this factory, founded in 1457, mustard is prepared according to traditional methods using small wooden barrels.

> If you want to take some time out for a cup of tea, Croissanterie La Fleur *(Kerkstraat 16)* is a cosy coffee shop/restaurant with a garden terrace. Access is through an old sweet shop .

157

EXCURSION 22km/14mi to the southeast

Doetinchem – This town, situated in the heart of the Achterhoek (see ZUTPHEN), formerly belonged to the Zutphen earldom. It was badly damaged by a bombardment in 1945. Today, it is a modern industrial and commercial town.

's-Heerenberg – This village close to the German border is dominated by the imposing castle, **Huis Bergh**★★ ⊘. Built in the 13C by the Van den Bergh family, this moated castle has undergone much alteration work, mainly in the 17C, and has burnt down twice. In 1946 its last owner, a keen collector, bequeathed the castle and its contents to a trust. The interior comprises a valuable **collection of antique furniture**★★, Old Dutch and Flemish paintings, illustrated manuscripts and carvings of wood and ivory. Particularly notable is the collection of Early Gothic Italian paintings including a work by Duccio. The coin collection and the weapons room can also be viewed.

The roof of the tower affords a fine view of the outwork and the steward's house (now a teashop), the 15C **Mint** and the Medieval parish church.

DOKKUM

Fryslân

Michelin maps 908 J 2 and 210 V 3 – Local map see LEEUWARDEN

The small town of Dokkum, in the north of Friesland, was once a flourishing port. Today it hides behind the remains of its tree-covered ramparts, from which only a few bell-towers and tall mills emerge. As the town is built on a mound, it has several steeply sloping streets.

St Boniface and his 52 companions were murdered here in 754. This English-born missionary came to Friesland in 716 to convert the people to Christianity; he then attached himself to St Willibrord in Utrecht. He was killed during his second mission to Friesland, and is buried in Fulda, Germany, where he had founded a monastery.

SIGHTS

ZIJl – From this wide bridge, there is a fine **view** over Klein Diep (meaning small canal) bordered by a mill, and the Groot Diep (large canal). The simple 17C **stadhuis**, or town hall, has a white clock tower and a 19C neo-Classical façade. On the other side of the canal are three lovely early-17C houses with crow-stepped gables which have been well restored.

Follow Diepswal to reach the museum.

Museum Het Admiraliteitshuis ⊘ – This regional museum is installed in the former Admiralty House (1618) and a neighbouring 18C house; note the Admiralty House's small Renaissance-style portal. The collections are varied: Dokkum silverwork, a Frisian sledge of carved wood, paintings, antique chests, items excavated from ancient burial mounds, local costumes, 19C toys, and Frisian folk art.

Waag – _Grote Breedstraat._ This small weigh-house (1754) has two decorated pediments, one of which bears the town's coat of arms (a crescent moon and three stars).

Grote Kerk or St.-Martinuskerk ⊘ – A mound and a church were erected here to commemorate the murder of St Boniface. The present building in the Gothic style has a chancel dating from the 15C. Inside the elevation over the side aisles includes a very tall gallery. A great number of tombstones are embedded in the floor; note the Frisian pulpit with elegant carved panels portraying a lion, a pelican and a falcon.

Bonifatiuskapel ⊘ – _Leave Dokkum to the south in the direction of Leeuwarden and once beyond the lever bridge take the second road on the left._ In the middle of the square stands the statue (1962) of the bearded monk, St Boniface, shielding his head with his Bible from his Frisian attackers. The chapel dedicated to St Boniface (1934) in the small park is the centre for a popular annual pilgrimage (see Calendar of events).

Michelin Route Planning on www.michelin-travel.com.
Michelin, your companion on the road, invites you to visit our web site and discover European route planning on the Internet.
Whether you just want to know the distance between two points, or need a detailed itinerary, for a holiday or on business, we provide all the information necessary for accurate travel planning.

DORDRECHT*

Zuid-Holland

Population 119 462

Michelin map 908 F 6 or 211 N 12

Plan of the conurbation in the current edition of The Red Guide Benelux

In the south of the province of Zuid-Holland, Dordrecht, which the Dutch familiarly call Dordt, is an important river centre between the Beneden Merwede, a branch of the Rhine, the Noord, the Dordtse Kil and the Oude Maas. It is also a great pleasure boat harbour with many yachts anchored at quaysides, both within the town and outside. The old town has kept its colourful quays, its canals and its old façades, while the southern quarters are noted for their bolder constructions.

It inspired many painters including Van Goyen (1596-1656); a number of 17C and 18C artists were born here *(see below)*. **Ary Scheffer** (1795-1858), painter of biblical and religious scenes, was Louis-Philippe's court painter.

Boat trips ⊘ – Dordrecht is the departure point for boat trips through the Biesbosch.

HISTORICAL NOTES

In 1220 it acquired city rights from the Count of Holland, William I, and because of this, it is considered the oldest town in the earldom.

The 14C was a period of great prosperity for Dordrecht due to the privilege of applying stop-over tolls, which from 1299 were levied on goods coming from the Rhine. The 15C, on the contrary, was a time of disaster: there was the unsuccessful siege in 1418 by Count John of Brabant as part of the struggle between the Hooks and Cods; the St Elisabeth's Day Flood of 1421 which isolated the town making it an island; the great fire of 1457 and then its capture in 1480 by John of Egmont. In the 16C the town recovered its splendour.

The cradle of independence – It was in the Dordrecht Court of Justice (Het Hof) that the first free assembly of the Holland and Zeeland States was held in July 1572. The capture of Brielle by the Sea Beggars in April of that same year had precipitated this event. In Dordrecht the delegates of the twelve confederate states of Holland and the nobility decided to deliver the country from the Duke of Alba's armies, and they proclaimed William the Silent as stadtholder. In this way they laid the foundation for the future United Provinces *(see Introduction, Historical table and notes)*.

Synod of Dort – Dordrecht was also the meeting place in 1618-19 of the great synod of Protestant theologians who came to settle the controversy that had arisen between the moderate **Remonstrants** or Arminians, supporters of Arminius, and the **Gomarists**, supporters of **Gomarus**. The latter group won, with the help of Maurice of Orange, and carried out bloody persecutions on their opponents, such as Oldenbarnevelt *(see AMERSFOORT)* and Grotius *(see DELFT)*. At this synod the union of all Protestant churches in the country took place, except for the Remonstrants, and a joint doctrine (canons of Dort) was established.

Birthplace of 17C painters – A number of 17C painters were born in Dordrecht. Some of them were Rembrandt's students. **Ferdinand Bol** (1616-80) went to live in Amsterdam where he worked in Rembrandt's studio. His works, notably the

---

The De Witt brothers

Dordrecht was the birthplace of the De Witt brothers, distinguished 17C statesmen.

Johan de Witt (1625-72) became the Grand Pensionary of Holland in 1653. Although he was an excellent administrator, he had less success in foreign affairs. He was unable to avoid the defeat of the Dutch fleet by England in 1654, which marked the end of the First Anglo-Dutch War. In addition he was hostile to the predominance of the House of Orange, and as a result he was quite unpopular for being out of step with popular opinion. After having won the Second Anglo-Dutch War (1665-67) and withstood the War of Devolution led by Louis XIV (1667-68), Johan de Witt managed to get approval for the **Perpetual Edict** of 1667, which abolished the Stadtholdership and thus the Orangist power in the province of Holland.

However, in the same year (1672) that Louis XIV and Charles II united against the United Provinces in the Third Dutch War, the people, feeling threatened, repealed the Perpetual Edict; William of Orange was elected Stadtholder as William III and army commander. Finally, **Cornelis**, the brother of Johan de Witt and burgomaster of Dordrecht in 1666, was wrongly accused of conspiring against William III and was imprisoned in the Prison Gate in The Hague. While visiting him, Johan de Witt was the victim of an uprising and was murdered with his brother near the prison *(see Den HAAG)*.

numerous portraits tinged with seriousness, are very like those of his master, for their chiaroscuro, the abundance of impasto and the harmony between warm colours.

Nicolaes Maes (1634-93) was also influenced by Rembrandt, whose pupil he was from 1648-52 in Amsterdam. More realist than the latter, he chose ordinary people, modest subjects and scenes in which he was able to evoke a degree of endearment. Towards the end of his life he changed to painting fashionable portraits.

Samuel van Hoogstraten (1627-1678) studied with Rembrandt, then after having travelled a great deal in Europe, returned to his birthplace. He painted mainly portraits and interior scenes. **Godfried Schalcken** (1643-1706) was one of his pupils.

Aert van Gelder (1645-1727) was first a pupil of Van Hoogstraten, then of the ageing Rembrandt in Amsterdam. His biblical scenes owe a lot to the technique of the great master, notably the sumptuous clothes and the slightly theatrical composition.

Albert Cuyp (1620-91) was influenced by Jan van Goyen and painted landscapes with luminous backgrounds, immense skies and in the foreground horsemen or peaceful herds of cattle.

From the 17C to the present – In the early 17C Dordrecht was first eclipsed by Amsterdam, and then by Rotterdam. The town became French in 1795.

Today Dordrecht has a flourishing industrial sector as firms are particularly attracted by its good location. Industries include chemicals, construction and the tertiary sector.

★ **OLD TOWN** *half a day*

★ **Grote Kerk or Onze-Lieve-Vrouwekerk** ⊙ – Legend has it that the church was started by a young girl, St Sura, who, wishing to build a chapel to the Virgin and possessing only three *daalders*, saw each time she prayed that three new coins were miraculously added to her treasure. The present church, which is Protestant, was built between 1460-1502 in Brabant Gothic style. The massive tower has remained unfinished because of subsidence on the north side. It ends in a terrace with four clock faces. The **carillon** (1949) consists of 53 bells.

J. Bouman/TRAVEL PICTURES

Grote Kerk, Dordrecht

Interior – It is very large (108m/354ft long) and imposing with its 56 pillars topped with typical Brabant crocket capitals. The oak **choir stalls**★ were finely carved by the Fleming Jan Terwen between 1538 and 1542 in the Renaissance style, and are among the most beautiful in the country. The low reliefs above the backs of the last row on the north side depict secular triumphs, notably those of Emperor Charles V; those on the south side portray religious triumphs. Also worthy of note are the cheekpieces and misericords. The Baroque chancel screen (1744) is elegant. In a chapel of the ambulatory on the east side, three stained-glass windows depict episodes in the town's history: the flood of 1421, the fire of 1457 and the capture of the town in 1480. The pulpit (1756) with a marble base is in the Rococo style, and the **organ** was built in 1671. Fine old tombstones are embedded in the church floor.

Tower ⊙ – *279 steps*. On the way up, take the chance to get a closer look at the 1626 clock. From the top terrace, there is a superb **view**★★ over the old town where the houses huddle together alongside the canals and docks. Note the length of the roofs; land bordering the canals was so expensive that houses were built backwards from the canal with façades as narrow as possible. Further in the distance are the rivers that surround the town.

DORDRECHT

To the right of the tower, the Leuvebrug over the Voorstraathaven has four **low reliefs** sculpted in stone in 1937 by **Hildo Krop** (1884-1970); they depict a prisoner, a baker, a dairywoman and an apothecary-surgeon in a naive style.

Blauwpoort or Catharijnepoort – Near this very plain gateway, dating from 1652, there are warehouses and a beautiful patrician house with a perron, the 18C **Beverschaep**: its door is topped by a naiad and a triton embracing one another; on the pediment a sheep *(schaap)* and a beaver *(bever)* support the coat of arms.

Nieuwehaven – Pleasure boats find shelter in this dock with tree-lined quaysides.

★ **Museum Mr Simon van Gijn** ⊙ – This lovely residence (1729) and its contents were bequeathed to the town by the banker **Simon van Gijn** (1836-1922), a great art collector. It contains rooms with rich furnishings, paintings, silver, glass and porcelain. Flemish wall hangings dating from 1730 hang in the reception hall. The living areas on the lower floor (the red drawing room, the dining room and the garden room) were furnished in 1886. The kitchen features copper utensils and a fine fireplace adorned with glazed earthenware tiling, all dating from around 1800. On the 1st floor are an Old Dutch study and library, and a bedroom and bathroom. The scale model in the passage is from 1740. There is also a very fine gold leather room from c 1686, the only fully preserved one of its kind. The 2nd floor has temporary exhibitions and a selection of prints and drawings from the Gijn Atlas. On the top floor is a collection of 19C toys, including dolls, dolls' shops and houses, and children's dinner services.

From the quay on the north side, there is a fine **view** of Nieuwehaven and part of the Grote Kerk. There is also a lovely view in the other direction over Kuipershaven, which is lined with warehouses.

Kuipershaven – Numerous barges are crammed into the coopers' quay, which specialised in the wine trade. At nos 41-42, a barrel is shown on the grill above the door. In the transom window of no 48 a basket is depicted.

Groothoofdspoort – This was the main gate (1618) to the town. It is topped by a dome.

From the quay, situated on the north side, there is a fine **view**★ over the wide confluence of the Merwede, the Noord and the Oude Maas Rivers.

On the other side of the gate near the lever bridge, the **Wijnhaven** (wine port), a harbour for pleasure boats, and the small bell-tower make a colourful picture.

Wijnstraat – This unevenly paved street lined with picturesque houses, all lop-sided, is another association with the wine *(wijn)* trade. Some houses are Renaissance, still with crow-stepped gables (nos 73-75; with the emblem of a cock: no 85), while others are in the Louis XIV style (no 87).

Cross the canal.

The city's oldest residences line this canal in the central area.

Voorstraat – In this busy shopping street are some interesting façades: note the lovely Rococo décor at no 178 and the **Muntpoort** at no 188, dating from 1555. At the beginning of the pedestrian precinct, on the left near the Augustijnenkerk, at no 214 a porch gives on to **Het Hof**, the former Court of Justice where the States General met in 1572.

Opposite Het Hof, at the corner of an alley leading to a bridge, there is a fine Renaissance façade.

Scheffersplein – This is the market place; in it is a statue of the painter Ary Scheffer.

Visstraat – This street, whose name means Fish Street, leads to Dordrecht's very modern commercial quarter. At no 7 there is a lovely small Renaissance house, **De Crimpert Salm** (1608), with an elaborate façade with a stone depicting a salmon *(zalm)* and a gable topped with a lion.

Cross the bridge towards Groenmarkt.

Views over the canal, which is narrow here, and the old town hall, a white neo-classical building. On the bridge there is a monument (1922) to the De Witt brothers.

Groenmarkt – Former vegetable market. On the right, at no 39, the **De Sleutel** house has a façade decorated with a key *(sleutel)* and tympana with recessed orders. Dating from 1550, it is reputedly the oldest in the town. At no 53, there is a fine façade with ogee-shaped tympana.

Grote Kerksbuurt – The house at no 56 has a charming façade.

ADDITIONAL SIGHTS

Dordrechts Museum ⊙ – This museum contains works by 17C artists who were born in the town, namely Albert Cuyp, Nicolaes Maes and Samuel van Hoogstraten. Dutch Romanticism is present, as well as pictures illustrating The Hague School and the Amsterdam School. In the section on 18C and 19C art, special attention should be given to the biblical scenes and portraits of **Ary Scheffer**: *Self-portrait at the Age of 43* (1883) and especially *Frédéric Chopin*, a remarkable picture of the great composer (1847). Scheffer's illustrations for *Histoire de la Révolution française*, a book written by the French politician Adolphe Thiers (1797-1877), are also on display. Various 20C artistic movements, such as magic realism and Cobra, are also represented in the museum's collections.

Arend Maartenshof – This old almshouse (1625) has kept its original character with small low houses surrounding a courtyard.

EXCURSION

Hollandse Biesbosch – *8km/5mi east of Dordrecht. Via the N 3, take the Hollandse Biesbosch turn-off.* This is the northern section of De Biesbosch National Park *(see BREDA, Excursions).* In the **visitor centre** ⊙, an exhibition and slide show give an account of the origins of the area and its inhabitants. Outside the visitor centre there is a special place from which visitors can watch beavers at work and at play. Biesbosch also has plenty to offer walking and boating enthusiasts.

EDAM

Noord-Holland

Population (with Volendam) 27 136
Michelin maps 908 G 4 and 210 P 7

An important cheese centre, Edam is a small, quiet and charming town, criss-crossed by canals still lined with a few fine 17C houses.

It is overlooked by the **Speeltoren**, a tall tower with a carillon, all that remains of a church demolished in the 19C. The town was formerly a busy port on the Zuiderzee, known for its shipyards.

Edam cheese – Originally made in Edam, it Is now made in several other regions. It is prepared with slightly skimmed milk and is similar in texture to Gouda, but differs in its easily identifiable shape: a ball with a yellow crust, covered with a thin red coating if it is for export. Dutch Edam has been exported since the 16C.

SIGHTS

Damplein – The main square on either side of the Damsluis is overlooked by the 18C **stadhuis**, or town hall, with its clock tower.
A lovely 16C house with a shop at the front contains the small local museum, the **Edams Museum** ⊙. It has a quite exceptional feature: a cellar that floats on groundwater.

Kaasmarkt – This square is the site of the former cheese market. The **Kaaswaag** ⊙, where cheese was weighed, is decorated with painted panels and now houses an **exhibition** on cheese-making. A traditional cheese market is held here on Wednesdays in July and August *(see Practical information at the front of the guide)*.

Grote Kerk or St.-Nicolaaskerk ⊙ – The 15C church has lovely early 17C stained-glass windows and a fine organ.

EINDHOVEN

Noord-Brabant

Population 199 877
Michelin map 908 H 7 and 211 M 14
Town plan in the current edition of The Red Guide Benelux

This industrial centre continues to grow. In 1900 Eindhoven had barely 5 000 inhabitants; now it is the fifth largest city in the Netherlands. Textile and cigar factories began appearing here in the early 19C, but by the end of the century they had been supplanted by Philips and, in 1928, by Van Doorne's Aanhangwagen Fabrieken, better known as DAF. Because of its industrial importance, Eindhoven was bombed several times during the Second World War, and hardly any historic buildings survived.

The "city of light" – Eindhoven owes its spectacular expansion mainly to Philips *(see below)*, which expanded from a simple light bulb factory into an international electronics giant. Apart from lighting, Philips also makes audio and video and medical equipment, household appliances and all kinds of electronic components, as well as equipment used in the professional field. **Philips Natlab**, the world's second largest laboratory, is where the video recorder, the CD and the CD-I were developed.
On the eastern edge of the city, on Noord-Brabantlaan, stands the **Evoluon**, a huge building (1966) supported by 12 V-shaped concrete pillars and resembling a large flying saucer. It was designed for Philips' 75th anniversary by the two architects, Kalff and De Bever, and is currently used as a conference centre.

A modern city – Although industrial and laid out to a modern urban plan, Eindhoven is a pleasant city, with particularly attractive pedestrian precincts. As the visitor drives into the city from a northerly direction, the sculptural installation entitled **Flying Pins** by Claes Oldenburg and Coosje van Bruggen, situated at the top of the Kennedylaan and Fellenoord, is a real eyecatcher. It consists of 10 tenpins (7m/23ft high) that fly around. The city is well provided with recreational activities, with parks like the **De IJzeren Man**. The environment education centre **Milieu Educatiecentrum Eindhoven** ⊙ *(Genneperweg 145)* is also worth a visit
The Eindhoven carnival is always a lively and popular event *(see Calendar of events)*. The city also has one of Europe's leading technical universities.

★ STEDELIJK VAN ABBEMUSEUM ⊙

This building opposite the town hall was bequeathed to the city in 1936 by the industrialist HJ van Abbe. The museum has a rich collection of paintings and sculpture from 1900 to the present, concentrating especially on contemporary art since 1945.

The museum is currently being rebuilt and expanded, and the work is scheduled for completion during the course of 2001. In the meantime, its collections are housed in the former shop for Philips employees on Vonderweg opposite the stadium. **Entr'acte**, as this short-term accommodation is called, holds temporary exhibitions of modern art.

The collection itself consists of an overview of modern art: the Cubism of Picasso, Braque and Juan Gris; Orphism or poetic interpretation of the real with Delaunay, Chagall and Fernand Léger; the De Stijl movement with Mondrian and Van Doesburg; Constructivism with a great number of works by El Lissitzky; the Expressionism of Kokoschka, Kandinsky and Permeke; and Surrealism with Miró, Ernst, Pieter Ouborg, and Francis Bacon.

Postwar artists include French abstract painters such as Bazaine, Sam Francis (born in California), and Serge Poliakoff (1906-1969) of the École de Paris.

The CoBrA movement is represented by Karel Appel, Asger Jorn and Corneille. Apart from painters such as Dubuffet and Tàpies, who revolutionised the use of materials in painting, there are also works by Vasarely, Lucio Fontana, Klein, the Zero group (Mack, Piene and Uecker), and the Americans of Pop Art including Morris Louis, Robert Indiana and Frank Stella.

Conceptual Art (Kosuth, Barry, Brouwn, Kawara), Minimal Art (Judd, André, Sol LeWitt) and contemporary German painting (Kiefer, Baselitz, Penck) are also represented.

ADDITIONAL SIGHTS

The centre – The area between Vestdijk and Keizersgracht houses the modern **Muziekcentrum Frits Philips** and the **De Heuvel Galerie** shopping centre. The **town hall** (1949-1955) was designed by J van der Laan and J Kirch. The **Liberation Monument** (1954) on the square in front of it is by Paul Grégoire.

Museum Kempenland ⊘ – *St-Antoniusstraat 5-7*. This museum, housed in the old Steentjeskerk, evokes the history and customs of the town and its hinterland, Kempenland. The collections concern archaeology, beliefs, textiles and handicrafts. The museum holds temporary exhibitions of Brabant painting and sculpture.

DAF Museum ⊘ – *Tongelresestraat 27*. A collection of some 50 lorries, buses and semi-trailers, and some 40 cars, chronicles DAF production from 1928 to the present day. The workshop where the brothers Hub and Wim van Doorne produced their very first trailers and semi-trailers is open to visitors. Their firm – in 1932 given the name of Van Doorne's Aanhangwagen Fabriek or DAF for short – together with Philips, represented Eindhoven's most important industry. A permanent exhibition is devoted to Charles Burki who worked as a freelance designer for DAF for 30 years.

Philips and Eindhoven: a company town

In 1891, Gerard Philips set up a light bulb assembly plant on Emmasingel. After five difficult years his brother Anton (whose statue now stands at the railway station) came to his aid, and from then onwards the business took off in a big way. The factory began making radio valves, X-ray tubes and medical equipment, and exporting them across Europe. In 1914 Gerard set up the natural sciences laboratory Natlab, which has since been responsible for many important forms of new technology *(see above)*. Later, in collaboration with DAF, Philips established the Technical College (1955), now Eindhoven Technical University.

By 1929, Philips had 20 000 employees and provided jobs for 70% of the local workforce. It opened new factories and offices on Emmasingel and Mathildelaan with names like De Witte Dame (The White Lady), De Bruine Heer (The Brown Man) and De Lichttoren (The Lighthouse). The city council could not keep up with this dramatic expansion, and Philips began building its own facilities for employees and their families: a theatre, library, schools, and most importantly housing, such as the Philipsdorp garden village on Frederiklaan *(see Introduction, Industrial heritage)*. The company also set up its own sports club, Philips Sportvereniging, whose football team is one of the country's best-known.

However, the close ties between Philips and Eindhoven ended in 1998, when the company moved its headquarters to Amsterdam. Now new uses are being sought for its many buildings. De Witte Dame and De Bruine Heer will house offices, apartments, small businesses, the Design Academy, the European Design Centre and the public library. The small light bulb factory opposite, where it all began, is now open to the public.

Horse and Flautist (1951) by Karel Appel

Stedelijk van Abbemuseum

Prehistorisch Openluchtmuseum Eindhoven ⊘ – *Boutenslaan 161b.* This settlement from the Iron Age (750-50 BC) has been reconstructed on the basis of excavations in Noord-Brabant and Kempen, using simple tools and natural materials. Enactors represent the daily activities of the Iron Age: there is a forge with a blacksmith at work, a weaving-shed where wool is being dyed, ovens where pots are being fired and bread baked, people working in the fields, and a cattle pen where pigs are being reared. Other aspects of this ancient society are also brought to life with pagan images and even prehistoric musical instruments. This museum project is an example of experimental archaeology, which attempts to answer questions about people in earlier times by living in the same way as they did. The museum particularly comes to life at weekends and when special events are held.

Het Witte Dorp – *Geldropseweg and St.-Jorislaan.* The White Village, a complex of 264 white homes with red roofs, was designed by **WM Dudok**. This fine example of functionalist residential building was built between 1937 and 1974. It is a listed monument.

EXCURSIONS

Nuenen – *8km/5mi north-east of Eindhoven.* This town preserves the memory of **Vincent van Gogh** *(see AMSTERDAM, Museum district)* who, after having spent several months in Drenthe, came to live in the presbytery where his parents lived. He lived here from December 1883 to November 1885, and it was then that he made a large number of studies of peasants' heads which he would later use in his great canvas *The Potato Eaters.* Two monuments and the **Van Gogh Documentatiecentrum** ⊘, containing some hundred photographs of paintings and drawings from the years Van Gogh spent in Nuenen, preserve the memory of his time here. At no 26 Berg is the **presbytery** where Vincent van Gogh's father died in March 1885.

Kasteel Heeze ⊘ – *12km/7.5mi southeast of Eindhoven.* This 17C castle, designed by Pieter Post, has been the home of the Van Tuyll family for more than 200 years. Behind the castle lies the original 15C castle Eymerick. Inside, the drawing rooms with their fine tapestries, a bedroom and a bathroom can be viewed.

Helmond – *38km/24mi. Leave to the northeast by the A 270.* This is an active textile manufacturing centre.
Kasteel Helmond★ is an imposing medieval **castle** consisting of a quadrilateral building with an inner courtyard, an encircling moat and a park. The castle houses the **Gemeentemuseum** ⊘ (municipal museum).

Asten – To the northwest of this village lies the **Beiaard- en Natuurmuseum Asten** ⊘, a museum of carillons and natural history.

The **carillon section**★ has information on bell-making, a collection of bells from all over the world, and clocks, carillons and chiming mechanisms, some of which can be played.

The natural history section displays dioramas with stuffed animals, butterflies and insects from De Groote Peel.

There is also a peat-bog garden and a bat cellar.

★ **Nationaal Park De Groote Peel** ⊙ – *Access to the south by Moostdijk, near Meijelse Dijk.* To the southeast of Asten stretches a large marshy area (1 400ha/3 460 acres) called **De Peel** (*peel* meaning marsh). This **peatland nature reserve** has been a **protected national park** since 1985. The varied and tranquil landscape, with large stretches of water, makes an ideal nesting place for waterfowl, and it has one of the most varied bird populations in western Europe. In the autumn, thousands of migratory birds use the Groote Peel as a resting or assembly place on their long trek south. In spring, around 95 bird species hatch here, including mainly **black-headed gulls**.

This gull, about 40cm/16in long, is normally white, although in summer its head becomes completely black. It can be found on the coasts in winter, but it often comes to nest inland, notably near the lakes. Males and females share the task of sitting on the eggs and jealously defend their nest.

The visitor centre, **Bezoekerscentrum Mijl op Zeven** ⊙, has documentation on the nature reserve itself and the local flora and fauna. Three nature trails make it possible to explore this fascinating natural environment.

EMMEN

Drenthe

Population 105 497
Michelin maps 908 L 3 and 210 AA 6
Local map see HUNEBEDDEN

The prosperous market centre of Emmen is a pleasant town bordered to the north and the east by fine forests. The southern end of the Hondsrug has numerous *hunebedden*, prehistoric funerary monuments.

SIGHTS

★ **Hunebed of Emmer Dennen (D 45)** – *Access by Boslaan, direction Emmer Compascuum. It is situated near a large crossroads and is well signposted.* This remarkable *hunebed*, an alleyway covered with six enormous slabs encircled by uprights, was erected on a mound right in the middle of the forest. Standing in an attractive setting it is popular with painters.

Hunebedden along the Odoorn road – *Coming from the centre of Emmen towards Odoorn, after the last farm, bear left on a path signposted "hunebed".* Between the trees there is a **long grave**★ (D 43); the shape of the burial mound has been reconstructed and two covered alleyways are hidden. The whole is surrounded by uprights between which are piles of rocks which hold up the earth. A few hundred yards further to the north, on the left side of the road, there is a small *hunebed* (D 41) covered with capstones.

On leaving Emmen, on the right, a lane marked *hunebedden* goes through the forest to a large clearing of heather. Three *hunebedden* (D 38/40) stand in this lovely setting: one is half buried, the second, also buried, was given the shape of a square, while the third is covered with fallen stones.

★ **Noorder Dierenpark** ⊙ – This zoo is particularly interesting for its great variety of species. The starting point is **Biochron**, where the beginning of life on Earth is explained. Visitors then walk from one continent to another. In the gigantic **AmeriCasa** there are colourful birds from South American tropical forests. A tropical garden is a haven for more than 1 500 fluttering butterflies. The seal pool and the **African House** with crocodiles and naked mole-rats are other attractions. A 1.5ha/4 acre area of **African Savannah** is home to giraffes, zebras, antelopes, rhinoceroses, cranes, and impalas, and beneath the children's farm there is also a new "sewer" full of rats.

EXCURSIONS

★ **Noorsleen, Schoonoord and Orvelte** – *40km/ 25mi to the west – local map see HUNEBEDDEN.*

Noordsleen – This charming village of the Drenthe, with a restored mill, has two *hunebedden. Access by the small road to Zweeloo and a lane on the right signposted "hunebedden" (D 51).* On the left, is a small covered alleyway still topped by three capstones (four have disappeared). Further on the right, the *hunebed*★ (D 50) shaded by a large oak which grows in its centre is better preserved. Five slabs are still in place as well as the oval crown of upright stones. The entrance pillars are on the south side.

Schoonoord – 3.5km/2mi to the south of the locality, in the woods near a riding centre, a *hunebed* (D 49) has been partially reconstructed. Above, the heather-covered ground forms a mound and hides the large slabs which form the *hunebed's* roof. This *hunebed* is called **De Papeloze Kerk** (church without a priest); congregations met here at the beginning of the Reformation.

Orvelte, museum-village

★ **Orvelte** – This **museum-village** ⊘ in the heart of the Drenthe comprises a collection of typical farmhouses and barns with thatched roofs. Cars are not permitted. Many of the villagers still go about the traditional agricultural activities of cattle and sheep rearing and cereal growing. Others keep alive traditional crafts and trades, including miller, blacksmith, clog-maker and potter.

Coevorden – *21km/13mi to the south-west.* An old fortified town designed by **Menno van Coehoorn**, Coevorden has kept several interesting monuments. The **castle** is a fine building flanked by a corner turret, with walls of rose-coloured roughcast and pierced in the left part of the façade (15C) by tall narrow windows. Part of it is occupied by the town hall; in the basement there is a restaurant. Near Markt *(Friesestraat no 9)*, there is a picturesque late-Renaissance **house** with voluted gables and ornamentation: bright red shells, heads of women, cherubs, Moors, and inscriptions. On Marktplein, facing the docks are the three 17C roofs of the Arsenal (restored), which contains the local museum, **Gemeentemuseum Drenthe's Veste** ⊘.

To the east, beyond Weyerswold *(6km/4mi)* typical thatched cottages of the Drenthe stand beside innumerable small oil wells; the **Schoonebeek** region was once rich in petroleum.

ENKHUIZEN★

Noord-Holland

Population 16 713

Michelin maps 908 G 3 and 210 Q 6

Enkhuizen was the main Frisian settlement and seat of their chiefs until 1289 when West Friesland passed to the counts of Holland. The town had one of the largest herring fishing fleets which brought great prosperity; three herrings figure on the town's coat of arms. Enkhuizen was fortified in the mid 16C, and it was one of the first towns to revolt against the Spanish in 1572. In the 17C the town had approximately 50 000 inhabitants, but as the port began to silt up in the 18C, Enkhuizen's maritime activities started to dwindle. Once they had ceased entirely with the building of the Barrier Dam in 1932, the town looked to its rich agricultural hinterland for a living and today it is an important market town and centre for bulb-growing. The marina is also an important asset of the town.

ENKHUIZEN

Enkhuizen is linked to Lelystad, the main town of Flevoland, by the dike road *(31km/19mi)*. This was originally to have enclosed the fifth and last polder around the edge of the IJsselmeer *(local map see IJSSELMEER)*, but the Markerwaard project was abandoned in 1986.

Boat trips ⊘ - Boats leave from Spoorhaven for Stavoren, Urk and Medemblik (in combination with the steam tram).

★ OLD TOWN 5hr

Enkhuizen has numerous 17C façades in Renaissance style, their fine decoration bearing witness to its former prosperity.

Westerstraat - This is the town's main street. There are lovely façades, notably that of no 158 to the north, dating from 1617 with the town emblem on a gable: a young girl bearing a coat of arms depicting three herrings.

Westerkerk or St.-Gomaruskerk ⊘ - This hall church was completed in 1519. Its free-standing wooden tower built in the 16C on a stone base was rebuilt in the 19C in the neo-Classical style. Inside, the three naves are covered with a wooden vault. There is also a fine wooden **rood screen**★ with six richly carved panels (16C), a pulpit (16C), which is a replica of the one found in the Grote Kerk in The Hague, and a 1547 organ case.
Opposite the church is the former Mint of West Friesland, **West-Friese Munt**, with a lovely, finely decorated façade dating from 1617. Further on at no 109 the façade of the Orphanage or **Weeshuis** has been rebuilt in the style of the original façade (1616).

Turn right to take Melkmarkt and Venedie.

Dijk - At no 32, a house (1625) displays the motto: "Contentement passe rychesse" (happiness is worth more than riches).

★ Drommedaris

- This imposing and well-known building (now a café and restaurant) which was part of the town walls was, like the one in Hoorn, intended for keeping watch over the entrance to the port. It consists of a circular tower and an adjoining gatehouse. Note the decoration above the doorway. It has a carillon cast by Hemony, which is one of the best in the country. From the top there is a **panorama**★ of Enkhuizen, its port, the IJsselmeer lake and in the distance Friesland.

From the quay to the south of the tower, there is a fine **view**★ to the east over the docks (Zuiderspui) and the backs of houses with picturesque wooden oriels overlooking flowered gardens.

Zuiderspui – This short street has some interesting façades: no 1 has five coats of arms, from left to right can be seen those of Hoorn (a horn), the House of Orange, West Friesland, Enkhuizen and Medemblik. This is the home of the **Flessenscheepjesmuseum** ⊘, which contains over 500 large and small bottles with ships inside. A video film shows how the ships were put inside the bottles.

Breedstraat – Several houses have interesting façade stones, notably no 81, called Den Kuiser Maegt (the young girl from Enkhuizen), depicting the town's coat of arms; no 60, an old boat, and no 59, a young girl also holding the town's coat of arms.

Stadhuis – The town hall is an imposing building dating from 1686. The interior is decorated with painted ceilings, tapestries and murals.

On the corner of Zwaanstraat stands the **old prison**, a small building, which today functions as exhibition space and whose picturesque façade dates from 1612.

★★ **Zuiderzeemuseum** – The Zuiderzee Museum is made up of two sections: an indoor and an outdoor museum.

Zuiderzeemuseum

★★ **Binnenmuseum** ⊘ – The indoor museum consists of twelve linked buildings around three courtyards. Some are 17C houses and warehouses formerly belonging to the Dutch East India Company. The covered reception hall is reached via the first courtyard, which preserves much of the atmosphere of the Golden Age, and the second, where the ship collection is visible through a glass wall.

The museum has a variety of permanent **exhibitions**. One, entitled **Walvisvaart**, uses maps, paintings (including the life-size *Catching a whale off the coast of Spitsbergen*, Storck, 1690), tools and various objects to evoke the whaling industry, highly active in the region from the 17C to the 19C. The ship collection in the **Schepenhal** has a number of old vessels, including wooden sailing boats which used to cruise along the Zuiderzee, a flat-bottomed fishing boat and a vessel from Urk which was pulled along the ice.

The beautifully restored **pepper store** looks and smells just as it did when it was owned by the East India Company in the 18C. Other exhibitions deal with fishing in the **North Sea and Zuiderzee**, the region's constant **battle against the water** (including a computer animation on the subject of the Afsluitdijk), and **water transport**. Together, they give a varied picture of seven centuries of Zuiderzee history.

★★ **Buitenmuseum** (Open-air Museum) ⊙ – *Entrance opposite the Binnenmuseum, or access by the ferry leaving the car park near the entrance to the dike linking Enkhuizen to Lelystad.* This museum is a reminder of daily life in the old Zuiderzee fishing ports between 1880 and 1932, completion date of the Barrier Dam (Afsluitdijk). More than 130 shops, houses and workshops from around thirty localities have been reconstructed to make up this charming **village-museum**. Everything in the museum conspires to evoke life in bygone days: the furniture, the tools, the layout of the gardens, the church from old Wierengen Island and the reconstruction of Marken port in 1830. Visitors may buy old-fashioned candy, go for a ride on an old boat, or see the sailmaker, ropemaker and fish curer at work. Shops and manufacturing are also well represented: there is a spice shop, a butcher's, a pharmacy, a steam laundry, an agricultural credit bank and even three lime kilns.

Children can dress up in a traditional costume during their visit, and there is a **children's island** where they can investigate how children lived in Marken around 1930.

There is also a **nature reserve** attached to the museum, containing plants, birds and a duck enclosure .

Return to Westerstraat.

Here, too, there are also lovely gables, shop signs and façade stones (a cooking pot, a bull's head, etc).

The gaper,
a typically Dutch phenomenon

In the Art Nouveau pharmacy De Grote Gaper, there is a colourful collection of heads with their tongues sticking out. These humorous images, known as *gapers*, were used as shop signs by Dutch pharmacists. They were a reminder that people had to open their mouths wide when taking the medicines they sold, and of course patients also had to show their tongues to the doctor.

Zuider Kerk or St.-Pancraskerk ⊙ – This church is flanked by a fine Gothic tower, the wooden cap of which was added in the 16C. Its carillon was cast by the Hemony brothers.

ENSCHEDE

Overijssel

Population 148 814

Michelin maps 408 L 5 and 210 AA 9

Enschede, situated in the green countryside of the Twente region, is the largest town in Overijssel province. An important industrial centre, it specialises mainly in textiles. Its rapid expansion due to the development of industry only started at the beginning of the 19C. Severely damaged by fire in 1862 and bombarded in 1944, it is, today, a modern city. On 13 May the town was hit by another disaster, when there was an explosion at a fireworks factory, killing 21 people and destroying nearly 400 homes.

The vast campus of **Twente University**, founded in 1964, lies to the north-west of the town.

★ RIJKSMUSEUM TWENTHE ⊙ 1hr 30min

The building erected in 1930 to plans by Muller and Beudt was extended by Ben van Berkel in 1995-1996. The museum boasts a large collection of art and decorative arts.

★ **Old Masters and Applied arts** – *Right-hand wing.* The pre-20C and decorative arts section in the right-hand wing is an atmospheric display in differently-coloured rooms. It includes superb medieval **manuscripts**, incunabula, gold and silver, and **sculpture**. The collection of **late-Medieval painting** contains altarpieces and portraits by such artists as Van Cleve, Cranach, and Holbein the Younger; there are also **16C and 17C landscapes** by Brueghel the Younger, Van Goyen, Ruysdael and Avercamp. There are works by Jan Steen, Teniers and Terborch, and etchings by Rembrandt. The **18C**, in which the museum plans to specialise in the future,

Twente and the textile industry

The ready availability of water made it possible to wash the fibres and work the looms. Twente formerly specialised in the processing of linen, which was cultivated, retted, spun and woven on the spot. **Almelo** was the centre of this activity. Twente linen was exported to Norway and to Russia where the Vriezenveen *(7km/4mi to the north of Almelo)* merchants had founded a colony near St Petersburg. In the 18C linen was replaced by cotton which was less costly; at the same time they produced in large quantities a twill of linen and cotton called bombasine *(bombazijn)*. In the early 19C weaving and spinning production were industrialised with the development of looms driven by steam power.

The metallurgical industry also developed greatly at this time; in 1960, together with the textile industry, it represented 86% of the town's industrial activity. Since then the development of artificial fibres, foreign competition and economic recession have caused the decline of the textile industry. Iron and steel manufacture and processing, the building industry, the tertiary sector and technology are currently the region's developing industries.

is represented with works by De Wit and Troost. There is also a collection of glass, silver and furniture from this period. The museum has paintings by the **Romantics** (Koekkoek, Schelfhout and Leickert), and there is a separate room devoted to the Barbizon School (Daubigny, Troyon) and to the **Hague and Amsterdam Schools** (the Maris brothers, Mauve, Israëls, Breitner). This section ends with **Impressionism** (Jongkind, Monet, Sisley) and an early work by Mondrian.

*Return to the entrance via the passageway alongside the courtyard, where there is a collection of **delftware and grandfather clocks**. From here, the collection of modern and contemporary art can be viewed in chronological order in the left-hand wing.*

Modern and contemporary art – *Left-hand wing.* Here, the emphasis is on the development of Dutch art, with works by Toorop, Redon, pre-war **expressionists** (Sluiters, Gestel), the **Cobra group** (Appel, Constant, Corneille, Lucebert), the **Hague experimental** and **informal artists** such as Ouborg and Wagemaker. **Systematic, serial and fundamental art** from the 1960s and 70s is also represented. Contemporary painters from the Netherlands include Sjoerd Buisman, Marlene Dumas, Cornelis Rogge and Henk Visch. The museum also stages interesting **temporary exhibitions**.

Portrait of a six-year-old girl (1594), attributed to Jan Claesz

Rijksmuseum Twenthe

ADDITIONAL SIGHTS

Museum Jannink ⊙ – This museum is located in a renovated textile mill dating from 1900. Until 1964 there were 30 000 spindles here, plus 567 looms in an adjoining single-storey building which has now disappeared. The museum's collections illustrate the history of the Twente since 1600, with the emphasis on the textile industry over the past 150 years. Workers' interiors, which have been recreated, show the effects of this evolution on living conditions (cottage industry and rural life; then the move to the city to be closer to the factory with all it entails, increased comfort...). Also displayed are the tools used through the different

171

ENSCHEDE

Beelden		
van Mari Andriessen	. . . .	X A
Hervormde Kerk	. . . .	Y D
Museum Jannink	. . . . . .	X
Natuurmuseum	. . . .	YZ M¹
Rijksmuseum Twenthe	. . . .	V
Stadhuis	. . . .	Z H
Volkpark	. . . .	X

periods: spinning wheels, winding machines and looms. An exhibition of aerial photographs shows how Enschede has grown, and on the first floor there is a display about daily life here in the past.

Natuurmuseum ⊙ - This natural history museum displays rocks, fossils, precious stones and minerals etc.; the invertebrate section features insects, shells and coral.

There is also a small exhibition on aspects of geology and minerals. The 1st floor is devoted to fauna: **dioramas** show the main species of mammals and birds found in the Netherlands, aquariums and small ponds for reptiles; one room has an exhibition on whales.

Volkspark – In the south-eastern part of this park, one of the many green areas of Enschede, there is a monument erected to the memory of victims of the Second World War: a group of bronze statues by the sculptor **Mari Andriessen**.

Stadhuis – The town hall was built in 1933 by G Friedhoff, who was influenced by Stockholm's town hall. This rather austere brick building is flanked by a tall square bell-tower with slightly bulging walls.

Hervormde Kerk – This sandstone Reformed Church stands on Markt, the town's main square. It was begun c 1200 and enlarged in the 15C but has kept its great Romanesque **tower** (13C), with its paired openings. The spire was added at the beginning of the 20C. There is a sundial dating from 1836 on the right-hand outer wall of the church, opposite the VVV.

THE VERDANT REGION OF TWENTE

Round trip 80km/50mi. Leave by ① on the town plan and allow about 5hr.

The route crosses the northern part of **Twente**. Known for its industrial activities, Twente is also a verdant region where the land, cut by waterways, is divided into pastures and magnificent forests. Scattered throughout the area are large farms with wooden gables and sometimes half-timbered walls.

Oldenzaal – This small industrial town, near the German frontier, is an old, once fortified settlement, which has kept its concentric streets round a lovely Romanesque basilica, the **St.-Plechelmusbasiliek** ⊙. It is dedicated to the Irish saint, St Plecheln, and dates from the early 12C. The square bell-tower is massive, a typical feature of this region. In 1950 the church was given the title of basilica. The interior is impressive, with the groined vaulting of the nave resting on great square piers. The chancel and the south aisle were rebuilt in the Gothic style in the 15C. The south arm of the transept has a triptych (Adoration of the Magi) attributed to the Fleming, Pieter Coecke van Aalst.
Not far away is **Het Palthe Huis** ⊙ *(on Marktstraat)*, now a museum. This 17C Baroque house displays traditional objects in period rooms. There is also a reconstructed apothecary's shop, and in the attic an 18C chair in which a murderer was held for 110 days.

Denekamp – This small town, situated in one of the loveliest parts of Twente, has kept its strange tradition of *midwinterhorens*, which translated means horns of mid-winter. They are horns of carved wood which are blown at the approach of Christmas *(see Calendar of events)* in Twente villages; their origin remains mysterious.
Near the town stands a castle, **Kasteel Singraven** ⊙. A lovely road runs alongside the Dinkel, a calm tree-lined waterway where there is a lovely 15C **watermill**; grain is still ground here and wood is sawn; the building on the left houses a restaurant. The 17C **castle** flanked by a square tower is reflected in the Dinkel, one of whose branches waters the magnificent park. The furniture, tapestries, porcelain, paintings all add to the refined atmosphere of the 18C interior.

★ **Ootmarsum** – This charming village with concentric streets is built on a mound, round a Gothic church. Some of the houses have beautiful, elaborately decorated Renaissance façades and wooden gables. On Kerkplein stands the **Church of St Simon and St Judas**. This church is in the Romanesque-Gothic transitional style, which is reminiscent of Westphalian churches by the use of stone and by its thick square tower to the west (partly demolished). The apse is Gothic as is the fourth bay. Inside, the polychrome colours highlight the lines of the pointed arches and ribs. Worthy of note are the wooden statue of the Virgin (c 1500) at the end of the north side aisle and the modern stained-glass windows. In the display cabinets are silver liturgical plate and a lovely chasuble (1749) embroidered with the effigy of the church's patron saints. On the south side aisle a tomb is used as a columbarium, to store cinerary urns.
Ootmarsum also has two small museums: the **Onderwijsmuseum Educatorum** ⊙, which deals with the history of education, and the open-air **Openluchtmuseum Los Hoes** ⊙. This includes a number of barns and a carriage works around an old farmhouse of the "los hoes" type *(see Introduction, Traditions and folklore)*. This gives a fine picture of how local farmers lived and worked around 1900, and an exhibition, "Ootmarsum in its historical perspective", describes the town's rich past.
Take the road to Almelo.

Kuiperberg – From the belvedere on top of the Kuiperberg (alt 65m/213ft) there is a **view** over Ootmarsum and the wooded countryside. Next to it stands an old Jewish cemetery.

Continue to Delden via Almelo and Borne.

Delden – Delden is an important agricultural market centre. **Kasteel Twickel**, the former residence of the Counts of Wassenaar, stands to the north of the town. Founded in the 14C, it was altered in the 16C (main door) and the 17C. It is surrounded by moats and lovely **gardens** ⊙.

The **Grote Kerk or St.-Blasiuskerk**, a Gothic-style sandstone hall-church, has a heavy square tower.

The old town hall *(Langestraat 30)* houses both the VVV and a small salt museum, the **Zoutmuseum** ⊙. Located not far from the country's main rock salt deposits, it explains the origin, extraction and use of salt, as well as its importance to humans, animals and plants.

Hengelo – This commercial and industrial town has modern buildings, in particular the **town hall**, the work of Berghoef (1963). Since 1972, to the east of town, a new experimental residential quarter is being built by the architect Piet Blom.

Return to Enschede by ⑥ on the town plan.

FLEVOLAND★

Flevoland

Michelin maps 908 G 4, H 4, 5, I 4, 5
and 210 P 8, Q 8, 9, R 7, 8, 9, S 7, 8, 9, T 7, 8, U 7,8 –
Local map see IJSSELMEER

Flevoland is in fact two polders (Oostelijk Flevoland and Zuidelijk Flevoland) which represent the most recent achievements in the Zuiderzee reclamation project *(see IJSSELMEER).*

Oostelijk Flevoland – This was the third polder created on the IJsselmeer, after Wieringermeer Polder and the Noordoost polder. An area of 54 000ha/133 380 acres, it was diked and drained between 1950-57. The largest part of this polder is destined for agriculture (75% of the area; mainly oilseed rape and bulbs) while 11% of the land has been turned into meadows and woods, 8% for housing and the rest alloted to canals, roads and dikes. Before being exploited, the land was first sown with reeds. Farmhouses hidden behind screens of poplars and enormous barns are scattered over this flat countryside, criss-crossed by clusters of young trees. Tall trees indicate an already old dwelling-place. In the fields drained by ditches, sheep, cattle and ponies graze. There are numerous lapwings, golden pheasants and water birds such as the coot, a small dark wader whose black head has a white spot.

Since 1960 towns and villages have sprung up: Lelystad, Dronten, Swifterbant, Biddinghuizen; piles placed on a sand bed ensure the stability of the construction. Wide straight roads cut across the polder. Some have been built on the ring dikes. Lakes such as the **Veluwemeer**, separating the polder from the Zuiderzee's former coast, act as regulators and have become recreational lakes with bathing areas.

Zuidelijk Flevoland – It is separated from the Oostelijk Flevoland Polder by a security dike, the Knardijk, parts of the road being forbidden to traffic. It is surrounded by a dike built between 1959-67. In 1968 this polder of 43 000ha/106 210 acres had largely been drained. Half the area is devoted to agriculture, 25% to dwelling areas, 18% for meadows and woods. The rest is taken up by canals, dikes and roads. To the north, near Oostvaarders dike, there is a nature reserve, **De Oostvaardersplassen**. This marshland is a refuge for birds including some very rare species. The polders are at their best in May and June, when the oilseed rape fields are in flower.

LELYSTAD

Lelystad, capital of Flevoland, bears the name of the engineer Cornelis Lely *(see IJSSELMEER).* and consists mainly of individual houses and bungalows interspersed amid the greenery. The **Agora** community cultural centre, comprising a cinema and library, marks the centre of town.

Lelystad is linked to Enkhuizen by a dike, Markerwaarddijk *(31km/19mi)* with a road running along the top. The Oostvaardersdiep, a canal 300m/985ft wide, forms a waterway stretching between Amsterdam and the northern part of the country. The Houtribsluizen, two large locks spanning the Oostvaardersdiep, separate the Markermeer from the IJsselmeer.

Nieuw Land Poldermuseum ⊙ – This museum stands near the locks, and houses a permanent exhibition on the reclamation work carried out on the Zuiderzee. The history of the region's relationship with water is chronicled using historic film and sound recordings, models, interactive computer programs etc, and deals with subjects as varied as fishing, trade, geology and early cultures. The construction of dikes, the creation of polders and their first inhabitants are all covered. The large "Playing with Water" model is specially designed for children.

* Batavia-dock – Nationaal Scheepshistorisch Centrum ⊙ – Set up next to the information centre is the **Batavia***, a replica of a merchant ship belonging to the Dutch East India Company. The original vessel was built in Amsterdam in 1628. During her maiden trip, she ran aground on some reefs off the west coast of Australia; some of the 341 crew managed to survive the shipwreck. The wreck itself has since been salvaged, and is now on display in the West Australian Maritime Museum in Fremantle. The reconstruction of the ship was the work of a group of young people undergoing specialised training, and began in 1985. Since the launch of the replica the dock has expanded into a shipbuilding centre using traditional techniques. Apart from the Batavia, two other vessels are on display: the Flevo-aak, a modern version of a traditional barge, and a replica of De Zeven Provinciën, begun in 1995. This was the famous flagship of Admiral Michiel de Ruyter, built in 1665 and one of the largest of its time. The guided tour begins with a film in the visitor centre, and then takes visitors to see the boat and the workshops where the pulleys, sails and carved wooden sculptures are made; these recreate the atmosphere of Holland's Golden Age. The tour ends with a visit to the Batavia itself, showing how a 17C merchant vessel was a combination of a warehouse, a fortress and a community of individuals.

The **Nederlands Instituut voor Scheeps- en Onderwaterarcheologie** (Dutch Institute for Maritime Archaeology) and the **Nederlands Sportmuseum** are located beside the dock. In the **Expertisecentrum**, which looks like a ship's hull turned upside down, sections of shipwrecks – some excavated, others simply found – are examined and preserved. In time, a number of "pavilions" will be erected between this centre and Batavia dock which will deal with a variety of maritime topics. The first of these is the **Beurtvaarderspaviljoen**, which gives an insight into the life and work of bargemen assigned to regular service and has a 17C wreck on display.

Nederlands Sportmuseum ⊙ – This museum is dedicated to sports. Photographs and films as well as medals, shirts, shoes and skates worn by famous Dutch sportsmen and women have been brought together to recall

Morand-Grahany/HOA QUI

The Batavia

some major sporting achievements. Anyone who is keen to try out a new sport is given the opportunity to do so here.

Zepp/allon ⊙ – *To the north of Lelystad on the Airship Plaza site.* This museum chronicles the history of hot-air ballooning and aviation from 1783 to the present day. Exhibits include a gondola from an airship, hot-air balloon baskets and items from the Graf Zeppelin. Note also the prototypes for the new airship due to be built by the local firm Rigid Airship Design.

Natuurpark Lelystad – *To the east of Lelystad.* One of the exhibits in this park is the **wreck** of a ship dating from 1878. It has been left where it was found during drainage of the polder in 1967 and part of its cargo of bricks can be seen nearby. Elsewhere in the park, a prehistoric settlement has been reconstructed.

Lelystad aerodrome – Two museums have been created here: **Vliegend Museum Lelystad** ⊙, which comprises more than thirty vintage and modern aircraft, and **Uiverdome** ⊙, where the Uiver is on show, the only DC-2 in the world that still flies. In 1934 this KLM aircraft won the London-Melbourne Race.

ADDITIONAL SIGHTS

Almere – This town, to the south of Flevoland and bordering the Gooimeer, was founded in 1975. Since then it has expanded rapidly and is estimated to have 185 000 inhabitants by 2005. Almere is particularly known for its architecture, which gives every district and neighbourhood its own individuality. A number of well-known architects, including Cees Dam and Rem Koolhaas have contributed and continue to contribute to the project. In **ACHK – De Paviljoens** ⓥ *(Odeonstraat 5)* three wagon-like pavilions on stilts house temporary exhibitions of contemporary art.

Six Flags Holland ⓥ – This amusement park is located on the Veluwemeer in the district of **Biddinghuizen**. The many attractions offer plenty of choice for thrill-seekers, including a variety of **roller coasters**, a white-water ride, the rotating G-Force ride and the blood-curdling Space Shot. In **Bugs Bunny World** children are welcomed by Looney Tunes cartoon characters. There are also a variety of shows, including stunt shows, and other family attractions. Six Flags Holland also has a holiday village with chalets.

Dronten – This new town, standing right in the heart of the polder, was planned round a church with an openwork tower and a community centre, **De Meerpaal**. This immense glass hall, built in 1967 by Frank van Klingeren, is effectively an extension of Marktplein.

FRANEKER★

Fryslân

Michelin maps 908 H 2 and 210 S 3

This charming small Frisian town (Frjentsjer) had a famous university which was founded in 1585, where Descartes became a student in 1629. It was closed in 1811 during the reign of Louis Bonaparte.

SIGHTS

★ **Stadhuis** ⓥ – The town hall is a splendid building in the Dutch mannerist style, dating from 1591, with a double gable; it is topped by an elegant octagonal tower. The Council Chamber or Raadzaal and the Registrar's Office, Trouwzaal, are hung with 18C painted leather, in rich colours.

★ **Eise Eisinga Planetarium** ⓥ – At a time when a number of his contemporaries feared the end of the world due to the exceptional position of the stars, the Frisian **Eise Eisinga** decided to prove that the situation was not dangerous. This wool-comber, who had been interested in astronomy since childhood, built in 1774-81 an ingenious system whereby the movement of the stars was depicted on his living

Eise Eisinga Planetarium

room ceiling. Eisinga represented with surprising precision the celestial vault as known by 18C astronomers. This planetarium, whose movement can be seen in the attic, is the oldest European one in working order.

The charming House of the Corn Porters, **Korendragershuisje**, can be seen at the end of Eisingastraat.

Museum 't Coopmanshûs ⊙ - *Voorstraat 49-51*. The exhibits in this museum, installed in the Waag (weigh-house) and the large adjoining 17C and 18C houses, include a tribute to **Anna Maria van Schurman** (1606-1678). A celebrated entomologist and draughtsman, who belonged to the Labadist community founded by the French émigré **Jean de Labadie** (1610-1674), she advocated bringing Protestantism back to Primitive Christianity. The history of the former university is illustrated by portraits of professors and a "xylotheque" - an outstanding collection of wood samples presented in the form of books, presented to Franeker University by Louis Bonaparte in about 1810. The museum also displays several splendid collections of Frisian silver, porcelain and glass. Note the miniature charity fête by J Kooistra. It also holds temporary exhibitions on modern art.

In the same street, at no 35, the **Martenahuis** was built in 1498.

Martinikerk - This Gothic church has 15C paintings, and figures of saints on the pillars. The floor is strewn with finely sculptured tombstones in the Frisian style.

Weeshuis - The former orphanage's door is topped with 17C inscriptions.

Nearby, the **Cammingha-stins** is a lovely 15C and 16C residence, now housing the **Kaatsmuseum** ⊙, which uses photographs, prizes, emblems and a variety of documents to give visitors an insight into the popular Frisian ball game - similar to fives - called *Kaatsen*.

GIETHOORN**

Overijssel

Michelin maps 908 J 3 and 210 V 6

The picturesque town of Giethoorn stands in the middle of the vast bogland area known as De Wieden.

Peat used to be dug here on a massive scale, creating the many lakes in this region. To transport the turf, long canals and ditches were cut, along which thatched farmhouses and peat-cutters' houses were subsequently built. Giethoorn owes its name to the great number of goats' horns *(geitehoorns)* discovered by the original settlers when they started to dig for peat.

A lakeside village - The pretty thatched cottages of Giethoorn face onto the canals spanned by hump-backed bridges or simple footbridges. Well-tended lawns and gaily planted flowerbeds slope down to the water's edge. The bicycle is the most popular form of transport although many locals use flat-bottomed punts (punters). Even bridal processions can be seen punting along the canals.

No cars are allowed into the village and it must be explored on foot (a path runs alongside the main canal) or by boat. Punts, motor boats, canoes and sailing boats can be hired at various points in the village and there is a large choice of boat excursions available. The village stretches along both sides of the Dorpsgracht, which is almost 7km/4mi long. The busiest part during the tourist season lies between the Centrum-Dorp turn-off and the Zuid turn-off. If you want to avoid the crowds of day-trippers - particularly in the summer months - then seek out the nearby village of Dwarsgracht and hamlet of Jonen on the other side of the canal.

The newly restored working farm museum, **Museumboerderij 't Olde Maat Uus** ⊙, tells the story of life in Giethoorn during the 19C.

Kameeldak roofs - The *hallenhuizen* or hall-houses *(see Introduction, Farmhouses)* are remarkable for their thatched hump-backed roofs. When more and more land was reclaimed the grain yields increased and the farmers had to extend their storage space. Since land was at a premium they extended upwards and as a consequence the farm buildings became taller than the farmhouse. Roofs with this change in level were called camel-backed *(kameeldak)*. Another characteristic of these farms is that they have no carriage entrance as everything was transported by water. Hay was stored in the barn above the boat house.

Giethoorn's Planet Hollywood

The best-known café in Giethoorn is undoubtedly **Eetcafé Fanfare** *(Binnen-pad 68)*. The vast array of musical instruments and photographs on the walls vouch for Giethoorn's brush with fame back in 1958 when Bert Haanstra shot his famous film *Fanfare* here.

The lakes – The meres which stretch to the east and south of the village are vast stretches of water scattered with small reed-covered islands. The entire area is a unique ecological habitat rich in birdlife and is a haven for recreation.

Giethoorn

EXCURSIONS *26km/16mi*

Wanneperveen – In this small town which, like many peat-bog villages has a name ending in *veen* (peat-bog or fen), thatched cottages run for several miles alongside the road. Not far from the village's west entrance lies the **cemetery**; its free-standing bell-tower, scantily built with a few beams, is characteristic of Southern Friesland. In the main street, at no 83, note a lovely house with a crow-stepped gable, the **old town hall** (1612).

Vollenhove – This was another of the historic ports on the Zuiderzee, before the Noordoostpolder was reclaimed. The bastions of the old town ramparts are visible near the church, where pleasure boats now lie moored. On **Kerkplein** stand a few fine buildings: **St.-Nicolaaskerk**, a Late Gothic church with two naves and its free-standing bell-tower, the **Klokketoren** which was used as a prison; adjoining the bell-tower is the **old raadhuis** (town hall), a brick and sandstone porticoed building dating from 1621 and now converted into a restaurant; finally the lovely façade

The legend of Kaatje

Kaatje (Little Kate) was an innkeeper who made her fortune back in the 18C. Her bronze statue stands by the lock in Blokzijl, and it is said that stroking her head with your left hand will bring you luck. If it is wealth you are after then you must stroke her head with your right hand. But beware, anyone who tries to be too clever and uses both hands can expect punishment from Vrouwe van Blokzijl.

Kaatje bij de Sluis

If you are hoping for some culinary luck, then try the gourmet restaurant Kaatje bij de Sluis.

of the **Latin School** – dating from 1627 and now used as a bank – has crow-stepped gables and an entrance with two carved stelae in front. The new town hall is housed in the 18C **Oldruitenborgh** manor house, set in the park of the same name. Opposite the town hall the church, Kleine Kerk, stands in the midst of a fine garden, the **Historische tuin Marxveld**. In the adjoining Bisschopstraat is Vollenhove's antiquities collection, **Oudheidkamer**.

* **Blokzijl** – This was also one of the prosperous old ports on the Zuiderzee and a member of the Hanseatic League. The Dutch East India Company used the port as a haven for its East Indiamen when storms arose. Today it is pleasure boats which cruise past the lovely 17C houses on the water-front, making their way to the lock.

The **Gildenhuys** ⊙, in the picturesque Kerkstraat, displays the handicrafts that used to be practised in the town. A little further on the 17C **Grote Kerk** ⊙ was one of the country's first Protestant houses of prayer. The **interior**★ with its wooden ceiling and pulpit – equipped with its very own hourglass to remind the preacher that the patience of the congregation did have limits – is also well worth a visit.

GOES

Zeeland

Population 35 381

Michelin map 908 C 7 and 211 I 13 – Local map see DELTA

The former port of Goes owed its prosperity to salt mining and the madder industry (the production of a red dye). Through the location of its canals it has preserved the layout of its 15C ramparts. Today Goes is the main centre of Zuid Beveland. The town is surrounded by meadows and orchards and it is linked to the Oosterschelde by a canal. A historic **steam train** ⊙ runs between Goes and Oudelande (south of Goes).

Jacqueline of Hainaut or Jacoba – Goes was one of the ancestral seats of the Counts of Zeeland and the town is closely associated with the turbulent Jacoba, daughter of William VI. On William's death in 1417 Jacoba inherited the earldoms of Hainaut, Holland and Zeeland, and was envied by many. She was a fierce opponent of the **Cods** (see GORINCHEM). In 1421 she had left her second husband John IV, Duke of Brabant, who dispossessed her of the Holland earldom by giving it to John of Bavaria, Jacoba's uncle and supporter of the Cods. The following year she married Humphrey, Duke of Gloucester, fourth son of King Henry IV, brother to King Henry V of England. Later, to escape from the intrigues of Philip the Good, who had invaded her territories, she took refuge in Goes. She was forced by Philip to sign an agreement in Delft in 1428, the **Treaty of Delft**, in which she recognised him as heir and promised never to remarry. The promise was soon broken (1432) and Jacoba lost her title of countess (1433); three years later she died in Slot Teylingen, near Sassenheim (see KEUKENHOF).

Market day – The weekly market on Goes's Grote Markt (Tuesdays; see Introduction, Traditions and folklore) gives the occasional opportunity of seeing the Zeeland costumes of Zuid-Beveland. The head-dresses are very beautiful, with square lace caps worn by the Catholic women and oval ones by the Protestants.

SIGHTS

Grote Markt – The town's main square is overlooked by the 15C **stadhuis** (town hall) which was altered in the 18C in the Rococo style. Inside on the left is a café which opens at lunchtime.

* **Grote Kerk** ⊙ – Part of the church dates from the 15C and was altered and refitted between 1619 and 1621 after a fire. The main nave is very high. The **north portal** is finely decorated in the Flamboyant style and has a wide window topped by an open-work gable. Inside, the church has a remarkable 17C **organ**, crowned with an 18C canopy.

Opposite, the neo-Gothic church, **Marie Magdalenakerk**, dates from 1908.

Museum voor Zuid- en Noord-Beveland ⊙ – Singelstraat 13. Housed in a former orphanage, this museum has a varied collection including traditional Beveland costumes and 17C paintings depicting archers. On the right of the museum is the former almshouse, **Oude Mannen- en Vrouwenhuis** (1665). The depictions above the portals bear witness to the building's former use.

Turf- en Kleine Kade – To the north of Grote Markt. These quays are lined with some fine houses.

EXCURSIONS *15km/9mi east - local map see DELTA*

Kapelle - The **Dutch Reformed Church** with its imposing 14C brick bell-tower and corner pinnacles is visible from afar, across the low-lying polderland.
In the nave, note the decorated balusters and heads of satyrs from the 15C. The chancel, decorated with blind arcading, contains a 17C tomb.

Yerseke (or **Ierseke**) - This small port on the Oosterschelde specialises in the culture and trade of oysters, mussels and lobsters and boasts the only mussel auction in the world. On the third Saturday in August the annual mussel festival, **Mosseldag Yerseke**, takes place, where everyone can sample the mussels free of charge.

GORINCHEM

Zuid-Holland

Population 33 248

Michelin maps 908 F 6 and 211 O 11

On the borders of three provinces (Zuid-Holland, Noord Brabant and Gelderland), Gorinchem, often called **Gorkum**, is an important waterway junction, at the confluence of two large rivers, the Waal (branch of the Rhine) and the Maas, as well as the Merwedekanaal and a small river, the Linge. It has a large marina to the west.

Hooks and Cods - Gorkum dates from the 13C and because of its strategic position it has suffered numerous sieges.
In 1417 it was the site of a ferocious fight between the Hooks (Hoeken), supporters of **Jacoba** (*see GOES*) who had inherited the town, and **Willem van Arkel**, on the side of the Cods (Kabeljauwen). Van Arkel wished to reconquer the town, which had belonged to his father. He lost his life during a skirmish in the city.

GORINCHEM

		Gasthuisstraat	12	Peterburg	27
		Groenmarkt	13	Pompstraat	28
		Hoge Torenstraat	15	Robberstraat	30
		Hoogstraat	16	Tolsteeg	31
Appeldijk	3	Kelenstraat	18	Torenstraat	33
Blauwe Torenstr.	4	Kruisstraat	19	Vijfde Uitgang	34
Boerenstraat	6	Langendijk	21	Visbrug	36
Bornsteeg	7	Lombardstraat	22	Walstraat	37
Burgstraat	9	Molenstraat	24	Westwagenstr.	39
Dalembolwerk	10	Nieuwe Waalsteeg	25	Zusterhuis	40

Burgerkinderenweeshuis	A
Gorcums Museum	M

Hugo de Grootpoortje	S
Huis' t Coemt al van God	V

Gorkum was one of the first strongholds wrested from the Spanish by the Beggars in 1572. Among the prisoners taken by the Beggars there were 16 priests who were executed at Brielle the same year; they are known as the martyrs of Gorkum.

Gorinchem was the birthplace of the 16C painter **Abraham Bloemaert**, who spent most of his life in Utrecht.

HISTORIC CENTRE *45min*

The historic core is girdled by the star-shaped outline of the bastions and ramparts which have been transformed into an esplanade. It is crossed by the River Linge, which forms a picturesque harbour, the **Lingehaven**.

Grote Markt – The old neo-Classical **town hall** (1860) houses the VVV tourist information office and the **Gorcums Museum** ⊙, which has a collection of paintings, sculptures, models, toys and silver chronicling the town's history. The town's collection (Stadscollectie) consists mainly of works by modern and contemporary local artists, including Ad Dekkers, which are displayed in temporary exhibitions.

At no 23 Grote Markt is the **Hugo de Grootpoortje**, a small Baroque structure which is all that remains of the house where the famous jurist and scholar Hugo Grotius fled after escaping from prison in Slot Loevestein *(see Excursions)*.

Groenmarkt – The 15C **Grote Kerk or St.-Maartenskerk** is located in this square. The church's tall early-16C Gothic tower, **St.-Janstoren** ⊙, is particularly worth seeing. The builders realised during its construction that the tower was leaning over to one side, but all they could do was adjust the top part of the tower accordingly.

Burgerkinderenweeshuis – On the 18C façade of the old orphanage, also called **Huize Matthijs-Marijke**, a carved stone depicts Christ and children, between the founders of the orphanage.

Huis "'t Coemt al van God" – A narrow-fronted house with a crow-stepped gable, decorated with Renaissance-style medallions (1563).

Dalempoort – This lovely, small rampart gateway, square with a high roof topped by a pinnacle, dates from 1597. It is the only one of the town's four gateways to remain. From here, the tall wall mill called **De Hoop** (meaning Hope – 1764), is visible.

Buiten de Waterpoort – This tree-lined esplanade stretches from the south of the old water-gate (Waterpoort), which was closed in 1894 to enlarge the road. Boat trips leave from this landing stage. There is a fine **view** over Dalempoort, the mill and the river. To the south-east, on the opposite bank, the tall bell-tower of the church of Woudrichem and the pink brick Slot Loevestein rise above the greenery.

EXCURSIONS

Leerdam – *17km/11mi to the north-east. Leave via Spijksedijk.*
This town, situated on the Linge, has been the main glass-making centre in the Netherlands since the first glassworks was established here in 1795. To the south-west, in a villa on the Oosterwijk road *(Lingedijk 28)*, is the **Nationaal Glasmuseum** ⊙. This displays interesting collections of glass and crystal from Leerdam (19C and 20C) and from various other countries (18C, 19C, and 20C). Leerdam also has a number of glass galleries.

Woudrichem – *21km/13mi to the south. Leave Gorinchem by Westwagenstraat.*
At the confluence of the Rhine (Waal) and the Maas, this small fortified town, commonly called **Workum**, is still enclosed in its encircling bastioned ramparts. Through the Peace of Woudrichem in 1419, John of Bavaria obtained important rights over the territories of his niece, Jacoba *(see GOES)*. Workum has a small pleasure boat harbour with a ferry to Slot Loevestein for foot passengers. To the south one enters the town by **Koepoort**. On the right is the squat **tower** of the Late Gothic church, the walls of which are decorated with medallions. Near the 15C prison gate, **Gevangenpoort**, in Hoogstraat, the **Oude Raedthuys** *(no 47)* has a graceful Renaissance-style façade with a crow-stepped gable. In the same street, at no 37, note a façade stone depicting an axe chopping wood, and opposite, two twin houses of 1593 and 1606, whose façade stones are sculpted to depict a golden angel and a salamander. Note also the inscriptions, "In the Golden Angel" and "In the Salamander", their respective names.

★ **Slot Loevestein** ⊙ – *Catch the ferry in Woudrichem (for footpassengers only).*
This solid fortress in pink brick is flanked with four square towers and surrounded by moats and ramparts. Slot Loevestein was built between 1357 and 1368 by Dirk

Slot Loevestein

Loef van Horne. The Count of Holland, Albrecht van Beieren (of Bavaria), seized it in 1385 and surrounded it with an enclosure. In the 15C the castle was transformed into a prison by **Jacoba van Beieren** who had just seized Gorkum. In 1619 **Hugo de Groot** *(see DELFT)*, who had been taken prisoner the previous year, was imprisoned in Loevestein. There he devoted himself to the preparation of legal and theological works. His escape remains legendary. He managed to escape in March 1621 by hiding in a chest which had been used to bring him books. Inside the castle, it is possible to visit large rooms with lovely chimneypieces. In one of these rooms is the chest used by Hugo de Groot for his escape.

GOUDA*

Zuid-Holland

Population 71 576

Michelin maps 908 F 5 and 211 N 10

Gouda (pronounced how-dah) owes its fame to the stained glass in the church, its cheese, its syrup waffles, its pipes and its pottery. Situated at the confluence of the Hollandse IJssel and the Gouwe, this peaceful town is criss-crossed by several canals. In the Middle Ages, Gouda, then called Ter Gouwe, developed under the protection of its castle, which was destroyed in 1577. In the 15C, brewing and trading brought great prosperity to Gouda, while the 16C marked a decline. The town picked up again in the 17C due to the cheese trade and the manufacture of pipes introduced by English mercenaries.

Today there is also the production of candles, Gouda having the biggest factory in the country, and pottery.

Gouda is the home town of **Cornelis de Houtman** (c 1565-99), who was in charge of an expedition to the East (1595-7) and founded the first Dutch trading post in East India (Indonesia) on the island of Java.

Boat trips ⊙ – Tours are organised to the Reeuwijk Lakes.

*THE OLD TOWN CENTRE 3hr

Markt – In the centre of the main square stands the stadhuis with its picturesque tall silhouette. Several markets take place in this square, particularly the **cheese and craft markets** ⊙ (Goudse Kaas- en Ambachtenmarkt).

No 27, the Arti Legi, houses the tourist information centre.

* **Stadhuis** ⊙ – The lovely mid-15C Gothic town hall was restored in the 19C and 20C. It has a very decorative sandstone façade on the south side with a gable, flanked by turrets and adorned with a small balcony. The staircase in front is in the Renaissance style (1603). On the east side is a **carillon**, whose small figures

come to life every half hour; it depicts the scene of Count Floris V of Holland granting the city charter to Gouda in 1272. The interior of the Registrar's Office (Trouwzaal) is worth visiting; it is decorated with tapestries woven in Gouda in the 17C.

Waag – The Classical-style weigh-house was built in 1668 by **Pieter Post**. The façade is decorated with a low relief depicting the weighing of cheese which formerly took place here. It now houses the **Kaasexpo-seum** ⊘, a museum tracing the development of the cheese and dairy industry in the Netherlands as a whole, and Gouda in particular. Behind the Waag the lovely **Agnietenkapel** has been restored.

Stadhuis

Ch. Sappa/CEDRI

★ **St.-Janskerk** ⊘ – Founded in the 13C, the church of St John was destroyed by fire three times. Each time it was rebuilt and extended, and it is now the longest church in the Netherlands, measuring some 123m/135yd. Fronted by a small tower – the remains of the original church – it is surrounded by numerous pointed gables enhanced by large stained-glass windows. The interior of this Late Gothic cruciform basilica with wooden barrel vaulting is very light, and sober in the extreme.

★★★ **Stained glass** (Goudse Glazen) – The church is renowned for its magnificent collection of 70 stained-glass windows. Forty were spared by the Iconoclasts, the others were made after the Reformation. The largest, of which there are 27, were donated by the king, princes, prelates or rich bourgeois. The 13 most remarkable stained-glass windows, in both the eastern and the central parts of the church, are attributed to the **Crabeth brothers** (Dirck and Wouter) who made them between 1555 and 1571 when the church was Catholic. They illustrate biblical subjects. The works of the Crabeth brothers are numbered:

5: The Queen of Sheba pays a visit to Solomon

6: Judith beheading Holofernes

7: Dedication of Solomon's temple and the Last Supper (a present from Philip II, king of Spain, and Mary Tudor, queen of England)

8: Heliodorus, temple thief, chastened by the angels

12: Nativity

14: Sermon of St John the Baptist (Gouda's patron saint; his colours, white representing purity and love, and red symbolising suffering, appear in the town's coat of arms)

15: Baptism of Jesus (the oldest window, 1555)

16: First sermon of Jesus

18: Jesus's message to St John in prison

22: The purification of the temple (window donated by William the Silent and symbolising the Church's fight for purification)

23: Elijah's sacrifice and the Ablutions, donated by Margaret of Parma, governor of the Low Countries at the time of the revolt

30: Jonah cast up by the whale *(tall window above the ambulatory, to the left of the chancel)*.

More recent stained-glass windows which date from the Protestant period were added between 1594 and 1603 on the western side. Donated by the free towns of Holland, they depict armorial bearings, historical events, allegories and a few biblical scenes. They include:

25: the raising of the siege of Leiden (in 1547) in the middle of floods; portrait of William the Silent; silhouette of Delft *(Illustration; see Introduction, Historical table and notes)*

27: the Pharisee in the temple

28: the adulteress

28A *(right aisle)*: Stained-glass window by Charles Eyck placed in 1947 and evoking the Liberation of the Netherlands.

The seven stained-glass windows in the **chapel** *(door under window 14 in the chancel)* depict the Arrest of Jesus, Christ Mocked, the Scourging, the *Ecce Homo* at Pontius Pilate's House, the Bearing of the Cross, the Resurrection, Ascension and the feast of Pentecost; they come from a nearby convent.

The organ at the end of the church *(west side)* dates from 1736. The new organ in the chancel dates from 1974. Interesting tombstones are strewn over the floor of the building.

Walk round the church to the right, to the north entrance of the Museum Het Catharina Gasthuis.

GOUDA

★ **Museum Het Catharina Gasthuis** ⊙ – Installed in the former St Catherine's Hospital (Gasthuis), this municipal museum has a varied collection of paintings, period rooms and items illustrating the history of the hospital and the town. To the north of the museum, there is a gateway dating from 1609, the **Lazaruspoortje**, leading to the garden and the museum entrance. It has a polychrome low relief depicting Lazarus the leper at the table of a rich man, and comes from the former lepers' home. The old part of the hospital (1542), where the wards once were, is now used for temporary exhibitions. A 19C municipal pharmacy is on display in an adjoining room.

Behind the 17C-19C period rooms is the **Great Hall** (Ruim) devoted to the Gouda civic guard; the schutterstukken, group portraits of companies of the civil guard, include one by Ferdinand Bol. Next door are the boardrooms, the kitchen and pantry, and the chapel. The latter is devoted to **religious art**: 16C altarpieces, silver, and a chalice given to the town by Jacoba of Bavaria in the 15C.

A small cellar contains old torture instruments and a "lunatics' cell", the only surviving one of its kind in the Netherlands.

On the upper floor there are collections of toys, the reconstruction of the surgeons' Guild Room, and paintings by the Barbizon School and The Hague School (Anton Mauve, Isaac Israëls, Jacob Maris) as well as Jan Toorop.

Museum De Moriaan ⊙ – Under the sign of the Blackamoor *(moriaan)* evoking a tobacco shop, this Renaissance-style house built c 1625 has a lovely façade overlooking the picturesque Gouda canal. The tobacco shop of 1680 has been

Gouda cheese

Gouda is one of the most famous cheeses in the Netherlands (the other is Edam). Marketed in Gouda, it is either factory-made or from farms (its name then becomes *boerenkaas* meaning farm cheese).

Gouda is made with fresh or pasteurised (when it is factory-made) cow's milk. It is either young, medium or old. The indication *volvet 48+* means that its fat content is at least 48%.

Other specialities of the town are *siroopwafels* (syrup waffles).

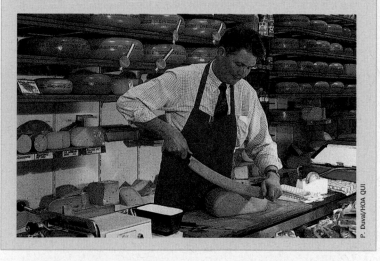

P. Duval/HOA QUI

reconstructed. Fine collections of clay pipes and decorated **Gouda pottery** (*Gouds plateel*) are displayed in elegant settings, bearing witness to the town's rich tradition as a centre of the pottery industry, which began producing the famous Gouda clay pipes in the 17C. In about 1900, it began making ornamental ceramics instead (*see Introduction, The arts*).

Jeruzalemstraat – At the corner of Patersteeg is the **Jeruzalemkapel**, a 15C chapel. Opposite, on the other corner is the former orphanage, **Weeshuis** of 1642, now a library, with a lovely façade with a voluted gable, and beside it, a doorway topped by a low relief depicting two orphans. On the opposite pavement at no 2 an old people's home, **Oude Mannenhuis**, opens by a door (1614), altered in the 18C.

At the far end of Spieringstraat is the **municipal park** with an 1832 windmill, **Walmolen 't Slot**, which was formerly used for milling grain. In the park there is a tree which was planted when Queen Wilhelmina came of age in 1898.

★THE REEUWIJKSE PLASSEN AND WOERDEN

30km/19mi to the north. Leave Gouda by Karnemelksloot. After the canal, take the 2nd road on the left in the direction of Platteweg.

★ **Reeuwijkse Plassen** – The intensive use of these vast stretches of water by water sports enthusiasts has done nothing to spoil the captivating landscape through which the road passes, winding between the lakes.

After Sluipwijk, go in the direction of Bodegraven then Woerden.

Woerden – Woerden was an important stronghold on the Oude Rijn and was for long considered "the key to Holland", as those who occupied Woerden had access to the rest of the country. In 1672 Louis XIV's armies, commanded by the Duke of Montmorency-Luxembourg, defeated William III's Dutch army.

The 15C **castle**, beside the town's southern gate, has served as a quartermaster's store since 1872. The old town hall is now occupied by the municipal museum, or **Stadsmuseum** ⊙. This delightful small building dating from 1501 is flanked by a turret and has a lovely façade with voluted gables above. The windows along the entire width of the first floor provide the outlook for the 17C council chamber. An old pillory takes up the right part of the façade. Woerden also has a stage mill (1755), De Windhond (The Greyhound).

185

FROM OUDEWATER TO SCHOONHOVEN

34km/21mi. Leave Gouda by Nieuwe Veerstal and follow the very narrow dike road; passing is difficult.

This road, which follows the Hollandse IJssel, offers picturesque **views**★ of the river with its marshy banks and its farmhouses.

Oudewater – Oudewater is one of the Netherlands' oldest small towns and was the birthplace of **Jacob Arminius** (c 1560-1609) *(see DORDRECHT)*, and the Primitive painter **Gerard David** (c 1460-1523), who moved to Bruges in 1483. Oudewater is famous for its witches' scales or **heksenwaag** ⊘ (1482), which can be seen in the Waag, or weigh-house; the small Witches Museum in the attic retraces the history of witchcraft with engravings, documents and a video film. This fine Renaissance building with crow-stepped gables is near Markt, which spans a canal. In the 16C women accused of witchcraft came from afar to be weighed at Oudewater in the presence of the burgomaster of the town. If the woman was not underweight for her size she was too heavy to ride a broomstick, so she was not a witch. She was then given a certificate of acquittal. All the people weighed in Oudewater were acquitted. The last certificate was issued in 1729. Next to the weigh-house, at no 14, note the Renaissance façade (1601) of Arminius's birthplace. Other attractive façades are to be admired in the surrounding streets of Oudewater (Wijdstraat). At no 3 Donkere Gaard, near Markt, there is a fine house.

Near Markt, the Renaissance **stadhuis** (town hall, 1588) has a side façade preceded by a flight of steps and topped with a crow-stepped gable.

Take the Gouda road to Haasrecht, then follow the valley of the Vlist towards Schoonhoven.

It is a picturesque **route**★. The road, shaded by willows, runs alongside the river banks with their abundant vegetation. Beautiful farmhouses with reed-covered roofs and conical haystacks topped with a small roof line the road.

Vlist – Lovely wooden windmill.

On leaving Vlist, cross the river.

Bracket clock (c 1715) by A Witsen;
Nederlands Goud-, Zilver- en
Klokkenmuseum, Schoonhoven

Collectie Nederlands Goud-, Zilver- en Klokkenmuseum

Schoonhoven – This charming small town at the confluence of the Vlist and the Lek is known for its traditional gold and silverware; a few smiths continue the craft today. The town is traversed by an attractive canal and linked to Lek's south bank by a ferry. Close to the ferry terminal stands the town's south gate, **Veerpoort**, which was built in 1601.

At the near end of the picturesque canal is the **Edelambachtshuys** ⊘, housing a large collection of antique silver, and an old workshop. A little further along, the **Stadhuis**, dating from 1452, overlooks the canal. Although it has been modernised it retains a tall roof topped by a pinnacle (carillon). On the left is the **Grote Kerk** with its characteristic leaning tower. On the Dam, in the centre of the canal, is the **Waag** or weigh-house, a building of 1617 in its original state, with a hipped roof. Nearby is the **Nederlands Goud-, Zilver- en Klokkenmuseum** ⊘, or Netherlands Gold, Silver and Clock Museum. This has a fine **collection**★ of wall clocks from Friesland and the Zaan, French dial cases, 18C timepieces, a large number of watches, a collection of silverware, an assay office for gold and silver testing, and a silversmith's workshop. Since 1996 the picturesque, 50m-high neo-Gothic **water tower** (1901) has been the centre of the Zilver in Beweging initiative. Some lovely houses can be seen in the town, notably no 37 Lopikerstraat; the 1642 façade is decorated with a double crow-stepped gable and red shutters.

The most important sights in this guide can be found on the Principal Sights map, and are described in the text. Use the map and plans, the Calendar of events, the index, and read the Introduction to get the most out of this guide.

GRONINGEN

Groningen Ⓟ
Population 171 193
Michelin maps 908 K 2 and 210 Y 3
Plan of the conurbation in the current edition of The Red Guide Benelux

Groningen is the dynamic provincial capital and the main town in the north of the Netherlands. The town is located at the northern extremity of the Hondsrug with polderlands to the north and peat bogs to the south-west.
The town's university and various other colleges mean that it has a young population and is dominated by students, who fill the many outdoor cafés in summer. Groningen also has a remarkably large number of cyclists; over half the population travels to school and work by bike.

HISTORICAL NOTES

A settlement already existed by the year AD 1000. By the beginning of the 13C Groningen belonged to the Hanseatic League. A convention concluded in 1251 with the neighbouring cantons made Groningen the only grain market in the region, bringing it six centuries of prosperity.
Under the Bishop of Utrecht's authority the town passed into the hands of the Duke of Geldern in 1515. Then, having tried to escape from the Habsburg authority, it finally gave in to Charles V in 1536. It joined the Union of Utrecht in 1579 and was taken by the Spanish in 1580 and then by Maurice of Nassau in 1594. An era of prosperity followed with the construction of a new town rampart.
The university was founded in 1614; it very quickly acquired a great reputation and students came from all over Europe. Descartes chose it in 1645 to arbitrate in his conflicts with Dutch theologians. Today it still plays an important part in the life of the town.
In 1672 the town resisted against the troops of the Bishop of Münster, ally of Louis XIV. The fortifications were strengthened in 1698 by Coehoorn and razed to the ground in 1874 to allow for the extension of the city. A few remains in **Noorderplantsoen** have been transformed into a garden.
The town of Groningen is the homeland of the painters **Jozef Israëls** (1827-1911), head of The Hague School, and **Hendrik Willem Mesdag** (1831-1915), who was one of its members.

A dynamic town – Groningen is an important communications junction and also has two harbours. It is linked to the sea by means of important canals. Groningen is a large industrial centre (high-technology, tobacco, asphalt and steel). The town is Western Europe's number one sugar-beet centre.

Groningen has an important congress and exhibition centre, the **Martinihal**, near the racecourse in the new districts which are developing to the south. Other important examples of modern architecture include the Groninger Museum, the Waagstraat complex and the head office of Nederlandse Gasunie.

AROUND GROTE MARKT 1hr 30min

Grote Markt – Prolonged by Vismarkt, the fish market, this vast and busy square, lined by the town's main buildings, forms the city centre. Grote Markt gives onto the different pedestrian precincts; the main shopping street is Herestraat. Various markets take place here (see Travellers' addresses).

> ### Groningen gas
>
> Groningen has been the oil capital of the Netherlands and nerve centre of its power supply ever since oil was found in the Drenthe near Schoonebeek (see EMMEN, Excursions) in 1945. In 1960 large deposits of natural gas were also discovered in the province of Groningen. The reserves are estimated at c 1 800 billion m^3, which makes it one of the largest deposits in the world. The region features 29 extraction centres which all have several winding shafts. One of these centres is located in **Slochteren**, east of Groningen. Nearly half the country's production of natural gas is channelled through pipelines towards Belgium, France, Germany and Italy.

Stadhuis – The neo-Classical town hall (1810) is linked by a glassed-in footbridge to a modern annexe.

★ **Goudkantoor** – This gracious Renaissance Gold Office, built in 1635, has elegant façades with finely worked gables; the windows are topped by shell motifs. Originally the provincial tax collector's office, it is now a café and restaurant (see Travellers' addresses).

WHERE TO STAY

Groningen is best known for the futuristic Groninger Museum, but it also has a number of attractive hotels in historic buildings.

MID-RANGE

Auberge Corps de Garde – *Oude Boteringestraat 74, 9712 GN,* ☎ *(050) 314 54 37, Fax (050) 313 63 20, www.corpsdegarde.nl. 24 rooms.* A 17C guardhouse and an adjoining building on the Boteringebrug are now a cosy hotel, with large, comfortable rooms and antique furniture.

Schimmelpennick Huys - *Oosterstraat 53, 9711 NR,* ☎ *(050) 318 95 02, Fax (050) 318 31 64, www.schimmelpennickhuys.nl. 38 rooms.* A pleasant hotel in an old mansion close to Grote Markt, with a choice of suites or rooms overlooking the courtyards. There are rooms of various sizes with modern decor; the main emphasis, as in the rest of the hotel, is on white. Breakfast is served in the Baroque Room, the conservatory or the garden.

Hotel De Ville – *Oude Boteringestraat 43, 9712 GD,* ☎ *(050) 318 12 22, Fax (050) 318 17 77. www.deville.nl. 45 rooms.* Behind the simple exterior of these restored mansions is a chic but charming hotel. Quietly located in the old town centre, it has a classically styled interior and spacious modern rooms. The bar in the conservatory looks out onto an attractive courtyard garden.

WHERE TO EAT

De Pauw - *Gelkingestraat 52,* ☎ *(050) 318 13 32.* This centrally located restaurant has an unusual formula: the main course consists of a trolley buffet placed beside your table, with starters and desserts to order.

Martinitoren

Restaurant Grand Café Schimmelpennick Huys - *Oosterstraat 53,* ☎ *(050) 311 18 72.* Enjoy a cup of coffee, a light meal or a full dinner, and rub shoulders with the great and good of Groningen. You can eat in the conservatory, the Jugendstil or Empire Rooms, or the pleasantly green courtyard. *See also Hotel Schimmelpennick Huys above.*

Bistro 't Gerecht – *Oude Boteringestraat 45,* ☎ *(050) 589 18 59.* French-inspired bistro next to (and part of) the Hotel De Ville. Long benches, wooden panelling and mirrored walls; traditional, mainly French, cuisine.

Muller - *Grote Kromme Elleboog 13,* ☎ *(050) 318 32 08.* This restaurant in one of Groningen's busiest areas for nightlife serves excellent food to a smart clientele.

Ni Hao – *Hereweg 1,* ☎ *(050) 318 14 00.* Chinese restaurant near the station.

BRASSERIES, CAFÉS, BARS, COFFEE SHOPS...

De Apedans – *Verlengde Oosterstraat 1.* This trendy bodega restaurant has a tastefully designed interior and serves simple food.

Het Goudkantoor – *Waagplein 1.* An elegant building housing one of the town's busiest café-restaurants; a must if you're in the Waag area.

Newscafé – *Waagplein 5.* Besides a cocktail bar and reading table, this café also has computers for anyone wanting to do some Internet-surfing. International dishes are served on the first floor.

't Feithhuis – *Martinikerkhof 10.* This trendy town-centre café provides day-long sustenance: breakfast, lunch, salads, afternoon tea and dinner.

PRACTICAL INFORMATION

General information – The tourist office, **VVV Groningen** (Grote Markt, ☎ (0900) 202 30 50 or www.vvvgroningen.nl), can help with information on sights, tours and accommodation. It also offers special accommodation packages and can book hotels and tickets for plays, concerts and other events.

Transport – If yours is a short visit, there are many clearly **signposted car parks** in the centre of Groningen. If you are staying for longer, park at one of the **Park and Ride sites** on the outskirts of town and take the Citybus to the centre, which is largely car-free and not accessible to through traffic. **Public transport timetables** and tickets are available from the VVV. Groningen is an ideal cycling town, with an extensive network of cycle paths. You can hire a **bicycle** in the Central Station or under the library.

Walks and tours – The VVV sells street maps and suggested **walking routes**, and **guided walks** depart from here on Monday afternoons in summer.

Boat trips – **Canal tours** leave from opposite Groningen's Central Station from May to September. Information: Rondvaartbedrijf Kool ☎ (050) 312 83 79 or from the VVV.

Shopping – Groningen's main shopping street is **Herestraat**, but there are other good areas for shopping. These include the historic **Korenbeurs** or corn exchange, at A-Kerkhof 1, and the modern **Waagstraat complex** on Grote Markt.

Markets – On Good Friday, Vismarkt becomes a blaze of colour as the annual **flower market** takes over. There are also **weekly markets**: one on Tuesdays, Fridays and Saturdays selling **general** items on Grote Markt and Vismarkt; an **organic food market** and small **flea-market** on Vismarkt on Wednesdays, and a **non-food market** on Grote Markt on Thursdays. Various Sunday markets are also held.

Theatre and concerts – The VVV publishes a newspaper (Uitgaanskrant Groningen) giving details of all the events, concerts and exhibitions taking place in Groningen; it also sells tickets. The main theatres are the **Stadsschouwburg** (municipal theatre) at Turfsingel 86, ☎ (050) 312 56 45, and **De Oosterpoort**, Trompsingel 27, ☎ (050) 313 10 44.

Nightlife – Groningen's thriving nightlife centres on the areas around Grote Markt and the Waag, Gedempte Zuiderdiep and Kromme Ellebogen. Most of the discos are in Poelestraat and Peperstraat. Unlike many other towns and cities there are no fixed closing times, and most cafés are open until 3am. Other attractions include **Holland Casino**, Gedempte Kattendiep 150 (☎ (050) 312 34 00), and cinemas; the VVV publishes a weekly film listing every Thursday.

Events – The **Groningen Liberation Festival** takes place on 5 May each year, and consists of music and theatre events. In June, **Swingin' Groningen** sees live jazz and other music on stages in and around Grote Markt. The high point of the summer is **Noorderzon** (Northern Sun), a very lively theatre and music festival in August offering something for young and old alike. The **raising of the siege of Groningen** is celebrated on 28 August, and for a weekend in September Groningen is transformed into an African, American or Asian city in the **Landenfestival**, or Countries Festival.

Martinikerk ☉ – This church, the second on this site, was rebuilt in the 15C. It is known for its **tower**★ ☉, which is the pride of Groningen. 96m/315ft high with six storeys, this bell-tower is topped by a weathervane in the shape of a horse depicting St Martin's mount. It has a carillon cast by the Hemony brothers and affords a fine **view** over the canals, the square, the roofs of Martinikerk, and the Prinsenhof and its gardens. Inside the church, the chancel is decorated with 16C frescoes depicting scenes in the life of Christ.

ADDITIONAL SIGHTS

★ **Groninger Museum** ☉ – *Illustration: see Introduction, The arts.* The highly original, **polymorphous building**★★ (1992-94) housing the Groninger Museum lies opposite the station, on a small island in the Verbindingskanaal. Because the museum's collections were very diverse, different architects and designers were asked to work together on the design. Each of the three main buildings has its own distinctive character, and uses different materials, colours and forms. The museum is entered through a golden tower designed by Alessandro Mendini (b 1931), which is used as a store. The lower part of the west pavilion is clad in red brick, and is the work of Michele De Lucchi (b 1951); this houses the archaeological and historical collections, which are shown in rotation. The round room above it was designed by Philippe Starck (b 1949); in the display case that follows the sloping wall and in the maze of curtains, there is a particularly fine **Oriental porcelain collection**★, including pieces from the wreck of the East India Company vessel *De Geldermalsen*. Mendini designed the first of the two pavilions one above the other on the east side, in which temporary exhibitions of contemporary art are held. The upper one, a superb example of Deconstructivism, was designed by Coop Himmelb(l)au. It houses the collection of visual art from 1500-1950, which includes works by the local artists' group "De Ploeg", or temporary exhibitions.

★ **Noordelijk Scheepvaartmuseum en Niemeyer Tabaksmuseum** ⊙ – These museums are located in two beautifully restored medieval merchants' houses: the Gotisch Huis *(on the left)* and the Canterhuis *(on the right)*.

The **Noordelijk Scheepvaartmuseum**★ is devoted to inland water transport and coastal shipping in the northern part of the Netherlands since the 6C. The scale models of ships, navigational instruments, charts, paintings and ceramics are particularly well displayed and retrace the brilliant period of the Hanseatic League, the Dutch East and West India Companies, the activities relative to peat extraction and its transportation by boat, the coastal shipping of bricks, and schooners which replaced the traditional galliots.

The **Niemeyer Tabaksmuseum** (tobacco museum) is located at the rear of the Gotisch Huis. A fine collection of pipes, snuffboxes and jars illustrate the use of tobacco over the centuries. A 19C tobacco merchant's shop has been reconstructed.

Groninger Museum

GRONINGEN

Gevelsteen met hert	**Y**	**A**
Goudkantoor	**Z**	**B**
Groninger Museum	**Z**	**M¹**
Huis Cardinaal	**Y**	**C**
Kortegaard	**Y**	**D**
Noordelijk Scheepvaartmuseum en Niemeyer Tabaksmuseum	**Z**	**M²**
Patriciërshuis	**Y**	**N**
Prinsenhof	**Y**	**R**
Provinciehuis	**Z**	**P**
Stadhuis	**Z**	**H**
Zonnewijzer	**Y**	**S**
17de-eeuwse huizen	**Y**	**V**

Martinikerkhof – This lovely square, laid out on the site of a 19C cemetery (*kerkhof*), is surrounded by houses which have been attractively restored.
To the north-east is the **Provinciehuis**, rebuilt in 1916 in neo-Renaissance style and flanked by an onion-shaped turret. On its left, Cardinaal house has a small Renaissance façade (1559), whose gable is decorated with three heads: Alexander the Great, King David and Charlemagne. This façade has been reconstructed from that of a house which no longer exists. To the north of the square, the Prinsenhof, originally built for the Brethren of the Common Life (*see* DEVENTER), became the Bishop of Groningen's residence in 1568. Preceded by a courtyard and a 17C portal, it is built onto the Gardepoort, a small gateway (1639).

Behind the **Prinsenhof** there is a small 18C garden, the **Prinsenhoftuin**, with hedges, roses and herbs. It opens on to the Turfsingel, a canal where peat (*turf*) was transported, via a gateway called the Zonnewijzerpoort which has an 18C **sundial** on the garden side.

Ossenmarkt – At no 5 there is a fine 18C **patrician house**; it is a good example of the local architectural style, having a wide façade with rows of rather narrow windows.
Not far away, at the corner of Spilsluizen and Nieuwe Ebbingestraat, stand two 17C houses. The one on the left is also characteristic of the Groningen style.
On the other side of the canal a sculptured stone depicting a stag juts out from the wall of a house.
At the corner of Spilsluizen and Oude Boteringestraat is the former guard room, **Kortegaard**, with a covered gallery (1634) where cannons once stood (*see Travellers' addresses*).

EXCURSIONS

Hortus Haren ⊙ – *6km/3mi south. Leave Groningen via Hereweg; Hortus Haren is to the south of Haren.* Hortus means "botanical garden", and this 21ha/52 acre area contains various **themed gardens** such as sculpture and rose gardens, with others focusing on particular countries and regions such as Great Britain, France, or Bengal. Exotic trees and plants grow in the greenhouses, while the denizens of the vivarium include grisly bird-eating spiders. Beside the Hortus is **Het Verborgen Rijk van Ming**, or The Hidden Empire of Ming. This recalls the time of the Ming Dynasty (1368-1644), and includes rocks, bridges, pagodas, hundreds of red carp and many flowering plants, all brought to the Netherlands from China. There are also demonstrations of calligraphy, tai chi and silk painting, and tea ceremonies are held in a traditional teahouse.

North-west Groningen

27km/17mi north-west by motorway.

Aduard – Of the old Cistercian abbey founded in 1192 only the infirmary remains. Later it became a Dutch reformed church, or **Nederlandse Hervormde Kerk** ⊙, and was incorrectly referred to as the abbey church (Abdijkerk). Although the façade is sober, the interior has interesting decorative details: Gothic bays alternating with blind arches depicting geometric motifs, bays on the ground floor surrounded by ceramic cable moulding. The 18C furnishings are elegant: pulpit decorated with coats of arms, pews with carved backs, the lords' pews topped by a canopy with heraldic motifs, copper lecterns.

Leens – **Petruskerk**, a church built in the 12C and 13C, houses a lovely Baroque **organ**★ built by Hinsz in 1733.

Lauwersoog – *Local map see WADDENEILANDEN.* Departure point for ferries to Schiermonnikoog. Lauwersoog is situated near the **Lauwersmeer**, a former arm of the sea, which like the Zuiderzee, has been closed off by a dike completed in 1969 and around which polders are being reclaimed.
The scale models, photographs and illuminated maps in the **Expozee exhibition** ⊙ give an interesting presentation on the Lauwersmeer polders and the protection of the Waddenzee. There is also a tank containing animals from the Waddenzee.

* Rural churches

Round tour of 118km/73mi to the north-east. Leave Groningen by Damsterdiep.

Every village in the province of Groningen has its brick church which dates from the 12C and 13C and is usually in the transitional Romanesque-Gothic style. Architecturally they are quite simple but they are often adorned with attractive decorative brickwork both inside and outside. Sometimes they are built on a terp, and the saddleback roof of the bell-tower often emerges from behind a screen of tall trees. Characteristic features of the interiors are the frescoes, lovely carved furnishings and hatchments. The farmhouses of the region are also quite imposing *(see Introduction: Farmhouses).*

Garmerwolde – The nave of this 13C **village church** was demolished in the 19C, so it has a free-standing **bell-tower**★. The flat east end has bays outlined by recessed arches and a gable with blind arcading. The interior still has some 16C frescoes on the vaults and an 18C carved pulpit.

Ten Boer – On a terp, a 13C **church**, topped by a pinnacle, has some lovely decoration, especially on the north side: bays outlined by recessed arches, medallions, multifoil blind arcading and gables both with reticulate brickwork.

Stedum – Built on a terp surrounded by moats, this typical **church** with its tall saddleback-roofed bell-tower is picturesque. A frieze runs above the modillions sculptured with characters or heads of animals.

Loppersum – This large Gothic **church** has two transepts with blind arcading on the gables. The interior is interesting for its **frescoes**★, which decorate the chancel vaults and the Lady Chapel. In the chapel south of the chancel there are numerous memorial slabs.

Zeerijp – Next to its free-standing bell-tower, the **church** dating from the 14C has a gable in two parts with blind arcading and a brick mosaic. The interior is remarkable for its **domes**★ with brick decoration which varies in each bay. Blind arcading decorates the end of the nave. The organ, the Renaissance pulpit, and hatchments are also worth seeing.

Leermens – This 13C **church** has a flat east end decorated with blind arcading and a background decorated with brick motifs.
On arriving at Oosterwijtwerd, there is a large farmhouse with four roofs.

Krewerd – This **church**, built on a terp, has vaults decorated with brick motifs. The organ dates from 1531.

Appingedam – This town is renowned for its twice-yearly agricultural market (April and October).
From the footbridge (Vrouwenbrug) over the canal there is a fine **view**★ of the overhanging kitchens and the town hall's pinnacle. Appingedam's marina is nicely situated in the town centre.
The **old raadhuis**, flanked by a 19C bell-tower, dates from 1630. The façade is decorated with shell motifs, a facing brick with a pelican, a statue of Justice and a voluted pediment. The 13C **Nikolaikerk** has some lovely frescoes.

Menkemaborg

Delfzijl – Delfzijl is an industrial city and a busy shipping port on Dollard Gulf; it is linked to Groningen by Eemskanaal. The town's main activities are petrochemicals and the manufacture of soda. To the south of the town, at **Farmsun**, an aluminium smelting works, supplied with alumina from Surinam, was the first of its kind in the Netherlands, when it was built in 1956. Delfzijl also has a large pleasure boat harbour; **boat trips** ⊘ are organised.

From the dike on Dollard, there is a **view** over the harbour and the town, overlooked by a tall wall mill, called **Molen Adam** (1875). On a square near the station, a monument topped by a swan, **Het Zwaantje**, commemorates the Resistance. A small **statue of Maigret** on the lawns of the Damsterdiep *(600m/0.3mi from the pumping station to the west of Eemskanaal, opposite the RWR warehouses)* is a reminder that **Georges Simenon** (1903-89) was a visitor in 1929. It is believed that he created his most famous character, police inspector Maigret, while in Delfzijl.

Bierum – On a terp there is a small 13C **church**, whose bell-tower was reinforced by a flying buttress. The semicircular east end of the chancel dates from the 14C. The interior is roofed with geometrically decorated ribbed domes on which a few traces of frescoes remain. The organ dates from 1792-93, the baptismal font from the early Middle Ages. Around the church the cemetery has remarkable 19C sculptured memorial slabs depicting symbols of life (trees) and time (hour glasses).

Eemshaven – This port was built on reclaimed polderland of Emmapolder and Oostpolder. The port started trading in 1973 and has given rise to an important industrial zone. To the east the imposing **Eemscentrale** power station has been powered by natural gas since 1976.

Uithuizermeeden – The **church** with a 13C nave and a transept (1705) has a white tower rebuilt in 1896-97. The pulpit was sculptured in the 18C.

Uithuizen – The small **Hervormde Kerk** contains a remarkable organ built in 1700 by Arp Schnitger and a noble's pew from the same period.

To the east of Uithuizen, **Menkemaborg Castle★★** ⊘ is surrounded by a moat and a typically Dutch garden laid out in Renaissance and Baroque tradition; the grounds also feature a maze, an orchard and a vegetable garden. The oldest part (14C) of the building, with only a few small windows, was extended by the addition of two wings in the 17C and 18C. The interior is pleasantly furnished and decorated and gives some idea of how the local nobility lived during the 17C and 18C. Note the 1777 orchestrion, portraits of past owners, a four-poster bed by Daniël Marot and lovely pieces of 17C Chinese porcelain.

Opposite the castle, the **1939-1945 Museum** ⊘ contains vehicles, weapons and documents from the Second World War.

Oldenzijl – The small Romanesque **church** and its churchyard stand on a terp encircled by a moat and a screen of trees. Inside the plainness of the brick walls is broken by several small round windows trimmed with mouldings and the decorative effect of the blind arcading in the chancel.

Return to Groningen by Garsthuizen, the N 46, Ten Boer and the N 360.

Oldenzijl – Romanesque church

Den HAAG**

THE HAGUE or 's-GRAVENHAGE – Zuid-Holland Ⓟ
Population 440 743
Michelin maps 908 D 5 and 211 K 10 and folds 1 and 2 (inset)
Plan of the conurbation in the current edition of The Red Guide Benelux

Although The Hague, whose official name is 's-Gravenhage (generally shortened to Den Haag), is home to the Dutch government and Parliament, as well as many foreign embassies, it is only the provincial capital. Dutch monarchs have been enthroned in Amsterdam since 1813. This coastal town is a pleasant and quiet residential community, with a multitude of squares, parks (more than 700 public gardens) and several canals.

The Hague sprawls over a large area and has a relatively small population, earning itself the title of "the biggest village in Europe". It is marked by a certain aristocratic charm and is considered to be the most worldly and elegant town in the Netherlands; in fact, some of its 19C colonial atmosphere still remains.

However, the city also has some important modern architecture, such as Rem Koolhaas's Lucent Danstheater and H Hertzberger's transport and planning ministry building. The "De Resident" development between the Binnenhof and the station has involved a large number of international architects, including Richard Meier, who designed the new city hall.

HISTORICAL NOTES

A meet – Up to the 13C, The Hague was just a hunting lodge built by Count Floris IV of Holland in the middle of a forest which stretched northwards to Haarlem. About 1250 his son William II built a castle on the site of the present Binnenhof. Floris V completed the work of his father by adding the Ridderzaal.

At the end of the 14C, abandoning Haarlem, the Count of Holland Albert of Bavaria and his retinue came to live in The Hague.

A village... – 's-Gravenhage, the Count's Hedge or Die Haghe, the hedge, rapidly developed without being more than a place of residence and rest. The cloth trade, which started in the 15C, was not enough to make it a mercantile town.

Benedictus de Spinoza

The great philosopher Spinoza spent the last seven years of his life in The Hague; he died here in 1677. Born in Amsterdam in 1632, this Jew of Portuguese origin was a brilliant scholar. In 1656 Spinoza was excommunicated and banished from Amsterdam by the synagogue authorities for questioning the orthodox Jewish doctrines and interpretations of scripture. He took refuge for a time in Ouderkerk aan de Amstel, then went to live in Rijnsburg near Leiden in 1660. For three years he devoted himself to philosophy and polishing lenses to earn a living. After a few years spent in Voorburg, a suburb of The Hague, in 1670 he moved into a modest residence in Paviljoensgracht.

ROGER-VIOLLET

It was only after his death that his *Posthumous Works* published in 1677 appeared in Latin; it included the **Ethics**, which became universally famous.

Den HAAG

The confederation of cities which constituted the Low Countries at the time refused to admit The Hague to their governing council. However, it was in The Hague in 1432 and 1456 that Philip the Good held the chapters of the Order of the Golden Fleece. The absence of fortifications brought destruction upon the city, as in 1528 when it was attacked by Maarten van Rossum, famous captain of a Gelderland troop of mercenaries. In 1581, the act declaring Philip II of Spain's disavowal by the States General of the United Provinces was posted on the door of the Ridderzaal.

...which develops – In the 17C The Hague found peace and prosperity again. Seat of the States General of the United Provinces, then the government, it became an important centre of diplomatic negotiations. From the middle of the 17C to the end of the 18C substantial mansions in Renaissance and Baroque styles were built round the medieval centre of the Binnenhof.
The French entered The Hague in 1795. Eleven years later the town had to cede its rank of capital to Amsterdam where Louis Bonaparte had installed his government.
In 1814 the government and the Court returned to The Hague. But the title of capital remained with Amsterdam, where the king was enthroned in 1815.
The 19C confirmed the residential character of the town, which had become the favourite residence of colonials returning from Indonesia. This period marked it so profoundly that it is sometimes referred to as "the widow of the Indies". Even today, The Hague has a sizeable Indonesian community.

The Hague School – Between 1870 and 1890 a group of painters in The Hague tried to renew painting, and notably the art of landscapes, in the manner of the Barbizon School in France.
A group of artists gathered around the leader, **Jozef Israëls**, a painter of fishing scenes and portraits: **JH Weissenbruch** (1824-1903); **Jacob Maris** (1837-99), painter of dunes and beaches; **HW Mesdag**, painter of numerous seascapes and the famous *Mesdag Panorama (see below)*; **Anton Mauve** (1838-88), painter of the Gooi heathland; **Albert Neuhuys** (1844-1914), painter of household interiors; **Johannes Bosboom** (1817-91), painter of church interiors; and **Blommers** (1845-1914), painter of the life of fishermen. Neuhuys and Mauve, having worked in Laren, are sometimes attached to the Laren School. The Hague painters did not set out to achieve brilliant colours nor great draftmanship. Greys and browns were the dominant colours and their works nearly always expressed a certain melancholy.

Morning ride along the beach (1876), Anton Mauve;
Rijksmuseum, Amsterdam

The diplomatic town – The Hague was chosen several times as a centre for international negotiations, including the peace conferences of 1899 and 1907. Finally the construction of the Peace Palace (1913) established its vocation as a diplomatic town. It is the seat of the International Court of Justice, an organisation dependent on the UN, the Permanent Court of Arbitration and the Academy of International Law.

WHERE TO STAY

As The Hague is the country's diplomatic, administrative and commercial centre, hotels are mostly modern business-oriented ones. However, it does have two unusually good 19C hotels (see Luxury).

YOUTH HOSTEL

NJHC City Hostel Den Haag – Scheepmakerstraat 27, 2515 VA Den Haag, ☎ (070) 315 78 78, Fax (070) 315 78 77. 220 beds. Close to the station, and has its own brasserie.

MODERATE

Petit – Groot Hertoginnelaan 42, 2517 EH Den Haag, ☎ (070) 346 55 00, Fax (070) 346 32 57. 20 rooms. This hotel is located in an elegant mansion near the Haags Gemeentemuseum. It has comfortable rooms and its own car park.

Sebel – Zoutmanstraat 40, 2518 GR Den Haag, ☎ (070) 345 92 00, fax (070) 345 58 55. 27 rooms. Simple family hotel in a row of terrace houses within walking distance from the city centre. Car-parking spaces available.

MID-RANGE

Corona – Buitenhof 42, 2513 AH Den Haag, ☎ (070) 363 79 30, Fax (070) 361 57 85. 26 rooms. Right in the heart of the city, close to the Binnenhof, and thus the ideal base for a visit to The Hague. The comfortable rooms are decorated in Louis XVI style or Art Deco.

Parkhotel – Molenstraat 53, 2513 BJ Den Haag, ☎ (070) 362 43 71, fax (070) 361 45 25. 114 rooms. This modern business hotel borders the gardens of Paleis Noordeinde. The rooms are functional yet comfortable, some looking out over the park and others overlooking the beautiful inner courtyard. The hotel has a fine staircase in the style of the Amsterdam School.

LUXURY

Des Indes – Lange Voorhout 54, 2514 EG Den Haag, ☎ (070) 361 23 45, fax (070) 361 23 50. www.interconti.com. 76 rooms. This stately hotel, formerly the residence of a wealthy baron, is a journey back in time to the 19C. It has red carpets, high ceilings, grand staircases, marble and stucco, obviously in combination with every modern facility. For a taste of bygone days, there's none better, but be warned: it doesn't come cheap.

Kurhaus – Gevers Deynootplein 30, 2586 CK Scheveningen, ☎ (070) 416 26 36, Fax (070) 416 26 46. www.kurhaus.nl. 255 rooms. This imposing 19C Scheveningen beach hotel offers a choice of royal suites or luxury rooms. The hotel is full of character, with the huge domed Kurzaal (see below), the outside terrace overlooking the sea and of course the thermal baths which gave this stylish hotel its name.

WHERE TO EAT

THE HAGUE

It Rains Fishes – Noordeinde 123, ☎ (070) 365 25 98. Trendy fish restaurant offering "fusion cuisine": western produce prepared in eastern style, with sometimes surprising but always delicious results.

Saur – Lange Voorhout 47, ☎ (070) 346 25 65. A French restaurant in a beautiful location opposite the Paleis. Food is served at the bar downstairs.

The Raffles – Javastraat 63, ☎ (070) 345 85 87. Indonesian cuisine.

Shirasagi – Spui 170, ☎ (070) 346 47 00. Japanese restaurant with food prepared at the table (teppan-yaki).

Brasserie Buitenhof – Buitenhof 39, ☎ (070) 363 79 30. Atmospheric brasserie restaurant of the Corona hotel (see above). A good place for a genteel cup of coffee; covered terrace.

SCHEVENINGEN

Westbroekpark – Kapelweg 35, ☎ (070) 354 60 72. Once you've had enough of the sea, sample the delicious cuisine of this restaurant in the park, overlooking the famous rose garden.

Seinpost – Zeekant 60, ☎ (070) 355 52 50. A circular restaurant offering excellent fish dishes and a wonderful view of the North Sea.

Kurzaal – Gevers Deynootplein 30, ☎ (070) 416 26 36. Lunch or dine in style at this buffet restaurant in the imposing old concert hall of the Kurhaus.

BRASSERIES, CAFÉS, BARS, COFFEE SHOPS...

't Goude Hooft – *Dag. Groenmarkt 13, Den Haag*. International cuisine in one of The Hague's best-known brasseries, with its own sun terrace.

Zeldenrust – *Bankastraat 32, Den Haag*. Brasserie with a café and terrace located between Madurodam and Panorama Mesdag. Tasty sandwiches and salads and a pleasant atmosphere.

Deining Brasserie de la mer – *Stevinstraat 80 (at the corner of Badhuisweg), Scheveningen*. Quiet brasserie away from the buzz of the boulevard; particularly ideal if you get peckish late at night, as the kitchen is open till midnight. Meals are served in the garden on warm summer's nights.

Museumcafé Het Paleis – *Lange Voorhout 74, Den Haag*. This café in the basement of the Museum Het Paleis has the original Art Deco interior of the Krul coffee house in The Hague, and is a good place for a drink before or after a visit to the museum.

Slagerij P.G. Dungelman – *Hoogstraat 34, Den Haag*. Not a bar or café, but a butcher's serving wonderful hot croquettes!

PRACTICAL INFORMATION

General information – The **VVV tourist offices** in **The Hague** (*Koningin Julianaplein 30, Winkelcentrum Babylon, 2595 AA Den Haag*) and **Scheveningen** (*Gevers Deynootweg 1134, Palace Promenade shopping centre, 2586 BX Scheveningen*) both have the same telephone number, ☎ (0900) 340 35 05. Also at www.denhaag.com. They can provide information on sights, events, cultural activities and accommodation packages, and publish an annual information guide including a list of bars, restaurants, hotels, youth hostels, apartments and campsites. Hotel rooms can be booked by the reservations department of the **Stichting Promotie Den Haag**, ☎ (070) 363 56 76.

Emergencies – The Hague's **Tourist Assistance Service (TAS)** offers help to foreign tourists who are victims of crime or road or other accidents. It is open daily from 9am to 9pm, ☎ (070) 310 32 74.

Transport – Parking in the centre of The Hague or Scheveningen is difficult and expensive. Most **parking is metered**, and if you don't put enough into the meter or park illegally you are likely to be clamped. If this happens, go to the payment office in the multi-storey car park behind the Central Station. Alternatively, use one of the many well-signposted **car parks**.
The main sights in the city centre are within walking distance of one another, but you can also take a **bus** or **tram**. You can buy individual tickets from the driver, but it is cheaper to buy a **strippenkaart** or strip of tickets beforehand. These are available from VVV offices, post offices, nearly all tobacconists and newsagents, and in many hotels. If you will be in The Hague for several days, a **meerdagenkaart** (multi-day travelcard) is a good idea.

Tours and walks – In summer, the VVV organises two **guided bus tours** of the town: a royal tour of the palaces of The Hague and Scheveningen, and an architectural tour of the city's buildings, both ancient and modern. For bookings, ☎ (0900) 340 35 05. The VVV also sells booklets giving details of **self-guided walking tours** on various themes.

Boat trips – Depart daily from **Scheveningen harbour** between June and September. **Fishing trips** are also possible. Information: Rederij Groen, Dr. Lelykade 1d, ☎ (070) 355 35 88; Rederij Fortuna, opposite Dr. Lelykade opposite 62, ☎ (070) 355 54 61; *Rederij* Trip, Dr. Lelykade 3, ☎ (070) 354 11 22; Rederij Vrolijk, Dr. Lelykade, ☎ (070) 351 40 21.

Shopping – The Hague is a great place to shop. In addition to the big **city-centre department stores** and chain stores there are lots of excellent small shops in the streets and squares around the palaces. Indoor shopping is available at the stylish Passage (Hofweg 5-7/Buitenhof 4-5) and at the Babylon shopping centre next to the Central Station. But The Hague is best known for its countless **antique shops** and **commercial art galleries**; the VVV publishes brochures full of useful shopping suggestions. Late-night shopping is on Thursdays, when the shops are open until 9pm.
The best places to shop in **Scheveningen** are Palace Promenade, Gevers Deynootplein and the boulevard. Late-night shopping day is Friday, except in Palace Promenade, where the shops are open every day from 10am to 10pm.

Markets – The Hague has excellent markets several days a week. There are **general goods markets** in Herman Costerstraat (Monday, Wednesday, Friday and Saturday) and on Markthof (daily except Sundays). A **farmers' market** takes

Herring seller

place by the Grote Kerk on Wednesdays. A lively **art and antiques market** is held on Lange Voorhout on Thursdays and Sundays from May to September, and on Thursdays on the Plein during the rest of the year.

Theatres and concerts – **Classical music:** Dr. Anton Philipszaal, Spuiplein 150, ☏ (070) 360 98 10; Sunday morning concerts in the Circustheater, Circusstraat 4, ☏ (070) 416 76 00. **Pop, rock, blues:** 't Paard, Prinsegracht 12, ☏ (070) 360 16 18. **Theatre and dance:** Koninklijke Schouwburg, Korte Voorhout 3, ☏ (0900) 345 67 89; Lucent Danstheater, Spuiplein 152, ☏ (070) 360 49 30 (home of the world-famous Nederlands Dans Theater); Nederlands Congres Centrum, Churchillplein 10, ☏ (070) 306 63 66; Theater aan het Spui, Spui 187, ☏ (070) 346 52 72; Diligentia, Lange Voorhout 5, ☏ (0900) 410 41 04.

Nightlife – **Scheveningen's Boulevard** is the place to be: crowded and boisterous with something for everyone, including shops, street cafés, restaurants, bars and discos. If the weather drives you indoors, you might opt for a musical at the **Circustheater**, a night at the movies, or a flutter at the **Holland Casino**.

Events – An annual Indonesian fair, **Pasar Malam Besar**, is held on the Malieveld in June, and includes theatre performances, lectures, stalls and music. The famous **North Sea Jazz Festival**, in July, is a magnet for jazz and blues fanatics from all over the world. Modern dance enthusiasts make a beeline for the annual **CaDance Festival** at the Theater aan het Spui, and the international **Holland Dance Festival** takes place in alternate

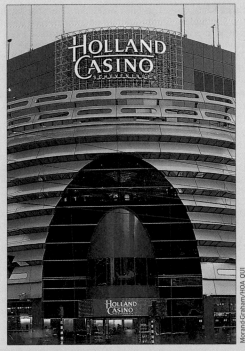

Scheveningen – Holland Casino

years. Scheveningen has its own annual **Sand Sculpture Festival** in May/June, and the traditional **Herring Festival** is in late May/early June, when the first batch of new Dutch herring is auctioned. In early June the **kite-flying festival (Vliegerfeest)** is held on the beach.

CENTRE *half a day*

Stately mansions line the wide avenues around the Binnenhof, the centre of the country's political life. Nearby, shops are grouped in the pedestrianised area: the town has a great many antiques dealers and luxury boutiques.

Buitenhof – This is the "outer courtyard" of the old castle which once belonged to the Counts of Holland. A statue of King William II stands in the centre.

★ **Binnenhof** – Enter by the Stadtholder doorway to reach the inner courtyard (Binnenhof) in the centre of which stands the Ridderzaal, or Knights' Hall. The buildings all around date from different periods in Dutch history. They now house the Upper House of Parliament and the Ministry of General Affairs *(north wing)*, part of the State Council *(west wing)* and the Lower House *(south and east wing, as well as the new extensions)*. Van Oldenbarnevelt *(see AMERSFOORT)* was executed in this courtyard on 13 May 1619.

Binnenhof Visitor Centre ⊘ – This has a **model** of the Binnenhof and a historical timescale showing the political history of the Low Countries over the past twelve centuries. It is also the starting point of a tour, which begins with a video about the Binnenhof and continues through the Ridderzaal and the Upper and Lower Houses of Parliament.

★ **Ridderzaal** ⊘ – An **exhibition** in the cellars of the Ridderzaal *(no 8a)* explains the origin and workings of the two chambers and the roles of the head of state and the monarch.
The Ridderzaal, built as a banqueting hall for Count William II of Holland, was completed c 1280 by his son Count Floris V. The building, which looks very much like a church, was located in the prolongation of the old castle. Its façade with a pointed and finely worked gable is flanked by two slender turrets. Inside, the great hall, restored c 1900, has recovered its vault with open-work beams. Since 1904 the two chambers of the States General have gathered in the Ridderzaal for a ceremonial opening session and to listen to a speech made by the Queen.
The back of the building, visible from the Binnenhof's second courtyard, consists of the old castle built c 1250 by Count William II. The main hall became, in 1511, the hall of sessions of the Holland and West Friesland Court, and was called the Roll Court.

Eerste Kamer ⊘ – The First or Upper Chamber is situated in the north wing, in the **Stadtholders' Quarters**, bordered by a covered gallery. It is the former assembly hall of the Holland and West Friesland States (17C). Since 1848 it has been used as a place of assembly for the Upper House or Senate, which consists of 75 members elected for four years by the twelve Provincial States. It has a wooden ceiling painted in the Baroque style by two of Rubens' pupils: A de Haan and N Wielingh.

Trêveszaal – *Not open to the public.* The Truce Hall, where in 1608 a twelve-year truce with Spain was prepared, is now used by the Council of Ministers. It was rebuilt in 1697 by Marot in the Louis XIV style.

Tweede Kamer ⊘ – The Second or Lower Chamber is composed of 150 representatives, elected for four years by universal suffrage.
Between 1815 and 1992 the former **ballroom** *(presently undergoing restoration)*, situated in the wing added by the Stadtholder William V in the late 18C, was used to accommodate the deputies; decorated in the Louis XIV style, the ballroom has a balcony and several boxes. In 1992 the members of the Lower Chamber moved to **modern buildings** *(Entrance Plein 2A)* based on plans by the Dutch architect Pi de Bruijn and set up among the existing buildings to the south of the Binnenhof. The central hall, whose glass roofing lets in the daylight, houses an original work of art by Lex Wegchelaar, made with marble elements taken from a low relief (1938) by RN Roland Holst. The plenary sessions are held in the semicircular chamber. Behind the speaker's chair are painted panels by R van de Wint.

Plein – The Ministry of Defence overlooks this square; in the centre stands the statue of William the Silent (1848). No 23 is a splendid 18C building designed by Daniël Marot. In winter a market selling art and antiques is held on the square every Thursday.

★★★ **Mauritshuis** ⊘ – This museum is named after Count Johan Maurits of Nassau-Siegen, who in around 1640 commissioned **Pieter Post** to build this elegant residence to plans by Jacob van Campen. It was built in a strictly Classical style, with its height, width and depth all approximately the same (c 25m/80ft) *(Illustration: see Introduction, The arts)*. Since 1822 it has been the home of the royal painting collection, one of the finest in the world; the relatively small number of paintings makes for a most agreeable visit.

The collection is still expanding, and is displayed in the form of temporary exhibitions, each highlighting a particular aspect of this rich assemblage of artworks. The permanent collection as described below is therefore rarely all on show at the same time.

Ground floor – This is devoted to foreign schools and the Flemish School. The first room of the **Flemish School** is remarkable with the moving *Lamentation of Christ* (c 1450) by Rogier van der Weyden, the penetrating *Portrait of a Man* by Memling, and *Christ Carrying the Cross* by Quentin Metsys. There are lovely portraits by Holbein the Younger (16C), one of a young woman by the German Bartholomeus Bruyn; two portraits by Antonio Moro, including one of a goldsmith.

Two rooms are reserved for **Rubens** and his contemporaries. *The Adoration of the Shepherds* by Jordaens and canvases by David Teniers feature alongside a rich collection of works by Rubens: portraits of his two wives; *Michel Ophovius*, bishop of 's-Hertogenbosch; and finally the famous Garden of Eden with the Fall of Man (c 1615), where the two people painted by Rubens can be seen against a landscape executed with charming meticulousness by Jan Brueghel the Elder.

Index of street names and sights for maps of DEN HAAG

DEN HAAG
(`S -GRAVENHAGE)

0   300m

de Pier

OOSTDUINPARK

NOORDZEE

Sea Life
Scheveningen

Kurhaus

Deynootweg

Zwolse

straat

MUSEUM
BEELDEN AAN ZEE

CASINO

27

Harstenhoekweg

Gentsestr.

Stevins

BELGISCH
PARK

SCHEVENINGEN

Badhuisweg

Nieuw

Belgischepl.

Gen

M

T²

Stevinstr.

10

73

Park

laan

Badhuisw

Obelisk

121

Keizerstr.

21

Juriaan-Kokstr.

Haring

kade

Westbroekpark

HET KANAAL

Strandweg

110

36

94

Duin

straat

Kanaal

Duin

weg

Visafslagweg

1° HAVEN

112

112

De Haven

Zeesluisweg

Duin

weg

Scheveningse

weg

VAN STOLKPARK

weg

MADURODAM

VOOR
HAVEN

Lelykade

2° HAVEN

Duin

Doornstr.

93

slag

Hendrik

Prof. B. M. Teldersweg

M

Dr.

West

Boerzelaar

van

Franken

Staten

laan

STATENKWARTIER

93

Fred.

laan

Eisenhowerlaan

SCHEVENINGSE BOSJES

40

HOEK VAN HOLLAND
KIJKDUIN

Willem

de Zwijgerlaan

103

Nederlands
Congres Centrum

40

Het Catshuis

Zorgvliet

Scheveningse

9

Nieboerweg

Houtrust

Kranenburgweg

GEMEENTEMUSEUM
DEN HAAG

Museon

Omniversum

18

RIOOLGEMAAL

40

Jacob Catslaan

107

Vredespaleis

MUS
MES

HOUTRUST-
HALLEN

Pres. Kennedy laan

103

Conrad

Hertoginne

laan

van Meerdervoort

Prins
Hendrikpl.

str.

weg

laan

DUINOORD

Koningin

kade

Prins Hendrik

str.

Piet

Eland

Sport

Beeklaan

Laan

Emma

Segbroek

Fahrenheitstr.

Groot

Meerdervoort

Koningspl.

Regentesse

Weimarstr.

Gouderegenstr.

Thomson

laan

van

Thomsonlaan

laan

REGENTESSEKWARTIER

76

Laan van Eik en

Laan

Valkenbos

Valkenbos

kade

Weimarstr.

Fahrenheitstr.

weg

VALKENBOS

Mient

Mient

kade

Valkenbos

Beeklaan

Loosduinse

TRANSVAAL

Monstersestr.

Delft

Mient

Duinen

Loosduinse

Paul Kruger

laan

96

kade

Steijn

laan

125

N 213 ⟍ NAALDWIJK
VLAARDINGEN

DELFT

DEN HAAG

1st floor – Among the Dutch painters of the **Golden Age**, **Rembrandt** is the reigning master here. Between the portrait of the artist when he was 23 (1629; *Illustration, see LEIDEN*), which holds one's attention by its meticulous precision of detail and its taste for scrupulous observation, and the portrait of 1669, one of his last works, with an overwhelming depth, one can see the whole evolution of the painter.

The Anatomy Lesson of Doctor Nicolaes Tulp (1632), his first group portrait painted when he was 26, brought him glory; the research in composition, the contrasts of light give the scene a dramatic intensity already characteristic.

The same emotion appears in *Susanna* of 1637, one of the rare nudes by Rembrandt, the *Simeon in the Temple* (1631) with its subdued muted light, or in the more fiery works like the pathetic *Saul and David* (1658) and *The Two Negroes* (1661).

The museum also has two admirable paintings by **Johannes Vermeer**, the *View of Delft* and the *Girl with a Pearl Earring* both c 1660. To these two masterpieces one can compare the *Diana*, one of the first paintings already showing the limpid and serene poetry of the Delft master.

The museum has a number of genre paintings: some Jan Steens, where the verve, malice, and delicacy bring charming anecdotes to life *(Merry Company, Girl Eating Oysters)*, some Van Ostades with scenes of country life *(The Violinist)*, portraits by Frans Hals *(Head of a Child)*, some Ter Borchs and The *Young Mother* by Gerrit Dou. There are also landscape painters; painters of rivers (Van Goyen and Van de Velde), of the countryside (Salomon van Ruysdael and his nephew Jacob van Ruisdael), of skaters (Avercamp) and of domestic animals (Paulus Potter, *Young Bull*). There are also some small gems: the famous *Goldfinch* (1654) which Carel Fabritius, Rembrandt's pupil, painted in the year of his death at the age of 32.

Girl with a Pearl Earring, Johannes Vermeer

Stichting Vrienden van het Mauritshuis

Hofvijver – From Korte Vijverberg, there is a lovely **view**★ over this artificial lake in which are reflected the Mauritshuis, the octagonal tower of the Prime Minister's quarters, the windows of the Truce Hall and the Upper Chamber. In the middle of the lake, which has a fountain, there is an island planted with trees. Storks have nested here for many years, and the stork appears in the city's coat of arms.

Haags Historisch Museum ⊘ – The collections of the Hague Historical Museum, installed in the former premises of the Archers' Company of St Sebastian (1636), illustrate the history of the town and the life of its townspeople: furniture, eggshell porcelain, church silver, views of the city, a doll's house and other items.

Follow Lange Vijverberg.

G. Sioen/CEDRI

Hofvijver

★ Museum Bredius ⊙ – This museum has a privileged setting: a fine mansion built in 1757. The painting collection features many of the works left to the town by Abraham Bredius (1855-1946), an art historian and former director of the Mauritshuis. In the remarkable section on 17C art, you can admire the famous *Satyr among the Peasants* by Jan Steen, a fine *Christ's Head* by Rembrandt, *Festivities on the Ice* by A van der Neer, along with canvases by Albert Cuyp, Adriaen van Ostade, Willem Pieter Buytewech and JJ van de Velde. On the floor above, note the drawings by Rembrandt and Jacob van Ruysdael.

At no 8 there is a façade attributed to Daniel Marot.

★ Lange Voorhout – Along the tree-lined avenues of Lange Voorhout there are some of the most beautiful patrician residences in The Hague. Most of them are occupied by embassies. There is a large **art and antiques market** on Lange Voorhout in the summer and from the end of June to the beginning of September a large **open-air exhibition of modern sculpture** is also held here every year.

Museum Het Paleis ⊙ – The former palace of Queen Emma (1858-1934), wife of William III and mother to Wilhelmina, stands at the far end of the main avenue. Its elegant 18C façade was the work of Pieter de Swart. The municipal museum organises temporary exhibitions here.

In front of the **Hotel des Indes** *(nos 54-56; see also Travellers' addresses)*, there is a lovely statuette, **"The Stroller"** dedicated to the chronicler Elias.

The building at no 34 was constructed in 1734-36 by Daniël Marot. Between 1813 and 1814 William I, first king of the Netherlands, lived here. The building now houses the Supreme Court of Appeal.

At no 15, on the opposite side, stands the building bought by the painter Mesdag to house the **Pulchri Studio** association, of which he was the president from 1889.

Kloosterkerk – This former convent chapel built in the 15C and 16C is used for organ concerts and choral services.

Noordeinde – This busy street lined with antique shops crosses the square where the **Paleis Noordeinde** stands. Also called Het Oude Hof, this 16-17C building with two wings at right angles was occupied by Louise de Coligny, widow of William the Silent, by the Princes Maurice and Frederick Henry, sons of the latter, and by King William I. Queen Beatrix has installed her offices here. Opposite there is an equestrian statue of William the Silent.

Return via Noordeinde, past Heulstraat.

Waals-Hervormde Kerk – The Walloon Reformed Church built in 1807 by Louis Napoleon to be used by the French-speaking Protestant community of The Hague. After the mid-16C the Protestant refugees, fleeing persecution in the southern Netherlands (Belgium), established French-speaking parish communities. These increased in the 17C with the arrival of the Huguenots from France. Services are still held today in **Walloon churches** which are part of the Dutch Reformed Church.

De Plaats – In the centre of this square is the statue (1887) of Johan de Witt who was put to death here at the same time as his brother Cornelis *(see DORDRECHT)*.

Museum de Gevangenpoort ⊙ – This 13C gatehouse was part of the ducal castle on the Binnenhof. In the 15C it became a prison, where a number of famous figures including Cornelis de Witt *(see DORDRECHT)* were incarcerated. It is now a museum, with a collection of medieval instruments of torture and punishment.

★ Galerij Prins Willem V ⊙ – In 1773 the Stadtholder of the United Provinces William V converted the second floor of the house, adjoining the Prison Gate, into a picture gallery. This gallery was open to the public; it may be seen as the very first public museum in the history of the Netherlands. The prince's collection featured mainly 17C landscapes, genre scenes and paintings of still life. In 1815 King William I donated the collection to the state, and it was transferred to the Mauritshuis in 1821. The gallery has been restored and decorated in the manner of the 18C, the paintings entirely covering the walls.

Although it only features a few works belonging to the original collection, the present display of 17C paintings is extremely interesting. It includes landscapes by Philips Wouwerman, a number of works by Jan Steen, *The Bear Hunt* by Paulus Potter, *Girl with a lamp* by Gerard Dou, and a picture by Van de Velde the Younger: *The War Ship at Sunset*.

Groenmarkt – This is the central square of The Hague, home to both the town hall and the Grote Kerk. Numerous pedestrian precincts start from here, notably **Paleispromenade** to the north, and **De Passage**, the large covered passage built in 1880, to the south.

Grote Kerk or St.-Jacobskerk ⊙ – Flanked by a tower with a carillon of 51 bells, this great brick hall-type church (c 1450) is roofed with a wooden vault. In the chancel (c 1500), there is the tomb of Admiral Jacob van Wassenaar van Obdam and the coat of arms of the knights of the Order of the Golden Fleece, who held their chapter in this church in 1456. Several stained-glass windows are worth seeing in the ambulatory; on one Charles V is shown kneeling at the Virgin's feet. The pulpit of 1550 is beautifully sculpted. The church is now used for cultural and commercial events.

Oude Raadhuis – The old town hall has a lovely 16C façade with crow-stepped gables. The 18C side façade is elegantly decorated. At the top of the richly ornamented front is the motto Ne Jupiter Quidem Omnibus (Even Jupiter cannot please everyone). The statues above the centre section depict Justice and Prudence with the coat of arms of The Hague and a Latin inscription which, loosely translated, means "Wise men learn by other men's mistakes, fools by their own".

BEYOND THE CITY CENTRE

* **Panorama Mesdag** ⊘ – Installed in a rotunda on piles, this extraordinary landscape, 120m/394ft in circumference and 14m/46ft in height, shows Scheveningen as it was in 1880, and is the work of artist **Hendrik Willem Mesdag**. In 1879 from the top of the highest dune in Scheveningen he had already reproduced the landscape on a glass cylinder, a replica of which is shown here.

This work, which is very much in the tradition of the Hague School, took only three months. Mesdag painted the sky, the sea, the beach with boats; his wife, Sientje Mesdag-van Houten, did the village; Théophile de Bock, the dunes; Breitner probably painted the figures and Blommers the woman in costume and her child. Despite the differences in technique it remains a unit; the perspective is marvellous, the sky above the sea has a soft luminosity, while behind the village the bell-towers of The Hague can be picked out.

Since the spectator is 14m/46ft away from this painting and standing on flotsam-strewn sand, the effect is that of looking down on the panorama from the top of a high dune. In the entrance halls, paintings and watercolours by Mesdag and his wife are exhibited.

Museum voor Communicatie ⊘ – The communication museum uses interactive displays to tell the story of communication, from the first postage stamp to today's e-mails and from the hand-operated telegraphs and telephones of old to the latest mobile phones and the Internet. The collections consist of postage stamps, telephone cards, sorting and fax machines, telegraphs and so on.

* **Museum Mesdag** ⊘ – Using the fortune he inherited from his father, Mesdag constructed this building beside his house in 1887 to house his growing collection of arts and crafts. He bequeathed everything to the State in 1903. The original house is now part of the museum. On the ground floor, in the studio where his wife Sientje formerly painted, authentic objects recreate the atmosphere of Mesdag's former studio. The museum allows an interesting comparison to be made between the Barbizon School with Millet, Daubigny, Corot, Théodore Rousseau, Courbet, and The Hague School with Bosboom, Mauve, the Maris brothers, Jozef Israëls and obviously Mesdag, the painter of seascapes. In the paintings of the two schools one finds fairly sombre tones, often greys, and a distinct preference for nature and landscapes.

Vredespaleis ⊘ – The Peace Palace was inaugurated a year before the start of the First World War, on 28 August 1913. On the initiative of Czar Nicholas II the first **Peace Conference** took place in The Hague (at Huis Ten Bosch) in 1899. It was decided at that time to create a Permanent Court of Arbitration whose functions were defined in 1907 during the Second Peace Conference which took place in the Ridderzaal. In the meantime the American industrialist and philanthropist, Andrew Carnegie, donated the funds to house this Court, the Netherlands government donated the land and the French architect Cordonnier was put in charge of the construction. In 1922 the palace became, in addition, the seat of the Permanent Court of International Justice, which in 1946 became the **International Court of Justice** (the United Nation's main judicial organ). It also houses the Academy of International Law of The Hague, founded in 1923.

Each nation has contributed to the furnishings and decoration of the palace. The Japanese room, hung with sumptuous tapestries, is where the Administrative Council meets, and where French is the official language; the members sit round an immense table with seats decorated with the various countries' coat of arms. Walk alongside **Zorgvliet Park** to see **Het Catshuis**, the Dutch Prime Minister's house which belonged to **Jacob Cats**.

** **Gemeentemuseum Den Haag** ⊘ – The Hague's municipal museum is a masterpiece of 20C museum architecture. Designed by **HP Berlage** and built in 1935, it consists of a reinforced concrete skeleton with a brick facing. A gallery leads to the different exhibition rooms, designed to gain the maximum advantage from natural light. A major refurbishment completed in October 1998 has restored this, Berlage's last design, to its former glory; it also included the addition of a fashion gallery.

The rich and very varied collections consist of decorative arts, 19C and 20C visual arts, costumes, musical instruments, drawings and prints.

Decorative arts – This section includes ceramics from Italy and Spain, Venetian glassware, blue and polychrome delftware and glassware manufactured in the Netherlands (17C and 18C). The collections of local silverware (15C-19C) and porcelain and ceramics (1776-1790; 1885-1914) give a picture of the items made in The Hague. Other objects are on display in 17C and 18C period interiors. Decorative arts from c 1900 (including major examples of Dutch Art Nouveau) and modern design are well represented. The 15 new rooms around the fashion gallery feature masterpieces of decorative art from the Islamic world and the Far East.

Modern art – The museum houses works by great masters of the 19C and 20C. The **French School** is well represented, with paintings by Courbet, Sisley, Monet, Signac and Van Gogh (including *Garden at Arles* and *Poppy Field*). The museum also has three paintings by Picasso (*Woman With a Pot of Mustard, Harlequin, Sibyl*), and single works by Braque, Léger and Marquet. Like Van Gogh and Van Dongen, Jongkind worked in France for much of his life. The work of this artist, regarded as a precursor of French Impressionism, is well represented.

The collection of mainly German Expressionists includes works by Kirchner, Schmidt-Rottluff, Jawlensky and Kandinsky.

The museum offers an excellent overview of **Dutch painting** from the 19C to the present; the Romantics with W Nuyen, The Hague School (the Maris brothers, Jozef Israëls, Weissenbruch, Anton Mauve and Isaac Israëls), and Breitner, Verster and Toorop. However, the Gemeentemuseum is best known for its large collection of paintings and drawings by **Piet Mondrian**, including his last, uncompleted painting Victory Boogie-Woogie (1943-44, *see also AMERS-FOORT*). It also owns important works by other pioneers of abstract art, such as the **De Stijl** group *(see AMERSFOORT)*. Among the post-war Dutch artists represented are Appel, Corneille, Constant, Schoonhoven, Van der Heyden and the sculptor Carel Visser. There is also work by foreign artists such as Vasarely, Arp, Ernst, Henry Moore and Francis Bacon.

Music – In addition to an extensive collection of musical instruments from all over the world, there is an exceptional display of European instruments from the 16C to the electronic age. Exhibitions are held in the music print section.

Fashion gallery – This new gallery has temporary exhibitions on historic and contemporary clothing and the work of specific designers.

Print collection – This has an impressive selection of works by 19C French artists including Daumier, Bresdin, Redon and Toulouse-Lautrec. Works by modern Dutch artists include watercolours and drawings by the Hague School, prints by Werkman and a significant proportion of the work of **MC Escher** *(Illustration, see LEEUWARDEN)*. Temporary exhibitions are held.

Museon ⊙ – This broad-based science museum presents collections related to the history of the Earth, dealing with subjects such as geology, human evolution, the cultures of the world, science and technology. Photographs, film, sound and computers are used in both the permanent displays and temporary exhibitions, and visitors are invited to take an active part.

Evening dress (1997),
Yoshiki Hishinuma

Omniversum ⊙ – The films and other presentations shown on this huge screen (840m²/9 042sq ft), which also serves as a planetarium, are aimed at familiarising the viewer with the world of science, nature and culture. Two projection systems, around forty loudspeakers and a great many projectors for special effects make for a breathtaking visual experience.

Nederlands Congres Centrum – The Netherlands Conference Centre was built to plans of the architect JJP Oud by his son between 1964 and 1968. The conference centre is a vast building with walls of sky-blue tiles and yellow bricks, overlooked by a triangular 17-storey tower. The entrance, on the north side, is highlighted by a large composition by Karel Appel in red and blue mosaic. Among the many meeting rooms, the large conference centre (seating capacity 2 000) is three storeys high. In the basement the festival hall, which can hold 4 000 people, is used for banquets and exhibitions.

★★ **Madurodam** ⊘ – This miniature town was built in 1952, and was originally intended for children, but adults will also enjoy the superb 1:25-scale models. It is essentially a microcosm of the Netherlands, with buildings, monuments and typical scenes from all around the country, including bulb fields, windmills, and farmhouses from the different provinces. The miniature town was completely renovated during the 1990s. In addition to the old favourites such as the Sint-Janskathedraal in 's Hertogenbosch, the Domtoren in Utrecht,

Madurodam

Anne Frank's house and the Muiderslot, new buildings have been added, including the ING Bank in south-east Amsterdam, the "De Maas" office building and the Erasmus Bridge in Rotterdam, the environment ministry in The Hague, and the new Groninger Museum. Working trains, cars, buses and boats and night-time lighting add to the fascination of this living town.

ADDITIONAL SIGHTS

Heilige Geesthofje – Built in 1616, this almshouse is a charming enclosure with small low houses with crow-stepped dormer windows. Opposite, near the house (no 74) where Spinoza ended his days, stands the statue of the illustrious philosopher.

Museum van Het Boek/Museum Meermanno-Westreenianum ⊘ – On Prinsessegracht, lined with 18C mansions, this museum houses the Baron van Westreenen's collections. The ground floor is usually devoted to exhibitions about modern and antique books. On the 1st floor, in the library, there are **manuscripts and incunabula** from the medieval period. The museum also contains Greek, Roman and Egyptian antiquities.

Letterkundig Museum ⊘ – *Access via the library (Koninklijke Bibliotheek).* This museum of literature uses manuscripts, letters, curios, portraits and audio-visual material to give an overview of Dutch literature from 1750 onwards. There is also a **museum of children's books** and temporary exhibitions are also held.

Haagse Bos – Crossed by Leidsestraatweg, these woods surround the royal palace, **Huis ten Bosch**, where the first Peace Conference was held in 1899. This edifice was built in the 17C by Pieter Post for Amalia Van Solms, the widow of Stadtholder Frederick Henry. It is Queen Beatrix's official residence.

Clingendael – This extensive park, with its meadows shaded by majestic trees and strewn with lakes, was once private property; there is a splendid Japanese garden.

Westbroekpark – This park surrounded by lakes (rowing) is famous for its **rose garden** *(early July to late September)* where an international exhibition is held annually.

⌂⌂ SCHEVENINGEN

Belonging to The Hague administrative district, Scheveningen is an elegant seaside resort with a very large and busy beach. It has often been devastated by storms: the storm of 1570 submerged part of the village. The church, originally located in the town centre, is now near the beach. Today Scheveningen is protected by many breakwaters and a high dike.

The **Circustheater**, dating from 1904, is the only theatre in the Netherlands capable of staging very large-scale productions of operas, musicals and the like. It was refurbished in 1993.

The beach – *Illustration, see Admission times and charges at the back of the guide.* – This long and wide stretch of fine sand is lined for 3km/2mi by a boulevard, Strandweg, which is the continuation to the east of a promenade where many café terraces are opened up during the summer months. Some substantial transformations have recently occurred on this seafront. Overlooking the beach, the imposing restored **Kurhaus** (1885; *see also Travellers' addresses*) is now home to a casino; special events are also held here.

Kurhaus, Scheveningen

The **Pier**, with its long promenade, leads to four constructions built on piles offering entertainment. An observation tower 45m/148ft high offers a panoramic view of Scheveningen, The Hague, the dunes towards Wassenaar and out to sea.

The port – Beyond the lighthouse, towards the west, the fishing port remains very busy. Two inner docks have coasting vessels, pleasure boats and a fleet of trawlers. The **obelisk** commemorates the place where William I landed from England to take possession of his throne in November 1813. First situated to the east of the port near the dunes, around Dr. de Visserplein as shown on the Panorama Mesdag, the fishing village has grown with new quarters to the south and west of the port; they are large quadrilateral brick buildings arranged round a courtyard with wide porches.

Some of the older women remain faithful to the traditional costume: black dress and apron. The headdress, placed on a metal headband fixed with two hairpins, is distinctive; the end of the headband is adorned with two oval buckles of filigree gold. On Sundays the bonnet is of lace.

★★ **Museum Beelden aan Zee** ⊘ – This seaside sculpture museum is located in a pavilion on the Boulevard, built by King William I in 1826 to provide rest and sea air for his ailing wife, Queen Wilhelmina. The museum around the pavilion was designed by the Dutch architect **Wim Quist** and opened in 1994. On display is the exceptionally varied collection of Mr and Mrs Scholten-Miltenburg. It consists of works by contemporary artists from all over the world, such as Karel Appel, Fritz Koenig, Francisca Zijlstra, Shinkichi Tajiri, Waldermar Otto, Man Ray and Igor Mitoraj. The theme of the collection is the **universality of the human figure**, with all its different experiences, feelings and moods. On the **south patio** there is a magnificent bronze sculpture of the royal family by Arthur Spronken. There is a fine view of the North Sea from the **sea room**.

Sea Life Scheveningen ⊘ – This aquarium features life forms from the beach to the deepest depths of the sea, and includes sharks, rays, crabs, conger eels and jellyfish. There is also an underwater observatory, a tropical reef adventure and an underwater tunnel.

EXCURSIONS

Voorburg – *3km/1.5mi to the east via the A12 exit 4.* **Hofwijck Manor** stands quite near Voorburg station, and today it houses the **Huygensmuseum** ⊙. This small manor surrounded by water was designed by **Constantijn Huygens** (1596-1687) and built by the architect **Pieter Post** in the years 1641-43. Part of the symmetrical garden still exists today. Constantijn Huygens, who acted as first secretary to the stadtholders Frederick Henry, William II and William III, was also a poet and a composer. He decided to have Hofwijck built as a refuge from his busy life in The Hague; "hof wijk" means "refuge from the court". His son **Christiaan Huygens** (The Hague, 1629-95) invented the pendulum clock. This great astronomer and physicist enjoyed a worldwide reputation. After a long stay in London and Paris, Christiaan returned to the Netherlands. He settled in Hofwijck, where he lived until his death. The collections in the museum retrace the history of the family: portraits, original editions of works by Constantijn Huygens and a replica made in Leiden of Christiaan Huygens' world-famous pendulum clock.

Wassenaar – *12km/7mi to the north; leave The Hague via Benoordenhoutseweg.* Wassenaar is one of the most attractive residential suburbs of the Randstad conurbation, and large numbers of people commute from here to The Hague. It has many substantial villas hidden among trees. The **Duinrell theme park** ⊙ is hidden amid the woods and dunes, and includes a large recreation area, roller coasters, numerous water attractions and a large tropical swimming-pool complex, the **Tikibad** ⊙.

Naaldwijk – *16km/10mi to the south via Oude Haagweg.* Cross the market-garden region of **Westland**, divided by canals, and covered with thousands of greenhouses, orchards and gardens between The Hague, Hoek van Holland and the coastal dunes; flowers are cultivated as well as vegetables. In the heart of Westland, Naaldwijk (sometimes called the Glass Town) is a large horticultural centre and has a major **auction** ⊙ of cut flowers and potted plants *(Dijkweg 66, Honselersdijk).* On Wilhelminaplein, the old 17C **town hall** has a Baroque voluted gable. Not far away, behind the Gothic church, the Holy Ghost Almshouse, **Heilige Geest Hofje**, forms a group with low, picturesque 17C houses with tall dormer windows arranged round a chapel of the same period.

The length of time given in this guide
 – for touring allows time to enjoy the views and the scenery;
 – for sightseeing is the average time required for a visit.

HAARLEM★★

Noord-Holland Ⓟ

Population 148 262
Michelin maps 908 E 4 and 211 M 8
Local map see KEUKENHOF
Plan of the conurbation in the current edition of The Red Guide Benelux

Situated on the Spaarne, Haarlem is the capital of the province of Noord-Holland. The town played an important role in the history of the earldom of Holland, and, being the birthplace of Dirk Bouts and Adriaen van Ostade as well as the residence of Frans Hals, it was also of great significance in the history of Dutch art. Today the town is the centre of a large bulb-growing region *(see Keukenhof)*. In spring, the Bloemen-corso or flower parade starts in Noordwijk and ends in Haarlem *(see Practical information at the front of the guide)*.
Although Haarlem is not situated very far inland, it is well protected from the North Sea winds by the dunes. And although it lies only about twenty kilometres from Amsterdam, it still has the typical atmosphere, tranquility and elegance of the towns in Holland's hinterland.

HISTORICAL NOTES

Haarlem was founded in the 10C and is therefore older than Amsterdam.
Haarlem was the residence of the Counts of Holland and it was fortified in the 12C. It obtained its city charter in 1245. In the 13C some of the townspeople took part in the Fifth Crusade and the capture of Damietta in Egypt in 1219. The bells of the Grote Kerk are still called *damiaatjes* in memory of this great deed. In the 14C Haarlem expanded, but all that remains of its fortifications is the late 15C gateway, Amsterdamse Poort, to the east.

A bloody siege – During the uprising against the Spanish, Haarlem was besieged for seven months (1572-3) by the troops of Dom Frederico of Toledo, son of the Duke of Alba. During the winter, William the Silent managed to provide the town with supplies through the Beggars, who came on skates over Haarlemmermeer, but despite the heroic defence by the whole population, the town capitulated in June 1573. In 1577 Haarlem decided to side with the States General, who had been designated stadtholder of Holland and Zeeland by William in November 1576 with the Pacification of Ghent.

The 17C marks the peak of Haarlem; the town took advantage of the fall of Flemish cities by developing the linen industry and made a fabric sold all over Europe under the name of holland (a plain weave linen).

Haarlemmermeer – Formed by peat exploitation, this great lake of about 18 000ha/44 460 acres was a threat to Amsterdam and Leyden due to storms. As early as 1641, the famous hydraulic engineer **Jan Adriaenszoon Leeghwater** had suggested draining it by using windmills and making polders. The work was not undertaken until two centuries later, when steam powered **pumps** took the place of windmills. Three pumping stations were installed, one being the one invented by Cruquius. When the work was completed in 1852 some 88 million m³/3 107 million cu ft had been pumped out.

The present territory of Haarlemmermeer, which has become a district borough, is an average 4m/13ft below sea level, and Schiphol Airport, which is located there is 4.5m/15ft below. The silty marine deposits found under the peat bogs are very fertile.

A hot-bed of artistic genius – Haarlem is probably the birthplace of **Claus Sluter** (c 1345-1406), a sculptor who produced works of great realism, working for the Dukes of Burgundy in the Charterhouse of Champmol near Dijon. The painters **Dirk Bouts**, who went to live in Leuven (Belgium), and **Jan Mostaert**, who painted religious scenes and was painter to Margaret of Austria, were both born in Haarlem during the 15C, while **Geertgen tot Sint Jans** lived here for a time *(see LEIDEN)*.

In the 16C **Maarten van Heemskerck** (1498-1574) was the pupil of **Jan van Scorel** during his stay in Haarlem from 1527-29. **Cornelis van Haarlem**, Mannerist painter (1562-1638), and **Willem Claeszoon Heda** (1594-1680), famous for his still-life paintings, were born in this town. The engraver **Hendrick Goltzius** (1558-1617), **Pieter Claeszoon** (1597-1661), another still-life painter, and **Pieter Saenredam** (1597-1665), painter of serene church interiors, all ended their days here. **Hercules Seghers** (1589/90-1638), a remarkable landscape painter, was probably born here. **Lieven de Key** (c 1560-1627), who was part of the "brain drain" from Flanders to the Netherlands and who became the town's architect in 1593, was one of the great Renaissance architects. *For information about Frans Hals, see text box below.*

Portrait painter **Bartholomeus van der Helst** (1613-70), **Philips Wouwerman** (1619-68), a painter of horses, imitated by his brother Pieter, and **Nicolaes Berchem** (1620-83) who, unlike his father Pieter Claeszoon, painted landscapes, were also born in Haarlem. Another native of Haarlem, **Adriaen van Ostade** (1610-84), was principally a genre

The Banquet of the Officers of the Civic Guard of St Adrian by Frans Hals

Frans Hals

This painter was born in Antwerp c 1582, but his family moved to Haarlem around 1591. Frans Hals became the portrait painter of the town's bourgeois at a time when the portrait and particularly group portraits (guilds, brotherhoods) were in fashion. Of the 240 works ascribed to Hals, no fewer than 195 are portraits.

Hals abandoned the tradition of rigid poses and stilted compositions and introduced, especially in his commissioned works, a certain vitality and more natural attitudes for his subjects. In some cases he went so far as to catch them unawares. His bold and fluent brushwork was considered sloppy at the time. He enlivened his canvases with bright splashes of colour on scarves and flags. His rapid but expressive brush strokes, which foreshadowed modern art and especially Impressionism, gave his models a life, a mobility which made his portraits real snapshots.

For a long time a frank cheerfulness radiated from his paintings, but after 1640 there was no longer the verve and fantasy in his works. In the famous group of regents and regentesses the return to black and white, verticality, expressionless faces, even disenchantment, left a sinister impression, almost a forewarning of his death two years later (1666) at the age of 84.

Frans Hals's many pupils included **Judith Leyster** (1609-60), the Fleming **Adriaen Brouwer** and **Adriaen van Ostade** (1610-85), painter of village scenes. The latter's pupils were his brother Isaack as well as Jan Steen.

painter whose work is characterised by extreme realism. **Salomon van Ruysdael**, who was born in Naarden (c 1600-70) but who settled in Haarlem, was one of the foremost pioneers of Dutch landscape painting together with Jan van Goyen. His nephew and pupil **Jacob van Ruysdael** (1628/9-82) was born in Haarlem. He painted more tormented landscapes, already romantic with dark cliffs, waterfalls, trees menaced by storm, and disquieting chiaroscuros.

AROUND GROTE MARKT *1hr 30min*

★ **Grote Markt** – This great square is bordered by the Grote Kerk, the Stadhuis and the former meat market. In the square there is a statue of **Laurens Coster** (1405-84) (his real name was Laurens Janszoon) considered in the Netherlands to be the inventor of printing in 1423, that is to say about ten years before Gutenberg.

★★ **Grote Kerk or St.- Bavokerk** ⊙ – *Entrance: Oude Groenmarkt 23*. This large 15C church, which should not be confused with the Catholic St Bavo's *(Leidsevaart)*, has an elegant wooden lantern tower covered with lead sheeting, 80m/262ft high over the **transept crossing**★. The entrance to the church is surrounded by booths, erected against the southern façade. These booths were rented out by the clergy to pay for the maintenance of the sacrarium.

Inside, admire the short nave and, in the long chancel *(illustration: see Architecture, p 55)*, a lovely cedar-wood stellar **vault**★. The gravestones on the floor include that of **Pieter Saenredam**, and **Frans Hals** is also buried here *(in the chancel)*. Note also a 17C pulpit with a Gothic sounding board, choir stalls (1512) carved with amusing subjects, the copper lectern in the shape of a pelican (1499), and above all the lovely early 16C **chancel screen**★, backed by finely worked brass. The great **organ**★ *(illustration: see Introduction, The arts)* built by Christiaen Müller in 1738 was decorated according to the drawings of Daniël Marot. It has long been considered one of the best organs in the world, and it is said that Handel and Mozart (as a child) came to play this instrument. An international organ festival is organised every two years in Haarlem *(see Calendar of events)*.

Vishal ⊙ – The fish market was built in 1769, up against the northern façade of St-Bavokerk; like the meat market, it is an annexe of the Frans Hals museum.

★ **Vleeshal** ⊙ – The Meat Hall is an ornamental building in the Mannerist style, built by Lieven de Key between 1602 and 1604. It has richly decorated dormer windows and a façade decorated with the heads of oxen and sheep. The building is part of the Frans Halsmuseum, and is used for temporary exhibitions. The basement houses the **Archeologisch Museum Haarlem** ⊙.

Verweyhal ⊙ – This hall, also part of the Frans Halsmuseum, is named after the Haarlem-born Impressionist painter Kees Verwey; some of his work is on display in the museum.

HAARLEM

The most important sights in this guide can be found on the Principal Sights map, and are described in the text. Use the map and plans, the Calendar of events, the index, and read the Introduction to get the most out of this guide.

* Stadhuis ⊙ – The town hall, with its slim tower, is a 14C Gothic building to which numerous alterations have been made; the protruding section on the right has a gallery on the ground floor and a 15C and 17C voluted façade, while on the left there is a Renaissance-style loggia above the flight of steps. The **Gravenzaal** or Counts' Hall on the 1st floor has kept its original appearance; the paintings which hang here are copies of old murals from the Carmelite convent and depict the Counts of Holland.

*** FRANS HALSMUSEUM ⊙ 1hr 30min

Since 1913, this museum has occupied a **former almshouse for old men** built between 1607 and 1610; it is said to have been designed by the architect Lieven de Key. Prior to being used as a museum the building was an orphanage (1810-1908). It has undergone many alterations over the years.

The façade is characteristic of this type of institution with a row of low houses on either side of the entrance, topped with a crow-stepped gable and window. Behind this façade is an inner courtyard around which the rooms are arranged.

The group of houses with crow-stepped gables opposite the museum used to be part of the **St.-Elisabeths Gasthuis** *(see below)*, whose regents were the subject of portraits painted by Frans Hals.

Works by Frans Hals – The eight paintings of civic guards (room 21) and regents by Frans Hals constitute a remarkable collection making it possible to follow the evolution of the master's style.

The first painting which marks the already brilliant beginnings of the painter dates from 1616 when Hals was about 34 years old. It is the **The Banquet of the Officers of the Civic Guard of St George**. The mobility of the characters and their personality are shown in an extraordinary way. The atmosphere is less restrained in the *The Banquet of the Officers of the Civic Guard of St George* and *The Officers of the Civic Guard of St Adrian*, both painted in 1627 and rich in spontaneity and colour. In **The Officers of the Civic Guard of St Adrian** of 1633, Frans Hals displays the height of his virtuosity. **The Officers of the Civic Guard of St George** of 1639, with a self-portrait of the artist (figure no 19 in the top left-hand corner) is the last of this genre. In 1641 a tendency for restraint and solemnity appears in Frans Hals' work and predominates in the *Regents of St Elizabeth's Hospital* (room 25). The sombre colour of the garments underlines the expression on the faces and the very studied attitude of the hands. In 1664, Hals was over eighty when he produced *Regents of the Old Men's Home* (room 28); in this daring, somewhat cynical study of six characters, Hals had the cheek to portray one of them as being quite tipsy with his hat perched on the back of his head. Painted the same year, the painting of the **Regentesses of the Old Men's Home** (room 28) with furrowed hands, bony faces, and severe looks, communicates a sentiment of anguish and discomfort.

The Haarlem School – A distinction is usually made between the first and the second Haarlem School. The **first Haarlem School** (15C and first half of the 16C) is particularly associated with religious art, characterised by strong realism. The Mannerist works of Jan van Scorel *(Baptism of Christ in the River Jordan)*, Maarten van Heemskerck, Karel van Mander and Cornelis Corneliszoon van Haarlem *(Baptism of Christ)* are perfect examples of this movement. The **second Haarlem School**, which flourished in the second half of the 17C, saw the development of the various types of subject into separate genres. Frans Hals was the master of the group portrait; Esaias van de Velde, Salomon and Jacob van Ruysdael, and Van Goyen specialised in landscapes; Terborch, Van Ostade and Judith Leyster painted mainly genre scenes; Verspronck produced very fine portraits; Wouwerman and Cuyp specialised in painting animals; Pieter Saenredam and Jacob Berckheyde painted mainly church interiors; and Floris van Dijck and Willem Claeszoon Heda founded a distinguished tradition of still-life painting *(as can be seen in the 18C regents' room)*.

Crafts – Apart from paintings, the museum contains collections of furniture, Haarlem silverware (in the former ward); a **book of tulip drawings** by Judith Leyster, the reconstruction of an **apothecary** with delftware jars and, in a room with Dutch gilded leather, an 18C **doll's house**.

Modern art – In a new wing there are **modern and contemporary Dutch paintings**, notably by Isaac Israëls, Jan Sluyters, Piet Mondrian (figurative period) and members of the Cobra Group.

ADDITIONAL SIGHTS

* **Teylers Museum** ⊘ – This is now the oldest public museum in the Netherlands, built after the Haarlem wool and silk merchant Pieter Teyler van der Hulst (1702-78) wrote a will leaving all his money to the furtherance of the arts and sciences. Construction began in 1779.

The old rooms, and particularly the beautiful stucco-decorated **Ovale Zaal** (1784), have kept their attractively antiquated appearance. They contain displays of early fossil finds, minerals and scientific instruments, including the largest electrostatic generator ever built, dating from 1791.

Teylers Museum – the Ovale Zaal (1784)

The Aquarellenzaal, or **Watercolour Room**, was converted in 1996 to house a changing selection from the superb **collection of drawings**★★. This consists of around 2 500 works by Dutch masters such as Goltzius, Rembrandt and Schelfhout, some 1 500 Italian works by artists including Michelangelo, Raphael, Pietro Testa and Annibale Carracci, many of which formerly belonged to Queen Christina of Sweden, and drawings by Dürer, Watteau, Boucher and others.

The two rooms of paintings contain interesting examples from the Romantic era, and works from the Hague School and the Amsterdam School, including *Summer Landscape* by Barend Cornelis Koekkoek, *The River Lek at Elshout* by J Weissenbruch, *Evening at Sea* by Hendrik Willem Mesdag, and *Children in the Dunes* by George Hendrik Breitner.

The **numismatic collection** contains examples of Dutch medals from the 16C to the 20C, and coins from Gelderland and West Friesland.

The new wing (1996) is used for temporary exhibitions.

Waag – At the corner of Damstraat and Spaarne stands the **Waag**, or weigh-house, built in 1598 in the Mannerist style and attributed to Lieven de Key. This is where the ships' cargo used to be weighed.

Waalse Kerk – The Walloon Church is Haarlem's oldest place of worship, and was the chapel of the Beguine convent until 1586.

Amsterdamse Poort – This late 15C gateway, preceded on the town side by two turrets, was also a water-gate commanding the Spaarne.

Haarlem Station – The Netherlands' first railway line, between Amsterdam and Haarlem, was built in 1839 *(see also Introduction, Industrial heritage)*. The elegant Art Nouveau station, dating from 1908, is still in use.

Former Sint-Elisabeths Gasthuis – *Groot Heiligland 47, diagonally opposite the Frans Hals Museum.* This former hospital now houses the following:

Historisch Museum Zuid-Kennemerland ⊘ – This small museum tracing the town's history includes a model of Haarlem in 1822. The story of the town is told by Laurens Janszoon Coster in an audio-visual presentation.

ABC Architectuurcentrum ⊘ – This centre of architecture holds temporary exhibitions on historic and modern architecture.

Spaarnestad Fotoarchief ⊘ – *First floor.* These photo archives, the largest in the Netherlands, contain more than three million press photographs, spanning the period from 1870 right up to the end of the 20C. The temporary exhibitions provide a good insight into the archives' full collection.

Oude hofjes (Almshouses) – Among the numerous charitable institutions which the people of the wealthy town of Haarlem had from the 15C on are the **Proveniershof** of 1592 which has a large doorway opening on Grote Houtstraat, the **Brouwershofje** (1472) in Tuchthuisstraat and the charming **Hofje van Loo** of 1489, visible from Barrevoetestraat.

Kathedrale Basiliek St.-Bavo ⊙ – *Leidsevaart 146*. The sacristy of this very large neo-Gothic basilica, built between 1895 and 1906 by JT Cuypers, son of PJH Cuypers *(see Introduction, Industrial heritage)*, contains the **treasury**: a large collection of liturgical objects, mainly gold and silverware (15C-20C). Note the early 16C robes which come from an old Beguine convent in the town.

OUTSKIRTS

★ **Museum De Cruquius** ⊙ – *7km/4mi to the south-east via the Dreef, north-east of a large bridge on the road to Vijfhuizen. Local map see KEUKENHOF. Illustration: see Introduction, Industrial heritage.* This museum, on the edge of the old Haarlemmermeer, is installed in one of the three pumping stations, which were used between 1849 and 1852 to drain it. The station bears the name of the hydraulic engineer Nicolaas de Kruik, alias **Nicolaas Cruquius** (1678-1754), instigator of a project (1750) to drain the lake. The museum presents interesting material on the technical developments in the history of man's fight against the sea, and on the creation of polders, including a scale model illustrating the theory of a polder and an animated scale model showing the part of the Netherlands which would be flooded by the sea in the absence of dikes and dams.

Visitors may also admire the station's original **steam engine★**, fitted with eight beam engines and eight pumps, in the neo-Gothic engine room. Built in Cornwall, this unique machine was inaugurated in 1849.

Stoomgemaal Halfweg ⊙ – *8km/5mi east via the A 5 towards Amsterdam (Zwanenburg exit)*. This is the world's oldest working steam-driven pumping station, built in 1853. It originally had a capacity of 25 000l of water a second. One of the two steam boilers has been dismantled to show the mechanism of the pumping station.

Spaarndam – *8km/5mi to the north-east via Spaarndamseweg, which becomes Vondelweg, then after a bend take Vergierdeweg on the right.* The houses of this picturesque village – a wonderful place to enjoy some smoked eel and a glass of beer – huddle up along both sides of the dike. This is interspersed with several locks making it possible to link the Spaarne and the IJ. On one of these locks there is a statue of **Hans Brinker**. According to legend the young boy plugged a hole he had discovered in a protecting dike with his finger for a whole night and thus saved the town from being flooded. The origin of this anecdote is a children's book written in 1873 by the American novelist Mary Mapes Dodge, *Hans Brinker or the Silver Skates*. Beyond this small monument is the marina; a path makes it possible to walk alongside the water to reach the Oost- and Westkolk docks to see some beautifully restored houses.

Zandvoort – *11km/7mi in a westerly direction via Leidsevaart. Town plan in the current edition of The Red Guide Benelux.* This is one of the busiest seaside resorts in the Netherlands. A large avenue runs along the dunes which overlook the beach. Since 1976 Zandvoort has had a **casino**. The **Circus Zandvoort** *(Gasthuisplein 5)* is a fine example of modern architecture by Sjoerd Soeters, built in 1991 and including a cinema and a theatre. The famous Zandvoort **racing circuit** lies to the north of the town. The Dutch Formula 1 Grand Prix was held here until 1985, and today it is the Formula 3 racing circuit.

EXCURSIONS

★★★ **Bulb fields** – *See KEUKENHOF, Bulb fields.*

From Bloemendaal aan Zee to Beverwijk – *35km/22mi to the north via Verspronckweg.*

Bloemendaal aan Zee – This is Haarlem's family beach.

Nationaal Park Zuid-Kennemerland ⊙ – *Visitor centre at the south-east entrance to the park in Overveen.* This national park, 3 800ha/9 390acres in area, is situated on the long line of dunes edging the North Sea, and criss-crossed by footpaths and cycling tracks. Large numbers of migratory birds pass through here.

Bloemendaal – Behind the chain of dunes, this is an elegant residential centre where the villas stretch over wooded hills. In the open-air theatre or Openluchttheater *(Hoge Duin en Daalseweg 2)* theatrical performances are given in summer. Nearby is the highest dune in the country, **Het Kopje** (50m/164ft). Further to the north are the ruins of **Kasteel Brederode**, destroyed by the Spanish in 1573.

IJmuiden – IJmuiden, at the far end of the North Sea canal, is famous for its locks, but it is also a seaside resort and ranks as the country's biggest fishing port and the seventh largest in Western Europe. The catch is sold by auction in the huge halls of the busy fish market. Three sea **locks★** make it possible for seagoing ships of up to 80 000 tonnes to sail up to Amsterdam. The north lock, the most recent, was inaugurated on 29 April 1930. It is 400m/1 312ft long, 40m/131ft wide and 15m/49ft deep.

IJmuiden has a very industrial landscape because it has been a major steel and aluminium producing centre since 1924; the blast furnace and steel works, Koninklijke Nederlandsche Hoogovens en Staalfabrieken, are located here. The local beach is therefore somewhat marred by chimney stacks and plumes of smoke.

Beverwijk – Together with Heemskerk, this community forms the residential area of the IJmond, one of the country's leading industrial zones. The **Beverwijkse Bazaar**, a large covered market *(only open at weekends)*, has some 3 000 stalls. The blast furnaces between Beverwijk and the seaside resort **Wijk aan Zee** are hidden from view by a green belt.

HARDERWIJK

Gelderland
Population 39 204
Michelin maps 908 H 4 and 210 S 8

Harderwijk was another of the Hanseatic League ports on the old Zuiderzee. It has retained a few picturesque lanes, the remains of its brick ramparts and its port, where you can eat excellent smoked eel. Situated on the edge of **Veluwemeer** *(see FLEVOLAND)*, Harderwijk has two pleasure boat harbours and a beach, and attracts many tourists. The hinterland, which is part of the Veluwe with great stretches of dunes, forests and heathland, is very attractive and includes several nature reserves. **Carolus Linnaeus** (Carl von Linné, 1707-78), the famous Swedish botanist and pioneer of scientific classification, is closely associated with Harderwijk, having attended the university here. Founded in 1647, this institution was abolished by Napoleon in 1811.

Boat tours ⊙ of the Flevoland polders depart from Harderwijk.

SIGHTS

* **Dolfinarium** ⊙ – This very popular attraction is the largest marine mammal park in Europe, with dolphins, sea lions and walruses, all of which take part in the performances. Other highlights include the touch-tank, Roggenrif; the Laguna, where visitors can wonder at life above and below the surface of the water; the three-dimensional Pirate film; and the exciting SOS Barracuda. Fort Heerewich is a sanctuary for stranded dolphins.

Old town – A number of well-restored Renaissance houses and 18C patrician residences are the heritage of a prosperous past.
Enter the old town through the charming 14C-16C **Vischpoort** (near Strandboulevard) which leads to the old fish market (Vischmarkt).
The Kleine Marktstraat on the right and the Hondegatstraat lead to the main square, Markt.

Markt – In the main square stands the old town hall or **stadhuis**, which dates from 1837. The stadhuis is recognisable by its portico crowned with a pinnacle.
Donkerstraat is a pedestrian street lined with numerous grand 18C mansions with Rococo doorways. Looking up Academiestraat on the left, note the 16C tower, **Linnaeustorentje**, which marks the site of the university's botanical gardens. At the far end of Donkerstraat *(no 4)*, an 18C mansion is now home to the **Veluws Museum** ⊙, which is devoted to the history of the Veluwe (coins, costumes, model ships) and to the old college of Harderwijk. The rostrum of the former Nassau-Veluws Gymnasium illustrates the importance of education in the town's past; the low seat was occupied by examination candidates, while the upper seat was reserved for the rector. Apart from Carolus Linnaeus *(see above)*, both Herman Boerhaave *(see LEIDEN)* and Constantijn Huygens *(see Den HAAG, Excursions)* received doctorates in Harderwijk.
Taking Smeepoortstraat on the right, pass in front of the **Grote Kerk** ⊙, a tall 14C church. At the far end of the street, Bruggestraat returns to Markt.

EXCURSION

Elburg – *20km/12mi to the north-east.*
In the 14C Elburg was a busy mainland port looking out on the Zuiderzee and even belonged to the Hanseatic League. Today this small town encircled by its square walls (14C) and canals retains its medieval character, but now looks out across the polders of Flevoland. The streets are laid out in a regular grid pattern and often fronted by attractive houses as in the row alongside the Beekstraat Canal. The only town gate to remain is the one that faced northwards onto the

sea, the 14C **Vischpoort** ⊙. At the other end of the street the former convent (Agnietenklooster) dates from 1418. The collections of the **Gemeentemuseum** ⊙, or Municipal Museum, are displayed in the Gothic chapel and other conventual buildings. The council chamber and wedding room are also housed here. The 14C **St.-Nicolaaskerk** ⊙ has a massive square tower. In the neighbouring street, Van Kinsbergenstraat, there is a series of interesting houses, including the 15C Arent thoe Boecophuis.

Boat trips ⊙ are organised on the lakes (Veluwemeer and Drontermeer).

HARLINGEN

Fryslân

Population 15 438

Michelin maps 908 H 2 and 210 R 3

Local map see WADDENEILANDEN

Harlingen (Harns in Frisian) was formerly a great whaling port, with its boats sailing as far as Greenland until c 1850. Today this town at the mouth of Harinxma Canal is a centre of shrimp and prawn fishing, and exports dairy products to Britain. It is also the departure point for boats to the islands of Terschelling and Vlieland *(see WADDENEILANDEN).*

Harlingen has a school of fluvial navigation and a college for shipbuilding. The town now also has two pleasure boat harbours.

Each year there are Fishing Days (**Visserijdagen** – *see Calendar of events*) and ring tournaments *(ringrijderij)* as well as a naval review.

SIGHTS

The charm of its old streets makes Harlingen an attractive town. It is pleasant to stroll along the main street, Voorstraat, and along the quays of the two old ports, the Noorderhaven and the Zuiderhaven. There are some interesting 16C to 18C façades.

* **Noorderhaven** – This dock, which has become a marina, is lined with picturesque houses and warehouses. On the north quay there are some lovely façade stones. On the south side stands the 18C **stadhuis**, topped by a low relief depicting the archangel St Michael; the rear of the building giving on to Voorstraat is flanked by a tower with a carillon.

Gemeentemuseum Het Hannemahuis ⊙ – *Voorstraat 56.* Installed in the Hannemahuis, an 18C residence, this museum is devoted to the history of Harlingen and its maritime past. The furniture, the seascapes by Nicolaas Baur, a painter born in Harlingen (1767-1820), engravings, collections of Chinese porcelain, Frisian silverware and scale models of ships, are all beautiful. A room looking on to the garden has a lovely collection of earthenware tiles.

At the far end of the street, near the canal, there is the statue of a schoolboy, Anton Wachter, hero of a series of novels by **Simon Vestdijk** (1898-1971), a famous writer born in Harlingen; his works describe middle-class provincial life.

De Stenen Man (Stone Man) – At the top of a dike to the south of the port there is a monument crowned with two bronze heads, erected in 1774 in memory of the Governor Caspar de Robles who had the dike rebuilt in 1573. Behind the dike is Harlingen's beach, with a beautiful view of the harbour.

HEERLEN

Limburg

Population 95 367

Michelin map 908 I 9 and 211 U 17

This town was the main centre of the Netherlands' coalfields which cross Limburg, continue into Belgium in the Maaseik region, and the Aachen basin in Germany. Mining started in 1896 *(see Introduction, Industrial heritage)* and was abandoned in 1975. However, a number of industries have been established in the region and Heerlen is becoming an important commercial centre. The city possesses a modern quarter built round a vast pedestrian precinct, **Promenade**.

The Romanesque St.-Pancratiuskerk has for a tower the old castle keep built in 1389 by the Duke of Burgundy, Philip the Bold.

Coriovallum – Heerlen, ancient Coriovallum, was a Roman camp on the great route going from Boulogne-sur-Mer to Cologne via Maastricht. In 1C AD another route (Xanthus-Trier) passed this Roman camp. Important Roman baths (2C to 4C) were found in Heerlen.

SIGHT

Thermenmuseum ⊘ – This museum houses the remains of the Roman baths, which can be seen from an elevated walkway. It also contains objects found during excavations: coins, bronze statuettes, pottery. Models, reconstructions and a light show give an impression of the building as it once was.

EXCURSION

* **Kasteel Hoensbroek** ⊘ – *5km/3mi in a northerly direction.* This impressive moated castle in Maasland Renaissance style is made up of a 14C round tower and 17C and 18C living quarters built round three inner courtyards. The bedrooms, workrooms and tower-rooms are open to visitors, as are the kitchen and cellars. The medieval tower affords a fine view of the surrounding area.

Kerkrade – *10km/6mi east of Heerlen.* This border town has been a centre of mining activity since the Middle Ages. Since mining ceased Kerkrade has diversified its industrial sector. Every four years *(see Calendar of events)* an International Music Competiton **(Wereld Muziek Concours)** is held here; it attracts groups of amateur musicians.

* **Industrion** ⊘ – This modern museum traces the development of industry and the way in which it has influenced society. In the past, Limburg was particularly important for its minerals: marl for making cement, clay as a raw material for the ceramics industry (particularly in Maastricht) and of course gravel and coal. Life was tough for workers in these industries, as the reconstruction of a street and a single-room home shows, and a miner describes his work underground. This interactive, hands-on display gives a vivid picture of life in the past, and there is also a working metal factory.

* **Abdij Rolduc** ⊘ – *Go towards Herzogenrath and turn left before the railway.* This former abbey stands to the east of the town high on the valley slope overlooking the River Wurm, which marks the frontier. The abbey buildings have been transformed to serve as a cultural centre, a gymnasium, and a seminary. The **abbey church** (abdijkerk) is surrounded by 17C and 18C buildings. Started in the early 12C, it has been restored several times, in particular in the 19C by Cuypers who replaced the Gothic chancel with a Romanesque one. On the west side, it has a façade with a massive porch tower flanked by two square towers. Inside, level with the first and third bays of the nave, pseudo-transepts have been built in the side aisles. The **capitals*** in the nave are very varied. Note also the bases of certain engaged columns in the side aisles. The heightened apse is trefoil in shape and built above a Romanesque crypt (remarkable capitals).

Den HELDER

Noord-Holland
Population 59 590
Michelin maps 908 F 3 and 210 N 5 – Local map see WADDENEILANDEN

Den Helder owes its importance to its position on the Marsdiep Channel, which separates it from Texel Island. It grew from the small fishing village **Huisduinen**, which expanded eastwards. In 1500 the new town took the name of Den Helder.
In 1811 Napoleon made Den Helder a stronghold. He called it the Gibraltar of the North, and visited it in October of that year. Today it is the **Netherlands' chief naval base**, and also the departure point for boats to Texel. **Navy Days** are held here in July of each year.

SIGHTS

Marinemuseum ⊘ – This museum evokes the history of the Dutch navy from the 17C onwards with a selection of scale models, instruments, photos, uniforms, emblems, maps, paintings, and films. The collection includes a submarine, a Second World War minesweeper and a 19C ram-type vessel, the "Schorpioen". The Maintenance and Technical Department is located on the site of the former Rijkswerf Willemsoord, at walking distance from the museum.

Nationaal Reddingmuseum Dorus Rijkers ⊘ – The national maritime rescue museum includes lifeboats, equipment, prints and models, as well as a ship's bridge and numerous hands-on exhibits which are ideal for children.

Fort Kijkduin ⊘ – This is one of Den Helder's six forts. It has been extensively restored, and now contains a **museum** and a marine aquarium. The tour of the underground passageways and vaults brings the fort's history to life, and the **North Sea Aquarium** in the former bunkers has a particularly interesting glass tunnel. In clear weather, the fort has a fine **view** of the De Razende Bol sand flats, the North Sea and the island of Texel.

TO CALLANTSOOG AND SCHAGEN *27km/17mi to the south*

The road runs along a dike behind which there are several beaches.

Callantsoog – To the south there is a nature reserve, **Het Zwanenwater** ⊘. The reserve stretches over 573 ha/1 415 acres among coastal dunes and the moors round two lakes which attract many birds. The best time to visit is around mid-May during nesting time. The breeding grounds can be seen from a distance, generally among the reeds. Spoonbills *(illustration see WADDENEILANDEN)* arrive from West Africa at the end of February and leave again in July and August.

Schagen – On Thursdays in summer *(see Calendar of events)* a colourful **market** (Westfriese markt) is held in this town where the costumes of West Friesland are worn.

's-HERTOGENBOSCH

DEN BOSCH – Noord-Brabant ℗
Population 128 009
Michelin maps 908 H 6 and 211 Q 12
Plan of the conurbation in the current edition of The Red Guide Benelux

Capital of the Noord-Brabant province, 's-Hertogenbosch is also the seat of a Catholic bishopric. It differs from other towns in the country in its almost Mediterranean character, which can be seen in its noisy carnival *(see Calendar of events)*. An annual art and antiques market is held here at Easter.

HISTORICAL NOTES

The great forests of the area were the hunting grounds of Duke Godefroy of Brabant, hence the name 's-Hertogen Bosch, the Duke's Wood. Today the town is usually called **Den Bosch**, the Woods. But marshland has replaced the forests. 's-Hertogenbosch received its city charter about 1185 from Henry I, Duke of Brabant. The town owes its prosperity to the wool and cloth trades.

A magician's art

's-Hertogenbosch was the birthplace of **Hieronymus Bosch** (c 1450-1516) whose real name was Jeroen van Aeken. The life of this painter is not well known, except that he lived a comfortable life in this town.

A solitary genius, Hieronymus Bosch did not belong to any school. Flemish influence is discernible only in his landscapes with distant perspectives, the naturalistic tone given to the scenes he paints and in the somewhat archaic outline drawings of his characters. But with this visionary painter, reality is placed at the disposal of a prodigious imagination. Objects and animals take strange shapes, men and beasts fill fantastic

Museum Boijmans Van Beuningen, Rotterdam

The Prodigal Son, Hieronymus Bosch

scenes of a dream-like, even nightmarish, universe where it is often difficult to distinguish hell from paradise. Condemning evil, denouncing the ravages of sin was probably the intention of this mysterious artist, who was as passionately interested in alchemy as ethics judging by the presence of numerous symbols in his works.

His early works were mostly simple and sober, then later the compositions became more complex and the subjects more and more strange, as in the most extraordinary of his works, the *Garden of Earthly Delights*, where the painter would have had no cause to envy the Surrealists. This last painting is in the Prado Museum in Madrid, but one can see several fascinating works by Hieronymus Bosch in the Museum Boijmans Van Beuningen in Rotterdam.

's-HERTOGENBOSCH

In 1561 Philip II of Spain, who reigned over the Low Countries, made 's-Hertogen-bosch a bishopric, dependent on the Archbishop of Mechelen. Taken by the Spanish in 1579, the town only surrendered to the Prince of Orange Frederick Henry, son of William the Silent, in 1629 after a long siege. Its 17C fortified wall is still clearly marked by a line of bastions and canals in the old moats. The **Citadel** (1637) currently houses the Provincial Public Records Office.

The modern town – 's-Hertogenbosch, an important road and rail junction, is well situated on the Zuid-Willemsvaart Canal near the Maas. Numerous commercial and industrial establishments have developed here. The weekly cattle market, which takes place on Wednesdays in the **Brabanthallen**, is a particularly important one. There is a horse market on Thursdays.

The town has several recreational areas, including two lakes (the **Zuiderplas** and **Oosterplas**) and the **Prins Hendrik Park** where there is a deer park and another large lake.

The **Provincial House** (Provinciehuis) was built in 1968-71 to the south-east of the town.

★★ SINT-JANSKATHEDRAAL ⊙ *45min*

St John's Cathedral is one of the most beautiful churches in the Netherlands. It was assigned to the Protestant faith from 1629-1810, after which Napoleon returned it to the Catholic faith. In 1985 it was given the status of basilica.
It was built between 1380 and 1530 in the Brabant Gothic style. It has a 13C belfry porch whose **carillon**, placed in 1925, has become famous.
The cathedral *(plan: see Architecture, p 55)* seen from **Parade**, the square to the south, has impressive proportions and a wealth of ornamentation. The fantastic world of grotesque personages astride the **flying buttresses**★ may have inspired Hieronymus Bosch. Other amusing figures decorate the side chapels' gable spandrels. The apse is superb with its numerous radiating chapels round the ambulatory. A squat tower with five lantern turrets rises above the transept crossing.

Sint-Jansmuseum De Bouwloods ⊙ – The site next to the cathedral has been turned into a museum containing some of the original sculptures that have been replaced during successive periods of restoration work. There are also plaster casts, a scale model of the church and a model of a flying buttress.

St.-Janskathedraal

's-HERTOGENBOSCH

Interior – The very luminous interior has a grandiose appearance with its five naves and 150 columns which, in the characteristic style of Brabant Late Gothic, are a cluster of slender pillars without capitals. The last restoration, completed in 1985, has brought to light the vault frescoes, which are very varied. The oldest, in the chancel, date from the first half of the 15C.

Note the canopy, slightly turned and finely worked, above a statue leaning against a pillar of the transept crossing.

The pulpit with its 16C Renaissance low reliefs, the restored 15C stalls and the 17C Renaissance-style organ case by Florens Hocque are worth seeing. The copper baptismal font (1492), in the chapel on the left of the great organ, is a masterpiece by a Maastricht coppersmith.

In 1629 when Frederick Henry, Prince of Orange, seized 's-Hertogenbosch, the canons left the town for Brussels, taking with them the altarpieces which Hieronymus Bosch had painted for the cathedral. The rood screen (1610) is now in the Victoria and Albert Museum in London. The stained-glass windows were all made after 1850.

St Anthony's Chapel in the south arm of the transept has a fine **15C altarpiece**★ by the Antwerp School which came from a local village. The six small scenes of the lower part, depict in rather naive fashion the birth and childhood of Jesus, but the main theme of the altarpiece is the Passion of Christ, with the Calvary in the centre. The figures carved in wood are particularly remarkable for their expressions.

The Chapel of Our Lady, on the right of the great organ, has a miraculous 14C statue of the Virgin.

ADDITIONAL SIGHTS

Markt – This very busy triangular market square is in the heart of the city, where one of the main shopping pedestrian precincts, **Hinthamerstraat**, starts. A general market is held on the square on Wednesdays and Saturdays. In front of the Stadhuis stands a statue (1929) of Hieronymus Bosch.

Stadhuis ⊙ – Dating from the 15C , the town hall was given a classical façade in 1670. Part of its **carillon** was cast by the Hemony brothers. On the ground floor, the Trouwkamer (marriage room) has lovely Cordoba leather hangings. The Gothic cellar has been transformed into a café and restaurant.

De Moriaan – This building, which houses the tourist information centre (VVV), has, to the north of the Markt, a brick façade with a 13C crow-stepped gable.

* **Noordbrabants Museum** ⊙ – The North Brabant Museum is set up in the old governor's mansion (1768-1769, Pieter de Swart) and two new wings built by Wim Quist.
The museum sheds light on various aspects of the history, art and culture of the North Brabant province, focusing on several themes: the medieval town, the guilds, the Eighty Years' War, the Church, popular art, and archaeology. The highly interesting collection features objects excavated from various sites, including an **amber statue of Bacchus** (c AD 200). The painting collection includes the admirable *Study of a Brabant Peasant* by Van Gogh and *The Four Seasons* by David Teniers the Younger. One can also see sculptures, costumes and ornamental *objets d'art* (guild silverware and rustic jewellery).
The museum also holds temporary exhibitions on contemporary art.

Museum Slager ⊙ – This houses works by a family of painters, from Petrus Marinus Slager (1841-1912) to Tom Slager, born in 1918.

Museum Het Kruithuis ⊙ – This hexagonal brick edifice, dating from 1617-1621, is located in the northern part of town. It is built around a courtyard and was once circled by a moat. Until 1742 it was used as a powder magazine. Today the rooms on the ground floor are the setting for exhibitions on design and contemporary art. The first floor presents collections of modern jewellery and ceramics, from 1950 up to the present day.

Boat trip on the Binnendieze ⊙ – A trip along this river, which in places flows under the houses and streets, is a pleasant introduction to the different facets of the city.

EXCURSIONS

Autotron Rosmalen ⊙ – *6km/4mi north-east by N 50.*
This automobile theme park has a wide variety of attractions for young and old. The collection on the first floor of the **AutoDome**★ automobile museum retraces over 115 years of motor car history. On display are a replica of the petrol-powered three-wheeler car designed by Benz in 1885; a Ford Model T (1909); American-built limousines (1940s); a 1947 Tatra 600 which was ahead of its time; a 1958 Daf; an Austin Mini and a Fiat 500 from the 60s-70s; and more. The ground floor features the magnificent products of the Dutch manufacturer Spijker (1899-1925); a number of dream cars and limousines; and a selection of sports and racing cars. In the **Philips Automotive On The Road Experience** visitors can acquaint themselves with the latest developments in the field of car lighting.
In the theme park itself, children can obtain their own "driving licence" and drive a Ferrari or a 4x4 jeep; there is also an old-jalopy ride and a go-carting track.

Heeswijk-Dinther – *14km/8mi to the south-east via Maastrichtseweg.* North-west of this village stands the 14C **Kasteel Heeswijk** ⊙, set in the woods and surrounded by moats. It contains beautifully furnished rooms and interesting *objets d'art.*
At Heeswijk, a farmhouse museum, **Meierijsche Museumboerderij** ⊙ *(at Meerstraat 28)* recreates the life of Brabant peasants in 1900.

Kasteel Ammersoyen ⊙ – *In Ammerzoden. 11 km/7mi to the north. Leave 's-Hertogenbosch via Orthenseweg.* This imposing 14C moated castle is built up in a square around an inner courtyard with vast towers in each of the four corners. Formerly (1876-1945) a convent of the Poor Clares, part of the building is now the town hall. The great hall, the ladies' apartments and the tower rooms are all open to the public.

Zaltbommel – *15km/9mi to the north. Leave 's-Hertogenbosch via Orthenseweg.* The walls of this old stronghold beside the Waal have largely been preserved. On Markt, the **stadhuis** dates from 1763. At no 18 Boschstraat, next to a chemist's shop, there is a Renaissance house with caryatids. This, the main street, leads to the 14C water gate, **Waterpoort**.

In Nonnenstraat, the **Huis van Maarten van Rossum** ⊙ has been converted into a regional museum, the Maarten van Rossummuseum. It has a picturesque façade (c 1535), corner turrets and crenellations. Inside is a varied collection of historical objects.

At the far end of Nieuwstraat is the 14C **Grote- of St.-Maartenskerk**, abundantly decorated, where the imposing 15C belfry porch is 63m/207ft high.

Heusden – *19km/12mi to the north-west via Vlijmenseweg.*
On the banks of the Maas, which here becomes the Bergse Maas, Heusden is an old stronghold fortified in 1581. Inside its ramparts, which have been transformed Into an esplanade, it has some fine façades. Worth seeing is no 4 Hoogstraat (main street), a 17C house with very elaborate scrolls.

The **stadhuis**, rebuilt in 1956, has an automatic **carillon** and a jack-o' the-clock.

The **Vismarkt** (fish market) near the dock is surrounded by 17C houses. A covered market (Visbank) of 1796 still stands.

Heusden has three **post mills**.

Drunen, Waalwijk and De Efteling – *25km/16mi to the west. Leave 's-Hertogenbosch by Vlijmenseweg.*

Drunen – To the south of the locality stretch the **Drunen dunes**, part of a large area of drifting sand.

The **Land van Ooit** ⊙ (Land of Yesteryear) amusement park has been designed with children in mind. It features giants, knights and maidens who speak their own language and have their own currency. Storytelling sessions, tournaments, a puppet theatre and a fountain garden make for an exciting visit.

Waalwijk – Main centre of the Netherlands' leather and shoe industry, Waalwijk has an interesting leather and shoe museum, the **Nederlands Leder- en Schoenenmuseum** ⊙. An important collection of shoes from all over the world; a reconstruction of a c 1930 shoe factory and a 1870 tannery. Other display cases show the evolution of the European shoe.

★★ **De Efteling** ⊙ – *South of Kaatsheuvel.*
The Efteling theme park has something for everyone, children and adults alike: a world of fairy tales and elves in the Fairy Tale Wood (Sprookjesbos), Dream Flight (Droomvlucht), Fairy Tale Show (Sprookjesshow) and the House of the Five Senses (Huis van de Vijf Zintuigen); excitement in Vogel Rok, Pegasus, Python, Piraña and the Half Moon; spine-chilling encounters in Villa Volta and the Haunted Castle (Spookslot); and a voyage to exotic places in Fata Morgana and Carnival Festival. Other highlights include a small steam train, a carrousel, gondolas, a hotel and a golf course.

HILVERSUM

Noord-Holland
Population 82 308
Michelin maps 908 G 5 and 211 Q 9
Town plan in the current edition of The Red Guide Benelux

Hilversum in the picturesque moors and woods of the Gooi is, in a way, a large residential suburb of Amsterdam: it is an extensive residential area with villas scattered among the trees. Because Hilversum is relatively high, it has long been the country's main centre of broadcasting.

WM Dudok (1884-1974), the Netherlands' main exponent of Cubic Expressionist architecture, worked for Hilversum council from 1915 onwards. His creations included the town hall, the municipal sports ground, various residential areas and some 20 schools.

★ **Raadhuis** – *To the north of town. Illustration: see Architecture, p 59.* Built between 1927 and 1931, the town hall is the work of **WM Dudok** and is considered to be his *magnum opus*. For the most part it is a harmonious juxtaposition of cubic masses in which the different volumes create a play of horizontal and vertical lines and give the building a different appearance from every side. The tall clock tower is reflected in a lake on the south side. The bare walls are of a soft-yellow tinted brick. The horizontal lines of the brickwork are emphasised by putting the mortar bed of the bed joints further back from the brick face, producing an effect of rows of horizontal stripes. Inside all is functional and rational. The furniture, clocks, lighting, even the burgomaster's gavel were designed by Dudok. The **Dudok Centrum** in the basement documents Dudok's life and work.

Goois Museum ⊙ – *Kerkbrink 6.* This museum in the old town hall uses archaeological finds, objects and photographs to chronicle the history of Hilversum and the Gooi region. It also has a collection of Loosdrecht porcelain.

★THE GOOI

Round tour of 62km/39mi – allow one day.

Leave Hilversum via Soestdijkerstraatweg.

Soestdijk – To the north of town is the Royal Palace, **Koninklijk Paleis**, residence of the Queen Mother (Princess Juliana). This former hunting lodge was used in the summer by the Dutch sovereigns.

Baarn – A pleasant, leafy residential area. **Kasteel Groeneveld** ⊘ (c 1710) is now home to the nature conservation centre, Nationaal centrum voor Bos, Natuur en Landschap. The landscaped park is also open to visitors.
Near Laren lies the **Gooi**. This densely wooded region of Noord-Holland is in fact an immense residential suburb with many substantial houses tucked away in lovely parks where Amsterdamers have chosen to live. There are still several tracts of heathland in the vicinity.

Laren – A picturesque village, Laren is a painter's haven. At the end of the 19C the **Laren School** gathered together several painters under the guidance of Neuhuys and Anton Mauve. Several of the artists were also members of The Hague School.
In the centre of the village, around the villa of the American painter William Henry Singer (1868-1943), stands the **Singer Museum** ⊘, built in 1956 by Singer's widow. The museum holds temporary exhibitions on modern art as well as showing its permanent collection on a rotational basis. This collection includes works by Singer himself, 19C and 20C French painters, the Amsterdam and Hague Schools (Maris, Bosboom and Isaac Israëls), the Laren School and Modernists. There is also a sculpture garden.

Blaricum – Lovely residential town in the heart of the Gooi.

Huizen – Since the closing of the Zuiderzee, this town has become industrialised and has a large marina.

★ **Naarden** – *See NAARDEN.*

Muiden – Near this small harbour used frequently by pleasure boats is a castle, the **Muiderslot**★ ⊘, standing on the banks of the IJmeer and at the mouth of the Vecht. It is an old brick fortress with stout corner towers, surrounded by a moat, and its massive silhouette is visible from afar. Built c 1204 to defend the mouth

The Muiderslot

of the Vecht, it was rebuilt by Floris V, Count of Holland. He was assassinated here in 1296 by the nobles, who felt he granted too many privileges to the common people. As of 1621 the castle became the meeting place for the **Muiderkring** (Muiden Circle), an intellectual and literary circle which gathered around the then owner of the premises, the historian and poet **PC Hooft** (1581-1647). The distinguished participants included the jurist Hugo Grotius, the poets Joost van den Vondel and Constantijn Huygens and the writer Maria Tesselschede. When Hooft died the castle fell into neglect but today the rooms have been refurbished to show their former 17C glory.

Bussum – An important residential town on the edge of the Gooi.

On leaving Bussum, turn right towards 's-Graveland.

's-Graveland – In the vicinity of this town, there are a number of fine manor houses. **Trompenburg** *(not open to the public)* is probably the most elegant with its gracious silhouette reflected in the waters of the lake. Built by Admiral Cornelis Tromp, it consists of a rectangular house and a domed pavilion.

Return to Hilversum via ④ on the town plan.

A new concept in travel planning.
When you want to calculate a trip distance or visualise a detailed itinerary;
when you need information on hotels,
restaurants or campsites, consult Michelin on the Internet.
Visit our web site to discover our full range of services for travellers:
www.michelin-travel.com

HINDELOOPEN

Fryslân

Michelin maps 908 H 3 and 210 R 5 – Local map see SNEEK

This small town (Frisian name: Hylpen), on the banks of the IJsselmeer, is one of the eleven towns of Friesland. It was once very prosperous due to its trade with Norway and was a member of the Hanseatic League. The main road bypasses Hindeloopen which is a quiet and peaceful town with lanes winding between houses and gardens, its footbridges spanning small canals; the presence of many pleasure boats in summer tends to disturb the calm.

Furniture and costumes – Since the 18C Hindeloopen has specialised in hand-painted furniture, where red and dark green prevail. The colours as well as the motifs and shapes are inspired by Scandinavian styles seen by sailors during their long journeys. Hindeloopen was a close-knit community, and each drawing was symbolic. The cotton fabrics used in the costumes came from the Far East. Large foliage motifs in reds, greens or blues on a white background were particularly popular *(see Introduction, Traditions and Folklore).*

Hindeloopen - Dike and clock tower

* **Museum Hidde Nijland Stichting** ⊘ – Located near the church, this museum (formerly the town hall [1683]) captivates by its reconstructed interiors, collections of fine traditional costumes, the series of tiles or earthenware pictures and its images of the great sailing ships of the past.

Het Eerste Friese Schaatsmuseum ⊘ – *Kleine Weide 1-3.* The First Frisian Skating Museum is a treasure trove for lovers of this sport; it includes skates, sledges, medals, photos, trophies and a detailed display on the famous Elfestedentocht, or Eleven Towns Race *(see LEEUWARDEN).*

Nationaal Park De HOGE VELUWE★★★

Gelderland
Michelin maps 408 I 5 and 211 U10

The Hoge Veluwe National Park, which covers 5 500ha/13 585 acres, is the Netherlands' largest nature reserve. It contains the famous Kröller-Müller Museum, the St.-Hubertus hunting lodge, the Museonder underground museum, and countless sculptures and monuments. The park is a unique combination of nature and culture.

★★★ PARK ⊘ *Half a day*

History – This site was purchased in 1914 by an industrialist couple, Mr and Mrs Kröller-Müller, as a country residence. Mr Kröller wanted a place to hunt, and his wife wanted a culture park. The St-Hubertus hunting lodge was designed by **HP Berlage,** who had already designed office buildings for the couple, and was built between 1914 and 1920. Under Mrs Kröller-Müller's influence, sculptures and monuments were added to the northern part of the park. In 1938, the couple decided to donate the site and their valuable art collection to the state, on condition that the state built a museum, the Kröller-Müller Museum. These two great patrons of the arts lived in the park until they died, and were buried on the Franse Berg, the area of high dunes behind the museum.

Landscapes – A desolate landscape of heathlands, grass, sand dunes and lakes is interspersed with clusters of tall oak and beech trees, pine and birch woods. These are the many faces of the Hoge Veluwe, and it is worth a visit at any time of year. The rhododendrons flower in May and June, while in August there are great expanses of purple heather. In autumn, the deciduous trees are brilliantly coloured, and the park looks magical under a coating of snow.

Fauna – The park has a rich wildlife ranging from red deer, moufflons, wild boar and roe deer to a wide variety of birdlife. Mid-September to mid-October, during the **rutting season** of the red deer, is a particularly interesting time to visit. The best time to observe the animals is in the late afternoon when they are searching for food, in winter and spring (ie until the end of May).

A DAY IN THE HOGE VELUWE

● The park is served by **public transport** from Arnhem, Ede and Apeldoorn. Bus route 12 (from Arnhem) runs through the park from late March to late October; the driver provides a commentary.

● The park has three **entrances**, at Otterlo, Hoenderloo and Schaarsbergen.

● There are large car parks at the three entrances, the Kröller-Müller Museum, the St.-Hubertus hunting lodge and the visitor centre. The maximum speed in the park is 50kph/30mph. Only the surfaced roads (marked in white on the plan) may be used by cars.

● The **white bicycles** at the entrances to the park, the Kröller-Müller Museum and the visitor centre may be used free of charge and ridden anywhere on the paths. They should be returned to the place where they were issued at the end of the day.

● There are 42km/26mi of **signposted cycle paths**, including three routes (10, 18 and 26km/6, 11 and 16mi). Brochures detailing routes taking in most of the park's monuments and works of art are on sale in the visitor centre.

● Apart from certain areas reserved for game, visitors are free to walk anywhere in the park, and walking tours of various lengths are marked by **wooden poles** with coloured tops. Information and maps are available in the visitor centre.

● The park also has **five game observatories**. The most accessible of these are De Klep and the Vogelvijvers (bird lakes). The visitor centre has information on where and when to see specific animals.

● **Restaurants and toilets** are located at the visitor centre, the Kröller-Müller Museum and at the Schaarsbergen entrance. **Picnicking** is allowed anywhere, and there is a picnic area at the visitor centre. Cooking and fires are not allowed.

● **Dogs** and other animals are not allowed inside the buildings, and must be kept on a lead in the park.

● **Camping** in the park is permitted only on the camp site at the Hoenderloo entrance. There are also various camp sites outside the park.

● Tickets on sale at the entrances to the park provide entry to all sights except the Kröller-Müller Museum, entrance to which costs an extra 7fl.

Visitor Centre ⊘ – This snail-shaped building is linked to the Museonder, and offers detailed information about the park and its sights and recreation facilities. It also sells details of cycling and walking paths, and has an excellent display, including films, on the history, landscapes, flora and fauna of the park. The centre makes an ideal starting point for a visit to the park.

★★★ KRÖLLER-MÜLLER MUSEUM ⊘ *3hr*

The Kröller-Müller Museum was built to the designs of **Henry van de Velde** and is named after its founder, Helene Kröller-Müller. The museum was inaugurated in 1938 and then in 1961 a Sculpture Garden was created. In 1977 **Wim Quist** was commissioned to build a new wing. The museum houses an important collection of paintings, sculptures and drawings, including works by Van Gogh.

To the right of the main entrance is the **Beeldenzaal** or sculpture room, displaying *The Rider and Horse* by Marini (1952) and works by Zadkine. Early 20C paintings are hung in the six rooms that follow. There are a number of canvases by **Mondrian** showing his diversity of style. The paintings by **Van der Leck** are followed by works of the **Constructivists** (Strzeminski, Schlemmer) and **Futurists** (Ballà, Severini and Boccioni). **Cubism** is represented by Picasso, Braque, Gris and Léger (*Soldiers Playing Cards*, 1917). Another room is dedicated to the work of **Charley Toorop**. One of the most important works in this section is *The Beginning of the World*, a bronze sculpture (1924) by Brancusi, regarded as marking the beginning of modern sculpture. Further on there are works by James Ensor and Pointillist canvases by Seurat (*Le Chahut*), Van Rijsselberghe and Signac.

A selection of works by **Van Gogh** is arranged in chronological order from right to left around a patio. Looking at them in this order brings out the contrast between the sombre early works (*The Potato Eaters, Weavers*), and the later, more brightly coloured and dynamic paintings. The latter include *The Olive Grove, Road with Cypress and Star, Evening Café, The Bridge at Arles, Old Man in Sorrow, The Good Samaritan* (after Delacroix) and superb portraits such as *Postman Roulin, L'Arlésienne* (after a drawing by his friend Gauguin), and the *Self-Portrait*. There are also works of 1887 like the *Faded Sunflowers*, which was Mrs Kröller-Müller's first acquisition, and *Still-life with Plaster Statue*.

Nationaal Park De HOGE VELUWE

APELDOORN

Jachthuis
★ St.-Hubertus

Hoenderloo

N 304

Otterlose
Monument

Zand

Hertenbos

Bezoekerscentrum
Museonder ★

Landschappentuin
Beeldenbos

Deelense
Veld

★★★ KRÖLLER-MÜLLER
MUSEUM

Vogelvijvers

Plijmen

Deelense Zand

Wildbaan

Otterlo

Houtkamp weg

Wildbaanweg

Oud-
Reemster
Zand

Oud-
Veld

Reemster

Oud-
Reemst

Kemperberg

Rijzenburg

KNOOPPUNT
GRIJSOORD

A 12-A 50

Schaarsbergen

N 224

A 12

N 310

N 311

UTRECHT   ARNHEM   'S-HERTOGENBOSCH   ARNHEM

NATIONAAL PARK
DE HOGE VELUWE

Information	
Birds	
Game observation hide	
Cycling track	
Waymarked trail	
Campsite	
Restaurant	
Car park	
One way	
Quicksand	
Heathland	
Woodland	

Houtkamp weg

★★★ KRÖLLER-MÜLLER
MUSEUM

Rietveld paviljoen

F

B

Beeldentuin ★

E

C   D

Jardin
d'Email

Wildbaanweg

G

★ Beeldenpark

In the rooms behind the patio, along with **French Impressionists** (Cézanne, Renoir and Monet), there are landscapes by Jongkind, Millet and Corot. **Symbolism** is represented by the work of artists such as Jan Toorop and Johannes Thorn Prikker. Other 19C paintings include works by Israëls and Breitner. Then come the **Dutch painters** of the Golden Age (Avercamp, Van Goyen and Van de Velde the Younger) and masters of the 16C such as Bruyn the Elder (*Portrait of a Woman with a Carnation*, with a vanitas on the reverse side), a *Venus and Cupid* (1525) by Hans Baldung Grien and a *Venus and Cupid as a Honey Thief* by Cranach. There are also works from 15C Italy and France.

Also on display are Greek ceramics, Chinese and Japanese porcelain, Mexican and African sculpture and 20C ceramics (Csàsky).

The **new wing** is used for displaying the collection of **contemporary sculpture** (Minimal Art, Zero Group and Arte Povera) in the form of temporary exhibitions. Giacometti's *Striding Man* (1960) is in the passage leading to one of the rooms.

★★ **Sculpture garden and sculpture park** ⊙ – *Go through the museum to reach the sculpture garden.* This pleasant tree-shaded garden is the setting for some 20 sculptures by contemporary artists.

On leaving the museum note the floating polyester sculpture by Marta Pan (1961) (B), *Reclining Niobe* by Permeke (1951) (C), *The Great Penelope* by Bourdelle (1912) (D) and *The Air* by Maillol (1939) (E). Further on is a **pavilion** designed by Rietveld in 1953. The park contains many other works, including Dubuffet's **Jardin d'émail** (1975), a white construction so large that it is possible to walk around inside it; *Concetto Spaziale Nature*, five spheres by Lucio Fontana (1965) (F); the gigantic *Trowel* (1971) by Claes Oldenburg, *Igloo* by Mario Mertz and *Construction of 56 Barrels* by Christo. Finally, there is a very fine example of land art: Spin Out by Richard Serra (G), consisting of three steel discs in the hollow of a dune.

The **sculpture park**, on the steep slope of the Franse Berg, has another 10 sculptures.

Sculpture wood – *Enter via the road to the visitor centre.* This small site is dotted with contemporary sculptures: *Herbaceous Border* (1987) by F Morellet, the surprising *Otterlo Beech Tree* (1988) by Penone, André Volten's quadruple composition *1: 4 = 1 x 4* (1986) and *One* (1988), a bronze by Serra.

K-Piece, by Mark di Suvero

ADDITIONAL SIGHTS

★ **Museonder** ⊙ – The "museum underneath" is located underground next to the visitor centre, and is a very original display of the world beneath the surface of the soil. It includes the underground lives of plants and animals, the role of ground water, the effects of climatic change on the soil and the history of the Veluwe landscape, in a fascinating presentation which uses a wide variety of media.

Landschappentuin – This garden is actually a miniature version of the whole park, showing the many different landscapes of the Hoge Veluwe within the space of a short walk. There is a hut made of turf at the beginning of the route.

★ **Jachthuis St.-Hubertus** ⊙ – This hunting lodge is actually a large castle, the plan of which is in the shape of a pair of antlers. It was built by Berlage between 1914 and 1920, and is regarded as one of his masterpieces. Both the building, with its 31m/102ft tower, and the two lakes and surrounding gardens are highly geometric. The interior and furnishings were also designed by Berlage. As in the rest of the building, every shape, colour and detail has symbolic significance, referring to the legend of St Hubert, the patron saint of hunters. This ingenious aspect of the building is described in detail on the tour *(free; booking at visitor centre compulsory)*. Helene Kröller-Müller died here in 1939, and her husband two years later. Today, the hunting lodge is used as a residence for guests of the government.

EXCURSION

Otterlo – *1km/0.5mi from the west entrance to Hoge Veluwe National Park*. Otterlo is the home of the **Nederlands Tegelmuseum** ⊙, or Dutch Tile Museum, which gives a history of Dutch wall and floor tiles from 1510 to the present day. Tile production was introduced to the northern Netherlands from Italy and Antwerp in the early 16C, and was initially influenced by Italian earthenware and Chinese porcelain. Around 1620, multicoloured patterns were replaced by the typical blue, followed in the 18C by Rotterdam purple. Dutch tiles were highly popular at this time and were exported all over the world. Popular subjects included landscapes, children playing, artisans, flowers, animals and Bible scenes. The latter were often found on fireplaces, where they were used as illustrations when telling stories. After a steep decline in tile production in the 19C, there was a revival around 1900 with the advent of Art Nouveau. Large colourful tableaux were all the rage at that time.

HOORN★

Noord-Holland
Population 63 405
Michelin maps 908 G 4 and 210 P 7
Plan of the conurbation in the current edition of The Red Guide Benelux

On the banks of the IJsselmeer, Hoorn is one of the most typical of the old Zuiderzee ports. The town played a part in the foundation of the East India Company and today remains a thriving commercial centre. Hoorn has a busy marina and, with its period buildings and winding streets, is a pleasant place for visitors to walk round.
An old-fashioned **steam tram** ⊙ runs from Hoorn to Medemblik where the journey can be continued by boat to Enkhuizen *(further information is available from the tourist information office [VVV])*.

HISTORICAL NOTES

A town was founded c 1300 on the shores of the natural haven and it grew rapidly to become the main settlement of Western Friesland. Overseas trade and fishing brought great prosperity to Hoorn.
It was in Hoorn that the first large herring-net was made in 1416, marking the beginning of what was to become a flourishing industry.
To the north of the town centre, gardens mark the course of the moats of the early 16C fortifications.
In October 1573 the famous naval engagement, the Battle of the Zuiderzee, took place just outside the harbour; the combined fleets of the towns of Hoorn, Enkhuizen, Edam and Monikendam – all towns already in the hands of the Sea Beggars – defeated the Spanish under Admiral **Bossu**. However Hoorn's hour of glory came in the 17C when it served as the administrative and commercial centre of all Holland north of Amsterdam.
The town had one of the six "chambers" which comprised the federal organisation of the Dutch East India Company *(see Introduction, Historical table and notes)*.
In 1616 **Willem Schouten** (1580-1625) was the first to round the southernmost tip of South America, 96 years after Magellan had discovered the Magellan Strait. Schouten named the southernmost rocky headland of Tierra del Fuego Cape Horn, after his native town.
Jan Pieterszoon Coen (1587-1629), also a native of Hoorn, was the enterprising Governor General of the Dutch East Indies from 1617 to 1623 and again from 1627 to his death in 1629. He founded Batavia, today Jakarta, and is generally considered to be the founder of the Dutch commercial empire in the Dutch East Indies (Indonesia).
Like the rest of the country Hoorn declined in the 18C, and it was two centuries later before it was to experience a recovery.

★ OLD TOWN 3hr

This was the original site of Hoorn and today a succession of old façades, many with lovely sculptured stones with a seafaring theme, can still be seen.

Achterstraat – The **Doelengebouw** (target building) at no 2 was formerly used for practice by the town's company of archers. The scene above the doorway (1615) shows the martyrdom of St Sebastian, the patron saint of archers.

Onder de Boompjes – On the corner of this canal and Pakhuisstraat an old storehouse of 1606 is decorated with a sculptured **façade stone** depicting two sailing ships of the United East India Company. To protect spices and other costly goods from enemy attack, these storehouses were usually located on the far side of town from the harbour.

Korte Achterstraat – At no 4 in this street is the old orphanage or **Weeshuis** (1620). A commemorative plaque recalls that Admiral Bossu was imprisoned in Hoorn for three years after his naval defeat *(see above)*.

Nieuwstraat – In this shopping street stands the old **stadhuis** with its double crow-stepped gabled façade (1613).
The house at **no 17** has a façade with Poseidon and his wife Amphitrite accompanied by dolphins; along with Poseidon's trident, these animals symbolised free trade and sea power.

Kerkplein – At no 39 opposite a church (secularised) is **De Boterhal** (the butter market), formerly St John's almshouse (St-Jans Gasthuis). The building, which dates from 1563, is a fine residence with a gable decorated with sculptures.

Kerkstraat – At no 1 there is an attractive 1660 façade.

★ **Rode Steen** – This picturesque square is overlooked by the Westfries Museum and by the Waag, or weigh-house. The name Rode Steen, red stone, refers to the blood that was shed here during public executions. In the centre stands a 19C statue of Jan Pieterszoon Coen *(see above)*.
The house at no 2 has a façade stone depicting a blacksmith, hence its name: *In Dyser Man* (The Iron Man).

Westfries Museum ⊙ – The West Friesland Museum is an elegant Baroque edifice dating from 1632. Its tall **façade**★ is imposing with its large windows, very colourful coats of arms (House of Orange and West Friesland) and cornices topped by lions bearing the coats of arms of seven local towns: Alkmaar, Edam,

Westfries Museum

J. P. Lescourret/EXPLORER

Enkhuizen, Hoorn, Medemblik, Monnickendam and Purmerend. It was the seat of the States' College consisting of delegates from seven important towns, which governed West Friesland and the Noorderkwartier (Northern Quarter). In the entrance note a lovely gate (1729).

Worthy of note on the ground floor are the ceiling in the Louis XVI drawing room, and the fine hall (Grote Voorzaal) decorated with a lovely chimney and group portraits of marksmen's guilds. The beams are supported by corbels carved with coats of arms of the region's towns. On the upper floors, the rooms decorated with lovely furniture and *objets d'art* reproduce the refined interiors of the 17C and 18C. The Admiralty Room contains scale models and weaponry and a portrait of Admiral Bossu. Also the painting by Hendrik Corneliszoon Vroom **View of Hoorn**★ (1622) is interesting; remarkably the view of the old harbour depicted in this painting shows that today the harbour has remained almost intact. The smell of cloves that still lingers in the East India Company Room (VOC-zaal) evokes the times when the large merchant ships sailed to the East. The attic still contains two cells dating from the time of the French occupation, when the building served as a court of law. In the basement there is an exhibition of finds from local excavation sites.

Waag – Probably the work of Hendrick de Keyser, the weigh-house is a fine 1609 building in blue stone, which today houses a restaurant. In a niche, a unicorn (the symbol of the town) holds a shield depicting a cornucopia.

Grote Oost - In this street the houses near the square are very steeply inclined and topped with imposing sculptured balustrades in the Rococo style.

Number 43, the imposing **Foreestenhuis**, is named after Nanning van Foreest, one of the town's best-known governors. The elegant Louis XIV-style façade dates from 1724, and the balcony is supported by Atlas figures.

Oosterkerk – This recently restored church was founded in 1453; a Renaissance façade, added in 1616, is topped with a charming wooden pinnacle. The church is now used mainly as a venue for cultural events.

When visiting Hoorn, don't forget to sample its wonderful smoked eel. Drop in on D Wormsbecher en Zoon's shop in Wildebrugsteeg and sample this delicacy at the counter or on the terrace.

Bossuhuizen – *Slapershaven 1-2*. The frontage of these houses has a frieze in relief depicting the sea battle of 1573, in which Admiral Bossu was defeated. The left façade is very typical of the old shops on the quayside, with a ground floor topped by tall narrow windows separated by carved wood pilasters.

Oude Doelenkade – On the picturesque **Binnenhaven**★ quay, or inner harbour, there is a row of old warehouses; note nos 21 and 17-19 with their façade stones depicting navigational scenes. In fine weather the harbour is often busy with elegant sailing ships and crowds of onlookers.

★ **Veermanskade** – This quay is lined with a series of fine restored houses. Most of them are old merchants' residences, some with the typical Hoorn façade, with carved wood pilasters. Others have lovely façade stones and are topped by crow-stepped or bell gables.

Note the birthplace of the navigator **Willem Bontekoe** (1587-1630); the façade displays a spotted cow (*koe*: cow; *bonte*: spotted).

Willem Ysbrantszoon Bontekoe – the hero of Hoorn

Willem Bontekoe (1587-1657) published his *Journael* in 1646. It was a great success, and was translated into a number of other languages. The book describes his adventures as the master of a United East India Company vessel from 1618 to 1625. The first part, describing his journey from Hoorn to Batavia (now Jakarta), became particularly famous. The voyage was a nightmare for the crew of 206; the mainmast broke not long after they set sail, there was an epidemic of scurvy on board, and the ship finally blew up not far from Batavia. Bontekoe describes how he and 54 other crew members survived this disaster and finally reached their destination.

The second part of Bontekoe's book is devoted to his years of sailing in Asian waters and fighting the Portuguese and Chinese, and the third section recounts his stay in Madagascar.

Bontekoe remains a source of inspiration even in the 20C: he was the subject of Johan Fabricius' 1924 bestseller, *De scheepsjongens van Bontekoe* (Bontekoe's Cabin Boys), though his role is not the heroic one portrayed in his own journal.

Hoofdtoren – Built in 1532 to keep watch over the port's main (*hoofd*) entrance; in 1651 it was topped by a wooden pinnacle. On the other side of the tower a sculpture depicts a unicorn, the symbol of the town. Since 1968 a trio of ship's boys – bronze sculpture by Jan van Druten – contemplate the port from the foot of the tower. They are the heroes of a children's novel by Johan Fabricius dedicated to Bontekoe.

Bierkade – This is the quay where beer brought by ship from Hamburg and Bremen was unloaded. Nos 10 and 13 have interesting façades.

At no 4, two cheese warehouses from 1903 now house the **Museum van de Twintigste Eeuw** ⊙, or Museum of the Twentieth Century. This gives an overview of the rapid pace of technological change and the many discoveries made during the past hundred years.

The numbers ① – ② etc indicate the main routes into and out of town.
They are the same on town plans and on Michelin Maps.

HULST

Zeeland

Population 19 568

Michelin maps 908 B D 8 and 211 J 15

At the frontier with Belgium, Hulst is a small town with cheerful, colourful houses and streets paved with pink brick. It is an old fortified town which was built in accordance with the Old Dutch system (see Introduction, The arts).

Hulst was once the capital of the Vier Ambachten, or Four Shires, comprising Hulst, Axel, Assenede and Boechout (these last two towns became Belgian in 1830). The 17C ramparts with their nine **bastions** and five ravelins, or triangular outworks, have been preserved. They are planted with fine trees and are still encircled by moats.

Reynard's city – The surroundings of Hulst are evoked in the Dutch version of the 13C epic Van den vos Reinaerde (Reynard the Fox). Near Gentsepoort is a monument (Reinaertmonument) in honour of Reynard.

SIGHTS

Grote Markt – The **stadhuis**, with a perron flanked by a square tower, dates from the 16C. The **St-Willibrordusbasiliek** is a fine building in the Brabant Gothic style. Its modern tower has an excellent carillon. For more than a century (1807-1931), the church was used by both Catholics and Protestants: the chancel and ambulatory being reserved for the former, the nave for the latter.

Keldermanspoort – This 16C gateway and water-gate were uncovered during excavations in 1952. The latter gave access to a military port.

The top of the nearby ramparts affords a view of the crow-stepped gable and octagonal turret of the **hostel** which belonged to Dunes Abbey, near Koksijde in Belgium. This hostel houses the **Streekmuseum De Vier Ambachten** ⊙, or Four Shires Local History Museum.

EXCURSION

Terneuzen – 24km/15mi to the north-west. This port at the mouth of the Scheldt commands the entrance to the Gent-Terneuzen canal. There are three **locks**, the largest being 290m/951ft long and 40m/131ft wide.

Admission times and charges for the sights described are listed at the end of the guide. Every sight for which there are times and charges is identified by the symbol ⊙ in the Sights section of the guide.

HUNEBEDDEN*

Drenthe and Groningen

Michelin maps 908 K 2, 3, L 2, 3 and 210 Y 4, Z 4, 5, 6, AA 5, 6

A hunebed is a prehistoric funerary monument, with a side entrance usually orientated to the south.

Megaliths of this type are found in the Netherlands, concentrated in the Drenthe where 53 have been registered and numbered. Only one is not included, that of Noordlaren which is in the province of Groningen.

Imposing dimensions – The smallest hunebedden are not less than 7m/23ft long and a length of 25m/82ft is not unusual. The biggest is near Borger: the slabs which form it weigh more than 20 tonnes. The megaliths used to build hunebedden are erratic boulders from the **Hondsrug** (Dog's back), an end moraine deposited by a Scandinavian glacier, which extended from Groningen to Emmen. The hunebedden we can see today have lost their original appearance. When first built, the hunebed was hidden under a small burial mound, the earth being held up by a ring of upright stones; the space between these uprights was filled in with rubble. In Emmen and especially south of Schoonoord one can see reconstructed hunebedden.

A funerary monument – Hunebedden prove that prehistoric man lived in the Drenthe from 3000 or 2000 BC. They were used as collective burial chambers. Dishes, plates, tools and even jewellery were placed next to the bodies. Consequently excavations in the vicinity of the *hunebedden* have been very fruitful. The objects discovered, notably pottery, have made it possible to connect *hunebedden* with the civilisation known as the Bell-Beaker culture.

★ HUNEBED TRAIL

52km/32mi from Emmen to Noordlaren – allow 1 day

Emmen – *See EMMEN.*

Klijndijk – *Go towards Valthe on the right.* On leaving the village turn right on to a sandy path, then left. Skirting the woods one reaches a long *hunebed* where two capstones remain.

Valthe – On leaving the village towards the north-east, on the right before a petrol station, a lane marked *hunebed (about 400m or 0.25mi)* leads to *hunebed* D 37, surrounded by oaks. It is in fact two covered alleyways, one of which has been knocked down by three large oaks.

HUNEBEDDEN

0   8 km

🐾 Most interesting

🐾 Interesting   🏛 Not described

Going towards Odoorn, on the left after a wood, there is a small lane marked hunebed *which leads to* hunebed *D 34.*

Set among heather, it is a small covered alleyway with two leaning slabs.

Odoorn – The town of Odoorn, at the heart of sheep-rearing country, organises an important annual sheep market. At **Exloo** *(4km or 2.5mi north of Odoorn)* a sheep-shearing festival and a traditional handicraft festival are held each year *(for these two events see Calendar of events).*
On leaving Odoorn, *hunebed* D 32, reached by a small path marked *"hunebed"*, is hidden behind a curtain of trees. It is topped by four capstones.

Borger – *In the main street, take the road to Bronneger.* The **Nationaal Hunebedden Infocentrum** ⊘ is devoted to *hunebedden* and life during prehistoric times.
A little further on, surrounded by trees, is the Borger **hunebed**★ (D 27), the biggest of all. It is still topped by nine enormous capstones. Its entry on the south side is clearly visible.

Bronneger – *In this hamlet, a path marked* hunebed *leads to an oak wood.* There are five small *hunebedden* (D 23/25 and D 21/22).

Drouwen – The *hunebedden* (D 19/20) are on a rather bare mound, near the main road (they are visible from the road). One is surrounded by a circle of stones.

6km/4mi to the north of Drouwen, go left towards Assen, then turn right towards Eext.

Hunebed in Eexterhalte

Eexterhalte – Shortly after the fork, on the right there is a **hunebed**★ (D 14) topped by six capstones. One can still see some of the stones encircling it.

Eext – In this village, in line with a bend, a path on the left leads to a *hunebed* (D 13), which has kept its original appearance; set in a cavity at the top of a mound, it consists of a square of uprights pressed closely together, and still has one of the capstones which served as the roof. Two stones set further apart mark the entrance, located, exceptionally, on the east side.

Annen – Small *hunebed* (D 9) on the left of the road.

Zuidlaren – This small town is an important tourist centre.

Midlaren – The village has two *hunebedden. Turn left, between two houses, on to a dirt track called* Hunebedpad. 200m/656ft away, after having crossed a road, and behind two houses shaded by large trees, there are two covered alleyways (D 3/D 4) each one made of several enormous slabs.

Noordlaren – *Before reaching the mill, take a lane on the left marked* hunebed *which leads to a grove.* This *hunebed* (G 1), where there still remain two capstones resting on five uprights, is the only one in the Groningen province.

IJSSELMEER

Flevoland – Fryslân – Gelderland – Noord – Holland – Overijssel
Michelin maps 908 G 2, 3, 4, 5, H 2, 3, 4, 5 and 210

IJsselmeer is the name that has been given to the Zuiderzee since it was cut off from the sea by the construction of a Barrier Dam in 1932.

HISTORICAL AND GEOGRAPHICAL NOTES

The old Zuiderzee – The IJssel river formerly flowed into a series of small lakes. Enlarged progressively they developed into a large lake called **Lake Flevo** by the Romans and known in the Middle Ages as **Almere** or Almari. In 1287 a tidal wave destroyed part of the north coast, enlarged the mouth of the lake and invaded the low-lying regions which surrounded it, turning it into a large gulf open to the North Sea. It owes its name of Zuiderzee or South Sea to the Danes.
From the 13C to 16C commercial ports developed such as Staveren, Kampen, Harderwijk, affiliated to the **Hanseatic League**, an association of towns in Northern Europe which had the monopoly of traffic in the Scandinavian countries. In the 17C and 18C, trade turned towards the Far East and brought prosperity to such towns as Amsterdam, Hoorn, Medemblik, Enkhuizen etc.

Creation of the IJsselmeer – The idea of closing the Zuiderzee by a dike goes back to 1667 when **Hendrick Stevin** published a work in which he proposed this means of combating the devastation caused by the North Sea. In 1825 a violent storm ravaged the coasts of the Zuiderzee. In 1891 a project was presented by the engineer **Dr C Lely** (1854-1929). It was only adopted by Parliament in 1918, following the terrible floods of 1916 and when Lely had become Minister of Public Works for the third time. The aim envisaged was triple: by the construction of a dike to put an end to the floods which menaced the banks of the Zuiderzee, create a reserve of fresh water to stop the increasing salinity of the soil, and with the formation of polders to gain 225 000ha/555 750 acres of fertile land. The work on the IJsselmeer started in 1919; in 1924 the small Amsteldiep dike linking **Wieringen Island** to the mainland was completed.

Wieringermeer Polder – From 1927 to 1930 this polder was reclaimed. It stretches over 20 000ha/ 49 400 acres in a former gulf of the Zuiderzee between Medemblik and Wieringen Island. Immediately after the drainage (700 million m³/24 720 million cu ft of water), the polder presented a surface of muddy clay. In 1945, two weeks before their surrender, the Germans blew up the Wieringermeer Polder dike and flooding ensued. The surging water created two funnel-shaped holes of more than 30m/98ft deep. These "gaping" holes could not be repaired and the dike had to be re-routed round what is now called **De Gaper**. Again drained and returned to its former state, the polder is now a flourishing agricultural region.

Construction of the dike – The barrier dam or Afsluitdijk *(see below)* was built in 1927 between the Frisian coast and the former Wieringen Island by creating an artificial island (Breezand) between the two points. With clay dredged from the bottom of the Zuiderzee, a dike was built, against which sand was deposited; the sand doubled by a layer of clay was collected on the spot by pumping. As the work advanced the current grew stronger and the remaining channel was sealed off with great difficulty.

The barrier dam was completed on 28 May 1932. 30km/19mi long and 90m/295ft wide at sea level, it is more than 7m/23ft above sea level and forms a new lake, the IJsselmeer.

Three large polders – Once the barrier dam was completed, the creation of the second IJsselmeer polder was undertaken, the **Noordoostpolder** *(see NOORDOOST-POLDER)* and then the two **Flevoland★** *(see Flevoland)* polders.
The project concerning the development of the very last IJsselmeer polder **(Markerwaard)** has been abandoned. Only the northern part of the surrounding dike has been completed: a road, the N 302, now links Enkhuizen to Lelystad.

★★ AFSLUITDIJK (BARRIER DAM) *30km/20mi*

On the **Den Oever** side, at the dam's entrance, stands a **statue** of the engineer Lely on the left. On the seaward side the barrier dam has a breakwater which protects a bicycle path and a dual carriageway. Below the barrier dam on the IJsselmeer side, fishermen come to place their nets on the bottom of the lake, mainly to catch eels.

The barrier dam

The **Stevin Lock** which bears the name of the engineer Stevin *(see above)*, forms the first group of locks for ships to pass through. They are also used to evacuate water.

At the point where the two sections of the barrier dam joined in 1932 there is now a **tower** with the inscription "A living nation builds for its future". From the top of this monument there is a **panorama** over Waddenzee and IJsselmeer. Near this edifice a footbridge spans the road.

Further on, a viaduct built in 1979 enables traffic to cross between the two ports of **Breezanddijk** and gives drivers the possibility of turning back.

The **Kazemattenmuseum Kornwerderzand** ⊘, or Kornwerderzand Bunkers Museum, is by the **Lorentzsluizen** *(access via Kornwerderzand turnoff)*. Some of the 17 wartime bunkers have been restored to their original condition (May 1940) and opened to the public. One can now see the jute sacks on which the soldiers slept, their mess tins in the kitchen, the working telephone switchboard, and cannons and machine guns ready for action. The museum also has displays on the period from 1932 to 1965, including the building of the Afsluitdijk, the German invasion in 1940, resistance and liberation, and the Cold War.

About 4km/2mi past Kornwerderzand, the Afsluitdijk reaches the east coast of the IJsselmeer and the province of Fryslân.

PLACE NAMES IN FRISIAN

You may encounter both Dutch and Frisian placenames on maps and roadsigns. The following are the names of some of the places described in this book:

Dutch	Frisian	Dutch	Frisian
Grou	Grouw	Rinsumageest	Rinsumageast
Harlingen	Harns	Sloten	Sleat
Hinderloopen	Hylpen	Sneek	Snits
Hoorn	Hoarne	Twijzel	Twizel
Leeuwarden	Ljouwert	West-Terschelling	West-Skylge
Oudkerk	Aldtsjerk	Workum	Warkum

KAMPEN★

Overijssel

Population 32 188
Michelin maps 908 I 4 and 210 U 7
Town plan in the current edition of The Red Guide Benelux

Kampen extends along the IJssel's west bank, near the mouth of the river. In the Middle Ages it was a very prosperous port due to the herring trade. It was a Hanseatic League city *(see IJSSELMEER)* with commercial ties extending over the whole Baltic area. In the 16C there was a very rapid decline in the town brought about by the wars, which ruined the hinterland, and by the silting up of the IJssel. In the 19C a channel was made leading to the Zuiderzee but the closing of this sea reduced Kampen to the state of a river port. This barrier to its development resulted in many of the town's old buildings being preserved, and the town centre is surprisingly attractive, with nearly 500 historic monuments.

One of Kampen's most renowned inhabitants is the painter **Hendrick Avercamp** (1585-1634), also called the Mute of Kampen, who settled in the town in the early 17C.

Kampen and the tobacco industry

In 1813 two small tobacco factories were set up in Kampen, followed by the first major cigar manufacturer in 1826. By 1880 almost 40% of Kampen's labour force worked in the cigar industry, with the town's 1 400 cigar makers producing 1.5 million cigars a week in their heyday. But the 1930s economic crisis, the Second World War and the increasing popularity of cigarettes brought this thriving industry to its knees. Some of the buildings that evoke the town's involvement with tobacco include the **Kamper Tabaksmuseum** ⊙, featuring tools used in the tobacco industry and smokers' implements; the tobacco factory **(tabaksfabriek)** in Voorstraat 102-106; and the tobacconist's shop **"De Olifant"** at no 101 Oudestraat.

Viewpoint – From the east bank of the IJssel there is an overall view of the town, which is particularly beautiful at sunset. In the centre, the onion-shaped turret of the Oude Raadhuis and the Nieuwe Toren stand out, to the right the 14C **Buitenkerk (1)**, to the left St.-Nicolaas and the large towers of the Koornmarktspoort. This is arguably the most attractive river bank in the Netherlands.

Kampen port

SIGHTS

* **Oude Raadhuis** ⊘ (2) – A little dwarfed by the new 18C town hall, the old town hall is a small brick edifice dating from 1543, crowned with galleries and flanked at the back by a slightly leaning tower with an open-work onion-shaped dome. Its gable, with a helical **chimney**★, is surrounded by bartizans. Note the iron cage by the façade, in which offenders used to be locked up and exposed to the public as a punishment. The **Magistrates' Hall**★ (Schepenzaal), with sombre 16C oak wainscoting forming the seats, has a **bench** richly decorated with Renaissance style reliefs, next to a monumental **chimneypiece**★ by Colijn de Nole (1545).

Oude Vleeshuys – *Oudestraat 119.* The town's coat of arms is engraved on the Renaissance stone façade (1596) of the old butcher's shop; it portrays two lions framing a fortified gateway.

Nieuwe Toren ⊘ – This tall square tower, erected in the 17C, has an octagonal bell-tower with a carillon cast by François Hemony. Next door a fine Art Nouveau building houses a bakery.

Gotische Huis – *On the right of the Nieuwe Toren.* This elegant residence with a tall façade, crowned with pinnacles and pierced with numerous windows, has been thoroughly restored and contains the municipal museum, the **Stedelijk Museum** ⊘. The museum houses a fine collection of silverware of the boatmen's guild, including a fine 1369 **goblet**★, and chronicles Kampen's past. At the rear the remnants of a horse mill are on display.

Pass under the Nieuwe Toren and follow Nieuwe Markt to Burgwal, a quay running alongside Burgel Canal, which crosses the town. Turn left.

Broederkerk (3) – This is the 15C former church of the Minorites (Franciscans).

Broederweg – On the right side of this street, there is a Gothic chapel, a former Walloon church which in 1823 became a **Mennonite church** (4).

Broederpoort (5) – This is a lovely gateway with a voluted gable (1465) flanked by graceful turrets.

After the gateway, turn left.

Plantsoen – This is the name of the pleasant park which follows the old ramparts: the moats form the Singelgracht.

* **Cellebroederspoort** (6) – An elegant building flanked by steeply-pitched roofed towers, this gateway, which was part of the 15C walls, was altered in 1617 in the Renaissance style.

Go through the gateway and follow Cellebroedersweg then Geerstraat. By Boven Nieuwstraat, on the right you reach Muntplein.

St.-Nicolaaskerk or Bovenkerk ⊘ (7) – This imposing Gothic edifice (14C) is overlooked by a tower 70m/230ft high. The interior consists of a nave and four aisles, a wide transept and a large ambulatory with radiating chapels. Note the 16C chancel screen and a Late Gothic stone pulpit. The **organ** ⊘ has 3 200 pipes and was built in 1741 by Hinsz.

Koornmarktspoort (8) – This is the oldest gateway to the town. Dating from the 14C and situated on the old corn market, Koornmarkt, near St-Nicolaas, the gateway has retained its defensive character with a massive central keep flanked, since the late 14C, by two squat towers.

KEUKENHOF and BULB FIELDS***

Zuid-Holland and Noord-Holland

Michelin maps 908 E 5 and 211 L 9, M 9

Bulbs have been grown in the region around the Keukenhof for hundreds of years. In spring, the fields between Leiden and Haarlem resemble a vividly coloured chessboard *(illustration: see Admission times and charges at the back of the guide)*.

An original speculation – The tulip is said to have been brought from Turkey by Augier Ghislain de Busbecq (1522-92), the Imperial envoy. Busbecq gave bulbs to Charles de l'Ecluse (1526-1609), a scientist better known under the name of **Carolus Clusius**, who at the time was in charge of the Emperor's garden of medicinal plants in Vienna. Professor at the University of Leiden in 1593, Clusius started to cultivate tulips on the sandy and humid soil which stretched along the North Sea between Leiden and Haarlem. This experiment was a great success.

Other flowers such as hyacinths and gladioli had also been introduced, but it was the tulip which attained the highest prices. Between 1634 and 1636 speculation was rife and "tulipmania" reached insane proportions. A rare tulip bulb was sold for 6 000 florins. Buyers even went so far as to exchange one bulb for a coach and two horses, for acres of land or for a house. The Dutch States put an end to this speculation in 1636 and the flower industry was regulated. At the end of the 17C the tulip craze gave way to that of the hyacinth.

**THE KEUKENHOF

The **Keukenhof National Flower Exhibition** ⊘ has been held every spring since 1949.

When a group of bulb-growers was looking for an exhibition site, Keukenhof was chosen as the ideal location and has ever since served as the showcase for Dutch growers. Each year this extraordinary garden attracts nearly 900 000 visitors.

The tulip vase

The tulip vase was a 17C Dutch invention. It was usually spherical or fan-shaped, and sometimes took the form of a pagoda. There were holes or tubes around the outside, each holding a single flower. Despite their name, the vases were not just used for tulips. Whole vases full of one type of flower were not fashionable in the 17C, particularly as tulips were so expensive. Instead, people preferred to show off a selection of different flowers. The vases were often made as pairs, so that they could be placed at either end of a table or shelf in a similar way to candlesticks.

In the 15C the site was Jacoba van Beieren's *(see GOES)* kitchen garden (*keuken*: kitchen and *hof*: garden); the countess used the castle, which still stands nearby, as her hunting lodge. The castle grounds are landscaped in the English style, contrasting with the geometric shapes of the surrounding bulb fields, and include fountains, water features, lakes with swans, themed gardens and works of art. The layout is changed each year, so there is always something new to see, and the brilliant colours of the tulips, hyacinths and narcissi form a striking contrast with the cool greens of the grass and trees. Three layers of bulbs are planted one on top of the other, providing new blooms throughout the entire season. The less hardy plants are displayed in large greenhouses, and changing flower shows are held in the various pavilions. There is a permanent **orchid display** in the Koningin Beatrix Paviljoen. Flowering shrubs, themed gardens (including a wild garden, a music garden and a historical garden), fountains and water features all add to the splendour of the park. The **beeldenroute** is a trail that takes in some 50 art works. The Groningen windmill on the north side of the park has a splendid **view★** of the surrounding bulb fields.

Since 1999 a summer exhibition has been held on the newly acquired site, the **Zomerhof** ⊘ (7ha/17 acres), which comprises a dune landscape and a terp planted with summer blooms, as well as themed gardens, water features and a Japanese garden. The annual bulb market (Bloembollenmarkt) takes place in October.

***BULB FIELDS

A few figures – Today bulbs cover an area of 14 400ha/36 000 acres in the country. The main production areas are in the south of Haarlem and to the north of the line formed between Alkmaar and Hoorn. Flevoland is also a bulb-growing area. More than a billion guilders' worth of bulbs are exported all over the world each year.

Bulb-growing – The most widespread species in the Netherlands are the tulip, narcissus, hyacinth, iris and crocus, but numerous other flowers are cultivated such as the gladiolus, lily, grape hyacinth, dahlia, anemone and freesia.

Towards mid-March the bulb fields take on their first colour with the blossoming of orange and violet **crocuses**, which are followed by white and yellow **narcissi** (end March). In mid-April the **hyacinths** flower, as well as the early **tulips**. A few days later

HAARLEM / HILLEGOM

KEUKENHOF

🛈	Information desk	🍺	Cafe	✉	Post office
●	Bulb and flower shop	🚌	Bus station	✚	First Aid
✗	Restaurant	🚐	Exchange bureau		

the most beautiful tulips open out. It is, therefore, at the end of April that the fields are usually at their most beautiful. Divided into multicoloured strips separated by small irrigation canals, they look like an immense patchwork. It is the time of the Bloemencorso, the flower parade from Haarlem to Noordwijk *(see Calendar of events)*. The fields are then covered by **irises**, and **gladioli** in August. Another floral float procession takes place in September between Aalsmeer and Amsterdam *(see Calendar of events)*.

Shortly after blossoming the stems are cut off by mechanical means, in order to strengthen the bulb. Once harvested, the large bulbs are sold. The bulbules are replanted in autumn.

Crossing the bulb fields by railway from Leiden to Haarlem offers lovely views; flying over them in an **aeroplane** ⊘ is even better.

★★ EXCURSION THROUGH THE BULB FIELDS

Circular tour from Haarlem – allow one day

★★ Haarlem *- See HAARLEM.*

Leave Haarlem to the south via Van Eedenstraat.

Going through the outskirts of Haarlem there is a succession of fine houses in spacious grounds, before the first bulb fields appear. On the right is a 17C-18C mansion, **Huis de Manpad**.

245

Take the first road on the right and once over the level crossing turn left.

Vogelenzang – The village is pleasantly set amid woods not far from the coastal dunes. Once again there are some prestigious villas in well-tended grounds.
To the south of De Zilk the pale tints of the sand dunes contrast with the brightly coloured carpet of flowers.
Beyond Noordwijkerhout the road starts climbing to the junction with the road to Sassenheim, which offers splendid **views**★ of the bulb fields.

Noordwijk aan Zee – See LEIDEN, Excursions.

Continue towards Lisse/Sassenheim. Just past the Voorhout sign on the right, turn left into Loosterweg.

★★ **Keukenhof** – See p 243.

Lisse – One of the main villages in the bulb-growing area. The **Museum de Zwarte Tulp** ⊙ (Black Tulip Museum), located in an old house in the centre, offers information about the bulb-growing industry and has a collection of preserved tulips. Tours of the **Kagerplassen** lakes and the picturesque island village of **Kaagdorp** depart from Lisse.
Nearby, close to the important bulb-growing centre of **Sassenheim**, are the ruins of **Kasteel Teylingen**, where Jacoba or Jacqueline of Hainaut spent the last years of her life.

Hillegom – The **Den Hartogh Ford Museum**★ ⊙ (Haarlemmerstraat 36) has a display of 185 cars made by the Detroit manufacturer. They date from the period 1903-48, and form the world's largest private collection of Fords. They include the popular Model T, a Lincoln 160 from 1929 and a 1936 Ford 720 coupé. The last room contains lorries, buses and some fire engines, all made by Ford.

Continue towards Haarlem and follow the signs to Cruquius.

★ **Museum De Cruquius** – See HAARLEM, Outskirts.

For historical background on the region see the Historical Table and Notes in the Introduction

LEEUWARDEN*

Fryslân Ⓟ

Population 88 762
Michelin maps 908 I 2 and 210 T 3
Plan of the conurbation in the current edition of The Red Guide Benelux

Leeuwarden – Ljouwert in Frisian – is an attractive town of scenic canals and historic buildings. The former residence of the Frisian stadholders is now the dynamic capital and cultural centre of Fryslân.

The town is the centre of a thriving dairy farming industry and herds of the famous black and white cattle are a regular feature of the surrounding countryside. The famous Frisian cow has been Immortalised by a larger than life bronze statue on the Harlingersingel-Harlingerstraatweg roundabout. The locals affectionately refer to it as **Us Mem**, Our Mother.

The Friday cattle markets in the huge Frisian Expo Centre and the annual cattle inspection *(see Practical information at the front of the guide)* reflect the importance of this industry. Fryslân is also well known for its beautiful black horses.

Famous figures who have lived in Leeuwarden include **Mata Hari**, JJ **Slauerhoff** and **MC Escher**. The writer **Simon Vestdijk** also spent his youth here.

HISTORICAL NOTES

Founded from the linking of three mounds located on the edge of the old **Middelzee**, a sort of gulf, drained between the 14C and 18C, Leeuwarden gained some importance in the 12C when it was fortified.

Capital of Friesland – Friesland was a bone of contention between the Counts of Holland and the Dukes of Saxony, whose feudal lord was the German emperor. In 1499 the Emperor Maximilian gave the fief to **Duke Albert of Saxony**, who elected to reside in Leeuwarden which had become the provincial capital. In 1516 the Emperor Charles V gave the town a new set of fortifications.

After the independence of the United Provinces, Leeuwarden became the residence of the **stadholders** of Friesland and Groningen in 1584. The first was **William Louis** of Nassau (1560-1620), son of John of Nassau (brother of William the Silent). In 1675, under Henry Casimir II (1657-96), the Frisian stadholdership became hereditary.

John William Friso (1648-1711) received the title of Prince of Orange as a legacy from the Holland stadholder (and King of England) William III. Friso's son **William IV** (1711-51), stadholder of Friesland, was chosen as the first hereditary stadholder of the whole country in 1747. The present dynasty in the Netherlands stems from him, the first king being his grandson William I.

In 1580 Leeuwarden received its new curtain wall and, at the beginning of the 17C, a few bastions to the north and west. These were razed in the 18C and today have been converted into the Prinsentuin, or Princes' Garden, bordered by the Stadsgracht.

Since 1909, Leeuwarden has been the departure point of the famous **Eleven Towns Race** (Elfstedentocht).

Mata Hari – In 1876 Margarethe Geertruida Zelle was born here. Having learnt to dance in the Dutch Indies (Indonesia), she went to Paris in 1903 and became famous as a dancer under the name of **Mata Hari** (In Malayan: Eye of the Day). She was shot in 1917 for spying for the Germans.

SIGHTS

** **Fries Museum/Verzetsmuseum** ⊙ – The Frisian Museum and Resistance Museum is housed in two historic buildings on Turfmarkt, linked by an underground tunnel. The museum has a very varied collection of items relating to Frisian culture.

Kanselarij – This former courthouse in the Renaissance style (1566), on Turfmarkt, has a wide, heavily decorated façade with a flight of steps, and a statue of Charles V at the top of the façade.

On the second floor there is a collection of the **top items** from each collection, including archaeological finds, Frisian silver, Indian chintz, a chest from Hindeloopen, and portraits. Objects from 16C Friesland are displayed in the adjoining rooms.

The first floor is mainly devoted to **17C painting**: still-life paintings, historical paintings, landscapes and, most importantly, portraits. This genre was particularly popular during the Golden Age; the wealthy middle classes liked to immortalise themselves and their families for posterity. The best-known Frisian portrait painter of this period was Wijbrand de Geest. There is also a portrait from the studio of Rembrandt depicting Saskia van Uilenberg, the daughter of Leeuwarden's mayor and later Rembrandt's wife.

The Elfstedentocht

In winters when it is cold enough for the Frisian canals to freeze over, the whole country is gripped by Elfstedentocht fever. Once the ice reaches an average thickness of 15cm/6in, the green light is given for the preparations to begin. The organisers then have only 48hr to get the course ready and make arrangements for thousands of participants and tens of thousands of spectators from the Netherlands and abroad. At 5.30am on the third day, the starting signal is given and this 200km/125mi tour of 11 towns begins. It starts and finishes in Leeuwarden, and passes through Sneek, IJlst, Sloten, Stavoren, Hindeloopen, Workum, Bolsward, Harlingen, Franeker and Dokkum. All entrants completing the course within the regulation time receive a small silver cross. The current record, set in 1985, is 6hr 47min. The last Elfstedentocht took place on 4 January 1997, for only the 15th time since the first official race on 2 January 1909, though the tradition is believed to date from the 18C.

A visit to Het Eerste Friese Schaatsmuseum (The First Frisian Skating Museum) in Hindeloopen *(see HINDELOOPEN)* is a must for anyone interested in the history of the Elfstedentocht.

The 15th Elfstedentocht, 4 January 1997

The **silverware**★★★ department in the vaulted cellars is one of the biggest and finest in the country. It includes a superb collection of 16C drinking horns and goblets, and the 17C and 18C Frisian ornamental silver is also particularly fine: the Baroque Popta treasure, the finely engraved boxes with knots symbolising the marriage vows, and oval brandy bowls with ornamental handles.

The top floor houses the **Frisian Resistance Museum**, with photographs and other objects evoking the atmosphere of the Second World War. It follows four families illustrating the different attitudes to occupation: collaboration, adaptation, resistance and persecution.

The tunnel and the modern section of the museum are used for temporary exhibitions of **modern Frisian art**.

Eysingahuis – This late 18C house is the former residence of the aristocratic Eysinga family. Its **period rooms** give a fascinating picture of life at the time, and include Louis XVI- and Empire-style furniture and Chinese porcelain. On the lower floor, there is a room devoted to the life of **Mata Hari**.

The room of paintings on the first floor contains portraits, landscapes, seascapes and still-life paintings giving an overview of 19C **Frisian painting**. Well-known artists from that time include Laurens Alma Tadema and Christoffel Bisschop, who was also a collector of silver, porcelain, furniture, costume and paintings. His collection is on display in the **Bisschop rooms**. There are also two **Hindeloopen rooms** with furniture decorated with the typically colourful motifs of the region *(see Introduction, The arts)*. Samplers and 18C and 19C Frisian clothing are exhibited in the **costume and textile room**.

The **archaeology department** on the second floor focuses on three periods: the Stone Age, the terp period and the late Middle Ages.

WHERE TO STAY

Although Leeuwarden has only a few hotels, some of them are particularly characteristic.

MODERATE

Wyswert – *Rengerslaan 8, 8917 DD*, ☏ *(058) 215 77 15, Fax (058) 212 32 11. 28 rooms*. This hotel school to the north of the centre also offers inexpensive rooms. Service is provided by students under professional supervision.

MID-RANGE

Van den Berg State – *Verlengde Schrans 87, 8932 NL*, ☏ *(058) 280 05 84, Fax (058) 288 34 22. 6 rooms*. This small hotel and restaurant (*see below*) is located in a 19C country house in a quiet residential area south of the centre. The rooms are very spacious, with their own lobbies and luxurious bathrooms. The suite has a waterbed and jacuzzi.

het Stadhouderlijk Hof – *Hofplein 29, 8911 HJ*, ☏ *(058) 216 21 80, Fax (058) 216 38 90. www.stadhouderlijkhof.nl 25 rooms*. This town-centre hotel is the former residence of the Frisian stadholders. The only room where there are still traces of this aristocratic past is the Nassau-Zaal, where portraits of princes and counts from the Van Nassau-Dietz dynasty hang on the walls; it is now used for weddings. The rest of the hotel, including the large bedrooms, is decorated in tasteful and very modern style.

WHERE TO EAT

Van den Berg State – *Verlengde Schrans 87*, ☏ *(058) 280 05 84*. This hotel and restaurant outside the centre of town (*see above*) offers excellent food, classic decor and a view of the garden; meals are served outdoors in clement weather.

Kota Radja – *Groot Schavernek 5*, ☏ *(058) 213 35 64*. Asian cuisine served in agreeable surroundings.

BRASSERIES, CAFÉS, BARS, COFFEE SHOPS...

Het Haersma Huis – *Tweebaksmarkt 49*. This grand café lies a stone's throw from the Fries Museum and is an ideal venue for a snack before or after a visit to the museum. It has classic modern decor in a historic building, and there is also a terrace.

De Koperen Tuin – *Prinsentuin 1*. Watch the world go by from the terrace of this garden tearoom as you enjoy lunch or just a drink or ice cream. There are free concerts on Sundays, and much of Simon Vestdijk's book De Koperen Tuin was set in the garden. However, the café is open only from early April to late September.

't Pannekoekschip – *Willemskade 69*. This delightful ship moored on Willemskade, between the station and the old town, offers a choice of 90 kinds of pancake.

PRACTICAL INFORMATION

General information – The **VVV tourist office** at Stationsplein 1, ☏ (0900) 202 40 60, www.vvvleeuwarden.nl is the place to go if you need information about sights, tours, excursions or accommodation. It also offers special packages, and publishes an annual tourist guide to Leeuwarden.

Transport – There are two indoor **car parks**, De Klanderij and Zaailand, and a park and ride point next to the station. **Bicycles** are available for hire from the Zaailand car park.

Tours and walks – For information, contact the VVV.

Shopping – Leeuwarden is a pleasant place to shop, and has an extensive **pedestrian area**. Late-night opening is on Thursdays, and shops also open on the first Sunday of the month. The VVV sells a booklet on interesting places to shop in Leeuwarden.
Apart from all these modern shops, Nieuwesteeg, in the heart of town between Nieuwestad and Bagijnestraat, has authentic old shops practising traditional crafts. These include a 19C corn chandler's, a barber's, a coppersmith's, a wine cellar and a coffee room; we defy you to leave empty-handed.

Night-life – There are two theatres, the modern glass **Stadsschouwburg De Harmonie**, Ruiterskwartier 4, ☏ (058) 233 02 33, and **Theater Romein**, Bagijnestraat 59, ☏ (058) 215 82 15. There are also cinemas, and lots of lively bars in the town centre.

Events – There are numerous variations on the famous Elfstedentocht in summer, using such modes of transport as bicycles, cars (veteran and otherwise) and Shanks's pony. The annual **cattle stud inspections** at the Frisian Expo Centre are also well worth seeing. In November the town hosts the film festival **Noordelijk Filmfestival**.

Over de Kelders – One of the quays on this canal is dug out of cellars (*kelders*). From the bridge to the north there is a fine view over the quays of Voorstreek and the bell-tower of St Boniface. The small **statue of Mata Hari** was erected in 1976 for the 100th anniversary of her birth.

Waag – On Waagplein, in the centre of the town, this weigh-house is a 1598 building of red brick, the first floor decorated with heraldic lions. Above them is a frieze sculptured with various motifs. The weighing of butter and cheese took place here up to 1880. The large awning was to protect the goods from sunlight.

Weerd – This narrow street plunges into Leeuwarden's old quarter.

Hofplein – The **stadhuis** (town hall) is on this square, a sober, classical building (1715) topped by a 17C carillon. At no 34 note a fine façade stone (1666) depicting Fortune. In the stadhuis annexe, added in 1760, the Council Room (*Raadzaal*) has a side façade with Rococo decoration topped by the lion which appears on the town's coat of arms.
Opposite this is the **Stadhouderlijk Hof** *(see Travellers' addresses)* or former residence of the Frisian stadtholders. The building itself dates from 1881, and has medieval remains underneath. In the centre of the square there is a statue of William Louis, first hereditary stadtholder, called by the Frisians **"Us heit"** (Our Father). At no 35 a façade stone depicts a stork.

Eewal – This wide main road is lined with elegant 18C residences. Some still have lovely façade stones (nos 52 and 58).

Grote Kerk or Jacobijnerkerk ⊘ – Dating from the 13C, the Jacobin Church was reconstructed in the 15C and 16C and devastated by the revolutionaries in 1795.

Since 1588 it has been the Nassau Frisian mausoleum. The great **organ** ⊙ was built in 1724-7 by Christian Müller. The Oranjepoortje (1663) on the south side of the church was the entrance for the stadtholder's family, and the copper orange tree above it refers to this fact.

Fries Natuurmuseum ⊙ – The former 17C municipal orphanage is now the home of the Frisian Natural History Museum, which has displays on the soil and the various landscapes of the region and the plants and animals that live there. The basement has an excellent exhibition, **Friesland onder Water**, in which visitors can explore the bottom of a drainage ditch. The whales and dolphins exhibition on the first floor includes the skeleton of a 15m/50ft **sperm whale** beached near Ameland in 1994.

Grote Kerkstraat – The tall house where Mata Hari is believed to have lived has been converted into the **Frysk Letterkundich Museum en Dokumintaasjesintrum**, or Frisian literary museum and documentation centre. Further on at no 43 there is a fine façade stone depicting a lion and a fortified castle, then near the corner of Doelestraat, at no 17, a lovely Baroque portal is decorated with garlands in the Frisian style.

★★ **Museum Het Princessehof, Nederlands Keramiek Museum** ⊙ – During the 18C, this 17C palace (hof) was the official residence of Princess Marie-Louise of Hessen-Kassel (known familiarly as Maaike-Meu), widow of the Frisian stadtholder John William Friso, Prince of Orange. Her dining and music room on the ground floor is richly decorated: stucco ceiling, gold curtains, portraits and Chinese porcelain.

This palace and adjoining buildings are now the home of the Netherlands Ceramics Museum, containing collections of porcelain, pottery and stoneware pieces from many different countries (illustrations: see Introduction, The arts).

The exhibits from **Asia** are displayed in chronological order (five rooms).

Some samples of the **Japanese production** are on show but the most splendid of all are the **Chinese porcelain**★★. They illustrate the development of the industry from the terracotta pieces made in the 3rd millennium BC up to the objects manufactured under the Ching dynasty (1644-1912), renowned for its famille verte, famille noire and famille rose, much sought after by European collectors. There is also a room devoted to "chine de commande", earthenware commissioned from China by Europeans.

European ceramics are the subject of a beautiful display: majolica from Italy, Delftware, Wedgwood, porcelain, Art Nouveau and Art Deco ceramics (1900-1930).

The museum also presents an extensive collection of **earthenware tiles**★★, mainly from Spain, France, Portugal and the Netherlands. The colourful tile pictures used on floors, walls and fireplaces are particularly interesting. There is also an Islamic collection with tiles from Turkey, Iran and elsewhere.

Two rooms are devoted to the JWN van Achterbergh collection, giving an overview of Dutch ceramics between 1950 and 1985. The De Prins van Leeuwarden gallery shows contemporary **European ceramics**.

Museum Het Princessehof – Nationaal Keramiek Museum Leeuwarden

Iranian tile (Lagwardina, c 1300)

Oldehove ⊙ – This massive Gothic tower in brick was never completed due to the instability of the ground, which explains why it leans sharply. The plan of the adjacent church, which was destroyed in 1595, is indicated on the square by coloured paving. From the top of the tower (40m), there is an overall **view** of the town and the surrounding area; the Waddeneilanden are visible in fine weather.

Prinsentuin – Near the tower, a footpath leads across the old, tree-covered quays of **Stadsgracht**, a wide canal which follows the outline of the fortifications. The garden contains the **Pier Pander Museum** ⊙, mainly devoted to the work of this Frisian sculptor (1864-1919).

ADDITIONAL SIGHTS

Otterpark Aqualutra ⊙ – 7km/4mi northeast via the N 355 towards Groningen. In 1988, when the last otter in the Netherlands died after being run over, the Netherlands Otter Station Foundation decided to set up a breeding centre (not open to the public) and a nature park. This now provides an opportunity to encounter a wealth of freshwater fauna, centring on the otter which, because it is at the top of the food chain, is a good way of gauging water quality. Otters are mainly active at night, so the best time to see them is at **feeding time**. The park also contains mink, polecats, beavers, deer, storks and waterfowl, while the central exhibition building has aquariums, vivariums, exhibitions and films.

Marssum – *5km/3mi to the west via Harlingerstraatweg*. The **Poptaslot** ⊙, or Heringa State, preceded by a gatehouse with voluted gables, is a 16C-17C manor house containing 17C and 18C furnishings. Nearby, the old almshouse, **Popta-Gasthuis**, founded in 1712 is a picturesque group of low buildings with a monumental portal.

Drachten – *27km/17mi to the south-east via Oostergoweg*. The great apartment complexes and brick houses of Drachten extend over the Frisian countryside with rich meadows bordered by poplar trees. This town is a commercial and industrial centre with busy streets and pedestrian precincts, adorned with statues.

TERP REGION

Round tour of 118km/73mi. Leave by Groningerstraatweg. Turn left after 9km/6mi.

From the beginning of 5C BC and up to 12C AD in the low regions liable to sea or river flooding, the Frisians established their farmhouses and later their churches on manmade mounds called **terps**.

About a thousand of these terps still exist today, two thirds of which are in the province of Friesland and the rest in the province of Groningen, where they are called *wierden (illustration: see GRONINGEN, Excursions)*. Their average height is between 2 and 6m/6.5 and 19.5ft, and their area between 1 and 12ha/2.5 to 29.5 acres. The excavations have been very successful.

The tour covers a region where most of the villages have a *terp* with a church of tufa and brick with rustic charm, whose tower with a saddleback roof rises from a curtain of trees indicating its presence. The typical Frisian countryside is scattered with lovely farmhouses with gables decorated with an *"uilebord" (see Introduction, Traditions and folklore; illustration, see Admission times and charges at the back of the guide)*. Windmills and beautiful black Frisian horses are also a common sight.

Oentsjerk (Oenkerk) – This lovely forest-like castle park, **Stania State**, is open to the public.

Aldtsjerk (Oudkerk) – This village, known as **Oudkerk** in Dutch, has a castle and a church on a *terp*.

J.P. Lescouret/EXPLORER

Farmhouse and Frisian horses

Rinsumageest – The church, built on a *terp*, has a Romanesque crypt with two elegantly sculptured capitals. The interior is typical of Frisian churches.

Dokkum – *See DOKKUM.*

Follow the canal to the south-east.

The road soon climbs.

Turn right towards Kollumerzwaag.

Veenklooster – Charming village with thatched cottages round a *brink*. A leafy avenue leads to **Fogelsangh State** ⊙, built on the site where an abbey once stood; there is a **museum** in the garden.

Twijzel – All along the main road, which passes through this town for a couple of miles, stand a row of magnificent **farmhouses**★. Behind the pleasant façades stand enormous barns, often with thatched roofs *(illustration: see Introduction, Traditions and folklore).*

At Buitenpost, turn left.

Kollum – This town has a 15C Gothic church with a 13C tower. The nave is separated from the side aisles by stocky columns. The vaults with painted ribs are decorated with naive frescoes, as is the north wall where one can see a St Christopher.

Oostmahorn – From the top of the dike, there is an overall view of **Lauwersmeer** *(see GRONINGEN, Excursions).* Like the Zuiderzee, this low-lying region was flooded by the sea in the 13C. To avoid floods and create new polders a barrier dam has been built, creating the lake, a popular centre for watersports.

Anjum – This village has kept an 1889 windmill. On a small *terp* there is a Romanesque church, enlarged in the Gothic style.

Take the road to Dokkum, then turn right towards Metslawier.

Metslawier – Grouped round the Gothic church, the old, remarkably well-restored houses form a harmonious whole.

Wierum – This is a small harbour with modest homes; its church is built on an oval *terp* and surrounded by a cemetery. The top of the dike affords a fine **view** over the Waddenzee, which at low tide forms an immense beach. The islands of Ameland and Schiermonnikoog are visible on the horizon.

Holwerd – It is the departure point for boats going to Ameland Island.

After Blija, turn left to Hogebeintum.

Hogebeintum – This village on the highest *terp* in Friesland (nearly 9m/30ft above sea level) has a **church** ⊙ with a bell-tower with a saddleback roof and surrounded by a cemetery. It offers a fine view over the neighbouring countryside. The interior is interesting for the series of **16 hatchments**★ (from the 17C to the early 20C) which decorate the walls. On each carved wood panel, there is a coat of arms adorned with Baroque motifs, symbols of death (scythe, hour-glass, skulls and bones) and heads of cherubs in naive and rustic styles. There are also some lovely seignorial pews in wood, and on the floor numerous memorial slabs.

Reach Birdaard to the south and follow the Dokkumer Ee Canal towards the south. Via the village of Lekkum, Prof. Mr PS Gerbrandyweg and Groninger-straatweg, one returns to Leeuwarden.

LEIDEN★★

LEYDEN – Zuid-Holland
Population 117 389
Michelin maps 908 E 5 and 211 L 10
Plan of the conurbation in the current edition of The Red Guide Benelux

Built on the Oude Rijn, Leiden is an agreeable, lively town criss-crossed by canals. It is famous mainly for its university, the oldest in the country, but also for being the place where the first Dutch tulips were grown. It is also the birthplace of Rembrandt. Leiden has a number of exceptional museums and many idyllic "hofjes" or alms-houses.

HISTORICAL NOTES

In Roman times Leiden was called Lugdunum Batavorum. The medieval town grew at the foot of a fortified castle, the Burcht, erected in the 9C on an artificial mound. It owed its prosperity to its location on the Oude Rijn, which was then the main branch of the river, but the displacement of the mouth of the estuary towards Rotterdam reduced the town's role to that of an inland market. In the 14C Leiden regained a certain prosperity with the linen industry introduced by weavers from Ieper (Belgium) taking refuge from the Black Death.

John of Leiden was born here in 1509. He was the leader of the Anabaptists, members of a religious sect, who took refuge in Münster, Germany, in 1534. The town was seized in 1535 and John of Leiden died the following year.

A heroic siege – In the 16C the town was besieged twice by the Spanish. The first siege (end 1573 – March 1574) failed. The second, started a month later was terrible. The population, reduced to half due to plague and starvation, revolted against the burgomaster Van der Werff, who offered his body to the famished. Revived by the courage of their leader, the inhabitants continued their resistance.

Finally, William the Silent had the idea of breaching the dikes to flood the surrounding countryside. On 3 October the Spanish were attacked by the Sea Beggars, who had sailed in over the flooded land on flat-bottomed boats; the Spaniards raised the siege, abandoning, at the foot of the ramparts, a big pot of beef stew (hutspot). The inhabitants of Leiden were then supplied with bread and herring. Since that time a commemorative feast, **Leidens Ontzet**, has taken place annually with a historical procession, distribution of herring and white bread and eating of beef stew (hutspot) in memory of the pot left by the Spanish. To reward the town, William the Silent founded a university here in 1575.

Leiden University – It was the first in the Low Countries liberated from Spain and for a long time rivalled that of Leuven, which had remained Catholic; it very quickly acquired a European reputation due to its relatively tolerant spirit and the great minds it drew there: the Flemish humanist Justus Lipsius (1547-1606); the philologist Daniël Heinsius (1580-1655); the famous theologians Gomarus, Arminius and Episcopius (see DORDRECHT); the French philologists Saumaise (1588-1653) and Joseph Scaliger (1540-1609); the physician and botanist **Boerhaave**, master of clinical education (1668-1738); and **Van Musschenbroek** (1692-1761), inventor in 1746 of the Leiden jar, the first electrical condenser. In 1637 **René Descartes** (1596-1650) published anonymously in Leiden his Discourse on Method written in Utrecht, where he had formerly lived. The influence of the university was increased by the fact that Leiden had become a great centre of printing in the 17C due to the illustrious **Elzevier** family; the first member of the family to settle here was Louis, who came from Leuven (Belgium) and moved to Leiden in 1580.

The Protestant refuge – In the 16C and 17C Leiden welcomed numerous Flemish and French Protestants (who fled in 1685 because of the Revocation of the Edict of Nantes) as well as English. In 1609 a hundred or so English Puritans arrived via Amsterdam, led by their spiritual leader **John Robinson** (c 1575-1625). They had left their country under the threat of persecution. Former farmers, they had to adapt themselves to their new urban condition and applied themselves to various handicraft trades. A printing press published religious works which were exported to England and Scotland. Their stay became difficult and the Puritans decided to leave Leiden and go to America. Sailing from Delfshaven on the Speedwell they reached England and embarked on the Mayflower in Plymouth. The 102 emigrants among which there were 41 Puritans or **Pilgrim Fathers** landed in December 1620 on the coast south-east of present-day Boston and founded Plymouth Colony, the first permanent settlement established in New England.

WHERE TO STAY

As a student town Leiden has few really special hotels, but here are some suggestions.

MODERATE

Het Haagsche Schouw – *Haagse Schouwweg 14, 2332 KG, ☏ (071) 531 57 44, Fax (071) 576 24 22. www.valk.com 62 rooms.* This modern hotel, part of the Van der Valk chain, is outside the centre near the A 44 motorway. It is linked by a covered footbridge to a 17C inn, Het Haagsche Schouw, where the restaurant and dining rooms are located.

MID-RANGE

Nieuw Minerva – *Boommarkt 23, 2311 EA, ☏ (071) 512 63 58, fax (071) 514 26 74. www.nieuwminerva.nl 40 rooms.* Fourteen of the forty rooms in this centrally located hotel have their own name and individual style. There is for instance the Angel's Paradise (Engelenbak) with a canopy bed; the Keukenhof Room, named after the famous bulb fields and decorated with tulip motifs; the Safari Room with a mosquito net and the Posh Room with a wooden bedstead. There is also an unusual bridal suite.

De Doelen – *Rapenburg 2, 2311 EV, ☏ (071) 512 05 27, Fax (071) 512 84 53. www.dedoelen.com 15 rooms.* This small hotel is located in a historic building a stone's throw from many of the main sights, and thus an ideal base for a visit to the town. Start your day in style in the beautiful breakfast room.

WHERE TO EAT

't Pannekoekenhuysje – *Steenstraat 51-53, ☏ (071) 513 31 44.* Here delicious pancakes are served on delft plates.

De Poort van Leyden – *Haven 100, ☏ (071) 513 31 44.* This brasserie, located in the Zijlpoort (1667), one of two remaining town gates of Leiden, has a good atmosphere, and a fine view of the town ramparts from the conservatory. In the summer months the terrace by the water's edge is opened up. Good for a quick lunch, an extensive evening meal, or just a drink.

Anak Bandung – *Garenmarkt 24a, ☏ (071) 512 53 03.* Indonesian cuisine, including rijsttafel. Meals served on the terrace in summer. Open evenings only.

Stadscafé/Restaurant Van der Werff – *Steenstraat 2, ☏ (071) 513 03 35.* A stylish place for a drink or snack when visiting the Rijksmuseum voor Volkenkunde.

De Knip – *In Voorschoten, 5km/3mi from the centre of Leiden, Kniplaan 22 (4km/2mi via Veurseweg). ☏ (071) 561 25 73.* Wonderful meals served on a shaded waterside terrace. Closed Mondays.

PRACTICAL INFORMATION

General information – The VVV tourist information office (Stationsweg 2d, 2312 AV Leiden, ☏ (0900) 22 22 333 or www.leiden.nl) has information on sights, tours, cultural events, excursions etc.

The staff can also help with finding accommodation. The VVV publishes an annual brochure listing hotels, pensions and camp sites in and around Leiden.

Transport – **Car**: a 24hr parking permit (dagkaart) for the centre of Leiden costs 16 guilders and can be purchased from meters or the VVV. The Haagweg car park on the edge of town costs 7.5 guilders a day, including the shuttle-bus fare to the town centre. **Bicycles** can be hired at the Rijwielshop (bicycle shop) behind the station, ☏ (071) 512 00 68.

Tours and walks – The VVV sells leaflets detailing two walking tours: one of Leiden's almshouses and the other following in the footsteps of Rembrandt. It also organises tours.

Boat trips – **Canal tours** of the town centre depart from Beestenmarkt (operated by Rederij Rembrandt, ☏ (071) 513 49 38). Trips along the **Oude Rijn** to Avifauna leave from Oude Singel *(see Excursions)*; there are also **tours to Braassem** and the **polders** and **windmills** leaving from the harbour opposite no 14 (Rederij Slingerland, ☏ (071) 541 31 83).

Shopping – The historic town centre is a pleasant place to shop. Late-night shopping (until 9pm) is on Thursdays.

Markets – A large **general market** is held on the waterside in the town centre every Wednesday and Saturday from 9am to 5pm. This tradition dates back 900 years.

Nightlife – Being a university town, Leiden has a very lively nightlife, and the bars and cafés are particularly crowded on Thursday evenings. **Theatre and concert halls**: information and bookings from the VVV.

Events – The **Leidse Blues & Jazzweek** is held in January in the town centre. The **Leidse Lakenfeesten** is a ten-day cloth festival held in July, featuring a cloth market, a parade, a street musicians' competition and other events. The raising of the **siege of Leiden** is commemorated on 2 and 3 October.

Admission times and charges for the sights described are listed at the end of the guide. Every sight for which there are times and charges is identified by the symbol ⊘ in the Sights section of the guide.

LEIDEN

The most important sights in this guide can be found on the Principal Sights map, and are described in the text. Use the map and plans, the Calendar of events, the index, and read the Introduction to get the most out of this guide.

LEIDEN SCHOOL

From the 15C to the 17C a great number of painters were born in Leiden, including the illustrious Rembrandt.

Geertgen tot Sint Jans (c 1465-c 1495), who died in Haarlem, is the most gifted painter of the late 15C. Although still turned towards the Middle Ages, he showed virtuosity in the treatment of fabrics *(illustration: see Introduction, The arts)*. **Cornelis Engebrechtszoon** (1468-1533) also retained a Gothic style, with crowded compositions and rather tormented linear painting. His pupil **Lucas van Leyden** (1489 or 1494-1533) is the great Renaissance painter. Influenced by Italian art his *Last Judgement*, which can be seen in the Lakenhal, is a very fine work, with its balance of composition, sense of depth, elegant draughtsmanship and fine colours.

At the beginning of the 17C a few artists of the Leiden School painted *vanitas*, still life paintings where certain specific objects representing the arts and sciences (books, maps etc), wealth (jewellery), earthly pleasures (goblets, playing cards) or death (skulls) are depicted with great precision, often with a moralistic message. These subjects were much used by Jan Davidszoon de Heem *(see UTRECHT)* when he stayed here before going to Antwerp.

Jan van Goyen, born in Leiden in 1596, went to live in Haarlem in 1631 where he died (1656). He was a great painter of pale, monochromatic landscapes with immense skies covered with clouds. Son of **Willem van de Velde the Elder** (c 1611-93), **Willem van de Velde the Younger** (1633-1707), specialised like his father in painting pictures of naval battles, in which the light formed an integral part of the composition. The Van de Veldes ended their lives in London, where they became court painters to Charles II. **Gerrit Dou** (1613-75) is perhaps the most conscientious of all the intimate genre painters of Leiden. He took to chiaroscuro when a pupil of the master, Rembrandt, but he produced mainly scenes of bourgeois life *(Young Woman Dressing*, Museum Boijmans Van Beuningen in Rotterdam). His pupil **Frans van Mieris the Elder** (1635-81) depicted smiling people in refined interiors. **Gabriel Metsu** (1629-67) was a genre painter and a master in his manner of treating fabrics and the substance of objects; he treated with great sensitivity slightly sentimental subjects .

Unlike his contemporaries, **Jan Steen** (1626-79) depicts very busy scenes with humour. His paintings display the whole human comedy where somewhat dishevelled people indulge in various pleasures; they play music, drink, eat and play in a very unruly atmosphere *(illustration: see AMSTERDAM)*.

★★ THE OLD TOWN AND ITS MUSEUMS

★★ **Rijksmuseum voor Volkenkunde** ⊙ – This ethnology museum is famous for its collections of non-Western civilisations. These ethnographic collections were started by King William I (1772-1843), who sent scholars all over the world to build a collection of rarities. Later three significant Japanese collections were acquired (including the PF von Siebold collection), and the Indonesian collection also grew. Today the museum collection covers the entire world and is divided into ten areas: **Africa** (bronze from Benin, masks, sculptures), the **Arctic regions** (ivory, leather coats), **China** (earthenware, wooden Bodhisattva sculptures, roller paintings), **Indonesia** (gamelans, wajang marionettes, basalt Hindu figures, Kris daggers, textiles), **Japan and Korea** (bronze Buddha figures, lacquerware, prints, porcelain), **Latin America** (mummies from Peru, Mexican earthenware, headdresses), **North America** (fighting implements, Kachina masks), **Oceania** (tree-bark paintings, women's figures), **Southern and South-East Asia** (Indian prints, Nepalese spinning wheel) and **South-West and Central Asia** (objects used in Tibetan worship, Turcoman amulets). The museum was extensively renovated and extended between 1997 and 2001 and is now beautifully presented. Visitors can either walk from one continent to another or choose to follow an itinerary taking in all the major exhibits. The park in which the museum is set contains sculptures by contemporary non-Western artists.

Molenmuseum De Valk ⊙ – This tower mill, the last in Leiden and built in 1743, bears the name of a bird of prey (*valk*: falcon). It has seven floors and the first ones were the living quarters. The mill was in operation until 1964. Today the repair workshop, the forge and the drawing room (zondagskamer) are all open to visitors. There is also an exhibition retracing the history of Dutch windmills.

★★ **Stedlijk Museum De Lakenhal** ⊙ – Installed in the old cloth merchants' hall (lakenhal) of 1640, this is a museum of decorative arts (furniture, silverware, pewterware), which also contains a fine section of paintings.

The 1st floor focuses on the **textile industry** that has been so important to Leiden. The various stages of wool production are shown in a 16C series of paintings by Isaac van Swanenburgh. On the 2nd floor the town's history is evoked, including the raising of the **siege of Leiden** on 3 October 1574. Its religious past is also chronicled; there is a chapel from the old Catholic church *(see UTRECHT)* and a display on the persecution and execution of the Remonstrants *(see DORDRECHT)* in 1623. All over the museum are objects from the collections of glassware, silver, tin and tiles, as well as **painting and decorative arts** from the 16C to the 20C, including numerous Leiden masters.

By Cornelis Engebrechtszoon (room 16) there are two admirably detailed triptychs: *Crucifixion* and *Descent from the Cross*, as well as a small *Carrying of the Cross*. But the works of **Lucas van Leyden** dominate. In his luminous triptych of the **Last Judgement** (1527) painted with assurance of draughtsmanship, the painter knew how to free the figures from constraint and rigidity. The central panel shows the Son of Man enthroned in thick clouds for the Supreme Judgement. On the panels heaven and hell are painted, and on the back, St Peter and St Paul, the town's patron saints. Among the 17C Leiden painters exhibited are Gerrit Dou, Jan Steen and some of the highly polished works of Mieris the Elder as well as an early work by Rembrandt. The museum also possesses some fine 17C paintings: a still-life by J Davidszoon de Heem, *Horse Market at Valkenburg* by Salomon van Ruysdael and landscapes by Van Goyen. The period from the 18C to the early 20C is also represented. The collection of contemporary art is shown in temporary exhibitions.

To the south of **Turfmarkt** there is a lovely **view** over the harbour and the mill. Further on, on **Prinsessekade** an old warehouse has been restored, which looks on to Galgewater harbour.

* Rapenburg – This is the most beautiful canal in Leiden, spanned by triple-arched bridges and lined with trees. On the west side there are some fine houses dating from the town's golden era.

** Rijksmuseum van Oudheden ⊘ – The national museum of antiquities has important collections of Items from Egypt, the Middle East, Greece and Rome, as well as a Dutch archaeology section. The museum has recently been extensively rebuilt and extended and now boasts a covered inner courtyard and air-conditioned rooms. The **Egyptian collection****, including sarcophagi, mummies, funerary amphora and other funerary objects, is particularly interesting. The sculpture collection includes two burial chapels, reliefs, the splendid stele from Hoey and the famous figures of Maya and Merit. Bronze figurines, jewellery, amulets, earthenware, etc. are brought together to give a good overall picture of ancient Egyptian handicrafts. Egyptian art from the time of the Roman emperors and Coptic art also feature. The **Classical Antiquity** section includes glassware and ceramics, but is primarily known for its sculptures and its amphorae decor-

Stele (detail), c 1300 BC from Hoey

ated with mythological figures. The rooms devoted to the **Middle East** contain archaeological finds from Mesopotamia, Syria-Palestine, Turkey and Iran, and include examples of cuneiform script and utensils and decorative objects made of stone, ivory, bronze, gold and silver. The **Dutch archaeology section** provides detailed coverage of the Netherlands' early history from 250 000 years ago to the early Middle Ages and includes the gold brooch from Dorestad and the silver Viking treasure from Wieringen.

In the Taffeh hall is the **Temple of Isis from Taffeh** in Nubia, dating from the Augustan age (27 BC to AD 14). It was given to the Netherlands in 1969 by the Egyptian government as a gesture of thanks for its contribution to UNESCO's international campaign in connection with the Aswan dam. The building of the dam involved flooding a large part of Nubia, and various monuments had to be dug up and moved.

The **Koninklijk Penningkabinet** ⊘ (Royal Coin Collection) is shown in temporary exhibitions.

Rembrandt

Rembrandt Harmenszoon van Rijn was born in Leiden in 1606. Son of a miller he lived near the Rhine, hence his name Van Rijn. His childhood remains mysterious. In 1620 he enrolled at Leiden University, but attracted by painting

Foto © Mauritshuis

he soon became an apprentice to Jacob van Swanenburgh, then in 1623 in Amsterdam to **Pieter Lastman** (1583-1633), a great admirer of Italy and Caravaggio. Although he painted numerous portraits and even self-portraits, Rembrandt right from the start showed a penchant for biblical history, which he first painted with minute detail typical of the Leiden School.

Unlike other great painters of his time the artist never studied in Italy, and adopted a very personal style. His chiaroscuro was not that of Caravaggio, where strong contrasts between light and shade existed, but showed an imperceptible change from shadow to people suffused with a warm light who occupied the centre of the painting. His works are steeped in a mysterious atmosphere from

Rembrandt, Self portrait aged 23,
Mauritshuis, The Hague

which an intense emotion and profound spirituality emanate. Beginning in 1628 he took up etching and drawing, sometimes seeking inspiration from ordinary people, such as beggars.

At the end of 1631 he settled in Amsterdam; it was then that he painted the famous **The Anatomy Lesson of Doctor Tulp** (1632). This group portrait brought glory to the young painter of 26. Orders started flowing in. Rembrandt met Saskia whom he married in 1634. Several children were born, one of whom, Titus, was born in 1641. In 1639 he moved to a house in the Jewish quarter, the present Rembrandthuis. In 1642 he painted his greatest work, the **Night Watch**, a group portrait of members of the civic guard. This genre, which had already been revived by Frans Hals, is treated by Rembrandt with daring and complexity of technique up to then unequalled. However, not much interest was shown in this painting at the time, although it was to become his most famous. In addition, 1642 marked the beginning of the painter's misfortune: he lost his wife Saskia, having already seen his parents die in 1630 and 1640. He painted numerous portraits including that of the young Titus (1655) and a solemn *Self-Portrait* (1652), but the wealthy art patrons began to abandon him with the exception of the burgomaster Jan Six. In 1657 and 1658 he was unable to pay his debts and had to sell his house and goods. In 1661 his *Conspiracy of Julius Civilis*, commissioned for the town hall, was refused (National Museum in Stockholm).

In 1662 he lost his mistress Hendrickje Stoffels. **The Sampling Officials of the Drapers Guild** (1662) was his last group painting, but he still did some marvellous paintings such as the *Jewish Bride* before passing away, forgotten, a year after his son Titus, in 1669. He had just completed his last self-portrait.

The Rijksmuseum in Amsterdam has an exceptional collection of the master's works.

Among Rembrandt's numerous pupils in Amsterdam, were the landscape painter **Philips Koninck** (1619-88) and several painters who came from Dordrecht *(see DORDRECHT)* or Leiden, such as Gerrit Dou.

Academiegebouw – Since the 16C the administrative offices of the university have been housed in the chapel of a former convent. Upstairs on the first floor there is a "sweating room" where the nervous students waited to take their exams. The **Academisch Historisch Museum** ⊙, housed in the vaulted room, retraces the history of the university since 1575.

Hortus Botanicus ⊙ – The botanical garden was founded by the university in 1590 for the purpose of cultivating and studying plants from all over the world, but more particularly from Asia. In 1593, Clusius brought the first Dutch tulips into flower here. The Clusiustuin (Clusius garden) is a reconstruction of the original garden. The orangery and greenhouses contain tropical and subtropical plants, such as Victoria Amazonica, the giant water-lily that flowers at night. The garden also contains centuries-old trees and a Japanese garden. A new addition is the Winter garden, where a footbridge affords a fine view over the trees and plants below.

Latijnse School – The Latin School was founded in 1324, and in 1599 it was given a Renaissance frontage.

Continue to Breestrat via Pieterskerkkoorsteeg.

Gravensteen – This former prison is now home to the Law Faculty and has a lovely classical front on the church side.

Pieterskerk ⊙ – St Peter's, a large and heavily built Gothic church with a nave and four aisles, stands in the middle of the churchyard (Pieterskerkhof). There are memorial slabs to the painter Jan Steen and Professor Boerhaave as well as the Puritan leader, John Robinson *(see above)*. The church is now a multi-purpose centre.

Jean Pesijnhofje – Built in 1683 on the site of John Robinson's house and intended for the members of the Walloon church, this almshouse took the name of its founder, Jean Pesijn, a French merchant of Huguenot origin. There is a memorial slab to John Robinson.

Breestraat – This, the town's main shopping street, is very busy. At the point where the itinerary crosses it, there is a **blue stone** where executions took place.

Stadhuis – Built in 1600 and damaged in a fire in 1929, the town hall was rebuilt in its original style. It has a perron in front and is topped with a very decorative gable.

Burcht – At the beginning of Nieuwstraat one can see the 17C entrance doorway of the **Burcht** topped by a lion with the town's coat of arms (two keys). This fortress was built on an artificial mound at the confluence of the Oude Rijn and the Nieuwe Rijn. There remains a stout curtain wall with crenellations and loopholes. Its watchpath offers a panorama over the town.

St.-Pancraskerk or Hooglandsekerk – This 15C church has interesting Flamboyant sculptured portals at the transepts.

Leiden American Pilgrim Museum ⊙ – In this small 16C house is a collection of objects and documents associated with the Pilgrim Fathers during their time in Leiden (1608-1620) *(see above)*.

Hooglandse Kerkgracht – Alongside this filled-in canal is the old orphanage, **Weeshuis**, with a decorative panel above the doorway depicting foundlings. At nos 19-21 is the centre for visual arts, the **CBK** (Centrum Beeldende Kunst Leiden), where exhibitions and other activities are held.

Waag – The weigh-house was built in 1657-59 by Pieter Post.

Leiden's "hofjes"

Hofjes are almshouses built round a central courtyard or garden; Leiden has 35 of them, and they are primarily a Dutch phenomenon. They were originally intended as homes for the elderly poor, and were mostly set up by wealthy church elders hoping to gain a place in heaven through the prayers of the occupants, who received free accommodation and sometimes food, drink and clothing. In return, they had to comply with a strict set of rules laid down by the regents, or governors, who were usually descendants of the dead founder. Sometimes the regents had a separate meeting room, or regentenkamer, in the almshouses.

Most hofjes have only one entrance from the street, consisting of a passageway (sometimes with a gatehouse) or entrance hall. In the past, the gate would be opened and closed by a porter at fixed times of day.

Today, the hofjes are oases of tranquillity amid the hubbub of the city, and are therefore very popular places to live. When you visit, please respect the peace and privacy of the people who live there.

ADDITIONAL SIGHTS

★ **Museum Boerhaave** ⓥ – This well-appointed museum is located in the former hospital Caeciliagasthuis (1596), where the famous scientist and doctor Herman Boerhaave *(see above)* taught his medical students from his sickbed. Its very varied collection of instruments and documents is one of the most important in the world, giving an overview of five centuries of natural sciences and medicine. It includes the collection of astronomical and surgical instruments formerly owned by Christiaan Huygens, inventor of the pendulum clock, and the microscopes of the naturalist, Antonie van Leeuwenhoek. The reconstructed Anatomy Theatre (1596) contains a collection of human and animal skeletons.

Loridanshofje – The 1656 almshouse at no 1 Oude Varkenmarkt has a simple inner courtyard. At Noordeinde 2a, the former nautical college houses a **model-making museum** ⓥ. At the far end of Oude Varkenmarkt is the 1645 gateway, **Doelenpoort**, crowned with an equestrian statue of St George, the patron saint of the archers' guild.

★★ **Naturalis** ⓥ – *Follow Plesmanlaan towards The Hague; turn right into Darwinweg after the Academisch Ziekenhuis (Leiden teaching hospital).* The entrance to this natural history museum is located in the 17C pest-house, which was built outside the centre because of its function. The buildings around the attractive courtyard include a **Nature Information Centre**. The glass **zebra bridge** leads to the modern part of the museum, which contains seven permanent exhibitions. These bring the complexity and richness of the natural world to life in an exciting and interactive way.

The **Oerparade** (prehistoric parade) exhibition includes hundreds of fossils, dinosaur skeletons and a mosasaur, an extinct aquatic lizard. Don't miss the million-year-old remains of Java Man, discovered in 1891 by the Dutch anthropologist Eugène Dubois. The lights in the central tree trunk trace the 3.8-billion-year evolution from the first life forms to the animals of today. The top of the tree is in the floor of the **Natuurtheater**, where hundreds of (stuffed) animals run, fly, swim and crawl. The rich variety of plants, fungi, algae and bacteria are displayed in an original way, followed by stones and minerals. **Aarde**, or Earth, shows how earthquakes and volcanoes occur, why the Earth's crust and the weather and the atmosphere are in a constant state of change, and what happens at the centre of the planet. **Leven** (life) explores how humans and animals obtain food, protect themselves and reproduce. On the walls of the **Ecosystemen** room, videos show the different types of ecosystems, such as the polar seas, deserts, tundra and tropical rainforests, and the relationships between animals, plants and the environment. The history of how different periods and cultures (Islam, 18C Enlightenment, Tao culture, ancient Egypt) have viewed life and nature is explored in **Visies op natuur**. Another unmissable attraction is the

© Naturalis - Ger van der Vlugt

Natuurtheater

Schatkamer (treasury), which includes King William I's collection of precious stones, as well as unusual minerals and extinct animals such as the Cape lion and the Tasmanian wolf. In view of the fragility of the objects, the Treasury is open only from 1.30pm to 4.30pm. **Kijkje Aarde**, a look at the Earth, is ideal for children, with stones, trees and animals talking about the various cycles that exist in nature.

The museum also holds **temporary exhibitions**, showing selections from the huge collection of 10 million mammals, insects, birds, butterflies, fossils and minerals normally held in the tower.

EXCURSIONS

★★ **Keukenhof** – *See KEUKENHOF and BULB FIELDS.*

Alphen aan den Rijn – *17km/11mi to the east via the Hoge Rijndijk. Can be reached by boat.* Alphen aan den Rijn is a small industrial town on the banks of the Oude Rijn.

Vogelpark Avifauna ⊘ is a substantial bird park (over 3 000 birds), with large cages for rare birds, a tropical aviary with waterfall, a pool complete with penguins, and ponds with pink flamingos. It also has a large playground and is the departure point for **boat trips** to the Braassemermeer, the lake to the north of Alphen.

★ **Archeon** ⊘ – *On the south side of Alphen.* This archaeological theme park is divided into three areas showing what life in the Netherlands was like during the prehistoric, Roman and medieval periods, with people dressed in authentic costumes bringing the past to life.

In the park, where the planting is designed to be appropriate to each particular historical era, there are excellent reconstructions of settlements, camps and homes. The prehistory section, for example, includes the settlements of the early agriculturists, the Vlaardingen culture and the builders of the prehistoric funerary monuments known as *hunebedden*. The Roman section includes a bath-house where visitors can obtain a massage, while gladiator fights are held in the arena. The medieval section is bustling with people: the civic guard keeps an eye on visitors as they enter, and the basket-maker, baker and shoemaker give demonstrations of their work. The monastery of Gravendam has been reconstructed based on excavations in Dordrecht, and here you can obtain a medieval meal prepared by the Friars Minor.

Katwijk aan Zee and Noordwijk aan Zee – *18km/11mi to the north-west; leave Leiden by Oegstgeesterweg. Local map see KEUKENHOF, Bulb fields.*

⌂ **Katwijk aan Zee** – This is a popular resort not far from the bulb fields. The long sandy beach is backed by lines of dunes.

⌂⌂ **Noordwijk aan Zee** – This fashionable seaside resort has excellent amenities for the visitor. Again a wide sandy beach stretches seawards from the chain of high dunes. Several flower parades (Bloemencorso) pass through Noordwijk *(see Calendar of events)*.

Behind the dunes of Noordwijk is ESTEC, the technical branch of the European Space Agency, where satellites are tested and European space projects are managed. A little further on is **Noordwijk Space Expo** ⊘ *(Keplerlaan 3)*, where model rockets, real satellites, space suits, photographs, a slide show and other items tell the story of mainly European space flight. There is also a discovery trail for children, the reward for which is an astronaut's diploma signed by Wubbo Ockels, the first Dutchman into space.

Nationaal Museum Paleis Het LOO★★★

Gelderland

Michelin maps 908 15 and 211 U 9

Het Loo Palace and its gardens were opened to the public in 1984 following an extensive restoration programme. The palace and gardens are surrounded by a 650-ha/1 626-acre park ⊙ in the heart of the Veluwe, which abounds in game.

HISTORICAL NOTES

When **William III** (1650-1702), Prince of Orange and Stadtholder of the United Provinces, bought the 14C-15C castle, Het Oude Loo in 1684, this ardent huntsman was fulfilling a lifetime's dream. In 1685 the first stone of Het Loo Palace was laid, about 300yd/275m from the site of the old castle, by William's wife Princess **Mary II**, daughter to James II. Het Loo Palace was intended for the princely couple with their court and guests, as well as their large hunt.

The palace was built by **Jacob Roman** (1640-1716), pupil of Pieter Post. The interior decoration and the design of the gardens were commissioned by **Daniël Marot** (1661-1752), a Parisian Huguenot, who probably arrived in the Netherlands shortly after the Revocation of the Edict of Nantes (1685).

In 1689 William III was proclaimed King of England after his father-in-law and uncle, James II, had fled the country. Het Loo Palace was to become a royal palace, and had to be enlarged: the colonnades which linked the main part of the building to the wings were replaced by four pavilions and the gardens were further embellished.

1684	**William III**, Prince of Orange and Stadtholder of the United Provinces, buys Het Oude Loo.
1685	Building starts at Het Loo. Revocation of the Edict of Nantes.
1688-97	War of the League of Augsburg.
1689	William and Princess Mary crowned King and Queen of England.
1692	An extension is made to the palace.
1694	Queen Mary dies in England.
1702	The King-Stadtholder William III dies without a successor.
1747-51	**William IV**, son of John William Friso, hereditary Stadtholder of the United Provinces.
1751-95	**William V**, son of the precedent stadtholder.
1795	Conquest of the country by the French army. William V flees to England. Het Loo seized by the French, suffers from the destructive rage of the soldiers.
1795-1806	The Batavian Republic.
1806-10	Louis Bonaparte, King of Holland, puts rough-cast on the palace façade and commissions an English-style park.
1810	The Kingdom of Holland becomes part of the French Empire.
Oct 1811	Emperor Napoleon stays briefly at Het Loo Palace.
1815	Het Loo, now State property, is offered to **King William I** as a summer residence.
1840	At Het Loo Palace, William I abdicates in favour of his son **William II**.
1849-90	Reign of **William III**.
1890-8	Regency of **Queen Emma**.
1898	Reign of **Wilhelmina**, only daughter of William III and Emma.
1901	Marriage of Queen Wilhelmina to Duke Henry of Mecklenburg-Schwerin.
1904-14	The State decides to extend and refurbish the palace.
1948	Abdication of Queen Wilhelmina, who retires to Het Loo Palace.
1962	Death of Queen Wilhelmina.
1967-75	Princess Margriet, daughter of Queen Juliana, and her family are the last members of the royal family to live at Het Loo.
1969	Queen Juliana donates the palace to the nation and it is decided to create a museum.
1977-84	Restoration of the palace and gardens.
June 1984	Opening of the **National Museum**.

HET LOO-APPARTEMENTEN
1st FLOOR
0   10 m

KING-STADHOUDER
WILLIAM III'S SUITE

Slaapkamer van Willem III ★

★ Kamer van
koning Willem III

to ground floor

Cabinet van Mary ★★

QUEEN
MARY II'S SUITE

★ Grote of
Audiëntiezaal

★ Bibliotheek

Hek van verguld smeedijzer ★★★   Grotto

GROUND FLOOR

King's Garden

★ Werkkamer van
koningin Wilhelmina

★ Zitkamer van koningin Wilhelmina

Queen's Garden

Nieuwe Eetzaal ★

to 1st floor

Chapel

TOUR ⊘ about 3hr

Since the rooms are lit as they were in days gone by, some of the rooms can be fairly dark. It is therefore advisable to choose a sunny day on which to visit the palace.

After having walked alongside the **royal stables** (fine series of vintage cars and sleighs, late 19C-early 20C), the visitor comes to a wide avenue, where the beech trees form a magnificent vault. Beyond this is a vast brick building flanked with long wings which surrounds the main courtyard. A grille, painted blue and gold, encloses the main courtyard, where a fountain decorated with dolphins was used to water the horses.

The finely proportioned building, built on a north-south axis, is impressive for its severe sobriety, characteristic of the Dutch Baroque style. The only decorative elements are the tympana (sandstone) of hunting scenes, and the window sills. The east pavilions were intended for Queen Mary while those situated to the west included those of the King-Stadtholder William III. The sash windows of the main part of the building and the pavilions were a novelty often believed to be a Dutch invention and characteristic of English Georgian style.

East Wing – The east wing contains a collection of historic documents, ceramics, paintings and prints as well as *objets d'art* regarding the most illustrious members of the House of Orange. Many of the documents were written in French, the language used by the Dutch court until the regency of Queen Emma (1890).

West Wing – On the ground floor there is a video film show on the history of the palace and its restoration. On the first floor the **Museum of the Chancery of the Netherlands Orders of Knighthood** (Museum van de Kanselarij der Nederlandse Orden) exhibits insignia, uniforms, Dutch and foreign Orders.

★★★ **Apartments** – *Access by a staircase on the side of the steps leading to the main building.*

From the vaulted cellars a staircase leads up to the **great hall** (**1**) where two 17C garden vases, after drawings by Daniel Marot, are exhibited.

The **old dining room** (**2**) is hung with 17C Antwerp tapestries. Note the cabinet (Antwerp, 1630), with biblical scenes painted by Frans Francken the Younger. The remarkable **new dining room**★★★ (**3**) (c 1692) is a very good example of Marot's contribution to the palace's interior decoration. The white columns and pilasters, decorated with gold bands, combine with the coffered ceiling to give this room, hardly bigger than the old dining room, a majestic character. On the walls, the Brussels tapestries (c 1690) depict the armorial bearings and monograms of William III and his Queen, as well as a mirror (1689), in finely carved gilded wood, which came from Honselersdijk Kasteel (south of The Hague; the castle has since been demolished).

Here, as in other rooms, there are some admirable Dutch chairs (late-17C) with their high backs of finely worked wood.

At the end of the **white hall** (**4**), which has portraits of members of the Nassau family who lived in Friesland, a staircase leads up to the **chapel** (**5**) where **organ concerts** ⊙ are held. The coffered stucco ceiling is by Marot. The Bible exhibited is a gift from the Dutch people to their King, William III, who had shown generosity during the 1861 floods. It was in this chapel that many Dutch filed past to bid farewell to Queen Wilhelmina (her funeral took place in Delft).

Go back down the stairs and take the left corridor.

At the end of the corridor on the left, **Prince William IV's Chamber** (**6**), a luminous room due to the yellow silk damask, has, apart from portraits of the stadtholder and his wife Anne of Hanover, Princess of England, daughter of George II, a crystal chandelier (c 1747) and a ceiling decorated with Chinese motifs. The walls of the **Frisian Cabinet** (**7**), opposite, are covered with gilded leather (18C). Note also the portraits of the Frisian Nassaus.

The **library**★ (**9**), on the first floor, was laid out after Marot's drawings and decorated with a stucco ceiling inlaid with mirrors. Beyond the library, the **gallery** (**10**), decorated with panelling and green damask, has some magnificent chandeliers and contains a fine collection of paintings. Next to the window giving on to the main courtyard, there are portraits of René de Chalon and his wife Anne of Lotharingia (1542); William the Silent (two first portraits on the left) inherited the Principality of Orange from René de Chalon. Adriaen van de Venne (1589-1662) has depicted the sons and nephews of William the Silent on horseback. On either side of the chimney there are William III and Mary, King and Queen of England, Ireland and Scotland, by G Kneller, a German artist working at the English court. The portrait above the chimney showing the King-Stadtholder on horseback, is a study for a large painting exhibited in Hampton Court in London. After crossing the **drawing room** of the **Stadtholder William V** (**11**) where a porcelain chandelier from Berlin hangs from the stucco ceiling – note also portraits (1795) of William V and his wife, Princess Wilhelmina by John Hoppner – the visitor comes to the drawing room of the first Dutch King, **William I** (**12**). The Empire chairs, covered in blue and gold cloth, were made in the Dutch workshop of A Eeltjes (1751-1836) for Het Loo Palace at the request of Louis Napoleon. On the walls there are portraits of the king and his daughter Marianne.

Move on to visit the apartments of Queen Mary and the King-Stadtholder William III, reconstructed in their 17C layout.

In **Mary Stuart's Bedroom** (**13**) the sumptuous canopied four-poster bed (c 1685) is covered in Genova velvet; it comes from Kensington Palace in London, where Mary lived. The table, the two pedestal tables and the mirrors in silver and gilt silver (c 1700) are the work of an Augsburg gold and silversmith, J Bartermann. The decoration on the ceiling, where the four elements and the four cardinal virtues are depicted, is by the painter Gerard de Lairesse (1641-1721).

Mary Stuart's Dressing Room (**14**), the walls of which are covered with 17C Dutch tapestries, adjoins the **Queen's Antechamber**★★★ (**15**), which is decorated mainly in red and green. This lovely little room, where Mary had a splendid view over the gardens, has a lacquer cabinet (1690) made in England as well as Delft and Chinese porcelain.

The **great staircase** (**17**), designed by Marot, has been reconstructed by W Fabri at the request of Queen Wilhelmina.

The landscapes on the walls of the **great hall**★ (**18**) were painted by J Glauber (1646-1726); this room with lovely grisailles on a golden background is where King William I abdicated in 1840. At certain times visitors have access to the roof (entrance located between room 18 and 19) which affords a splendid **view**★★★ of the gardens

A **passage** with gilt leather hangings (**19**) leads to the **King-Stadtholder William III's Closet** (**20**). There is a fine Dutch writing-desk (late-17C). In **William III's Bedroom**★ (**21**) the wall hangings are carmine red.

The next room (22) was laid out according to the taste of **King William II**, with neo-Gothic rosewood furniture (c 1845). To the right of the king's portrait, there is a portrait of his wife, Grand Duchess Anna Pavlovna, by JB van der Hulst.

When reconstructing **Sophia's Drawing Room (23)** the watercolours painted at the queen's request, which depict the rooms she occupied, were an excellent reference. The 19C German artist Franz Xaver Winterhalter painted the portrait of Queen Sophia in a dark green dress.

The small room (24) which gives on to the King's Garden was the **King-Stadtholder William III's Closet**. At the request of the sovereign, Melchior d'Hondecoeter (1639-c 1695) painter of still-life paintings and animals, decorated the mantelpiece. The furnishings in **King William III's Bedroom★** (1817-90) **(25)** are in walnut and ebony, inlaid with ivory, brass, mother-of-pearl and semi-precious stones.

The following three small rooms contain, respectively: objects relating to **Prince Henry (1820-79) (26)**, brother of William III; a **collection of 19C watercolours (27)**; toys and furniture which had belonged to **Queen Wilhelmina** as a child **(28)**.

On the ground floor **Queen Sophia's Closet (29)** has been fitted out in Moorish style. There is also the **trophy room (30)** of Prince Henry, husband of Queen Wilhelmina. On the left of the windows there is the prince in hunting costume (1917) by J Kleintjes. **Queen Emma's Drawing Room (31)** – Emma was second wife of William III – and that of **Prince Henry (32)** are furnished according to the tastes of the time (1900). The palace visit ends with **Queen Wilhelmina's Drawing Room and Office★ (33** and **34)** arranged as they were when she was alive. The statuette on the chimney in the second room is of Gaspard de Coligny (father to William the Silent's fourth wife, Louise) who led the Huguenot army in the 16C.

Go down to the vaulted cellars, then pass between the two staircases and turn right, then left to reach the gardens.

Statue of Venus, central fountain

Ch. Bastin et J. Evrard

On the way, do not miss the **small kitchen** covered in Delft tiles. Queen Mary used this kitchen when she prepared jam, with fruit from her garden. The **small grotto** has shells, fine stones and marble decoration.

★★ **Gardens** – *Go up to the terrace.*

The superb **garden gate**★★★ in gilded wrought iron at the rear of the palace used to provide access to the terrace. It took one year for a Dutch craftsman to recreate this masterpiece (designed by D Marot) by resorting to the techniques used in those days. Under the crown the initials of William and Mary (W and M) are visible, and in the lower part, orange trees and acanthus leaves.

The terrace, flanked by two statues in sandstone symbolising the rivers which edge the Veluwe, affords a fine **view**★ over the gardens (6.5ha/16 acres).

Documents of the time, as well as traces discovered under the layers of sand in the 19C English garden, have made it possible to reconstitute the 17C gardens. In addition the choice of plants decorating the flower beds has been limited to species known at the time.

There are four gardens:

The **lower garden**, surrounded on three sides by terraces, consists of four *parterres de broderie* (embroidery-like pattern) and four English-style *parterres* decorated with statues representing Flora and Bacchus *(east side)* and Apollo and Venus receiving a golden apple from Paris *(west side)*. The Venus adorning the central fountain is the replica of a statue by Gaspar Marsy (1625-81) which is in Versailles. Note the terrestrial and celestial globes; the first *(on the left)* reflects the world as it was known in Europe at the end of the 17C, whereas the positioning of the second *(on the right)* corresponds to that of the sky above Het Loo at the birth of Princess Mary Stuart. The waterfall in the middle of the slope on the right is decorated with a very graceful statue of Narcissus gazing at himself in the water, the copy of a work by the Belgian sculptor Gabriel de Grupello (1644-1730).

Beyond the path lined with a double row of oak trees which led to Het Oude Loo (a few turrets can be seen) extends the **upper garden**. This is delimited by colonnades – go up the staircase to see the view – and among the large trees in the English-style garden, there is a tulip tree, recognisable by its leaves ending not in a point but in a V-shaped notch. The king's fountain symbolises the power of the sovereign William III who wished it to shoot water higher into the air than those of his rival Louis XIV.

Distinguished people have witnessed the qualities of the water: contrary to the water of Versailles, that of Het Loo was limpid and odourless.

The **King's Garden** *(to the west of the palace)*, where blue and orange are the dominant colours, has a lawn which was once a bowling-green. The lovely Canadian maple tree in the corner of the lawn was a present from Queen Juliana to her mother Wilhelmina.

Flowers in pastel shades and fruit trees (orange, apricot, cherry-plum, morello cherry trees) were chosen for the **Queen's Garden** *(to the east of the palace)*. This garden has a more intimate character, with its arbour of greenery.

MAASTRICHT★★

Limburg

Population 121 479

Michelin map 908 and 211 T 17

Plan of the conurbation in the current edition of The Red Guide Benelux

Once prized for its strategic location on the borders of Belgium and Germany, Maastricht is now the bustling cosmopolitan provincial capital of Limburg. The city has developed on the banks of the great Maas river from which it takes its name. The town is quite distinct from the rest of the country. Its houses built of Namur limestone are more typical of the Maasland than of Limburg, and its hilly hinterland is equally atypical of the Netherlands.

A university town since 1976, Maastricht has seven faculties. Its student population gives this historic town a vibrant feel, and its somewhat exuberant character reveals itself in the many restaurants, cafés and annual carnival festivities.

HISTORICAL NOTES

The original settlement grew around a fortified bridge built by the Romans on the Roman road from Bavay (in northern France) to Cologne, hence its name which means the Maas crossing (Mosae Trajectum).

St Servatius, finding it safer than Tongeren (Belgium), transferred his bishopric here in 382. In 722 St Hubert moved it to Liège. The town already belonged to the Frankish kings. In 1204 it passed into the trusteeship of the Duke of Brabant who, in 1283, shared his power with the Prince-Bishop of Liège.

It was given its first defensive walls in 1229.

The sieges of Maastricht – Maastricht having rallied to the Revolt of the Netherlands, the Spanish besieged the town in 1579, took it by surprise, devastated it and left only 4 000 people alive. The United Provinces annexed the town in 1632. In 1673, 40 000 French, commanded by Louis XVI appeared before the walls of Maastricht. The siege was terrible, the Dutch defence fierce. England contributed some 6 000 troops under the command of the Duke of Monmouth. But Vauban, who was directing the operations, won a victory for the French who lost 8 000 men on the battlefield, among them **D'Artagnan**, officer of the musketeers.

The French captured Maastricht again in 1748, due to a clever move by Maurice de Saxe, Marshal of Saxony. Taken by Kleber in 1794, Maastricht was annexed to France, as was Breda.

In 1814 the town became part of the Netherlands kingdom. In 1830 the garrison resisted against the Belgians, thus obtaining the right to remain part of the Netherlands, but this was only confirmed by the Treaty of London in 1839. The fortifications were partly demolished in 1867.

During the occupation, Maastricht was one of the first towns liberated, in September 1944; only its bridges were damaged.

The Maastricht Treaty – On 10 December 1991, the governments of the twelve EC members reached agreement in Maastricht on political, monetary and economic union. The Treaty on European Union was signed by the heads of government involved in February 1992, again in Maastricht.

Maastricht today – Continuing its tradition as a busy medieval centre on an important trading route, Maastricht is an active industrial centre specialising in ceramics, papermaking and cement.

The annual **carnival**★ *(see Calendar of events)* is a highly popular event which draws large crowds of townspeople and visitors to the general merry-making. The town is also known for its male voice choir, the **Mastreechter Staar**, founded in 1883.

★ OLD TOWN *half a day*

Vrijthof – This square is the heart of the town, with a large number of pedestrianised shopping streets radiating out from it. It has many outdoor cafés and restaurants, and is overlooked by two churches.

Museum Spaans Gouvernement ⊙ – To the south there is the Gothic façade of the 16C Spanish Government House, where William the Silent was declared an outlaw by Philip II of Spain. This former chapter-house has a number of period rooms around an attractive courtyard, with furniture, silverware, porcelain, glass and ceramics dating from the 17C and 18C.

★★ **St.-Servaasbasiliek** ⊙ – This imposing monument, one of the oldest in the Netherlands, although often altered, was begun c 1000 on the site of a 6C sanctuary. It then had one nave and side aisles, a transept and a flat east end. In the 12C it was enlarged on the one hand by the present chancel, flanked by two square towers and an apse, and, on the other hand, by a monumental **westwork**. The westwork is characteristic of the Rhenish-Mosan style *(see Introduction: Architecture and Sculpture)*; the basilica is one of the first examples of this style. Topped by two towers, it is decorated with Lombard arcading. There is a carillon in the south tower of the westwork.

In the 13C the lovely south portal or **royal portal**★ (Bergportaal) was built and is now painted with vivid colours; the tympanum illustrates the death, ascension and crowning of the Virgin.

In the 15C the side chapels and the north portal were added. The north portal gives on to cloisters also built in the 15C.

Interior – On the basilica's entrance portal there is a 15C statue of St Peter.

The **chancel**★ vaults (restored) have recovered their 16C paintings. With its tall pillars and the gallery above the ambulatory, the chancel forms a harmonious whole.

St. Servatius with a model of the basilica

I. Hendrikx/GLOBAL PICTURES

269

WHERE TO STAY

Maastricht is known as the most "Burgundian" town in the Netherlands, the term Burgundian evoking the times of Burgundian dominion when life, food and wine were enjoyed at their fullest. Maastricht's ebullient, exuberant character particularly reveals itself in its wide array of places to eat and stay, offering delicious food and delightful accommodation.

MODERATE

De Dousberg – *Dousbergweg 4, 6216 GC,* ☎ *(043) 346 67 77, Fax (043) 346 67 55. 52 rooms.* Budget hotel with simple rooms. On bus routes 55 and 56. Has its own café.

MID-RANGE

Dis – *Tafelstraat 28, 6211 JD,* ☎ *(043) 321 54 79, fax (043) 325 70 26. www.hoteldis.nl 6 rooms.* This small hotel enjoys a central position and occupies the upper floor of a historic building. The rooms are spacious, tastefully decorated (contemporary art and modern furniture) and adequately appointed. Breakfast is served downstairs in the vaulted room, which also functions as an art gallery.

Les Charmes – *Lenculenstraat 18, 6211 KR,* ☎ *(043) 321 74 00, fax (043) 325 85 74. www.hotellescharmes.nl 15 rooms.* This delightful small hotel is housed in an inconspicuous patrician's house dating from 1725. The informal atmosphere of the bedrooms, each one with its own individual character, echoes the relaxed personal welcome on arrival. The breakfast room has a conservatory overlooking the garden.

Botticelli – *Papenstraat 11, 6211 LG,* ☎ *(043) 352 63 00, Fax (043) 352 63 36. www.botticellihotel.nl 18 rooms.* As its name suggests, the atmosphere in this quiet hotel a stone's throw from the Vrijthof is very much an Italian one. The panelled walls of this 18C house are decorated with *trompe-l'oeil* paintings, and some of the rooms have fresco-style wall decorations. The furnishings are modern, and the spacious rooms are tastefully decorated. There is a beautiful courtyard garden between the front and back of the building.

d'Orangerie – *Kleine Gracht 4, 6211 CB,* ☎ *(043) 326 11 11, Fax (043) 326 12 87. 33 rooms.* This charming hotel is located in two historic buildings near the Maas. The rooms of various sizes still bear traces of the original interior, such as stucco ceilings, marble fireplaces and thick beams. The rest of the decor is in classic English and French style, and there is an enclosed garden at the back.

LUXURY

Derlon – *O.L.-Vrouweplein 6, 6211 HD,* ☎ *(043) 321 67 70, Fax (043) 325 19 33. www.goldentulip.nl/hotels/gtderlon 41 rooms.* This modern hotel near the Onze Lieve Vrouwebasiliek has a unique feature: Roman remains in the cellar. Important relics of a town square, a well and a road from ancient Maastricht were found here during rebuilding. This hotel is literally full of history.

WHERE TO EAT

TOWN CENTRE

Le Petit Bonheur – *Achter de Molens 2,* ☎ *(043) 321 51 09.* This restaurant lies hidden in the heart of the town, and has a rural French feel to it. In summer, you can dine at the little tables in the courtyard.

Sukhotai – *Tongersestraat 54,* ☎ *(043) 321 79 46.* Excellent Thai dishes served in suitably oriental surroundings. The patio terrace is used in summer.

Au Coin des Bons Enfants – *Ezelmarkt 4,* ☎ *(043) 321 23 59.* Housed in a 16C building, this restaurant serves culinary delights inspired by French cuisine. Meals are served on the terrace in fine weather.

Beluga – *Havenstraat 19,* ☎ *(043) 321 33 64.* This small restaurant in the Stokstraat quarter serves fine French cuisine. The quiet terrace overlooks a small square, Op de Thermen.

Toine Hermsen – *St.-Bernardusstraat 2,* ☎ *(043) 325 84 00.* The culinary high point of this "Burgundian" town; a truly excellent restaurant near the Onze Lieve Vrouwebasiliek.

RIGHT BANK (Wyck)

Gadjah Mas – *Rechtstraat 42,* ☎ *(043) 321 15 68.* Affordable, high-quality Indonesian cuisine.

Mediterraneo – *Rechtstraat 73,* ☎ *(043) 325 50 37.* An Italian restaurant further along this busy street.

't Pakhoes – *Waterpoort 4-6*, ☎ *(043) 325 70 00*. As the name suggests, this restaurant was once a warehouse (pakhuis). It serves Belgian-French cuisine and has a downstairs bar and its own terrace in the summer.

OUTSIDE MAASTRICHT

Château Neercanne – *5 km south of Maastricht along Bieslanderweg. Cannerweg 800*, ☎ *(043) 325 13 59*. The delicious French cuisine, the view over the Jeker valley, the Baroque gardens and the marl caves make a meal at this 17C castle an experience to remember. The 1611 chapel now houses l'Auberge, a lunchtime restaurant.

BRASSERIES, CAFÉS, BARS, COFFEE SHOPS...

Eetcafé Rilette – *St.-Pietersstraat 54*, ☎ *(043) 325 52 84*. A welcoming café with art on the walls and a French and Italian menu.

Café Sjiek – *St.-Pietersstraat 13*, ☎ *(043) 321 01 58*. Despite its trendy-sounding name, a relaxed kind of place serving food like grandmother used to make. The terrace in the municipal park is a great place to sit in summer.

Café Bistro 't Liewke – *Grote Gracht 62*, ☎ *(043) 321 04 59*. This attractive old house near the Vrijthoftheater makes an excellent venue for an evening out, with its intimate decor and Italian-inspired food.

PRACTICAL INFORMATION

General information – The **VVV**, or tourist information office, is at Het Dinghuis, Kleine Staat 1, 6211 ED Maastricht, ☎ (043) 325 21 21. It offers details of local sights, events, cultural activities, concert and theatre tickets and bargain accommodation packages. The **reservations department** on ☎ (043) 321 78 78 will book you a hotel room.

Transport – Parking is not allowed in the centre of town except where expressly stated. All **parking spaces** are either metered or **pay-and-display**, and if you do not pay the right amount you risk being clamped. Alternatively use one of the many well-signposted **multi-storey car parks**. The main town-centre sights are within walking distance of one another; another option is to hire a **bicycle** from Rijwielshop "Aon de Stasie" on Stationsplein.

Tours and walks – The VVV organises walks in the historic town centre during the summer months. Leaflets with details of **self-guided walks** covering particular themes and areas are also available.

Boat trips – From April to early December, **Rederij Stiphout**, ☎ (043) 351 53 19, organises various trips on the Maas, including day trips to Liège and dinner cruises.

Pavement cafés in the old town

Shopping – The best area is between Vrijthof and the station, where late-night shopping is on Thursdays. The best-known (and most expensive) shopping street is the picturesque **Stokstraat**. There are also a large number of art galleries and antique shops.

Markets – There is a **small market** in Marktplein on Wednesdays and a larger one on Fridays.

Theatre and concerts – **Uit in Maastricht** includes detailed listings of all plays, concerts and other events, and is available from the VVV, which also sells tickets. **Theater aan het Vrijthof**, Vrijthof 47, ☎ (043) 350 55 55, is the home of the Limburg Symphony Orchestra. The **Mastreechter Staar**, the town's well-known male-voice choir, usually rehearses in the Staargebouw (the former Augustinian church) on Monday and Thursday evenings.

Night-life – Maastricht has various districts, each with its own distinct atmosphere, and all with plenty of bars and restaurants. **Rechtstraat**, on the right bank, is Maastricht's answer to the Rue des Bouchers in Brussels; the **Jekerkwartier** (around the stream called the Jeker) is the town's "Latin Quarter", full of students, artists, theatres, art galleries and bars; while the **historic old town** between Markt, Vrijthof and O.L.-Vrouweplein has numerous bars and places to eat.

Events – There is always something going on in Maastricht. It all starts with the **Grand Carnival**, followed by **Easter in Maastricht**, featuring international big bands, brass bands and choirs. Early May is the time of the **St-Servaasfeest**, or festival of St Servatius, which includes processions and a fair. The **programme of summer events** includes organ and carillon concerts, a pop festival, and street theatre, and in late August a lavish culinary feast, the **Preuvenmint**, takes place on the Vrijthof. The year ends with the **Festival Musica Sacra** (September) and the town-centre **Christmas market**.

For sports lovers, there is the **Amstel Gold Race**, a cycling event that takes place in spring and begins and ends in Maastricht, and a showjumping event in autumn, **Jumping Indoor Maastricht**.

A number of trade fairs are held at the **MECC** exhibition centre, including the internationally renowned art and antiques fair **TEFAF** in March. This specialises in 16C and 17C Dutch and Flemish painting.

Inside the westwork, on the first floor, is the Emperor's Room (Keizerszaal), topped by a dome. The **capitals**★ of the westwork are interesting for their rich decoration.

The last chapel on the north aisle, towards the transept, has a Sedes Sapientiae (Seat of Wisdom) and a seated Virgin and Child, of 13C Mosan type. Nearby is a doorway, formerly the main access to the church, opening onto cloisters. Outside it is topped by a lovely tympanum depicting Christ in Majesty.

The **crypt**, which is under the nave, contains the tomb of St Servatius behind a grille, the sarcophagus of Charles the Simple and the sarcophagus of the Bishops Monulfus and Gondulfus, founders of the primitive church in the 6C, as well as two other bishops, Candidus and Valentinus. The neighbouring crypt with square pillars, under the chancel, belonged to the 6C primitive church.

★★ **Treasury** (Kerkschat) – The collegiate chapel (12C) houses the treasury: a rich collection of liturgical objects, mainly gold and silversmiths' work, ivory, sacerdotal ornaments, paintings, altarpieces and statues. There is notably a bust of St Servatius, a symbolic silver key decorated with foliated scrolls which would have been given to him by St Peter, the pectoral cross said to have belonged to St Servatius (late 10C), pieces of oriental cloth, as well as a great number of reliquaries and shrines of the late 12C. The most remarkable object is **St Servatius's shrine** called Noodkist (*illustration: see Introduction, The arts*). In oak, covered with gilded copper, enamelled, chased and decorated with precious stones, it is an important work of the Mosan School (c 1160); at each end Christ and St Servatius are depicted, with the apostles on the sides.

St.-Janskerk – This Gothic church, Protestant since 1632, was built by the canons of St Servatius to be used as a parish church. Since 1987, it has been used by the Reformist community. Dating from the 12C, it was enlarged in the 15C with a chancel and a tower 70m/230ft high, decorated in the Utrecht style.

Take a few steps along Bonnefantenstraat.

From this street there is a fine view looking over a **17C house** with crow-stepped gables and the gardens of the Natural History Museum, located on the other side of the canal.

Turn back and take Looiersgracht.

Grote Looiersstraat – On this charming shaded square surrounded by old houses, a sculptured group depicts children listening to the popular Maastricht storyteller, Fons Olterdissen.

★ **Natuurhistorisch Museum** ⊙ – This natural history museum focuses on the region of Zuid-Limburg. In the **geology** section visitors are taken on a journey of discovery going back 350 million years, starting with the Carboniferous period and ending with the arrival of the first Romans. Particular attention is given to the **fossils** which were found in the Maastricht limestone beds. Many date from the Upper Cretaceous (74-65 million years ago), a period which is also referred to as the Maestrichtian. Note also the remains of the enormous Mosasauri and giant tortoises, found in Sint-Pietersberg *(see below)*. In the **biology** section, **dioramas** give explanations about the flora and fauna that thrive in the area today and the aquariums give visitors an insight into life under water. In the basement are reconstructions of a flint mine and a marlpit. Also worthy of note are the fine collection of precious stones, the Kabinet, and the period room. The botanical garden features wild plants specific to the local area.

★ **Walmuur** – The defensive walls still preserved to the south of town are dominated by numerous towers. Shaded by beautiful trees they are surrounded by pleasant gardens. On the two sections which survive one can follow the rampart walk from where there are fine views.

Follow the rampart walk, then leave it to take a footbridge crossing the small river.

Monseigneur Nolenspark – A lovely park laid out at the foot of the ramparts. Animals such as deer are kept in enclosures.

Take the rampart walk again.

From the top of the first tower one overlooks the lakes where swans and ducks swim. On the north side of the ramparts one can see the **Bejaardencentrum Molenhof** building. Beside it, near the Jeker, hides an old watermill. Continuing, one reaches the semicircular tower, **De Vijf Koppen**, where one overlooks a large lake.

Helpoort – This gate, flanked by two round towers, was part of the 13C curtain wall. It is the oldest town gate in the country.

★ **Onze Lieve Vrouwebasiliek** ⊙ – This is the oldest building in town. It is thought that it is on the site of an old Roman temple where a cathedral was built at the time when Maastricht was the episcopal see. The edifice already existed in the year 1000. The very tall **westwork** in front of the church, as at St.-Servaasbasiliek, dates from this period. It is flanked by two round turrets; its upper part, added c 1200, is decorated with Romanesque blind arcading. The nave and the beautiful apse date from the 12C.

Among interesting sculptures grouped under the left porch of the westwork, note the effigy of a bishop (c 1200). Inside, the **chancel★★** with an ambulatory

Ph. Gajic/MICHELIN

. Westwork of Onze Lieve Vrouwebasiliek, Maastricht

topped by a gallery, thus forming two rows of superimposed columns, like that at St.-Servaasbasiliek, is remarkable. Furthermore, the richly decorated capitals are very varied. The nave, like that of Rolduc Abbey near Kerkrade, has alternating thick and thin pillars supporting the vault, restored in the 18C. The transept was given pointed vaulting in the 15C. The organ case dates from 1652.

The church has two Romanesque **crypts**, one under the transept crossing (1018), the other under the westwork, and 16C cloisters.

Index of street names and sights for maps of MAASTRICHT

Treasury (Kerkschat) ⊘ – The treasury has precious reliquaries and shrines, ivory, and liturgical ornaments including Bishop Lambert's early 8C dalmatic.

Stokstraat – This is a pleasant pedestrian precinct where the lovely 17C and 18C restored houses, decorated with pediments, façade stones and signs, are now art, antique and print shops.
At no 28 there is a façade decorated with sculptured friezes.
To the west, on a small square called **Op de Thermen**, paving stones indicate the site of remains of old Roman baths discovered here in 1840.

Dinghuis – This picturesque narrow-fronted building in the Mosan Renaissance style was formerly the courthouse. It now houses the tourist information office.

Markt – On this busy main square a market takes place on Wednesdays and Fridays.
The **Stadhuis** (town hall), built 1659-65 by **Pieter Post**, is an imposing quadrilateral building preceded by a large perron and topped by a bell-tower with a **carillon** ⊘.
Return to Vrijthof by the pedestrian precinct crossing the shopping quarter.

Maastricht – the picturesque Stokstraat

J.P. Lescouret/PIX

The numbers ① – ② etc. indicate the main routes into and out of town.
They are the same on town plans and on Michelin Maps.

THE RIGHT BANK (WYCK AND CÉRAMIQUE-WIJK)

The monumental **St.-Servaasbrug** (1280-1298) is one of the oldest bridges in the country. It crosses to the "other" Maastricht: the narrow streets of the **historic Wyck district** were once the commercial centre of the town. There are still many elegant 17C and 18C mansions, particularly on the long Rechtstraat; most of these are now bars and restaurants. There are also many commercial art galleries and antique shops here.

Further on is a new commercial and residential area, **Céramique-wijk**, still partly under construction, which shows no traces of the area's rich past. It is home to the Bonnefantenmuseum, the **Maastricht Exhibition and Congress Centre** or MECC, the **Centre Céramique** (town hall, library, city archive, the European Journalism Centre) and the **Gouvernement** or government building, built partly on an island, where the European Council met in December 1991. This meeting led to the signing of the Maastricht Treaty on 7 February 1992 in the Statenzaal of the building.

★★ **Bonnefantenmuseum** ⊙ – This museum re-opened in a new building on the site of a former ceramics factory beside the Maas in 1995. The simple, E-shaped stone and brick building was designed by Aldo Rossi (1931-1977). It has a prominent silver-coloured domed tower, 28m/90ft high. The museum has very varied collections of pre-20C and modern art. The **Wiebengahal** opposite the museum is all that remains of an industrial complex dating from 1912 *(see Introduction, Industrial heritage).*

Bonnefantemuseum, Maastricht

The **pre-20C art section** *(first floor)* includes Southern Flemish works by studios and masters such as Pieter Brueghel the Younger *(Census at Bethlehem)* and Harry Met de Bles *(Landscape with the Repudiation of Hagar)*, and Italian panel paintings from 1300-1600. There is an important collection of medieval sculpture from the Maas region (c 1400-1550), dominated by the works of the Master of Elsloo and of the early 16C Maastricht sculptor Jan van Steffeswert. Also worthy of particular attention is the superb **Neutelings**★★★ collection. The collection of medieval art amassed by Willem Neutelings (1916-1986) is of exceptionally high quality, consisting of complete domestic altars, wood and alabaster altar fragments, delicate ivory diptychs, sculpture groups and free-standing copper and bronze figurines. There is a beautifully expressive late 15C alabaster "St John's charger" from Nottingham (the name refers to the beheading of St John the Baptist) and a statue of the Assumption and Coronation of the Virgin Mary, which still bears traces of red and blue paint; also a bishop's crozier (c 1240) from Limoges, ornamented with enamel, and a 16C Antwerp domestic altar with a centre panel showing Mary and Joseph with the infant Christ in a setting of Gothic

Ch. Bastin et J. Evrard

architecture, and wings painted by Jan van Dornicke. The collection also includes a movingly simple 12C bronze of Christ Crucified, probably from near Mechelen in Belgium. There is also a collection of 18C Maastricht silverware.

Selections from the museum's **modern art collection** are displayed in rotation on the second floor. This includes works by artists who made a name for themselves in the 1960s and 70s, such as Luciano Fabro, Bruce Nauman, Marcel Broodthaers, Robert Mangold, Mario Merz and Sol Le Witt, as well as contemporary artists such as Imi Knoebel, Jan Dibbets, René Daniëls, Didier Vermeiren and Marien Schouten. The museum also organises modern art exhibitions with an international flavour and aimed more specifically at the young viewer.

ADDITIONAL SIGHTS

Kazematten ⊙ – The casemates are to be found in Waldeckpark. They belonged to a system of fortifications which was built between 1575 and 1825. Most of the fortifications above ground were razed in 1867, but the network *(10km/6mi)* of underground galleries remains. Some of these galleries are open to the public, and visitors who are able to tackle the labyrinth of corridors and stairs can visit the **Waldeck Bastion** with its domed vaults, gunpowder stores and lookout posts. Not far away, near the fortified walls there is a bronze statue of D'Artagnan.

* ST.-PIETERSBERG

2km/1mi to the south via Sint-Hubertuslaan and Luikerweg.

Between the valleys of the Maas and the Jeker, St Peter's Mount rises to more than 100m/328ft high. It is above all famous for its **caves**, old quarries which have been worked since Roman times *(see also VALKENBURG)*. The stone, a sort of marl that hardens on exposure to the air, was used for numerous buildings in Maastricht.

Today the galleries extend for more than 200km/124mi with a height of up to 12m/39ft high, and are decorated with charcoal drawings. They were excavated by lowering the floor level so that now the oldest drawings covering the walls are near the roof. The sedimentary rock contains a large number of fossils. In 1780 the head of a Prehistoric animal was found; it was called Mosasaurus (*Mosa*: the Maas). This was confiscated by the French in 1795 and is now on display in the Musée d'Histoire Naturelle in Paris. A second head was found in 1998 and can be seen in the Natural History Museum.

During troubled times the caves were used to shelter the people of Maastricht; they retain traces of these periods of refuge. This was not always a pleasant experience, since the temperature is about 10°C/50°F and it is very damp.

Fort St.-Pieter ⊙ – From the fort's (1701) terrace, there is an overall view of the town. The innermost part of the fort is linked to the system of tunnels inside the hill.

Marl caves (Grotten Noord) ⊙ – During the Second World War these caves sheltered **Rembrandt**'s painting *The Night Watch*. There are graffiti here and a bas-relief of the Mosasaurus.

Continue along the road then take the second on the left to reach other caves.

Grotten Zonneberg ⊙ – These caves are very similar to the preceding ones, steeped in history and a maze of corridors covered with graffiti.

OUTSKIRTS

Cadier and Keer – *5km/3mi to the east via ④ on the town plan.*
The **Afrikacentrum** ⊙ exhibits interesting collections of art (figures and masks) and utensils from Africa.

FROM MEERSSEN TO SUSTEREN

35km/22mi. Leave via ① on the town plan.

Meerssen – Former residence of the Frankish kings. In 870 a treaty was signed sharing Lotharingia, the domain of King Lothair II (855-869) between the two brothers Louis the German and Charles the Bald, the King of France. In the 13C Meerssen attracted the monks from the Abbey of St-Rémi in Reims. They built the fine **basilica** of the Blessed Sacrament (13C-14C). The chancel has a richly decorated stone tabernacle in the Flamboyant Gothic style (early 16C).

Elsloo – This small village with its rich history of lords and Goat Riders has retained much of its old charm. The former **Schippersbeurs** ⊙ houses a small regional museum. The **castle gardens** and the nearby wood **Bunderbos** make for a pleasant walk. The old watermill near **Kasteel Elsloo** dates from 1552.

Stein – Stein is the home of the small **Archeologie Museum** ⊙. Built around a megalithic communal grave, the museum also has collections associated with Prehistoric, Roman and Merovingian sites in the region. A little further on stands the **Witte Toren** or white tower, a remnant of Kasteel Stein.

Sittard – Sittard, which obtained its charter in 1243, was a much disputed stronghold. A large part of the town is still surrounded by ramparts **(Fort Sanderbout)**. It is a busy commercial and industrial town, known in particular for its carnival *(see Practical information at the front of the guide)*.

On the **Markt**, the main square, there stands St.-Michielskerk in the 17C Baroque style, and a picturesque half-timbered house with a corbelled gable built c 1500. In Rosmolenstraat, **Kritzraedthuis** is a lovely bourgeois house which dates from 1620. The 14C **Grote Kerk or St.-Petruskerk** ⊙ has carved wood Gothic stalls, which are probably the oldest in the country.

Stedelijk Museum Het Domein ⊙ *(Kapittelstraat 6)* is a museum of local history and archaeology as well as a contemporary art museum. The art section focuses mainly on work by young artists and includes photography and new media. Exhibits in the history section relate to pre-historic times, Limburg and multi-media.

Susteren – **St.-Amelbergakerk** ⊙, an old abbey church, was built in the Romanesque style probably during the first half of the 11C. The nave, very simple and covered with a flat ceiling, leans on square pillars alternating with squat columns. The crypt outside the apse was probably inspired by that of Essen Cathedral in Germany. It contains an 8C sarcophagus and a 13C calvary. The **treasury** ⊙ next door to the church houses an evangelistary, the Amelberga shrine from 1100 and silverware.

MARKEN*

Noord-Holland

Michelin maps 908 G 4 and 210 P 8

Separated from the continent in the 13C during the formation of the Zuiderzee, Marken was an island 2.5km/1.5mi from the shore until 1957. Now connected to the mainland, it is on the edge of the Gouwzee, a sort of inland sea. Marken, whose population is Protestant, has from the beginning formed a close community. It has kept its atmosphere of days past with its wooden houses and townspeople who, in season, wear the traditional costume.

Before the IJsselmeer was created, the population earned its living from fishing; today tourism is a major source of income, although Marken has not made as many concessions as Volendam in this respect.

* The village – The village consists of two quarters: Havenbuurt, near the port and Kerkbuurt, around the church. In the past, it was subject to regular flooding, so the houses were grouped on small mounds and built on piles. When there was a threat of flood, the openings under the houses were closed. Most of the houses are painted dark green, with slightly corbelled side gables; some are tarred and have roof tiles.

Ph. Galir/MICHELIN

Traditional costume, Marken

The **interiors**, painted and polished, are richly decorated with ceramics and ornaments. The box beds have a drawer which was used as a cradle.

★ **Costumes** – The women wear a wide skirt and a black apron over a striped petticoat. The striped blouse, worn in summer, is covered with a corselet and a printed front. The headdress is just a gaily coloured lace and cotton skullcap, from which a fringe of starched hair sometimes sticks out like a peak. The men wear a short waistcoat, baggy trousers tightened at the knees and black socks. The children wear a costume more rarely; boys and girls wear a skirt and bonnet, only the shapes and colours differ. The costume worn on feast days, and particularly at Whitsun, is more elaborate.

Marker Museum ⊙ – *Kerkbuurt 44*. This small exhibition on the history of Marken is located in four smoke-houses, once used for smoking herrings and eels.

MEDEMBLIK

Noord-Holland

Michelin maps 908 G 3 and 210 P 6

Medemblik received its charter in 1289, when it became the capital of West Friesland. It was then part of the Hanseatic League. Today it is one of the "ghost towns" of the former Zuiderzee region. The dike that marks the eastern end of the Wieringermeer Polder starts at Medemblik. To the north of the town, the **Ir. Lely** pumping station is the most important one used to dry out the polder.

An old **steam tram** links the town to Hoorn and a boat service operates between Medemblik and Enkhuizen.

SIGHTS

Nieuwstraat – One of the most charming features of Medemblik is its main street, Nieuwstraat, which still has several old houses with pretty stone façades. No 8 is the **Bakkerijmuseum** ⊙, a bakery museum. At no 26 stands an unusual house: its 1613 façade presents a lintel decorated with four coats of arms. The **Waag**, or weigh-house, at the end of the street boasts a façade with crow-stepped gables, embellished with a carved façade stone depicting a pair of scales.

Westerhaven – This quay, stretching along one of the port's two main basins (Westerhaven means western basin) retains several fine houses: nos 9 to 14, with crow-stepped gables, and nos 16 to 20.

In **Torenstraat**, which begins at Westerhaven, the old orphanage, **Weeshuis**, has a gateway surmounted by a low relief depicting four orphans (18C).

★ **Oosterhaven** – Along the quay skirting this basin – Oosterhaven means eastern basin – stand a great many old façades: nos 22, 43 and 44 have carved stones. The far end of the quay affords a pleasant **view** of IJsselmeer.

Kasteel Radboud ⊙ – *On the opposite side of Oosterhaven*. Around 1288 the Count of Holland Floris V fortified and altered this castle to keep the newly subjugated Frisians in check. Only two wings have been preserved, surrounded by moats, the rest having been destroyed in the 17C and 18C. In the attic above the great hall an exhibition retraces the history of the castle and the surrounding area.

Nederlands Stoommachinemuseum ⊙ – *Oosterdijk 4*. The steam pumping station that houses this museum was used to drain the polder behind it until 1976. Today, it has an interesting collection of steam-operated machinery *(see Introduction, Industrial heritage)*. The machines can be seen working one weekend a month from April to October.

MIDDELBURG★

Zeeland Ⓟ

Population 44 481
Michelin map 908 B 7 or 211 G 14
Local map see DELTA

Middelburg, the capital of the province of Zeeland, is an old fortified town, with canals marking what used to be its outer limits. Two 18C wall mills still stand.

HISTORICAL NOTES

Formerly Middelburg was a prosperous commercial city, with its cloth trade and its imports of French wine from Argenteuil and Suresnes shipped from the port of Rouen to Rouaansekaai.

The Sea Beggars captured it in 1574. In 1595 and 1692 the town was given its first line of fortifications with bastions. These have remained more or less intact up to the present, but the only old gate which remains is **Koepoort** (1735) to the north.

It is said that a spectacle manufacturer of Middelburg, Zacharias Jansen, invented the microscope in 1590 and the telescope in 1604. However, some people prefer to attribute the invention of the microscope to Van Leeuwenhoek.

Middelburg continued to prosper in the 17C and 18C due to the United East India Company which had a trading post here. In 1940 heavy German bombing destroyed the historic centre of the town. Its old buildings have been rebuilt and it remains the great market of the Walcheren peninsula. In July and August, on the Molenwater, visitors can watch a **ringrijderij**, a sort of tournament where the aim is to unhook a ring. On Vismarkt, in summer, there is an antiques market *(Thursdays)*.

THE HEART OF TOWN

* **Stadhuis** ⊙ – Overlooking the **Markt** or main square *(market every Thursday)*, this imposing building, begun in 1452 by two members of the Keldermans family from Mechelen in Belgium, is inspired by the Hôtel de Ville in Brussels. Almost wholly destroyed by fire in May 1940, it has been rebuilt in the Late Gothic style.

The main façade is remarkable with its 10 first-floor Gothic windows. Between each window double niches have statues, remade in the 19C, depicting the Counts and Countesses of Zeeland back to back. The roof is decorated with 24 dormer windows. The finely decorated octagonal turret on the right dates from the 17C.

A highly distinctive belfry, 55m/180ft high, has a pinnacle at each corner and dominates the whole. The interior contains antique furnishings, in particular the immense **Burgerzaal**, the former cloth hall. On the left is the **Vleeshal** ⊙, the former meat hall which is now used as exhibition space.

In front of the town hall stands a bronze **fountain** by Ilya and Emilia Kabakov. Anyone who sits on one of the chairs and looks through the hole in the plinth is in for a surprise.

Behind the town hall there is a lovely restored chapel called the English Church, **Engelse Kerk**.

J. P. Lescourret/PIX

Stadhuis, Middelburg

* **Abbey** – Today the seat of the provincial government of Zeeland, this vast monastic building was a Premonstrant abbey, which was built in the 12C on the site of a Carolingian castle; the circular shape of this castle is still visible on the town map. The abbey was secularised after the capture of the town by the Sea Beggars.

To the east, one of the defensive gates, the **Gistpoort** on Damplein, has a lovely Late Gothic façade.

Head in the direction of Abdijplein.

Provinciehuis – On the east side of the main square, on the site where the old hostelry of the abbey once stood, is the new provincial government building.

* **Zeeuws Museum** ⊙ – The Zeeland Museum, on the site of the former clergy houses and the Gravenhof, has very varied collections relating to the history of the province of Zeeland. The Celtic goddess **Mehallenia** features prominently with several votive steles dating from Roman times, which were found in Domburg and in Noord-Beveland. The goddess is usually shown sitting, wearing a long dress and a pelerine, accompanied by a dog and carrying a basket of fruit. There is also an 18C collection of rarities where notably an orrery can be seen. Several of the fine series of local 16C **tapestries** illustrate Zeeland's naval victories over the Spanish. There are also collections of decorative art, including antique furniture, Zeeland silverware, Chinese porcelain and delftware, and of local **costumes**. There is a

MIDDELBURG

painting collection, comprising work by old masters and by artists who found inspiration in Zeeland, including Jan and Charley Toorop and Jacoba van Heemskerck. Contemporary art from Zeeland is also represented.

Kloostergang – On the south side of the monastery, the cloisters enclose a **herb garden**. In the Medieval crypts the **Historama Abdij Middelburg** ⊘ shows the history of the abbey and its inhabitants with a 20-minute video and pictures, and the bones of a **mammoth** that lived in Zeeland 10 000 years ago are displayed in a corner section of the cloisters. The adjoining former chapter-room is now part of the **Roosevelt Studiecentrum**. This famous American family is said to have its roots in Zeeland.

Abbey churches ⊘ – Adjacent to the cloisters, standing side by side, are three churches. The **Koorkerk** (left), with a 14C nave and apse, has a 15C organ whose case was renovated in the 16C. The 16C **Nieuwe Kerk** (right) holds organ concerts in the summer. In between these two churches is the **Wandelkerk**, against which the tower known as **Lange Jan** ⊘ (Tall Jan) leans. This 14C octagonal stone construction, crowned with a small 18C onion-shaped dome, is 85m/279ft high. From the top there is a fine view over the abbey, the town and its canals.

ADDITIONAL SIGHTS

St.-Jorisdoelen – These old premises of the civic guard dating from 1582 were rebuilt in the original style in 1970. The building's voluted gable is topped by a statue of St George (Sint Joris).

★ **Miniatuur Walcheren** ⊘ – This is an open-air scale model of Walcheren Peninsula with its dikes, ports and main buildings, made to a scale of 1:20. A little further on stands the **Koepoort** (1735).

Oostkerk – This octagonal church with an onion-shaped dome is fairly typical of 17C Protestant buildings. **Pieter Post** was one of the architects who built it between 1646-67.

The quays – The **Rotterdamsekaai**, **Rouaansekaai** and **Londensekaai** are lined with fine rows of 18C merchants' houses and storehouses, witness to the prosperity of that time.

Kloveniersdoelen – This is the former arquebusiers' mansion, built between 1607 and 1611 in the Flemish Renaissance style. Since 1795 it has been used as a military hospital. It has a very wide brick façade streaked with white stone and brightened by painted shutters. The central voluted gable bears a sculptured low relief of arquebuses and cannon balls, topped by an eagle. Behind is an octagonal turret with an onion-shaped dome.

ROUND TOUR OF THE WALCHEREN PENINSULA

49km/30mi – allow 2hr – local map see DELTA. Leave by ③ on the town plan.

≅≅ **Domburg** – This seaside resort with a large beach situated at the foot of high dunes is very popular. To the west, the top of the highest dune offers an interesting **view** over Domburg and the coast. Just outside Domburg (on the road to Oostkapelle) is **Kasteel Westhove**, a 13C moated castle which is now a youth hostel

The route follows the dunes which isolate Walcheren Peninsula from the sea. A few farmhouses, each surrounded by a curtain of trees, line the route.

Westkapelle – This town is on the western point of Walcheren, where the dunes are not strong enough to hold out against currents and are reinforced by a **dike**. This extends over 4km/2.5mi and its highest crest is 7m/23ft above sea level. In 1944 it was bombarded by the Allies, which caused flooding of the island and made it possible to evict the Germans. Westkapelle, a family seaside resort, has a beach facing south. The **lighthouse** is on the top of the bell-tower of an old Gothic church which was destroyed by fire.

Zoutelande – Small seaside resort.

The beach at Zoutelande

Vlissingen – *See VLISSINGEN.*
Return to Middelburg by ② on the town plan.

The length of time given in this guide
   – for touring allows time to enjoy the views and the scenery;
   – for sightseeing is the average time required for a visit.

NAARDEN*

Noord-Holland

Population 16 875
Michelin maps 908 G 5 and 210 P 9
Local map see HILVERSUM

Naarden used to be the capital of the Gooi *(see HILVERSUM)*. It was formerly situated about 3km/2mi to the northeast of its present position, but was burned down in the civil war between the Cods and the Hooks in 1350. As it had been prone to flooding, it was rebuilt further inland. Naarden became an important stronghold, taken by the Spanish in 1572, then by the French in 1673. Today it is a small, peaceful town, still circled by its extensive 17C **fortifications★**, shaped as a 12-pointed star with six bastions surrounded by a double ring of walls and canals.

The educational reformer, Jan Amos Komensky, better known as **Comenius** (1592-1670), was buried in Naarden. The town is also the birthplace of **Salomon van Ruysdael**, the famous 17C landscape painter.

SIGHTS

★ **Stadhuis** ⊙ – The fine Renaissance-style town hall with crow-stepped gables dates from 1601. The interior is embellished with old furniture; it contains 17C paintings and a scale model of the 17C fortifications.

Grote Kerk ⊙ – This Gothic church is dedicated to St Vitus. Inside, the wooden barrel vaulting is decorated with beautiful 16C **paintings★**. From the top of the 45m/150ft tower (235 steps) there is an impressive **view★** of the fortifications and, in fine weather, of Amersfoort, Amsterdam and Hilversum in the distance.

Comenius Museum ⊙ – *Kloosterstraat 33*. The collections displayed here illustrate the life and work of the Czech humanist. Born in Moravia, Comenius belonged to the Bohemian Brotherhood *(see UTRECHT, Excursions)*. He was persecuted and in 1628 he fled to Poland. He spent the last 14 years of his life in Amsterdam. He devoted himself primarily to educational research and was a strong advocate of the theory that education should seek to develop the child's individual powers of observation through teaching by illustration. Comenius was also one of the first to advocate education for all. His tomb can be seen in the former Walloon chapel, which has been turned into a mausoleum.

Het Spaanse Huis – *Turfpoortstraat 27*. The façade stone of this building (1615) depicts the massacre of the townspeople by the Spanish in 1572, hence its name, The Spanish House.

★ **Nederlands Vestigingmuseum** ⊙ – *Westwalstraat 6*. The five pillboxes of one of the bastions *(Turfpoort)* have been transformed into a fortress museum. Cannons and other weapons, uniforms, engravings and an audiovisual presentation retrace the eventful history of Naarden. One of the highlights of the visit is the 61m/206ft long passageway intended to be used to listen to the enemy at night.

Exclusive shopping in a military arsenal

If you're interested in art, design and/or fine food, don't miss Het Arsenaal (Kooltjesbuurt 1). This 17C complex, formerly used to store weapons and ammunition, was converted into a design centre by the furniture designer Jan des Bouvrie in 1993. An elegant courtyard garden is surrounded by exclusive shops, a restaurant and a gallery of modern art. Elsewhere, there are many interesting small shops in Marktstraat and Cattenhagestraat.

NIJMEGEN*

Gelderland

Population 151 864
Michelin maps 908 I 6 and 211 T 11
Plan of the conurbation in the current edition of The Red Guide Benelux

The only town in the Netherlands built on several hills, Nijmegen is the gateway to the delta region, due to its location on the Waal, main branch of the Rhine, and near the canal, the Maas-Waalkanaal. **Boat trips** ⊙ are organised on the Waal.
Nijmegen is a lively university town with a booming night life. On the sporting front, Nijmegen is involved in the **Wandelvierdaagse**, the four-day walking event which starts and finishes in the town.

HISTORICAL NOTES

An old Batavian oppidum, Nijmegen was conquered by the Romans under Emperor Augustus then burnt down in AD 70 by the Roman, Cerialis, General of Emperor Vespasian who was trying to quell the **Batavian revolt** stirred up the year before by **Gaius Julius Civilis**. It subsequently became a prosperous Roman city called Ulpia Noviomagus.

Nijmegen was one of Charlemagne's favourite places to stay, and he built himself a castle on the present Valkhof. In the Middles Ages the town expanded west of this castle. In the 14C it became a member of the Hanseatic League. In 1585 it was taken by Alessandro Farnese, Duke of Parma, but recaptured in 1591 by Maurice of Nassau. Nijmegen is the birthplace of **St Peter Canisius** (1521-97); he was named doctor of the church, when he was canonised in 1925.

The peace of Nijmegen – After the French, under the leadership of Turenne, captured it without difficulty in 1672, Nijmegen gave its name to three treaties which were signed there between France, the United Provinces, Spain (1678) and the German Empire (1679). They mark the peak of Louis XIV's reign who, at the outcome of the war against the United Provinces, which had started in June 1672, annexed to France the Franche-Comté and a part of Flanders. The United Provinces remained intact. It was during the preliminary conferences for these treaties that the French language began to impose itself as the diplomatic language (despite this the treaties were written in Latin as was customary).

Nijmegen in the 20C – In February 1944 the town was bombarded by the Americans. At the time of the Battle of Arnhem in September, Nijmegen was in the midst of heavy fighting. The bridge over the Waal, Waalbrug, built in 1936, which the Germans were threatening to destroy, was saved by a young inhabitant of the town, Jan van Hoof. A tablet to his memory has been put up in the centre of the bridge, on the east side. A **monument** at the southern end of the bridge commemorates the liberation of the town.

The Netherlands Catholic University founded in 1923 has been installed in a campus to the south of the town on the road to Venlo since 1949.

SIGHTS

Grote Markt – In the centre of the square the **Waag**★ (weigh-house), built in 1612 in the Renaissance style, has a lovely façade with a perron where the red and black colouring of the shutters and the sombre red brick make an attractive combination. The ground floor is now a restaurant.

There is also a bronze statue of **Mariken van Nieumeghen**, heroine of a late 15C religious drama in which, seduced by the devil, she followed him for seven years before repenting. The hands of the statue have three iron rings with which the Pope had ordered Mariken to chain her neck and arms. They loosened themselves when she had atoned for her sin. Near the weigh-house there is a group of four **17C houses**. One, the **Kerkboog** is identifiable by its decorated gable (1605) above a vaulted passage; the passage leads to St.-Stevenskerk.

Near the east end of the church, the old **Latijnse School** is a fine building of 1554.

St.-Stevenskerk ⊘ – This large 13C Gothic church, enlarged in the 15C, is flanked by a massive square tower with an octagonal onion-shaped domed pinnacle (1604) which has an 18C **carillon**. The interior contains some lovely **furnishings**: the back of the door of the south arm of the transept (1632), the local gentry's pews in the Renaissance style by Cornelis Hermanszoon Schaeff of Nijmegen and the Renaissance pulpit by Joost Jacobs. Note also the 18C princes' pew decorated with the armorial bearings of the town (eagles) and the province (lions), the **organ** built in the 18C by König and the copper chandeliers. From the **tower** (access by the west façade, 183 steps) there is a panorama over the town and the Waal.

The church's precinct has been restored; a large market takes place here on Monday mornings. To the north are lovely houses with gabled **Kannunikenhuizen** or canons' houses.

Emblem of the bargemen's guild, Museum Het Valkhof

Commanderie van St.-Jan – This 15C and 16C brick building (restored) overlooking the Waal, is an old hospital. Founded in the 13C to shelter pilgrims going to the Holy Land, it came into the possession of the Order of the Hospital of St John of Jerusalem in the following century. Today it houses the **Museumbrouwerij De Hemel** ⊘, where the brewing and distilling processes are explained and visitors are shown how vinegar and mustard are made.

Stadhuis ⊘ – This fine 16C and 17C town hall, partly destroyed by the bombardments, was restored in 1953. It is flanked by an onion-shaped turret. The exterior is decorated with statues carved by Albert Termote depicting the emperors who were Nijmegen's benefactors or who had played a part in its history. On the corner is a statue of the Virgin.

NIJMEGEN

Inside there are lovely rooms decorated in the old style, the Aldermen's Room *(Schepenhal)* and the Marriage Room *(Trouwzaal)*. In the Truce Hall, **Trêveszaal**, where the walls are covered with verdure tapestries, the treaties of 1678 and 1679 were signed. In the Council Room *(Raadzaal)* and the Great Hall *(Burgerzaal)* hang other tapestries.

Valkhof – This park has been laid out on the site of a castle built by Charlemagne. It took the name of "falcon's court" because Louis the Pious, son of Charlemagne and heir to his father's empire, bred falcons here for hunting. The castle rebuilt by Frederick Barbarossa in the 12C was destroyed in the 18C.

St.-Maartenskapel – In the centre of the park are the remains of the Romanesque chapel of Frederick Barbarossa's castle. There remains a finely decorated apse, two columns with foliated capitals at the chancel's entrance, and blind arcades outside.

★ **St.-Nicolaaskapel** – Near a terrace from where there is an interesting **view** over the Waal, this old chapel of the Carolingian castle stands hidden behind trees. It was probably modified in the 11C. It has 16 sides and is topped by an octagonal turret. Inside one can see the pillars which encircle a central octagonal-shaped space. Upstairs there is a gallery with twin bays.

Belvedere – It is the name of a watch tower (1640) in the old curtain wall, now converted into a restaurant, the terrace offers a fine **view** over the Waal.

★ **Museum Het Valkhof** ⊙ – This modern glass-clad museum, designed by Ben van Berkel, deals with the history, art and culture of Nijmegen and Gelderland. In addition to one of the country's largest collections of **Roman artefacts and works of art**, it also has a fine collection of prehistoric and early medieval antiquities, mostly found during excavations in Nijmegen and the surrounding area. They

285

include a bronze head of Emperor Trajan, silverware, jewellery, coins, glassware, bronze and all kinds of everyday objects. Prints, drawings and paintings help to bring the history of the town to life. There is an interesting triptych by an unknown master showing Christ on the cross with the parents of St Peter Canisius, Jan Van Goyen's *View of the Valkhof at Nijmegen*, and *The peace of Nijmegen*, painted in 1678 for Louis XIV. The museum also has an interesting collection of **modern and contemporary art** (Pop-Art, Expressionism) and holds temporary exhibitions.

* Nationaal Fietsmuseum Velorama ⊙ – The national bicycle museum has more than 250 examples from Britain, France, Germany and the United States, illustrating the progress made from the first dandy-horse to today's mountain bikes and reclining bicycles. Velocipedes with wooden wheels, penny-farthings and the American Star with its small front wheel were followed by the British "Rover", an ordinary-sized bike with two wheels the same size. Bicycles became much more comfortable to ride after pneumatic tyres were introduced in the late 19C, and shortly afterwards the bicycle began to enjoy unprecedented and growing popularity. On the second floor, there is a small room devoted to old and new Dutch bicycles.

Museum De Stratemakerstoren ⊙ – In the underground passageways of this 16C curtain wall tower, temporary exhibitions are held which recount the town's rich past.

Natuurmuseum Nijmegen ⊙ – This museum is housed in a former synagogue dating from 1912. The permanent exhibition entitled "Het Rijk te Kijk" invites visitors to take a closer look at the natural riches of Nijmegen and the surrounding area. Temporary exhibitions are also organised.

Kronenburgerpark – The **15C ammunition tower** in this park is all that remains of the old town walls. In the basement of the nearby **Paddestoelentoren Het Rondeel**, or mushroom tower, mushrooms are grown.

ADDITIONAL SIGHTS

Heilig Land Stichting (Holy Land Foundation) – *4km/2mi to the south-east via Groesbeekseweg.* The Open-air Bible Museum, the **Bijbels Openluchtmuseum Heilig Land Stichting** ⊙, takes you back to the Palestine of biblical times. In the main building the origin of the Bible and the Koran is recounted and the history of Judaism, Christianity and Islam is retraced. The open-air section contains reconstructions of a Palestinian village with its synagogue, a fishing village, an inn and the Via Orientalis, a depiction of Jerusalem with its Jewish, Roman, Greek and Egyptian houses.

Berg en Dal – *6km/4mi to the east via Berg en Dalseweg.* This village (whose name means Hill and Valley) is located in a region appreciated for its woodlands and undulating countryside. The **Afrika Museum** ⊙ is installed to the south (*Postweg 6*). It contains a collection of sculpture including masks and everyday objects, laid out in a modern building, and reconstructions in the open-air (Ghana and Mali dwellings, houses on piles).

The **Duivelsberg** (76m/249ft high) is criss-crossed with paths. By following the signs "Pannekoeken" (restaurant) one reaches a car park. From there a signposted path leads to a belvedere with a **view** over the German plain and Wijlermeer.

Groesbeek – **Nationaal Bevrijdingsmuseum 1944-1945** ⊙ (*Wijlerbaan 4*). The Liberation Museum is located in the place where Major-General James M Gavin landed with the 82nd Airborne Division on 17 September 1944. Original films, dioramas, photographs and models show events before, during and after the war; they focus on Operation **Market Garden** (*see ARNHEM*). In the **Dome of Honour**, shaped like a stylised parachute, is a roll of honour bearing the names of the 1 800 American soldiers who died at Nijmegen.

Doornenburg – *18km/11mi to the north-east. Leave by Waalbrug and turn towards Bemmel and Gendt.* This village has a 14C **castle** which was rebuilt after the Second World War. It is a tall square fortress surrounded by water and is linked by a footbridge to a fortified courtyard where there is a chapel and a farmhouse.

Admission times and charges for the sights described are listed at the end of the guide. Every sight for which there are times and charges is identified by the symbol ⊙ in the Sights section of the guide.

NOORDOOSTPOLDER

Flevoland
Population 43 160
Michelin maps 908 H 3, 4, I 3, 4 and 210 S 6, 7, T 6, 7, R 6, 7
Local map see IJSSELMEER

The Noordoostpolder was the second area to be reclaimed in the process of draining the Zuiderzee, but only once the sea had become a freshwater lake.

Drainage – The polder covers more than 48 000ha/118 560 acres. The 55km/34mi long enclosing dike was built between 1937 and 1940. From 1941 on three pumping stations at Vollenhove, Urk and Lemmer evacuated 1.5 billion m³/52 971 billion cu ft of water. Collection and drainage ditches completed the draining process.
The polder includes the former island of Schokland, the highest point at 3.5m/11ft).

Development – Once the land had been drained 500km/310mi of roads were built, and the future capital **Emmeloord** was built in the middle of the polder. After years (1942-62) of improving and fertilising the soil, the Noordoostpolder is now mainly devoted to agriculture and over 1 650 farmhouses have been built. The smaller units are clustered round the villages while the larger farms are dispersed in the outlying areas. The main crops are wheat, potatoes and sugar beet with an occasional field of flowers. Cattle and sheep graze the meadows.

SIGHTS

Emmeloord – The capital of the polder was laid out according to town planning concepts of the time. Right in the centre of the town the **water tower** ⊙ built in 1957 provides water for the whole polder and true to Dutch traditions has a carillon of 48 bells. The **view** from the top stretches north to the Frisian coast, south-west to Urk and the power station on the Oostelijk Flevoland Polder.

Schokland – This former island in the Zuiderzee was low-lying and difficult to protect from the sea. Its three villages were abandoned in 1859. The former church (1834) and a modern building have been converted into the **Museum Schokland** ⊙ (between Ens and Nagele) which relates the island's past: geology, prehistory and more recent times. Items on display include archaeological finds made during reclamation work on the polder.
Behind the presbytery there are remains of the stockade which protected the island from the onslaught of the sea. Steles set into the walls of the church and the presbytery indicate the levels of past floods.

Schokland and UNESCO

Since the end of 1995, the former island of Schokland has been a UNESCO world heritage site. It was chosen as an international symbol of the centuries of struggle between man and the sea.
Schokland, now part of an artificial polder and previously surrounded by the Zuiderzee, has not always been an island. In prehistory it was an area of dry land, and the small lake did not appear until Roman times. This gradually expanded into a sea, and ensured that the subsoil remained untouched for centuries until the polderisation process began in 1941 and archaeologists made excavations. They found the remains of ancient houses built on piles and artificial mounds, and dozens of shipwrecks. Ceramics, stone tools, furrows and even a burial site containing 20 skeletons, all dating from the period between 4500 and 1800 BC, were unearthed. But the really important feature of this area is the large quantity of prehistoric remains such as fossils and bones of mammoth, aurochs and woolly rhinoceros, as well as large quantities of geological material. The huge and rare erratic boulders deposited here by glaciers during the ice ages are internationally renowned.

---

* **Urk** – The former island of Urk has been joined to the mainland since the creation of the polder, though it still forms a distinctive community with an island feel. Its traditions have been retained, including strict Calvinism and keeping Sunday as a day of rest. A few of the older people still wear the traditional costume: for the men a black suit with a striped shirt; for the women a black skirt with a floral or embroidered panel on the front of the blouse and a head brooch.
Urk's fishing activities once centred around eel-fishing, but today sole and plaice are also fished. Its fish auction has become one of the largest on the European mainland, dealing in fish from the IJsselmeer and the North Sea. The busy **harbour** makes an attractive picture with the gaily painted eel-fishing **boats**.

Urk

Urk is also popular with watersports enthusiasts and tourists, the latter often crossing by **boat** ⊘ from Enkhuizen.

From beside the church (1786) on its mound there is a **view** of the enclosing dike and IJsselmeer beyond. The names of local fishermen who have drowned since 1815 are written around the edges of the terrace. In the maze of narrow streets that make up the old village centre many typical fishermen's cottages can still be seen.

ROERMOND

Limburg

Population 44 708
Michelin maps 908 J 8 and 211 V 15
Town plan in the current edition of The Red Guide Benelux

Roermond, the most important city of central Limburg, is an industrial town at the confluence of the Maas and the Roer, near the German and Dutch frontier. Due to its bisphoric founded in 1559, it is also the religious capital of this very Catholic province.

It was granted its city rights in 1232, and was soon given a fortified wall of which only the 14C **Rattentoren** on the Buitenop remains. Roermond was one of the first towns captured in 1572 by William the Silent coming from Dillenburg, but was recaptured by the Spanish in October of the same year. Roermond then passed to first Austria, then France, and was only returned to the Kingdom of the Netherlands in 1815. The town, which suffered greatly in the last war, has been partly rebuilt. It includes two marinas and vast stretches of water between the Maas and a side canal.

SIGHTS

Onze Lieve Vrouwe Munsterkerk ⊘ – *In the town centre.* This is the old church of a Cistercian abbey. It was started in 1218 in Rhenish style, and shows the transition between Romanesque and Gothic style; the church was restored at the end of the 19C by **Cuypers** (who was born here in 1827). To the west it has a massive porch framed by two towers with spires, and it is topped by a dome flanked by two turrets at the transept crossing. The trefoil plan of the western part with the transept arms ending in apsidals, the apse's outside gallery, the roofs of the towers and turrets in the shape of bishops' mitres, and the decoration of Lombard arcading are typical features of Rhenish buildings.

The church has a Brabant altarpiece (c 1530) in carved and painted wood, and at the transept crossing there is the tomb of the abbey's founders, the Count of Gelderland Gerald IV and his wife Margaret of Brabant.

Near the church, at the corner of Pollartstraat, the Prinsenhof, built 1660-70, was once the palace of the stadtholders of Upper Gelderland during Spanish rule.

Take Steenweg, the main shopping street and a pedestrian precinct.

Kathedrale Kerk ⊘ – Dedicated to St Christopher, it stands near Markt. Built in 1410 in the local Gothic style, it was damaged during the last war, but since restored.

Opposite the cathedral there is a 1764 **Baroque house**.

THORN, THE WHITE VILLAGE

14km/9mi south-west of Roermond. Leave Roermond via the A 68. Not far from the Belgian frontier, this large village built of pink brick, often painted white, has a certain charm.

Abdijkerk ⊘ – Near Plein de Wijngaard, its paving decorated with geometric motifs, stands the abbey church fronted by a high brick tower striped with white stone. This is the old church of a women's abbey founded at the end of the 10C by Ansfried (who became Bishop of Utrecht in 995) and his wife Hilsondis. Rebuilt at the end of the 13C in the Gothic style, it has preserved from Romanesque times two staircase turrets and a crypt on the west side.

Thorn

It was enlarged in the 15C, and remodelled in the Baroque style at the end of the 18C. It was restored by Cuypers at the end of the 19C. The interior is surprisingly white. The eastern chancel, raised and adorned by a Baroque altarpiece stands over a Gothic crypt which comprises the treasury (reliquaries, crowns). The chapels in the aisles have interesting low reliefs. In the south aisle there are charming 17C and 18C statues of saints in the folk art tradition. At the end of the nave, a double flight of stairs leads to the canonesses' chancel. From here one reaches a small **museum** installed in the old chapter-house containing the archives both of the 14C and 15C: engravings, portraits and scale models of the abbey. In the western crypt, which is Romanesque, there is a sculptured stone baptismal font (15C).

Take the main street (Akkerwal, Akker, Boekenderweg). At the second chapel (St.-Antoniuskapel) turn left.

On a small shady square, the 1673 **Chapel Under the Lime Trees** (Kapel onder de Linden), was enlarged in 1811. Inside, the oldest part on the east side has fine Baroque decoration (stucco work, paintings), while the 19C part was decorated in the Empire style.

ROTTERDAM★★

Zuid-Holland

Population 592 665
Michelin maps 908 E 6, folds 25 and 26 (inset) and 211 L 11
and folds 37 to 40 (inset)
Local maps see DELTA and ROTTERDAM
Plan of the conurbation in the current edition of The Red Guide Benelux

The Netherlands' second most populated city, Rotterdam is one of the world's largest ports, located on the **Nieuwe Maas**, 30km/19mi from the North Sea. It is near the mouth of two important waterways – the Rhine and the Maas – leading into the industrial heartland, and is thus the meeting point of sea and river traffic. The city of Rotterdam sprawls over both banks of the river and is linked by tunnels, bridges and the underground. It is part of the **Rijnmond**, a group of 23 municipalities forming part of **Randstad Holland**.

Almost completely destroyed during the last war, Rotterdam has been entirely rebuilt. During the 1980s and 90s, radical changes have been made to the city's skyline, and Rotterdam's many new buildings have earned it the nickname of Manhattan on the Maas; it also has a great deal of important modern architecture. The latest challenge is the development of the **Kop van Zuid** on the other side of the Maas, where the city council intends to create a second centre for Rotterdam by around 2010. The Erasmus Bridge (Erasmusbrug), completed in 1996, links the two halves.

Erasmus Roterodamus

This was the way the great humanist Geert Geertsz signed his name throughout his life. Erasmus was born in Rotterdam in 1469. As a child, he lived in Gouda, Utrecht and Deventer, where he attended the school of the Brethren of Common Life.

Both his parents died c 1484. At his guardians' insistence, Erasmus became a monk in 1488 at the convent of Steyn, near Gouda, where he was able to continue studying.

In 1493, having left the convent, he became secretary to the Bishop of Cambrai, whom he accompanied on his travels. He was, however, attracted by learning, and succeeded in getting a scholarship to study theology at the Sorbonne. During a stay in England in 1499 he met Thomas More, the author of *Utopia*, who was to become a close friend. In 1502, fleeing the plague which had spread through France, he arrived at the University of Leuven and soon became a professor there.

A tireless traveller, Erasmus was in Italy in 1506, where his **Adagia**, the commentary on

Giraudon

quotations and proverbs from Antiquity he wrote in Paris in 1500, was reprinted. He was then in London in 1509 where he wrote and published his *In Praise of Folly* two years later. In Basle in 1514, Erasmus met Holbein who in 1515 illustrated an edition of *In Praise of Folly* and made several portraits of the humanist.

When, in 1517, Luther put up the theses which triggered the Reformation, Erasmus was in Leuven. He at first refused to take part in religious quarrels, but when the Faculty of Theology condemned Luther's Theses, his neutrality created problems. After spending some months at Anderlecht near Brussels in 1521, he left for Switzerland and published, in 1526, an enlarged edition of his satirical dialogues, **Colloquia Familaria**, which was very successful. The Prince of Humanists died in Basle in 1536.

Rotterdam University was named after him in 1973.

WHERE TO STAY

Rotterdam is a city of modern architecture, so this is not the place to go looking for quaint old hotels.

Youth Hostel

NJHC City Hostel Rotterdam – *Rochussenstraat 107-109, 3015 EH,* ☎ *(010) 436 57 63, Fax (010) 436 55 69. 22 rooms. Near the Museumpark.*

Hotels

MODERATE

Breitner – *Breitnerstraat 23, 3015 XA,* ☎ *(010) 436 02 62, Fax (010) 436 40 91. 32 rooms.* Small, central hotel in a quiet street. The simple rooms of different sizes all have shower/bath and toilet.

MID-RANGE

New York – *Koninginnehoofd 1, 3072 AD,* ☎ *(010) 439 05 00, Fax (010) 484 27 01. 72 rooms.* Once the former headquarters of the Holland-Amerika shipping line, this is one of the few Rotterdam hotels to be located in a historic building. It is on the other side of the Maas, and therefore not particularly central, but highly recommended nevertheless.

Inntel – *Leuvehaven 80, 3011 EA,* ☎ *(010) 413 41 39, Fax (010) 413 32 22. www.hotelinntel.com. 149 rooms.* This business hotel is next to the IMAX theatre and has a view over the Nieuwe Maas, the Erasmusbrug and Leuvehaven. It has a pool, sauna and gymnasium, and an underground car park.

Parkhotel – *Westersingel 70, 3015 LB,* ☎ *(010) 436 36 11, Fax (010) 436 42 12. www.bilderberg.nl. 187 rooms.* The rooms in the modern, silver-coloured tower of this hotel have a magnificent view of the city. It is within walking distance of the shopping and entertainment areas, and has its own garden, sauna, solarium, fitness and massage room, and parking.

WHERE TO EAT

Boompjes – *Boompjes 701,* ☎ *(010) 413 60 70.* The pavilion in which this restaurant is located is one of Rotterdam's architectural highlights, with big glass walls allowing diners to watch the busy shipping traffic on the Nieuwe Maas; the terrace is open in summer.

Brasserie La Vilette – *Westblaak 160,* ☎ *(010) 414 86 92.* Chic but lively brasserie offering good food that won't break the bank.

Café Rotterdam – *Wilhelminakade 699,* ☎ *(010) 29 08 42.* This café-restaurant is right by the Hotel New York and located in the magnificent departure lounge of the Holland- Amerika Line. The glass wall on the Nieuwe Maas side provides a wonderful view of the city and the Erasmusbrug, which is lit at night.

Chalet Suisse – *Kievitslaan 31,* ☎ *(010) 436 50 62.* Besides fondue and raclette, this Swiss chalet style restaurant near Museumpark serves ordinary dishes as well. A large terrace looks out over the park.

De Engel – *Eendrachtsweg 19,* ☎ *(010) 413 82 56.* One of the places to be in Rotterdam, serving good food in an informal setting.

De Tijdgeest – *Oost-Wijnstraat 14-16,* ☎ *(010) 233 13 11.* Trendy brasserie in a set of old merchant's houses and warehouses near the old port (Oude Haven). Good value for money. Terrace.

Morand-Grahame/HOA QUI

The old port

Kip – *Van Vollenhovenstraat 25,* ☎ *(010) 436 99 23.* A pleasant brasserie near Museumpark. Its name means "chicken", but it serves lots of other things too. There is a small garden at the back.

Parkheuvel – *Heuvellaan 21,* ☎ *(010) 436 07 66.* This top-class restaurant is one of the city's finest, with a view of the ships on the Nieuwe Maas thrown in for good measure.

Zeezout – *Westerkade 11,* ☎ *(010) 436 50 49.* This modern seafood restaurant is very popular, so booking is advisable.

PRACTICAL INFORMATION

General information – The tourist office, **VVV Rotterdam** (Coolsingel 67, 3012 AC, ☎ (0900) 403 40 65, www.vvv.rotterdam.nl) can help with just about anything you need to know, including sights, tours, cultural events, excursions, and bookings for hotels, theatres and concerts. It also publishes a handy guide to Rotterdam.

Transport – Park in one of the **multi-storey car parks** in the centre (charge payable) or the free **Park & Ride** sites on the edge of the city. **RET**, the city's public transport company, has an extensive network of metro, bus and train lines. Most of the main sights are easy to reach from Rotterdam Central Station. In summer the tourist tram, **route no 10**, crosses the whole of the city. RET's service point in front of the train station or at Coolsingel 141, ☎ (0900) 92 92 sells tickets valid for one, two or three days. **Bicycles** are available for rent in the cycle shop in the station, ☎ (010) 412 62 20.

Blaak metro and train station

Walks and tours – The **VVV** organises a wide variety of guided and unguided bus tours, walks and cycle tours, as well as taxi tours of the city or port. If you have a specific interest in architecture, contact **ArchiCenter** on ☎ (010) 436 99 09. The organisation **Gilde Rotterdam** offers walking tours of specific parts of the city and on particular themes such as architecture; ☎ (010) 436 28 44.

Boat trips – **Flying Dutchman**: harbour tours by hydrofoil, departing from Parkkade opposite the Euromast, ☎ (010) 436 12 22. **Spido Havenrondvaarten**: tours of the port and the Delta project, departing from Leuvehoofd, ☎ (010) 275 99 88. **Stichting De Crossboot**: trips to the Rottemeren lakes and Delfshaven leaving from Zaagmolenbrug, ☎ (010) 414 97 51.

Rotterdam from the air – Get a bird's-eye view of the city from the **Euromast** *(see description below),* or do it in style with an air tour operated by **Kroonduif Air**, ☎ (010) 415 78 55.

Shopping – Rotterdam has many shopping centres, including the **Lijnbaan**, Europe's first pedestrian area; the **Beurstraverse**, one of the city's architectural highlights; the Plaza, opposite the station (Centraal Station); and the 2km/1mi long **Zuiderboulevard**. The **Vrij Entrepot** is a new shopping area in the Kop van Zuid district. The area in and around the former warehouse De Vijf Werelddelen has all kinds of shops and numerous restaurants and bars.

There is late-night shopping on Fridays, when most shops stay open until 9pm. Shops in the town centre also open on Sundays from 12pm to 5pm. The many commercial art galleries are centred around **Witte de Withstraat**, the cultural hub of Rotterdam. The VVV sells a guide to some of the more interesting places in which you can be parted from your money.

Markets – The **Centrummarkt**, one of the biggest markets in the country, takes place on the Binnenrotteterrein on Tuesdays and Saturdays. On Fridays there is a market here from 12pm to 9pm and from April to December a **Sunday market** is held. An **antiques market** is held on Sundays during the summer on Schiedamsdijk. Other large markets include **Markt Zuid** on Wednesdays and Saturdays on the Afrikaanderplein, and **Markt West**, with a wide variety of exotic foreign products, on Grote Visserijplein on Thursdays and Saturdays.

Theatres and concerts – **R'Uit Magazine** gives a full monthly summary of all exhibitions, dance and theatre performances, concerts and other events. It is available free from the VVV and elsewhere. The easiest way to book tickets is at the **VVV's art and culture counter**. Leading venues include the Doelen concert and conference building, Schouwburgplein 50, ☎ (010) 217 17 00; **Rotterdamse Schouwburg**, Schouwburgplein 25, ☎ (010) 404 41 11; **Theater Zuidplein**, Zuidplein 60, ☎ (010) 481 65 00; **Lantaren/Venster**, Gouvernestraat 133, ☎ (010) 277 22 77; and **Luxor Theater**, Posthumalaan 29, ☎ (010) 413 83 26.

Nightlife – For an evening with a difference, try the **Holland Casino** in the Plaza complex opposite Centraal Station. Cinemas include the huge **IMAX** screen at Leuvehaven, **Cinema Pathé** on Schouwburgplein, and **Lantaren/Venster** (Gouvernestraat) for cinephiles.

Events – There always seems to be some kind of festival going on. Annual events include the **International Film Festival** (January), the multicultural **Dunya Festival** (early June), the tropical-style Summer **Carnival Street Parade** (July), the **Wereldhavenfestival**, or World Port Festival, in early September, and the arts and cultural event **September in Rotterdam**. The **World Tennis Tournament** and the **Rotterdam Marathon** take place in March and April.

HISTORICAL NOTES

Rotterdam was originally a small village built on the dike (dam) on the small river Rotte. The town was still of little importance when Erasmus was born there.

Expansion – In 1572 the Spaniards pursued by the Sea Beggars, who had just captured Brielle, pleaded with the inhabitants of Rotterdam to be allowed to enter. Once inside, Admiral Bossu allowed his troops to pillage the town. After this betrayal, Rotterdam joined the revolt.

From 1576 to 1602 ports were constructed which were used by the Sea Beggars' fleet; the town rapidly surpassed its rival, Dordrecht, and became the second largest in Holland. Nevertheless, when Rotterdam was captured by the French in 1794, its trade suffered severely.

Major dock work – It was only after Belgium and the Netherlands separated in 1830 that Rotterdam once again became a transit port for the Rhine. As the depth of the river in the estuary (Brielse Maas) had become inadequate for the increasingly large ships, an access canal had to be built across the island of Voorne in 1830, the Voornsekanaal. The Voornsekanaal also became insufficient, and in 1863 the Minister Jan R Thorbecke approved the plans drawn up by the young hydraulic engineer **Pieter Caland** for the construction of a waterway crossing the sandy plains separating Rotterdam from the North Sea. The **Nieuwe Waterweg**, a waterway 18km/11mi long and 11m/36ft deep at low tide, was dug between 1866 and 1872, and is comparable to Amsterdam's Noordzeekanaal, without locks. The port of **Hoek van Holland** was built at the sea end for passenger traffic. In 1997, the final project of the Delta Plan was completed: the gigantic storm surge barrier near Europoort (see DELTA, and below).

New docks started to be built on the south bank of the river towards 1870 (Binnen Dock, Entrepot Dock, Spoorweg Dock) which were bigger than the old ones and linked to the railway. Between 1876 and 1878 two bridges were built across the Maas (Willemsbrug and Koninginnebrug) as well as a railway viaduct 1 400m/4 598ft wide spanning the river. Three docks were built, the Rijn Dock (1887-94), the Maas Dock (1988-1909) and the Waal Dock (1907-31), which together formed the largest artificial harbour in the world. Subsequently the port was extended to the west along the north bank of the Nieuwe Maas (Merwe Dock, 1923-1932).

Delfshaven, the small outer harbour that had been part of Delft since 1400, was incorporated into Rotterdam in 1886.

A martyred city – On 14 May 1940 Rotterdam suffered German bombing that destroyed almost all of the old town. Only the town hall, the central post office, the stock exchange and Erasmus' statue were spared. In March 1943 Allied bombing completed the destruction. 280ha/692 acres were razed, 30 000 houses and buildings set on fire. The port was also very badly bombed during the last war, and was then sabotaged in 1944 by the Germans who destroyed 7km/4mi of docks and 20% of the warehouses.

THE NEW CITY

Reconstruction of the city – Immediately after the war Rotterdam began rebuilding. Rational urban planning was adopted, which allowed for more open spaces and a cultural and commercial city centre.

Large numbers of people moved to the suburbs, which led to the spectacular development of the built-up area. Many communities were set up almost overnight, such as **Hoogvliet** in the south and **Alexanderpolder** in the east, and Prins Alexanderpolder (1971). The quarter south of the Maas was given a shopping centre, the **Zuidplein**; a theatre and a vast sports complex, the **Ahoy** (concerts, exhibitions). Numerous recreational areas were created on the city outskirts to meet the needs of the ever-growing suburban population. The most important are located to the west on the island of Voorne, not far from Brielle, and to the north-east along the Rotte.

The new port – *See the insets on Michelin maps 908 and 211.* In 1945 the reconstruction of the port began. It was decided that national industry should be developed. A new port, **Botlek**, was built in 1954 on the island of Rozenburg, where refineries and petro-chemical plants were subsequently set up. When these facilities became inadequate, the new **Europoort** was added. Finally, to accommodate the giant tankers, open-sea docks were built to the south of the Nieuwe Waterweg, in the **Maasvlakte** region, where an industrial zone was created around the port and its installations. Due to the continued growth of the port, plans for a **second Maasvlakte** are currently underway.

Port activity – With a total goods traffic of 303.4 million tonnes in 1999, Rotterdam is one of the world's largest ports. This gigantic concern employs altogether 60 130 people.

Port of Rotterdam

Index of street names and sights for maps of ROTTERDAM

Petroleum and its by-products account for 114.5 million tonnes, or around 35% of the total activity. Four important refineries (Shell, Esso, Kuwait Petroleum and Nerefco) have been set up between Rotterdam and the sea. They have led to the creation of a powerful chemical industry (ICI, AZCO, DSM, ARCO, Shell etc).

The port of Rotterdam enjoys a privileged situation at the mouth of two big European rivers and within easy reach of major road and railway networks, not to mention the presence of two nearby airports: Schiphol and Zestienhoven (a mile or so north of the town).

Both a home port and a port of transit, Rotterdam is used by over 300 regular international shipping lines; in 1999 it received 30 199 deep-sea ships.

The port facilities have had to adapt to the remarkable increase in **container traffic** (6 343 000 containers in 1999, as against only 242 325 in 1970). Transhipment centres *(distriparken)* have been set up, offering storage, distribution and reassembling services; they are located near the huge shipping terminals designed to receive the container vessels.

Bridges and tunnels – There are a number of tunnels and bridges spanning the Nieuwe Maas.

Maastunnel – Opened in 1942, the Maas Tunnel is 1 070m/3 510ft long, of which 550m/1 804ft are under the river. It has four separate galleries: two one-way roads for cars placed side by side, and two upper levels for cyclists and pedestrians with eight escalators.

Beneluxtunnel – This was built in 1967 to relieve some of the traffic from the Maastunnel and to allow a crossing between the two banks while avoiding the city centre. It is 1 300m/4 265ft long and the river bed was dredged 22.5m/74ft deep.

★★ **Willemsbrug** – This cable-stayed bridge, recognisable by its red gateway-shaped pylons, was designed by C Veerling and opened in 1981. The dual carriageway across this bridge forms an important traffic artery.

Van Brienenoordbrug - This bridge to the east was inaugurated in 1965. It has a single span 297m/974ft long, rising 25m/82ft above the water. It ends in a bascule bridge on the north side. Since 1992 the twelve-lane Tweede Brienenoordbrug (Second Bridge) has regulated traffic flow in the area.

★★ **Erasmusbrug** – *Illustration: see Architecture, p 59*. Ben van Berkel designed this bracket-constructed single-pylon bridge, which is 800m/2 600ft long. It was officially opened in 1996, and has become known among local people as "The Swan". The bridge consists of two approach ramps with a fixed steel cable bridge and a movable steel bascule bridge between them. The bridge links the city centre with the **Kop van Zuid**, where 125ha/300 acres of former port area has been redeveloped for residential and business use. There are also plans for recreational and other facilities.

1 THE CENTRE *about 2hr*

The centre of Rotterdam is a mass of high-rise office blocks, shops and banks.

Stationsplein – If you turn your back to **Centraal Station** (1957), the **Delftse Poort**★ office building (1986-91) is on your left. This was designed by A Bonnema, and houses the Nationale Nederlanden insurance company. The two mirror-glazed towers are 93m/300ft and 150m/487ft high. On the right, the **Groot Handelsgebouw** or **Wholesale Building** (1949-51), built by architect H Maaskant and covering an area of 2ha/5 acres, symbolises the reconstruction of the city of Rotterdam.

Kruisplein – To the right is the former **Bouwcentrum** or **Building Centre** (today the **Weena Point** office building). On the corner of Weena is an enormous reproduction of Picasso's **Sylvette**. On the left, the elegant **Millennium Tower**★ was completed in the year 2000. This glass tower, reminiscent of the Empire State Building, is 149m/489ft high and houses a luxury hotel and offices.

★ **De Doelen** – This immense concert hall and conference centre is home to the Rotterdam Philharmonic Orchestra. The original building dates from 1966; the new conference wing was built on in 2000.
To the north of Westersingel stands a deeply moving statue symbolising the Rotterdam Resistance.

Schouwburgplein – This square has been completely redesigned by Adriaan Geuze. The esplanade has been clad in metal plates, some of which can be raised to serve as a podium. The four huge desk lamps that light the area can be controlled by members of the public. The **Cinema** Pathé on the western side, clad in corrugated metal, was designed by K van Velsen. The Schouwburg, or theatre, was designed by **W Quist** and opened in 1988.

★ **Lijnbaan** – This shopping promenade may not look particularly modern now, but it was ahead of its time in the 1950s. The architects, Van den Broek and Bakema, designed adjoining low-rise shops with tall flats behind them. The idea of a traffic-free shopping centre provided inspiration for cities all over the world.

Cross Lijnbaan to reach the town hall.

Opposite the town hall is the **War Memorial**. It was designed by Mari Andriessen in 1957; three generations are depicted.

Coolsingel – This is the city's main thoroughfare, and the town hall, the post office and the stock exchange are situated here.

Built between 1914-20, the **town hall** is one of the few buildings to have survived the bombings. It has an excellent **carillon**. Among other statues in front of the building is one of the great jurist, Grotius (1970).
Inside the **post office**, dating from the same period as the town hall, the remarkable concrete framework of the building is visible. Facing the Stock Exchange, in front of the department store De Bijenkorf (The Beehive), stands a gigantic metal "**Construction**"; it is the work of Naum Gabo (1957) and illustrates the reconstruction of the town.
The Stock Exchange, **Beurs**, was built in 1936-1940 and designed by JF Staal. The **World Trade Center**★ (1983-86), a 23-storey block built through the roof of the Stock Exchange hall, is a distinctive landmark. Designed by the architect RB van Erk, it has the shape of a flattened ellipse with green glass façades.

Beursplein – The rebuilding of this square to the designs of Pi de Bruyn was carried out in 1994. The plan includes the **Beurstraverse** (an underground shopping mall below Coolsingel), department stores, an apartment block and a car park.

Behind the Stock Exchange (Beurs) turn left and walk across the pedestrian bridge spanning the Rotte Canal.

The **Statue of Erasmus** on Grotekerkplein is the work of Hendrick de Keyser and was finished in 1622.

Grote Kerk or St.-Laurenskerk ⊙ – Completed in 1646, with its truncated tower built into the transept, this late-Gothic church was destroyed in 1940, then restored. It now has, once more, a fine façade with a new bronze door (1968) by Giacomo Manzù.

ROTTERDAM

The **interior**⋆ consists of a wide nave, the severity of which is attenuated by the warm colours of the panelled vaults, the copper chandeliers, the great red and gold organ (1973), and the 18C gilded ironwork of the sanctuary. The slightly protruding transept contains 17C admirals' tombs and a fine 16C organ. The bronze baptismal font (1959) is by Han Petri.

Go back to Beursplein and follow Korte Hoogstraat.

★ **Historisch Museum Het Schielandhuis** ⊙ – Built between 1662-65 to house the administrative centre of the Schieland dikes. The carefully balanced Classical façade is richly decorated with sculpture.

The three period rooms on the first floor contain paintings by local artists and other items made in Rotterdam, including silver, glass and furniture. The Regency room is devoted to the works of Adriaen van der Werff (1659-1722); his fine technique and the quality of his works brought this painter international recognition.

This floor is also used for temporary exhibitions, including a display of prints and drawings from the **Atlas Van Stolk collection**, covering the history of the Netherlands. In addition, there is a section on the history of Rotterdam showing its growth from a small 13C settlement to a major international port. It includes items such as medieval pilgrims' insignia, the oldest surviving Dutch clog, portraits of directors of the Dutch East India Company, and the white flag with which Rotterdam capitulated in 1940.

The top floor contains items from **everyday life** in times gone by (doll's house, a reconstruction of a dairy, a toy kitchen from 1853) and a collection of clothes dating from 1900 to the present day.

The Schielandhuis is surrounded by three towers: on the right is the Schieland-toren (Schieland Tower), one of Europe's tallest residential buildings; on the left W Quist's **Robecotoren**; and opposite the museum the modern glass tower of the Fortis Bank head-office.

Cross Coolsingel and turn left into Binnenwegplein.

Binnenwegplein – Upon entering the square one finds the **City Informatiecen-trum** ⊙, which provides information about the new developments in the city centre. **Het Ding** *(The Thing; 1969)* is a giant kinetic sculpture by the American artist George Rickey.

Turn left by Doormanstraat, cross Westblaak and turn right into Witte de Withstraat.

Witte de Withstraat – This street is often referred to as the cultural district of the city because it has many art galleries and is close to the Museumpark. Places of interest include the **Witte de With Centrum** ⊙, which focuses on contemporary art – in particular experimental art and new art movements – with exhibitions dedicated to fine art, architecture, design and theatre. Diagonally across from there is the **Nederlands Foto Instituut (NFI)** ⊙, dedicated to photography and new media. In addition to an archive, a restoration workshop and a school for photography and video, there are exhibition halls where temporary exhibitions are held.

Westersingel – The public garden in front of the Parkhotel contains a headless statue by Rodin, **Man Walking**. On the other side of Westersingel, at no 22 on Mauritsweg, the façade of the reconstructed **Café de Unie** was designed by JJP Oud in 1925. Its lines and colours recall compositions by members of the abstract movement, De Stijl.

★★ 2 THE MUSEUMPARK

In the space of only a few years, the area around the **Museumpark** has become the cultural heart of Rotterdam.

The park (1988-93) was designed by French landscape architect Yves Brunier and architect **Rem Koolhaas**, who was born in Rotterdam in 1944. They created three areas, each with its own distinct character; one paved with white shell grit and small apple trees, one consisting of a black asphalt podium, and one with a lake and a winding path, creating a romantic effect.

A number of important museums adjoin the park.

★★★ **Museum Boijmans Van Beuningen** ⊙ – *Because of building work scheduled for completion in late 2001, only part of this museum is open. In the meantime temporary exhibitions are being held.* Located on the edge of the park, this fine art museum is in a building inaugurated in 1935, to which a wing was added in 1972. Besides an excellent collection of Old Masters, the museum contains a large number of modern and contemporary works of art, engravings and drawings and a decorative arts section.

Old Masters – This includes a remarkable collection of pre-Renaissance art. The *Three Marys at the Open Sepulchre* is a major work by the **Van Eycks**. There are admirable paintings by **Hieronymus Bosch**, *The Marriage at Cana, St Christopher*, and in particular *The Prodigal Son* where one can appreciate the painter's poetic humour, his flights of imagination, and his mastery of colour. Note a Virgin and Child surrounded by angel musicians, *The Glorification of the Virgin*, a masterpiece by **Geertgen tot Sint Jans**. The Prophet Isaiah is shown on the left panel of the famous altarpiece by the **Master of the Annunciation of Aix**. *The Tower of Babel* by **Bruegel the Elder**, the delightful *Portrait of a Young Scholar in a red beret* (1531) by **Jan van Scorel**, and works by **Pieter Aertsen** etc represent the 16C. The 17C painting collection is particularly interesting. There are two portraits by **Frans Hals**; church interiors by **Pieter Saenredam** and **Emmanuel de Witte**; a portrait by **Rembrandt** of his young son Titus; landscapes by **Hercules Seghers**, **Van Goyen**, **Hobbema** and **Jacob van Ruisdael; and** also interior scenes by **Jan Steen** and **Gerrit Dou**. The **Rubens** collection has, among other sketches, a remarkable series on the theme of Achilles' life. In the fine group of Italian paintings from the 15C to 17C, there are works by the Venetians: Titian, Tintoretto and Veronese.

Willem Van der Vorm Collection – It includes, notably, an interesting series of 17C paintings with Rubens, Van Dyck, Rembrandt *(Tobias and his Wife)* and many Dutch masters such as Gerrit Dou, Ter Borch *(Woman Spinning)* and Van de Velde with two seascapes. 19C French painting is represented by the Barbizon School. There are works by Daubigny, Théodore Rousseau and Corot. For the 18C, Hubert Robert, Chardin and Watteau and the Venetian Francesco Guardi should be mentioned.

Prints and Drawings – This important collection, a part of which is exhibited during temporary exhibitions, covers the 15C to the present day. It includes works by Albrecht Dürer, Leonardo da Vinci, Rembrandt, Watteau, Cézanne and Picasso.

Modern and Contemporary Art – It covers the period from 1850 to the present. The Impressionist artists Monet, Sisley and Pissaro are represented as well as Signac, Van Gogh, Mondrian and Kandinsky. Note the small 14-year old ballet dancer, a graceful statuette by Degas.

Among the Surrealist works there are paintings by Salvador Dali and René Magritte. The collection also includes works by Kees van Dongen, who was born in Delfshaven.

The contemporary art collection is exhibited by rotation; it includes sculptures by Richard Serra, Oldenburg, Joseph Beuys, Bruce Nauman and Walter De Maria, and Donald Judd, and paintings by the Germans Kiefer and Penck, the Italians Cucchi, Clemente and Chia.

Finger on cheek, Kees van Dongen

Museum Boijmans Van Beuningen, Rotterdam/(c) ADAGP PARIS 1999

Dutch contemporary art is represented by Van Elk, Carel Visser, Rob van Koningsbruggen and René Daniels.

Among the contemporary trends are works by Milan Kunc and Salvo as well as sculptures by Thomas Schütte, Bazilebustamente and Niek Kamp.

Decorative Arts – The museum also has a very rich collection of objets d'art; glassware, silverware, majolica and Persian, Turkish, Spanish, Dutch and Italian ware.

★ **Nederlands Architectuurinstituut** ⊙ – The Dutch architect Jo Coenen designed this complex, known as NAi, which opened in 1993. A number of other architects, including the Czech, Borek Sipek, were involved in designing the interior of the complex, which consists of four buildings, each serving a different function and with its own style.

As you enter from the Museumpark side, you will see a sculpture by Auke de Vries in the pond on the left. The tall, transparent section of the institute houses the offices and a library of some 35 000 books and journals on Dutch and foreign architecture and related subjects, which is open to museum visitors. Underneath the transparent section, level with the pond, are an auditorium and the foyer.

After the reception desk, a ramp leads to the different levels of the exhibition wing, recognisable from the outside by its purplish-brown brick walls. This wing is used to stage temporary exhibitions on various aspects of architecture, urban planning, landscape architecture and related disciplines.

Nederlands Architectuurinstituut, Jo Coenen

The curved wing on concrete pillars on Rochussenstraat is known as the collection wing *(accessible only on group tours)*. This houses archives of items relating to Dutch architecture from 1800 to the present day, including working drawings and models by leading architects such as Cuypers, Berlage, Rietveld, Coenen, Koolhaas and Weeber. The outer walls have no windows, and are clad in red-painted corrugated steel. At night, the colonnade is lit in changing colour combinations in a light installation designed by Peter Struycken.

Chabot Museum ⊘ – The Chabot Museum building dates from 1938; the architects GW Baas and L Stokla created a functional-looking villa of glass, steel frames, a flat roof and whitewashed walls in the spartan Nieuwe Bouwen style of the 1920s, 30s and 40s. Since 1993, the **villa**★ has been an appropriate home for the drawings and paintings of the local expressionist artist Hendrik Chabot (1894-1949). Chabot was also a graphic artist and sculptor.

Kunsthal ⊘ – This building beside the Westzeedijk holds important temporary exhibitions of the visual arts, architecture, design, photography and non-Western cultures.

The architect, **Rem Koolhaas**, has made ingenious use of the difference in level between the Museumpark and the dike. A series of exhibition spaces are grouped around a slope linking the two areas. The fa çade on the park side is made of travertine and glass; on the dike side, a service road runs underneath the building. The figures of the camel driver and his camel on the roof by the artist Henk Visch are a reminder of the temporary, nomadic nature of the exhibitions.

Natuurmuseum ⊘ – This monumental villa dating from 1852 features stuffed mammals and birds, insects and shells. The new glass pavilion houses a 15m/50ft whale skeleton. A permanent exhibition entitled **RegioNatuur** looks at the flora and fauna of the Rijnmond area.

★ ③ CITY OF WATER *about 3hr*

A walk through this part of the city gives a good overview of the city's links with the sea.

★ **Maritiem Museum Rotterdam** ⊙ – This museum is located on Leuvehaven, Rotterdam's first artificial sea harbour. An interactive exhibition entitled *WereldHaven/HavenWereld* chronicles the history of the port of Rotterdam through film, time navigators and large scale-models. The exhibition *I name you...* – *Shipbuilding in the Netherlands* covers the rich history of this industry in the Netherlands since the 17C. The *Mens aan boord* exhibition illustrates the hard lives of seafarers on board ship during the 17C and 18C. *De Collectie* gives an insight into the riches contained in the museum collection, with ship models, navigation instruments, maps, globes and other objects. *Professor Plons* is an interactive exhibition for children.

Leuvehaven is also the home of an old armoured vessel, the **Buffel** (1868), which belongs to the museum. Cabins belonging to the different crew members are on view, as well as the prison cells and the well-appointed captain's cabin.

Maritiem Buitenmuseum ⊙ – The historical ships and cranes in this outdoor maritime museum illustrate how the port operated in earlier times. The pavilions contain workshops and two exhibitions.

IMAX – From the comfort of your seat, enjoy the 70mm images projected by the IMAX system onto a screen measuring 23m/75ft high and 17m/56ft across. Combined with six-channel sound, the effect is sensational.

At the end of Schiedam-sedijk, turn left across the Nieuwe Leuvebrug.

The Nieuwe Leuvebrug offers an excellent view of the **Erasmusbrug★★** *(see above)*. Harbour tours depart from Leuvehoofd, which is dominated by the 50 m/115 ft high **Nationaal Monument voor de Koopvaardij**, a monument dedicated to merchant shipping.

★ **Boompjes** – In the 17C, this was an elegant promenade with a double row of lime trees; hence its name, which means "little trees". Now, it is a modern boulevard with a variety of places to eat and drink, and residential and office buildings. The three towers, the **Boompjestorens**, were designed by the architect Henk Klunder and are lit in red, blue and yellow at night.

Continue along Boomp-jeskade until it widens out; turn left into Scheepmaker-shaven and follow the quay to the right.

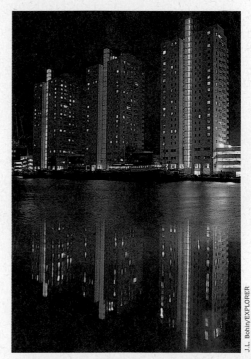

The three Boompjestorens, Henk Klunder

The 92m/300ft-high white office block, **Willemswerf★**, is the headquarters of the shipping company Nedlloyd. The architect, **Wim Quist**, built it in two sections; the other, beside the Nieuwe Maas, is wedge-shaped.

Follow the Boompjes under the Willemsbrug approach road.

★ **Oude Haven** – The old port was Rotterdam's first harbour, built in 1325. It is now a pleasant place for a stroll, and visitors can sit out on one of the busy terraces in fine weather. The **Witte Huis**, or White House, on the south-west side, is the only remnant of the pre-war period. This 11-storey office block dates from 1897-1898, and was the Netherlands' first high-rise building. The old Dutch commercial sailing ships of the Inland Waterways Museum, **Openlucht Binnenvaart Museum**, can be seen moored in Oude Haven. Nearby the impressive form of the cable-stayed **Willemsbrug★★** *(see above)* spans the Nieuwe Maas.

Overblaak - The architect **Piet Blom** built his **kubuswoningen**★★★ (cube-shaped apartments) over a pedestrian bridge between 1978 and 1984. One **apartment** ⊙, no 70, is open to the public. The so-called "Pencil" or Het Potlood apartment block towers above the area.

Behind the cube apartments is the entrance to the **Blaak metro** and railway station (1983-93; *illustration, see Travellers' addresses*). The architect, H Reijnders, placed a huge canopy of coloured tubes over the street-level part of the station.

Go back to the Oude Haven and follow Gelderskade to the Wijnhaven.

Mariniersmuseum ⊙ - This museum, next door to the Witte Huis, chronicles the history and work of the Marine Corps. Opposite is the Houtepen, a shallow-water mine sweeper dating from 1961.

Follow Wijnhaven and then turn right to reach Plein 1940.

A sculpture by the Franco-Russian artist Zadkine, **Monument to a Devastated City** (1953) is located to the north of the Leuvehaven; the man's heart has been torn out, and he gestures in despair, symbolising Rotterdam's suffering during the war.

★ 4 DELFSHAVEN

From Delfshaven, Delft's old port, the Pilgrim Fathers embarked in 1620 for England from where they sailed for the New World.

Piet Hein was born here in 1577, the Admiral who distinguished himself in Mexico in 1628 against the Spanish. The painter **Kees Van Dongen** was born here in 1877 (d 1968). He portrayed violently coloured female figures.

★ **Zakkendragershuisje** ⊙ - To the north of Voorhaven, beside the lock, this renovated 17C building is where porters used to gather when ships had to be loaded or unloaded. It contains a tin smelting workshop where traditional methods are still used.

★ **Voorhaven** - By the lever bridge at the front end of this picturesque quay stands a 15C chapel with a pinnacle known as the Pilgrim Fathers' Church.

★ **Museum De Dubbelde Palmboom** ⊙ - The "Double Palm Tree" Museum is attractively installed in a converted warehouse dating from 1825. It chronicles the long history of Rotterdam as a place where people meet, ideas are exchanged and goods are traded. On the first floor, archaeological finds show that goods were being imported here as early as 2400 BC. Goods that were being traded in the port of Rotterdam included tiles, majolica, tinware and luxury items imported by the United East India Company. Industrialisation and the history of the port from 1870 to 1970 is the theme of the second floor, which focuses on the first steam engines and the storage of goods. The third floor contains reconstructions of Rotterdam shops and other interiors from the 1930s to the 1950s. Finally, the top floor is devoted to the history of Delfshaven, including the Pilgrim Fathers and the sea hero Piet Hein, of whom there is a statue (1870) not far from the museum, opposite Coolhaven.

Molen De Distilleerketel - This tower mill dates from 1727 and is still operational.

★ 5 KOP VAN ZUID

This former dockland area (125ha/300 acres) south of the Maas has become a permanent building site over the past few years. The local authorities plan to create a second city centre here, with 5 300 new homes and 435 000m²/525 000 sq yd of office space and industrial units. Some of the projects already completed are the **Wilhelminahof** (lawcourt, offices, underground, etc) opposite Erasmusbrug, the **Belvédère** (KPN Telecom), the new **Luxor Theater** and the **World Port Center** on Wilhelminapier and the **Ichthus Hogeschool** in Posthumalaan. New buildings will stand alongside renovated and converted dockland buildings. Some splendid examples include the **Vrij Entrepot** (shopping and entertainment), the **Hotel New York** (once the head-office of the transatlantic shipping company Holland-Amerika Lijn) and the **Café Rotterdam** (the former departure hall of Holland-Amerika Lijn). Further information about this gargantuan project (scale models, film, walks) is available from the **Kop van Zuid Information Centre** ⊙. Nearby, the former railway bridge **De Hef**★, which dates from 1927, is left permanently open.

ADDITIONAL SIGHTS

Het Park – This park is an oasis of peace and tranquillity amid the hustle and bustle of Rotterdam. It comprises the small wooden church **Noorse Zeemanskerkje** (Westzeedijk) and **Euromast**.

★ **Euromast** ⊘ – This tower was built in 1960 and is situated close to Parkhaven. From the viewing platform, which is 100m/328ft up, there is a remarkable **view**★ of the city and the port. The Space Tower was added in 1970, bringing the total height of Euromast to 185m/607ft. The **panorama**★★ stretches 30km/19mi in all directions and includes the Europoort.

Euromast

Wereldmuseum ⊘ – This Ethnography Museum is housed in the old Royal Yacht Club building. In Hotel Het Reispaleis, where guests from all over the world stay, children are given an insight into multi-cultural society in an interactive way. The *Rotter-dammers* exhibition tells the stories of 10 families in an attempt to give visitors an insight into migration patterns in the 20C and the effects on society in Rotterdam today. In the treasury some splendid items of the museum's rich collections are on display, including objects from Africa, America, the Islamic world, Indonesia, Oceania and Asia. There is also a collection of textiles and some contemporary art from foreign cultures.

Opposite the museum is the **Clubgebouw van de Koninklijke Roei- en Zeilvereniging De Maas** (1908-09), a fine building which is home to the Royal rowing and sailing club De Maas.

Belasting & Douane Museum ⊘ – This museum uses prints, paintings and other objects to chronicle the history of tax levying in the Netherlands since the Middle Ages. The examples of the ingenuity of smugglers illustrates how unpopular taxation has always been.

Nationaal Schoolmuseum ⊘ – The national school museum is a small but interesting museum housed in the **former town library**★, dating from 1923. Half a dozen classrooms retrace the history of education since the Middle Ages. Exhibits include some fine horn-books, pencil boxes and other school requisites.

Opposite the museum, the fountain **De Maagd van Holland** dates from 1874.

★ **Diergaarde Blijdorp** ⊘ – In a floral park, this zoo contains an interesting collection of over 2 000 animals. The large Riviera Hall includes aquariums, terrariums containing reptiles and amphibians, a tropical hothouse and aviaries. **Taman Indah** is a reconstructed rainforest, with its own hot, wet climate, and is home to elephants, rhinoceroses and tapirs. The new **Oceanium** houses sea-lions, sharks, turtles, penguins, jelly-fish and thousands of tropical fish. The zoo also has a bat cave, a nocturnal animal house and a monkey island (Gorilla-eiland).

Arboretum Trompenburg ⊘ – The oldest part of this botanical garden (6ha/15 acres) is an English landscaped garden dating from 1820. Other features include a rose garden, hothouses with cacti and succulents and a nursery.

Kralingsebos – This wood surrounds a big lake (Kralingseplas) and has two windmills on the east side. One of them, the **Ster** (Star), is an old spice mill dating from 1740 and rebuilt in 1969.

★★ THE PORT

See also above and the insets on Michelin maps 908 and 211

Boat tours *departing from Leuvehoofd (see Travellers' addresses)*

Short harbour tour ⊙ – The boat sails west, down the Nieuwe Maas to Eemhaven. It follows the north bank, past Het Park and Euromast on the right (below the ventilation towers lies the Maastunnel) and then **Delfshaven**, **Merwehaven** (specialising in fruit), **Schiedam** *(See SCHIEDAM)*, **Wilhelminahaven** (naval repairs on a floating dock) and **Wiltonhaven**. The boat then turns round and crosses the river to sail back up the opposite bank towards Rotterdam, past **Eemhaven** (specialising in container traffic and transhipment of goods), **Waalhaven**, **Maashaven** (previously mainly grain but now handling miscellaneous goods) and **Rijnhaven**. This dock is lined by quays, where in the past the great transatlantic liners of the **Holland-Amerika Line** moored. Elegant cruise ships still dock here.

Longer tour of the port ⊙ – This tour goes all the way to Botlek.

Europoort tour ⊙ – The tour allows one to grasp the sheer size of the port installations and takes in the Nieuwe Waterweg storm surge barrier (Storm-vloedkering in de Nieuwe Waterweg) *(see DELTA)*.

Car tour to Europoort and Maasvlakte

79km/49mi to Maasvlakte. Leave Rotterdam towards Schiedam and take the Beneluxtunnel on the left.

At the south exit there is a fine view of the Pernis oil terminal.

Take the motorway on the right, running alongside a railway line.

Botlektunnel – Opened in 1980 under the Oude Maas which comes from Dordrecht, this tunnel has a single carriageway 500m/1 640ft long and 21m/69ft below sea level. It was built to relieve the traffic congestion on the old bridge.

Botlek – It is a grain port and oil terminal. Moreover, it has installations for chemical products, bulk transport and naval repairs.

Leave the Europoort road opposite, and continue right to rejoin the river.

Rozenburg – On Het Scheur, the river's opposite bank, is the Maassluis *(see below)* industrial sector. Near the Rozenburg church there is a windmill called "De Hoop" (Hope).

Shortly afterwards leave the Europoort road on the left to take Noordzeeweg which runs between the Nieuwe Waterweg and the Calandkanaal.

On the left unloading facilities for oil tankers of different companies can be seen. The end of the road goes around an old radar station, where there is a **view** of the Hoek van Holland, Europoort and the estuary which is divided by a dike; towards the north, there is the entrance to the Nieuwe Waterweg leading to Rotterdam, and to the south, the entrance to Europoort – 30 000 ships pass through the estuary every year.

Return by the same route and take the Calandbrug, then go under Brielsebrug to reach Europoort.

Europoort – The vast installations of Europoort, built between 1958 and 1975, cover 3 600ha/8 892 acres on the south bank of Nieuwe Waterweg. To the right one passes the oil terminals which have already been seen, and to the left the **Hartelkanaal**, which has recreational areas on either side of it; and then along the edge of **Brielse Meer**, an artificial lake for pleasure boats that was once a branch of the Maas, the Brielse Maas.

Dintelhavenbrug – A bridge over an access canal to Dintelhaven, the mineral port. From this bridge one can occasionally see a ferry in **Beneluxhaven**, which like Hoek van Holland is a port for ferries between England (Kingston upon Hull) and the Netherlands.

Once over the Suurhoffbrug, turn right towards Maasvlakte.

Oostvoornse Meer – This lake was created by the closing of the Brielse Gat in 1965; swimming, surfing and sailing facilities have been provided.

Maasvlakte (Maas Plain) – A stretch of sandy land reclaimed from the North Sea in 1965-1971 to accommodate the inevitable extension (around 1 200ha/3 000 acres) of Rotterdam's port. At present it houses an oil terminal (Maasvlakte Olie Terminal), a container terminal (Europe Container Terminus BV), an electric power station (EZF), facilities for the storage and transhipment of minerals (EMO) and a branch of Holland's national gas board (Nederlandse Gasunie).

A new lighthouse has replaced that of Hoek van Holland as the Maasvlakte development had left it stranded inland. Due to the continuing expansion of the port of Rotterdam, plans are under discussion for a second Maasvlakte, which would lie in front of the current Maasvlakte and would also be reclaimed from the sea.

EXCURSIONS

☐ From Schiedam to Hoek van Holland

31km/19mi by the A 20 motorway going west.

Schiedam - *See SCHIEDAM.*

Vlaardingen - This major river and sea port used to specialise in herring fishing. Today it is also an important industrial and commercial centre. From the banks of the Nieuwe Maas one can look at the unending traffic of ocean-going ships toing and froing from Rotterdam. Downstream along the south bank is the Botlek oil terminal.

Maassluis - This port is on the Scheur, between the Nieuwe Maas and the Nieuwe Waterweg. To protect Rotterdam from flooding, a **storm surge barrier**★ has been built in the Nieuwe Waterweg between Maassluis and Hoek van Holland. This opened in May 1997, and consists of two immense white gates that are able to close off the 360m/1 200ft Nieuwe Waterweg completely. Both gates have steel trusses resembling horizontal versions of the Eiffel Tower. Control of the whole complex is largely automatic, and is the only one of its kind in the world. The **Keringhuis** ⊙ information centre has a permanent exhibition about the barrier.

Hoek van Holland - At the mouth of the Nieuwe Waterweg, the Hook of Holland is the passenger port for Rotterdam and for ferries going to England (Harwich). It is an impressive sight to see the ships heading for Rotterdam or the North Sea. Opposite are the Europoort installations. An artificial beach was created north of Hoek van Holland in 1971.

☑ Brielle and Oostvoorne

41km/26mi to the south-west. Leave Rotterdam via Dorpsweg.

Brielle - *See BRIELLE.*

Oostvoorne - This is a seaside resort situated near a chain of dunes. A 311-ha/768-acre nature reserve, the **Duinen van Voorne**, has been laid out in the dunes; the reserve is criss-crossed by paths. A visitor centre provides information about the reserve's flora and fauna.

☒ Windmills and polders

Round tour of 81km/50mi - about 3hr - leave Rotterdam via Maasboulevard, go towards Gorinchem and turn off towards Alblasserdam.

The narrow dike road follows the Noord, a stretch of water frequently used. Between the Noord and the Lek lies the **Alblasserwaard**. This old **waard** (low land surrounded by rivers) has a ring of dikes around it and has been made into a polder.

Alblasserdam - This town on the Noord has naval shipyards.

Kinderdijk - Kinderdijk means children's dike, for it is said that during the great floods which occurred on St Elisabeth's feast day in 1421, the sea washed up on the dike a crib with a crying baby and a cat.
Towards the end of the village an opening between houses on the right gives a pretty view of the windmills which dot the plain.

★★ **Kinderdijk windmills** ⊙ - *Illustration: see cover*. Near the Nederwaard pumping station, along the "boezems" or drainage pools for the polderland, stand 19 windmills. Their exceptional number, their size and the beauty of the marshy plain have made them famous, and they were designated as a UNESCO World Heritage Site in 1997. Up to 1950 they helped drain the Alblasserwaard, which is below sea level; today, their sails turn for tourists only on Windmill Days *(see Practical information at the front of the guide)*.
One can walk along the dikes or take a **boat tour** ⊙.
The eight windmills of the Nederwaard are round stone polder mills *(see Introduction, Windmills)* dating from 1738 (1 to 8). The interior of the second **mill** can be visited. A little further on there is a smaller hollow post mill *(see Introduction, windmills)* called De Blokker or Blokweerse Wip. There are also eight windmills dating from 1740 with rotating caps along the other canal, but which are octagonal in shape and thatched (1 to 8). Hidden behind them are two other windmills built in 1761.

Continue by car along the dike road which follows the Lek.

From Nieuw-Lekkerland on, just down to the right of the dike, large T-shaped farmhouses can be seen; they are thatched and have haystacks beside them protected by a little roof *(illustration: see Introduction, Farmhouses).* Orchards surround these farmhouses.

Other windmills can soon be seen.

At Groot-Ammers take the Molenaarsgraaf road.

Soon four **windmills** appear in a single row along the canal. Three are hollow post mills, the fourth is an octagonal polder mill.

Further on rejoin the large canal which crosses the Alblasserwaard and follow the south bank until you come to Alblasserdam.

The **road**★ which is almost at water level is picturesque. There are large hall-farmhouses *(see Introduction, Farmhouses)* and windmills along the way. Some of these farmhouses have a safety exit a little above ground level, which led into the living room and which was used during floods.

Return to Rotterdam via Maasboulevard.

SCHIEDAM

Zuid-Holland
Population 75 169
Michelin maps 908 E 6, fold 24 (inset) and 211 L 11

Although it is part of the Rotterdam conurbation, Schiedam (pronounced Sreedam) is a typical small town whose centre is surrounded by canals, lined with several windmills. Shipbuilding yards and numerous industries make it a busy town but its main claim to fame is its genever industry (genever is similar to gin).

About 1260 a castle was built in Schiedam and one of its towers still stands near the new town hall. In 1574 the castle was destroyed by the inhabitants so that it would not fall into the hands of the Spanish.

SIGHTS

Stedelijk Museum ⊘ – *Hoogstraat 112.* Located in the town's pedestrianised area, the museum is housed in the former hospital, St Jacobs Gasthuis, an impressive 18C building with a portico. Its collections relate to the history of the town, and (mainly Dutch) contemporary art such as the CoBrA group, systematic painting, Pop Art and New Figurative Art.

In the basement, there is the National Distillery Museum, **Nederlands Gedistilleerd Museum De Gekroonde Brandersketel** ⊘. Old labels, advertisements, miniatures and stills illustrate the making of genever in the 18C, and a wide variety of genever, liqueurs and bitters can be sampled.

Windmills – The town was formerly surrounded by 19 huge mills, mainly used for milling grain intended for the distilleries. Five stage mills stand along Noordvest, the canal marking the course of the old ramparts; these are among the tallest in Europe.

De Walvisch (The Whale) – This is the southernmost of the five mills, and dates from 1794.

Continuing along the quay towards the north, one can see the four other mills.

De Drie Koornbloemen (The Three Cornflowers) – This mill of 1770 was used to grind cattle food.

De Vrijheid (Freedom) – Started in 1785, it still mills grain.

The home of genever

The Dutch started to distil grain c 1600. As time went on, they narrowed their production down to malt spirit, finally specialising in making genever, using the juice of juniper berries to give the "gin" its particular flavour. At one time Schiedam had four hundred distilleries, and the monumental 18C and 19C mansions, warehouses, windmills and former distilleries along the canals bear witness to the industry's importance. Today, only about five remain, producing young genever *(jonge jenever)* and old genever *(oude jenever)*, the latter having a fuller flavour. Each distillery has its own recipe, which is kept a closely-guarded secret. The locals have a variety of ways of ordering a genever: a *"hassebassie"*, a *"neut"*, a *"pikketanissie"* or a *"schiedammertje"*, but whatever it is called, it is always genever and it always tastes good.

De Noord (The North) – This mill of 1803 is 33.33m/109ft tall including the cap, maximum height of sails 44.56m/146ft. Its premises are used for tasting sessions by an important distillery, whose buildings are opposite.

De Nieuwe Palmboom (The New Palm Tree) – This is the home of the **Nederlands Malend Korenmolenmuseum** ⊙, or Netherlands Corn-Milling Museum. The windmill is still in operation and used for milling rye and malt for the De Gekroonde Branderssketel distillery. The museum shows what it was like to live and work in a windmill.

Take the road opposite the Stedelijk Museum and cross the Lange Haven, the town's central canal.

A fine view over the picturesque quays.

Then follow the quay (Oude Sluis) on the right.

Behind the old Corn Exchange or Korenbeurs there is the gracious 1725 guild-house of the Porters' Guild, the **Zakkendragershuisje**, with a curving gable topped by a turret.

Maasboulevard – From this boulevard near the pleasure boat harbour, there is an interesting **view** of the heavy maritime traffic between Rotterdam and the sea.

The port of Pernis is on the opposite bank.

SLUIS

Zeeland

Population 6 477 (Sluis-Aardenburg)
Michelin maps 908 B 8 and 211 F 15

This small town, situated near the Belgian border, was together with Damme an outer harbour of Bruges in the 14C when it was at the mouth of the Zwin, which is now silted up. Today it is a pleasant and busy tourist town, owing part of its appeal to its numerous sex shops. The grassy mounds visible on entering the town are remains of the old ramparts. Sluis is also the birthplace of **Johan Hendrik van Dale** (1828-72), the founder of the great Dutch monolingual dictionary *Van Dale Groot Woordenboek der Nederlandse Taal.*

SIGHTS

Stadhuis ⊙ – The town hall is overlooked by a tall 14C **belfry**, the only one existing in the Netherlands. It is decorated with turrets and a jack-o'-the-clock. From the top of the bell-tower there is a fine panoramic **view**. The Council Room has among other things a lovely 18C grille.

Molen de Brak – This wall mill, destroyed in 1944, was rebuilt in 1951. From the gallery the **view** extends over the surrounding countryside and the Zwin nature reserve *(see The Green Guide Belgium, Grand Duchy Of Luxembourg).*

OUTSKIRTS

St.-Anna ter Muiden – *2km/1mi to the northwest, near the frontier*. At the foot of the church's imposing 14C brick tower, the small triangular **square**, the rustic houses and the water pump form a charming picture. Note a thatched wooden barn at the far end of the square.

Aardenburg – *8km/5mi to the southeast*. The fine Gothic church, **St.-Bavokerk**, with characteristics of the Scheldt Gothic style (which developed in Belgium), contains 14C and 15C sarcophagi with interesting paintings on their inside panels.

EXCURSIONS

IJzendijke – *22km/14mi to the east*. This old stronghold only has a small halfmoon-shaped bastion or ravelin remaining from its ramparts, covered with earth and surrounded by water. Nearby there is a lovely windmill. The spire topped with a golden cock belongs to the oldest Protestant church (1612) in Zeeland. At no 28 Markt is the Regional Museum, **Streekmuseum WestZeeuws-Vlaanderen** ⊙. Apart from a rustic interior typical of Cadzand around 1850 there are implements used in the cultivation of flax and madder and a section devoted to the Zeeland plough horses.

Breskens – *29km/18mi to the north*. A fishing port at the mouth of the Westerschelde, Breskens is the departure point for the **ferry** ⊙ to Vlissingen. It also has a pleasure boat harbour. From the promenade laid out on top of the dune between the fishing port and the ferry terminal, there are fine views over the beaches and the Scheldt, and of Vlissingen.

SNEEK

Fryslân

Population 31 104
Michelin maps 908 I2 and 210 T4
Town plan in the current edition of The Red Guide Benelux

Sneek (Snits in Frisian) is a small, active and very popular tourist centre. In the Middle Ages it was a port on the Middelzee, an inland sea, which has since disappeared. Sneek is situated in the centre of a region much admired for its lakes, in particular Sneekermeer which is used for various water sports. Sneek has a marina and several sailing schools. One can hire motor boats, sail boats, or take boat trips in season (apply to the VVV).

Every year regattas are organised during the great **Sneek-week**. In addition, every summer for a fortnight the *skûtsjesilen* are held on the Frisian Lakes and IJsselmeer. These are regattas with **skûtsjes**, old trading boats with dark brown sails and a wide and flat hull flanked by two leeboards, still found in several Frisian towns. *For information about both events and an illustration, see Practical information at the front of the guide.*

SIGHTS

★ **Waterpoort** – This elegant 1613 gateway in brick decorated with sandstone protected the entrance to the port. Its central part pierced with arcades and forming a bridge over the Geeuw is flanked by two turrets.

Stadhuis ⊙ – Dating from the 16C, modified in the 18C, the town hall has a lovely Rococo façade with tall windows and green shutters and a richly carved perron guarded by heraldic lions.

G. Guittot/DIAF

Waterpoort

Fries Scheepvaart Museum/Sneker Oudheidkamer ⊘ – *Kleinzand 14*. This museum is devoted to Frisian navigation, both fluvial and maritime, with a large collection of models of ships used in the 18C and 19C, reconstructed pleasure-boat interiors, paintings, sail and mast workshops, and navigational instruments. There is also a display dedicated to ice sports (ice skating, Eleven Towns Race) and to skûtsjes (reconstruction of a deckhouse). In the Antiquities Room, admire the lovely collection of Frisian silverware, especially from Sneek. Several (nine) interiors have been recreated including the delightful room, from a neighbouring farm, decorated with naive 18C Frisian landscape paintings.

EXCURSION

Heerenveen – *23km/14mi to the south-east*, Heerenveen was founded in the 16C by Frisian lords, hence its name which means the Lords' Peat or Fen. About 4km/2mi to the south the flowered houses of **Oranjewoud** are hidden among the hundred-year-old trees of a 17C Nassau Frisian property, crossed by small canals. Two manor houses, **Oranjewoud** ⊘ and **Oranjestein** ⊘, adorn this magnificent landscape *(access by Prins Bernhardlaan)*. The lovely municipal park, De Overtuin, and paths in the woods make it a pleasant place for walks.

★ FRIESE MEREN (FRISIAN LAKES)

Round tour of 134km/83mi – about 1 day – leave Sneek in the direction of Bolsward.

The most attractive part of Friesland is without doubt this area of broads and canals with picturesque and historic villages. Here and there one can catch a glimpse of a church standing high on an artificial mound (terp) behind a screen of trees. In summer the waterways are alive with pleasure boats.

★ **Bolsward** – *See BOLSWARD.*

Near the Workum crossroads, take a minor road towards Exmorra.

Exmorra, Allingawier and Ferwoude are situated on the tourist route **(Aldfaers Erf)**.

Exmorra – This **Fries Landbouwmuseum** ⊘ (Frisian agricultural museum) uses machinery, tools and photographs to illustrate the development of agriculture in Friesland. A country grocer's shop of 1885 and a village school can also be viewed. Further on, the charming 13C church on a terp, surrounded by a cemetery, has been restored.

Allingawier – Near the church with a saddleback-roofed bell-tower is a typical old **Friesland farmhouse** ⊘: a large building contains the huge barn and the stable, while the living quarters are on the first floor of the annexe to leave room underneath for the dairy. A bakery, a forge and a painter's workshop can also be viewed.

Makkum – This is a picturesque fishing port on the edge of the IJsselmeer and on a canal. Since the 17C tin-glazed earthenware has been made here and above all tiles similar in style to those of Delft, but more rustic *(see Introduction, The arts)*.
On the main square, the **Waag** (weigh-house) is a fine construction of 1698. It houses the Museum of Frisian Ceramics, **Fries Aardewerkmuseum DeWaag** ⊘, in the attic and in the adjacent house. The museum displays objects used daily or for decorative purposes (plates, platters, hot plates) from 1600-1880. Note especially the objects with blue painting on a white background from Makkum and Harlingen dating from the 18C, the period when Frisian earthenware was at its peak.
Among the painted tile scenes note the one on the chimneypiece from a wealthy Makkum farmhouse.
In Tichelaar's Royal Pottery and Tile Factory, **Tichelaars Aardwewerk- en Tegelfabriek** ⊘, founded in 1594, one can see an exhibition of earthenware and visit the workshops to see the different stages in pottery-making.
Take the narrow road in the direction of Workum. The road runs parallel to the dike on one side and the canal on the other. Keep your eyes open for herons.

In Gaast, turn left to reach Ferwoude.

Ferwoude – In this locality an old farmhouse and its carpentry **workshop** ⊘ (1845) is open to the public. Opposite is the village church, topped by a pointed spire.

Workum – *See WORKUM.*

Hindeloopen – See HINDELOOPEN.

Stavoren – *8.5km/5mi from Koudum.* A fishing village, Stavoren (Starum in Frisian) has two pleasure boat harbours. It is linked to Enkhuizen by a boat service *(see ENKHUIZEN).* In the past Stavoren was the capital of the Frisian kings and a member of the Hanseatic League. Evangelised in the 9C by St Odulphus, it flourished in the 11C. Its harbour was excellent in the 14C. Then it silted up, as legend has it, because of a rich widow of Stavoren who ordered one of her ships' captains to bring her a precious cargo. The latter returned to Stavoren with wheat and the furious widow had all the wheat thrown into the harbour.
After Koudum there is a fine **view** from the lever bridge over the two lakes on either side of the road. One soon crosses the wooded region of **Gaasterland**, which stretches southwest of Balk.

Balk – Near Slotermeer, this town is on a canal bordered with several lovely 18C houses, witness to its former prosperity due to the butter trade, for which Balk was the centre.

★ Sloten – Near Slotermeer and on the fringe of the wooded Gaasterland region, Sloten (Sleat in Frisian), an old fortified town, seems to have been built on a reduced scale, which accentuates its charm; narrow streets with tiny 17C and 18C houses run alongside the small canal lined with lime trees. Following the quays, one reaches **Lemsterpoort**, an old water-gate and its **mill** of 1755 with a lovely view over the canal and the lakes where yachts sail in season. From the lever bridge near Spannenburg, there are also fine views over a wide canal.

Joure – Since the 17C this town has specialised in clock-making. Joure is also the birthplace of Egbert Douwes, founder of the well-known brand of coffee. The **Museum Joure** ⊘ (housed in the first Douwe Egberts factory) deals with all the old trades of the town, ie coffee, tea and tobacco trade, clock-making, gold and silversmithing, copper casting, and the baking and printing trade, as well as the local wildlife and countryside. In the garden is a reconstruction of the labourer's cottage where Egbert Douwes was born in 1723. A little further along at Midstraat 97 an early 20C shop is open to visitors.
A few miles north of Joure, the road runs along a narrow strip of land between two lakes; there are some fine **views**. On the left **Sneekermeer** is one of the most frequented Frisian lakes.

Grou – Near a lake, it is a very popular water sports centre.

Wieuwerd – The village has a **crypt** with strange powers. Built in the 14C on a small terp surrounded by a cemetery and altered in the 19C, this small **church** was used as a tomb in the 17C and 18C for eleven people. The corpses were protected from decomposition by an antimonious gas which rose from the ground: four of the mummies are exhibited under a sheet of glass. To illustrate this phenomenon several birds, one of which was a parrot (1879), were suspended from the vault.

Bozum – This charming village has a restored 12C and 13C **Romanesque church** built of tufa and brick in front of a tower with a saddleback roof. To the west is a semicircle of lovely low houses. The church interior is rustic and the paintings in the chancel (c 1300) are very faded.

Return to Sneek via ① on the town plan.

Michelin Route Planning on www.michelin-travel.com.
Michelin, your companion on the road, invites you to visit our web site and discover European route planning on the Internet.
Whether you just want to know the distance between two points, or need a detailed itinerary, for a holiday or on business, we provide all the information necessary for accurate travel planning.

STADSKANAAL

Groningen
Population 32 838
Michelin maps 908 L 2 and 210 AA 5

In this former fenland area, which has been reclaimed as agricultural land, the villages are linear settlements strung out along the main canals, giving the impression of being one long village. Stadskanaal (canal town) is one of these, as are Veendam and Musselkanaal.

EXCURSIONS

Ter Apel – *20km/12mi to the south-east.* Ter Apel's **former convent, Museum-Klooster Ter Apel** ⊙, is pleasantly situated in a park which boasts some splendid oak trees. The church and two ranges of the cloisters are all that remain, and the visitor can visit the cloisters, the refectory and the cellar, where the sarcophagi that were found during excavations in the cloister garth are now on show. A herb garden has been planted in the inner courtyard. The **church** has a Gothic rood screen of carved wood (1501), and stalls of the same period which are quite plain but have misericords carved with quaint figures.

Bourtange – *25km/16mi in an easterly direction. See BOURTANGE.*

Nieuweschans – *35km/22mi to the north-east.*
This small quiet village lies in the eastern part of the province of Groningen quite near to the German border. The low houses have been tastefully restored.

STAPHORST★

Overijssel
Population 15 227
Michelin maps 908 J 4 and 210 W 7

The neighbouring villages of Staphorst and **Rouveen** form a world of their own. The townspeople belong to a strict form of Protestantism, a bastion against the innovations of modern life: even now no cars are allowed to drive through the village while Sunday services are in progress. Some of the women, both young and old, wear the traditional costume but categorically refuse to be photographed.

★ **Farmhouses** – The two villages stretch out along the road for over 8km/5mi. The thatched hall-type farmhouses *(see Introduction, Traditions and folklore)* are all identical with neatly painted green shutters and doors, blue window frames and milk churn racks, and a tree of life in the window of the front door. Another characteristic of these farmhouses is the line of doors along one of the side walls. The racks for the empty milk churns are often finely carved and painted. Two **working farm museums** ⊙ are open to visitors.

Staphorst local costume

★ **Costumes** – The attractive woman's costume is worn quite often. Although rather sombre (black shoes, stockings and pleated skirt with a blue or black apron), it is brightened up by a floral bodice-front *(kraplap)* with a matching bonnet.
A red (blue if in mourning) tartan fichu is sometimes worn over the shoulders. In winter a blue cardigan is worn over the costume.
The older women still wear the head band with spiral antennae *(see Introduction, Traditions and folklore)*. The bonnet is reserved for small girls. When the children come out of school (around noon and 4pm), young girls prettily attired in their local costumes are often seen pedalling past on their bicycles.

TIEL

Gelderland
Population 37 436
Michelin maps 908 H 6 and 211 R 11

Tiel is well situated on the banks of the Waal in the centre of the fruit-growing region of the **Betuwe**; the orchards make a magnificent sight when the trees are in blossom. It lies at the centre of the river plain situated between the Lek, Nederrijn (Lower Rhine), Waal and Maas rivers. Tiel was another of the Dutch towns that belonged to the Hanseatic League back in the 15C. Every second Saturday in September a procession, the **Fruitcorso**, celebrates the end of the **fruit-picking season**.

EXCURSIONS *19km/12mi to the northwest*

Buren – This small town hemmed in by its walls became the seat of an earldom in 1492, which passed to the House of Orange when Anne of Buren married William the Silent.
The **old orphanage**, founded by Maria of Nassau in 1613, is a well preserved Renaissance building and has a porch with heavy ornamentation. It contains the **Museum der Koninklijke Marechaussee** ⊙, which tells the story of the Dutch police. Not far away, part of the curtain wall bordering the river has been turned into a promenade and affords lovely **views** over the river and the Betuwe orchards. In the main street, Voorstraat, is a **church** with a 15C bell-tower crowned by an octagonal Renaissance upper section, itself topped out with a pinnacle turret. The **stadhuis**, recognisable by its Rococo doorway, was rebuilt in the 18C. Nearby is a small cart museum, the **Boerenwagenmuseum** ⊙ *(Achter Boonenburg 1)*. At the end of Voorstraat is a brick town **gateway** and a 1716 **wall mill**.

Culemborg – This historic village received its charter in 1318 and became the seat of an earldom in 1555. Some sections of its old walls still stand. It was the birthplace of **Jan van Riebeeck** (1619-77), who in 1652 founded the Cape Colony (now Cape Town) for the Dutch East India Company as a stopping place on the way to the East Indies. In **Marktplein** stands the **stadhuis**, built in the Flamboyant Gothic style. The only gateway to remain of Culemborg's old walls is the **Binnenpoort**. The **Museum Elisabeth Weeshuis** is housed in a 16C orphanage and relates the history of Culemborg and the building. A number of original rooms (kitchen and trustees' room) have been preserved, and in the cellar a fine silver collection is on display.

TILBURG

Noord-Brabant

Population 190 559

Michelin maps 908 G 7 and 211 P 13

Tilburg is one of the Netherlands' largest towns in terms of population. Located on the Wilhelminakanaal, it is known as the "Modern Industrial Town" and is a flourishing business and retailing community. Tilburg has a student population of over 25 000, with educational institutions including the Catholic University of Brabant and the Tilburg Theological Faculty. The country's first and only rock academy opened here in September 1998.

The economy of the town was long dominated by the **textile industry** *(see Introduction, Industrial heritage)*, and in 1871 there were 125 woollen mills employing 4 600 people. These were mainly family businesses with a low degree of specialisation, but they failed to keep abreast of change and were therefore unable to keep pace with increasing competition from the rest of Europe in the 1960s. The main industries now are chemicals, photographic products, paper and printing.

The town was also the birthplace of the artist **Cornelis van Spaendonck** (1756-1840) and his brother Gerardus (1746-1822), both of whom specialised in flower paintings and worked in Paris.

King William II regularly stayed in Tilburg, and the distinctive neo-Gothic palace he had built on Willemsplein now houses the tourist office. The king died in Tilburg in 1849. Tilburg is proud of its annual two-week July **fair**, the largest in Europe. It is also the venue for the **Festival Mundial**, focusing on the third world, which is held in Leijpark every year in June and is the largest of its kind in the Netherlands.

SIGHTS

Stadhuisplein – There are quite a number of recenly-constructed buildings in Tilburg's main square. The shopping streets leading off to the north are now pedestrian zones.

Stadsschouwburg – The 1961 municipal theatre was the work of the architects Bejvoet and Holt. Glass curtain walls adjoin curved surfaces of bare brick.

Stadhuis – The sober lines of the black granite-clad town hall (1971) were the work of Kraayvanger. The town hall adjoins the neo-Gothic palace of King William II.

Noordbrabants Natuurmuseum and Scryption ⊙ – The natural history museum is located diagonally opposite the station and deals with the flora and fauna of North Brabant and the relationship between nature and man. Next door is the Scryption, a museum of written communication. Its collection includes typewriters, calculators, office machines, inkstands and pens.

★★ **De Pont (Stichting voor Hedendaagse Kunst)** ⊙ – Jan de Pont (1915-87) was a local businessman who asked that part of his estate should be used to promote modern art. A foundation was therefore set up, and at the beginning of the 1990s a former woollen mill was converted into a 4 200m²/45 000sq ft exhibition space. This magnificent space is flooded with natural light, and is used to display a selection of the foundation's very varied art collection. This includes works by Richard Serra, Marlene Dumas, Thierry De Cordier, Gerhard Merz, Anish Kapoor, James Turrell, Jan Dibbets, Marien Schouten, Rob Birza, Guido Geelen and Richard Long. Alongside the large central hall are the former woolsheds, which are ideally suited to works requiring a more intimate display area. The museum holds temporary exhibitions, and makes its garden available to an artist in the summer.

★ **Nederlands Textielmuseum** ⊙ – This museum is very appropriately housed in one of the last textile factories to survive in Tilburg. The main hall, built for large, heavy machinery, has a distinctive sawtoothed roof to maximise the amount of natural light.

The central focus of this working museum is a permanent exhibition on the textile industry in the Netherlands, which shows the technological and social changes wrought upon the industry by the advent of the steam engine. The museum's impressive working steam engine dates from 1906. There are a number of other machines of the kind used by the Tilburg wool industry. The wool arrived in the factory in large sacks, and first had to be washed. The fibres were mechanically untangled, blended, and carded to make the fibres lie parallel. The wool could then be taken to the spinning machine. Demonstrations of some of the textile machines are given, and the museum presents various aspects of the industry: knitting, dyeing, linen manufacture and fabric-printing. The four-storey building that used to house the spinning machines is now a braid-weaving mill. There is also a visual arts section with works in which textiles play an important part, a tufting workshop and an interesting display of Dutch household textiles since 1890.

EXCURSIONS

★ **Safari Beekse Bergen** ⊙ – *4km/3mi to the south-east via ② on the town plan. North of Hilvarenbeek.* The **safari park** (110ha/272 acres) is home to over 1 000 animals. Lions, rhinoceroses, cheetahs, giraffes, antelopes, zebras and baboons are just some of the residents of the drive-through area, which can be toured by bus or boat, or in the visitor's own car. The section with the penguins, flamingos, squirrel monkeys and other rare species can be visited **on foot**. There is also an African village, and for the children there is an adventure **safari trail**. Demonstrations with birds of prey are given from May to October. Adjacent to the safari park is **Speelland Beekse Bergen**, an amusement park offering a variety of pursuits including sailing, rowing, swimming, crazy golf, trampolining, and more. There is a cable-car to take visitors over to the other side of the water.

★ **Oisterwijk** – *10km/6mi to the east via ① the town plan.* This pleasant holiday centre offers a choice of excursions in its immediate vicinity, where wooded dunes, heather-clad moors and numerous lakes are to be found. In the town itself the **house** at nos 88-90 Kerkstraat, dating from 1633, has an elegant gable. **De Lind**, the charming square in front of the town hall, is planted with lime trees to form an avenue traditionally followed by wedding processions.

UTRECHT★★

Utrecht P

Population 232 718
Michelin maps 908 G 5 and 211 P 10
Plan of the conurbation (showing motorway network with access roads)
in the current edition of The Red Guide Benelux

Utrecht is a lively but intimate town with a maze of streets and numerous old buildings testifying to its long and rich history. Its picturesque canals, wharves and terraces give it a unique character; it is also a university town and a commercial centre well-known for its trade fair, which was first held in 1917. The Catholic church also plays an important role.

Every year a **Festival of Ancient Music**★ is held here. And during the annual **Dutch Film Festival** the Gouden Kalf (golden calf) awards are held *(see Calendar of events).*

HISTORICAL NOTES

Utrecht was founded at the beginning of our era on the Rhine, which passed through the town at that time. Under the Roman Empire the town was called Trajectum (ford) from which it gets its present name. In the 7C it was chosen as the seat of Friesland missions. **St Willibrord** (658-739) was made Bishop of the Frisians in 695 but settled in Utrecht, Friesland then being considered a dangerous place.

At the time of Charlemagne, who extended his empire northwards, the area became part of the Carolingian Empire. After the Treaty of Meerssen, Utrecht became a fief of the German emperors. Under their domination, Bishop Balderik (918-976) succeeded in enlarging the bishopric's jurisdiction. Having become very powerful, the bishops extended their sovereignty over the present-day provinces of Utrecht, Overijssel, Drenthe and Groningen: their territory was called the **Sticht**. Born in Utrecht in 1459, **Adrian VI**, tutor to Charles V and then a professor in Leuven (Belgium), was the only Dutch pope (1522-23). Charles V took possession of the Sticht in 1528. Made an archbishopric by Philip II of Spain in 1559, the bishopric of Utrecht from that time covered all the main towns of the area, except 's-Hertogenbosch. However the town's prosperity was coming to an end as the commercial centre of the Low Countries had moved towards the coast. In 1577 the inhabitants expelled the Spanish garrison.

The Union of Utrecht – In January 1579 the representatives of the states of Holland and Zeeland and the territories of Groningen and Utrecht, and the stadtholder of Gelderland united to sign the **Union of Utrecht**; they decided that no separate agreement would be made with Philip II, and that the Protestant religion would be the only one authorised in Holland and Zeeland, but in the other regions, practice of the Catholic religion would not lead to prosecution. In the same year signatures were added by representatives from Overijssel, Friesland and Drenthe and some southern towns such as Antwerp.

This treaty, following the Union of Arras by which the Duke of Parma had forced the southern states to submit to Spain, was the cause of the split between South and North Low Countries (which later became the United Provinces).

In 1635, **René Descartes** stayed in Utrecht and wrote the *Discourse on Method* which was published in Leiden. The year 1636 was marked by the founding of Utrecht University, the second in the country after the one in Leiden.

The schism of the Old Catholics – In the 15C a first schism shook the bishopric of Utrecht, where the chapter had retained the privilege of electing its bishops. In 1423, opposition to a pontifical candidate caused a bitter conflict between the partisans of the two opposing bishops. In 1702 the Archbishop of Utrecht, Petrus Codde was accused of Jansenism and dismissed from his duties by the pope. In 1723 the Chapter of Utrecht elected a successor without pontifical agreement. Thus, in 1724, the Old Catholics Church was formed in Utrecht. A large number of French Jansenists, fleeing to the Netherlands after the condemnation of their religion by the papal bull *Unigenitus* in 1717, became members of this independent church with Jansenist tendencies. In 1870 a group of Germans, refusing the dogma of pontifical infallibility, joined the Church of Old Catholics in Utrecht. In 1889 a great meeting of members of this Church, coming from several countries, took place in Utrecht. This religion is still practised in the Netherlands where it has about 7 000 followers.

The Utrecht School of painting – In the 16C a school of painting with a strong Italian influence developed in Utrecht. **Jan van Scorel** (1495-1562) was born near Alkmaar, but lived in Utrecht apart from a visit to Italy and a stay in Haarlem. He helped spread the Italian influence in the Netherlands; *The Baptism of Christ* (in the Frans Halsmuseum in Haarlem) is one of his best works. His pupil, **Maarten van Heemskerck** his pupil, was also a Romanist painter (a 16C Northern European artist greatly influenced by the Italian Renaissance). An excellent portrait painter, Jan van Scorel also had as a pupil **Anthonis Mor** (1517-76) who made his career under the name of **Antonio Moro**, particularly in Spain, where he showed his talent painting the court of Philip II. In the beginning of the 17C, **Abraham Bloemaert** (1564-1651), born in Gorinchem, passed on his admiration for Italian painting to many of his pupils, including **Hendrick Terbrugghen** (1588-1629) who, born in Deventer, worked mostly in Utrecht and who on his return from Italy was one of the first to take his inspiration from Caravaggism (those artists greatly

317

WHERE TO STAY

Utrecht is primarily a university and business town, and there are few hotels with much in the way of old-world charm.

Youth Hostel

NJHC Ridderhofstad – *Rhijnauwenselaan 14, 3981 HH Bunnik,* ☎ *(030) 656 12 77, Fax (030) 657 10 65. 137 beds.* 6km/4mi east of the centre by no 40/41 bus towards Rhijnauwen.

Hotels

MODERATE

Ouwi – *F.C. Dondersstraat 12, 3572 JH,* ☎ *(030) 271 63 03, Fax (030) 271 46 19. www.hotel-ouwi.nl 28 rooms.* This small hotel consists of a row of houses in a quiet street on the edge of town. The rooms are small but clean, with en-suite bathrooms. Good value for money.

MID-RANGE

Mitland – *Ariënslaan 1, 3573 PT,* ☎ *(030) 271 58 24, Fax (030) 271 90 03. www.mitland.nl 82 rooms.* Modern hotel in a leafy location on the outskirts, with a waterside restaurant and leisure facilities including a pool, sauna, tennis and bowling.

Malie – *Maliestraat 2, 3581 SL,* ☎ *(030) 231 64 24, Fax (030) 234 06 61. www.maliehotel.nl 45 rooms.* This hotel is located in a 19C building near the centre. The rooms are comfortable, with modern furnishings, and there is a terrace in the large garden.

WHERE TO EAT

Wilhelminapark – *Wilhelminapark 65,* ☎ *(030) 251 06 93.* This pavilion in the park is an ideal way of escaping the hustle and bustle of Utrecht. The food is excellent, there is a view of the lake, and you can eat outside in summer.

Bistro Chez Jacqueline – *Korte Koestraat 4,* ☎ *(030) 231 10 89.* Friendly bistro near the tourist office.

BRASSERIES, CAFÉS, BARS, COFFEE SHOPS...

Toque toque – *Oudegracht 138.* Pleasant corner café serving delicious international cuisine.

Stadskasteel Oudaen – *Oudegracht 99.* This medieval castle is now home to a brewery, complete with copper brew-kettles, a tasting room, a waterside terrace, a restaurant, and theatre performances too.

Canalside terraces, Oudegracht

Winkel van Sinkel – *Oudegracht 158*. A meal or drink in this old warehouse provides an opportunity to admire the attractive central atrium with its glass roof and balustraded gallery.

Film-theatercafé 't Hoogt – *Slachtstraat 5*. Busy arts café where you can watch a play or film and then have a drink afterwards.

Stairway to Heaven – *Mariaplaats 11-12*. A rock café with a restaurant. Live concerts on Wednesdays, and dancing on Thursdays, Fridays and Saturdays.

PRACTICAL INFORMATION

General information – The VVV tourist office is in the same complex as the Muziekcentrum Vredenburg (Vredenburg 90, 3501 DC Utrecht, ☎ (0900) 414 14 14 or www.tref.nl/utrecht/VVV). It offers information on sights, cultural and other events, accommodation packages, and tickets for theatre and other performances. For hotel bookings, contact **Utrecht Hotel Service** on ☎ (030) 231 75 76.

Transport – Parking in the streets of Utrecht is difficult and expensive; it is free only after 11pm. If you want to avoid getting ticketed or clamped, use one of the many **multi-storey car parks**, which are signposted. It is actually not possible to drive across the centre of town; instead, use the ring road. There is a park and ride site at the Galgenward stadium east of the centre.

All the main sights are within walking distance of one another.

Tours and walks – The VVV sells brochures giving details of **walking routes** on various themes. It also offers a **guided walk around town** on Sundays from mid-May to mid-September. Tours by **horse-drawn carriage** leave from Domplein.

Boat trips ⊘ – Tours of the canals, and further afield on the **Vecht**, the **Kromme Rijn** and to the **Loosdrechtse Plassen**. Rederij Schuttevaer, Oudegracht opposite no 85, ☎ (030) 272 01 11; Rederij Lovers, Nieuwekade opposite no 269, ☎ (030) 231 64 68.

Shopping – **Hoog Catharijne** is the Netherlands' largest indoor shopping precinct; another is **Shoppingcenter La Vie**, though shopping is much more interesting in the large pedestrian area in the old town. Late-night shopping is on Thursdays. For a truly authentic shopping experience, try the **Museum voor het Kruideniersbedrijf** ⊘ (Grocer's Shop Museum) in a small street behind the Statenkamer. This attractive shop dating from 1873 sells all kinds of old-fashioned delicacies, such as sweets, liquorice and peppermint, all measured out using copper weights. For antiques lovers the Oudegracht is the place to be.

Markets – There is a **general market** on Vredenburg every Wednesday and Saturday, and a **farmers' market** on Fridays. On Saturdays, one **flower market** takes place on the Bakkerbrug and part of the Oudegracht, and another on Janskerkhof. Finally, a **fabrics market** is held in Breedstraat on Saturday mornings.

Specialities – **Boterspritsjes**, delicious butter shortbread biscuits, are a local delicacy.

Theatres and concert halls – **Uitloper**, a free weekly publication available in many cafés, restaurants and theatres, lists all the films, theatres and exhibitions on offer. **Vredenburg**, Vredenburgpassage 77, ☎ (030) 231 45 44; **Stadsschouwburg** (municipal theatre), Lucas Bolwerk 24, ☎ (030) 230 20 23; **'t Werftheater**, Oudegracht aan de werf 60, ☎ (030) 231 54 40; **Huis aan de Werf**, Boorstraat 107, ☎ (030) 231 53 55.

Nightlife – Utrecht is a university town, and has countless bars and cafés. There are large numbers on Janskerkhof, Neude and of course the canalside cellars where you can eat and drink outdoors in summer.

Events – **Bluesroute**, held on the third weekend in April, offers free concerts throughout the town centre. The international **Springdance** festival takes place in April every other year. The **Festival aan de Werf** is an international theatre and visual arts event, while at Whitsun, the Maliebaan is the venue for **Stoom** (Steam), a nostalgic event featuring a wide variety of steam-driven vehicles and an old-fashioned fair. The prestigious **Holland Festival Oude Muziek** (late August-early September) includes a large number of concerts of music from the 11C to the 19C. The **Netherlands Film Festival** in late September is when the country's top film prize, the Golden Calf, is awarded.

influenced by Caravaggio's chiaroscuro); **Gerard van Honthorst** (1590-1656), born in Utrecht and who also became a faithful imitator of Caravaggio after a visit to Italy; and **Cornelis van Poelenburgh** (c 1586-1667), who painted with precision luminous landscapes. One who remained uninfluenced by the problems of chiaroscuro was **Jan Davidszoon de Heem** (1606-83/4). He was born in Utrecht and lived in Leiden and then in Antwerp, and specialised in the *vanitas* still-life paintings.

From the 17C to the 19C – In the 17C Utrecht was a very important fortified town; today a ring of canals marks the course of the fortifications. The town was occupied by the armies of Louis XIV from 1672-74 and in 1712. Prepared in Utrecht's town hall in January 1712, the **Treaty of Utrecht** was signed in 1713 in Het Slot van Zeist *(see Excursions)* and brought an end to the Spanish War of Succession which had broken out in 1701, caused by the accession to the throne of Philip V, Louis XIV's grandson. In 1806 the King of Holland, Louis Bonaparte, stayed with his court in a private mansion in Utrecht *(at no 31 Drift)*.

Utrecht was once famous for **Utrecht velvet**, which was used for covering walls and furniture.

Modern Utrecht – Utrecht has been expanding since the middle of the century and has many new quarters and buildings. Among many achievements there is a very large indoor shopping mall, the **Hoog Catharijne**, a municipal theatre (1941) by Dudok, the **Rietveld-Schröderhuis** (1924) by Rietveld and the **Kanaleneiland** (or island of canals) quarter (1962) to the west near the Amsterdam-Rijnkanaal and the **Muziekcentrum** (1979) on the Vredenburg, designed by the architect Hertzberger.

The University of Utrecht has a new campus to the east, **De Uithof**. Its **Educatorium**, or educational centre, was designed by the leading Dutch architect **Rem Koolhaas**.

There are many statues in the town. Among them are the *Fountain of the Muses' Feast* (1959) by JC Hekman in front of the theatre, and *Queen Wilhelmina* by Mari Andriessen in Wilhelmina Park (1968).

★★ OLD TOWN *half a day*

The tree-lined **canals**★★ (Oudegracht and Nieuwe Gracht) of Utrecht's city centre are edged by canalside quays which are much lower than the street and on to which open vaulted cellars.

Vredenburg – This large square, which links the old town with the new quarters, is the heart of Utrecht. The old fortress of Charles V stood here; the foundations were discovered during the laying out of the square. A Music Centre (**Muziekcentrum**) with an original design by the architect Herzberger was built here in 1979. The main auditorium seats 1 700 people. The VVV tourist office is also located in this complex.

Ph. Gajic/MICHELIN

The Oudegracht

To the west, the new **Hoog Catharijne** shopping mall extends to the station. This vast urban complex includes shopping galleries with air-conditioning in the basement, a large hotel, and the **Beatrixgebouw**, the main building of the Exhibition Palace (Jaarbeurs) where there are international fairs and a permanent commercial exhibition.

From Oudegracht bridge, there is a fine **view** over the canal (reach via Lange Viestraat). On the left is the open dome of the neo-Classical **Augustinuskerk** (1839).

★ **Oudegracht** – Narrow and spanned by numerous bridges, this old canal passes through the town from one side to the other, originally linking the Rhine to the Vecht. It includes some of the city's liveliest areas, both on the upper and the lower quays, which are lined with shops and restaurants.

At the point where it forms a bend one can see the **Drakenborch**, a house rebuilt in 1968 in the old style. Opposite at no 99, the 14C **Huis Oudaen** *(see Travellers' addresses)* has a tall façade topped by crenellations.
Cross the first bridge (Jansbrug).

The quay on the opposite side is reserved for pedestrians. Walking along, one soon has a lovely **view**★ of the cathedral's tall tower (Domtoren).
Return to the other quay.

On this bridge and along Oudegracht there is a flower market on Saturdays. The **Winkel van Sinkel** (1839) at the end of Oudegracht is one of the country's oldest warehouses. Both the large caryatids in the portico and the four white sculptures at the top are made of cast iron.

Pass in front of the **stadhuis** with its neo-Classical façade (1826) which conceals ruins dating from the Middle Ages. From here, there is a fine **view**★ of the continuation of the Oudegracht and of the Domtoren.

Vismarkt – In the days when this was still a fish market, fish was kept in large baskets in the canal to keep it fresh. Numerous antique shops line the canal further along from Vismarkt.

★★ **Domtoren** ⊙ – This bell-tower was formerly linked by an arch to the nave of the cathedral, which was destroyed shortly after a church service in 1674 by a hurricane which also devastated the town. Built between 1321-82 in the Gothic style, restored at the beginning of the 20C, it influenced many other bell-towers in the country, of which it is the highest. Its three storeys, of which the first two are square and of brick and the last octagonal and of stone, soar up to 112m/367ft in height. It has a fine carillon, most of the bells having been cast by the Hemony brothers. From the tower (465 steps, tickets available from RonDom at Domplein no 9), there is an immense and magnificent **panorama**★★ over the town and the surrounding area.

Domplein – This square lies between the Domtoren and the Domkerk. A line of paving stones indicate the nave's old layout.

★ **Domkerk** ⊙ – The tall silhouette of its transept stands miraculously preserved from the hurricane of 1674; hidden behind it is the chancel. Both are Gothic, built between 1254 and 1517 on the site where St.-Maartenskathedraal once stood. The chancel with five chapels radiating round the ambulatory was inspired by that of Doornik Cathedral. The bronze **doors** (1996) are by Theo van de Vathorst; they are decorated on the outside with evangelical texts in seven languages: Dutch, Frisian, English, Japanese, Greek, Latin and Syrian. The relief at the top shows St Martin dividing his cloak. Inside, the doors depict the works of charity. Inside there are **funerary monuments**, in particular in the second chapel on the south side of the ambulatory, the tomb of Bishop Guy of Avesnes, who died in 1317. The neo-Gothic organ dates from 1831. The stained-glass windows (1926, 1936) are by Roland Holst. The Domkerk was formerly a cathedral, but this title is now held by the Catharijnekerk next to the Museum Catharijne Convent.

Utrecht University – Built at the end of the 19C in the neo-Renaissance style, the university incorporates the cathedral's old **chapter-house** (1409), now used as the main lecture hall or **Aula**. The Union of Utrecht was signed in this room on 15 January 1579. The seven coats of arms on the stained glass windows recall the provinces and the regions that were signatories to the union. On the wall seven tapestries woven in 1936 bear the emblems of the various faculties.
The statue (1887) on the square outside the university depicts **Jan van Nassau**, the brother of William the Silent, who instigated the Union of Utrecht.

Kloostergang – A replica of a 10C runic stone from Jelling (Denmark), evoking the conversion of the Danes to Christianity, stands at the entrance to the 15C cathedral cloisters. Around the cloisters, the gables have low reliefs illustrating the life of St Martin, patron saint of the old cathedral and of the city. The **view** of the transept and the apse of the cathedral from this intimate cloister garden is very pretty. Go past a fountain with a statue of a canon writing to reach the south side of the cloisters. In the street called Achter de Dom (meaning behind the cathedral) is the back of the old chapter-house. The medieval building beside it is a cloister-house where canons lived.

Pausdam – At the junction of two canals, this is a beautiful square where the **Paushuize** stands. This elegant house, intended for Pope *(paus)* Adrian VI was only completed in 1523, the year of his death. The stepped gable on the canal has a statue of the Saviour.

Nieuwegracht – This canal is similar to the Oudegracht, but is lined with elegant residences. One can see Hofpoort, a 17C Baroque doorway of the Law Courts, and no 37, a lovely old house. Further on, at no 63, is the Museum Catharijneconvent *(see below)*. From the bridge, a fine **view** over the canal and Domtoren can be had.
Walk back to Pausdam and turn into the picturesque Kromme Nieuwegracht. The houses on the left side all have their own little bridges.

Pieterskerk ⊙ – This early-Romanesque church was built in 1048. Pieterskerk is one of the four churches Bishop **Bernulphus** had built to form the shape of a cross round what was then St.-Maartenskathedraal. Two of these churches have disappeared: abbey church of St.-Paulusabdij and St.-Mariakerk, where only the cloisters remain. The two others, Pieterskerk and Janskerk are all that remain of the famous **Bernulphus's Cross** of Churches. The vaults in the transept are Gothic, but the nave with its wooden barrel vault supported by ten red columns is Romanesque. Four **Mosan low reliefs**★ (c 1170), found during the church's restoration, are embedded in the wall in front of the raised chancel. They show the Judgement of Christ by Pilate, the crucifixion, the angel outside the empty tomb and the three Marys with the herbs. The Romanesque baptismal font has corners decorated with heads. In the chapel to the left one can see the remains of Romanesque frescoes showing the Virgin on the moon's crescent. **Concerts** are given on the new organ at the far end of the church.

★ **Crypt** – The groined vaulting is supported by stout fluted columns. In the apse there is a red sandstone sarcophagus which contains the remains of Bishop Bernulphus, founder of the church.

At no 8, on the corner of Achter St.-Pieter and Keistraat, there is a lovely 17C house, **De Krakeling**; the front is decorated with festoons and the door with a palm tree.

Janskerkhof – On Saturdays, the beautiful 17C and 18C houses around this square provide a picturesque backdrop to the colourful flower market. In the middle of the square is the Romanesque-Gothic **Janskerk**, founded by Bishop Bernulphus as the northern end of the cross of churches. The building has undergone major restoration and houses, among other things, an early music performance centre. The small building (1683) with a coat of arms opposite the church is the **main guardhouse** of the States of Utrecht, whose members met in the Statenkamer opposite. In front of it is a **statue of Anne Frank**, and to the right an equestrian statue of **St Willibrord**.

To the south of the square is the old restored **Statenkamer**, where the States General of the province met. This building, which originally belonged to a monastery of Friars Minor, is now the law faculty of Utrecht University.

Post Office – Despite what its exterior might suggest, this building on Neude is pleasantly well lit inside. It was designed in the style of the Amsterdam School by J Crouwel and built between 1918 and 1924. The extraordinary **parabola vaulting**★ is made up of lines of glazed yellow brick and glass, and the imposing black statues symbolise the five continents, trade and prosperity. The statue in the vestibule represents mail sent by land (horses), sea (fish) and air (birds).

Huis De Coninck van Poortugael – Dating from 1619, the "House of the King of Portugal" has a charming Mannerist façade with a crow-stepped gable; above the ground-floor windows are the coats of arms of Nijmegen and Portugal. The man in the centre with a sceptre is King Philip III of Portugal and Spain.
The heads of an ox and two rams on the façade on the other side of the street belong to the former **Grote Vleeshuis**, or meat market (1637).

THE MUSEUM DISTRICT

The Utrecht Museum District, established in 1995 in the old town and comprising the following museums, forms the historic cultural heart of Utrecht.

★ **Nationaal Museum van Speelklok tot Pierement** ⊙ – Located in an old five-aisled Gothic church, the Buurkerk, this museum has a magnificent collection of 18C to 20C **mechanical musical instruments**★★. The guide operates a number of these during the tour. Exhibited are old clocks and music boxes, pianolas and orchestrions made for cafés and dance halls, a Steinway player piano (1926) and a Hupfeld automatic violin (1910). The museum also houses a superb collection of barrel organs, small street organs and enormous fair or dance organs *(see Introduction, The arts)*.

Aboriginal Art Museum ⊙ – This new museum contains collections of contemporary Aboriginal art, including paintings (some on bark), ceremonial sculptures, memorial stones, didgeridoos and utensils.

★★ **Museum Catharijneconvent** ⊙ – This large museum of religious art is housed in the Late Gothic convent of St Catherine (originally a monastery belonging to the Knights of St John) and an 18C canalside house. It is devoted to the history of Christianity in the Netherlands, and has the country's largest collection of **medieval art**★★★. The very varied collections are beautifully displayed. They include magnificent liturgical robes (such as the 15C cope of David of Burgundy), manuscripts and miniatures (including the finely worked evangeliarum of Lebuinus, gold and silver objects, sculptures, altarpieces and paintings by such artists as Geertgen tot Sint Jans, Jan van Scorel, Rembrandt, Frans Hals, and Pieter Saenredam. The history of the Catholic and Protestant churches, and events such as the Iconoclasm and the Reformation, are inextricably tied up with that of the country as a whole. The differences between the two churches are explored in the canalside house, focusing on such themes as church interiors, the different church services, the role of religion in everyday life, and the relationship between church and state. The **St.-Catherinakerk** can also be visited from the museum (subject to certain conditions).

★ **Universiteitmuseum** ⊙ – This museum is the home of the collections built up by Utrecht University since it was established in 1636. The visit begins with the **Bleulandkast**★, dating from 1816, which contains an impressive collection of medical preparations and wax models. A permanent exhibition, **Geleerd in Utrecht** (Learned in Utrecht), retraces 360 years of university education and includes the standard metre and kilogram, which the Netherlands received from France's Metre Committee in 1799 to bring an end to the differences between weights and measures in different countries. On the second floor are **collections**★ relating to dentistry and ophthalmology, with often bizarre instruments and models displayed in rotation. The **Rarities collection** between the two includes stuffed animals, skeletons and fossils. The museum also organises temporary exhibitions. **Jeugdlab** is a laboratory specifically designed for the younger visitors.

Behind the museum is the **Old Botanical Garden** (1724), with greenhouses, orangeries, a seed-house, a herb garden and ginkgo trees.
The **Beyerskameren**, a late 16C almshouse with a courtyard, is located at the end of Lange Nieuwstraat on the left. The impressive Baroque building in Agnietenstraat is the **Fundatie van Renswoude**, built in 1756 as a school for orphans. Around the corner to the left is a row of beautiful small almshouses, the **Kameren Maria van Pallaes**, founded in 1651.

★★ **Centraal Museum** ⊙ – This museum is housed in the former monastery of St Agnes and contains rich collections relating mainly to Utrecht. The **pre-20C painting collection** *(main building, ground floor)* includes work by Jan van Scorel, Abraham Bloemaert and the Utrecht School, Pieter Saenredam, and the Utrecht Caravaggists Hendrick Terbrugghen and Gerard Honthorst. This section also includes a fine 17C **doll's house**. The **modern painting collection** *(main building, first floor)* is dominated by the Utrecht surrealist **Moesman** and the magic realists **Pyke Koch** and **Carel Willink**. The **Van Baaren collection** *(medieval wing, first floor)* contains work by late 19C and early 20C Dutch and French artists (Breitner, Van Gogh, Isaac Israëls, Daubigny, Maris and Verster). The **Kids Centraal** exhibitions *(medieval wing, top floor)* are specifically for children. The most important exhibit in the archaeology department *(medieval wing, basement)* is the **Utrecht Ship**, which is made from one single tree trunk. It dates from 997 and was excavated in Utrecht in 1930. The Chapel contains **medieval sculptures** from the time when Utrecht was the main religious centre in the Northern Netherlands. And finally, the Stables house a display devoted to the **topography of Utrecht** and contain a Louis XVI drawing-room and the 1926 Rietveld Harrenstein bedroom. The museum also holds major temporary exhibitions.

The wing on the opposite side of Agnietenstraat contains the **Rietveld collection**, which uses scale models and chairs (including the red and blue chair) to give an overview of the work of this famous architect. There is also a room dedicated to **Dick Bruna**, the creator of the popular picture books for toddlers.

Christ entering Jerusalem – central panel of the Lochorst Triptych
by Jan van Scorel, Centraal Museum, Utrecht

* **Nederlands Spoorwegmuseum** ⊘ – The former Maliebaan Station is the setting for the Dutch Railway Museum, which illustrates the history of the Dutch railways, beginning with the evolution from horse-drawn carriages to the first steam train. The Netherlands' first railway was built between Amsterdam and Haarlem in 1839. Excellent scale models and films give an idea of the subsequent history of railways, from the steam locomotive to the high-speed train.

Outside on the tracks (no longer used) there are more than 60 locomotives, carriages and tramcars. One of the museum's highlights is a reconstruction of the engine *De Arend* (the eagle) which in 1839 with another engine *(De Snelheid)* drew the first train to run in the Netherlands. There is also a signal box, an evocative reconstruction of a station, a children's railway, and an exciting multimedia display called **HollandRailShow**.

ADDITIONAL SIGHTS

Bruntenhof – The main entrance to this picturesque 1621 **almshouse** has a Baroque portal. The Leeuwenberchkerk (1567) on the left was once part of a pest-house, used for victims of the plague.

Kloostergang van St.-Marie – Only the Romanesque cloisters in brick remain of this church built in the 11C, one of the four churches of Bernulphus's Cross *(see Pieterskerk)*.

Waterleidingmuseum ⊘ – This fine water-tower, dating from 1895, chronicles the history of the mains water supply and of washing and ironing. It also has a fine view of the town.

Moluks Historisch Museum ⊘ – This museum deals with the history and culture of the Moluccan people of Indonesia, from their war with Japan to the arrival of the first immigrants in the Netherlands in 1951. Temporary exhibitions are also held.

** **Rietveld Schröderhuis** ⊘ – Restored after the owner's death (Mrs Schröder, in 1985), this world-famous house, built in 1924, illustrates perfectly the architectural theories of the **De Stijl** movement to which **Gerrit Rietveld** (1888-1964) belonged. In response to Mrs Schröder's demands (she attached a great deal of importance to communicating with nature; every room has a door to the outside) Rietveld created an open plan where the different elements placed at right angles determined the space. Rietveld limited himself to neutral tones – white and grey

Rietveld Schröderhuis, Utrecht

– for the large surfaces and primary colours for the linear details. Visiting the interior enables one to appreciate the originality of the layout, which is both simple and clever. On the ground floor the rooms are clearly divided, while the first floor is a large open space with sliding partitions to close off the living room and bedrooms.

EXCURSIONS

Zeist – *10km/6mi. Leave Utrecht by Biltsestraatweg.*
Zeist is a charming and elegant holiday resort nestling among lush woods. From the centre of the town a path leads to the **stately home of Slot Zeist**, built between 1677 and 1686 by Willem van Nassau-Odijk with interiors designed by Daniël Marot. **The Treaty of Utrecht** *(see above)* was signed here in 1713. The building was originally surrounded by magnificent grounds. It is now used as a conference and exhibition centre. The 18C buildings on **Broeder- en Zusterplein**, on either side of the drive, belong to the **Moravian Brotherhood** community, refugees from Moravia and Bohemia and disciples of Jan Hus, who was burned at the stake in 1415. Some house the national agency for the preservation of places of historic interest, which has its headquarters in Zeist.

★★ Loosdrechtse Plassen
Round tour of 70km/44mi – allow 1 day. Leave Utrecht via Sartreweg.

Set between lush green strips of land, these lakes cover about 3 600ha/ 8 900 acres producing an unspoilt landscape known as the Water Garden of the Netherlands. The **Loosdrechtse Plassen**★★ are flooded peat workings that go back to the 14C. Particularly favourable for water sports, they are served by numerous pleasure boat harbours. Authentic farmsteads and splendid villas line the road.

Westbroek – The picturesque route is edged by canals spanned by small bridges, each one leading to a house surrounded by a charming garden.

After **Breukeleveen** the road follows the lakeshore; there is a fine **view**.

Kasteel-Museum Sypesteyn ⊙ – This castle is located just outside **Nieuw-Loosdrecht**; it was rebuilt based on old illustrations between 1912 and 1927, and was later turned into a museum. Displayed inside are furniture, portraits, sculptures, weapons, silverware, clocks and especially Loosdrecht porcelain.

The park has a rose garden, an orchard and a maze.

Oud-Loosdrecht – This is the main tourist centre in the region. It has a large pleasure boat harbour.
Turn right then left towards Vreeland.
The road soon returns to the lake; it has lovely **views**.

Vreeland – An attractive **lever bridge** makes it possible to cross the Vecht, which is then rejoined at Loenen aan de Vecht. The **Vecht**, formerly a busy waterway, was replaced in 1952 as the main link from the Rhine to Amsterdam (Amsterdam-Rijnkanaal). The road runs along this peaceful and winding river, on whose banks are charming villas and small manor houses surrounded by magnificent parks.

Loenen – This small town with trim houses bedecked with flowers has a tall stage mill with a handrail called De Hoop (hope).

Breukelen – In the 17C this locality gave its name to a quarter in New York founded by Dutch settlers: Breukelen, pronounced in English as Brooklyn.
To the south of Breukelen, there is a pleasant **route**★ which offers views of lovely estates on the banks of the Vecht.
To the right of the road the 17C castle **Kasteel Nijenrode** now houses Nijenrode University.

★ **Kasteel De Haar** ⊘ – Standing to the west of **Haarzuilens** in the middle of a large park, this moated castle is the largest

In the Netherlands. It was built in 1892 by PJH Cuypers, the architect of the Rijksmuseum in Amsterdam, in neo-Gothic style. The enormous brick construction was erected on the site of the old medieval castle and on soil consisting partly of clay and partly of sand, and as a result is gradually being damaged by subsidence. It is hoped that extensive restoration work will remedy this problem.

The main building, with pepper-pot roof towers, is surrounded by wide moats and linked to a large fortified gateway by a covered bridge. The pentagonal inner courtyard has a steel roof, exacerbating the subsidence. The interior, which is still inhabited in summer, contains the exceptional **collections**★ of Baron van Zuylen van

Haarzuilens – Kasteel De Haar

327

> ### Belle, the rebel of the Vecht
>
> Isabella Agneta Elisabeth van Tuyll van Serooskerken, known for short as Madame de Charrière or Belle van Zuylen, still appeals to the modern imagination. This feminist before her time was born at Slot Zuylen on 20 October 1740, and spent her summers there and winters at the family's canalside house in Utrecht. She caused a great stir in the salons of Utrecht and The Hague with her interest in literature, science, philosophy and music, her unconventional attitudes and above all her satirical view of the aristocracy. When her first novel *Le Noble* was published in Paris and Amsterdam in 1763, her enraged father bought up all the copies and had them destroyed.
>
> Belle van Zuylen's independent attitude was perhaps best illustrated when the famous Scottish writer James Boswell asked for her hand in marriage. Her reply was short and to the point: "I have no talent for subservience." At the age of 31, however, she escaped the stifling atmosphere of her parents' home by marrying a Swiss, Charles-Emmanuel de Charrière de Penthaz. She moved to Neuchâtel in Switzerland, where she died in 1805. Belle wrote of her marriage: "I still feel that my thoughts, words and deeds are unhindered. I have a different name and do not always sleep alone, but that is all that has changed."

Nijevelt, notably lovely old furnishings, Flemish tapestries, Persian carpets, paintings and porcelain. The 19C bathroom, still in working order, is also worthy of note.

Return to Haarzuilens, cross over the motorway and the canal, then turn right, then left to reach Oud-Zuilen.

Slot Zuylen ⊘ - Situated near the Vecht at **Oud-Zuilen**, this castle is a solid medieval moated castle; it was rebuilt c 1751 and four octagonal towers were added. **Belle van Zuylen** was born here in 1740. The castle houses ancient objects illustrating the daily life of the past, lovely furniture, a richly endowed library and a Chinese porcelain collection. One room is decorated with a large tapestry (1643) woven in Delft. In the modest rooms where Belle van Zuylen lived, a bust of her, a few books and some engravings evoke the life of the writer.

Belle's sophistication is reflected in her many letters, including her 11 years of passionate correspondence with the Baron d'Hermenches, and in her novels and plays. She was a friend of Benjamin Constant and Madame de Staël, and wrote in French, the international language of 18C culture.

The **garden wall**, dating from 1740, is also interesting; sheltered bays are used to grow grapes, peaches, figs and other Mediterranean fruit.

Return to Utrecht by Amsterdamsestraatweg.

VALKENBURG AAN DE GEUL*

Limburg – Population 18 170
Population 17 908
Michelin maps 908 I 9 and 211 U 7

Valkenburg is a small old town situated in the charming Geul Valley, between two branches of the river. It is a bustling and fairly fashionable holiday resort with a casino and a health spa, the Thermae 2000. The town has preserved two fortified gateways: 14C **Grendelpoort** and 15C **Berkelpoort** with its footbridge.

Marl stone, a sort of limestone, predominates in the surrounding hilly countryside as at St.-Pietersberg not far from Maastricht. Yellow marl-stone has been quarried locally for centuries as a building stone. A certain number of the caves and galleries (70km/44mi) can now be visited, and quite a number have been transformed into museums or other tourist attractions.

SIGHTS

Castle ruins ⊘ - The ruins of the castle of the lords of Valkenburg dominate the town. Only parts of walls and broken arches still remain. The castle was built in c 1115 and was subjected to a great number of sieges. In 1672 it was blown up by order of the King-Stadtholder William III. From the top of the ruins there is a fine **view** of the town and the Geul valley.

Fluweelengrot ⊘ – This system of caves, which is connected to the castle by secret passages, is named after the former owner, Fluwijn. Like the Gemeente-grot (municipal cave), the Fluweelengrot *(temperature inside:10°C)* is an old marl-stone quarry where refugees sought shelter, as the many drawings and low-reliefs witness.

★ **Steenkolenmijn Valkenburg** ⊘ – A coal mine has been reconstructed in the galleries of an old quarry *(see Introduction, Industrial heritage)*. The visit provides information on the methods of coal extraction as practised in Limburg before the last workings were closed. A film from 1966 provides a realistic picture of a coal mine. Then walk along the galleries to see the trains for the transportation of miners or coal, the water pumps, the shaft supports, the systems for evacuating the coal and the safety systems. A number of fossils are also on display.

★ **Gemeentegrot** ⊘ – These are ancient marl quarries (14 °C) which were already known to the Romans. They sheltered the population in time of war, notably in September 1944 on the town's liberation.
The walls are covered with charcoal drawings and low reliefs, some representing the animals whose fossils have been found in the sedimentary marl-stone, such as the Mosasaurus *(see MAASTRICHT: Excursions)*; others represent artistic (Mona Lisa) or religious subjects. The stone was gradually quarried downwards, leaving some drawings placed very high up.

Wilhelminatoren – *Access either by car from Daalhemerweg, then turn left, or by chairlift.*
From the top of the tower (160 steps), 30m/98ft high, there is a good view of the town's wooded surroundings. There are also two toboggan runs.

Roman Catacombs ⊙ – In the old quarries 14 Roman catacombs have been reconstructed. They were designed by the architect of the Rijksmuseum PJH Cuypers, based on drawings by archaeologists.

Streekmuseum ⊙ – Objects found during excavations of the castle and reconstructed workshops and mementoes of marksmen's guilds are exhibited here.

Station – The oldest in the Netherlands, this neo-Gothic station dates from 1853.

★ ZUID-LIMBURG

Round tour of 58km/36mi – about half a day

Southern Limburg is a transitional region between the Dutch plains and the Ardennes hills jutting out between Belgium and Germany. It is a rural area whose appearance is not marred by the region's coal mines. Its fertile plateaux, lush valleys, its fields shaded by apple trees, its hilltops from which can be seen vast stretches of countryside, form a pleasant landscape dotted with fine manor houses and white half-timbered farms *(see Introduction, Traditions and folklore)*.

Leave Valkenburg by ② on the town plan, going eastwards in the direction of Gulpen.

The road follows the verdant Geul Valley.

Oud-Valkenburg – On the left is the fine 17C **Kasteel Schaloen**, restored in the 19C by Cuypers. The park is watered by a branch of the Geul. A little farther on, behind a chapel, is **Kasteel Genhoes**, built in the 16C and 18C and surrounded by moats.
After Wijlre, notice on the left **Huis Cartils**, in the middle of a fine park.

Wittem – On the right, the **Kasteel Wittem** is a 15C building, restored in the 19C in the neo-Gothic style. It is now a hotel and restaurant. A road over the plateau leads to Vaals.

Vaals – This busy resort owes its lively atmosphere to the proximity of the German frontier and Drielandenpunt.
A winding road climbs through the woods to Drielandenpunt. 500m/550yd before the end of the road, on the left, there is a fine **view**★ of Aachen.

An orchard in Southern Limburg

Ph. Roy/EXPLORER

★ **Drielandenpunt** – This site is the meeting point *(punt)* of three *(drie)* countries' *(landen)* frontiers: Germany, Belgium and the Netherlands. It is also the highest point in the Netherlands being at 321m/1 053ft. From the top of the **Boudewijntoren** there is a **panorama**★ over the region, with Aachen close by, Germany's Eifel forests, and in the distance to the west, Maastricht. There is also a maze.

Vijlen – This village still has a few half-timbered houses.

By a road through the woods one reaches the road from Vaals to Epen: pretty **view** over the hills to the south.

Epen – Resort where several houses still have half-timbered walls. On the edge of the village *(turn left before the church)* is a fine half-timbered farmhouse The climb gives fine **views**★ over the frontier hills to the south.

After Heijenrath there is a fine **view** on the right over Gulp Valley which one crosses at **Slenaken**, a small frontier village. Then follow the river towards Gulpen. This is a pleasant drive through a landscape of lush fields.

Euverem – In pools near the Gulp, trout are farmed; some of them are sent to nearby fishing waters.

At the junction of the N 278, on the right there is a **view** of **Kasteel Neuburg**, which is now a hotel.

Gulpen – A resort at the confluence of the Gulp and the Geul.

Margraten – To the west of this town lies the **Netherlands American Military Cemetery**. On the walls the names of the 1 722 missing are engraved. In the cemetery lie the graves of 8 301 soldiers marked out by crosses.

VEERE★

Zeeland

Michelin maps 908 B 7 and 211 G 13 – Local map see DELTA
Town plan in the current edition of The Red Guide Benelux

Veere is situated on **Veerse Meer**, a former branch of the sea closed by a dam which links Walcheren to Noord-Beveland *(see DELTA)*. From 1541 to 1799 Veere was a trading centre for Scottish wool and in that time developed into a prosperous port. This special relationship with Scotland dated from the 15C and had arisen through the marriage of Wolfert van Borsele, lord of Veere, to the daughter of King James I of Scotland.

With no outlet to the North Sea for its fishing boats (the dam was built in 1961), Veere has become a sailing centre and a holiday resort. With its paved alleyways and monuments, Veere is a charming town full of character.

Veere – Campveerse Toren

SIGHTS

Campveerse Toren – This 15C tower is part of the town's old fortifications. It is built of brick and decorated with bands of white stone and has a crow-stepped gable. It has been a tavern for the past five centuries.

★ **Schotse Huizen (Scottish houses)** ⊘ – *Kade 25 and 27*. Built in the 16C in the Flamboyant Gothic style, these two buildings were used as offices and warehouses by the Scottish-wool merchants who lived in Veere. At no 25 the façade stone depicts a lamb, symbol of the wool trade, and at no 27 an ostrich; both illustrate the name of the house. Inside there are Zeeland costumes and a reconstruction of a typical back room. In the fine Gothic room there are the original statues of the lords and ladies of Veere, which once decorated the stadhuis.

★ **Oude Stadhuis (Old Town Hall)** ⊘ – This two-storey Gothic building, made of sandstone, was started in 1474. The windows on the first floor are separated by recesses surmounted by canopies, under which are the statues of the four lords and three ladies of Veere. These statues (1934) replace the original ones, which are now kept in the Schotse Huizen. The roof is dominated by a 1599 onion-shaped belfry with a **carillon** of 48 bells.

In the **courtroom** *(ground floor)*, one of the oldest in the Netherlands, there is the silver gilt goblet which **Emperor Charles V** gave to Count Maximilian of Buren in 1548. The portraits displayed in the **council chamber** depict marquesses and marchionesses from Veere, members of the house of Orange-Nassau.

Grote Kerk or Onze Lieve Vrouwekerk ⊘ – A massive 15C structure in the Brabant Gothic style, with a large tower which was never completed. In the 19C it became a hospital and barracks; traces of that time are still visible in the windows. Today it houses a cultural centre. Opposite the church is the **Cisterne fountain** (1551), a lovely octagonal rotunda with diagonal arches and small columns.

The most important sights in this guide can be found on the Principal Sights map, and are described in the text. Use the map and plans, the Calendar of events, the index, and read the Introduction to get the most out of this guide.

VENLO

Limburg

Population 64 580

Michelin maps 908 J 7 and 211 W 14

Plan of the conurbation in the current edition of The Red Guide Benelux

In the northern part of the province of Limburg, near the German-Dutch frontier, Venlo is a small industrial town on the banks of the Maas.

A legend of the Middle Ages gives AD 90 as the date of Venlo's foundation by Valuas, chief of a Germanic tribe, the Bructeri. The name of the town's founder is commemorated in all the celebrations, parades and processions; the effigies of two giants representing Valuas and his wife are carried through the town.

In 1364, Venlo, by then a prosperous town, became a member of the Hanseatic League.

Today it is the centre of a large market gardening area (asparagus, mushrooms, flowers, tomatoes, gherkins), which stretches north to the outskirts of Grubbenvorst. The town's immediate surroundings are covered with hothouses.

The carnival *(see Calendar of events)* is a very lively one.

Boat trips – Boat trips are organised on the Maas. Landing stage: Maaskade.

SIGHTS

★ **Stadhuis** – In the middle of Markt, the town hall is a fine quadrilateral Renaissance building (c 1600). The façade is flanked by two octagonal corner towers topped with onion-shaped spires and has steps leading up to a perron at the centre.

St.-Martinuskerk ⊙ – The tower of this church, which dates from the beginning of the 15C, has a carillon of 48 bells. The interior has interesting **furnishings** ★ and *objets d'art*.

The 15C Gothic **stalls** are carved to represent about twenty scenes of the Old and New Testaments; the misericords are decorated with various subjects (heads, evangelist symbols, foliage, proverbs, fables, etc). On the left of the triumphal arch note a 16C *Virgin and Child*; on the right a 17C Christ; in the chancel of Sacraments, north of the high altar, a carved 16C oak bench; in the chancel of Our Lady on the right of the high altar, a 15C limestone *Pietà* and an *Ecce Homo* painted by Jan van Cleef, a painter born in Venlo (1646-1716). A beautiful brass **baptismal font**, dating from 1621, stands at the back of the south side aisle.

In the same street (Grote Kerkstraat), at nos 19-21, there is the interesting façade of the **Huize Schreurs** built in the Renaissance style (1588), topped by a voluted gable; on the 1st floor, blind arcades lean on two corbels carved with the head of a lion.

* **Limburgs Museum** ⊙ – A modern construction of glass, wood, concrete, steel
and brick, this museum building was designed by Jeanne Dekkers. Inside, a long
corridor, three storeys high, leads from an area of glass-walled office space to the
exhibition halls. The brick wall measuring over 100 m/110 yd in length recalls the
rampart that occupied this site until the 19C. The museum illustrates the history
and traditions of the province of Limburg and local trends in an original and
interesting way. The starting point is **Historoscoop**, a multimedia show giving
information on the region and the River Maas in particular. The other 11 rooms
take visitors on a voyage of discovery into the past, from prehistoric man mining
flint to today's high-tech society. Displays with lifelike figures, smell, light and
sound effects, skeletons and scale models all bring the exhibitions to life, while
interactive computer programs give more in-depth explanations. The museum
also organises temporary exhibitions.

The museum's **information centre** is housed in a nearby 1930s petrol station.

Museum Van Bommel-Van Dam ⊙ – This museum of 20C and contemporary
Dutch art mainly holds temporary exhibitions.

Romerhuis – A 16C house with crow-stepped gable and pinnacles.

EXCURSION

Tegelen en Steyl – *4km/3mi to the south-west via Prof Gelissensingel.*
Tegelen is a small industrial town well-known for its **Passion Plays** (Passiespelen)
enacted every five years at De Doolhof open-air theatre *(see Calendar of events).*
The Tiendschuur is a barn which now houses a ceramics museum.
In Steyl the **Missiemuseum Steyl** ⊙ contains artefacts collected from all over
the world by Dutch missionaries. Butterflies and stuffed animals are also on
display.
Not far from the museum, there is a botanical garden, **Jochum-Hof** ⊙.

Arcen Castle gardens ⊙ – *9km/5mi north of Venlo via the N 271.* The
32-ha/80-acre gardens of this castle dating from 1653 include a Rosarium, lakes,
a wood containing deer, oriental gardens and the Casa Verde, a large subtropical
glasshouse.

VENRAY

Limburg

Population 37 571

Michelin maps 908 I 7 and 211 U 13

On Grote Markt, **St.-Petrus Bandenkerk** ⊙, a large Gothic church, contains some
interesting furnishings. Apart from the Baroque pulpit, note a fine late 15C brass
lectern and a remarkable series of wooden **statues** and the one of St Paul in stone; the
oldest is of St James (15C). The Apostles, with their attributes, stand against the
pillars of the nave. In the aisles there is a series of saints, including a beautiful St Lucy,
which come from old altars no longer in existence. At the entrance there is a Baroque
statue of St Peter, shown as pope.

EXCURSION

Overloon – *7km/4mi to the north.* For three weeks in the autumn of 1944 the
British and Americans fought a battle round this village to support Operation
Market Garden *(see ARNHEM)*, one of the biggest tank battles of the war, often
compared to that at Caen because of the terrible artillery bombardment and the
number of tanks involved.
The **Nationaal Oorlogs- en Verzetsmuseum** ⊙, or National War and Resistance Museum,
is to the east of Overloon in the woods where the fighting occurred. A
15ha/37 acre enclosure and large exhibition hall contain an interesting collection
of German and Allied equipment: tanks, planes, a one-man submarine, guns,
bombs, torpedoes, etc. In the Documentation Centre the history of the Second
World War is told by means of photographs, models, maps, weapons, uniforms,
and so on. In a building devoted to concentration camps in Europe and Asia
(Kampengebouw), a permanent exhibition illustrates the tragic plight of the
victims through photographs, films, documents and various other objects.

The length of time given in this guide
* – for touring allows time to enjoy the views and the scenery;*
* – for sightseeing is the average time required for a visit.*

VLISSINGEN

FLUSHING – Zeeland

Population 44 530

Michelin maps 908 B 7 and 211 G 14 – Local map see DELTA

Flushing, on the Westerschelde estuary and commanding the entry to the Walcheren canal, is both a fishing port and an industrial centre with large naval shipyards. Flushing also has a Naval College and warships are moored here. From the ferry terminal there are car ferry services to England (Sheerness) and across the estuary to Breskens *(see SLUIS, Excursions)*.

Boat trips ⊙ – Flushing is the starting-point for boat trips along the coast of Walcheren Peninsula.

HISTORICAL NOTES

Flushing became important in the 14C on account of its commercial activities (mainly with England) and herring fishing industry. Flushing became a trading centre for herring in 1444. Philip II embarked here in 1559 when he finally left the Low Countries for Spain. From 1585 to 1616 the town was pledged to the English as a guarantee of the costs incurred by the Earl of Leicester's army to uphold the United Provinces after the assassination of William the Silent.

Admiral de Ruyter (1607-76), born in Flushing, distinguished himself during the third war against England (1672-74) and was fatally wounded during a battle near Syracuse. The French draughtsman **Constantin Guys** (1802-92), nicknamed "the painter of modern life" by the poet Charles Baudelaire, was also a native of Flushing.

The Boulevard – The town's seafront is a long avenue known as the Boulevard, flanked by an esplanade.

The 15C **Gevangentoren** or Prison Tower stands here. Down below stretches a wide beach sheltered from northern winds. At the far end of the Boulevard, on an old bastion, note the little lighthouse and the statue of Admiral de Ruyter. From there you have a nice view of the port below and the **Old Exchange** (1635), a fine building with green shutters surmounted by a pinnacle.

Maritiem Attractiecentrum Het Arsenaal ⊙ – *Arsenaalplein 1*. This former arsenal (1823) now provides an exciting introduction to the seafaring world for children in particular. It includes a parade of ships, a **pirates' cave**, and a chance to experience the sinking of a ship and be washed up on Treasure Island. The 65m/215ft crow's-nest gives a view across Zeeland and the Westerschelde. The tour ends with a visit to the world beneath the sea.

Stedelijk Museum ⊙ – *Bellamypark 19*. This museum tells the story of the town's rich maritime past. It focuses particularly on the famous admiral Michiel de Ruyter and the East India Company, and the local pilotage service. The display also includes items of cargo from ships that have run aground on the sandbanks.

Reptielenzoo Iguana ⊙ – *Bellamypark 35*. Over 500 living reptiles, amphibians and insects are on view here. There is also a "baby room" in which eggs are hatched and young animals are kept.

EXCURSION

Fort Rammekens ⊙ – *On Rammekensweg by Ritthem, east of Flushing*. This sea fort is the oldest in Western Europe and was built in 1547 to defend the ports of Middelburg and Antwerp. The casemates added in 1809 by Napoleon now house exhibitions on the history of the fortress and on the surrounding countryside.

VOLENDAM★

Noord-Holland

Michelin maps 908 G 4 and 210 P 8

Volendam, like Marken, stands on a small land-locked sea, Gouwzee. It is one of the best known ports of the old Zuiderzee. Its townspeople – who, unlike the people of Marken, are mostly Catholic – wear the traditional costume in summer, and it has become a symbol of the Netherlands for foreigners, though any sense of authenticity has long since been lost. Tourism is an important activity.

Village – The long street, which runs along the top of the high dike, is just a line of shops, but behind and below the dike there are picturesque narrow alleyways winding between small brick houses with wooden gables.

★ **Traditional costume** – The men wear black trousers with silver buttons, short black jackets over striped shirts, and round caps. The women's costume consists of a black skirt with a striped apron or a striped skirt with a black apron, a shirt with a flowered front under a black short sleeved overblouse, and a necklace of

---

The Cartographers of 17C Europe

The daring and enterprise of Dutch merchant-seamen and navigators led to the rise of the United Netherlands as a maritime power. Amsterdam became not only the centre of international commerce but also of commercial cartography. The map-makers of the period were often equally at home as engravers, publishers or cartographers.

Great names of Dutch cartography included Petrus Plancius; Mercator (of the projection and Atlas 1606); Hondius who revised Mercator's Atlas and mapped Sir Francis Drake's round-the-world voyage; Blaeu (Willem Jansz) publisher of the poet and dramatist Vondel and cartographer to the East India Company from 1634; his arch rival Johannes Jansonius, son-in-law to Hondius and successor to the family firm; and Van Keulen, founder of a publishing house famous for its nautical charts.

---

large coral beads with a gold clasp, hidden in winter by a blue and white shawl. When they are not wearing a pointed black bonnet they wear a lace cap for feast days, very tall with turned-up wings, whose shape is famous. Visitors should watch the congregation leaving church when the couples cross the little wooden bridge in front of the Catholic church.

Volendams Museum ⊙ – *Zeestraat 37*. This museum is located in a small shop and classroom. The exhibits include traditional costumes and jewellery, fishing equipment and cigar bands.

De WADDENEILANDEN★★

Wadden Islands

Michelin maps 908 F 2, 3, G 2, H 1, I 1, J 1
and 210 N 4, 5, O4,5, P3, Q2, R2, S2, T2, U2, V2, W1,2.

The Wadden Islands are a unique nature reserve in the north of the country. There are five inhabited islands, extending between the North Sea and the Waddenzee. The largest, **Texel**, is part of the province of Noord-Holland; the others, **Vlieland**, **Terschelling**, **Ameland** and **Schiermonnikoog**, are part of Fryslân. There are also smaller islands and sandbanks, such as the bird island of **Griend**, and **Rottumeroog** and **Rottumerplaat**, both in Groningen province. The belt of islands continues northwards along the coasts of Germany and Denmark.

The formation of the islands and the Waddenzee – Along with the German and Danish islands, the islands are the remains of an ancient chain of dunes which stretched as far as Jutland in Denmark. As far back as the Roman period the sea had breached the chain of dunes and invaded the flat hinterland forming the **Waddenzee**. In the 13C this was connected to a vast gulf which had just been formed, the Zuiderzee *(see IJSSELMEER)*.

Tides and currents – The islands are still subject to the action of strong currents and the North Sea continues its insidious undermining process to the **west** of the islands. Kilometer posts are planted in lines along the beaches to record the movement of the sand, and the **breakwaters** are built to reduce this movement.

To the **east**, the strong currents displace the sand which then silts up the Waddenzee. At low tide, the sea leaves huge stretches of mudflats or sand called *wadden* (because they can be waded across). These are popular with birds, but cause ships to make large detours to follow the marked channels. The Waddenzee can be walked with a guide, at certain times of year and when weather permits *(see below)*.

The power of the wind – The constant strong west wind has always been the greatest enemy of the Wadden region. Over the course of time, it has gradually "turned" the islands round to the east; villages on the islands' west sides, such as Westerburen on Schiermonnikoog and Westervlieland on Vlieland, have been swallowed up by the sea. Even today, huge areas of sand are forming on the south-west sides of the islands. Since 1900, large-scale conifer planting has been carried out in an attempt to prevent the spread of these areas, and this, combined with breakwaters, dikes and careful maintenance of the dunes, has kept the large islands more or less in place. Some of the sandbars, such as **Noorderhaaks** (better known as De Razende Bol, the fast-moving ball) are constantly on the move.

The strong wind does have one advantage: because it makes the clouds move faster, the Wadden Islands have less rain than other parts of the country.

Battling against the sea – Time and time again, the low-lying islands have been flooded by big storms as the dunes and dikes prove unable to resist the power of the sea. For example, the small island of Griend, between Vlieland and Harlingen, was a prosperous place in the 13C; little by little it was eroded by the high tides, and had to be abandoned in the 18C; what remains of it now is an important breeding ground

Dunes on Ameland

for birds. Likewise the dike built between Ameland and the Frisian coast in 1871 was destroyed by storms eleven years later, and Rottumerplaat was regularly under water until 1950.

Landscape – The northern and western sides of the islands have wonderful **beaches** of very white sand bordered by **dunes**. The dunes have been planted with marram grass to prevent them from being carried along by the wind. They are particularly high and wide on Texel, but the highest dunes are on Ameland and Terschelling, where they reach a height of over 30m/100ft.

The **coniferous forests** planted inland in the early 20C radically changed the appearance of the islands, which had hitherto been largely treeless.

The very flat south coasts of the islands are protected by **dikes**. The countryside is generally subdivided into several **polders** separated by small dikes, where numerous herds of cows and a few horses graze. Texel specialises mainly in sheep-raising.

There are also several small **harbours** on the Waddenzee. They were once the departure point for fishing and whaling; today they are mostly marinas.

Fauna – All these islands form a vast sanctuary for **seabirds**. Some come to lay their eggs, including gulls of all kinds, spoonbills, and pintail ducks.

In the autumn a great number of **migratory birds** from northern Europe (Scandinavia, Iceland) and from Siberia stop for a time on the Waddenzee, which is rich in food (fish and shellfish), then continue on their way to warmer climates (France, Spain, North

Spoonbill

Sheldrake

Grey heron

Silver seagull

Lapwing

Stork

Oyster catcher

THE WADDEN ISLANDS:
PRACTICAL INFORMATION

Getting there by boat – The ferry situation varies from one island to another; some are high-speed and others are not; some allow cars and others do not. Ferries are quite frequent in the high season, but in the low season they may be limited to one a day, or even none in bad weather. It is therefore a good idea to check the appropriate ferry company's 24hr information line a few days before you go. Cars can be left in the large harbour car parks on the mainland. *(For more information on each island, see below and the Admission times and charges at the back of the guide).*

Exploring the islands – The best way to get about is by **bicycle**, and on Vlieland and Schiermonnikoog, where cars are forbidden, it is the only way. Cycling or walking are also the best ways of seeing the nature reserves and dunes. Bikes can be hired on each island and in most villages. However, in the summer they can be hard to come by and it is highly advisable to bring a bicycle with you from the mainland. **Cycling and walking maps** are available from the VVV tourist office.

Most islands have **bus** services; another alternative is to travel by **taxi**, which is not only comfortable, but has the added bonus that the driver may tell you all about the area. Having your own car might be useful on Texel.

Accommodation – In season, it is best to reserve rooms through the island's tourist information centre. There are a few hotels, but many islanders take in visitors. The VVV publishes an annual guide listing these, along with camp sites and holiday cottages.

Tours – The VVV can provide information on tours of the nature reserves or the mudflats, and birdwatching, seal-watching and beachcombing trips.

Walking across the mudflats ⊘ – These exciting trips, for which a guide is compulsory, take place from early April to late October. Most leave from Wierum (Fryslân) or Pieterburen (Groningen); *for addresses, see Admission times and charges at the back of the guide.* VVVs also organise shorter trips of this kind.

Sports – Sailing, surfing, fishing, parachuting, horse riding, golf, skating, cross-country skiing: the islands have them all, and the VVV can provide you with further information. **De Ronde om Texel**, the world's biggest catamaran race, is held in June.

The Wadden Islands on the internet – http://www.vvv-wadden.nl

Africa). This is the case with the avocet. Others spend winter on the Waddenzee: they include among the waders a large number of different types of dunlins and oyster catchers.

Nature reserves have been designated on each island, and in some cases visitors can only visit when accompanied by a guide. The largest reserves are usually on Forestry Commission (Staatsbosbeheer) land. Many areas are closed to the public during the nesting season, from mid-March to mid-August.

Seals used to come in great numbers to the sand banks on the north side of the islands, but their numbers were seriously depleted in the 1980s by a virus. Fortunately, there are now signs that the numbers are on the increase again, and you may be lucky enough to see them basking in the sun on one of the many sandbanks as you cross to the islands.

Flora – The **plant life** on the dunes, which are interspersed with small pools, is exceptionally varied. The most common species include the sea buckthorn with its edible orange berries, the Burnet rose, and grasses such as scurvy grass, Parnassus grass with white flowers and succulent plants such as milkwort. Terschelling is also the only place in Europe where cranberries are cultivated.

Tourism on the islands – Even if you are not interested in ornithology or botany, you will enjoy the natural beauty of the islands, an unpolluted environment (clear seas, the wild open expanses of dunes and a healthy climate), and the peace and quiet, though they do get very busy in summer. The islands also have a great deal to offer in autumn and winter.

The drawbacks – Tourism has taken its toll, and the Wadden Islands are also used by the army; aircraft noise from the military bases on Texel and Vlieland has scared away some of the birdlife. In addition rich reserves of natural gas have been found under the Waddenzee: a drilling platform has already been built between Den Helder and Texel.

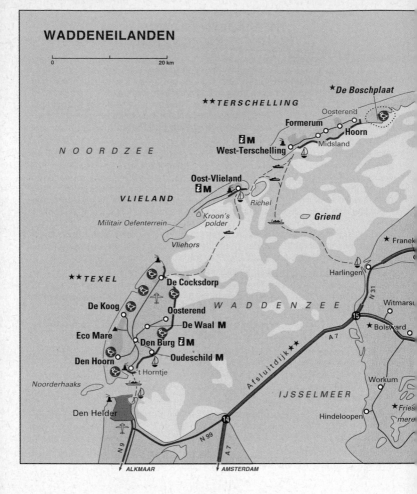

WADDENEILANDEN

0   20 km

★ *De Boschplaat*

★★ *TERSCHELLING*

Oosterend

Formerum

Hoorn

NOORDZEE

☑ M
West-Terschelling

Midsland

Oost-Vlieland
☑ M

Richel

VLIELAND

★ Franek

Kroon's polder

Militair Oefenterrein

Griend

Harlingen

Vliehors

N 31

★★ TEXEL

De Cocksdorp

WADDENZEE

Witmarsu

De Koog

Oosterend

Bolsward

De Waal M

Eco Mare

15

A 7

Den Burg ☑ M

Den Hoorn

Oudeschild M

Workum

't Horntje

Noorderhaaks

IJSSELMEER

★ Fries mere

Den Helder

Afsluitdijk ★★

Hindeloopen

14

N 9

N 99

A 7

↗ ALKMAAR   ↗ AMSTERDAM

AMELAND

Fryslân – Population 3 477

Ferry ⊘ – From Holwerd. Operated by Wagenborg Passagiersdiensten; information line ☎ (0519) 54 20 01 or www.wagenborg.nl

VVV (tourist office) – In Nes, ☎ (0519) 546 546 or www.ameland.nl

This long island covering about 5 800ha/14 326 acres with its large stretches of dunes, fine sandy beaches on the North Sea, and woods, is very popular with tourists, including a large number of Germans who come here in the summer. Nearly 100km/60mi of bicycle tracks cross the island passing through woods and over dunes. Like the other Wadden Islands, Ameland has its **nature reserves** for birds, including **Het Oerd** at the far eastern end of the island.

The inhabitants of Ameland specialised in **whaling** in the 17C and 18C. This activity was discontinued in the mid 19C, but the captains' houses can still be seen here and there on the island, and in some places whale bones are still used as fences. The four picturesque villages are all conservation areas.

Nes – This is the island's chief village, overlooked by an isolated **bell-tower** with a saddleback roof, dating from 1664. In Rixt van Doniastraat there are several old captains' houses, **Commandeurshuizen**, one-storey houses with a small lean-to on the side, and an entrance door that is slightly off-centre. A cordon of bricks or a geometric frieze outlines each floor, and there is often an iron anchor on the façade bearing the date when the house was built.

To the east on the road to Buren, past the new Catholic cemetery, the old **cemetery** is accessible by a small road on the left. It still has ancient tombstones, some decorated with a weeping willow, others very narrow and nearly 2m/6ft high. Several graves of British airmen whose planes crashed here during the war are to be found in this cemetery.

A visit to **Natuurcentrum Ameland** ⊙ will give you a much greater appreciation of the island's natural environment. Slides, photographs, sound recordings and models are used to give an impression of the different landscapes: mudflats, salt marshes, polders, woodland, dunes and beaches. There is an aquarium of North Sea fish, and the skeleton of one of four whales which were stranded here in November 1997.

Buren – This is the island's easternmost village; further east is Het Oerd nature reserve. The village square has a bronze statuette of a hook-nosed woman with a storm lantern, **Rixt van het Oerd** *(see below)*.

The **Landbouw en Juttersmuseum Swartwoude** ⊙ (Swartwoude Agriculture and Beachcombing Museum) uses photographs and other items to bring to life the harsh existence led by people on Ameland as recently as 1900. They eked out an existence from farming, fishing, poaching and beachcombing; the latter was made illegal in 1529, but was practised by poor coast-dwellers until late in the 18C. It was sometimes very lucrative when the cargoes of stranded ships were washed ashore, yielding such items as firewood, tins of food, alcohol and suitcases.

Ballum – The old tower amid the trees in the centre of this little village told the villagers the time and also sounded the alarm when danger threatened. Take Smitteweg, next to the new town hall, to the south-east to reach the **cemetery** where some of the beautiful old tombstones depict sailing ships or weeping willows.

How Het Oerd got its name

Long ago, a widow called Rixt and her son Sjoerd lived at the eastern end of Ameland. They had virtually no contact with the other islanders, and lived off the land; the only thing of any worth that they possessed was a cow. Every day, Sjoerd would go poaching and Rixt would walk along the beach looking for useful objects that had been washed ashore. Everything went well until Sjoerd grow up and left home to become a seaman. At first Rixt managed on her own, but after a long period of finding nothing on the beach, she hatched a cunning plan. One dark and stormy night, she tied a storm lantern to the cow's head and led it up to the top of the highest dune. A ship in distress just off the coast of Ameland thought it had found a safe haven, and set a course towards the light. But it broke up on the rocks and all the crew drowned. Rixt hurried to the beach, full of expectation, but when she saw one of the bodies lying on the shore she screamed: it was her son Sjoerd. Ever since then, if you listen carefully as the stormy winds blow across the island, you can still hear her heart-rending cry: Sjoooerd, Sjoooerd...

Hollum - tombstone in the churchyard

Hollum – To the south of the village stands a typically attractive church with a saddleback-roofed bell-tower. In the surrounding **cemetery** there are more 18C tombstones showing sailing ships.

Hollum was home to many of the captains of the whaling ships which operated out of Ameland, and one of their houses has been converted into a museum, the **Cultuur-Historisch Museum Sorgdrager** ⊙. Pieces of local furniture and tiled walls grace the interiors, which make an ideal setting for the collections of earthenware, pottery, costumes and other objects related to whaling, fishing and the dairy industry.

A lifeboat museum, **Reddingsmuseum Abraham Fock** ⊙, is located in Oranjeweg. This is the home of the famous **Ameland lifeboat** ⊙, which is drawn down to the water by a team of horses. The museum traces the evolution from beachcomber to lifeboatman, and a video describes how the latter have operated now and in the past.

Ameland's red and white lighthouse is further to the north-west (*illustration: see p 8*).

SCHIERMONNIKOOG

Fryslân - Population 1 004

This is the smallest of Waddenzee's inhabited islands: covering an area of 4 000ha/9 880 acres, it is 16km/10mi long and 4km/2mi wide, and has recently been designated a national park. The only village, Schiermonnikoog, has two large beaches and a small lake (pleasure boats), the Westerplas. To the east are the **Kobbeduinen** (dunes) and a nature reserve of 2 400ha/5 928 acres, **De Oosterkwelder**. With its wild scenery, its dunes, woods, beaches and its tranquillity, Schiermonnikoog is one of the most pleasant islands in the group.

The island became Frisian in 1580 before passing into the hands of several land-owning families from 1639 to 1858 and finally becoming state property in 1945.

Ferry ⊙ – From Lauwersoog. Operated by Wagenborg Passagiersdiensten; information line ☎ (0519) 34 90 79 or www.wagenborg.nl

VVV (tourist office) – ☎ (0519) 53 12 33 or (0519) 53 19 00, www.schiermonnikoog.net

Schiermonnikoog – The houses of this village are built among the trees. It developed after Cistercian monks from Friesland settled here c 1400. The name of the island derives from *schier* meaning grey, *monnik* monk and *oog* island. A statue of a monk on the green in the town centre is a reminder of its past.

Nearby, an arch made of two huge whale bones recalls the whaling of earlier times. The **visitor centre** ⊘ is housed in an old power station and contains an exhibition about the island's different landscapes. It also has the bones of one of four whales which were stranded on the island in 1997, and a small cultural and historical section.

In Middenstreek, a street which runs towards the west, and in the parallel Langestreek, there are interesting **old houses** with asymmetrical roofs.

★ **The Rif** – Past the Westerplas, at the south-western extremity of the island, lies a vast stretch of immaculate white sand reaching 1.5km/1mi in width. From Westerburenweg, a path which ends in the dunes, there is an excellent **view**★ of the Rif.

TERSCHELLING★★

Fryslân – Population 4 761

Ferry ⊘ – From Harlingen. Operated by Rederij Doeksen; information line ☏ (0562) 44 27 70 or 44 32 20 (express service). www.rederij-doeksen.nl

VVV tourist office – In West-Terschelling, ☏ (0562) 44 30 00 or www.terschelling.net

This very long island (28km/17.5mi) covers 11 000ha/27 180 acres and is the second largest of the Wadden Islands, after Texel. Terschelling is an island with many faces: wide sandy beaches, tall dunes, salt marshes and mudflats with hundreds of birds, dense coniferous forests, broad polders and a few small villages. The ideal way to explore it is by the many cycle paths that criss-cross the island.

It welcomes many holidaymakers in summer, who enjoy its huge sandy beaches. Terschelling (pronounced Ter-srelling) still has a wild aspect. It is covered with vast areas of dunes where an abundant vegetation of grasses, flowers and moss grow. It also has several **nature reserves**, of which the largest is De Boschplaat.

Terschelling is the homeland of **Willem Barents** or Barentsz (c 1555-97), the navigator who, while trying to find a north-east passage to India, discovered Novaya Zemlya in 1594 and Spitsbergen in 1596 *(see Introduction, Historical table and notes)*. The portion of the Arctic Ocean which lies between these two archipelagos, the Barents Sea, bears his name. On his third expedition (1596-97), his boat was caught in the ice. He spent the winter in Novaya Zemlya in a hut made from boat planks, and died in an attempt to return to civilisation. In 1876 the ship's log was found.

The ten-day **Oerol festival** takes place every June, with events and performances being held all over the island, on beaches, in the dunes and in barns.

Terschelling and its cranberries

Cranberry wine is a speciality of Terschelling, and the damp valleys between the dunes are almost the only place in Europe where cranberries grow. According to tradition it all started in about 1840, when a beachcomber, Pieter-Sipkes Cupido, found a barrel full of cranberries that had washed ashore from a ship. He took it into the dunes, opened it, and then left it there, disappointed that the barrel did not contain anything more valuable. But Terschelling had gained a new crop as a result.

The centre of the industry is in Formerum, but all over the island you can taste tarts, ice creams, jam, liqueur, wine and meat dishes prepared using local cranberries.

West-Terschelling – The capital of the island (known in Frisian as West-Skylge) is a small but lively port well situated in a large bay. It is overlooked by a square tower 54m/174ft high, the **Brandaris**, a lighthouse built in 1594 to replace the bell-tower of St Brandarius Chapel which had till then done sterling service as a lighthouse. The bell-tower was engulfed by the waves.

West-Terschelling – The marina at the foot of the Brandaris

At the foot of the tower lies a large **cemetery**. The 19C and early 20C tombstones, engraved with naively depicted boats, recall the maritime past of its inhabitants. One of the stones, in the middle of the cemetery, recalls the episode during which five of the island's lifesavers tried to rescue the survivors from the wreck of the *Queen of Mistley*, on 3 January 1880.

Terschelling Museum 't Behouden Huys ⊙ – *Commandeurstraat no 30*. This regional museum is housed in two dwellings belonging to captains (commandeurshuizen) (1668). It bears the name of the hut in which Willem Barents was forced to spend a winter on Novaya Zemlya. At the entrance, note the fine sculptured paving stones.

The top floor of the left-hand house tells the story of Terschelling; the rooms on the ground floor are furnished in 19C style. A new section of the museum contains a reconstruction of part of Willem Barents' ship, with a wide variety of objects and a panorama show recounting his voyages to the far north. The first floor is dedicated to pilotage and whaling. The other house contains model ships and related objects, together with a collection of flotsam and jetsam.

Centrum voor natuur en landschap ⊙ – *Burg. Reedekkerstraat 11*. This centre is devoted to the island's rich plant and animal life, with films and other media being used to show how dunes form, how dikes are built, how water is managed, and the role of forestry. It places particular emphasis on the "bird island" of Griend, and the De Boschplaat nature reserve. The centre also has large aquariums of fish, crabs and shellfish.

Formerum – A small windmill, **De Koffiemolen** (the coffee mill) is worth seeing. It has a thatched roof and dates from 1876; it is now used to mill grain.

Hoorn – The Frisian name of this village is Hoarne. The 13C church built of brick in the Frisian style is surrounded by gravestones. The oldest date from the 19C and are topped by a low relief depicting a ship.

★ **De Boschplaat** ⊙ – *No cars allowed; cycling paths in the western part*. Haycart tours and guided walks are organised. This nature reserve is the only **European natural monument** in the Netherlands, and a paradise for nature lovers. It covers 4 440ha/10 868 acres of the island's eastern end, which is uninhabited. Large numbers of birds come to nest on the dunes and estuaries. What makes it special is the large number of transitional zones between different ecosystems, for example between salt and fresh water, dry and wet, wind and shelter, and acid and alkaline soils. The vegetation is quite remarkable, as orchids and unique types of halophyte plants (those growing on salty soil) can be found. A large part of the Boschplaat is closed to visitors during the nesting season.

TEXEL★★

Noord-Holland – Population 13 343

Ferry ⊙ – From Den Helder. Operated by Teso; information line ☏ (0222) 36 96 91 or www.teso.nl

VVV (tourist office) Emmalaan 66, Den Burg, ☏ (0222) 31 47 41 or www.texel.net

---

Texel (pronounced Tessel) is 24km/15mi long and 9km/6mi wide, and is the largest of the Wadden Islands. If therefore has less of an island feel than its neighbours, but this "Netherlands in miniature" still has much to offer.

The capital, **Den Burg**, is roughly in the centre. **De Koog**, to the west, gives access to the main beach. **Oudeschild** is a small fishing and pleasure port. **Oosterend**, **De Waal** and **Den Hoorn** are small, picturesque villages; **De Cocksdorp** is the most northerly, and its lighthouse has a view of Vlieland on a good day.

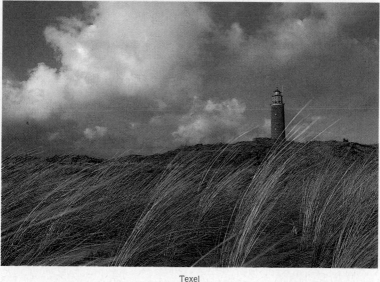

Texel

Bird Island – Birds are one of the most interesting features of Texel. Some 300 species nest and breed on the dunes or on the banks of the freshwater lakes. Texel has several state-owned **nature reserves**★ ⊙. *The waymarked nature trails are for walkers only.*

De Eijerlandse duinen – These dunes belonged to an island, Eyerlandt, which has been joined to Texel since 1629 by a sand bar. Numerous birds nest here from the end of March to the end of July, especially eiders which provide the down to make eiderdowns.

Texel and its sheep

The island's main activity, after agriculture and tourism, is sheep-breeding (there are about 16 000 sheep on the island, and some 20 000 lambs are born each spring). There are a particularly large number of sheep sheds around the ironically named Hoge Berg or "high hill" (15m/50ft) in the middle of the island. These are like small half-barns with thatched roofs, used to store hay and feed as well as to protect the sheep against the bitter west wind and the snow. They also take shelter behind the garden walls of the farmhouses, but Texel sheep always spend the winter outdoors.

Apart from their extremely fine meat, which has a natural salty taste from the grass they eat, the sheep also provide excellent wool and milk; it is said that the wool has a healing effect on muscle pain and rheumatism. The milk is also used to make cheese and even soap.

De Slufter – This is a large area surrounded by dunes, linked to the sea by a gap. The vegetation growing here is impregnated with salt. About forty different species of birds nest here. From the top of the dunes, at the end of the Slufterweg, which can be reached by a stairway, there is a **view*** over this amazing wild landscape which is covered in July and August with a mauve flower called sea lavender.

De Muy – This is a partly marshy area in the hollow of the dunes, where nearly fifty species of birds nest, especially white spoonbills with their characteristic beak and the grey heron. There are interesting plants (orchids, pyrola, and Parnassus grass).

De Westerduinen – Herring gulls nest on these dunes near the beach.

De Geul – This lake was formed in the dunes at the end of the last century. Several other small lakes have formed since. In the reeds one can see the spoonbill, the grey heron and the pintail duck. Nearby a wealth of interesting plants grow on the dunes and marshes. A fine viewpoint can be had over the reserve from the belvedere built on the **Mokweg**.

Eco Mare ☉ – *Ruyslaan 92. Access by De Koog road and the road numbered 13.*
A building, set in the dunes to the north-west of Den Burg, houses this centre devoted to the Wadden Islands and the North Sea, as well as a small Natural History Museum, **Natuurhistorisch Museum**, with collections on Texel, the Wadden-zee region and the North Sea. The first section is about the island's evolution, from its geological formation during the Ice Age up to its transformation into polders, and from its prehistoric inhabitants to the present-day tourist invasion. In another section, the nature reserves' flora and fauna can be studied with the help of dioramas, show cases with stuffed birds and photographs of plants. The underground **Waterzaal** (Water Hall) contains many aquariums, providing an interactive discovery tour of the world above and below the surface of the sea. It covers such subjects as seals, the beach, the effects of tides, the fishing industry, and the Waddenzee. There is also a tank in which visitors can touch tame rays. Young **seals**, and others recovering from illness and injury, cavort in the **salt water pools** outside; birds contaminated by pollution are also looked after here.
The **Duinpark** (dune park) contains three waymarked walks.

Oudheidkamer ☉ – *In Den Burg, in Kogerstraat, on a small shady square called Stenenplaats.* The "chamber of antiquities" is a former poorhouse, built in 1599; it is now a museum of paintings, costumes and everyday objects recalling local life. There is a tiny herb garden at the back.

Maritiem en Jutters Museum ☉ – *In Oudeschild, south-east of Den Burg.*
The Maritime and Beachcombing Museum is located in the seaweed sheds around the De Traanroeier windmill. It contains lifeboats, a shipyard and a smithy. One of the sheds is fitted out as a beachcombers' store-room, full of hundreds of often bizarre finds from the beach. The various floors of the 19C grain warehouses deal with the pilotage and rescue services, and the history of the roadsteads where East India Company ships had to await fair winds so that they could sail into the Zuiderzee; these brought great prosperity to the island in the 17C and 18C. Finally, a room on the ground floor explores the subject of underwater archaeology and the many shipwrecks in the Waddenzee.

Agrarisch en Wagenmuseum ☉ – *At De Waal, north of Den Burg.* The Agricultural and Cart Museum contains items formerly used on the island. On the top floor is a display showing the development of agriculture on Texel, and regular demonstrations are given in the smithy.

Oosterend – This picturesque village of green and white houses has four small churches, including one dating from the 11C which is the oldest on the island. The village is a conservation area.

VLIELAND

Fryslân – Population 1 150

Ferry ☉ – From Harlingen or Terschelling. Operated by Rederij Doeksen; information line ☎ (0562) 44 29 69 or 44 32 20 (express service), www.rederij-doeksen.nl

VVV (Vlieland) – ☎ (0562) 45 11 11 or www.vlieland.nl

This island, composed of dunes and woods, covering 5 100ha/12 597 acres is 20km/12.5mi long with a maximum width of 2.5km/1.5mi. There is only one small village, Oost-Vlieland. A single surfaced road crosses it from east to west. Only the army, at the western end, and tourists in season come and disturb the peace of this unspoilt countryside. The island is also beautifully quiet, because only the islanders are allowed to use cars.

Oost-Vlieland – In Dorpsstraat, the main street, there are a few old houses. On the south side of the street a house has been converted to create the **Museum Tromp's Huys** ⊙. This is a typical island home, with fine furniture and collections of antiques and paintings, including works by the Norwegian artist Betzy Berg who lived here at the beginning of the 20C.

A small visitor centre, **De Noordwester** ⊙, has been fitted out near the church. Photographs provide documentation on the island's flora and fauna; there are also some aquaria and a beachcombers' store-room. The 17C **church** on the other side of the square contains some whale jawbones from the adjoining **churchyard**. This has some interesting tombstones carved with hourglasses, anchors and ships, as well as the graves of soldiers from the Second World War.

To the left of the church is the beautiful 17C poorhouse or **deacons' house**, used to accommodate orphans, old people, and widows. There were quite a large number of these, despite the island's relatively small population, since the sea claimed many men's lives.

From the top of the **lighthouse** to the west of the village, there is a **view**★ over Oost-Vlieland, the dark green woods forming a contrast with the pale colour of the dunes, and the Waddenzee, where at each low tide vast stretches of mud flats appear, covered with flocks of birds.

WORKUM

Fryslân
Michelin maps 908 H 3 and 210 R 5
Local map see Sneek

This small town (Warkum in Frisian) was once a prosperous seaport where the eel trade flourished. Now it is a large holiday and water sports centre.

It is well known for its glazed pottery which is brown in colour and often decorated with a frieze of notched white scrolls. Workum still has several interesting houses with crow-stepped or bell-shaped gables (kolkgevel).

Merk – It has a picturesque collection of old buildings.

Stadhuis – The town hall has a tall 18C façade. On the left is the old town hall, a small Renaissance-style building decorated with a carved stone.

St.-Gertrudiskerk ⊙ – This large Gothic church was built in the 16C and 17C and has an imposing separate **bell-tower** crowned with a tiny onion-shaped dome. Inside the church there is a fine 18C pulpit and nine painted **biers** (gildebaren) illustrating the activities of the guilds. They were used during funerals to carry the bodies of guild members to the cemetery. The organ dates from 1697.

Waag – The former weigh-house is a fine 17C building with dormer windows. Inside is **Warkums Erfskip** ⊙ (Workum's Heritage), a museum of local history with the accent on shipping and the town's distinctive domestic ceramics (see above).

★ **Jopie Huisman Museum** ⊙ – Opposite the VVV (tourist information office). This small but attractive museum has a collection of paintings and drawings by the self-taught Frisian artist Jopie Huisman, born in Workum in 1922. Huisman also worked as a dealer in rags and scrap metal. His often moving canvases show a warm interest in ordinary people and everyday objects; the impressive precision with which he painted shoes, dolls, household objects and clothes often makes them more tangible than the real objects in the display cases beside the pictures. Apart from oil paintings, the museum also includes fine ink drawings, luminous watercolours, Frisian landscapes and caricature village scenes.

Self-portrait, Jopie Huisman

Stichting Jopie Huisman Museum

ZAANSTREEK★

Noord-Holland

Michelin maps 908 F 4 and fold 27 (inset) and 210 N 8

The Zaanstreek or Zaan Region is an area bordering the River Zaan to the north of Amsterdam. The succession of riverside towns were regrouped in 1974 to form the district of **Zaanstad** (pop 5 126). This is now an important dormitory town for people working in Amsterdam.

Originally the inhabitants gained a living from fishing. Then in 1592 Cornelius Corneliszoon built the first wind-powered saw-mill. Many other windmills were subsequently built for industrial purposes *(see Introduction, Industrial heritage)*, and it is thought that c 1760 there were some 600 in operation, making the Zaanstreek one of the first industrial regions in the world.

Saw mills made working the wood considerably easier, and as a result the shipbuilding industry started to flourish. The shipyard's reputation was such that in 1697 the **Czar Peter the Great** paid a visit incognito to undergo a period of training with a local shipbuilder.

Many of the windmills still exist. These industrial mills are usually very tall as they were built over the workshop. They were used in the manufacture of mustard, paper, oil, paint and tobacco. Another feature typical of the region are the **wooden houses**; houses could not be built of stone because the ground was too soft. Most of these houses have now been reassembled in the Zaanse Schans *(see below)*.

★ZAANSE SCHANS

The museum-village takes its name from fortifications which were built in the late 16C against possible attacks from the Spanish. There is no longer any trace of the redoubt.

This living museum was established in the 1960s and 70s when structures from all parts of Zaanstreek and especially from the town of Zaandam were re-erected here. The buildings have all been restored and arranged to form a replica village where people live and work. The aim of the villagers is to give visitors an impression of the Dutch way of life in earlier centuries.

The village is laid out along a dike, **Kalverringdijk**, alongside which runs a narrow canal spanned by several little humpbacked bridges. Some of the houses line secondary canals which are themselves followed by paths (such as Zeilenmaker-spad). Most of the houses are timber-built and they display an amazing variety of gables. The houses are generally green in colour, or are tarred black, while the gables, window and doors are outlined in white. Each gable is topped out with a small wooden ornament *(makelaar)*.

Several of the houses, shops and windmills are open to the public. There are demonstrations of the traditional crafts practised in Holland, and typical local products are on sale. Inevitably this has meant that the picturesque character of the Zaanse Schans has been somewhat overshadowed by commercial enterprise. **Boat trips** ⊙ on the River Zaan are also organised *(information from the visitor centre)*.

Industrial windmills, Zaanse Schans

ZAANSTREEK

- Windmill
- Tourist information
- Shop
- Toilets
- Restaurant

Zaans Museum ⊘ – This modern museum is devoted to the history of the Zaanstreek. The audio tour starts with a life-size model of the area and takes the visitor past several "squares", where everyday objects such as clogs, horn-books, ploughs and signs are displayed. Each "square" has a specific theme (wind, wood, industry, etc.) and films, computers and chat stations have been set up to give visitors more in-depth information. *Z-watch* on the top floor gives a good view of nearby factories, watercourses and windmills.

Ambachtencentrum ⊘ – This crafts centre is housed in the old De Lelie warehouse from Westzaan and contains a glassworks and a delftware workshop.

Klompenmakerij ⊘ – The clog-making workshop, located in the De Vrede warehouse (where grain and tobacco were stored and which dates from 1721), organises demonstrations of this traditional craft.

Scheepswerf – This late 18C barn is the boat-yard, where wooden boats are made and repaired.

Tinkoepel – Small pavilions like these, usually erected at the bottom of the garden, were used as a place in which to have tea. Today it houses a **pewter workshop** ⊘.

Museum van het Nederlandse uurwerk ⊘ – The clock museum, housed in a 17C weaver's house, has a varied collection of timepieces made in the Netherlands between 1500 and 1850.

Museumwinkel Albert Heijn ⊘ – This delightful old shop is a reconstruction of the very first **Albert Heijn** shop (today a large supermarket chain), which opened in Oostzaan in 1887, and sells old-fashioned items such as sugar candy, peppermint and liquorice.

De Hoop op d'Swarte Walvis – This reconstructed 18C orphanage from Westzaan is now a famous restaurant.

Het Noorderhuis ⊘ – The reception room of this merchant's house (1670) is open to the public, along with another room containing costumed figures and old dolls.

Mosterdmolen De Huisman – This octagonal smock windmill (1786) is used for making the much-sought-after local coarse-grain mustard.

Bakkerijmuseum In de Gecroonde Duyvekater ⊘ – This 17C house is named after a local speciality, *duivelskater*, a sweet loaf of bread. Note the marbled floor.

Weidemolen De Hadel – This small smock windmill stands at the far end of the Zeilenmakerspad (sailmakers' path).

Het Jagershuis – This merchant's house dating from 1623 is the oldest building in the Zaanse Schans. Today it is an antiques shop.

Kaasboerderij Catharina Hoeve ⊘ – Cheese is made in the traditional manner in this dairy, a 1988 replica of a farmhouse from the east of the Zaanstreek.

Houtzaagmolen De Gekroonde Poelenburg – This postmill used for sawing wood dates from 1869; it is built above the big workshop which turns with the mill when the sails are oriented to face the wind.

Verfmolen De Kat ⊘ – This mill, called The Cat, was used for grinding raw materials such as tropical woods into pigments for paints. In the 17C, there were 55 of these mills in the Zaanstreek.

Oliemolen De Zoeker ⊘ – In this mill which dates from 1610, salad oil is made by grinding many types of seeds.

Oliemolen De Bonte Hen – This oil mill has been here since 1693.

Oliemolen De Ooievaar – This oil mill, to the south of the Zaanse Schans, is called The Stork.

ADDITIONAL SIGHTS

Zaandijk – The town of Zaandijk, on the opposite bank of the Zaan and forming part of the Zaanstad conurbation, has a local museum of antiquities, the **Honig Breet Huis** ⊘. The museum is housed in the brick-built home of a wealthy 18C merchant. The inside is lavishly decorated with woodcarvings, murals and tiled chimney pieces. The museum also has a fine collection of furniture and porcelain. The Zaankamer, a room added in the 19C, affords a lovely view over the River Zaan. To the south is a 17C flour mill called **De Bleeke Dood** (Pale Death).

Koog aan de Zaan – In this small town there is an interesting Windmill Museum, the **Molenmuseum** ⊘. It is located in an attractive park, and shows different types of **scale models★**, ladders, tools, documents and engravings of the 17C to 19C. There is also a large map showing the locations of the remaining 1 000 windmills in the Netherlands. In 1850 there were still 9 000.

Zaandam – This industrial town on the Zaan has been served by the North Sea Canal (Noordzeekanaal) since 1876. The **Czaar-Peterhuisje** ⊘, where Czar Peter the Great lived can be seen at Krimp 23. The Czar spent some time here incognito in 1697, learning the craft of shipbuilding. It was built of wood in 1632, but in order to stop it from falling into disrepair, it was enclosed in 1895 by a brick construction, a gift of Czar Nicholas II.

The numbers ① – ② etc indicate the main routes into and out of town. They are the same on town plans and on Michelin Maps.

ZIERIKZEE★

Zeeland

Michelin maps 908 C 7 and 211 I 13

Zierikzee is the main town on the island of **Schouwen-Duiveland** (population 33 591) and in the past it was a prosperous port on the Gouwe, a strait which separated Schouwen from Duiveland. The town maintained good relations with the Hanseatic League and later it became the residence of the Counts of Holland and Zeeland.

The town is particularly remembered for an episode in its history when in 1576 the Spanish waded in water up to their shoulders across the Zijpe, separating Schouwen-Duiveland from the mainland, before taking the town. Decline set in from the 16C; however the town has been able to preserve its heritage of 16C to 18C houses.

Schouwen-Duiveland is linked to Goeree Overflakkee in the north by the Brouwersdam and the Grevelingendam, and to Noord-Beveland in the south by the Oosterschelde storm barrier and the Zeelandbrug *(see DELTA)*.

Boat trips ⊘ – Zierikzee Harbour is the departure point for boat trips on the Oosterschelde.

SIGHTS

★ **Noordhavenpoort** – This double gateway presents two 16C Renaissance gables on the town side and an older crow-stepped gable on the outside.
The **Zuidhavenpoort** takes the form of a square tower with four 14C corner turrets and is linked to the previous gateway by a lever bridge.

Oude Haven – Rows of elegant 17C and 18C houses line the quaysides of the old harbour. There are still some old ships to be seen.

Havenpark – On the north side of this square the house called **De Witte Swaen** dating from 1658 has a lovely Baroque gable. The house itself was rebuilt after the 1953 floods.
Adjoining the Gasthuiskerk is a former market, the **Beurs**, consisting of a Renaissance-style arcaded gallery with Tuscan columns.

's-Gravensteen – This onetime prison has a 1524 crow-stepped gable with ornamental wrought-iron grilles on the first floor windows. It is now home to the **Maritiem Museum** ⊘.

Stadhuis – The town hall was formerly the meat market. The outstanding feature of the building, which has been altered several times, is the unusual wooden **tower** topped with an ornamental onion-shaped dome (1550) surmounted by a statue of Neptune. The tower has a **carillon**. Two decorative gables provide further ornamentation to the façade. The decorative pieces of wrought iron were for holding lighted torches.

The **Stadhuismuseum** ⊘ inside is a local history museum. Most of the exhibits are displayed in the Harquebusiers' Hall with its fine timber ceiling.

ZIERIKZEE

Across from the stadhuis the 14C Huis De Haene, often called the **Tempellershuis**, is the oldest building in town. The influence of Bruges (Belgium) architecture can be seen in the ogee-shaped mouldings of the windows.

St.-Lievensmonstertoren ⊘ - This is the clock tower of the old Gothic cathedral, which was destroyed by fire in 1832. Building work on the tower started in 1454 and was supervised by a member of the Keldermans family, who were also responsible for Middelburg town hall. The tower rises to a height of 56m/184ft, but it remains unfinished. Next door is a large neo-Classical church (1848) with a portico.

Nobelpoort - The outside of this 14C square town gate is flanked by two tall towers, both later additions, topped by tall tapering pepperpot roofs.
Further on is a tall 19C **tower mill** called De Hoop (Hope).

ZUTPHEN*

Gelderland
Population 34 447
Michelin maps 908 J 5 and 211 W 10

Zutphen lies at the confluence of the IJssel, Berkel and Twentekanaal, not far from the heathlands of Veluwe. This pleasant historic city is the capital of the beautiful wooded region **Achterhoek** *(see below)*. It is an important commercial centre and its pedestrian precincts come alive on market days.

HISTORICAL NOTES

The county town of Zutphen became part of Geldern in 1127. In 1190 the town received its burgh charter, but in 1200 it was transferred to the see of Utrecht. In the 14C the town belonged to the Hanseatic League and built an enclosing wall which was extended the following century. Zutphen was then recognised as an important strategic point due to its easily defendable position in the surrounding marshland (the name Zutphen, sometimes spelt Zutfen, comes from Zuidveen, the southern peat bog). Zutphen became one of the richest towns in Gelderland and in the 16C it was given a second town wall of which several sections still remain. The town was captured by the Spanish in 1572 and only retaken by Maurice of Nassau in 1591. In 1586 the English poet Sir Philip Sidney died of wounds received in an action to prevent the Spaniards from sending supplies into the town. The French occupied Zutphen from 1672 to 1674 and recaptured it again in 1795.

* OLD TOWN *3hr*

's-Gravenhof - Both the St.-Walburgskerk and the stadhuis are to be found in this square. During excavations on the site in 1946 remains of the Counts of Zutphen's castle were uncovered and today the outline of the castle is marked out on the surface of the square.

St.-Walburgskerk ⊘ - This early 13C Romanesque church, dedicated to St Walburga, was given successive extensions in Gothic style up to the 16C. The church was damaged in 1945 and lost the upper storey of its tower three years later. The original tufa facing of the tower has been repaired with limestone. On the north side the 15C **Mariaportaal** has been recently restored.
Inside the vaulting is covered with 14C and 15C frescoes. The chancel has an extremely elaborate 15C ironwork **chandelier***. The plainer pulpit is 17C, like the organ case with its rich ornamentation. The **baptismal font** is a triumphant piece of copperwork cast in Mechelen, Belgium, in 1527. It is decorated with the figures of the evangelists and saints with a pelican at the summit. The **library*** dates from 1564 when it was built onto the ambulatory. The original appearance of the interior remains unchanged with low pointed vaulting and supporting columns. The ribs descend to sculpted consoles, and below in place of capitals are numerous small figures. The library houses around 750 titles, including eight manuscripts and 80 incunabula. About 100 books are displayed on wooden stands: illuminated missals, anthologies of texts written by St Thomas Aquinas and Luther. It is one of the few libraries in Europe which has retained its original appearance and furnishings.

Stadhuis - This 15C town hall was considerably altered in 1716 and again in 1729. It adjoins the former **Vleeshal**, or meat hall. Inside, the great hall *(Burgerzaal)*, has a lovely wooden ceiling.
Walk south along Lange Hofstraat.

Martinetsingel - From here there is an attractive **view*** of the town wall - with gardens sloping down to the green waters of the canal - and of the pointed towers of the Drogenapstoren away to the right and St.-Walburgskerk with its truncated tower in the background.

ZUTPHEN

★ Drogenapstoren – This splendid gateway dates from 1444-46. The change from square to octagonal is marked by crenellations and four octagonal turrets with pointed roofs. The tower itself is crowned by an even taller pointed roof.

Dat Bolwerck – This attractive Gothic house (1549) is surmounted by pinnacles. Next door are the 1639 cavalry barracks, **Ruiter Kortegaard**, with an attractive scrolled gable.

Zaadmarkt – This was the site of the grain market, and is now a general market. On the right at no 101 is the doorway of an **almshouse** dating from 1723.

Museum Henriette Polak ⊘ – The impressive **De Wildeman** mansion was altered in the 19C and today houses an interesting collection of paintings, sculptures and graphic arts by contemporary Dutch artists.
The secret chapel (1628) on the second floor was a refuge for Catholics.

Houtmarkt – The lovely 17C Renaissance tower, the **Wijndragerstoren**, stands on the site of the former timber market. It was made by the Hemony brothers. A market is held here every Thursday.

Stedelijk Museum ⊘ – The former Dominican convent is now the home of the municipal museum. The convent church stands to the south of a lovely garden and now houses a library. The exhibits on the ground floor include sections featuring clocks and watches, glasswork, silver **Hannema-de Stuers Fundatie** work as well as some paintings. The first floor is reserved for temporary exhibitions and gives access to the refectory (c 1500), where Medieval artefacts are on display. The local collections on the second floor cover Zutphen and its immediate region and include costumes from between 1780 and 1950. Pottery, old coins and stones are exhibited in the basement.

ADDITIONAL SIGHT

Berkelpoort – This 14C brick-built water-gate spans the Berkel with three arches. The entrances are flanked by watch turrets. There is a good **view** of the gateway from the footbridge to the west. Overlooking the footbridge is the **Leeuwenhuisje** with an overhang supported by lion-head brackets.

EXCURSIONS

59km/39mi south-east by the Doetinchem road.

Now known as the **Achterhoek**, the area from Zutphen to the German border was originally the earldom of Zutphen. It is an area of woodland (conifers, oaks and beeches) and pastures criss-crossed by quiet country roads and forest rides.

Bronkhorst – The picturesque town of Bronkhorst, which was chartered in 1482, is the smallest town in the Netherlands. At the intersection of the two main streets stand a 14C chapel, two taverns and an old Saxon farm.

Vorden – This town has two 19C **tower mills**. Vorden lies at the heart of a region where **eight castles** nestle in the surrounding woodlands: Vorden, Hackfort, Kiefskamp, Wildenborch, Bramel, Onstein, Medler and Wiersse. There are in actual fact 12 castles or small brick-built manor houses in all. Many were rebuilt in the 18C in a quite plain style. The nobility, attracted by the good hunting provided by the local forests, elected to build suitable residences locally. Some can only be reached on foot or by bicycle *(paths are signposted "opengesteld")*. **Kasteel Vorden** is L-shaped, with a slender octagonal tower in the angle. Today the castle serves as town hall. The most impressive castle is **Kasteel Hackfort**, flanked by two great round towers. Next to it is a **watermill** dating from about 1700.

Kasteel Vorden

Groenlo – The historic town of Groenlo stands on the banks of the Slinge and is still encircled by sections of its town walls. The town is famous for its beer, Grolsch, meaning "of Groenlo". The small **Grolsch Museum** ⊙ occupies a farmhouse dating from 1623.

Winterswijk – This town is also on the Slinge and is surrounded by tranquil forested areas dotted with impressive farmhouses.

Bredevoort – This historic town is famous for its many **bookshops**; it boasts more than 20 second-hand and antiquarian bookshops, and book markets are held here on a regular basis. Bredevoort is also the birthplace of **Hendrikje Stoffels**, Rembrandt's second wife.

ZWOLLE

Overijssel Ⓟ

Population 104 431
Michelin maps 908 J 4 and 210 V 7
Plan of the conurbation in the current edition of The Red Guide Benelux

Zwolle, capital of the province of Overijssel, has kept its special character in the historic centre within the ring of canals.

HISTORICAL NOTES

Zwolle was a member of the Hanseatic League in the 13C *(see IJSSELMEER)*, and linked to the Zuiderzee by the Zwarte Water; it was also a trading centre, for a long time servicing the traffic between the Netherlands and northern Germany.
After the Spaniards left in 1572, its 15C curtain wall was considerably strengthened due to its strategic position. The wall was destroyed in 1674 during the Third Dutch War and little remains, apart from the Sassenpoort in the south and, in the north,

One of the town's specialities are **Zwolse balletjes**, sweets shaped like a small cushion with different flavours. One of the places you can buy them is the Zwolse Balletjeshuis opposite the VVV tourist office. Another of Zwolle's specialities is **blauwvingers**. If you want to find out how these shortbread biscuits, shaped as fingers and dipped in chocolate, got their name, then go to Banketbakkerij Van Orsouw, the bakery on *Grote Markt 6*, where the legend of these biscuits comes free of charge with your purchase.

part of the late-medieval town wall. Today the ditches still surround the town and the pleasant gardens on the south and east sides mark the course of the ramparts and bastions.

Thomas à Kempis (1379/80-1471), who was a pupil at the School of the Brethren of the Common Life in Deventer and to whom is attributed the *Imitatio Christi* (The Imitation of Christ), entered the monastery of the order of Augustine monks near Zwolle, where he remained until his death.

Gerard Terborch (1617-81) was born in Zwolle. This painter, like his contemporary Gerrit Dou, is above all the meticulous painter of refined and peaceful interior scenes and excellent portraits and miniatures of the local notables.

SIGHTS

★ **Stedelijk Museum Zwolle** ⊙ – The municipal museum is located in an elegant 16C mansion, the Drostenhuis, and a new wing. The historic **Drostenhuis**★★ contains a display of items relating to the town's rich past, including a number of splendid period rooms with a fine collection of silverware from the Overijssel province and paintings by local artist Gerard Terborch. The kitchen is also worth a visit. The new wing, devoted to contemporary art and cultural history, is used for temporary exhibitions.

J.P. Lescourret/EXPLORER

Stedelijk Museum Zwolle – The kitchen of the Drostenhuis

Grote Kerk or St.-Michaëlskerk ⊙ – St Michael's is a hall-church with three naves, dating from 1406-1446. Unlike the neighbouring church of Our Lady, with its distinctive tower usually referred to as the **"pepper mill"**, it no longer has the traditional bell-tower, which did not survive the many disasters that befell the town. In 1690 an octagonal **vestry** was built on the site where the tower once stood. Inside, note a remarkable early 17C carved pulpit and an organ loft of 1721 comprising a splendid **organ**★ with 4 000 pipes, built by the Schnitger brothers. There is also a small 17C clock with a statue of St Michael which comes to life every half hour. Note also the segregated leper chapel next to the chancel.

Attached to the left side of the fine 16C north portal there is a picturesque little building, the **Hoofdwacht** or guard room, dating from 1614 with a decorated pediment.

Stadhuis ⊙ – Beside the old town hall (15C and 19C) which had become too small, a new one was built in 1976 by the architect JJ Konijnenburg. The old part on the left, covered with mustard-yellow roughcast, contains the **Aldermen's Hall** *(Schepenzaal)* dating from 1448. This old courtroom has a ceiling whose beams are held by 14 corbels with **sculptures**★ depicting grotesque figures. Legend has it that the artists of Zwolle, rival town of Kampen, carved these heads to hold the governors of Kampen up to ridicule. Note the executioner's swords and the picture of the *Last Judgement*, a reminder of the room's original use. On the terrace in front of the town hall there is a statue of Adam by Rodin.

Karel V-huis – This house, built in 1571, owes its name to the medallion of Charles V's head which can be seen on the gable. It has a fine Renaissance façade decorated with pilasters, friezes and a voluted gable. Further along is a church from 1309, the Bethlehemskerk, and the Refter (refectory).

★ **Sassenpoort** – Built in 1409, the Saxon Gateway is the only one which still exists from the fortified town wall. It has a machicolation and four octagonal corner towers. The pointed roofs were added in the 19C. The building was for a long time used as a prison, and now houses a **visitor centre** ⊘ providing information about the history of the town.

★ **Museum De Stadshof** – This museum of naive and "outsider" art is an international collection of paintings, drawings and sculptures by people from outside traditional artistic circles. The pieces, such as Hans Langner's *Requiem for my innocence (left of the entrance)*, have strong personal and expressive significance and are often highly imaginative and moving. In addition to the permanent collection, temporary exhibitions are also held.

Ecodrome ⊘ – *Willemsvaart 19, on the southern edge of Zwolle*. This theme park combines enjoyable displays on natural history, geology and the environment. The natural history museum contains skeletons of animals from the Ice Age and a colourful collection of birds, while the **Ecodrome pavilion** takes visitors through the story of the Earth's evolution. There are also plenty of attractions for children in the grounds.

EXCURSIONS

Hasselt – *11km/7mi north of Zwolle*. This small Hanseatic town boasts some interesting sights, including the Gothic church, Stefanuskerk, the fine old town hall, and two working limekilns.

Hattem – *7km/4.5mi south-west of Zwolle*. The rich past of this pleasant Hanseatic town is still evident in the medieval Dijkpoort, the tower mill De Fortuin and the Grote Kerk or St.-Andreaskerk. The **museum** ⊘ at Achterstraat nos 46-48 shows work by Anton Pieck and the two Jan Voermans, father and son.

* **Kasteel Het Nijenhuis** – *15km/10mi south-east of Zwolle. Take the* **Heino** *turn-off, towards Wijhe*. This medieval manor house is home to the international art collection of the foundation **Hannema-de Stuers Fundatie** ⊘. The house itself contains the collection of mainly 17C and 18C French and Italian art. The coach houses have been converted into exhibition space where the collection of 20C art (Permeke, Mondrian, Israëls and Appel), is shown in temporary exhibitions. The park has been turned into a **sculpture garden**.

Admission times and charges

As admission times and charges are liable to alteration, the information below is for guidance only.

⊘: Every sight for which times and charges are listed below is indicated by the symbol ⊘ after the title in the Sights section of the guide.

Order: The information is listed in the same order as in the Sights section of the guide.

Carnival: Several sights close at carnival-time. Carnivals take place during Feburary or March, around Lent.

Dates: Dates given are inclusive.

Last admission: Ticket offices usually shut 30min before closing time. Some places issue timed tickets owing to limited space and facilities.

Charge: The charge given is for an individual adult. Concessionary rates may be available for families, children, old-age pensioners and the unemployed. Prices are given in guilders (abbreviated to fl). Many places offer special rates for group bookings and some have special days for group visits. Large parties should apply in advance.

A **Museumjaarkaart** is an annual pass giving the holder free admission to 440 museums in the Netherlands *(see Practical Information at the front of the guide).*

Churches: Churches cannot be visited during services and are usually closed between noon and 2pm. They are included in the following list if the interior is of particular interest.

Sights with special disabled facilities are indicated by the symbol ♿.

The admission times and charges published in the previous edition are given where it has been Impossible to obtain the latest updated information; these entries are printed in italics.

Tourist offices (VVV): The addresses and telephone numbers of the local tourist offices, indicated by the symbol 🅱, are given below. The tourist offices provide information on local market days, early or late closing days as well as local events.

Guided tours: Most tours are conducted by Dutch-speaking guides but in some cases the term "guided tours" may cover groups visiting with recorded commentaries. Some of the larger and more popular sights may offer guided tours in other languages. Enquire at the ticket desk or bookstall.

Although admission prices are given in guilders (fl), visitors should be aware that in Jan 2002 the guilder will be replaced by the Euro, with 1€ equal to approximately 2.2fl. *See conversion table below.*

Fl	€	€	Fl
2.00	0.91	1	2.20
6.00	2.72	3	6.61
10.00	4.54	5	11.02
15.00	6.81	7	15.43
20.00	9.08	10	22.04
25.00	11.34	11	24.24
30.00	13.61	15	33.06
50.00	22.69	20	44.07

A

AALSMEER
🅱 Drie Kolommenplein 1 – 1431 LA – ☎ (0297) 32 53 74
fax (0297) 38 76 76

Bloemenveiling Aalsmeer – ♿ Open Mon-Fri, 7.30-11am. Closed Sat-Sun and public holidays. 7.50fl. ☎ (0297) 39 21 85. www.vba.nl

ALKMAAR
🅱 Waagplein 2-3 – 1811 JP – ☎ (072) 511 42 84
fax (072) 511 75 13

Boat trips – ♿ Open early Apr to late Oct. Information from Rondvaart Alkmaar B.V., ☎ (072) 511 77 50. www.rondvaartalkmaar.nl

Kaasmarkt – Open mid-Apr to mid-Sept, Fri, 10am-noon. ☎ (072) 511 42 84.

Hollands Kaasmuseum – Open Apr to Oct, daily, 10am (Fri 9am)-4pm. Closed Nov to Mar, Sun and public holidays. 2fl. ☎ (072) 511 42 84. www.kaasmuseum.nl

Nederlands Biermuseum De Boom – Open Oct to Mar, Tues-Fri, 10am-4pm, Sat-Sun, 1-4pm. Closed Mon, Easter Day, Whit Sunday, 25 and 26 Dec. 4fl. ☎ (072) 511 38 01.

Stadhuis – Guided tour or by appointment. ☎ (072) 511 42 84.

Grote Kerk or St.-Laurenskerk – Open June to mid-Sept, Tues-Sat, noon-5pm. Closed Sun and Mon. ☎ (072) 514 07 07.

Stedelijk Museum – Open Tues-Fri, 10am-5pm, Sat-Sun and public holidays, 1-5pm. Closed Mon, 1 Jan, 30 Apr and 25 Dec. 3fl. ☎ (072) 511 07 37.

Excursions

Broeker Veiling – ♿ Open Apr to Oct, Mon-Fri, 10am-5pm, Sat-Sun, 11am-5pm. Closed Nov to Mar, 30 Apr. 9.50fl. ☎ (0226) 31 38 07. www.broekerveiling.nl

Museum Betje Wolff – Open May to Sept, Fri, 11am-5pm, Sat-Sun, 2-5pm; Oct to Apr, Sun, 2-5pm. 4fl. ☎ (0229) 68 19 68.

Museum Kranenburgh – Open Tues-Sun, 1-5pm. Closed Mon, 1 Jan and 25 Dec. 7.50fl. ☎ (072) 589 89 27.

Noordhollands Duinreservaat – Open daily, dawn-dusk. 2fl. ☎ (0251) 66 22 66.

Zee Aquarium Bergen aan Zee – ♿ Open Apr to Sept, daily, 10am-6pm; Oct to Mar, daily, 11am-5pm. 11.50fl. ☎ (072) 581 29 28. www.zeeaquarium.nl

AMERSFOORT
🛈 Stationsplein 9 – 3818 LE – ☎ (0900) 112 23 64 fax (033) 465 01 08

O.L.-Vrouwe-Toren – *Open July and Aug, Tues-Fri, 10am-5pm, Sat, noon-5pm. Closed Sept to June. 5fl. ☎ (0900) 112 23 64 (VVV).*

Zonnehof – Open Tues-Sat, 10am-5pm, Sun, 1-5pm. 4fl. ☎ (033) 463 30 34.

St.-Joriskerk – *Open mid-June to mid-Sept, daily (except Sun), 2-4.30pm. Closed Sun and public holidays. 1fl. ☎ (033) 461 04 41.*

Armando Museum – Open Tues-Fri, 11am-5pm, Sat-Sun and public holidays, noon-5pm. Closed Mon and 1 Jan. 7.50fl. ☎ (033) 461 40 88.

Koppelpoort – ♿ *Open July and Aug, Tues-Fri, 10am-5pm, Sat-Sun and public holidays, noon-5pm. 2.50fl. Information from the tourist office, ☎ (0900) 112 23 64.*

Puppet theatre – Performances on Wed and Sat at 2.30pm. 8fl. ☎ (033) 470 01 53.

Museum Flehite – Open Tues-Fri, 11am-5pm, Sat-Sun, 1-5pm. Closed Mon and public holidays. 6fl. ☎ (033) 461 99 87.

Mannenzaal – Same opening times as Museum Flehite. ☎ (033) 461 99 87.

Museum Jacobs van den Hof – Open Sat-Sun, noon-5pm. 5fl. ☎ (033) 462 57 55. www.jacobsvandenhof.com.

Mondriaanhuis – Open Tues-Fri, 10am-5pm, Sat-Sun, 2-5pm. Closed Mon and public holidays. 6fl. ☎ (033) 462 01 80. www.modriaanhuis.nl

Excursions

Dierenpark Amersfoort – Open Apr to Oct, daily, 9am-6pm (9pm July and Aug); Nov to Mar, daily, 9am-5pm. 24fl. ☎ (033) 422 71 00. www.amersfoort-zoo.nl

Museum 't Vurhuus – ♿ Open Easter to autumn half-term holiday, Mon-Sat, 10am-5pm. Closed Sun and public holidays. 4fl. ☎ (033) 298 33 19.

Kasteel Huis Doorn – By guided tour only (1hr). Spring half-term holiday to autumn half-term holiday: Sun at 1.30pm, 2.30pm and 3.30pm; during school holidays: Tues-Thur at 11am, 2pm and 3.30pm, Fri and Sat at 2pm and 3.30pm, Sun at 1.30pm, 2.30pm and 3.30. 7fl. ☎ (0481) 421456.

Museum Dorestad – Open Tues-Sun, 1.30-5pm. Closed Mon, 1 Jan and 25 Dec. 4fl. ☎ (0343) 57 14 48.

Amerongs Historisch Museum – Open Apr to Oct, Tues-Thur, 1-5pm. Closed Nov to Mar. 2.50fl. ☎ (0343) 45 65 00.

Kasteel Amerongen – Open Apr to Oct, Tues-Fri, 10am-5pm, Sat-Sun and public holidays, 1-5pm. Closed Mon and Nov to Mar. 10fl. ☎ (0343) 45 42 12.

De Leersumse Plassen – Open mid-July to mid-Mar, dawn-dusk. Closed mid-Mar to mid-July. ☎ (030) 602 86 61.

AMSTERDAM   🛈 De Ruyterkade 5 - 1013 AA - ☎ (0900) 400 40 40 - fax (020) 625 28 69
www.visitamsterdam.nl

Cycle hire – Hire firms only; **Holland Rent-a-Bike**, Damrak 247, ☎ (020) 622 32 07; **Take-a-Bike**, Stationsplein 12, ☎ (020) 624 83 91; **MacBike**, Marnixstraat 220 and Mr Visserplein 2, ☎ (020) 620 09 85;, www.macbike.nl. **Yellow Bike**, Nieuwezijds Kolk 29, ☎ (020) 620 69 40, www.yellowbike.nl

Canal bikes – Near Anne Frank Huis, the Rijksmuseum, Leidseplein and Keizersgracht/Leidsestraat: information from Canalbike, Weteringschans 24, ☎ (020) 623 98 86, www.canal.nl

Museum boat – Leaves from Centraal Station. Seven stops near the main museums. Daily, 10am-5pm. Information from Rederij Lovers, ☎ (020) 530 10 90, www.lovers.nl

Canal Bus – Three different routes with 11 stops. The Blue Line between the Centraal Station and Nemo, the other two along a number of canals. Information: Canal Bus, Weteringschans 24, ☎ (020) 626 55 74, www.canal.nl

Beurs van Berlage Museum – Open daily (except Mon), 11am-5pm. 7fl. ☎ (020) 530 41 41. www.beursvanberlage.nl

Koninklijk Paleis – Open regular periods and during exhibitions. 9fl. Check details on ☎ (020) 620 40 60. www.kon-paleisamsterdam.nl

Nieuwe Kerk – Open daily, 11am-5pm. ☎ (020) 638 69 09. www.nieuwekerk.nl

Madame Tussaud Scenerama – Open daily, 10am-5.30pm; July and Aug 9.30am to 7.30pm. Closed 1 Jan, 30 Apr and 31 Dec. 19.95fl. ☎ (020) 522 10 10.

Amsterdams Historisch Museum – Open Mon-Fri, 10am-5pm, Sat-Sun and public holidays, 11am-5pm. Closed 1 Jan, 30 Apr and 25 Dec. 12fl. ☎ (020) 523 18 22. www.ahm.nl

Museum Amstelkring Ons' Lieve Heer op Solder – Open Mon-Sat, 10am-5pm, Sun and public holidays, 1-5pm. Closed 30 Apr. 10fl. ☎ (020) 624 66 04.

Oude Kerk – Open Apr to Dec, daily, 11am (Sun 1pm)-5pm. 7.50fl. ☎ (020) 625 82 84. www.oudekerk.nl

Self-portrait (1630) by Rembrandt,
Museum Het Rembrandthuis

Museum Het Rembrandthuis

Allard Pierson Museum – ♿ Open Tues-Fri, 10am-5pm, Sat-Sun and public holidays, 1-5pm. Closed Mon, 1 Jan, Easter Day, 30 Apr, Whit Sunday, 25 Dec. 9.50fl. ☎ (020) 525 25 56. www.uba.uva.nl/apm

Museum Het Rembrandthuis – Open Mon-Sat, 10am-5pm, Sun and public holidays 1-5pm. Closed 1 Jan. 12.50fl. ☎ (020) 520 04 00. www.rembrandthuis.nl

Holland Experience – Open daily, 10am-6pm. 17.50fl. ☎ (020) 422 22 33. www.holland-experience.nl

Zuiderkerk – ♿ Open Mon, 11am-4pm, Tues-Fri, 9am-4pm (Thur 8pm). Closed Sat-Sun and public holidays. No charge. ☎ (020) 552 79 87. www.dro.amsterdam.nl

Joods Historisch Museum – ♿ Open daily, 11am-5pm. Closed Yom Kippur. 10fl. ☎ (020) 626 99 45. www.jhm.nl

Portuguees-Israëlitische Synagoge – Open Sun-Fri, 10am-4pm. Closed Sat and Jewish festivals. 5fl. ☎ (020) 624 53 51.

Boat tours – Information from the various operators: **Rederij Lovers**, Prins Hendrikkade 25, ☎ (020) 530 10 90, www.lovers.nl; **Holland International**, Prins Hendrikkade 33a, ☎ (020) 622 77 88; **Rederij Kooij**, opposite Rokin 25, ☎ (020) 623 38 10; **Meyers Rondvaarten**, Damrak Steiger 4-5, ☎ (020) 623 42 08; **Amsterdam Canal Cruises**, Nicolaas Witsenkade 1a, ☎ (020) 626 56 36.

Theatermuseum – Open Tues-Fri, 11am-5pm, Sat-Sun, 1-5pm. Closed Mon, 1 Jan, 30 Apr, 25 Dec. 8.50fl. ☎ (020) 551 33 00. www.tin.nl

Bible Museum – Open Mon-Sat, 10am-5pm, Sun and public holidays, 1-5pm. Closed 1 Jan and 30 Apr. 8fl. ☎ (020) 624 24 36. www.bijbelsmuseum.nl

Kattenkabinet – Open Mon-Fri, 10am-2pm, Sat-Sun, 1-5pm. Opening times may vary in winter. Closed 1 Jan, 25 and 26 Dec. 10fl. ☎ (020) 626 53 78. www.kattenkabinet.nl

Museum Willet-Holthuysen – Open Mon-Fri, 10am-5pm, Sat-Sun and public holidays, 11am-5pm. Closed 1 Jan, 30 Apr, 25 Dec. 8fl. ☏ (020) 523 18 22. www.ahm.nl/willet

Museum Van Loon – Open Mon, Fri, Sat-Sun, 11am-5pm. Closed Tues-Thur. 7.50fl. ☏ (020) 624 52 55. www.musvloon.box.nl

Westerkerk – Open Apr to Sept, Mon-Fri, 11am-3pm. Closed Sat-Sun and Oct to Mar. ☏ (020) 624 77 66. www.westerkerk.nl

Anne Frank Huis – Open daily, 9am-7pm (Apr to Aug 9pm). Closed Yom Kippur. 10fl. ☏ (020) 556 71 00. www.annefrank.nl

Rijksmuseum – Open daily, 10am-5pm. Closed 1 Jan. 15fl. ☏ (020) 674 70 47. www.rijksmuseum.nl

Van Gogh Museum – ☕ Open daily, 10am-6pm. 15.50fl. ☏ (020) 570 52 52. www.vangoghmuseum.nl

Stedelijk Museum – ☕ Open daily, 11am-5pm. Closed 1 Jan. 10fl. ☏ (020) 573 27 37. www.stedelijk.nl

Filmmuseum – Performances: daily at 7pm, 7.15pm, 7.30pm, 9.30pm, 9.45pm and 10pm. Sun from 3pm. 12.50fl. ☏ (020) 589 14 00. www.nfm.nl

Hortus Botanicus – Apr to Oct: open Mon-Fri, 9am-5pm, Sat-Sun and public holidays, 11am-5pm. Nov to Mar: Mon-Fri, 9am-4pm, Sat-Sun and public holidays, 11am-4pm. Closed 1 Jan and 25 Dec. 7.50fl. ☏ (020) 625 90 21.

Nationaal Vakbondsmuseum – ☕ Open Tues-Fri, 11am-5pm, Sun, 1-5pm. Closed Mon, Sat and public holidays. 5fl. ☏ (020) 624 11 66. www.deburcht-vakbondsmuseum.nl

Artis – ☕ Open summer, daily, 9am-6pm; winter, daily, 9am-5pm. 28.50fl. ☏ (020) 523 34 00. www.artis.nl

Verzetsmuseum – ☕ Open Tues-Fri, 10am-5pm, Sat-Sun, noon-5pm. 8fl. ☏ (020) 620 25 35. www.verzetsmuseum.org

Hollandse Schouwburg – ☕ Open daily, 11am-4pm. Closed Yom Kippur. No charge. ☏ (020) 626 99 45. www.jhm.nl

Tropenmuseum – ☕ Open daily, 10am-5pm. Closed 1 Jan, 30 Apr, 5 May and 25 Dec. 12.50fl. ☏ (020) 568 82 15. www.kit.nl/tropenmuseum

Nederlands Scheepvaart Museum – Open Tues-Sun, 10am-5pm; mid-June to mid-Sept and during school holidays also open Mon, 10am-5pm. Closed 1 Jan, 30 Apr and 25 Dec. 14.50fl. ☏ (020) 523 22 22. www.scheepvaartmuseum.nl

Nemo – ☕ Open Tues-Sun and daily during school holidays, 10am-5pm. Closed Mon, 1 Jan and 30 Apr. 20fl. ☏ (0900) 919 11 00. www.e-nemo.nl

Heineken Brewery – Closed for rebuilding work; scheduled to re-open May 2001. Information: ☏ (020) 523 92 39. www.heineken.nl

Excursions

Cobra Museum voor Moderne Kunst – Open daily (except Mon), 11am-5pm. Closed Mon, and 1 Jan, 30 Apr and 25 Dec. 7.50fl. ☏ (020) 547 50 50. www.cobra-museum.nl

Aviodome – ☕ Open Apr to Sept, daily, 10am-5pm; Oct to Mar, Tues-Fri, 10am-5pm, Sat-Sun, noon-5pm. Closed Mon from Oct to Mar, 1 Jan, 25 and 31 Dec. 15fl. ☏ (020) 406 80 00. www.aviodome.nl

Molen van Sloten – ☕ Open daily, 10am-4pm. Closed 1 Jan, 30 Apr and 25 and 26 Dec. 6fl. ☏ (020) 669 04 12. www.molenvansloten.nl

Monnickendam: Museum De Speeltoren – Open June to mid-Sept, Tues-Sat, 11am-5pm, Sun, 2-5pm; mid-Apr to May, Sat, 11am-5pm, Sun, 2-5pm. 2.50fl. ☏ (0299) 65 22 03. www.ayllas.demon.nl

APELDOORN
🏢 Stationsstraat 72 – 7311 MH – ☏ (0900) 168 16 36
fax (055) 521 12 90

Veluwsche Stoomtrein – ☕ Departs June, Thur; mid-July to late Aug and during autumn half-term, Mon-Fri. 14fl (single), 20fl (return/round trip). ☏ (055) 506 19 89. www.stoomtrein.org

Historisch Museum Apeldoorn – Open Tues-Sat, 10am-5pm, Sun and public holidays, 1-5pm. Closed Mon, 1 Jan, Easter Day, Whit Sunday and 25 Dec. 2.50fl. ☏ (055) 578 84 29.

Gemeentelijk Van Reekum Museum – Open Tues-Fri, 10am-5pm, Sat-Sun, Easter Monday, Whit Monday and 26 Dec, 1-5pm. Closed Mon, 1 Jan, Easter, Whit Sun and 25 Dec. 2.50fl. ☏ (055) 521 91 55. www.apeldoorn.nl/vanreekum

Apenheul (Berg en Bos) – Open Apr to June, daily, 10am-5pm; July and Aug, daily, 9.30am-6pm; Sept and Oct, daily, 9.30am-5pm. Berg en Bos nature reserve closes 1hr after Apenheul. Closed Nov to Mar. 21.50fl. ☏ (055) 357 57 57. www.apenheul.nl

Excursions

Kasteel Cannenburch – By guided tour only (1hr): mid-Apr to Oct, Tues-Fri, 10am-5pm, Sat-Sun, 1-5pm; also Easter Monday, Whit Monday and 26 Dec, 10am-5pm. Closed Nov to mid-Apr and 30 Apr. 8fl. ☏ (0578) 57 12 92. www.hgl-vgk.nl

ARNHEM   🛈 Willemsplein 8 - 6800 AN - ☏ (0900) 202 40 75 - fax (026) 442 26 44

Boat tours: Depart mid-Apr to late Oct. Information from tourist office, ☏ (0900) 202 40 75.

Grote Kerk or Eusebiuskerk – Open Tues-Sat, 10am-5pm (4pm winter), Sun and public holidays, noon-5pm (4pm winter). Closed Mon. Tower: 10fl. ☏ (026) 443 50 68.

Historisch Museum Het Burgerweeshuis – Open Tues-Fri, 10am-5pm, Sat-Sun and public holidays, 11am-5pm. Closed Mon and 1 Jan. 5fl . ☏ (026) 442 69 00. www.hmarnhem.nl

Museum voor Moderne Kunst – Open Tues-Fri, 10am-5pm, Sat-Sun and public holidays, 11am-5pm. Closed Mon and 1 Jan. 7.50fl . ☏ (026) 351 24 31. www.mmkarnhem.nl.

Nederlands Openluchtmuseum – ♿ Open late Apr to Oct, daily, 10am-5pm. Closed Nov to late Apr. 22.50fl. ☏ (026) 357 61 00. www.openluchtmuseum.nl

Burgers' Zoo – Open summer season, daily, 9am-7pm; winter season, daily, 9am-dusk. 28.50fl. ☏ (026) 442 45 34. www.burgerszoo.nl

Kasteel Rosendael – Guided tours only: mid-Apr to Oct, Tues-Sat, 10am-5pm, Sun, 1-5pm (park 11am-5pm); Easter Monday, Whit Monday and 26 Dec, 10am to 5pm. Closed Mon, 30 Apr, Nov to mid-Apr. 8fl (12fl including park). ☏ (026) 364 46 45. www.hgl-vgk.nl

Veluwezoom visitor centre – Open Tues-Sun, 10am-5pm. Closed Mon, 25 and 31 Dec. ☏ (026) 497 91 00. www.veluwezoom.nl

Kasteel Middachten – Open July, Wed-Sun, 1-4pm; early Dec, noon-7pm. 12.50fl (castles and gardens). ☏ (026) 495 49 98.

Gardens – Open mid-May to mid-Sept, Wed-Sun, 10.30am-4.30pm. 7fl. ☏ (026) 495 49 98.

Airborne Museum – Open Apr to Oct, Mon-Fri, 10am-5pm, Sat-Sun, noon-5pm; Nov to Mar, Mon-Fri, 11am-5pm, Sat-Sun, noon-5pm. Closed 1 Jan and 25 Dec. 7.50fl. ☏ (026) 333 77 10. www.airbornemuseum.com

Museum voor Natuur- en Wildbeheer – Open Apr to Oct, Tues-Fri, 10am-5pm, Sat-Sun and public holidays, 1-5pm; Nov to Mar, daily (except Mon), 1-5pm, public holidays, 1-5pm. Closed Mon, 1 Jan, 30 Apr, 25 and 31 Dec. 10fl. ☏ (026) 339 06 98.

Ouwehands Dierenpark – ♿ Open Apr to Sept, daily, 9am-6pm; Oct to Mar, daily, 9am-5pm. 22fl. ☏ (0317) 65 02 00. www.ouwehand.nl

Cunerakerk – Information from VVV, ☏ (0317) 61 23 33.

ASSEN   🛈 Marktstraat 8-10 - 9401 JH - ☏ (0592) 31 43 24 - fax (0592) 31 73 06

Drents Museum – Open daily (except Mon), 11am-5pm. Closed Mon, 1 Jan and 25 Dec. 10fl. ☏ (0592) 31 27 41. www.drentsmuseum.nl

Herinneringscentrum Kamp Westerbork – ♿ Open Mon-Fri, 10am-5pm, Sat-Sun, 1-5pm. 7.50fl. ☏ (0593) 59 26 00. www.kampwesterbork.com

Excursions

Nationaal Rijtuigmuseum – Open May to Oct, Tues-Sat, 10am-5pm, Sun, 1-5pm. Closed Mon and public holidays, and Nov to Apr. 7.50fl. ☏ (0594) 51 22 60. www.rijtuigmuseum.nl

B

BERGEN OP ZOOM   🛈 Stationsstraat 4 - 4611 CC – ☏ (0900) 202 03 36 - fax (0164) 24 60

Stadhuis – *Open May to Sept, Tues-Sat, 1-4.30pm. Closed Sun, Mon, public holidays and Oct to Mar. 2fl. ☏ (0164) 25 18 59.*

Markiezenhof – Open Apr to Sept, daily (except Mon), 11am-5pm; Oct to Mar, daily (except Mon), 2-5pm. Closed Mon, 1 Jan, Easter Day and 25 Dec. 5fl. ☎ (0164) 24 29 30.

Wouw: Church – By guided tour only: Thur and Fri, 10am-noon and 2-4pm. ☎ (0165) 30 32 52 (VVV).

Streekmuseum De Ghulden Roos – Open Tues-Sun, 2-5pm. Closed Mon, 1 Jan, carnival, Easter, Whitsun and 25 Dec. 3.50fl. ☎ (0165) 53 69 16.

BOLSWARD 🅱 Marktplein 1 – 8701 KG – ☎ (0515) 57 27 27 – fax (0515) 57 77 18
www.friesland-vvv.net

Stadhuis – Open Apr to June and Sept to Oct, Mon-Fri, 9am-noon and 2-4pm; July and Aug, Mon-Sat, 10am-5pm. 2fl. ☎ (0515) 57 87 87.

Martinikerk – Open Mon-Fri, 10am-noon and 1.30-5pm. July and Aug also open Sat, 2-4pm. ☎ (0515) 57 22 74.

Excursion

Menno-Simonskerkje – Open daily, 10am-4pm by appointment. ☎ (0517) 53 19 59.

BOURTANGE 🅱 W. Lodewijkstraat 13 – 9545 PA – ☎ (0599) 35 46 00
fax (0599) 35 45 54

The fortifications may be visited at any time. The museums, exhibitions and slide show are open from Apr to Oct, Mon-Fri, 10am-5pm, Sat-Sun, 12.30-5pm. Information from Westerwolde Tourist Office (Bourtange fortress dept), ☎ (0599) 35 46 00.

BREDA 🅱 Willemstraat 17 – 4811 AJ – ☎ (076) 522 24 44 – fax (076) 521 85 30
www.bredadigitaal.nl/vvv

Grote Kerk or Onze-Lieve-Vrouwekerk – *Open mid-Apr to Oct, daily, 10am-5pm; Nov to mid-Apr, Mon-Fri, 10am-5pm.* ☎ *(076) 521 82 67.*

Het Spanjaardsgat: Castle – Guided tours only (2hr). Information from Breda Tourist Office, ☎ (076) 522 24 44.

Stadhuis – *Open Tues-Fri, 9am-4.30pm.* ☎ *(076) 529 40 55.*

De Beyerd – Open Tues-Fri, 10am-5pm, Sat-Sun and public holidays, 1-5pm. Closed Mon, 1 Jan and 25 Dec. 6fl. ☎ (076) 522 50 25.

Breda's Museum – Scheduled to open in Dec 1998. Information: ☎ (076) 529 93 00. www.breda-museum.nl

Kasteel Bouvigne – ♿ The castle itself is not open to the public. The gardens are open on Mon to Fri from 9am to 4pm, and closed at Sat-Sun and on public holidays. 1fl. ☎ (076) 564 10 00.

Excursions

Hoeven: Quasar – ♿ Open Sept to Apr, Wed, 2-5pm, Fri, 7.30-10pm, Sun, 1-5pm; May to Aug, Wed, 2-5pm and 7.30-10pm, Sun, 1-5pm. Closed 1 Jan and 25 Dec. 12.50fl. ☎ (0165) 50 24 39. www.quasarheelal.nl

Oudenbosch: Nederlands Zouavenmuseum – Open May to Sept, Tues, Thur and the first and third Sun of the month, 2-5pm; Oct to Apr, Tues and the first Sun of the month, 2-5pm. Closed on public holidays. 2.50fl. ☎ (0165) 31 34 48.

Raamsdonksveer: Nationaal Automobielmuseum – Open Easter to Oct, Tues-Sat, 10am-5pm, Sun and public holidays, 11am-5pm. Closed Mon and Nov to Easter. 16fl. ☎ (0162) 58 54 00.

De Biesbosch: Boat tours – By reservation only. Information: Biesbosch Informatie-centrum Drimmelen, ☎ (0162) 68 22 33. www.biesbosch.org

Biesbosch Museum – Open Tues-Sat, 10am-5pm, Sun and public holidays, noon-5pm. Closed Mon, 1 Jan and 25 and 31 Dec. 5.50fl. ☎ (0183) 50 40 09. www.biesboschmuseum.nl

BRIELLE 🅱 Markt 1 – 3231 AH – ☎ (0181) 47 54 75
– fax (0181) 475 470

Historisch Museum Den Briel – Open Apr to Oct, Tues-Fri, 10am-5pm, Sat, 10am-4pm, Sun, noon-4pm; Nov to Mar, Tues-Fri, 1-5pm, Sat, 10am-4pm. Closed Mon and public holidays; also Sun, Nov to Mar. 4fl. ☎ (0181) 47 54 75.

Grote Kerk or St.-Catharijnekerk – Open May to Sept, daily. Rest of the year by appointment, ☎ (0181) 47 54 75 (VVV).

D

DELFT   ☒ Markt 83-85 – 2611 GS – ☎ (015) 212 61 00 – fax (015) 215 86 95
www.vvvdelft.nl

Nieuwe Kerk – Open Apr to Oct, Mon-Sat, 9am-6pm; Nov to Mar, Mon-Fri, 11am-4pm, Sat 11am-5pm. 4fl. Closed Sun. ☎ (015) 257 02 98.

Tower – ♿ Same opening times as church.

Museum Paul Tetar van Elven – Open late Apr to late Oct, Tues-Sun, 1-5pm. Closed Mon and late Oct to late Apr. 4fl. ☎ (015) 212 42 06.

Legermuseum – Open Mon-Fri, 10am-5pm, Sat-Sun and public holidays, noon-5pm. Closed 1 Jan, 25 Dec. 6fl. ☎ (015) 215 05 00. www.legermuseum.nl

Prinsenhof – Open Tues-Sat, 10am-5pm, Sun and public holidays, 1-5pm. Closed Mon, 1 Jan and 25 Dec. 5fl. ☎ (015) 260 23 58.

Volkenkundig Museum Nusantara – ♿ Same opening times as Museum Lambert van Meerten. ☎ (015) 260 23 58.

Museum Lambert van Meerten – Open Tues-Sat, 10am-5pm, Sun and public holidays, 1-5pm. Closed Mon, 1 Jan and 25 Dec. 3.5fl. ☎ (015) 260 23 58.

Oude Kerk – Open Mon-Sat, 9am-6pm. Closed Sun. ☎ (015) 212 30 15.

Cultuurtuin voor technische gewassen – Open Mon-Fri, 8.30am-5pm, Sat, 10am-3pm. Closed Sun and public holidays. No charge. ☎ (015) 278 23 56.

Techniek Museum Delft – Open Tues-Sat, 10am-5pm, Sun and public holidays, noon-5pm. Closed Mon, 1 Jan and 25 Dec. 5fl. ☎ (015) 213 83 11.
www.museum.tudelft.nl

DELTA

WaterLand Neeltje Jans – ♿ Open Apr to Oct, daily, 10am-5.30pm; Nov to Mar, Wed-Sun, 10am-5pm. Closed Mon and Tues from Nov to Mar, 1 Jan, 25 Dec and 31 Dec. 21.50fl. ☎ (0111) 65 27 02. www.neeltjejans.nl

B. Rolland/EUREKA SLIDE

The Zeelandbrug, linking Zierikzee and Noord-Beveland

Haringvlietdam: Expo Haringvliet – Open Apr to Oct, daily, 10am-6pm. Closed Nov to Mar. 7.50fl. ☎ (0187) 49 99 13.

Brouwershaven: St.-Nicolaaskerk – Open Whitsun to Aug, Mon-Sat, 1.30-4.30pm. ☎ (0111) 69 19 40 (VVV).

DEVENTER   ☒ Keizerstraat 22 – 7411 HH; ☎ (0570) 61 31 00 – fax (0570) 64 33 38

Historisch Museum De Waag – ♿ Open Tues-Sat, 10am-5pm, Sun and public holidays 1-5pm. Closed Mon, 1 Jan, Good Friday, Easter Day, Whit Sunday, 25 Dec. 5fl. ☎ (0570) 69 37 80. www.deventer.nl

Speelgoed- en Blikmuseum – Same opening times as Historisch Museum De Waag. ☎ (0570) 69 37 86. www.deventer.nl

St-Nicolaaskerk or Bergkerk – Open Tues-Sun, 11am-5pm. Closed Mon, 1 Jan and 25 Dec. 2.50fl. ☎ (0572) 39 14 34. www.museumserver.nl/hannema.

Stadhuis – Open Mon-Fri, 9am-5pm. Closed Sat-Sun and public holidays. ☎ (0570) 64 99 59 (VVV).

Grote Kerk or St.-Lebuïnuskerk – Open during summer season, Mon-Sat, 11am-5pm; winter, Mon-Sat, 11am-4pm. ☎ (0570) 62 07 81. http://lebiunus.cjb.net

Tower – Open July and Aug, Mon-Sat, 1-5pm. Closed Sun and public holidays. 2.50fl. ☎ (0570) 62 07 81. http://lebiunus.cjb.net

Excursion

Natuurdiorama Holterberg – Open Apr to Oct, Mon-Sat, 9.30am-5.30pm, Sun and public holidays, 11am-5.30pm; Nov to Mar, Wed, Sun and school holidays, 1-5pm. 7.50fl. ☎ (0548) 36 19 79. www.museumholterberg.nl

DOESBURG
🛈 Kerkstraat 6 - 6981 CM - ☎ (0313) 47 90 88
fax (0313) 47 19 86

Grote Kerk or Martinikerk – Open Apr to Sept, Mon-Sat, 2-5pm. ☎ (0313) 47 90 88 (VVV).

Streekmuseum De Roode Tooren – Open Tues-Fri, 10am-noon and 1.30-4.30pm, Sat, 1.30-4.30pm; July and Aug also open Sun, 1.30-4.30pm. Closed Sun, Mon (except in July and Aug), 1 Jan, Easter Day, Whit Sunday and 25 Dec. No charge. ☎ (0313) 47 42 65.

Doesburgsch Mosterd- en Azijnmuseum – Open Tues-Fri, 10am-5pm, Sat, 11am-4pm. Closed Sun, Mon, 1 Jan, 30 Apr, Easter Day, 25 Dec. 2.50fl. ☎ (0313) 47 22 30.

Excursion

's-Heerenberg: Huis Bergh – By guided tour only: Apr, May and Oct, Sat-Sun at 2pm and 3pm; June and Sept, daily at 2pm and 3pm; July and Aug, Mon-Fri, 11am-3pm, Sat at 2pm and 3pm, Sun, 1-3pm; Nov to Mar, Sun at 2pm and 3pm. Closed 1 Jan, carnival, 25 and 31 Dec. 10fl. ☎ (0314) 66 12 81. www.huisbergh.nl

DOKKUM
🛈 Op de Fetze 13 - 9101 LE - ☎ (0519) 29 38 00
fax (0519) 29 80 15

Museum Het Admiraliteitshuis – Open Apr to Sept, Tues-Sat, 10am-5pm, Sun (July and Aug only), 2-5pm; Oct to Mar, Tues-Sat, 2-5pm. Closed Mon, Sun and public holidays. 4fl. ☎ (0519) 29 31 34.

Grote Kerk or St.-Martinuskerk – Guided tours only. Contact the verger, ☎ (0519) 29 20 65 or ☎ (0519) 29 34 40.

Bonifatiuskapel – Open June to Sept, daily, 2-5pm. ☎ (0511) 42 41 61.

DORDRECHT
🛈 Stationsweg 1 - 3311 JW - ☎ (078) 613 28 00 - fax (078) 613 17 83

Boat trips – For information and reservations, apply to the De Hollandse Biesbosch Visitor Centre *(see below)*.

Grote Kerk or O.-L.-Vrouwekerk – Open Apr to Oct, Tues-Sat, 10.30am-4.30pm, Sun and public holidays, noon-4pm. No charge. ☎ (078) 651 13 38.

Tower – Open Apr to Oct, Tues-Sat, 10.30am-4.30pm, Sun and public holidays, noon-4pm; July and Aug also open Mon, noon-4pm; Nov to Mar, Sat-Sun, 1-4pm. 2fl. ☎ (078) 651 13 38.

Museum Mr. Simon van Gijn – Closed for rebuilding; scheduled to re-open in 2001. ☎ (078) 613 28 00 (VVV).

Dordrechts Museum – Open daily (except Mon), 11am-5pm. Closed Mon, 1 Jan and 25 Dec. 8fl. ☎ (078) 648 21 48. www.museum.dordt.nl

Excursion

De Hollandse Biesbosch Visitor Centre – Open Sept to Apr, Tues-Sun, 9am-5pm; May and June, Mon, 1-5pm, Tues-Sun, 9am-5pm; July and Aug, daily, 9am-5pm. Closed 1 Jan and 25 Dec. No charge. Baanhoekweg 53, 3313 LP Dordrecht, ☎ (078) 630 53 53. www.dordt.nl/bezoekerscentrum or www.biesbosch.org

E

EDAM   🅴 Damplein 1 - 1135 BK - ☎ (0299) 31 51 25 - fax (0299) 37 42 36
www.vvv-edam.nl

Edams Museum - Open Apr to Oct, Tues-Sat, 10am-4.30pm, Sun and public holidays, 1.30-4.30pm. Closed Nov to Mar, Mon. 4fl. ☎ (0299) 31 51 25 (VVV).

Kaaswaag - ♿ Open Apr to Oct, daily, 10am-5pm. Closed Nov to Mar. ☎ (0299) 31 51 25 (VVV).

Grote Kerk or St.-Nicolaaskerk - Open Apr to Oct, daily, 2-4.30pm. Closed Nov to Mar. ☎ (0299) 31 51 25 (VVV).

EINDHOVEN   🅴 Stationsplein 17 - 5611 AC - ☎ (0900) 11 22 363
fax (040) 243 31 35 - www.vvveindhoven.nl

Milieu Educatiecentrum Eindhoven - Open Tues-Fri, 9am-5pm, Sat-Mon and public holidays, 1-5pm. Closed 1 Jan, Easter Day, Whitsun, 25 Dec and 26 Dec. No charge. ☎ (040) 259 47 00. www.mecehv.nl

Stedelijk van Abbemuseum - ♿ Temporary address: Entr'acte, Vonderweg 1. Open daily (except Mon), 11am-5pm. Closed Mon, 1 Jan and 25 Dec. Expected to re-open in spring 2002. 8fl. ☎ (040) 275 52 75. www.vanabbemuseum.nl

Museum Kempenland - Open Tues-Sun, 1-5pm. Closed Mon, 1 Jan, Easter Day and 25 Dec. 6fl. ☎ (040) 252 90 93. www.dse.nl/kempenland

DAF Museum - Open Tues-Sun, 10am-5pm; July and Aug and school holidays, daily, 11am-5pm. Closed Mon and public holidays. 10fl. ☎ (040) 244 43 64.

Prehistorisch Openluchtmuseum Eindhoven - Open daily, 10am-5pm. Closed 1 Jan, 25, 26 and 31 Dec. 5fl. ☎ (040) 252 22 81. www.dse.nl/eversham

Excursions

Nuenen: Van Gogh Documentatiecentrum - Open Mon-Fri, 8.30am-12.30pm and 1.30-4pm. Closed Sat-Sun and public holidays. 1.50fl. ☎ (040) 263 16 68.

Kasteel Heeze - By guided tour only: Mar to Oct, Wed at 2pm, Sun, Easter Day and Easter Monday and Whit Sunday and Monday at 2pm and 3pm. Closed Nov to Feb. 8fl. ☎ (024) 226 14 31.

Kasteel Helmond: (Gemeentemuseum) - Open Tues-Fri, 10am-5pm, Sat-Sun and public holidays, 2-5pm. Closed Mon, 1 Jan, carnival, 25 Dec. 3.50fl. ☎ (0492) 54 74 75.

Asten: Beiaard- en Natuurmuseum Asten - Open Tues-Fri, 9.30am-5pm, Sat-Mon, 1-5pm. Closed 1 Jan, carnival, 25 Dec. 7fl. ☎ (0493) 69 18 65. www.carillon-museum.nl

Nationaal Park De Groote Peel - Open daily, dawn-dusk. ☎ (0495) 64 14 97.

Bezoekerscentrum Mijl op Zeven - Open Mar, Apr, Sept and Oct, Tues-Sun, 10am-5pm; May to Aug, daily, 10am-5pm; Nov to Feb, Sun, noon-5pm; Christmas holidays, daily, 10am-5pm. ☎ (0495) 64 14 97.

EMMEN   🅴 Marktplein 9 - 7811 AM - ☎ (0591) 61 30 00 - fax (0591) 64 41 06

Noorder Dierenpark - ♿ Open daily from 9am. 27.50fl. ☎ (0591) 64 20 40. www.zoo-emmen.nl

Excursions

Orvelte: Museum-village - ♿ Open Apr to Oct, daily, 10am-5pm. Closed Nov to Mar. 12.50fl. ☎ (0593) 32 23 35.

Gemeentemuseum Drenthe's Veste - Open Apr to Sept, Tues-Sat, 11am-5pm. Closed Sun, Mon and public holidays, and Oct to Mar. 3fl. ☎ (0524) 51 62 25.

ENKHUIZEN   🅴 Tussen Twee Havens 1 - 1601 EM; ☎ (0228) 31 31 64
fax (0228) 31 55 31

Boat trips - Leave from Spoorhaven for Stavoren three times a day. Information from ☎ (0228) 31 31 64. To Urk (1hr 30min): late June to early Sept, Mon to Sat, three times a day. Information from ☎ (0527) 68 34 07.

Westerkerk or St.-Gomaruskerk - Closed for restoration.

Flessenscheepjesmuseum - Open daily, 10am-6pm. Closed 1 Jan, 25 Dec and 26 Dec. 5fl. ☎ (0228) 31 85 83.

Zuiderzeemuseum:

Binnenmuseum - ♿ Open Apr to Oct, Mon-Sat, 10am-5pm, Sun and public holidays, 10am-6pm (July and Aug, daily, 10am-6pm); Nov to Mar, daily, 10am-5pm. Closed 1 Jan and 25 Dec. 18.50fl (high season); 8fl (low season). ☎ (0228) 31 82 60. www.zuiderzeemuseum.nl

Buitenmuseum – Open Apr to Oct, Mon-Sat, 10am-5pm, Sun and public holidays, 10am-6pm (July and Aug, daily, 10am-6pm). Closed Nov to Mar. 18.50fl. ☎ (0228) 31 82 60. www.zuiderzeemuseum.nl

Zuider Kerk or St.-Pancraskerk – By appointment only. ☎ (0228) 31 31 64 (VVV).

ENSCHEDE   🛈 Oude Markt 31 – 7511 GB – ☎ (053) 432 32 00 – fax (053) 430 41 62
www.vvv-enschede.nl of vvv.twente.nl

Rijksmuseum Twenthe – ♿ Open Tues-Sun, 11am-5pm. Closed Mon, 1 Jan. 7.50fl. ☎ (053) 435 86 75.

Museum Jannink – Open Tues-Fri, 10am-5pm, Sat-Sun and public holidays, 1-5pm. Closed Mon, 1 Jan, Easter Day, 30 Apr, 5 May, 25 and 31 Dec. 3fl. ☎ (053) 431 90 93.

Natuurmuseum – Same opening times as Museum Jannink. 3fl. ☎ (053) 432 34 09.

St.-Plechelmusbasiliek – Open June to Aug, Tues and Thur, 2-3pm, Wed, 2-4pm; Sept, Wed, 2-4pm. ☎ (0541) 51 40 23 (VVV).

Het Palthe Huis – Open Tues-Fri, 10am-12.30pm and 1.30-5pm, Sat-Sun, 2-5pm. Closed Mon, Easter, Ascension Day, Whitsun and 25 Dec. 5fl. ☎ (0541) 513482.

Kasteel Singraven – Guided tours only (1hr): mid-Apr to Oct, Tues-Fri at 11am, 2pm and 3pm. Closed Mon, Sat-Sun and public holidays, Nov to mid-Apr. 9fl. ☎ (0541) 35 19 06.

Onderwijsmuseum Educatorum – Open Feb to Dec, Tues-Fri, 10am-5pm, Sat-Mon, 2-5pm. Closed Jan, Easter and 25 Dec. 5fl. ☎ (0541) 29 31 29. www.educatorium.nl

Openluchtmuseum Los Hoes – Open Feb to Dec, Mon, noon-5pm, Tues-Sun, 10am-5pm. Closed Jan. 5fl. ☎ (0541) 29 30 99.

Kasteel Twickel: Gardens – Open May to Oct, Mon-Fri, 11am-4.30pm. Closed Sat-Sun and Nov to Apr. 7.50fl. ☎ (074) 376 25 96.

Zoutmuseum – ♿ Open Mon-Fri, 11am-5pm, Sat-Sun, 2-5pm. Closed public holidays. 5fl. ☎ (074) 376 45 46.

F

FLEVOLAND   🛈 Stationsplein 186 – 8232 VT – ☎ (0320) 24 34 44
fax (0320) 28 02 18
🛈 Spoordreef 20 – 1315 GP – ☎ (036) 533 46 00 – fax (036) 534 36 65

Nieuw Land Poldermuseum – Open Mon-Fri, 10am-5pm, Sat-Sun and public holidays, 11.30am-5pm. Closed 1 Jan and 25 Dec. 8.50fl. ☎ (0320) 26 07 99. www.waterland.net/nieuwland.

Batavia dock – Nationaal Scheepshistorisch Centrum – Open daily, 10am-5pm (8pm July and Aug). Closed 1 Jan and 25 Dec. 17.50fl. ☎ (0320) 26 14 09. www.bataviawerf.nl

Nederlands Sportmuseum – Open Tues-Fri, 10am-5pm, Sat-Sun and public holidays, 11am-5pm. Closed 1 Jan and 25 Dec. 5fl. ☎ (0320) 28 00 00.

Zepp/allon – Open Tues-Sun, 10am-5pm. Closed Mon, 1 Jan and 25 and 31 Dec. 12.50fl. ☎ (0320) 24 77 50. www.airship-plaza.com

Vliegend Museum Lelystad – Open Apr to Sept, Sat-Sun, 11am-5pm. 4fl. ☎ (0320) 28 86 99. www.solcon.nl/vml

Uiverdome – Open July and Aug, daily, 10am-5pm; Sept and Oct, Wed-Sun, 10am-5pm. Closed Nov to June. 10fl. ☎ (0320) 28 41 63. www.aviodome.nl

ACHK – De Paviljoens – Open Tues-Sun, noon-5pm. Closed Mon, 1 Jan and 25 Dec. 2.50fl. ☎ (036) 545 04 00. www.achk-depaviljoens.nl

Six Flags Holland – Open May to June, daily, 10am-6pm; July and Aug, daily, 10am-10pm; Sept and Oct, Fri-Sun, 10am-6pm. Closed Nov to Apr. 41fl. ☎ (0321) 32 99 91.

FRANEKER   🛈 Voorstraat 51 – 8801 LA – ☎ (0900) 919 19 99 – fax (0517) 14 51 76

Stadhuis – Open Mon-Fri, 2-5pm. Closed Sat-Sun and public holidays. ☎ (0517) 38 04 80.

Eise Eisinga Planetarium – Open Tues-Sat, 10am-5pm; mid-Apr to mid-Sept also open Sun and Mon, 1-5pm. Closed 1 Jan and 25 Dec. 5fl. ☎ (0517) 39 30 70. www.planetarium-friesland.nl

Museum 't Coopmanshûs – Open Tues-Sat, 10am-5pm; Apr to Sept also open Sun, 1-5pm. Closed 1 Jan, 25 and 26 Dec. 3fl. Due to possible closure, it is advisable to check opening times in advance. ☎ (0517) 39 21 92.

Kaatsmuseum – Open May to Sept, Tues-Sun, 1-5pm. Closed Sun, Mon and public holidays. 2.50fl. ☎ (0517) 39 39 10.

G

GIETHOORN

🄴 Beulakerweg 114a - 8355 AL - ☎ (0521) 36 12 48
fax (0521) 36 22 81

Museumboerderij 't Olde Maat Uus – Open May to Oct, daily, 11am-5pm; Nov to Apr, Sun and during school holidays, noon-5pm. 5fl. ☎ (0521) 36 22 44.

Excursions

Gildenhuys – Open May to mid-Sept and during the autumn half-term holiday, Mon-Sat, 1.30-4.30pm; July and Aug, Mon-Thur, 7-9pm. Closed mid-Sept to Apr. 4fl. ☎ (0527) 29 13 81.

Grote Kerk – Information from VVV, ☎ (0527) 29 14 14.

GOES

🄴 Stationsplein 3 - 4461 HP - ☎ (0900) 168 16 66 - fax (0113) 25 13 50

Steam train – ♿ Departs Apr to June, Sun at 11am and 2pm; July and Aug, Sun-Fri at 11am, 2pm and 4pm; Sept and Oct, Sun at 2pm. 20fl 1st class, 15fl 2nd class. ☎ (0113) 27 07 05.

Grote Kerk – Open daily (except Sun), 9am-noon and 1-6pm. ☎ (0113) 21 67 68.

Museum voor Zuid- en Noord-Beveland – Open Tues-Fri, 10am-5pm, Sat, 1-4pm. Closed Mon, Sun and public holidays. 5fl. ☎ (0113) 22 88 83.

GORINCHEM

🄴 Grote Markt 17 - 4201 EB - ☎ (0183) 63 15 25
fax (0183) 63 40 40

Gorcums Museum – ♿ Open Tues-Sat, 10am-5pm, Sun, 11am-5pm (1pm Oct to Mar). Closed Mon, 1 Jan and 25 Dec. 3fl. ☎ (0183) 63 28 21.

St.-Janstoren – Information from VVV, ☎ (0183) 63 15 25

Excursions

Leerdam: Nationaal Glasmuseum – Open Tues-Fri, 10am-5pm, Sat-Sun and public holidays, 1-5pm. Closed Mon, 1 Jan and 25 Dec. 6fl. ☎ (0345) 61 27 14.

Slot Loevestein – Open Apr to Oct, Tues-Fri, 10am-5.30pm, Mon and public holidays, 11am-5.30pm; Nov to Mar, Sat-Sun only, 11am-5.30pm. Closed 1 Jan, 25, 26 and 31 Dec. 9.50fl. ☎ (0183) 44 71 71. www.slotloevestein.nl

GOUDA

🄴 Markt 27 - 2801 JJ - ☎ (0182) 51 36 66 - fax (0182) 58 32 10
www.vvvgroenehart.nl

Boat trips – Depart July and Aug. Information from VVV, ☎ (0182) 51 36 66.

Cheese and craft markets – Open June to Aug, Thur, 10am-12.30pm. ☎ (0182) 51 36 66 (VVV).

Stadhuis – Open Jan to May, Sept and Oct, Mon-Fri, 9am-noon and 2-4pm. Closed Sat-Sun. 1fl. ☎ (0182) 588758.

Kaasexposeum – Open Apr to Oct, Tues-Fri, 10am-5pm, Sat-Sun and public holidays, 1-5pm. Closed Mon, and Nov to Mar. 5fl. ☎ (0182) 52 99 96.

St.-Janskerk – Open Mar to Oct, Mon-Sat, 9am-5pm; Nov to Feb, Mon-Sat, 10am-4pm. Closed Sun, 1 Jan, 25 and 26 Dec. 3.50fl. ☎ (0182) 51 26 84.

Museum Het Catharina Gasthuis – Open Mon-Sat, 10am-5pm, Sun and public holidays, noon-5pm. Closed 1 Jan and 25 Dec. 4.75fl (also valid for Museum De Moriaan). ☎ (0182) 58 84 40.

Museum De Moriaan – Open Mon-Fri, 10am-5pm, Sat, 10am-12.30pm and 1.30-5pm, Sun and public holidays, noon-5pm. Closed 1 Jan and 25 Dec. 4.75fl (ticket also valid for Museum Het Catharina Gasthuis). ☎ (0182) 58 84 44.

Woerden: Stadsmuseum – Open Tues-Fri, 1-5pm, Sat-Sun, 1-4pm. Closed Mon, Easter, Whitsun, 25 and 31 Dec. 3fl. ☎ (0348) 43 10 08. www.woerdencentrum.nl

Heksenwaag – Open Apr to Oct, Tues-Sat, 10am-5pm, Sun and public holidays, noon-5pm. Closed Mon and Nov to Mar. 3fl. ☎ (0348) 56 34 00. www.heksenwaag.nl

Edelambachtshuys – Open Tues-Sat, 10am-5pm. Closed Mon, Sun, 1 Jan, 30 Apr, 25 and 26 Dec. 1fl. ☎ (0182) 38 26 14.

Nederlands Goud-, Zilver- en Klokkenmuseum – ♿ Open Tues-Sun, noon-5pm. Closed Mon, 1 Jan and 25 Dec. 6fl. ☎ (0182) 38 56 12.

GRONINGEN

Martinikerk – Open June to Aug, Tues-Sat, noon-5pm. Closed Sun and Mon. 1fl. ☎ (050) 311 12 77.

Tower – For opening times and admission charges contact VVV, ☎ (0900) 202 30 50.

Groninger Museum – Open Tues-Sun, 10am-5pm. Closed Mon, 1 Jan and 25 Dec. 12fl. ☎ (050) 366 65 55. www.groninger-museum.nl

Noordelijk Scheepvaartmuseum en Niemeyer Tabaksmuseum – Open Tues-Sun, 10am-5pm. Closed Mon, 1 Jan, 30 Apr, 28 Aug and 25 Dec. 6fl. ☎ (050) 312 22 02.

Excursions

Hortus Haren – ♿ Open daily, 9am-5pm (6pm Apr to Oct). 17.50fl. ☎ (050) 537 00 53. www.hortusharen.nl

Aduard: Nederlands Hervormde Kerk – Open Mon-Fri, 9am-noon and 2-5pm. ☎ (050) 403 17 24.

EXPOZEE exhibition – Open Apr, May, Sept and Oct, Wed and Sat-Sun, 11am-5pm; June, Wed-Sun, 11am-5pm; July and Aug, Wed-Sun, 10am-5pm. 6.50fl. ☎ (0519) 34 90 45.

Delfzijl: Boat trips – By arrangement. Information from VVV, ☎ (0596) 61 81 04.

Menkemaborg Castle – Open Apr to Oct, daily, 10am-noon and 1-5pm; Nov to early Jan, Feb and Mar, daily (except Mon), 10am-noon and 1-4pm. Closed Jan and Mon from Nov to Mar. 7.50fl. ☎ (0595) 43 19 70. www.borgen.nl

1939-1945 Museum – Open Apr to Oct, daily, 9am-6pm. 10fl. ☎ (0595) 43 41 00. www.museum1939-1945.nl

H-I

Den HAAG

Binnenhof Visitor Centre – Open daily (except Sun), 10am-4pm. Closed Sun and public holidays. No charge. ☎ (070) 364 61 44.

Ridderzaal, Eerste Kamer, Tweede Kamer – By guided tour only (45min): daily (except Sun), 10am-4pm. ☎ (070) 364 61 44.

Mauritshuis – ♿ Open Tues-Sat, 10am-5pm, Sun and public holidays, 11am-5pm. Closed Mon, 1 Jan and 25 Dec. 12.50fl (including Galerij Prins Willem V). ☎ (070) 302 34 56.
www.mauritshuis.nl

Haags Historisch Museum – Open Tues-Fri, 11am-5pm, Sat-Sun and public holidays, noon-5pm. Closed Mon. 6fl. ☎ (070) 364 69 40. www.haagshistorischmuseum.nl

Museum Bredius – Open Tues-Sun and public holidays, noon-5pm. Closed Mon, 1 Jan and 25 Dec. 10fl. ☎ (070) 362 07 29.
www.museumbredius.nl

Museum Het Paleis – Open daily (except Mon), 11am-5pm. Closed Mon, between exhibitions, 1 Jan, and 25 Dec. 10fl. ☎ (070) 362 40 61. www.gemeentemuseum.nl/paleis

H. Gyssels/DIAF

Museum de Gevangenpoort – By guided tour only, Tues-Fri, 11am-4pm, Sat-Sun and public holidays, noon-4pm. Closed Mon, 1 Jan and 25 Dec. 8fl. ☎ (070) 346 08 61. www.gevangenpoort.nl

Galerij Prins Willem V – Open Tues-Sun, 11am-4pm. Closed Mon, 1 Jan and 25 Dec. 2.50fl (free to holders of a ticket to Mauritshuis). ☎ (070) 302 34 35. www.mauritshuis.nl

Grote Kerk or St.-Jacobskerk – Open July and Aug, Mon-Fri, 11am-4pm; rest of the year by appointment. ☎ (070) 302 86 30.

Panorama Mesdag – Open Mon-Sat, 10am-5pm, Sun and public holidays, noon-5pm. Closed 25 Dec. 6fl. ☎ (070) 310 66 65. www.panorama-mesdag.com

Museum voor Communicatie – Open Mon-Fri, 10am-5pm, Sat-Sun and public holidays, noon-5pm. Closed 1 Jan and 25 Dec. 7.50. ☎ (070) 330 75 00. www.muscom.nl

Museum Mesdag – Open Tues-Sun, noon-5pm. Closed Mon, 1 Jan and 25 Dec. 5fl. ☎ (070) 362 14 34.

Vredespaleis – Open Mon-Fri, 10am-4pm (3pm Oct to Apr). 5fl. Closed Sat-Sun and public holidays. ☎ (070) 302 41 37.

Gemeentemuseum Den Haag – Open daily (except Mon), 11am-5pm. Closed Mon. 12.50fl. ☎ (070) 338 11 11. www.gemeentemuseum.nl

Museon – ♿ Open Tues-Sun and daily during school holidays, 11am-5pm. Closed Mon, 1 Jan and 25 Dec. 12.50fl. ☎ (070) 338 13 38. www.museon.nl

Omniversum – ♿ Open Mon, 1-5pm, Tues and Wed, 11am-5pm, Thur-Sun, public holidays and during school holidays, 11am-9pm. 17.50fl. ☎ (0900) 666 48 37. www.omniversum.nl

Madurodam – ♿ Open Mar to June, daily, 9am-8pm; July and Aug, daily, 9am-11pm; Sept to Feb, daily, 9am-6pm. 21fl. ☎ (070) 355 39 00. www.madurodam.nl

Museum van Het Boek/Museum Meermanno-Westreenianum – Open Tues-Fri, 11am-5pm, Sat-Sun and public holidays, noon-5pm. Closed Mon, 1 Jan and 25 Dec. 3.50fl. ☎ (070) 346 27 00.

Letterkundig Museum – Open Tues-Fri, 10am-5pm, Sat-Sun and public holidays, noon-5pm. Closed Mon, 1 Jan, 30 Apr, Easter Day, 5 May, Whitsun and 25 Dec. 6fl. ☎ (070) 333 96 66. www.letmus.nl

Scheveningen 🄴 G. Deynootweg 1134 – 2586 BX – ☎ (0900) 340 35 05 fax (070) 352 04 26 – www.denhaag.com

Museum Beelden aan Zee – ♿ Open Tues-Sun, 11am-5pm. Closed Mon, 1 Jan, 25 and 26 Dec. 7.50fl. ☎ (070) 358 58 57. www.beeldenaanzee.nl

The beach at Scheveningen

Sea Life Scheveningen – Open daily, 10am-6pm; July and Aug, daily, 10am-8pm. Closed 25 Dec. 15.50fl. ☎ (070) 355 87 81. www.sealife.nl

Excursions

Voorburg: Huygensmuseum – Open Wed, Thur and Sat-Sun, 1-5pm. Closed Mon, Tues, Fri and public holidays. 2.50fl. ☎ (070) 387 23 11.

Wassenaar: Duinrell theme park – Open early Apr to Oct, daily, 10am-5pm (6pm July and Aug). Closed Nov to early Apr. 29.50fl (including Tikibad). ☎ (070) 515 52 58. www.duinrell.nl

Naaldwijk: Flower auction (Bloemenveiling Holland) – Open Mon-Fri (except Thur), 8am-10am. Closed Thur, Sat-Sun and public holidays. 6fl. ☎ (0174) 63 21 58. www.bvh.nl

HAARLEM   ⓘ Stationsplein 1 - 2011 LR - ☎ (0900) 616 16 00 - fax (023) 534 05 37
www.vvvzk.nl

Grote Kerk or St.-Bavokerk – Open daily, 10am-4pm. 2.75fl.☎ (023) 532 43 99. www.grotekerk.nl

Vishal – ♿ Same opening times as Frans Halsmuseum. No charge. ☎ (023) 532 68 56.

Vleeshal – ♿ Same opening times as Frans Halsmuseum. 7.50fl. ☎ (023) 511 57 75. www.franshalsmuseum.nl

Archeologisch Museum Haarlem – Open Wed-Sun, 1-5pm. Closed Mon and Tues, 1 Jan and 25 and 26 Dec. No charge. ☎ (023) 531 31 35.

Verweyhal – Same opening times as Frans Halsmuseum. 7.50fl. ☎ (023) 511 57 75. www.franshalsmuseum.nl

Stadhuis – Guided tours by appointment only. ☎ (023) 511 31 58.

Frans Halsmuseum – Open Mon-Sat, 11am-5pm, Sun and public holidays, noon-5pm. Closed 1 Jan and 25 Dec. 10fl. ☎ (023) 511 57 75. www.franshalsmuseum.nl

Teylers Museum – Open Tues-Sat, 10am-5pm, Sun and public holidays, noon-5pm. Closed Mon, 1 Jan and 25 Dec. 10fl. ☎ (023) 531 90 10. www.teylersmuseum.nl

Historisch Museum Zuid-Kennemerland – Open Tues-Sat, noon-5pm, Sun, 1-5pm. Closed Mon, 1 Jan, 25, 26 and 31 Dec. No charge. ☎ (023) 542 24 27.

ABC Architectuurcentrum – Open Tues-Sat, noon-5pm, Sun, 1-5pm. Closed Mon and public holidays. No charge. ☎ (023) 534 05 84.

Spaarnestad Fotoarchief – Open Tues-Sat, noon-5pm, Sun, 1-5pm. No charge. ☎ (023) 518 51 52. www.spaarnefoto.nl

Kathedrale Basiliek St.-Bavo – Open Apr to Sept and during school holidays, Mon-Sat, 10am-4pm, Sun, 1-4pm. 2.50fl. ☎ (023) 553 33 77.

Museum De Cruquius – ♿ Open Mar to Oct, Mon-Fri, 10am-5pm, Sat-Sun and public holidays, 11am-5pm. Closed Nov to Feb. 6fl. ☎ (023) 528 57 04.

Stoomgemaal Halfweg – Open Apr to Sept, Wed and Thur, 1-4pm, Sat, 10am-4pm. Closed Nov to Mar. 4fl. ☎ (020) 497 43 96. www.rcz.com/stoomgemaal-halfweg

Excursions

Nationaal Park Zuid-Kennemerland Visitor Centre – Open Tues-Sun, 10am-5pm. Closed Mon, 1 Jan, Easter, Whitsun and 25 Dec. No charge. ☎ (023) 541 11 23.

HARDERWIJK   ⓘ Havendam 58 - 3841 AA - ☎ (0341) 42 66 66 - fax (0341) 42 77 13
www.vvveluwe.nl

Boat tours – Operate July and Aug. 8fl. Information from Rederij Flevo, ☎ (0341) 41 25 98. www.rederijflevo.nl

Dolfinarium – ♿ Open late Feb to early Jan, daily, 10am-6pm (last admission 4pm). Closed early Jan to late Feb, 1 Jan and 25 and 31 Dec. 32.50fl. ☎ (0341) 46 74 00. www.dolfinarium.nl

Veluws Museum – Open Mon-Fri, 10am-5pm, Sat, 1-4pm. Closed Sun and public holidays. 3.50fl. ☎ (0341) 41 44 68.

Grote Kerk – Open mid-May to mid-Sept, Mon-Fri. Closed mid-Sept to mid-May. ☎ (0341) 41 23 95.

Excursions

Elburg:

Vischpoort – Open mid-June to Aug, Mon, 2-4.30pm, Tues-Fri, 10am-noon and 1-4.30pm. Closed Sat-Sun and public holidays and Sept to May. 3fl. ☎ (0525) 68 13 41.

Gemeentemuseum – Open Apr, May and Sept, Mon, 2-5pm, Tues-Fri, 10am-noon and 2-5pm; June to Aug, Mon, 2-5pm, Tues-Fri, 10am-5pm; Oct to Mar, Tues-Fri, 10am-noon and 2-5pm. Closed Sat-Sun and public holidays; also Oct to Mar, Mon. 3fl. ☎ (0525) 68 13 41.

St.-Nicolaaskerk – Open June, Mon-Fri, 1.30-4.30pm; July and Aug, Mon, 1.30-4.30pm, Tues-Fri, 10am-noon and 1.30-4.30pm. Closed Sat-Sun and Sept to May. ☎ (0525) 68 15 20 (VVV).

Boat trips – ♿ Depart May to Sept, Tues-Sat, every 1hr from 10am to 5pm. 6fl. ☎ (0341) 41 41 59.

HARLINGEN

🛈 Voorstraat 34 – 8861 BL – ☎ (0900) 919 19 99
fax (0517) 41 51 76 – www.vvv-harlingen.nl

Gemeentemuseum Het Hannemahuis – Open Apr to June and mid-Sept to Oct, Mon-Fri, 1.30-5pm; July to mid-Sept, Tues-Sat, 10am-5pm, Sun and public holidays, 1.30-5pm. Closed Mon in summer, Nov to Mar, Easter Day and Whit Sunday. 2.50fl. ☎ (0517) 41 36 58.

HEERLEN

🛈 Bongerd 22 – 6411 JM – ☎ (045) 571 62 00 – fax (045) 571 83 83 – www.vvvzuidlimburg.nl

Thermenmuseum – Open daily, 10am-5pm. Closed 1 Jan, carnival, 25 Dec. 6fl. ☎ (045) 560 45 81. www.thermenmuseum.nl

Excursions

Kasteel Hoensbroek – Open daily, 10am-5.30pm. Closed 1 Jan, carnival, 25 and 31 Dec. 8.50fl. ☎ (045) 522 72 72. www.kasteelhoensbroek.nl

Industrion – ♿ Open Tues-Sun, 10am-5pm. Closed Mon, 1 Jan, carnival and 25 Dec. 8fl. ☎ (045) 567 08 09.

Abdij Rolduc – Open daily (guided tours available), 10am-5pm. ☎ (045) 546 68 88. www.rolduc.com

Den HELDER

🛈 Bernhardplein 18 – 1781 HH – ☎ (0223) 62 55 44
fax (0223) 61 48 88

Marinemuseum – Open Tues-Fri, 10am-5pm, Sat-Sun and public holidays, noon-5pm; also open Mon from May to Oct. Closed Mon (except May to Oct), 1 Jan and 25 Dec. 7.50fl. ☎ (0223) 65 75 34. www.marinemuseum.nl

Nationaal Reddingmuseum Dorus Rijkers – ♿ Open Mon-Sat, 10am-5pm, Sun and public holidays, 1-5pm. Closed 25 Dec. 5fl. ☎ (0223) 61 83 20.

Fort Kijkduin – Open daily, 10am-6pm. Guided tours at 11am, 1pm and 3pm. 13.50fl (includes aquarium). ☎ (0223) 61 23 66. www.fortkijkduin.nl

Callantsoog: Het Zwanenwater – Open Apr to July, daily, 7am-9pm; the rest of the year, dawn-dusk. 1.50fl. ☎ (0224) 58 15 41 (VVV).

's-HERTOGENBOSCH

🛈 Markt 77 – 5211 JX – ☎ (0900) 11 22 33 4
fax (073) 612 89 30

St.-Janskathedraal – Open daily, 10am-4.30pm.

Sint-Jansmuseum De Bouwloods – Open May to Sept, Tues-Sun, 1-4.30pm. Closed Mon; also Oct and Apr. 5fl. ☎ (073) 612 68 79.

Stadhuis – Open Mon, 11am-5.30pm, Tues-Fri, 9am-5.30pm, Sat, 9am-4pm; May to Sept also open Sun, 11am-3pm. Guided tours: Thur at 7pm, Sat at 2.30pm. Closed public holidays, and Sun from Oct to Apr. ☎ (073) 613 50 98.

Noordbrabants Museum – Open Tues-Fri, 10am-5pm, Sat-Sun, noon-5pm. Closed Mon, 1 Jan and 25 Dec. 2.500fl. ☎ (073) 687 78 77.

Museum Slager – Open Tues-Sun, 2-5pm. Closed Mon and public holidays. 6fl. ☎ (073) 613 32 16.

Museum Het Kruithuis – Closed for restoration. Scheduled to re-open in 2002. Information: ☎ (073) 612 21 88.

Boat trips on the Binnendieze – Open May to late Oct, Tues-Sun, 11am-5pm, Wed, 2-5pm. 8fl. ☎ (073) 612 23 34.

Excursions

Autotron Rosmalen – ♿ Open Epiphany to early Apr, Sat-Sun, 10am-5pm; Easter to Aug, daily, 10am-5pm; Sept, Thur-Sun, 10am-5pm; Nov to mid-Dec, Sat-Sun, 10am-5pm; Christmas to Epiphany, daily, 10am-5pm; during the spring and autumn half-term, daily, 10am-5pm. Closed Oct. 17.50fl. ☎ (073) 523 33 00. www.autotron.nl

Kasteel Heeswijk – Guided tours every first and third Sun of the month. Information: ☎ (0413) 29 23 52. www.kasteelheeswijk.nl

Meierijsche Museumboerderij – Open May to Sept, Wed, Sat-Sun and public holidays, 2-5pm. Closed Oct to Apr. 2.50fl. ☎ (0413) 29 15 46.

Kasteel Ammersoyen – By guided tour only: mid-Apr to Oct, Tues-Sat and public holidays, 10am-5pm, Sun, 1-5pm. Closed Mon, 30 Apr and Nov to mid-Apr. 8fl. ☎ (073) 594 95 82.

Huis van Maarten van Rossum – Open Tues-Fri, 10am-12.30pm and 1.30-4.30pm, Sat (except Oct to Mar) and Sun, 2-4.30pm. Closed Mon, also Sat from Oct to Mar, 1 Jan, Easter, Whitsun and 25 Dec. 3fl. ☎ (0418) 51 26 17.

Land van Oolt – Open late Apr to mid-Sept, daily, 10am-5pm; mid-Sept to mid-Oct, Sat-Sun, 10am-5pm; mid- to end Oct, daily, 10am-5pm. Closed Nov to late Apr. 27fl. ☎ (0900) 235 66 48. www.ooit.nl

Nederlands Leder- en Schoenenmuseum – ♿ Open Tues-Fri, 10am-5pm, Sat-Sun, noon-4pm. Closed Mon, 1 Jan, Easter, Whitsun and 25 Dec. 7.50fl. ☎ (0416) 33 27 38. www.tref.nl/waalwijk/schoenenmuseum

De Efteling – ♿ Open mid-Apr to Oct, daily, 10am-6pm; July and Aug, daily, 10am-9pm; second and third Sat-Sun in Dec, 11am-8pm; Christmas to Epiphany, daily, 11am- 8pm. 39fl. ☎ (0416) 27 35 35. www.efteling.nl

HILVERSUM
🛈 Noordse Bosje 1 - 1211 BD - ☎ (035) 624 17 51

Goois Museum – ♿ Open Tues-Sun, 1-5pm. Closed Mon, 1 Jan, 30 Apr and 25 Dec. 3fl. ☎ (035) 629 28 26.

Kasteel Groeneveld – Open Tues-Fri, 10am-5pm, Sat-Sun, noon-5pm. 5fl. ☎ (035) 542 04 46.

Singer Museum – ♿ Open Tues-Sat, 11am-5pm, Sun and public holidays, noon-5pm. Closed Mon, 1 Jan, 30 Apr and 25 Dec. ☎ (035) 531 56 56.

Muiderslot – By guided tour only (50min): Apr to Oct, Mon-Fri, 10am-5pm, Sat-Sun and public holidays, 1-5pm; Nov to Mar, Sat-Sun only, 1-4pm. Closed 1 Jan and 25 Dec. 10fl. ☎ (0294) 26 13 25. www.muiderslot.nl

HINDELOOPEN

Museum Hidde Nijland Stichting – Open Mar to Oct, Mon-Sat, 10am-5pm, Sun and public holidays, 1.30-5pm. Closed Nov to Feb. 3.50fl. ☎ (0514) 52 14 20.

Het Eerste Friese Schaatsmuseum – Open Mon to Sat, 10am-6pm, Sun, 1-5pm. 2.50fl. ☎ (0514) 52 16 83.

De HOGE VELUWE (National Park)

Park – Open Apr, daily, 8am-8pm; May, daily, 8am-9pm; June and July, daily, 8am-10pm; Aug, daily, 8am-9pm; Sept, daily, 9am-8pm; Oct, daily, 9am-7pm; Nov to Mar, daily, 9am-5.30pm. 8fl. ☎ (0900) 464 38 35. www.hogeveluwe.nl

Visitor Centre – Open daily, 10am-5pm. ☎ (0900) 464 38 35. www.hogeveluwe.nl.

Kröller-Müller Museum – ♿ Open daily (except Mon), 10am-5pm. Closed Mon (except public holidays) and 1 Jan. 8fl. ☎ (0318) 59 12 41. www.kmm.nl

Sculpture garden and sculpture park – Open daily (except Mon), 10am-4.30pm. Closed Mon (except public holidays) and 1 Jan. 8fl. ☎ (0318) 59 12 41. www.kmm.nl

Museonder – Same opening times as Visitor Centre. ☎ (0900) 464 38 35. www.hogeveluwe.nl.

Jachthuis St.-Hubertus – By guided tour only: Apr to Oct, daily, every 30min between 11am and 12.30pm and 2pm and 4.30pm; Nov to Mar (except Jan), daily, 2pm and 3pm. Closed Jan. ☎ (0900) 464 38 35. www.hogeveluwe.nl

Excursion

Nederlands Tegelmuseum – ♿ Open Tues-Fri, 10am-12.30pm and 1-5pm, Sat-Sun and public holidays, 1-5pm. Closed Mon, 1 Jan and 25 Dec. 6fl. ☎ (0318) 59 15 19.

HOORN
🛈 Veemarkt 4 - 1621 JC - ☎ (0900) 403 10 55 - fax (0229) 21 50 23

Steam tram – Departs: Apr to Oct and during Christmas period, Tues-Sun, 11am-3.30pm; July and Aug also on Mon. 23.50fl (return/round trip). ☎ (0229) 21 92 31. www.stoomtram.demon.nl

Westfries Museum – Open Mon-Fri, 11am-5pm, Sat-Sun and public holidays, 2-5pm. Closed 1 Jan, third Monday in Aug and 25 Dec. 5fl. ☎ (0229) 28 00 28. www.wfm.nl

Museum van de Twintigste Eeuw – Open Tues-Sun, 10am-5pm. Closed Mon, 1 Jan, 30 Apr, 25 and 26 Dec. 6fl. ☎ (0229) 21 40 01. www.hoorngids.nl/museumhoorn.

HULST   🛈 Grote Markt 19 - 4561 EA - ☎ (0114) 38 92 99 - fax (0114) 38 91 35

Streekmuseum De Vier Ambachten – Open Easter Day to Oct, daily, 2-5pm. Closed Nov to Easter Day. 2.50fl. ☎ (0114) 31 23 11.

HUNEBEDDEN

Nationaal Hunebedden Infocentrum – Open Feb to Dec, Mon-Fri, 10am-5pm, Sat-Sun and public holidays, 1-5pm. Closed Jan and 25 Dec. ☎ (0599) 23 63 74.

IJSSELMEER

Kazemattenmuseum Kornwerderzand – Open May to Sept, Wed and Sat, 10am-5pm; July and Aug also open Sun, 1-5pm. Closed Oct to Apr. 5fl. ☎ (0517) 57 94 53 or ☎ (0515) 23 14 22 (VVV Makkum).

K

KAMPEN   🛈 Botermarkt 5 - 8261 GR - ☎ (038) 331 35 00 - fax (038) 332 89 00
www.kampen.nl/vvv

Kamper Tabaksmuseum – By appointment only. ☎ (038) 331 58 68.

Oude Raadhuis – Open Mon-Thur, 11am-noon and 2-4pm; Apr to Sept also open Sat, 2-5pm. Closed Fri, Sun and public holidays. 1.50fl. ☎ (038) 331 73 61.

Nieuwe Toren – Open May to mid-Sept, Wed and Sat, 2-5pm; July and Aug also open Fri, 2-5pm. Closed public holidays. 1.50fl. ☎ (038) 339 29 99.

Stedelijk Museum – Open Feb to mid-June, Tues-Sat, 11am-12.30pm and 1.30-5pm; mid-June to mid-Sept, Tues-Sat, 11am-5pm, Sun, 1-5pm.; mid-Sept to Dec, Tues-Sat, 11am-12.30pm and 1.30-5pm. Closed Mon, Easter Day, Whit Sunday, 25, 26 and 31 Dec. 3fl. ☎ (038) 331 73 61.

St.-Nicolaaskerk or Bovenkerk – Open Easter Day to early Sept, Mon and Tues, 1-5pm, Wed to Fri, 10am-5pm; mid-Sept to autumn half-term, Mon-Fri, 1-4pm. ☎ (038) 331 36 08.

KEUKENHOF and BULB FIELDS

Keukenhof National Flower Exhibition – ♿ Open late Mar to late May, daily, 8am-7.30pm. 20fl. Closed late May to late Mar. ☎ (0252) 46 55 55.

Zomerhof – ♿ Open Aug to mid-Sept, daily, 9am-6pm. 15fl. ☎ (0252) 46 55 55. www.keukenhof.nl

Trips by plane – Information: Kroonduif Air B.V., Heathrowbaan 4, 3045 AG Rotterdam, Sun ☎ (010) 415 78 55. www.kroonduif-air.nl

Bulb fields

K. Tome/ALTITUDE/HOA QUI

Excursion

Museum de Zwarte Tulp – ♿ Open Tues-Sun, 1-5pm. Closed Mon, 1 Jan, 25, 26 and 31 Dec. 4fl. ☏ (0252) 41 79 00.

Den Hartogh Ford Museum – Open Wed-Sun, 10am-5pm. Closed Mon and Tues, 1 Jan, 30 Apr, 25 Dec and 31 Dec. 15fl. ☏ (0252) 51 81 18. www.fordmuseum.nl

L

LEEUWARDEN
🚉 Stationsplein 1 – 8901 AC – ☏ (0900) 202 40 60
fax (058) 215 35 93 – www.vvvleeuwarden.nl

Fries Museum/Verzetsmuseum – ♿ Open Tues-Sun, 11am-5pm. Closed Mon, 1 Jan and 25 Dec. 7.50fl. ☏ (058) 212 30 01. www.friesmuseum.nl or www.verzetsmuseum.nl

Grote Kerk or Jacobijnerkerk – Open June to Aug, Tues-Fri, 2-4.30pm. ☏ (058) 212 83 13.

Fries Natuurmuseum – ♿ Open Tues-Sat, 10am-5pm, Sun and public holidays, 1-5pm. Closed Mon, 1 Jan and 25 Dec. 6fl. ☏ (058) 212 90 85.

Museum Het Princesse-hof, Nederlands Keramiek Museum – Open Tues-Sun, 11am-5pm. Closed Mon, 1 Jan and 25 Dec. 7.50fl. ☏ (058) 212 74 38.

Oldehove – Open May to Sept, Tues-Sat, 2-5pm. 2.50fl. ☏ (0900) 202 40 60 (VVV).

Pier Pander Museum – Open Tues-Sat, 2-5pm. Closed Sun, Mon and public holidays. No charge. ☏ (058) 212 74 38.

Otterpark Aqualutra – Open Apr to Oct, daily, 9.30am-5.30pm; Nov to Mar, daily, 10.30am-4.30pm. 12.50 fl. ☏ (0511) 43 12 14. www.aqualutra.nl

Poptaslot – By guided tour only: Apr, May, Sept and Oct, Mon-Fri at 2pm; June, Mon-Fri at 11am, 2pm and 3pm; July and Aug, Mon-Sat, 11am-5pm. Closed Sun, and Nov to Mar. 6fl. ☏ (058) 254 12 31.

"Uilenbord", Frisian farmhouse

Morande-Grahame/HOA QUI

Fogelsangh State – Closed for renovation work. For information, ☏ (0511) 44 19 70.

Hogebeintum: Church – Open Apr to Oct, Tues-Sat, 10am-5pm, Sun, noon-5pm. ☏ (0518) 41 17 83.

LEIDEN
🚉 Stationsweg 2d – 2312 AV – ☏ (0900) 222 23 33 – fax (071) 516 12 27
www.leidenpromotie.nl

Rijksmuseum voor Volkenkunde – ♿ Closed for rebuilding work until mid-Apr 2001. ☏ (071) 516 88 00. www.rmv.nl

Molenmuseum De Valk – Open Tues-Sat, 10am-5pm, Sun and public holidays, 1-5pm. Closed Mon, 1 Jan, 3 Oct and 25 Dec. 5fl. ☏ (071) 516 53 53.

Stedelijk Museum De Lakenhal – ♿ Open Tues-Fri, 10am-5pm, Sat-Sun and public holidays, noon-5pm. Closed Mon, 1 Jan and 25 Dec. 8fl. ☏ (071) 516 53 60. www.lakenhal.demon.nl

Rijksmuseum van Oudheden – ₺ Open daily, 10am-6pm. Closed 1 Jan and 25 Dec. 7fl. ☎ (071) 516 31 63. www.rmo.nl

Koninklijk Penningkabinet – Open Tues-Fri, 10am-5pm, Sat-Sun and public holidays, noon-5pm. Closed Mon, 1 Jan, 3 Oct and 25 Dec. 7fl. ☎ (071) 516 09 99. www.penningkabinet.nl

Academisch Historisch Museum – Open Wed-Fri, 1-5pm. Closed during the summer holiday period. No charge. ☎ (071) 527 72 42.

Hortus Botanicus – Open during the summer holiday period, daily, 10am-6pm; winter, daily (except Sat), 10am-4pm. Closed Sat from Oct to Mar, 8 Feb, 3 Oct and 25 Dec to 2 Jan. 8fl. ☎ (071) 527 72 49. www.hortus.leidenuniv.nl

Pieterskerk – Open daily, 1.30-4pm. Closed during services. ☎ (071) 512 43 19. www.pieterskerk.com.

Leiden American Pilgrim Museum – Open Wed-Fri, 1-5pm, Sat, 10am-5pm. Closed Mon, Tues and Sun. ☎ (071) 512 24 13.

Museum Boerhaave – Open Tues-Sat, 10am-5pm, Sun and public holidays, noon-5pm. Closed Mon, 1 Jan and 3 Oct. 7.50fl. ☎ (071) 521 42 24. www.museumboerhaave.nl

Model-making Museum – Open Tues-Sat, 10am-5pm, Sun, noon-5pm. Closed Mon, 1 Jan and 25 and 26 Dec. 7.50fl. ☎ (071) 521 45 67. www.mostware.com/modelbouwmuseum

Naturalis – ₺ Open Tues-Sun, 10am-6pm; public holidays and school holidays, daily, 10am-6pm. Closed Mon 1 Jan and 25 Dec. 12.50fl. ☎ (071) 568 76 00. www.naturalis.nl

Excursions

Vogelpark Avifauna – Open daily, 9am-6pm. 16fl. ☎ (0172) 48 75 75. www.avifauna.nl

Archeon – Open Easter to July and Sept to Oct, daily (except Mon), 10am-5pm. Closed Nov to Easter and Aug. 24.50fl (includes meal). Opening times may vary, check latest details on ☎ (0172) 44 77 44. www.archeon.nl

Noordwijk Space Expo – Open daily (except Mon), 10am-5pm; also open Mon during school holidays, 10am-5pm. Closed Mon (except as stated), 1 Jan and 25 Dec. 15fl. ☎ (071) 364 64 46. www.12move.nl/space.

Het LOO

Palace and gardens – ₺ Open daily (except Mon), 10am-5pm. Closed Mon and 1 Jan. 15fl. ☎ (055) 577 24 00. www.hetloo.nl

Concerts – Last Friday of every month at 8.15pm. Reservations: ☎ (055) 577 24 48.

M

MAASTRICHT
🅱 Kleine Staat 1 - 6211 ED – ☎ (043) 325 21 21
fax (043) 321 37 46

Museum Spaans Gouvernement – By guided tour only (1hr): Wed-Sun, 1-5pm. Closed Mon, Tues and public holidays. 5fl. ☎ (043) 321 13 27.

St.-Servaasbasiliek – Enter via Vrijthof. Open daily, 10am-5pm (6pm July and Aug). Closed 1 Jan, carnival and 25 Dec. 4fl. ☎ (043) 321 04 90.

Natuurhistorisch Museum – Open Mon-Fri, 10am-5pm, Sat-Sun and public holidays, 2-5pm. Closed 1 Jan, carnival, Good Friday, Easter Day, Ascension Day, Whit Sunday and 25 Dec. 6fl. ☎ (043) 350 54 90. www.nhmmaastricht.nl

Onze Lieve Vrouwebasiliek – Open daily, 8am-5pm. ☎ (043) 325 18 51.

Treasury – Open Easter Day to autumn half-term, Mon-Sat, 11am-5pm, Sun, 1-5pm. 3.50fl. ☎ (043) 325 18 51.

Bonnefantenmuseum – Open Tues-Sun and public holidays, 11am-5pm. Closed Mon, 1 Jan, carnival and 25 Dec. 12.50fl. ☎ (043) 329 01 90. www.bonnefanten.nl

Kazematten – By guided tour only (1hr): Jan to Apr and Nov to Dec, Sun at 2pm; May, June, Sept and Oct, Sat-Sun at 2pm; July and Aug, daily at 12.30pm and 2pm; during school holidays, daily at 2pm. 6fl. ☎ (043) 325 21 21 (VVV).

Fort St.-Pieter – By guided tour only (1hr): June to Oct, Sun at 3.30pm; July and Aug and school holidays, daily at 3.30pm. 6fl. ☎ (043) 325 21 21 (VVV).

Marl caves – Grotten Noord – By guided tour only (1hr): Jan to mid-Mar, Wed-Fri at 2pm, Sat-Sun at 12.30pm and 2pm; mid-Mar to late Apr and Nov to Dec, Wed, Fri and Sat-Sun at 12.30pm and 2pm; late Apr to June and Sept to Oct, daily at 12.30pm, 2pm and 3.30pm; July and Aug, daily, 10.45am-3.45pm; during school holidays, daily at 12.30pm and 2pm. 6fl. ☎ (043) 325 21 21 (VVV).

Grotten Zonneberg – By guided tour only (1hr): Apr, daily at 12.45pm (except Sunday), 1.45pm and 2.45pm; May to mid-Sept, Mon-Sat, 10.45am-3.45pm (departing every hr), Sun, 1.45-3.45pm (every hr); autumn half-term, daily at 1.45pm (2.45pm on Sun); Nov to mid-Dec, Sat-Sun at 2.45pm. 6fl. ☎ (043) 325 21 21 (VVV).

Afrikacentrum – Open Tues-Fri, 1.30-5pm, Sat-Sun, 2-5pm. Closed Mon, 1 Jan, carnival, Easter, Whitsun and 25 Dec. 7.50fl. ☎ (043) 407 73 83. www.sma-nederland.nl/afrikacentrum.htm

Schippersbeurs – Open Tues-Thur, 1-4pm, Sun, 2-5pm. Closed Mon, Fri, Sat, 1 Jan, Easter Day, Whitsun and 25 Dec. 1fl. ☎ (046) 437 60 52.

Archeologie Museum – Open Wed and Fri, 9am-noon and 2-5pm, Sun, 2-5pm. Closed Mon, Tues, Thur, Sat and public holidays. 3fl. ☎ (046) 433 89 19.

Grote Kerk or St.-Petruskerk – Open June to Aug, Mon-Fri, 2-4pm. ☎ (046) 452 41 44 (VVV).

Stedelijk Museum Het Domein – Open Tues-Sun, 11am-5pm. Closed Mon, 1 Jan, carnival, Easter, Whitsun and 25 Dec. 3.50fl. ☎ (046) 451 34 60. www.hetdomein.nl

St.-Amelbergakerk – Open May to Oct, Tues and Sun, 2-5pm. ☎ (046) 449 46 15 (VVV).

Treasury – Open June to Sept, Sun, 2-5pm. 2.50fl. ☎ (046) 449 46 15 (VVV).

MARKEN

Marker Museum – ♿ Open Easter Day to Oct, Mon-Sat, 10am-5pm, Sun, noon-4pm. Closed Nov to Easter Day. 4fl. ☎ (0299) 60 19 04.

MEDEMBLIK
🛈 Dam 2 – 1671 AW – ☎/fax (0227) 54 28 52

Bakkerijmuseum – Open Apr to Oct, Tues-Sun (daily during school holidays), noon-5pm; mid-Feb to Mar and Nov to Dec, Sat-Sun, noon-5pm. 5fl. ☎ (0227) 54 50 14.

Kasteel Radboud – Open mid-May to mid-Sept, daily, 10am-5pm; the rest of the year, Sun, public holidays and school holidays, 2-5pm. Closed 1 Jan and 25 Dec. 5fl. ☎ (0227) 54 19 60.

Nederlands Stoommachinemuseum – Open Apr to Oct, Tues-Sun, 10am-5pm. The machines operate Sat-Sun. Closed Mon and Nov to Mar. 8fl. ☎ (0227) 54 47 32. www.stoommachinemuseum.nl

MIDDELBURG
🛈 Nieuwe Burg 40– 4331 AH – ☎ (0118) 65 99 00 fax (0118) 65 99 40– www.vvvmiddelburg.nl

Stadhuis – By guided tour only: Apr to Oct, Mon-Sat, 11am-5pm, Sun, noon-5pm; Nov to Mar, Sat-Sun at 1.30pm and 2.45pm. 6fl. ☎ (0118) 65 99 00.

Vleeshal – Open Tues-Sun, 1-5pm. ☎ (0118) 67 55 23. www.vleeshal.nl

Zeeuws Museum – Open Mon-Sat, 11am-5pm, Sun, noon-5pm. Closed 1 Jan and 25 Dec. 10fl. ☎ (0118) 62 66 55. www.zeeuwsmuseum.nl

Historama Abdij Middelburg – Open Apr to Oct, Mon-Sat, 11am-5pm, Sun, noon-5pm. Closed Nov to Mar. 6fl (including entry to Lange Jan). ☎ (0118) 62 66 55 (Zeeuws Museum).

Abbey churches – Open May to Sept, Mon-Fri, 10am-5pm. ☎ (0118) 62 66 55 (Zeeuws Museum).

Lange Jan – Open Apr to Oct, Mon-Sat, 11am-5pm, Sun, noon-5pm. Closed Nov to Mar. 6fl (including entry to Historama). ☎ (0118) 62 66 55 (Zeeuws Museum).

Miniatuur Walcheren – ♿ Open Apr to Oct, daily, 10am (9am July to Aug)-6pm. Closed Nov to Mar. 12.50fl. ☎ (0118) 61 25 25.

N

NAARDEN 🛈 Adr. Dorstmanplein 1b, 1411 RC – ☎ (035) 694 28 36
fax (035) 694 34 24

Stadhuis – Open Apr to Sept, Mon-Sat, 1.30-4.30pm. Closed Sun and public holidays, and Oct to Mar. ☎ (035) 695 78 11.

Grote Kerk – Same opening times as Comenius Museum.

Comenius Museum – Open Apr to Oct, Tues-Sat, 10am-5pm, Sun and public holidays, noon-5pm; Nov to Mar, Tues-Sun, 1-4pm. Closed Mon, 1 Jan, 25 and 31 Dec. 4.50fl. ☎ (035) 694 30 45.

Nederlands Vestingmuseum – ♿ Open Mar to mid-June and Sept to Oct, Tues-Fri, 10.30am-5pm, Sat-Sun, noon-5pm; mid-June to Aug, Mon-Fri, 10.30am-5pm, Sat-Sun, noon-5pm; Nov to Feb, Sun, noon-5pm; Christmas period, Tues-Fri, 10.30am-5pm, Sat-Sun and public holidays, noon-5pm. Closed 1 Jan, 25 and 31 Dec. 10fl. ☎ (035) 694 54 59. www.vestingmuseum.nl

NIJMEGEN 🛈 Keizer Karelplein 2 – 6511 NC – ☎ (0900) 112 23 44
fax (024) 329 78 79 – www.vvvnijmegen.nl

Boat trips – Operate July and Aug only. Information: Rederij Tonissen, ☎ (024) 323 32 85.

St.-Stevenskerk – *Open mid-June to Aug, Tues-Sat, noon-6pm. Closed Sept to mid-June. 1fl. ☎ (024) 3292607.*

Museum Brouwerij De Hemel – Open Tues-Sun from 12.20pm. Guided tours at 2pm and 4pm. Closed Mon. No charge for entry; guided tour 9fl. ☎ (024) 360 61 67.

Stadhuis – Guided tours by prior arrangement (2 weeks prior to visit) only, Mon-Sat. ☎ (024) 329 23 72.

Museum Het Valkhof – Open Tues-Fri, 10am-5pm, Sat-Sun and public holidays, noon-5pm. Closed Mon and 25 Dec. 7.50fl. ☎ (024) 360 88 05. www.museumhetvalkhof.nl

Nationaal Fietsmuseum Velorama – Open Mon-Sat, 10am-5pm, Sun and public holidays, 11am-5pm. Closed 1 Jan and 25 Dec. 6fl. ☎ (024) 322 58 51 www.velorama.nl

Museum De Stratemakerstoren – Open Tues-Fri, 10am-5pm, Sat-Sun, 1-5pm. Closed Mon. 6fl. ☎ (024) 323 86 90.

Natuurmuseum Nijmegen – Open Mon-Fri, 10am-5pm, Sun, 1-5pm. Closed Sat, 1 Jan, Easter, 30 Apr, the Friday of the Vierdaagse and 25 Dec. 4fl. ☎ (024) 329 70 70.

Bijbels Openluchtmuseum – Open mid-Mar to Oct, daily, 9am-5.30pm. Closed Nov to mid-Mar. 3.50fl. ☎ (024) 382 31 10.

Afrika Museum – Open Apr to Oct, Mon-Fri, 10am-5pm, Sat-Sun and public holidays, 11am-5pm; Nov to Mar, Tues-Fri, 10am-5pm, Sat-Sun and public holidays, 1-5pm. Closed 1 Jan and 25 Dec. 12.50fl. ☎ (024) 684 20 44. www.afrikamuseum.nl

Nationaal Bevrijdingsmuseum 1944-1945 – Open Mon-Sat, 10am-5pm, Sun and public holidays, noon-5pm. Closed 1 Jan and 25 Dec. 10fl. ☎ (024) 397 44 04.

NOORDOOSTPOLDER

Emmeloord: Water tower – Information from Emmeloord tourist office, ☎ (0527) 61 20 00.

Schokland: Museum Schokland – ♿ Open Apr to Oct, Tues-Sun, 11am-5pm (also Mon July and Aug); Nov to Mar, Sat-Sun, 11am-5pm. Closed Mon, 1 Jan and 25 Dec. 5fl. ☎ (0527) 25 13 96.

Urk: Ferry to Enkhuizen – Operates late June to early Sept, Mon-Sat, three times a day. Crossing takes 105 min. Information: ☎ (0527) 68 34 07.

R

ROERMOND 🛈 Kraanpoort 1 – 6041 EG – ☎ (0900) 202 55 88 –fax (0475) 33 50 68
www.roermond.com/toerisme/vvv

Onze Lieve Vrouwe Munsterkerk – Open Apr to Oct, daily, 2-5pm. ☎ (0900) 202 55 88 (VVV).

Kathedrale kerk – Open Apr to Oct, daily, 2-5pm. ☎ (0900) 202 55 88 (VVV).

Thorn: Abdijkerk – Open Apr to Oct, Mon-Fri, 10am-5pm, Sat, 10am-4pm, Sun, 11.30am-5pm; Nov to Mar, Sat-Sun, 1-4pm. 2.50fl. ☎ (0475) 56 19 62.

ROTTERDAM

Grote Kerk or St.-Laurenskerk – Open summer, Tues-Sat, 10am-4pm; winter, Thur, noon-2pm. Closed Sun and Mon. No charge. ☎ (010) 413 19 89.

Historisch Museum Het Schielandshuis – Open Tues-Fri, 10am-5pm, Sat-Sun and public holidays, 11am-5pm. Closed Mon, 1 Jan, 30 Apr and 25 Dec. 6fl. ☎ (010) 217 67 67. www.hmr.rotterdam.nl

City Informatiecentrum – Open Mon-Frid, 10am-6pm, Sat, 11am-5pm. Closed Sun and public holidays. No charge. ☎ (010) 413 40 11. www.cic.rotterdam.nl

Witte de With – Open Tues-Sun, 11am-6pm. Closed Mon, 1 Jan, Easter, Whitsun, 30 Apr and 25 Dec. 5fl. ☎ (010) 411 01 44. www.wdw.nl

Nederlands Foto Instituut – Open Tues-Sun, 11am-5pm. Closed Mon, 1 Jan, 30 Apr and 25 Dec. 5fl. ☎ (010) 213 20 11. www.nfi.2v.nl

Museum Boijmans Van Beuningen – Open Tues-Sat, 10am-5pm, Sun and public holidays, 11am-5pm. Closed Mon, 1 Jan, 30 Apr and 25 Dec. 10fl. Partially closed for rebuilding work until late 2002. Information: ☎ (010) 441 94 00. www.boijmans.rotterdam.nl

Nederlands Architectuurinstituut – Open Tues, 10am-9pm, Wed-Sat, 10am-5pm, Sun and public holidays, 11am-5pm. Closed Mon, 1 Jan, 30 Apr and 25 Dec. 7.50fl. ☎ (010) 440 12 00. www.nai.nl

Chabot Museum – Open Tues-Fri, 11am-4.30pm, Sat, 11am-5pm, Sun, noon-5pm. Closed Mon and public holidays. 6.50fl. ☎ (010) 436 37 13. www.chabotmuseum.nl

Kunsthal – Open Tues-Sat, 10am-5pm, Sun and public holidays, 11am-5pm. Closed Mon, 1 Jan, 30 Apr and 25 Dec. 15fl. ☎ (010) 440 03 00. www.kunsthal.nl

Natuurmuseum – Open Tues-Sat, 10am-5pm, Sun, 11am-5pm. Closed Mon, 1 Jan, 30 Apr and 25 Dec. 5fl. ☎ (010) 436 42 22. www.nmr.nl

Maritiem Museum Rotterdam – Open Tues-Sat, 10am-5pm, Sun and public holidays, 11am-5pm; July and Aug also Mon, 10am-5pm. Closed Mon (except July and Aug), 1 Jan, 30 Apr and 25 Dec. 7.50fl. ☎ (010) 413 26 80. www.mmph.nl

Maritiem Buitenmuseum – Open Mon-Fri, 10am-4.30pm, Sat-Sun, 11am-4.30pm. Closed 1 Jan, 30 Apr and 25 Dec. No charge. ☎ (010) 404 80 72. www.buitenmuseum.nl

Cube apartment – Open Mar to Dec, daily, 11am-5pm; Jan and Feb, Fri-Sun, 11am-5pm. 3.50fl. ☎ (010) 414 22 85.

Mariniersmuseum – Open Tues-Sat, 10am-5pm, Sun and public holidays, 11am-5pm. Closed Mon, 1 Jan, Easter, Whitsun, 30 Apr and 25 Dec. 6fl. ☎ (010) 412 96 00.

Zakkendragershuisje – Open Tues-Sat, 10am-5pm, Sun and public holidays, 1-5pm. Closed Mon, 1 Jan, 30 Apr and 25 Dec. No charge. ☎ (010) 477 26 64. www.hmr.rotterdam.nl

Museum De Dubbelde Palmboom – Open Tues-Fri, 10am-5pm, Sat-Sun and public holidays, 11am-5pm. Closed Mon, 1 Jan, 30 Apr and 25 Dec. 6fl. ☎ (010) 476 15 33. www.hmr.rotterdam.nl

Kop van Zuid Information Centre – Open Mon-Fri, 10am-5pm, Sat, noon-5pm. Closed Sun and public holidays. No charge. ☎ (010) 213 01 01. www.kopvanzuid.rotterdam.nl

Euromast – Open Apr to Sept, daily, 10am-7pm; July and Aug, Sun-Mon, 10am-7pm, Tues-Sat, 10am-10.30pm; Oct to Dec and Mar, daily, 10am-5pm; Jan and Feb, Sat-Sun, 10am-5pm 15.50fl. ☎ (010) 436 48 11. www.euromast.nl

Wereldmuseum – Open Tues-Fri, 10am-5pm, Sat-Sun and public holidays, 11am-5pm. Closed Mon. 7.50fl. ☎ (010) 270 71 72. www.wereldmuseum.rotterdam.nl

Belasting & Douane Museum – ⅙ Open Tues-Sun, 11am-5pm. Closed Mon, 1 Jan, Easter, 30 Apr, Whitsun and 25 Dec. No charge. ☎ (010) 436 56 29. www.belastingsdienst.nl/bdmuseum.

Nationaal Schoolmuseum – Open Tues-Sat, 10am-5pm, Sun, 1-5pm. Closed Mon and public holidays. 3.50fl. ☎ (010) 404 54 25. www.schoolmuseum.nl

Diergaarde Blijdorp – Open summer, daily, 9am-6pm; winter, daily, 9am-5pm. 27.50fl. ☎ (010) 443 14 95. www.diergaardeblijdorp.nl

Arboretum Trompenburg – ⅙ Open Apr to Oct, Mon-Fri, 9am-5pm, Sat-Sun, 10am-4pm; Nov to Mar, Mon-Fri, 9am-5pm, Sat, 10am-4pm. 5fl. ☎ (010) 233 01 66. www.trompenburg.nl

Short harbour tour (1hr 15min) – Tours Apr to Sept, daily, 9.30am-5pm; Mar and Oct, daily, 10am-4pm; Nov to Feb, daily, 11am-3.30pm. 15.50fl. ☎ (010) 275 99 88. www.spido.nl

Longer tour of the port (2hr 15min) – Tours June to Aug, daily, at 11am and 2pm. 25fl. ☎ (010) 275 99 88. www.spido.nl

Europoort tour (6hr 30min) – Tours July and Aug, Tues, at 10.30am. 40fl. ☎ (010) 275 99 88.

Excursions

Keringhuis – Open Mon-Fri, 10am-4pm, Sat-Sun and public holidays from 11am-5pm. No charge. ☎ (0174) 51 12 22. www.minvenw.nl/rws/projects/svk

Kinderdijk windmills – Open Apr to Sept, daily, 9.30am-5.30pm. Closed Oct to Mar. 3.50fl. ☎ (078) 691 51 79. www.kinderdijk.net

Kinderdijk Boat tour – Operates May to Sept, daily, 10am-5pm. Information from Rederij J.C. Vos & Zoon, ☎ (0180) 51 21 74.

S

SCHIEDAM
🛈 Buitenhavenweg 9 - 3113 BC - ☎ (010) 473 30 00
fax (010) 473 66 95

Stedelijk Museum – ♿ Open Tues-Sat, 11am-5pm, Sun and public holidays, 12.30-5pm. Closed Mon, 1 Jan and 25 Dec. 3fl. ☎ (010) 246 36 66.

Nederlands Gedistilleerd Museum De Gekroonde Brandersketel – Open Tues-Sat, 11am-5pm, Sun and public holidays, 12.30-5pm. Closed Mon, 1 Jan and 25 Dec. 8.50fl (includes tasting). ☎ (010) 426 12 91.

Nederlands Malend Korenmolenmuseum De Nieuwe Palmboom – Open Tues-Sat, 11am-5pm, Sun and public holidays, 12.30-5pm. Closed Mon, 1 Jan and 25 Dec. 4.50fl. ☎ (010) 426 76 75.

SLUIS
🛈 St-Annastraat 15 - 4524 JB - ☎ (0117) 46 17 00 - fax (0117) 46 26 84

Stadhuis – *Open May to Oct, Sun, 2-5pm; also Whit Sunday and Ascension Day, 2-5pm; July and Aug, daily, 1-5pm. Closed Nov to Apr. 2.50fl. ☎ (0117) 46 17 00 (VVV).*

Excursions

Ijzendijke: Streekmuseum West-Zeeuws-Vlaanderen – Open Tues-Sat, 1-5pm; mid-May to early Oct, also open Sun, 1-5pm. Closed Mon and public holidays. 2fl. ☎ (0117) 30 12 00.

Breskens-Vlissingen ferry – Leaves daily every 30min, Sun every 1hr. Further information: ☎ (0118) 46 59 05.

SNEEK
🛈 Marktstraat 18 - 8601 CV - ☎ (0515) 41 40 96 - fax (0515) 42 37 03
www.friesland-vvv.net

Stadhuis – By guided tour only (30min): early July to early Aug, Mon-Fri, 2-4pm. ☎ (0515) 48 53 71.

Fries Scheepvaart Museum/Sneker Oudheidkamer – Open Mon-Sat, 10am-5pm, Sun, noon-5pm. Closed public holidays. 4fl. ☎ (0515) 41 40 57. www.friesscheepvaartmuseum.nl

Excursions

Oranjewoud and Oranjestein – Open occasional Sat-Sun in July and Aug. Information from the tourist office, ☎ (0513) 62 55 55.

Fries Landbouwmuseum – Open Apr to Oct, daily, 10am-5pm. Closed Nov to Mar. 3fl. ☎ (0515) 57 59 95. www.frieslandbouwmuseum.nl

Friesland farmhouse – Open Apr to Oct, daily, 10am-5pm. 7.50fl. ☎ (0515) 23 16 31. www.aldfaerserf.nl

Fries Aardewerkmuseum "De Waag" – Open Nov to Apr, Mon-Fri, 10am-noon and 1-4pm; May, Mon-Sat, 10am-4pm, Sun and public holidays, 1.30-5pm; June and Sept, Mon-Sat, 10am-5pm, Sun and public holidays, 1.30-5pm; July and Aug, Mon-Sat, 10am-5.30pm, Sun and public holidays, 1.30-5pm; Oct, Mon-Sat, 10am-noon and 1-4pm. Closed 1 Jan, 25 and 26 Dec. 3fl. ☎ (0515) 23 14 22.

Tichelaars Aardwewerk- en Tegelfabriek – Open Mon-Fri, 9am-5.30pm, Sat, 10am-5pm. Guided tours every weekday at 11am, 1.30pm and 3pm. Closed Sun, 1 Jan, 25 and 26 Dec. 4fl. ☎ (0515) 23 13 41. www.tichelaar.nl

Ferwoude: Workshop – Open Apr to Oct, daily, 10am-5pm. 3.50fl. ☎ (0515) 23 16 31. www.aldfaerserf.nl

Museum Joure – Open May to Oct, Mon-Fri, 10am-5pm, Sat-Sun, 2-5pm; Nov to Apr, Mon-Fri, 10am-5pm, Sun, 2-5pm. Closed 1 Jan, Easter Day, Whitsun, last Thur in Sept, 25 Dec and 31 Dec. 4fl. ☎ (0513) 41 22 83. www.museumjoure.cybercomm.nl

STADSKANAAL

Excursion

Museum-Klooster Ter Apel – Open Apr to Oct, Mon-Sat, 10am-5pm, Sun, 1-5pm; Nov to Mar, Tues-Sat, 10am-5pm, Sun, 1-5pm. Closed Mon from Nov to Mar. 5.50fl. ☎ (0599) 58 13 70.

STAPHORST

Working farm – Open Apr to Oct, Mon-Sat, 10am-5pm. Closed Sun and public holidays. 3fl. ☎ (0522) 46 25 26.

Museum – Open June to Sept, Mon-Fri, 10am-5pm, Sat, 10am-noon. Closed Sun and public holidays. 2.50fl. ☎ (0522) 46 10 87.

T

TIEL

Excursions

Museum der Koninklijke Marechaussee – Open May to Sept, Tues-Fri, 10am-4.30pm, Sat-Sun and public holidays, 1.30-5pm. Closed Oct to Apr, Mon. 4.50fl. ☎ (0344) 57 12 56.

Boerenwagenmuseum – Open late Apr to Oct, Tues-Sun, 1-4.30pm. Closed Mon and Oct to late Apr. 4.50fl. ☎ (0344) 57 14 31.

TILBURG   🅱 Stadhuisplein 132 – 5038 TC – ☎ (0900) 202 08 15 – fax (013) 542 80 15
www.tilburg.nl/vvv

Noordbrabants Natuurmuseum – ♿ Open Tues-Fri, 10am-5pm, Sat-Sun, 1-5pm. Closed Mon, 1 Jan, Easter Day, 30 Apr and 25 Dec. 7fl. ☎ (013) 535 39 35 www.nbnm-mec.nl

Scryption – ♿ Open Tues-Fri, 10am-5pm, Sat-Sun, 1-5pm. Closed Mon, 1 Jan, Easter, 30 Apr, Whitsun and 25 Dec. 6fl. ☎ (013) 580 08 21.

De Pont – ♿ Open daily (except Mon), 11am-5pm. Closed Mon. 8fl. ☎ (013) 543 83 00. www.depont.nl

Nederlands Textielmuseum – ♿ Open Tues-Fri, 10am-5pm, Sat-Sun, noon-5pm. Closed Mon and public holidays. 7.50fl. ☎ (013) 542 22 41. www.textielmuseum.nl

Excursions

Safari Beekse Bergen – Open Jan and Dec, daily, 10am-4pm; Feb, Oct and Nov, daily, 10am-4.30pm; Mar to June and Sept, daily, 10am-5pm; July and Aug, daily, 10am-6pm. 23.50fl. ☎ (013) 536 00 35.

U

UTRECHT   🅱 Vredenburg 90 – 3511 BD – ☎ (0900) 414 14 14
fax (030) 233 14 17 – www.tref.nl/utrecht/VVV

Museum voor het Kruideniersbedrijf – Open Tues-Sat, 12.30-4.30pm. Closed Sun, Mon and public holidays. ☎ (030) 231 66 28.

Domtoren – By guided tour only (1hr): Mon-Sat, 10am-4pm, Sun, noon-4pm. Tickets from RonDom, Domplein 9. Closed 25, 26, 30 and 31 Dec. 5.50fl. ☎ (030) 233 30 36.

Domkerk – Open May to Sept, Mon-Fri, 10am-5pm, Sat, 10am-3.30pm, Sun, 2-4pm; Oct to Apr, daily, 11am-4pm. ☎ (030) 231 04 03.

X. Richer/HOA OUI

Pieterskerk – *Open July to the second Saturday in Sept, Tues-Fri, 11am-4pm, Sat, noon-4.30pm; the rest of the year, every first and third Saturday of the month, 11am-3pm.* ☎ *(030) 231 14 85.*

Nationaal Museum van Speelklok tot Pierement – ♿ Open Tues-Sat, 10am-5pm, Sun and public holidays, noon-5pm. Closed Mon, 1 Jan, 30 Apr and 25 Dec. 12fl. ☎ (030) 231 27 89. www.museumspeelklok.nl

Aboriginal Art Museum – For admission times and charges visit. www.aboriginalartmuseumutrecht.nl or phone ☎ (030) 238 01 00.

Museum Catharijneconvent – ♿ Open Tues-Fri, 10am-5pm, Sat-Sun and public holidays, 11am-5pm. Closed Mon and 1 Jan. 15fl. ☎ (030) 231 72 96. www.catharijneconvent.nl

Universiteitsmuseum – Open Tues-Sun, 11am-5pm. Closed Mon, 1 Jan, 30 Apr, 24, 25 and 31 Dec. 7.50fl. ☎ (030) 253 80 08. www.museum.uu.nl.

Centraal Museum – Open Tues-Sun, 11am-5pm. Closed Mon, 1 Jan, 30 Apr and 25 Dec. 15fl. ☎ (030) 236 23 62. www.centraalmuseum.nl.

Nederlands Spoorwegmuseum – ♿ Open Tues-Fri, 10am-5pm, Sat-Sun, Easter Monday, Whit Monday and 26 Dec, 11.30am-5pm. Closed Mon, 1 Jan, 30 Apr, Easter Day, Whit Sunday and 25 Dec. 15fl. ☎ (030) 230 62 06. www.spoorwegmuseum.nl

Waterleidingmuseum – Open Tues-Fri and Sun, 1.30-5pm, Sat 11am-4pm. Closed Mon and public holidays. 2.50fl. ☎ (030) 248 72 11.

Moluks Historisch Museum – Open daily (except Mon), 1-5pm. Closed Mon, 1 Jan, Easter Day, 25 Apr and 25 Dec. 4.50fl. ☎ (030) 236 71 16. www.museum-maluku.nl

Rietveld Schröderhuis – By guided tour only (1hr): Wed-Sat, 11am-3.30pm, Sun and public holidays, 12.30-3.30pm. Closed Mon, Tues, 1 Jan, 30 Apr and 25 Dec. 15fl. Reservations: ☎ (030) 236 23 10 (Centraal Museum). www.centraalmuseum.nl

Excursions

Kasteel-Museum Sypesteyn – By guided tour only (1hr): Apr and Oct, Sat-Sun and public holidays, noon-5pm; May to Sept, Tues-Fri, 10am-5pm, Sat-Sun and public holidays, noon-5pm. Closed Mon and Nov to Mar. 10fl. ☎ (035) 582 32 08. www.sypesteyn.nl

Kasteel De Haar – Guided tours only (hourly): mid-Mar to May and mid-Oct to mid-Nov, Tues-Sun, 1-4pm; June to mid-Aug, Mon-Fri, 11am-4pm, Sat-Sun, 1-4pm; mid- to end Nov and Jan to mid-Mar, Sun, 1-4pm. Closed mid-Aug to mid-Oct and Dec. 15fl. ☎ (030) 677 38 04. www.kasteelhaarzuilens.nl

Slot Zuylen – By guided tour only (1hr): mid-Mar to mid-May and mid-Sept to mid-Nov, Sat, 2-4pm, Sun, 1-4pm; mid-May to mid-Sept, Tues-Thur, 11am-4pm, Sat, 2-4pm, Sun, 1-4pm. 8.50fl. ☎ (030) 244 02 55. www.slotzuylen.com

V

VALKENBURG AAN DE GEUL

Th. Dorrenplein 5 - 6301 DV
☎ (0900) 97 98 - fax (043) 609 86 08
www.vvvzuidlimburg.nl

Castle ruins – Open daily, 10.30am-4pm (6pm July and Aug). Closed 1 Jan, carnival and 25 and 26 Dec. 5fl. ☎ (043) 609 01 10.

Fluweelengrot – By guided tour only (1hr): Jan to Easter, Mon-Fri at noon and 1.30pm, Sat-Sun and during school holidays, 11am-3pm; Easter to June, Sept and Oct, daily, 11am-4pm; July and Aug, daily, 11am-5pm; Nov and Dec, Sat-Sun, 11am-3pm. Closed 1 Jan, carnival and 25 and 26 Dec. 9fl. ☎ (043) 609 01 10.

Steenkolenmijn Valkenburg – Open Apr to Oct, daily, 10am-5pm; Nov, daily, 1-3pm; Dec to Mar, Sat-Sun and school holidays, 1-3pm. Closed 1 Jan, carnival and 25 Dec. 11.25fl. ☎ (043) 601 24 91.

Gemeentegrot – By guided tour only, on foot (1hr) or by miniature train (30min): daily, 10am-4pm. Closed 1 Jan and 25 and 26 Dec. 5.25fl (on foot), 6.75fl (train). ☎ (043) 601 22 71.

Roman catacombs – By guided tour only (50min): Apr to Sept and school holidays, daily, 10am-5pm; Oct to Mar, Sat-Sun at 2pm. Closed Nov to Mar (except Sat-Sun). 7.50fl. ☎ (043) 601 25 54.

Streekmuseum – Open daily (except Mon), 10am-5pm. Closed Mon, 1 Jan, Easter Day and 25 Dec. 3.50fl. ☎ (043) 601 63 94.

VEERE

Oudestraat 28 - 4351 AV - ☎ (0118) 50 13 65 - fax (0118) 50 17 92

Schotse Huizen – Open Apr to Oct, Tues-Sat, noon-5pm, Sun, 1-5pm. Closed Mon, 30 Apr and Ascension Day. 5fl. ☎ (0118) 50 17 44.

Oude Stadhuis – Open June to Aug, Mon-Sat, 1-5pm. Closed Sun and during weddings. 2fl. ☎ (0118) 50 60 64.

Grote Kerk or Onze Lieve Vrouwekerk – Open Apr to Oct, Mon-Sat, 10am-5pm, Sun, 1-5pm. Closed Nov to Mar. 5fl. ☎ (0118) 50 18 29.

VENLO

Koninginneplein 2 - 5911 KK - ☎ (077) 354 38 00
fax (077) 320 77 70

St.-Martinuskerk – Open daily, 9am-noon and 2-4pm. ☎ (077) 351 24 39.

Limburgs Museum – Open Tues-Sun, 11am-5pm. Closed Mon, 1 Jan, carnival and 25 Dec. 9fl. ☎ (077) 352 21 12. www.limburgsmuseum.nl

Museum Van Bommel-Van Dam – Open Tues-Fri, 10am-4.30pm, Sat-Sun, 2-5pm. Closed Mon and public holidays. 3.50fl. ☎ (077) 351 34 57.

Excursion

Missiemuseum Steyl – Open late Mar to late Oct, Tues-Sat, 10am-5pm, Sun and public holidays, 1-5pm; Nov to late Mar, daily (except Mon), 1-5pm. Closed Mon, 1 Jan, Good Friday and 25 Dec. 5fl. ☎ (077) 326 14 99.

Botanische tuin Jochum-Hof – Open Easter to Oct, daily, 11am-5pm. Closed Nov to Easter. 5fl. ☎ (077) 373 30 20.

Arcen Castle gardens – Open Apr to Sept, daily, 10am-6pm; Oct, daily, 11am-5pm; Christmas period, daily, 11am-6pm. Closed from Nov to the Christmas period, and from Jan to Mar. 19.50fl. ☎ (077) 473 18 82. www.kasteeltuinen.nl

VENRAY

Henseniusplein 13 - 5801 BB - ☎ (0478) 51 05 05 - fax (0478) 51 27 36

St.-Petrus Bandenkerk – Open Apr to Oct, daily (except Sun), 2-4pm. ☎ (0478) 51 05 05 (VVV).

Excursion

Nationaal Oorlogs- en Verzetsmuseum – ♿ Open June to Aug, daily, 9.30am-6pm; Sept to May; daily, 10am-5pm. Closed 1 Jan, 24, 25 and 31 Dec. 12.50fl. ☎ (0478) 64 18 20. www.oorlogsmuseum-overloon.nl

VLISSINGEN   🅵 Oude Markt 3 - 4381 ER - ☎ (0118) 42 21 90 - fax (0118) 42 21 91

Boat trips – Operate July and Aug. Information from the tourist office, ☎ (0118) 42 21 90.

Maritiem Attractiecentrum Het Arsenaal – ♿ Open Mar to May, Tues-Sun, 10am-7pm; June to Sept and during school holidays, daily, 10am-8pm; Oct to Dec, Tues-Sun, 10am-7pm. Closed Jan, Feb and 25 Dec and 31 Dec. 17.50fl. ☎ (0118) 41 54 00. www.arsenaal.com

Stedelijk Museum – Open Mon-Fri, 10am-5pm, Sat-Sun and public holidays, 1-5pm. Closed 1 Jan, 25 and 26 Dec. No charge. ☎ (0118) 41 24 98. www.lampsinshuis.com

Reptielenzoo Iguana – Open June to Sept, Tues-Sat, 10am-12.30pm and 2-5.30pm; Oct to May, daily, 2-5.30pm. Closed 1 Jan and 25 Dec. 9.50fl. ☎ (0118) 41 72 19.

Excursion

Fort Rammekens – Open Apr to Oct, Tues-Sun, 1-5pm. Closed Mon and Nov to Mar. 2.50fl. ☎ (0118) 41 24 98 (Stedelijk Museum). www.lampsinshuis.com

VOLENDAM   🅵 Zeestraat 37 - 1131 ZD - ☎ (0299) 36 37 47 - fax (0299) 36 84 84

Volendams Museum – ♿ Open Easter to autumn half-term, daily, 10am-5pm. 3.50fl. ☎ (0299) 36 92 58. www.volendam.com/museum

W

De WADDENEILANDEN

Guided walks across the mudflats – Early Apr to late Oct (weather permitting). Information and bookings: Stichting Wadloopcentrum Pieterburen, PB 1, 9968 ZG Pieterburen, ☎ (0595) 52 83 00, or Dijkstra's Wadlooptochten, Hoofdstraat 118, 9968 AH Pieterburen, ☎ (0595) 52 83 45.

Ameland

Ferry – From Holwerd. Departure times vary. Call the Wagenborg Passagiersdiensten recorded information on ☎ (0519) 542001 or www.wpd.nl. Crossing lasts about 45min. Reservations and other information: ☎ (0519) 54 61 11. 20.50fl (return), 138.80fl (car).

Natuurcentrum Ameland (Nes) – ♿ Open Jan to Mar and autumn half-term to the Christmas holidays, Wed-Sat, 1-5pm (spring half-term: Mon-Fri, 10am-noon and 1-5pm, Sat 1-5pm); Apr to June and Sept to autumn half-term, daily, 10am-noon and 1-5pm (Sat-Sun, 1-5pm only); July and Aug, daily, 10am-5pm and 7-9pm (except Sat-Sun); Christmas holidays, daily, 10am-noon and 1-5pm (Sat-Sun and public holidays, 1-5pm only). 4.25fl. ☎ (0519) 54 27 37.

Landbouw en Juttersmuseum Swartwoude (Buren) – Open mid-Nov to Mar, Wed-Sat, 1.30-5pm; Apr to June, Mon-Fri, 10am-noon and 1-5pm, Sat-Sun, 1.30-5pm; July and Aug, daily, 10am-5pm, Wed also 7-9pm; Sept to mid-Nov, Mon-Fri, 10am-noon and 1-5pm, Sat-Sun, 1.30-5pm. 4fl. ☎ (0519) 54 28 45.

Cultuur-Historisch Museum Sorgdrager (Hollum) – Open Nov to Mar, Wed-Sat, 1.30-5pm; Apr to June and Sept to Oct, Mon-Fri, 10am-noon and 1-5pm, Sat-Sun, 1.30-5pm; July and Aug, daily, 10am-5pm; Christmas and Easter holidays, Mon-Fri, 10am-noon and 1-5pm, Sat-Sun, 1.30-5pm. 4fl. ☎ (0519) 55 44 77.

Reddingsmuseum Abraham Fock (Hollum) – ♿ Open Jan to Mar and Nov to Dec, Mon-Fri, 1.30-5pm; Apr to June and Sept to Oct, open daily from 10am to noon and 1.30pm to 5pm (Sat-Sun 1.30pm to 5pm only). Closed public holidays. 3.50fl. ☎ (0519) 55 42 43.

Ameland Lifeboat (Hollum) – Demonstrations are given eight to ten times a year. Contact the museum for information. ☎ (0519) 55 42 43.

Schiermonnikoog

Ferry – From Lauwersoog. Departure times vary. Call the Wagenborg Passagiersdiensten recorded information line on ☎ (0519) 349079 or www.wpd.nl. The crossing takes about 45min and cars are not allowed on the island. Reservations and other information, ☎ (0519) 54 61 11. 21.70fl (return/round trip).

Visitor Centre – Open Apr to autumn half-term and during the Christmas holidays, Mon-Sat, 10am-noon and 1.30-5.30pm; rest of the year, Sat, 1.30-5.30pm. 1fl. ☎ (0519) 53 16 41. www.waterland.net/npschierm

Terschelling

Ferry – From Harlingen. Departure times vary. Call the Rederij Doeksen recorded information line on ☎ (0562) 44 27 70 (ferry) or ☎ (0562) 44 32 20 (express service). The ferry crossing takes about 1hr 30min and the express service 45min. Reservations and other information: ☎ (0562) 44 61 11; www.rederij-doeksen.nl. 42.25fl (return/round trip), 22.90fl (car).

Terschelling Museum 't Behouden Huys (West-Terschelling) – Open Jan to Mar, Wed and Sat, 1-5pm; Apr to mid-June, Mon-Fri, 10am-5pm; mid- to late-June and Sept, Mon-Fri, 10am-5pm, Sat, 1-5pm; July and Aug, Mon-Fri, 10am-5pm, Sat-Sun, 1-5pm; Oct and during school holidays, Mon-Fri, 10am-5pm. 6fl. ☎ (0562) 44 23 89.

Centrum voor natuur en landschap (West-Terschelling) – ᵬ Open Apr to Oct, Mon-Fri, 9am-5pm, Sat-Sun, public holidays and school holidays, 2-5pm. Closed Nov to Mar, 1 Jan, Easter, Whitsun and 25 Dec. 8.50fl. ☎ (0562) 44 23 90.

De Boschplaat – Open (limited access) mid-Mar to mid-Aug. Motor vehicles not allowed. Haycart tours: contact the tourist office, Willem Barentszkade 19a, ☎ (0562) 44 30 00.

Texel

Ferry – From Den Helder. Departure times vary. Call the TESO recorded information line on ☎ (0222) 36 96 91 or www.teso.nl The crossing takes about 20min; reservations not accepted. For more information, ☎ (0222) 36 96 92. 10fl (return), 48.50fl (car).

Nature reserves – For guided tours contact EcoMare or the tourist office. Boots and binoculars recommended. Limited access during nesting season.

EcoMare (De Koog) – Open daily, 9am-5pm. Closed 1 Jan and 25 Dec. 12.50fl. ☎ (0222) 31 77 41.

Oudheidkamer (Den Burg) – Open Apr to Oct and during Christmas holidays, Mon-Fri, 10am-12.30pm and 1.30-3.30pm. 3.50fl. ☎ (0222) 31 31 35.

Maritiem en Jutters Museum (Oudeschild) – Open Tues-Sun, 10am-5pm; July and Aug, daily, 10am-5pm. Closed 1 Jan and 25 Dec. 8fl. ☎ (0222) 31 49 56.

Agrarisch en Wagenmuseum (De Waal) – Open Easter to autumn half-term, Mon, 1.30-5pm, Tues-Fri, 10am-5pm, Sat, 10am-4pm, Sun and public holidays, 2-4pm. Closed from after autumn half-term until Easter. 5fl. ☎ (0222) 31 29 51.

Vlieland

Ferry – From Harlingen or Terschelling (May to Sept only, 30min). Departure times vary. Call the Rederij Doeksen recorded information line on ☎ (0562) 44 29 69 (ferry boat) or ☎ (0562) 44 32 20 (express service). The ferry boat crossing takes about 1hr 30min, and the express service about 45min. Cars are not allowed on the island. Reservations and other information: ☎ (0562) 44 61 11. 38.80fl (return).

Museum Tromp's Huys – Open Apr and Oct, Tues-Sun, 2-5pm; May-Sept, Tues-Sun, 11am-5pm; Nov to Mar, Wed and Sat, 2-5pm. Closed 1 Jan, Easter, Whitsun and 25 Dec. 5fl. ☎ (0562) 45 16 00.

De Noordwester – ᵬ Open Apr to Sept, daily (except Sun), 2-5pm; June, July and Aug, daily (except Sun), 10am-noon and 2-5pm; Oct to Mar, Wed and Sat-Sun, 2-5pm. 5fl. Closed 1 Jan and 25 Dec. ☎ (0562) 45 17 00.

WORKUM   🄱 Noard 5 - 8711 AA – ☎ (0515) 54 13 00 – fax (0515) 54 36 05
www.friesland-vvv.net

St.-Gertrudiskerk – Open Apr to Oct, daily (except Sun), 11am-5pm. ☎ (0515) 54 19 76.

Warkums Erfskip – Open Apr to Oct, Tues-Fri, 11am-5pm, Sat-Mon, 1-5pm. Closed Nov to Mar. ☎ (0515) 54 31 55.

Jopie Huisman Museum – Open Apr to Oct, Mon-Sat, 10am-5pm, Sun and public holidays, 1-5pm; Mar and Nov, daily, 1-5pm. Closed Dec to Feb. 5fl. ☎ (0515) 54 31 31.

Z

ZAANSTREEK
🏢 Gedempte Gracht 76 - 1506 CJ - ☎ (075) 616 22 21
fax (075) 670 53 81 - www.zaanseschans.nl

Boat trips - ♿ Operate Apr to Oct, daily, 11am-4pm (every hr on the hr); July and Aug, daily, 10am-5pm. b (075) 614 67 62.

Zaans Museum - Open Tues-Sat, 10am-5pm, Sun, noon-5pm. Closed Mon, 1 Jan, 30 Apr and 25 Dec. 10fl. ☎ (075) 616 82 18.

Ambachtencentrum - Open daily, 8.30am-6pm. ☎ (075) 635 46 22.

Klompenmakerij - ♿ Open daily, 8am-6pm. ☎ (075) 617 71 21.

Pewter workshop - Open Mar to Oct, daily, 10am-5pm; Nov to Feb, daily, 10am-4pm. Closed 25 Dec. ☎ (075) 617 62 04.

Museum van het Nederlandse uurwerk - Open Mar to Oct, daily, 10am-5pm; Nov to Feb, Sat-Sun, noon-4.30pm. 5fl. ☎ (075) 617 97 69.

Museumwinkel Albert Heijn - Open Mar to Oct, daily, 10am-1pm and 2-5pm; Nov to Feb, Sat-Sun, 11am-1pm and 2-4pm. No charge ☎ (075) 659 28 08.

Het Noorderhuis - Open Mar to Oct, Tues-Sun, 10am-5pm; July and Aug, daily, 10am-5pm; Nov to Feb, Sat-Sun and public holidays, 10am-5pm. Closed 1 Jan and 25 Dec. 2fl. ☎ (075) 617 32 37.

Bakkerijmuseum In de Gecroonde Duyvekater - Open Tues-Sun, 10am-5pm. Closed Mon. 1.50fl. ☎ (075) 617 35 22.

Kaasboerderij Catharina Hoeve - Open daily, 9am-6pm. ☎ (075) 621 58 20. www.henriwillig.com.

Verfmolen De Kat - Open Apr to Oct, daily, 9am-5pm; Nov to Mar, Sat-Sun, 9am-5pm. 4fl. ☎ (075) 621 04 77.

Oliemolen De Zoeker - Open Mar to Sept, daily, 9.30am-4.30pm. 4fl. ☎ (075) 628 79 42.

Honig Breet Huis - Open Tues-Sun, 1-5pm. Closed Mon, 1 Jan, Easter, Whitsun and 25 Dec. 250fl. ☎ (075) 621 76 26.

Molenmuseum - Open June to Sept, Mon, 1-5pm, Tues-Fri, 11am-5pm, Sat-Sun and public holidays, 1-5pm; Oct to May, Tues-Fri, 10am-noon and 1-5pm, Sat, 2-5pm, Sun and public holidays, 1-5pm. Closed Mon. 4.50fl. ☎ (075) 628 89 68.

Czaar Peterhuisje - Open Apr to Oct, Tues-Sun, 1-5pm; Nov to Mar, Sat-Sun, 1.30-5pm. Closed Mon and public holidays. 2.50fl. ☎ (075) 616 03 90.

ZIERIKZEE
🏢 Meelstraat 4 - 4301 EC - ☎ (0111) 41 24 50 - fax (0111) 41 72 73
www.vvvschouwenduivenland.nl

Boat trips - Operate July and Aug, Mon-Thur. Information: Rederij Gebhard, ☎ (010) 265 02 96.

Maritiem Museum - Open Apr to Oct and during school holidays, Mon-Sat, 10am-5pm, Sun and public holidays, noon-5pm. Closed 1 Jan and 25 Dec. 4fl. ☎ (0111) 45 44 64.

Stadhuismuseum - Open May to Oct, Mon-Sat, 10am-5pm, Sun, noon-5pm. Closed Nov to Apr and public holidays. 4fl. ☎ (0111) 45 44 64.

St.-Lievensmonstertoren - Information from VVV ☎ (0111) 41 24 50.

ZUTPHEN
🏢 Stationsplein 39 - 7201 MH - ☎ (0900) 269 28 88
fax (0575) 51 79 28 - www.achterhoektoerisme.nl

St.-Walburgskerk - Open May to Sept, Mon-Fri. 1.50fl. ☎ (0575) 51 41 78. www.walburgiskerk.nl

Museum Henriette Polak - Open Tues-Fri, 11am-5pm, Sat-Sun, 1.30-5pm. Closed Mon, 1 Jan, Easter Day, Whit Sunday and 25 Dec. 5fl. ☎ (0575) 51 68 78.

Stedelijk Museum - Open Tues-Fri, 11am-5pm, Sat-Sun, 1.30-5pm. Closed Mon, 1 Jan, Easter Day, Whit Sunday and 25 Dec. 5fl. ☎ (0575) 51 68 78.

Excursions

Grolsch Museum - Open Mon-Fri, 9am-12.30pm and 1.30-5pm, Sat, 9am-12.30pm and 1.30-4pm. Closed Sun and public holidays. 4fl. ☎ (0544) 46 12 47.

Index